Laughing Matters

Laughing Matters

A Celebration of American Humor

Selected and Edited
by Gene Shalit

BARNES
&NOBLE
BOOKS
NEW YORK

This edition published by Barnes & Noble, Inc.,
by arrangement with Doubleday Book and Music Clubs, Inc.

1993 Barnes & Noble Books

ISBN 1-56619-160-2

Printed and bound in the United States of America

M 9 8 7 6 5 4 3 2 1

A Salute

My gratitude to all of the artists and writers who gave their permission to have their work included . . . to the relentless Marian Reiner, who tracked down and secured those permissions . . . to Deb Woodin for her prodigious organization, patience, cheerfulness, suggestions, and remarkable endurance . . . to the good people at the Lenox, Massachusetts, Public Library, whose helpfulness is matched only by the glory of their building . . . to Joannie Kaplan, who laughed her way through private and public collections scouring books and magazines . . . to Willa Shalit, who joined me in crawling all over the living room floor trying to get pages in the right order . . . to Sam Gross, who must know the telephone number of every leading cartoonist in the country . . . to my editor, Barbara Greenman, who was polite when she mentioned that I was one year past my deadline, and almost as polite when she told me that I was two years past my deadline . . . to Casey Fuetsch, Meg Livingston, and Beth Margolis, who came to my aid in ways that I don't even know about . . . to Bluetooth and Vic & Sade . . . to Mark Hurst, copy editor, and Randall Mize, designer . . . to Maryellen Duffy . . . to Andrew Shalit, whose good taste was invaluable . . . to Sabrina Grigorian, too soon gone, so terribly missed . . . to Emily Griffith, who kept after me and provided so much incentive . . . to Garry Trudeau for leading me to special "Krazy Kats" . . . to Al Hirschfeld, who fetched his pen and created the "Overture" for the cover . . . and a bow to Sam Vaughan: Thanks for your support at the start.

My special gratitude to the indispensable Kurt Andersen, that prince of a person whose career has soared from presidential scholar to the *Harvard Lampoon* to *Time* to his very own *Spy*. He provided support, a keen mind, and essential advice, especially during the crucial formative stages; tipped me off to some pieces unfamiliar to me and to a number of younger off-the-path (and off-the-wall) humorists; and contributed the book's erudite and winning Afterword. I am lucky to be his friend.

Aside to Peter, Willa, Emily, Amanda, Nevin, and Andrew: And you thought it would never be finished.

G.S.

IN LOVING MEMORY OF

Robert W. Sink
Samson Raphaelson
Fritz Jauch
P. B. Cowan
R. Bruce Weirick

REQUIESCAT IN PACE

Contents

M. STEVENS

OVERCOMING DEPRESSION

A Useful Tip

In most anthologies, it doesn't matter which story, article, drawing, or poem you turn to first.

With *Laughing Matters,* it often matters.

You'll be rewarded if you read straight through. A good many of the drawings and verses will give you heightened pleasure if read in sequence because they comment on, or are a variation of, or are thematically related to a previous piece.

There are no section divisions or chapters. As you go along—except for an occasional U-turn—the shape of themes will become clear. Diaries, women vs. men, politics, dialect, ball games, literati, surrealism, satire, and the indefinable.

G.S.

Writing Humor Is a Funny Way to Make a Living

Almost everyone who cares about humor pays homage to E. B. White. Me too. After all, he and his collaborator-wife Katharine S. White did put together the best anthology of American humor of all time. However, "all time" ended in 1941, when their *A Subtreasury of American Humor* appeared, and a vast lode of humor has been written, filmed, and recited since then. This book was born of that book and, as Damon Runyon used to say, a story goes with it.

When I was seventeen, I was stricken with a curable ailment and sent to bed, missing not only dinner but my high school graduation. That summer passed outside of my bedroom window while I thrilled through the pages of the Whites' nothing-Sub-about-it-Treasury. And one dusk it actually happened: I fell out of bed laughing. It was Frank Sullivan's "A Garland of Ibids" that pushed me over the edge, and many years later, in Saratoga, New York, sitting on the edge of *his* bed toward the end of his life, I was able to tell him so, to our mutual delight.

The Whites' book did more for me that summer than all of Dr. Lester Graddick's aspirin and, ever since, I have cherished the humorists I was introduced to in its pages. So when Doubleday suggested that I do an anthology of humor, I couldn't wait to get started. That was in 1981, so I *have* waited to get started, which means that I am either a procrastinator or a reader whom Evelyn Wood would love to get her finger on.

So much good American humor has been written that it's impossible to include it all: Not everything funny is in this book, but everything in this book is funny. Some I have loved since youthhood. I have a near reverence for Benchley and Perelman and Sullivan and Samuel Hoffenstein and for many of their contemporaries. At their best that crowd was unsurpassed. But I have also embraced the younger humorists, the quirkier, wilder, darker, and more eccentric writers and artists.

Some laughing matters are very serious matters to me and I won't budge. There are certain people (and I don't want to have lunch with them) who will be offended by the dialect pieces in this collection. They ought to relax. They are often the sort of people who demand the removal of *Huckleberry Finn* from libraries. They should repeat after me: "Humor is a reflection of its time—a product of and a comment on the society, politics, and customs of the day." They ought to memorize Dr. Johnson's remark to Boswell: "A jest breaks no bones." Good-hearted ethnic humor in America has largely vanished. Too bad for America. Millions were once made merry (and millions more ought now to be) by Mr. Dooley and Mrs. Nussbaum, by Bella Gross and Hyman Kaplan, by the rural Lum and Abner, the urban Amos and Andy, by Dixie's Senator Claghorn, by Mr. Kitzel and Rochester and Billy Gilbert's sneezing Greek. The finest dialect humor has a *kindness* about it: You didn't have to send the children out of the room when Rochester approached Jack Benny. We were fractured by Chico Marx's fractured Italian, and by the Yiddish of Minerva Pius when her Mrs. Nussbaum answered the door in "Allen's Alley" (written by Fred Allen, a Catholic). Do I hear "But that time is past"? You'll still laugh as I do at Hyman Kaplan's immigrant version of Christopher Columbus if you put away your "all people are equal" speech. All people are *not* equal at speaking English, mine parents included. Yoo-hoo, Mrs. Goldberg, I love you. (Dear Gertrude Berg, rest in peace.)

And don't challenge me on "respect." Leo Rosten has towering respect for his Kaplanesque creation, and other dialect humorists respect *their* characters. You think Mark Twain had disdain for Jim? Respect we got. Plenty. What we do not want is cruelty, and you will find none in the good things I have chosen. Poking, yes. All humor pokes at something or someone. Veronica Geng ridicules "The Stylish New York Couples," leaving fashion magazine captions in tatters. ("Tatters by Sophie of Saks Fifth Avenue.") Benchley lampoons opera. Fran Lebowitz skewers teenagers. S. J. Perelman and Woody Allen and Philip Roth take on Jews and India and gangsters. So I point with enormous satisfaction to the inclusion of two ornaments of American humorous literature: "Green Pastures" from *Ol' Man Adam an' His Chillun* by Roark Bradford, and Marc Connelly's "A Fish Fry" from *The Green Pastures.*

I've been warned that some feminists will find Franklin P. Adams's "A Pair of Sexes" annoying, which annoys *me.* I find this early 1930s satire an apt companion to Dorothy Parker's "From the Diary of a New York Lady." F.P.A.'s lampoon is absolutely true of its time. Must we forget our past?

There are some things I have left out, and are you lucky! There's nothing here by Will Cuppy or Irvin S. Cobb. No tall tales and not a single piece included sheerly for posterity's sake. (Let posterity put out its own anthology.) There is hardly anything sadder than humor past its prime. A lot of it ought to be stamped with a date, like a carton of milk.

I'll tell you what I regret is not here: most of what made us laugh when we saw it *performed.* The humor of "I Love Lucy" that depended on Lucille Ball's clowning . . . Jack Benny's pauses . . . Fibber McGee's closet . . . the humor spoken in the distinctive voices of W. C. Fields, Mae West, Jerry Colonna, Ed Wynn, and Jimmy Durante . . . the silent scripts of Charlie Chaplin.

I laugh a lot. The world is a squirrel cage and I enjoy it. A television reporter for a Cincinnati paper once published a long attack on me (he had me down in the first paragraph but kept pummeling), asserting that his definition of unpleasant was being seated next to me at a Mel Brooks movie. I have been with Mel, having a normal (can that be the right word?) conversation, and I laughed so hard I almost strangled and had to be helped to recover my breath. George Burns once stopped in midstory, puffed his cigar, and said, "Stop laughing and listen." Carol Channing so convulsed me with a British dialect anecdote that I doubled over, my eyeglasses fell off, and I pushed my face into her shoulder, holding on to keep from collapsing.

I encountered a number of the pieces for this book during train rides between Manhattan and Hudson, N.Y. While reading Perelman's "No Starch in the Dhoti, *S'il Vous Plaît,*" I had to stuff my fist into my mouth. The concerned conductor leaned down to offer help. "A passenger says you're crying."

"I'm laughing," I choked, rubbing away my tears. "I'm *laughing.*"

What you are about to read made me smile, giggle, shriek, or laugh insanely—a range of sounds from pigeons cooing to a lunatic having a seizure.

I wish you the same.

GENE SHALIT

Laughing Matters

DOROTHY PARKER
LOUIS UNTERMEYER
ALEXANDER WOOLLCOTT

An Anthology
of Introductions
with Introductions by Gene Shalit

If *Laughing Matters* had been published in an earlier time, this ensemble might have been invited to provide its prelude. By happy chance, they *have* written what is exactly applicable to this collection. Dorothy Parker considers humor as a profession.   **G.S.**

It is a strange force that compels a writer to be a humorist. It is a strange force, if you care to go back farther, that compels anyone to be a writer at all, but this is neither the time nor the place to bring up that matter. The writer's way is rough and lonely, and who would choose it while there are vacancies in more gracious professions, such as, say, cleaning out ferry boats? In all understatement, the author's lot is a hard one, and yet there are those who deliberately set out to make it harder for themselves. There are those who, in their pride and their innocence, dedicate their careers to writing humorous pieces. Poor dears, the world is stacked against them from the start, for everybody in it has the right to look at their work and say, "I don't think that's funny."

I had thought, on starting this composition, that I should define what humor means to me. However, every time I tried to, I had to go and lie down with a cold wet cloth on my head. . . . Humor to me, Heaven help me, takes in many things. There must be courage; there must be no awe. There must be criticism, for humor, to my mind, is encapsulated in criticism. There must be a disciplined eye and a wild mind. There must be a magnificent disregard of your reader, for if he cannot follow you, there is nothing you can do about it. There must be some lagniappe in the fact that the humorist has read something written before 1918.

> Wit is one of the manners (or lack of manners) of launching laughter. Humor is different from wit—take it from Louis Untermeyer.   **G.S.**

Wit is sudden and startling and usually scornful; it leaps audaciously and wickedly. Humor is slower; it is rarely malicious; it does not fly to assault the mind but laughs its way into the heart. Satire is probing and critical; it cuts through pretention with quick corrosive acid; its purpose is coldly destructive. But humor seldom analyzes; it is warmly sympathetic, playful, sometimes high-hearted, sometimes hilarious. Unlike the poisoned barb of satire and the killing point of wit, humor is healing. It is not only wholesome, but recreative and rejuvenating. . . . As to the omissions which every reader will inevitably hold against the editor, there is this to say: Nothing is more personal than an anthology. Every anthologist says in effect: Here are some (though not all) of the things I've collected for years, and I hope you, the reader, will like them, too. If you ask me why I have left out some of your own favorites, I would offer these excuses: (a) Times change and taste changes with them. Some of the pieces I roared at in my youth still seem the best of their kind; some of the things that doubled me up last year seem pretty dull stuff to me today. (b) In spite of a lifetime spent reading and an acquired air of omniscience, it is just possible that I've never encountered your particular favorite.

> Alexander Woollcott is a hero of mine. Critic, anthologist, indefatigable letter writer, mesmerizer of vast radio audiences in the 1930s and 1940s, once dubbed Louisa May Woollcott, he enjoyed above all dropping a name while telling a good story.   **G.S.**

At a time when Helen Hayes was a new-risen star, she was escorted through Italy by a paternalistic *cicerone* who tacitly, at every point from the baptistry doors in Florence to the gaudy façade of the cathedral at Orvieto, exacted, as his fee, an expression of rapture. Finally he promised to show her, from an exceeding high mountain, the most beautiful view in all that storied countryside. Wherefore, when her already sated eyes had drunk their fill, she knew what was expected of her. Being an obliging creature and even then unique in her talent for expressing any emotion an occasion might call for, she gave a really superb performance of a woman entranced. But he turned away dissatisfied. "When I showed that to Eleanor Robson," he said, "she burst into tears."

Now while this book is another tour of certain bypaths in the realms of gold—for some it will often be a return visit—at least it is conducted by a guide less exigent. Indeed, the editor of any such anthology would do well to avoid an injudicious mannerism that in our time is threatening to become a national habit. With increasing frequency, the editor of this one is approached by some neighbor whose conversation has this alienating gambit. "Well," he will say, "I heard a story yesterday which you are sure to like." Or: "Here's something that will make you laugh your head off." Every now and again I am agile enough to cut in with some such comment as: "Perhaps you'd better let me be the judge of that." But when I do, the insensate raconteur only stares at me uncomprehendingly or gives a nervous laugh, and in either event then goes on with his story, which often as not proves to be one I can hear all the way through without once rolling on the floor in uncontrollable merriment. Wherefore, in the matter of liking the works in this anthology, let me begin by saying merely that I do and you may.

ROBERT BENCHLEY

Why We Laugh—or Do We?

In order to laugh at something, it is necessary (1) to know *what* you are laughing at, (2) to know *why* you are laughing, (3) to ask some people why *they* think you are laughing, (4) to jot down a few notes, (5) to laugh. Even then, the thing may not be cleared up for days.

All laughter is merely a compensatory reflex to take the place of sneezing. What we really want to do is sneeze, but as that is not always possible, we laugh instead. Sometimes we underestimate our powers and laugh and sneeze at the same time. This raises hell all around.

The old phrase "That is nothing to sneeze at" proves my point. What is obviously meant is "That is nothing to *laugh* at." The wonder is that nobody ever thought of this explanation of laughter before, with the evidence staring him in the face like that.*

We sneeze because we are thwarted, discouraged, or devil-may-care. Failing a sneeze, we laugh, *faute de mieux.* Analyze any funny story or comic situation at which we "laugh" and it will be seen that this theory is correct. Incidentally, by the time you have the "humor" analyzed, it will be found that the necessity for laughing has been relieved.

Let us take the well-known joke about the man who put the horse in the bathroom.† Here we have a perfect example of the thought-sneeze process, or, if you will, the sneeze-thought process. The man, obviously an introvert, was motivated by a will-to-dominate-the-bathroom, combined with a desire to be superior to the other boarders. The humor of the situation may *seem* to us to lie in the tag line "I want to be able to say, 'Yes, I know,'" but we laugh at the joke *subconsciously* long before this line comes in. In fact, what we are really laughing (or sneezing) at is the idea of someone's telling us a joke that we have heard before.

Let us suppose that the story was reversed, and that a *horse* had put a *man* into the bathroom. Then our laughter would have been induced by the idea of a landlady's asking a horse a question and the horse's answering—an entirely different form of joke.

The man would then have been left in the bathroom with nothing to do with the story. Likewise, if the man had put the *landlady* into the bathroom, the *horse* would obviously have been *hors de combat* (still another form of joke, playing on the similarity in sound between the word "horse" and the French word *"hors,"* meaning *"out* of." Give up?).

---

* Schwanzleben, in his work *Humor After Death,* hits on this point indirectly when he says, "All laughter is a muscular rigidity spasmodically relieved by involuntary twitching. It can be induced by the application of electricity as well as by a so-called 'joke.'"

† A man who lived in a boarding house brought a horse home with him one night, led it upstairs, and shut it in the bathroom. The landlady, aroused by the commotion, protested, pointed to the broken balustrade, the torn stair carpet, and the obvious maladjustment of the whole thing, and asked the man, confidentially, just why he had seen fit to shut a horse in the common bathroom. To which the man replied, "In the morning, the boarders, one by one, will go into the bathroom, and will come rushing out, exclaiming, 'There's a *horse* in the bathroom!' I want to be able to say, 'Yes, I know.'"

Any joke, besides making us want to sneeze, must have five cardinal points, and we must check up on these first before giving in:

(1) The joke must be in a language we can understand.

(2) It must be spoken loudly enough for us to hear it, or printed clearly enough for us to read it.

(3) It must be about *something.* You can't just say, "Here's a good joke" and let it go at that. (You *can,* but don't wait for the laugh.)

(4) It must deal with either frustration or accomplishment, inferiority or superiority, sense or nonsense, pleasantness or unpleasantness, or, at any rate, with some emotion that can be analyzed, otherwise how do we know when to laugh?

(5) It must begin with the letter "W."‡

Now, let us see just how our joke about the horse in the bathroom fulfills these specifications. Using the *Gestalt,* or Rotary-Frictional, method of taking the skin off a joke, we can best illustrate by making a diagram of it. We have seen that every joke must be in a language that we can understand and spoken (or written) so clearly that we an hear it (or see it). Otherwise we have this:

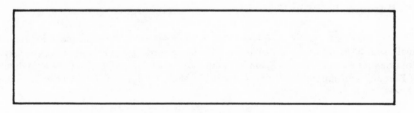

FIG. 1.
Joke which we cannot hear, see, or understand
the words of

You will see in Figure 2 that we go upstairs with the man and the horse as far as the bathroom. Here we become conscious that it is not a *true* story, something we may have suspected all along but didn't want to say anything about. This sudden revelation of *absurdity* (from the Latin *ab* and

‡ Gunfy, in his *Laughter Considered as a Joint Disease,* holds that the letter "W" is not essential to the beginning of a joke, so long as it comes in somewhere before the joke is over. However, tests made on five hundred subjects in the Harvard School of Applied Laughter, using the Mergenthaler Laugh Detector, have shown that, unless a joke begins with the letter "W," the laughter is forced, almost unpleasant at times.

surdus, meaning "out of deafness") is represented in the diagram by an old-fashioned whirl.

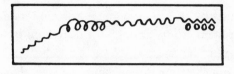

FIG. 2.

The horse-in-bathroom story under ideal conditions

Following the shock of realization that the story is not real, we progress in the diagram to the point where the landlady protests. Here we come to an actual *fact,* or factual *act.* Any landlady in her right mind *would* protest against a horse's being shut in her bathroom. So we have, in the diagram, a return to normal ratiocination, or Crowther's Disease, represented by the wavy line. (Whoo-hoo!)

From then on, it is anybody's joke. The whole thing becomes just ludicrous. This we can show in the diagram by the egg-and-dart design, making it clear that something has definitely gone askew. Personally, I think that what the man *meant* to say was "That's no horse—that's my wife," but that he was inhibited. (Some of these jokes even *I* can't seem to get through my head.)*

* A. E. Bassinette, in his pamphlet *What Is Humor—A Joke?,* claims to have discovered a small tropical fly which causes laughter. This fly, according to this authority, was carried from Central America back to Spain by Columbus's men, and spread from there to the rest of Europe, returning to America, on a visit, in 1667, on a man named George Altschuh.

DOROTHY PARKER

From the Diary of a New York Lady

During Days of Horror, Despair, and World Change

Monday. Breakfast tray about eleven; didn't want it. The champagne at the Amorys' last night was *too* revolting, but what *can* you do? You can't stay until five o'clock on just *nothing*. They had those *divine* Hungarian musicians in the green coats, and Stewie Hunter took off one of his shoes and led them with it, and it *couldn't* have been funnier. He is *the* wittiest number in the *entire* world; he *couldn't* be more perfect. Ollie Martin brought me home and we both fell asleep in the car—*too* screaming. Miss Rose came about noon to do my nails, simply *covered* with *the* most divine gossip. The Morrises are going to separate *any minute,* and Freddie Warren *definitely* has ulcers, and Gertie Leonard simply *won't* let Bill Crawford out of her sight even with Jack Leonard *right there in the room,* and it's all *true* about Sheila Phillips and Babs Deering. It *couldn't* have been more thrilling. Miss Rose is *too* marvelous; I really think that a lot of times people like that are a lot more intelligent than a lot of people. Didn't notice until after she had gone that the damn fool had put that *revolting* tangerine-colored polish on my nails; *couldn't* have been more furious. Started to read a book, but too nervous. Called up and found I could get two tickets for the opening of "Run like a Rabbit" tonight for forty-eight dollars. Told them they had *the* nerve of the world, but what *can* you do? Think Joe said he was dining out, so telephoned some *divine* numbers to get someone to go to the theater with me, but they were all tied up. Finally got Ollie Martin. He *couldn't* have more poise, and what do *I* care if he *is* one? *Can't* decide whether to wear the green crepe or the red wool. Every time I look at my finger nails, I could *spit. Damn* Miss Rose.

Tuesday. Joe came barging in my room this morning at *practically nine o'clock*. *Couldn't* have been more furious. Started to fight, but *too* dead. Know he said he wouldn't be home to dinner. Absolutely *cold* all day; couldn't *move*. Last night *couldn't* have been more perfect. Ollie and I dined at Thirty-Eight East, absolutely *poisonous* food, and not one *living* soul that you'd be seen *dead* with, and "Run like a Rabbit" was *the* world's worst. Took Ollie up to the Barlows' party and it *couldn't* have been more attractive—*couldn't* have been more people absolutely *stinking*. They had those Hungarians in the green coats, and Stewie Hunter was leading them with a fork—everybody simply *died*. He had *yards* of green toilet paper hung around his neck like a lei; he *couldn't* have been in better form. Met a *really new number*, very tall, *too* marvelous, and one of those people that you can *really* talk to them. I told him sometimes I get so *nauseated* I could *yip*, and I felt I absolutely *had* to do something like write or paint. He said why didn't I write or paint. Came home alone; Ollie passed out *stiff*. Called up the new number three times today to get him to come to dinner and go with me to the opening of "Never Say Good Morning," but first he was out and then he was all tied up with his mother. Finally got Ollie Martin. Tried to read a book, but couldn't sit still. *Can't* decide whether to wear the red lace or the pink with the feathers. Feel *too* exhausted, but what *can* you do?

Wednesday. The most terrible thing happened *just this minute*. Broke one of my finger nails *right off short*. Absolutely *the* most horrible thing I ever had happen to me in my life. Called up Miss Rose to come over and shape it for me, but she was out for the day. I do have *the* worst luck in the *entire* world. Now I'll have to go around like this all day and all night, but what *can* you do? *Damn* Miss Rose. Last night *too* hectic. "Never Say Good Morning" *too* foul, *never* saw more poisonous clothes on the stage. Took Ollie up to the Ballards' party; *couldn't* have been better. They had those Hungarians in the green coats and Stewie Hunter was leading them with a freesia—*too* perfect. He had on Peggy Cooper's ermine coat and Phyllis Minton's silver turban; *simply* unbelievable. Asked simply *sheaves* of *divine* people to come here Friday night; got the address of those Hungarians in the green coats from Betty Ballard. She says just engage them until four, and then whoever gives them another three hundred dollars, they'll stay till five. *Couldn't* be cheaper. Started home with Ollie, but had to drop him at his house; he *couldn't* have been sicker. Called up the new number today to get him to come to dinner and go to the opening of "Everybody Up" with me tonight, but he was tied up. Joe's going to be out; he didn't *condescend* to say *where, of course.* Started to read the papers, but nothing in them except that Mona Wheatley is in Reno charging *intolerable cruelty.* Called up Jim Wheatley to see if he had anything to do tonight, but he was tied up. Finally got Ollie Martin. *Can't* decide whether to wear the white satin or the black chiffon or the yellow pebble crepe. Simply *wrecked* to the *core* about my finger nail. Can't *bear* it. *Never* knew *anybody* to have such *unbelievable* things happen to them.

Thursday. Simply *collapsing* on my *feet.* Last night *too* marvelous. "Every-body Up" *too* divine, *couldn't* be filthier, and the new number was there, *too* celestial, only he didn't see me. He was with Florence Keeler in that *loathsome* gold Schiaparelli model of hers that every *shopgirl* has had since *God* knows. He must be out of his *mind;* she wouldn't *look* at a man. Took Ollie to the Watsons' party; *couldn't* have been more thrilling. Everybody simply *blind.* They had those Hungarians in the green coats and Stewie Hunter was leading them with a lamp, and, after the lamp got broken, he and Tommy Thomas did adagio dances—*too* wonderful. Somebody told me Tommy's doctor told him he had to absolutely get *right out of town,* he has *the* world's worst stomach, but you'd *never* know it. Came home alone, couldn't find Ollie *anywhere.* Miss Rose came at noon to shape my nail, *couldn't* have been more fascinating. Sylvia Eaton can't go *out the door* unless she's had a hypodermic, and Doris Mason *knows every single word* about Douggie Mason and that girl up in Harlem, and Evelyn North won't be *induced* to keep away from those three acrobats, and they don't *dare* tell Stuyvie Raymond *what* he's got the matter with him. *Never* knew anyone that had a more simply *fascinating* life than Miss Rose. Made her take that *vile* tangerine polish off my nails and put on dark red. Didn't notice until after she had gone that it's practically *black* in electric light; *couldn't* be in a worse state. *Damn* Miss Rose. Joe left a note saying he was going to dine out, so telephoned the new number to get him to come to dinner and go with me to that new movie tonight, but he didn't answer. Sent him three telegrams to *absolutely surely* come tomorrow night. Finally got Ollie Mar-tin for tonight. Looked at the papers, but nothing in them except that the Harry Motts are throwing a tea with Hungarian music on Sunday. Think will ask the new number to go to it with me; they must have meant to invite me. Began to read a book, but too exhausted. *Can't* decide whether to wear the new blue with the white jacket or save it till tomorrow night and wear the ivory moire. Simply *heartsick* every time I think of my nails. *Couldn't* be wilder. Could *kill* Miss Rose, but what *can* you do?

Friday. Absolutely *sunk; couldn't* be worse. Last night *too* divine, movie *simply* deadly. Took Ollie to the Kingslands' party, *too* unbelievable, everybody absolutely *rolling*. They had those Hungarians in the green coats, but Stewie Hunter wasn't there. He's got a *complete* nervous breakdown. Worried *sick* for fear he won't be well by tonight; will absolutely *never* forgive him if he doesn't come. Started home with Ollie, but dropped him at his house because he *couldn't* stop crying. Joe left word with the butler he's going to the country this afternoon for the week-end; *of course* he wouldn't *stoop* to say *what* country. Called up *streams* of marvelous numbers to get someone to come dine and go with me to the opening of "White Man's Folly," and then go somewhere after to dance for a while; can't *bear* to be the first one there at your own party. Everybody was tied up. Finally got Ollie Martin. *Couldn't* feel more depressed; never should have gone *anywhere near* champagne and Scotch together. Started to read a book, but too restless. Called up Anne Lyman to ask about the new baby and *couldn't* remember if it was a boy or girl—*must* get a secretary *next week*. Anne *couldn't* have been more of a help; she said she didn't know whether to name it Patricia or Gloria, so then of course I knew it was a girl *right away*. Suggested calling it Barbara; forgot she already had one. Absolutely *walking the floor* like a *panther* all day. Could *spit* about Stewie Hunter. Can't *face* deciding whether to wear the blue with the white jacket or the purple with the beige roses. Every time I look at those *revolting* black nails, I want to absolutely *yip*. I really have *the* most horrible things happen to me of anybody in the *entire* world. *Damn* Miss Rose.

GLUYAS WILLIAMS

RACONTEURS

"Well, good night again—this time we really are off. You know, Wallace scolds me. He says I never think of things I want to say until I have my wraps on and have said good night. Just last evening we got roped in for bridge at the Northrops', and you know how Wallace loathes bridge, though I must say he's a lamb about playing, but anyway I tried to break away early, and we got all ready to go, and . . ."

© 1938 The New Yorker Magazine, Inc.

HOWARD MOSS

The Ultimate Diary

(FURTHER DAILY JOTTINGS OF A CONTEMPORARY COMPOSER)

MONDAY

Drinks here. Picasso, Colette, the inevitable Cocteau, Gide, Valéry, Ravel, and Larry. Chitchat. God, how absolutely dull the Great can be! I know at least a hundred friends who would have given their eyeteeth just to have had a *glimpse* of some of them, and there I was bored, incredible lassitude, *stymied.* Is it me? Is it them? Think latter. Happened to glance in mirror before going to bed. Am more beautiful than ever.

TUESDAY

Horrible. After organ lesson at C's, he burst into tears and confessed that he loved me. Was mad about me, is how he put it. I was embarrassed. I respect him, he is a great *maître* and all that, but how could I reciprocate when I, myself, am so involved with L? I tried to explain. He said he thought it would be better if we discontinued our lessons. How am I ever going to learn to play the organ? Came home upset. Finished *Barcarolles, Gigue, Danse Fantastique,* and *Cantata.* Writing better than ever. Careful of self-congratulations. So somebody said. John Donne? Fresh mushrooms. Delicious.

WEDNESDAY

Drunk at the dentist's. He removed a molar, and cried when I said it hurt. *Très gentil.* I think he has some feeling for me. The sky was like a red blister over the Dome. Streaks of carmine suffused the horizon. Sometimes I wonder if I shouldn't have been a writer. Drunk as I was, I caught a glimpse of myself in a bakery window. No wonder so many people love me!

THURSDAY

Arletty said something profound at lunch. "The trouble with homosexuals is that they like men." She sometimes gets to the heart of the matter with all her superficiality. She is leaving M. Talked and talked about it. I found my attention wandering, and kept seeing the unfinished pages of the *Symphony*. It is a great hymn to world peace, a kind of apotheosis of calmness, though it has a few fast sections. Drank a lot, and can't remember much after lunch. Woke up in Bois. Think something happened. But what? To relieve depression, dyed my hair again. Must say it looks ravishing. *Ravissant.*

FRIDAY

Calls from Mauriac and Claudel. Why don't they leave me alone?

FRIDAY, LATER

Larry back from Avignon. Seems changed. Felt vague feeling of disgust. To camouflage, worked all day and finished *Pavane, Song Cycles,* and *Sonata.* Dedicated latter—last?—to Princesse de N. She sent me a Russian egg for my name day. How know? Malraux, Auric, Poulenc, and Milhaud dropped by.

SATURDAY

Stravinsky angry with me, he said over phone. I must never stop working, working. What about sex? L has left. Should I call C? Thinking of it. Press clippings arrived. Is there any other composer under seventeen whose works are being played in every capital of Asia? Matisse said, jokingly at lunch, that I was too beautiful to live. Genius is not a gift; it is a loan.

SATURDAY, LATER

At state banquet for de Gaulle, misbehaved. Slapped his wife in face during coffee. Drunk. Terribly depressed, but am I not also not a little proud? Contrite but haughty, sorry but pleased? Can't remember issue. Something about Monteverdi? Sent her a dozen white roses as apology. The Princesse says I should get out of town for a while. I WILL NOT RUN AWAY! C back. We are both more gorgeous than ever. Finished *War and Peace.* A good book.

SUNDAY

Pneumatique from Mallarmé. I will not answer. C and I had piquenique. Fell asleep on Seine bank. Dream: Mother in hippopotamus cage, crying. She said, "If music be the feast . . ." and then gobbled up by crowd of angry deer. What mean? Shaken. C bought me drink at Deux Magots. Sweet. Told me he thought there had never been a handsomer man placed on this earth. Forced to agree, after catching tiny glimpse of myself in café window. How often are genius and beauty united? They will hate me when they read this diary, but I tell the truth. How many can say as much?

MONDAY

A name even *I* cannot mention. . . . And he wants me to spend the summer in Africa with him! C angry. Finished *Concerto Grosso* and *Hymn to the Moon,* for female voices. Something new, a kind of rough susurration, here and there, a darkening of strings. It is raining. Sometimes I think we are more ourselves in wet weather than in dry. Bought linen hat.

TUESDAY

Gertrude, Alice, James, Joyce, Henry Green, Virginia Woolf, Eliot, Laforgue, Mallarmé (all is forgiven!), Rimbaud's nephew, Claudel's niece, Mistinguett, Nadia, Marais, Nijinska, Gabin, and the usual for drinks. I did it with Y in the pantry while the party was going on! Ashamed but exhilarated. I think if THEY knew they would have approved. Finished *Sixty Piano Pieces for Young Fingers.* Potboiler. But one has to live!

WEDNESDAY

Snow. Hideous hangover. Will never drink again. Deli dinner with Henry Miller.

THURSDAY

Half the Opéra-Comique seems to have fallen in love with me. I cannot stand any more importuning. Will go to Africa. How to break with C? Simone de Beauvoir, Simone Signoret, Simone Weil, and Simone Simon for drinks. They didn't get it!

FRIDAY

C left. Am bruised but elated. Dentist. I was right. I wonder if he'll dare send me a bill. *Now,* I mean. Tea with Anaïs. *Enchantant.*

SATURDAY

René Char and Dior for lunch. Interesting. Clothes are the camouflage of the soul. Leave for Africa with X tomorrow. Had fifty tiny Martinis. Nothing happened.

SUNDAY

Barrault, Braque, Seurat, Mayakovski, Honegger, and René Clair saw us off. Very gala. I think I am really in love for the first time. I must say I looked marvellous. Many comments. Wore green yachting cap and cinnamon plus fours. Happy.

WEDNESDAY

Dakar: Tangled in mosquito netting. Getting nowhere with *Chansons d'Afrique.*

SATURDAY

Back in Paris. God, what a fool I've been! Someday I will write down the whole hideous, unbelievable story. Not now. Not when I am so close to it. But I will forget *nothing.* Leaving tonight for Princesse de N's country place. Green trees, green leaves! The piercing but purifying wind of Provence! Or is it Normandy? Packed all afternoon. Long bath, many thoughts. Proust called. . . .

WOODY ALLEN

Selections from the Allen Notebooks

Following are excerpts from the hitherto secret private journal of Woody Allen, which will be published posthumously or after his death, whichever comes first.

Getting through the night is becoming harder and harder. Last evening, I had the uneasy feeling that some men were trying to break into my room to shampoo me. But why? I kept imagining I saw shadowy forms, and at 3 A.M. the underwear I had draped over a chair resembled the Kaiser on roller skates. When I finally did fall asleep, I had that same hideous nightmare in which a woodchuck is trying to claim my prize at a raffle. Despair.

I believe my consumption has grown worse. Also my asthma. The wheezing comes and goes, and I get dizzy more and more frequently. I have taken to violent choking and fainting. My room is damp and I have perpetual chills and palpitations of the heart. I noticed, too, that I am out of napkins. Will it never stop?

Idea for a story: A man awakens to find his parrot has been made Secretary of Agriculture. He is consumed with jealousy and shoots himself, but unfortunately the gun is the type with a little flag that pops out, with the word "Bang" on it. The flag pokes his eye out, and he lives—a chastened human being who, for the first time, enjoys the simple pleasures of life, like farming or sitting on an air hose.

Thought: Why does man kill? He kills for food. And not only food: frequently there must be a beverage.

Should I marry W.? Not if she won't tell me the other letters in her name. And what about her career? How can I ask a woman of her beauty to give up the Roller Derby? Decisions . . .

Once again I tried committing suicide—this time by wetting my nose and inserting it into the light socket. Unfortunately, there was a short in the wiring, and I merely caromed off the icebox. Still obsessed by thoughts of death, I brood constantly. I keep wondering if there is an afterlife, and if there is will they be able to break a twenty?

I ran into my brother today at a funeral. We had not seen one another for fifteen years, but as usual he produced a pig bladder from his pocket and began hitting me on the head with it. Time has helped me understand him better. I finally realize his remark that I am "some loathsome vermin fit only for extermination" was said more out of compassion than anger. Let's face it: he was always much brighter than me—wittier, more cultured, better educated. Why he is still working at McDonald's is a mystery.

Idea for story: Some beavers take over Carnegie Hall and perform "Wozzeck." (Strong theme. What will be the structure?)

Good Lord, why am I so guilty? Is it because I hated my father? Probably it was the veal parmigiana incident. Well, what *was* it doing in his wallet? If I had listened to him, I would be blocking hats for a living. I can hear him now: "To block hats—that is everything." I remember his reaction when I told him I wanted to write. "The only writing you'll do is in collaboration with an owl." I still have no idea what he meant. What a sad man! When my first play, "A Cyst for Gus," was produced at the Lyceum, he attended opening night in tails and a gas mask.

Today I saw a red-and-yellow sunset and thought, How insignificant I am! Of course, I thought that yesterday, too, and it rained. I was overcome with self-loathing and contemplated suicide again—this time by inhaling next to an insurance salesman.

Short story: A man awakens in the morning and finds himself transformed into his own arch supports. (This idea can work on many levels. Psychologically, it is the quintessence of Kruger, Freud's disciple who discovered sexuality in bacon.)

How wrong Emily Dickinson was! Hope is not "the thing with feathers." The thing with feathers has turned out to be my nephew. I must take him to a specialist in Zurich.

I have decided to break off my engagement with W. She doesn't understand my writing, and said last night that my "Critique of Metaphysical Reality" reminded her of "Airport." We quarrelled, and she brought up the subject of children again, but I convinced her they would be too young.

Do I believe in God? I did until Mother's accident. She fell on some meat loaf, and it penetrated her spleen. She lay in a coma for months, unable to do anything but sing "Granada" to an imaginary herring. Why was this woman in the prime of life so afflicted—because in her youth she dared to defy convention and got married with a brown paper bag on her head? And how can I believe in God when just last week I got my tongue caught in the roller of an electric typewriter? I am plagued by doubts. What if everything is an illusion and nothing exists? In that case, I definitely overpaid for my carpet. If only God would give me some clear sign! Like making a large deposit in my name at a Swiss bank.

Had coffee with Melnick today. He talked to me about his idea of having all government officials dress like hens.

Play idea: A character based on my father, but without quite so prominent a big toe. He is sent to the Sorbonne to study the harmonica. In the end, he dies, never realizing his one dream—to sit up to his waist in gravy. (I see a brilliant second-act curtain, where two midgets come upon a severed head in a shipment of volleyballs.)

While taking my noon walk today, I had more morbid thoughts. What *is* it about death that bothers me so much? Probably the hours. Melnick says the soul is immortal and lives on after the body drops away, but if my soul exists without my body I am convinced all my clothes will be too loose-fitting. Oh, well . . .

Did not have to break off with W. after all, for, as luck would have it, she ran off to Finland with a professional circus geek. All for the best, I suppose, although I had another of those attacks where I start coughing out of my ears.

Last night, I burned all my plays and poetry. Ironically, as I was burning my masterpiece, "Dark Penguin," the room caught fire, and I am now the object of a lawsuit by some men named Pinchunk and Schlosser. Kierkegaard was right.

FRANKLIN P. ADAMS

A Pair of Sexes

I. MAN TELEPHONES
"Ed? . . . Lunch at one. Whyte's. Right."

II. A WOMAN TELEPHONES
"Hello, operator. Operator? I want Caledonia five eight six seven,

please. Oh, this *is* Caledonia five eight six seven? Oh, I beg your pardon, I'm terribly sorry. I thought it was the operator. I've had so much trouble with the telephone lately. May I speak to Miss Lucille Webster, please? Oh, *speaking?* Oh, I'm terribly sorry. Is this Miss Webster? Is this you, Lucille? I didn't recognize your voice at first. First I thought it was the operator, and then I thought it was somebody answering for you, Lucille. I didn't recognize your voice at first. Got a cold or something? Oh, you sound as though you had. There's so much of it around this wretched weather. I never saw anything like it in my whole life. Well, I'm glad you haven't got a cold, though at first you certainly sounded like it. . . . I was just talking to Ethel for a second, and she had such a cold she could hardly talk. That's the reason I asked you. There's an *awful* lot of it around this wretched weather. . . . Oh, nothing particular. . . . Oh, yes, there is too. How silly of me! I was so interested in what you were saying, I almost forgot. Lucille, what are you doing tomorrow? . . . No, about lunch time. Or a little earlier. Or a little later. It doesn't matter. Because I expect to be in your part of town about that time, around lunch time, oh, maybe one or one-thirty or so, I have an appointment at twelve-thirty, and it oughtn't to take me more than half an hour, or at the most three quarters, surely not over an hour, I'm almost certain, and probably I'll be through in half an hour, but, anyway, I ought to be all through by one-thirty, and I could meet you anywhere you say. . . . Oh, I know, but Maillard's is pretty crowded about that time, and isn't there some place nearer? My appointment is on Forty-seventh Street near Madison—no, it's near Fifth, I guess. But that doesn't matter. I'll take a cab. If I can get one. Did you ever see anything like how hard it is to get a cab nowadays? My dear, last night I was twenty-five minutes trying to get one, and it got me late for dinner, and I *know* they didn't believe me. But if I can't get one I'll walk. It's only a block. And I guess a little exercise wouldn't do me any harm . . . Maillard's. . . . How about the Ritz? No, there's such a jam there. And it's hard to meet. Well, any place *you* say. . . . Oh, Lucille, that's a dreadful place. The food's so—oh, I don't know. You know. So—bad; if you know what I mean. Well, let's take a chance on Maillard's. Only it's so crowded. . . . Oh, no, I never heard that. . . . No, I haven't. I haven't read a thing in months, absolutely months. Where the time goes to I don't know. *I* simply do not know where the time goes to. Lucille, you're sure you've got tomorrow at lunch free? Because if you haven't, or there's something you'd rather do, just say so and we'll try again. Well, suppose we say at Maillard's at—oh, do you know that little tea shop on Forty-seventh? I think it's between Park and Madison on the—let's see—on the downtown, that's the south side of the street. I'll be there by one,

or anyway one-thirty, and if I'm there first I'll get a table, and you do the
same if you are. But I ought to be there by one. My appointment is for
half-past twelve, and it may take me only a few minutes. I might be there
before one. But surely by quarter past, and certainly by one-thirty. . . .
All right, then. Suppose we say about one, at Maillard's. . . . Oh, no,
what am I thinking of? We decided that would be too crowded, didn't we?
Unless you'd rather go there. That little tea shop is very nice. . . . Well,
yes, I'd just as soon go to Maillard's. It doesn't matter much. It's seeing
you I care about. There's a *lot* I want to talk to you about. These little
snatches at the telephone are so, well, so sort of unsatisfactory, if you
know what I mean. . . . All right, suppose we say Maillard's, then. And
then if we don't like the looks of things we can go somewhere else. . . .
All right, then, at . . . oh, let's go to the tea room. It's quieter. . . . All
right then. I'm longing to see you, Lucille. . . . Tomorrow, then. At the
tea shop, that's on Forty-seventh between Park and Madison, on the
downtown, that's the south side of the street. Tomorrow, then, about
one. That's Wednesday. . . . What? Is it Tuesday? . . . Well, I'm *all*
turned around. I thought it was Wednesday. I'm terribly sorry, Lucille. I
can't *possibly* meet you tomorrow if it's Tuesday. I've got a luncheon
appointment I've had for ages, simply for weeks, and I've postponed it so
often I don't dare do it again. . . . You can't Wednesday? I'm terribly
sorry. . . . Well, I'll try again. Ring me up. I'll be in all afternoon until
five twenty-five, and then I have to go uptown. . . . Yes. . . . Well, I'm
glad we had a nice little talk, anyway. . . . And I'll see you soon. . . .
What? No, *soon*—S for Sam. . . . Yes, soon. . . . Good-bye, Lucille.
. . . Good-bye. Good-bye. Good-bye."

DOROTHY PARKER

An Apartment House Anthology

THE GROUND FLOOR

Mr. and Mrs. Cuzzens much prefer living on the ground floor, they often say. Sometimes, when Mrs. Cuzzens is really warmed up to it, she puts the thing even stronger, and announces to the world that she would turn down flat all offers to live on an upper floor, in this or any other apartment house in New York City, even if you were to become desperate at her firmness and present her with an apartment rent free.

In the first place Mrs. Cuzzens is never wholly at her ease in an elevator. One of her liveliest anecdotes concerns an aunt of hers on her mother's side who was once a passenger in an elevator which stopped short midway between floors, and doggedly refused to move either up or down. Fortunately it all ended happily. Cries for help eventually caught the attention of the janitor—it seemed little short of providential that he had always had quite a turn for messing around with machinery—and he succeeded in regulating the power so that Mrs. Cuzzens' aunt reached her destination practically as good as new. But the episode made a terrific impression on Mrs. Cuzzens.

Of course it is rather dark on the ground floor, but Mr. and Mrs. Cuzzens regard that as one of the big assets of their apartment. Mrs. Cuzzens had a pretty nasty example of the effects of an oversunshiny place happen right in her own family. Her sister-in-law—not, Mrs. Cuzzens is careful to specify, the wife of the brother in the insurance business, but the wife of the brother who is on the road for a big tire concern, and is doing very well at it—hung some French-blue draperies at her living-room windows. And in less than a year the sunlight turned those curtains from their original color to an unwholesome shade of greenish yellow.

Why, the change was so marked that many people, seeing them in this state, almost refused to believe that they had ever been blue. Mrs. Cuzzens' sister-in-law, as is perfectly understandable, was pretty badly broken up about it. Naturally Mrs. Cuzzens would hate to have a thing like that happen in her own home.

There is another advantage to living on the ground floor. The rent there is appreciably smaller than it is on the stories above, although Mr. and Mrs. Cuzzens seldom if ever work this into the conversation. Well, it is easy to overlook it, in the press of more important reasons for occupying their apartment.

A MEAN EYE FOR FREAK NEWS

Mrs. Cuzzens has a fund, to date inexhaustible, of clean yet stimulating anecdotes, of which the one about the elevator and the one about the curtains are representative. She specializes in the unique. Hers is probably the largest collection in the country of stories of curious experiences, most of them undergone by members of her intimate circle. She is generous almost to a fault in relating them too. About any topic that happens to come up will be virtually certain to remind her of the funny thing that once happened to her Aunt Anna or the queer experience her Cousin Beulah had that time in Springfield.

Her repertory of anecdotes undoubtedly had much to do with attracting Mr. Cuzzens to her, for Mr. Cuzzens leans heavily to the out-of-the-ordinary himself. In his after-dinner reading of the newspaper he cheats a bit on the front-page items, just murmuring the headlines over, and gathering from them a rough idea—if you could really speak of Mr. Cuzzens as harboring a rough idea—of what is going on in the way of the conventional hold-ups and graft inquiries. But he casts a mean eye over the oddities in the day's news. He never misses the little paragraph about the man in Winsted, Connecticut, who intrusts a family of orphaned eggs to the care of a motherly cat, with gratifying results to one and all; or the report of the birth on an ocean liner, to a couple prominent in steerage circles, of a daughter, named Aquitania Wczlascki in commemoration of the event.

These specialties of Mr. and Mrs. Cuzzens work in together very prettily. They provide many an evening of instructive and harmless entertainment, while so far as expense goes, the only overhead is three cents for an evening paper.

Mr. Cuzzens puts on the slippers he got last birthday, and Mrs. Cuzzens unhooks a bit here and there as the evening wears on and she can feel reasonably sure that no one will drop in. As they sit about the grained-oak table in the glow of the built-in chandelier Mr. Cuzzens will read aloud some such fascinating bit of current history as the announcement of the birth, in Zanesville, Ohio, of a calf with two heads, both doing well. Mrs. Cuzzens will cap it with the description, guaranteed authentic, of a cat her mother's cousin once possessed which had a double set of claws on each foot.

CLEVER MR. CUZZENS

When the excitement of this has died down Mr. Cuzzens will find an item reporting that a famous movie star has taken a load off the public's mind by having her eyelashes insured for one hundred thousand dollars. That will naturally lead his wife to tell the one about the heavy insurance her Uncle David carried, and the perfectly terrible red tape his bereaved family had to go through before they could collect.

After twenty minutes or so passed in their both listening attentively to Mrs. Cuzzens' recital, Mr. Cuzzens' eye, sharpened by years of training, will fall on an obscure paragraph telling how an apple tree near Providence was struck by lightning, which baked all the fruit. Mrs. Cuzzens will come right back with the story of how her little nephew once choked on a bit of the core of a baked apple, and the doctor said it might have been fatal if he had got there half an hour later.

And so it goes, back and forth, all evening long.

But the Cuzzens have their light side too. They often make a night of it at the movies. In fact Mr. Cuzzens, who is apt to be pretty slangy at times, says that he and the little woman are regular movie fans. Mr. Cuzzens loses himself so completely in the display that he reads each subtitle aloud. If it seems to him worthy, and if the operator leaves it on long enough, he reads it through twice. Both he and his wife take deeply to heart the news pictures, showing a grain elevator destroyed by fire in Florence, Georgia; or the living head of Uncle Sam formed by a group of Los Angeles school children.

Any trick effects on the screen leave Mrs. Cuzzens bewildered. She can never figure out how, for example, they make a man seem to walk up the side of a house. However, Mr. Cuzzens is awfully clever at all that sort of thing—more than one person has told him he should have gone in for mechanical work—and he explains the process on the way home.

Occasionally Mr. and Mrs. Cuzzens patronize the drama. There is a theater near them to which come plays almost direct from their run lower down on Broadway. The casts are only slightly changed; just substitutions in five or six of the leading roles. Both the Cuzzenses prefer comedies of the wholesome type, setting themselves on record as going to the theater to be amused. They say that they wouldn't go around the corner to see one of those unpleasant plays, for there is enough trouble in this world, anyway. And after all, who is there that can give them any argument on that one?

Now and then they devote an evening to cards, playing a little interfamily game with Mr. Cuzzens' married sister and her husband. The sport is kept absolutely clean. No money changes hands.

In the daytime, while Mr. Cuzzens is busy at his office—he is with a firm that makes bathroom scales, and it's as good as settled that they are going to do something really worth while for him the first of the year—Mrs. Cuzzens is occupied with her own activities. She often complains that the days aren't half long enough for her, but nothing really satisfactory has been done to remedy this, as yet. Much of her time is devoted to shopping, for there are always button molds to be matched, or a strip of linoleum for the washtubs to be priced, or a fresh supply of trick paper for the pantry shelves to be laid in. She is almost overconscientious about her shopping. It is no unusual thing for her to spend an entire day in a tour of the department stores, searching for a particular design of snap fastener or the exact match of a spool of silk. She reaches home at the end of one of these days of toil pretty well done up, but still game.

And then there are her social duties. She is one of the charter members of a bridge club which numbers just enough to fill two tables comfortably. The club meets every fortnight, giving the players a chance to compete for the brocade-covered candy box—the winner must supply her own candy, which is no more than fair—or the six embroidered, guest-room-size handkerchiefs, which the hostess donates in the interest of sport.

During these functions Mrs. Cuzzens takes part in a great deal of tense conversation about the way the skirt was gathered over the hips and came down longer in front. She also gives, and receives, ideas on novel fillings for sandwiches, effective patterns for home-knit sweaters, and simple yet snappy dishes for Sunday-night supper.

Neither Mr. nor Mrs. Cuzzens is a native of New York. Up to a year or so after their marriage they helped swell the population of a town in Illinois which at the last census had upward of one hundred thousand inhabitants. They celebrate Old Home Week by a visit to the folks every year, but they congratulate themselves heartily that Mr. Cuzzens' business prevents their staying more than a week. For they agree that after eight years' residence in what Mr. Cuzzens aptly calls the big city they could never bring themselves to live in a small town again.

As Mrs. Cuzzens puts it, life in New York is so much broader.

THE SECOND FLOOR EAST

The Parmalees are always intending to move, but somehow they never get around to it. Several times Mrs. Parmalee has come out flat with the statement that the very next day she is going to look for an apartment farther downtown. But what with one thing and another coming up, she never seems to be able to make it.

Yet after all, as they argue, they might be a whole lot worse off than staying right where they are. Of course they are pretty far uptown, away from the theaters and restaurants; but everybody in their crowd, including themselves, has a car. So, to use Mr. Parmalee's very words, they should worry! It has often been remarked of Mr. Parmalee that it is not so much what he says as the way he says it.

Again, Mrs. Parmalee points out that it doesn't really matter much where they live, for they are hardly ever home, anyway. To which Mr. Parmalee retorts, just like a flash, that she has said a forkful!

And when you come right down to it, Mrs. Parmalee has seldom said a truer thing. It is indeed a cold night for the Parmalees when they have nothing to gather around but their own gas logs. The evening begins to hang heavy along around half past seven, and from then on things get no better rapidly.

The Parmalees are not ones to lose themselves in reading. Just let Mr. Parmalee see who won the first race, and give him a look at the financial page to ascertain whether Crucible Steel is plucking at the coverlet, and he is perfectly willing to call it a day as far as the pursuit of literature is concerned. As for Mrs. Parmalee, she masters the really novel murders and the better-class divorce cases, while for her heavier reading she depends on the current installment of the serial running in one of the more highly sexed magazines. That done with, she is through for the month.

Conversation could not be spoken of as a feature of the evening, either. Mr. Parmalee has been called, over and over again, a perfect scream when he is out on a party. But at home he doesn't really extend himself. A couple of half-hearted assents to his wife's comments on the shortcomings of the janitor and the unhealthful effects of such changeable weather —and that's, as someone has phrased it, that.

LIFE IN THE PARMALEE SET

So you can see for yourself about the only thing left in the way of parlor entertainment is to come to the mat. The Parmalees' battles are not mere family events; they come more under the head of community affairs. The entire apartment house takes an interest, almost a pride in them. Take them when they get going really strong and you won't miss a syllable, even as far off as the top-floor apartment on the other side of the house. On a clear night with the wind in the right direction the people living three houses down have been able to enjoy every word of it.

The bouts almost invariably end in a draw. Mr. Parmalee, it is true, has a somewhat broader command of language than his wife, but she has perfected a short contemptuous laugh which is the full equivalent of a nasty crack. It leaves Mr. Parmalee practically flat, with nothing more inspired to offer than an "Is that so?" or a "Yeah, you're perfect—you are!"

But these sporting events take place only rarely. The Parmalees have little time to indulge in home pleasures. Theirs is a full and sociable life. Mr. Parmalee is in what he jocosely calls the automobile game, and most of his friends are engaged in the same pursuit. And as their wives are Mrs. Parmalee's intimates, you can just imagine how nice and clubby that makes everything.

Their social day begins around five o'clock, when the dozen or so members of their set meet at one or another's apartment, for cocktails. The Parmalee coterie has been seriously inconvenienced since prohibition went into what has been called effect. It means that they can no longer meet at a hotel or a restaurant, as they used to in the old days. It is badly out of their way to gather at someone's house, for it often involves their having to go all the way downtown again for dinner. But they have to make the best of it, just like you or me.

And it is comforting to know that the gentlemen still manage, as a rule, to pick up a little something here and there before they are met by what Mr. Parmalee calls, with screaming effect, their better seven-eighths. The ladies, collectively, are usually referred to, by their husbands and by one another, as the girls—which is something of an understatement.

Up to the time of meeting, Mrs. Parmalee, like the rest of the girls, has put in a crowded afternoon at a matinee, the hairdresser's or the manicure's; a blinding polish on the finger nails is highly thought of by both the male and female members of the Parmalee's set. There is usually a great deal of trying on to be done, also, which does much toward taking up Mrs. Parmalee's time and Mr. Parmalee's money. He likes to see his wife dressed as elaborately as the wives of his friends. He is pretty fairly reasonable about the price of her clothes, just so long as they look as if they cost a lot. Neither of the Parmalees can see the point of this thing of paying high prices for unobtrusive garments. What they are after, Mr. Parmalee says, is their money's worth. As is only just.

Mrs. Parmalee and her friends dress with a soothing uniformity. They all hold the same ideas about style; really you'd seldom find a more congenial group in every way. All the girls, including Mrs. Parmalee, are fundamentally large and are increasing in weight almost daily. They are always going to start dieting next Monday.

In general style and get-up the girls resemble a group of very clever female impersonators. They run to rather larger and more densely plumed hats than the fashion absolutely insists upon, and they don't go in for any of your dull depressing colors. Always heavily jeweled, they have an adroit way of mingling an occasional imitation bracelet or necklace with the genuine articles, happily confident that the public will be fooled. In the warm weather their dresses are of transparent material about the arms and shoulders, showing provocative glimpses of very pink ribbons and of lace that you could hardly tell from the real.

There is a great deal of hearty gayety at the afternoon meetings of the crowd. You couldn't ask to see people among whom it is easier to get a laugh. Any popular line, such as "You don't know the half of it," or "You'd be surprised," is a sure-fire hit, no matter in what connection it is used. You might think that these jests would lose a little of their freshness after months of repetition, but you were never so wrong in your life. They never fail to go over big.

After a couple of hours of crackling repartee and whole-hearted drinking the Parmalees and their crowd set out for dinner. They dine at a downtown restaurant, if they plan going en masse to the theater afterwards. Otherwise they group themselves in their cars—most of the motors, like Mr. Parmalee's, are perquisites of being in the automobile game —and drive to some favorite road house, where they not only dine but get in some really constructive drinking during the evening. Mr. Parmalee is the life and soul of these parties. It is, his friends often say, as good as a show to hear him kid the waiter.

GUESS-WHAT-IT-COST-SPORTS

Dancing occurs sporadically after dinner, but most of the time is devoted to badinage. There is much good-natured banter, impossible to take in bad part, about the attentions paid by various of the husbands to the wives of various of the other husbands.

Often the conversation takes a serious turn among the men, as they tell about how much they had to pay for the last case of it. Stories are related of the staggering prices exacted for highballs at some restaurant where they will still listen to reason; and someone is sure to tell about the dinner he gave the night before, giving the menu in full detail, and as a climax calling upon his audience to guess what the grand total of the check was. These anecdotes are told with the pride that other sportsmen exhibit in telling about the size of the fish they caught.

The ladies spend what could be figured up to be the greater part of the evening in going out to the dressing room to keep their color schemes up to the mark.

In the warmer months the Parmalees make no radical change in their way of living. But though they do not go away for any long vacation they get a welcome glimpse of Nature by motoring to Long Beach for dinner three or four times a week with the rest of their crowd. They also manage to get a lot of wholesome country air and a refreshing eyeful of green grass down at the Belmont Park track.

What with all this talk of hard times and tight money wherever you go, it is cheering to see the Parmalees, who seem always to have it to spend. In his homey little chats with his wife Mr. Parmalee often gets quite worked up over where the money to meet their expenses is coming from; but he never lets it trouble him in his social life. Mr. Parmalee is a great advocate of being a good fellow when you have it. After all, as he has it figured out, the last places you can cut down are on theater tickets and restaurant checks and liquor.

It is also pleasant, in these days of change and restlessness, to think of the Parmalees going right along, never so much as thinking of wanting anything different. I wouldn't want to be the one to say that there is never just a dash of hard feeling between certain members of the crowd; the Parmalees never claimed to be any more than human. But such little differences as may spring up from time to time are easily dissolved in alcohol, and the crowd goes right on again, as usual.

After all, it takes Mr. Parmalee, with that wit of his, to sum up their whole existence in one clear-cut phrase. He says that it is a great life if you don't weaken.

THE SECOND FLOOR WEST

The minute you step into her apartment you realize that Mrs. Prowse is a woman of fine sensibilities. They stick out, as you might say, all over the place. You can see traces of them in the handmade candles dripping artistically over the polychrome candlesticks; in the single perfect blossom standing upright in a roomy bowl; in the polychrome bust of Dante on the mantel—taken, by many visitors, to be a likeness of William Gibbs

McAdoo; most of all in the books left all about, so that Mrs. Prowse, no matter where she is sitting, always can have one at hand, to lose herself in. They are, mainly, collections of verse, both free and under control, for Mrs. Prowse is a regular glutton for poetry. She is liable to repeat snatches of it at almost any time. There are heavier volumes, too, just as there are greater depths to Mrs. Prowse. Henry Adams, Conan Doyle in his latter manner, Blasco Ibañez, Clare Sheridan—all the boys and girls are represented.

Mrs. Prowse has not quite made up her mind as to whether it is more effective to have her books look well-thumbed or new and bright, though she rather inclines to the latter as being more decorative and less tiring. Most of the volumes are bound in red, which is, as Mrs. Prowse would put it, rather amusing with her orange curtains. If you were to pick up a book at random and go systematically through it you would find that, oddly enough, many of the pages, along after the middle, are uncut. But Mrs. Prowse's guests are not apt to go through her books, and the effect is, as I was saying only a minute ago, great.

It is not only literature that Mrs. Prowse patronizes. Beauty in any form gets a big hand from her. She can find it, too, in places where you or I would never think of looking. The delicate brown of a spoiled peach, the calm gray of a puddle on the sidewalk—such things never escape her.

Perhaps it is because she is so used to directing attention to things you might otherwise miss that Mrs. Prowse follows up the idea and coaxes you to notice those beauties which you couldn't very well avoid. She is always putting in a good word for the sunset or the sky or the moon, never letting slip an opportunity to get in a little press work for Nature.

She feels such things considerably more than most people. Sometimes, indeed, her appreciation of the beautiful stops just short of knocking her for what is academically called a goal. In the midst of a friendly conversation, or perhaps when it is her turn to bid in a bridge game, Mrs. Prowse will suddenly be rendered speechless, and lean tensely forward, gazing hungrily out the window at a lonely star or a wind-tossed cloud. She has quite a bad time in pulling herself together on these occasions. She must start perceptibly, look dazedly around the room, and press her hand against her eyes for a moment before she can return to the commonplace.

It is a blow to Mrs. Prowse and her husband that there has never been what Mrs. Prowse refers to as the patter of little feet about the house. But she manages to get a bit of comfort out of the situation. With no children to tie her down she is free to do all the worth-while things that beckon her. Look, for example, at what she accomplished during the past winter alone. She heard several lectures by visiting poets; went to two New

Thought meetings; had her horoscope read and learned that her name should have been Valda; attended the annual luncheon of a club devoted to translating Browning into English; went to tea in Greenwich Village three times; took a lesson in lampshade making; heard a debate on whether or not a woman should take her husband's name, and what of it; and had her hair permanently waved.

But at that, Mrs. Prowse does not feel that her time is fully occupied. What she would really like, she admits, is to work, and work hard. And there are several jobs for which she is forced to confess that she is just as well fitted at the next one.

She would consider, for instance, giving readings from the modern poets or doing selections from Maeterlinck to a soft accompaniment on the piano. She has thought, and pretty seriously, too, of the stage, which, she can't help feeling, she could do much to raise from its present commercialism. It is really just a matter of ethics that keeps her from rushing right out and going to work at one of these positions. She doesn't feel that it would be quite fair for her to take the job away from someone who might be in real need of the money.

You wouldn't want to say right out that Mr. Prowse is not in sympathy with his wife's ideas, but then again you would scarcely be justified in saying that he cheered her on. Mr. Prowse is apt to let things take their course, and not do any worrying about them.

He is fond of his business, golf, the Yankees, meat cooked rather rare, musical comedies and his friends. Mrs. Prowse accompanies him to the theater, and often tells his friends that they must come up sometime soon. But there is about her at these times an air of gentle martyrdom. You'd almost think you could hear the roar of the waiting lions, she does it so realistically.

Mr. Prowse's policy of going about just as cheerfully as if his wife had no sensibilities whatever is a uniquely annoying one to her. Some of her most effective moods are absolutely frittered away on him. Mrs. Prowse has feelings which are almost always being severely injured; you run a chance of stepping on them if you come within ten feet of her. She is too delicately strung to come bluntly out and say what has hurt her. She seeks refuge in a brooding silence, and you must guess what it is all about.

MISUNDERSTOOD BUT FAITHFUL

Mr. Prowse is particularly bad at the game. He never seems to realize that anything is wrong. Sometimes she even has to call attention to her mental suffering and its cause. Even then he cannot be drawn into a really satisfactory battle. And it is, you will agree, practically impossible to work up any dramatic interest in married life when one of the principals won't take part in the big scenes.

It is little wonder that Mrs. Prowse, though never actually saying that her marriage is anything but happy, sometimes intimates that she is not always understood.

She has always been somewhat taken with the idea of having an assortment of tame young men about her—nothing really out of the way, of course, just have them come to tea, and take her to picture galleries, and send flowers, and maybe write verses, which she could drop where her husband would find them. She has even gone so far, in the privacy of her room, as to invent a rather nice little scene, in which she mapped out what she would say to some smitten young tea-hound should he become too serious. It is a credit to Mrs. Prowse to report that her answer was to the effect that she could never forget the vows she made to Mr. Prowse at the altar.

In all the books, as it is useless to tell you, it is no trouble at all for a married woman to gather a flock of attentive young men about her. But Mrs. Prowse has found it rather rough going. The young men don't seem to fall in with the idea. There was, it is true, a young man she met at a tea who was interested in interior decoration. In answer to her invitation he did call one afternoon—it was just by luck that she was wearing her beaded Georgette crêpe—and told her all about how she ought to live with purples. But when he found out that she really didn't feel they could have the living room done over for another year anyway he faded gently out of her life.

And that, as a matter of fact, was about as far as Mrs. Prowse ever got along those lines.

As is no more than you would expect, Mrs. Prowse admits but few to her circle of intimates. She is constantly being disappointed in people, finding out that they have no depths. Perhaps the sharpest blow, though one frequently experienced, is in having people whom she had accepted as kindred spirits turn out to be clever on the surface, but with no soul when you came right down to it. Mrs. Prowse often says that somehow she can never bring herself to be intimate with people who are only clever.

And that really works out awfully well, for it makes it mutual.

THE THIRD FLOOR EAST

You couldn't find, if you were to take the thing really to heart and make a search of the city, a woman who works harder, day in and day out, than Mrs. Amy. She says so herself.

In the first place there are two young Amys to occupy her attention. Everyone in the building is conscious of the presence of the two young Amys, but the Parmalees, in the apartment below, are most keenly aware of it.

It is in the fresh morning, when the Parmalees are striving to fulfill a normal desire for sleep, that the young Amys seem particularly near. The Amy children are early risers, and they have none of that morning languor from which office workers are so apt to suffer. Mrs. Parmalee, whose bedroom is directly beneath theirs, has often said that she would be the last one to feel any surprise if at any moment they were to come right on through.

Of course there is a resident nurse who looks after the little ones, but Mrs. Amy seems to find little or no relief in this. The nurse watches over them all day, and sleeps in the bed between their cribs at night, but, as Mrs. Amy says, she cannot worry over them as a mother would.

It is in worrying that Mrs. Amy accomplishes some of her most strenuous work. She confesses that there is scarcely a minute when her mind is at rest. Her worries even cut in on her nights, and she describes graphically how, tossing from side to side, she hears the clock strike twelve, half past twelve, one, half past one—sometimes it goes on that way up to three.

The past months have been especially trying to her, for the older Amy child has lately started school. He attends the public school around the corner, where his mother cannot help but feel that his time is devoted less to acquiring education than to running a splendid chance of contracting diseases and bringing them home, to share with his sister. During his first term Mrs. Amy has at different times detected in him symptoms of mumps, measles, chicken pox, scarlet fever, whooping cough and infantile paralysis. It is true that none of these ever developed, but that's not the point. The thing is that his mother was just as much worried as if he had had record cases of them all.

Then there are her household cares to prey upon her. Annie, a visiting maid, arrives before breakfast and stays till after dinner, but Mrs. Amy frequently sighs that she is far from satisfactory. Twice, now, her gravy has been distinctly lumpy, and just the other day she omitted to address Mrs. Amy as "ma'am" in answering her. There may be those who can throw off such things, but Mrs. Amy takes them hard. Only the fact that she worries so over the prospect of not being able to get another maid prevents her from marching right out into the kitchen and formally presenting Annie with the air.

It seems as if there were some great conspiracy to prevent things' breaking right for Mrs. Amy. Misfortunes pile up all through the day, so that by evening she has a long hard-luck story with which to greet Mr. Amy.

All through dinner she beguiles him with a recital of what she has had to endure that day—how the milkman didn't come and she was forced to send out to the grocer's; how she hurried to answer the telephone at great personal inconvenience, only to find it was someone for Annie; how the butcher had no veal cutlets; how the man didn't fix the pantry sink; how Junior refused to take his cereal; how the druggist omitted to send the soap she ordered; how—but you get the idea. There is always enough material for her to continue her story all through dinner and carry it over till bedtime with scarcely a repetition.

Mr. Amy would be glad to do what he could to lighten her burdens, but Mrs. Amy, though she all but hints in her conversation that many of her troubles may be laid at her husband's door, refuses to let him crash in on her sphere.

He has a confessed longing, for instance, to take the children out on the nurse's Sundays off. But Mrs. Amy cannot be induced to see it. Her feeling is that he would be just as apt as not to take them in a street car, or to the zoo, where they would get themselves simply covered with germs. As she says, she would worry so while they were gone that she would be virtually no good by the time they got back.

Mr. Amy often seeks to persuade his wife to join him in an evening's revelry at the movies or the theater, but she seldom consents. Her mind cannot come down to the pleasures before her when it is all taken up with what might be going on at home at that very minute. The house might burn up, the children might run temperatures, a sudden rain might come up and spoil the bedroom curtains; anything is liable to happen while she is away. So you can see how much there is on her side when she tells Mr. Amy that she feels safer at home.

Occasionally the Amys have a few friends in to dinner. Mrs. Amy obliges at these functions with one of her original monologues on the things that have gone wrong in her household during that day alone. They would entertain oftener, but what with the uncertainty of Annie's gravy and the vagaries of the tradespeople, the mental strain is too great for Mrs. Amy.

Mr. Amy often has to take a man out for dinner, in the way of business. He used to bring his business acquaintances to dine with him at home, but it got on Mrs. Amy's nerves to that degree that she had to put a stop to the practice.

She said it just bored her to death to have to sit there and listen to them talk about nothing but their business.

THE THIRD FLOOR WEST

What is really the keynote of the Tippetts' living room is the copy of the Social Register lying temptingly open on the table. It is as if Mrs. Tippett had been absorbed in it, and had only torn herself from its fascinating pages in order to welcome you.

It is almost impossible for you to overlook the volume, but if you happen to, Mrs. Tippett will help you out by pointing to it with an apologetic little laugh. No one knows better than she, she says, that its orange-and-black binding is all out of touch with the color scheme of the room; but, you see, she uses it for a telephone book and she is simply lost without it. Just what Mrs. Tippett does when she wants to look up the telephone number of her laundress or her grocer is not explained. And few people have the strength to go into the subject unassisted.

Some day when you happen to be reading the Social Register and come to the T's, you will find that Mr. and Mrs. Tippett's names are not there. Naturally you will take this for a printer's error. But it is only too intentional. The Tippetts do not yet appear in the register, though they have every hope of eventually making the grade.

As soon as Mrs. Tippett feels that the one about using the Social Register as a telephone book has sunk in, she will begin to laugh off her apartment. She says that it is the greatest joke, their living way up here in this funny old house that has been made over into flats. You have no idea how the Tippetts' friends simply howl at the thought of their living up on the West Side.

Whimsically Mrs. Tippett adds that what with so many social leaders moving down to Greenwich Village and over by the East River, it seems to her that the smart thing to do nowadays is to live in the most out-of-the-way place you can find.

Mr. Tippett will enlarge on the thing for you, if you stay until he comes home from business. Mr. Tippett solicits advertising for one of the excessively doggy magazines. There is not much in it, but it gives him an opportunity to come in contact with some awfully nice people. He will put over some perfect corkers about living so far uptown that he goes to work by the Albany boat; or he may even refer to his place of residence as Canada for you.

He bears out his wife's statements as to their friends' amusement at the apartment; in fact you gather from the chat that the Tippetts' chief reason for occupying the place is the good laugh it affords their friends.

The Tippetts are exceedingly well connected, as you will learn just as soon as they get a chance to tell you. Mr. Tippett's own cousin is not only included in the Social Register but has been referred to in the society weeklies—oh, not a breath of scandal, of course!—and often figures in the morning papers under the head of "among those present were." The Tippetts are deeply devoted to her. She is seldom absent from their conversation. If she is ill their calls are more regular than the doctor's. When she is away they carry her letters about and read them aloud to you at a moment's notice. Way back in midsummer they start planning her Christmas present.

The Tippetts are kept busy the year round. Sometimes Mrs. Tippett says wistfully she almost wishes they were not quite so much in demand. Almost every day she has to keep an appointment with some friend, to have tea at one of the more exclusive hotels. She keeps a sharp lookout for any smart people that may be hanging around, so that at dinner she can breathlessly tell her husband whom they were with and what they had on.

It is great fun to be out with Mrs. Tippett. She can tell you who everybody is, where they originated, whom they married, what their incomes are, and what is going the rounds about them. From a close following of the society papers she really feels that she knows intimately all those who figure in their columns. She goes right ahead with the idea, and speaks of them by the nicknames under which they appear in the society press.

Mrs. Tippett is inclined to be a trifle overpunctual; haven't you heard it called a good fault? She often arrives rather early for her tea engagements, and so, not being one to waste time, she dashes off a few notes on the hotel stationery while waiting.

Mr. Tippett—it may be from three years of close association—has got from her this admirable habit of catching up with his correspondence at odd times. For instance, when he drops in at some club, as the guest of a member, he frequently finds a few minutes to sit down at a desk and scribble off a letter on the convenient paper.

The Tippetts have many obligations to fulfill. They are so fond of Mr. Tippett's cousin that they try never to disappoint her when she invites them to anything. This means they must spend two or three week-ends at her country place, dine with her several times during the winter, and use her opera tickets once or even oftener. You'd really be amazed at the

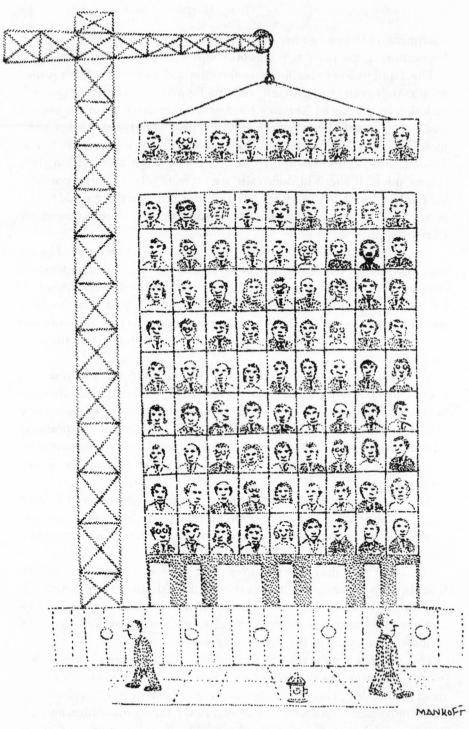

ROBERT MANKOFF

supply of subsequent conversation that the Tippetts can get out of any of these events.

Besides all this, they usually manage to attend one or two of the large charity affairs, for which tickets may be purchased at a not-so-nominal sum, and they always try to work in one session at the horse show.

This past season has been particularly crowded for Mrs. Tippett. Twice her volunteered aid has been accepted by a woman she met at Mr. Tippett's cousin's house, and she has helped arrange the counters at rummage sales. In short, things are coming along nicely with the Tippetts. They have every reason to be satisfied with their life.

Which is remarkably like Mr. Tippett's business, in that, though there is not much in it, it brings them in contact with some awfully nice people.

THE TOP FLOOR EAST

There was a time when Mrs. Huff kept her own carriage and lived in a three-story house with a conservatory between the dining room and the pantry. I don't feel that I am violating any confidence in telling you this, because Mrs. Huff would be the first one to say so.

All this was some time ago, when Mrs. Huff's daughter Emma was still in school—in private school, Mrs. Huff is careful to say. And one good look at Mrs. Huff's daughter Emma will convince you that her schooldays must have been indeed some time ago.

Shortly before Mr. Huff did what his widow refers to as passed on, the fortune began to meet with reverses, due mainly to Mr. Huff's conviction that he could put Wall Street in its place during his spare time. Mrs. Huff clung as long as possible to her own carriage and the three-story house with the conservatory, but she had eventually to let them go, in the order named. For a good many years, now, she has been settled in this apartment, in the midst of as much of her palmy-days furniture as could be wedged into the place.

But to Mrs. Huff those good old days are as yesterday. They are as fresh in her mind and her conversation. She can—does, even—go on for hours about how often they had to have the palms in the conservatory replaced, and how much they paid for the fountain, which represented a little girl and boy holding a pink iron umbrella over themselves—she can see it now. From there she drifts into reminiscences of all the trouble they had with drunken coachmen before they got their old Thomas, who was with them twelve years.

Mrs. Huff and her daughter live the calm and ladylike life befitting former conservatory owners. They are attended by one maid, Hannah by name, who was once Emma's nurse. She does the housework, washing, marketing and cooking; arranges Mrs. Huff's hair and corsets; remodels the ladies' clothes in the general direction of the styles; and is with difficulty persuaded to accept her wages each month—the same wages—which is rather a pretty touch of sentiment—as she was getting when she first entered Mrs. Huff's employ. As Mrs. Huff says, Hannah is really quite a help to them.

Mrs. Huff relies chiefly for her diversion on the funerals of her many acquaintances and connections. She reads the obituary column each morning in much the same spirit that other people look over the What Is Going on Today section. Occasionally if the day is fine and there is no really important funeral on hand she takes a little jaunt out to a favorite cemetery and visits various friends there.

Her minor amusements include calls on many sick and a few healthy acquaintances, and an occasional card party. Her stories of how often they had to change the palms and how much they paid for the fountain are the features of these affairs.

Miss Emma Huff suffers slightly from hallucinations; no, suffers is hardly the word. She manages to get quite a good time out of them.

She is under the impression that she is the desired of every man with whom she comes in contact. She is always arriving home fluttering from her adventure with the overzealous clerk in the shoe shop, or the bus driver who was too careful about helping her alight, or the floorwalker who almost insisted on taking her arm to direct her to the notions. Miss Huff never dares stay late at a friend's house, for fear some man may spring from the shadows and abduct her on the way home.

Between adventures Miss Huff does a good deal of embroidery. If there were ever a contest in putting cross-stitch baskets on guest towels she would be entered scratch. Also, she is a mean hand at copying magazine covers in water colors. Last year she made all her own Christmas cards, and if all goes well she plans doing it again next Christmas.

Once or twice it has been suggested by relatives or overintimate friends that it might be rather nice for Miss Huff to commercialize her talents. Or, if her feeling for art would not allow that, she might find some light and ladylike employment—just to pass the time, is always hastily added.

Mrs. Huff awards these advisers with what, in anybody else, would be a dirty look. She does not waste words to reply to any suggestion that a daughter of hers should enter the business world. For Mrs. Huff can never forget that she once kept her own carriage and lived in a three-story house with a conservatory between the dining room and the pantry.

THE TOP FLOOR WEST

There are, of course, a Mr. and a Mrs. Plank, but they sink indistin-guishably into the background. Mrs. Plank may be roughly summarized as a woman who always knows what you ought to do for that indigestion, while Mr. Plank is continually going into a new business where "none of us is going to get much money at first."

The real life of the Plank party is Arlette—Mrs. Plank let herself go, for the only time in her life, in the choosing of her daughter's name.

Arlette is, at the present writing, crowding nineteen summers, and she looks every day of it. As for her mode of living, just ask anybody in the apartment house.

Arlette stopped school three years ago by her own request. She had no difficulty in convincing her mother that she had enough education to get along with anywhere. Mrs. Plank is a firm believer in the theory that, unless she is going to teach, there is no earthly use of a girl's wasting her time in going all through high school. Men, says Mrs. Plank—and she has been married twenty-one years, so who could be a better judge—do not select as their wives these women who are all full of education. So for the past three years Arlette's intellectual decks have been cleared for matri-mony.

But Arlette has not yet given a thought to settling down into marriage. There was a short season when she thought rather seriously of taking up a screen career, after someone had exclaimed over the startling likeness between her and Louise Lovely. But so far she has taken it out in doing her hair in the accepted movie-star manner, to look as if it had been arranged with an egg-beater.

Most of Arlette's time is spent in dashing about in motors driven by young men of her acquaintance. The cars were originally designed to accommodate two people, but they rarely travel without seven or eight on board. These motors, starting out from or drawing up to the apartment house, with their precious loads of human freight, are one of the big spectacles of the block.

THE SKIDS FOR EDDIE

It is remarkable how without the services of a secretary Arlette prevents her dates from becoming mixed. She deftly avoids any embarrassing overlapping of suitors. Her suitors would, if placed end to end, reach halfway up to the Woolworth Tower and halfway back.

They are all along much the same design—slim, not too tall, with hair shining like linoleum. They dress in suits which, though obviously new, have the appearance of being just outgrown, with half belts, and lapels visible from the back.

The average duration of Arlette's suitors is five weeks. At the end of that time she hands the favored one a spray of dewy raspberries and passes on to the next in line.

The present incumbent, Eddie to his friends, has lasted rather longer than usual. His greatest asset is the fact that he is awfully dry. He has a way of saying "absotively" and "posolutely" that nearly splits Arlette's sides. When he is introduced he says, with a perfectly straight face, "You're pleased to meet me," and Arlette can hardly contain herself. He interpolates a lot of Ed Wynn's stuff into the conversation, and Arlette thinks it is just as good as the original, if not better.

Then, too, he knows a perfectly swell step. You take three to the right, then three to the left, then toddle, then turn suddenly all the way around and end with a dip; the effect is little short of professional.

But Arlette has lately met a young man who has his own car and can almost always get his father's limousine when he takes you to the theater. Also, his father owns a chain of moving-picture houses, and he can get a pass for her.

So it looks from here as if the skids were all ready to be applied to Eddie.

Mrs. Plank worries a bit over her daughter's incessant activities. She hears stories of the goings-on of these modern young people that vaguely trouble her, and she does wish that Arlette would take more rest. Naturally, though, she hesitates to bring the matter to her daughter's attention. Occasionally she goes so far as to hint that Arlette might take a little interest in watching her do the housework, so that she can pick up some inside stuff on household matters that might be useful in her married life.

For all Mrs. Plank wants, she says, is to live to see her daughter making some good man happy.

Arlette's ideas, now, seem to be more along the lines of making some good men happy.

ROBERT BENCHLEY

Opera Synopses

SOME SAMPLE OUTLINES OF GRAND OPERA PLOTS
FOR HOME STUDY

I

DIE MEISTER-GENOSSENSCHAFT

SCENE: *The Forests of Germany.*
TIME: *Antiquity.*

CAST

STRUDEL, *God of Rain* . . . . Basso
SCHMALZ, *God of Slight Drizzle* . . . . Tenor
IMMERGLÜCK, *Goddess of the Six Primary Colors* . . . . Soprano
LUDWIG DAS EIWEISS, *the Knight of the Iron Duck* . . . . Baritone
THE WOODPECKER . . . . Soprano

ARGUMENT

The basis of "Die Meister-Genossenschaft" is an old legend of Germany which tells how the Whale got his Stomach.

ACT 1

The Rhine at Low Tide Just Below Weldschnoffen.—Immerglück has grown weary of always sitting on the same rock with the same fishes swimming by every day, and sends for Schwül to suggest something to do. Schwül asks her how she would like to have pass before her all the wonders of the world fashioned by the hand of man. She says, rotten. He then suggests that Ringblatz, son of Pflucht, be made to appear before her and fight a mortal combat with the Iron Duck. This pleases Immerglück and she summons to her the four dwarfs: Hot Water, Cold Water, Cool, and Cloudy. She bids them bring Ringblattz to her. They refuse, because Pflucht has at one time rescued them from being buried alive by acorns, and, in a rage, Immerglück strikes them all dead with a thunderbolt.

ACT 2

A Mountain Pass.—Repenting of her deed, Immerglück has sought advice of the giants, Offen and Besitz, and they tell her that she must procure the magic zither which confers upon its owner the power to go to sleep while apparently carrying on a conversation. This magic zither has been hidden for three hundred centuries in an old bureau drawer, guarded by the Iron Duck, and, although many have attempted to rescue it, all have died of a strange ailment just as success was within their grasp.

But Immerglück calls to her side Dampfboot, the tinsmith of the gods, and bids him make for her a tarnhelm or invisible cap which will enable her to talk to people without their understanding a word she says. For a dollar and half extra Dampfboot throws in a magic ring which renders its wearer insensible. Thus armed, Immerglück starts out for Walhalla, humming to herself.

ACT 3

The Forest Before the Iron Duck's Bureau Drawer.—Merglitz, who has up till this time held his peace, now descends from a balloon and demands the release of Betty. It has been the will of Wotan that Merglitz and Betty should meet on earth and hate each other like poison, but Zweiback, the druggist of the gods, has disobeyed and concocted a love-potion which has rendered the young couple very unpleasant company. Wotan, enraged, destroys them with a protracted heat spell.

Encouraged by this sudden turn of affairs, Immerglück comes to earth in a boat drawn by four white Holsteins, and, seated alone on a rock, remembers aloud to herself the days when she was a girl. Pilgrims from Augenblick, on their way to worship at the shrine of Schmürr, hear the sound of reminiscence coming from the rock and stop in their march to sing a hymn of praise for the drying-up of the crops. They do not recognize Immerglück, as she has her hair done differently, and think that she is a beggar girl selling pencils.

In the meantime, Ragel, the papercutter of the gods, has fashioned himself a sword on the forge of Schmalz, and has called the weapon "Assistance-in-Emergency." Armed with "Assistance-in-Emergency" he comes to earth, determined to slay the Iron Duck and carry off the beautiful Irma.

But Frimsel overhears the plan and has a drink brewed which is given to Ragel in a golden goblet and which, when drunk, makes him forget his past and causes him to believe that he is Schnorr, the God of Fun. While laboring under this spell, Ragel has a funeral pyre built on the summit of a high mountain and, after lighting it, climbs on top of it with a mandolin which he plays until he is consumed.

Immerglück never marries.

II

IL MINNESTRONE
(Peasant Love)

Scene: *Venice and Old Point Comfort.*
Time: *Early 16th Century.*

Cast

ALFONSO, *Duke of Minnestrone* . . . . Baritone
PARTOLA, *a Peasant Girl* . . . . Soprano

CLEANSO		Tenor
TURINO	*Young Noblemen of Venice.*	Tenor
BOMBO		Basso
LUDOVICO	*Assassins in the Service of*	Basso
ASTOLFO	*Cafeteria Rusticana*	Methodist
	Townspeople, Cabbies and Sparrows	

Argument

"Il Minnestrone" is an allegory of the two sides of a man's nature (good and bad), ending at last in an awfully comical mess with everyone dead.

Act 1

A Public Square, Ferrara.—During a peasant festival held to celebrate the sixth consecutive day of rain, Rudolpho, a young nobleman, sees Lilliano, daughter of the village bell-ringer, dancing along throwing artificial roses at herself. He asks of his secretary who the young woman is, and his secretary, in order to confuse Rudolpho and thereby win the hand of his ward, tells him that it is his (Rudolpho's) own mother, disguised for the festival. Rudolpho is astounded. He orders her arrest.

ACT 2

Banquet Hall in Gorgio's Palace.—Lilliano has not forgotten Breda, her old nurse, in spite of her troubles, and determines to avenge herself for the many insults she received in her youth by poisoning her (Breda). She therefore invites the old nurse to a banquet and poisons her. Presently a knock is heard. It is Ugolfo. He has come to carry away the body of Michelo and to leave an extra quart of pasteurized. Lilliano tells him that she no longer loves him, at which he goes away, dragging his feet sulkily.

ACT 3

In Front of Emilo's House.—Still thinking of the old man's curse, Borsa has an interview with Cleanso, believing him to be the Duke's wife. He tells him things can't go on as they are, and Cleanso stabs him. Just at this moment Betty comes rushing in from school and falls in a faint. Her worst fears have been realized. She has been insulted by Sigmundo, and presently dies of old age. In a fury, Ugolfo rushes out to kill Sigmundo and, as he does so, the dying Rosenblatt rises on one elbow and curses his mother.

III

LUCY DE LIMA

SCENE: *Wales.*
TIME: *1700 (Greenwich).*

CAST

WILLIAM WONT, *Lord of Glennnn* . . . . Basso
LUCY WAGSTAFF, *his daughter* . . . . Soprano
BERTRAM, *her lover* . . . . Tenor
LORD ROGER, *friend of Bertram* . . . . Soprano
IRMA, *attendant to Lucy* . . . . Basso
Friends, Retainers, and Members of the local Lodge of Elks.

ARGUMENT

"Lucy de Lima," is founded on the well-known story by Boccaccio of the same name and address.

ACT 1

Gypsy Camp Near Waterbury.—The gypsies, led by Edith, go singing through the camp on the way to the fair. Following them comes Despard, the gypsy leader, carrying Ethel, whom he has just kidnapped from her father, who had previously just kidnapped her from her mother. Despard places Ethel on the ground and tells Mona, the old hag, to watch over her. Mona nurses a secret grudge against Despard for having once cut off her leg, and decides to change Ethel for Nettie, another kidnapped child. Ethel pleads with Mona to let her stay with Despard, for she has fallen in love with him on the ride over. But Mona is obdurate.

ACT 2

The Fair.—A crowd of sightseers and villagers is present. Roger appears, looking for Laura. He can not find her. Laura appears, looking for Roger. She can not find him. The gypsy queen approaches Roger and thrusts into his hand the locket stolen from Lord Brym. Roger looks at it and is frozen with astonishment, for it contains the portrait of his mother when she was in high school. He then realizes that Laura must be his sister, and starts out to find her.

ACT 3

Hall in the Castle.—Lucy is seen surrounded by every luxury, but her heart is sad. She has just been shown a forged letter from Stewart saying that he no longer loves her, and she remembers her old free life in the mountains and longs for another romp with Ravensbane and Wolfshead, her old pair of rompers. The guests begin to assemble for the wedding, each bringing a roast ox. They chide Lucy for not having her dress changed. Just at this moment the gypsy band bursts in and Cleon tells the wedding party that Elsie and not Edith is the child who was stolen from the summer-house, showing the blood-stained derby as proof. At this, Lord Brym repents and gives his blessing on the pair, while the fishermen and their wives celebrate in the courtyard.

S. J. Perelman

A platinum place in American humor belongs to Sidney Joseph Perelman. "In the dementia praecox field," said Robert Benchley, "he is in a class by himself."

He was also in a class by himself for self-description:

Button-cute, rapier-keen, wafer-thin and pauper-poor is S. J. Perelman, whose tall, stooping figure is better known to the twilit half-world of five continents than to Publishers' Row. That he possesses the power to become invisible to finance companies; that his laboratory is tooled up to manufacture Frankenstein-type monsters on an incredible scale; and that he owns one of the rare mouths in which butter has never melted are legends treasured by every schoolboy.

Retired today to peaceful Erwinna, Pennsylvania, Perelman raises turkeys which he occasionally displays on Broadway, stirs little from his alembics and retorts. Those who know hint that the light burning late in his laboratory may result in a breathtaking electric bill. Queried, he shrugs with the fatalism of your true Oriental. "Mektoub," he observes curtly. "It is written."

And *how* it is written when it is written by Perelman! In April 1978 I was invited to introduce him at Carnegie Hall, where he was to receive a Special Achievement Medal at the National Book Awards. He is a tough act to precede, but he was pleased by whatever was said and invited me out for a glass of water. Seated in a small café, I asked him, "Do you ever laugh when you write?"

"I think," he said, getting no argument from me, "that when one starts writing anything comic (that is, a *young* person), he literally rolls on the floor with enjoyment at his own skill. That disappears when you become professional and it turns into a very gloomy business. The creation of comedy is essentially a rather depressing business on the whole."

"Are there young humorists you admire?"

"Woody Allen. I think Woody is an enormously gifted man. I was so impressed with *Annie Hall* that I went to see it three times."

"Whom do you rank above all others?"

"James Joyce. I think he's the greatest comic writer that the language ever had. His writing is a dizzying flight of the comic imagination. I'm sorry to say that our particular kind of humor is a dying form."

Perelman had been a visiting lecturer at the University of California.

"That was a rather depressing experience. The questions leveled at me by the students in the journalism and drama classes fell into two categories. First, they all wanted to know how to get a good agent. They seemed to believe that getting a good agent was the way you licked anything. And the other question was: 'Could Harpo Marx really talk?' Beyond that I was unable to discuss very much. I must say I have no idea what they were thinking of doing."

We spoke of his pleasure in eviscerating clichés.

"I'm absolutely daffy about clichés. They are the consequence of a lifetime of reading absolutely abominable work, which I think is necessary for every writer. There's great stress placed upon children and young people to read the best books. I don't agree with this. I think you have to read an awful lot of mulch as a kind of foundation for your future life. And I think I have read more garbage, perhaps, than anybody should."

"Your vocabulary is often esoteric and sends me to my dictionary, which is good for me," I said, "but I've wondered if you carry carts of unusual words in your head."

"In a rather pompous way, I use the word *Flaubertian,* meaning that I do think there is an exact word for almost everything. And I do bother about words. Most of the words, in fact all of them, are in Roget's Thesaurus. That's perfectly obvious. And since I'm what is technically in the writing craft called a bleeder—that is, I write hard—I take the trouble to look up and hope to find the right word."

"And rewrite?"

"Rather than rewrite, I work slowly, sentence by sentence. Which has its pitfalls. James Thurber, for example, would write consecutive drafts swiftly. Innumerable drafts. I myself toil inch by inch, so to speak. It may surprise people to know that a man like Raymond Chandler, whom I knew quite well, produced writing with an admirable pace and swiftness. This was the product of unending toil. The myth that there are individuals so gifted that they can just spin the words off is one that should be destroyed."

"So how would S. J. Perelman describe the writing of S. J. Perelman?"

"The best description that I've ever heard was from A. J. Liebling. When he particularly liked someone's work he would say, 'He's a very careful writer.' And I think that's the ultimate compliment."

Reader, enjoy now S. J. Perelman, a very careful writer.   **G.S.**

S. J. PERELMAN

No Starch in the Dhoti, S'il Vous Plaît

Up until recently, I had always believed that nobody on earth could deliver a throwaway line with quite the sang-froid of a certain comedian I worked for in Hollywood during the thirties. You probably don't recall the chap, but his hallmark was a big black mustache, a cigar, and a loping gait, and his three brothers, also in the act, impersonated with varying degrees of success a mute, an Italian, and a clean-cut boy. My respect for Julio (to cloak his identity partially) stemmed from a number of pearls that fell from his lips during our association, notably one inspired by an argument over dietary customs. We were having dinner at an off-Broadway hotel, in the noisiest locale imaginable outside the annual fair at Nizhnii Novgorod. There were at least a dozen people in the party—lawyers, producers, agents, brokers, astrologers, tipsters, and various assorted sycophants—for, like all celebrated theatrical personages, my man liked to travel with a retinue. The dining room was jammed, some paid-up ghoul from Local 802 was interpreting the "Habanera" on an electric organ over the uproar, and, just to insure dyspepsia, a pair of adagio dancers were flinging themselves with abandon in and out of our food. I was seated next to Julio, who was discoursing learnedly to me on his favorite subject, anatomical deviations among showgirls. Halfway through the meal, we abruptly became aware of a dispute across the table between several of our companions.

"It is *not* just religious!" one was declaring hotly. "They knew a damn sight more about hygiene than you think in those Biblical days!"

"That still don't answer my question!" shouted the man he had addressed. "If they allow veal and mutton and beef, why do they forbid pork?"

"Because it's unclean, you dummy," the other rasped. "I'm trying to tell you—the pig is an unclean animal!"

"What's that?" demanded Julio, his voice slicing through the altercation. "The pig an unclean animal?" He rose from his chair and repeated the charge to be certain everyone within fifty feet was listening. "The pig an unclean animal? Why, the pig is the cleanest animal there is—except my father, of course." And dropped like a falcon back into his chow mein.

As I say, I'd gone along for years considering Julio pre-eminent in tossing off this kind of grenade, and then one Sunday a few weeks ago, in the *Times* Magazine, I stumbled across an item that leaves no doubt he has been deposed. The new champ is Robert Trumbull, the former Indian correspondent of the paper and a most affable bird with whom I once spent an afternoon crawling around the Qutb Minar, outside New Delhi. In the course of an article called "Portrait of a Symbol Named Nehru," Mr. Trumbull had the following to say: "Nehru is accused of having a congenital distaste for Americans because of their all too frequent habit of bragging and of being patronizing when in unfamiliar surroundings. It is said that in the luxurious and gracious house of his father, the late Pandit Motilal Nehru—who sent his laundry to Paris—the young Jawaharlal's British nurse used to make caustic remarks to the impressionable boy about the table manners of his father's American guests."

It was, of course, the utter nonchalance of the phrase "who sent his laundry to Paris" that knocked me galley-west. Obviously, Trumbull wasn't referring to one isolated occasion; he meant that the Pandit made a practice of consigning his laundry to the post, the way one used to under the academic elms. But this was no callow sophomore shipping his wash home to save money. A man willful and wealthy enough to have it shuttled from one hemisphere to another could hardly have been prompted by considerations of thrift. He must have been a consummate perfectionist, a fussbudget who wanted every last pleat in order, and, remembering my own Homeric wrangles with laundrymen just around the corner, I blenched at the complications his overseas dispatch must have entailed. Conducted long before there was any air service between India and Europe, it would have involved posting the stuff by sea—a minimum of three weeks in each direction, in addition to the time it took for processing. Each trip would have created problems of customs examination, valuation, duty (unless Nehru senior got friends to take it through for him, which was improbable; most people detest transporting laundry across the world, even their own). The old gentleman had evidently had a limitless wardrobe, to be able to dispense with portions of it for three months at a time.

The major headache, as I saw it, though, would have been coping with the *blanchisseur* himself. How did Pandit Motilal get any service or redress out of him at such long range? There were the countless vexations that always arise: the missing sock, the half-pulverized button, the insistence on petrifying everything with starch despite the most detailed instructions. The more I thought about it, the clearer it became that he must have been enmeshed in an unending correspondence with the laundry owner. I suggest, accordingly, that while the exact nature of his letters can only be guessed at, it might be useful—or, by the same token, useless—to reconstruct a few, together with the replies they evoked. Even if they accomplish nothing else, they should help widen the breach between East and West.

ALLAHABAD,
UNITED PROVINCES,
JUNE 7, 1903

Pleurniche et Cie.,
124, Avenue de la Grande Armée, Paris.
My dear M. PLEURNICHE:

You may be interested to learn—though I doubt that anything would stir you out of your vegetable torpor—that your pompous, florid, and illiterate scrawl of the 27th arrived here with insufficient postage, forcing me to disgorge one rupee three annas to the mailman. How symbolic of your character, how magnificently consistent! Not content with impugning the quality of the cambric in my drawers, you contrive to make me *pay* for the insult. That transcends mere nastiness, you know. If an international award for odium is ever projected, have no fear of the outcome as far as India is concerned. You can rely on my support.

And apropos of symbols, there is something approaching genius in the one that graces your letterhead, the golden fleece. Could any trademark be more apt for a type who charges six francs to wash a cummerbund? I realize that appealing to your sense of logic is like whistling an aria to the deaf, but I paid half that for it originally, and the Muslim who sold it to me was the worst thief in the bazaar. Enlighten me, my dear fellow, since I have never been a tradesman myself—what passes through your head when you mulct a customer in this outrageous fashion? Is it glee? Triumph? Self-approbation at the cunning with which you have swindled your betters? I ask altogether without malice, solely from a desire to fathom the dark intricacies of the human mind.

To revert now to the subject of the drawers. It will do you no good to bombinate endlessly about sleazy material, deterioration from pounding on stones, etc. That they were immersed in an acid bath powerful enough to corrode a zinc plate, that they were wrenched through a mangle with utmost ferocity, that they were deliberately spattered with grease and kicked about the floor of your establishment, and, finally, that a white-hot iron was appliquéd on their seat—the whole sordid tale of maltreatment is writ there for anybody to see. The motive, however, is far less apparent, and I have speculated for hours on why I should be the target of vandalism. Only one explanation fits the facts. Quite clearly, for all your extortionate rates, you underpay your workmen, and one of them, seeking to revenge himself, wreaked his spite on my undergarment. While I sympathize with the poor rascal's plight, I wish it understood that I hold you responsible to the very last sou. I therefore deduct from the enclosed draft nine francs fifty, which will hardly compensate me for the damage to my raiment and my nerves, and remain, with the most transitory assurances of my regard,

Sincerely yours,
PANDIT MOTILAL NEHRU

PARIS,
July 8, 1903

Pandit Motilal Nehru,
Allahabad, U.P., India.
Dear PANDIT MOTILAL:

I am desolated beyond words at the pique I sense between the lines in your recent letter, and I affirm to you on my wife's honor that in the six generations the family has conducted this business, yours is the first complaint we have ever received. Were I to list the illustrious clients we have satisfied—Robespierre, the Duc d'Enghien, Saint-Saëns, Coquelin, Mérimée, Bouguereau, and Dr. Pasteur, to name but a handful—it would read like a roll call of the immortals. Only yesterday, Marcel Proust, an author you will hear more of one of these days, called at our *établissement* (establishment) to felicitate us in person. The work we do for him is peculiarly exacting; due to his penchant for making notes on his cuffs, we must observe the greatest discretion in selecting which to launder. In fine, our function is as much editorial as sanitary, and he stated unreservedly that he holds our literary judgment in the highest esteem. I ask you, could a firm with traditions like these stoop to the pettiness you imply?

You can be sure, however, that if our staff has been guilty of any oversight, it will not be repeated. Between ourselves, we have been zealously weeding out a Socialist element among the employees, malcontents who seek to inflame them with vicious nonsense about an eleven-hour day and compulsory ventilation. Our firm refusal to compromise one iota has borne fruit; we now have a hard core of loyal and spiritless drudges, many of them so lackluster that they do not even pause for lunch, which means a substantial time saving and consequently much speedier service for the customer. As you see, my dear Pandit Motilal, efficiency and devotion to our clientele dominate every waking thought at Pleurniche.

As regards your last consignment, all seems to be in order; I ask leave, though, to beg one trifling favor that will help us execute your work more rapidly in future. Would you request whoever mails the laundry to make certain it contains no living organisms? When the current order was unpacked, a small yellow-black serpent, scarcely larger than a pencil but quite dynamic, wriggled out of one of your *dhotis* and spread terror in the workroom. We succeeded in decapitating it after a modicum of trouble and bore it to the Jardin d'Acclimatation, where the curator identified it as a krait, the most lethal of your indigenous snakes. Mind you, I personally thought M. Ratisborn an alarmist—the little émigré impressed me as a rather cunning fellow, vivacious, intelligent, and capable of transformation into a household pet if one had leisure. Unfortunately, we have none, so fervent is our desire to accelerate your shipments, and you will aid us materially by a hint in the right quarter, if you will. Accept, I implore of you, my salutations the most distinguished.

Yours cordially,
OCTAVE-HIPPOLYTE PLEURNICHE

ALLAHABAD, U.P.,
September 11, 1903

Dear M. PLEURNICHE:

If I were a hothead, I might be tempted to horsewhip a Yahoo who has the effrontery to set himself up as a patron of letters; if a humanitarian, to garrote him and earn the gratitude of the miserable wretches under his heel. As I am neither, but simply an idealist fatuous enough to believe he is entitled to what he pays for, I have a favor to ask of you, in turn. Spare me, I pray, your turgid rhetoric and bootlicking protestations, and be equally sparing of the bleach you use on my shirts. After a single baptism in your vats, my sky-blue *jibbahs* faded to a ghastly greenish-white and the fabric evaporates under one's touch. Merciful God, whence springs this compulsion to eliminate every trace of color from my dress? Have you now become arbiters of fashion as well as littérateurs?

In your anxiety to ingratiate yourselves, incidentally, you have exposed me to as repugnant an experience as I can remember. Five or six days ago, a verminous individual named Champignon arrived here from Pondichéry, asserting that he was your nephew, delegated by you to expedite my household laundry problems. The blend of unction and cheek he displayed, reminiscent of a process server, should have warned me to beware, but, tenderhearted ninny that I am, I obeyed our Brahmin laws of hospitality and permitted him to remain the night. Needless to say, he distinguished himself. After a show of gluttony to dismay Falstaff, he proceeded to regale the dinner table with a disquisition on the art of love, bolstering it with quotations from the Kamasutra so coarse that one of the ladies present fainted dead away. Somewhat later, I surprised him in the kitchen tickling a female servant, and when I demurred, he rudely advised me to stick to my rope trick and stay out of matters that did not concern me. He was gone before daylight, accompanied by a Jaipur enamel necklace of incalculable value and all our silver. I felt it was a trivial price to be rid of him. Nevertheless, I question your wisdom, from a commercial standpoint, in employing such emissaries. Is it not safer to rob the customer in the old humdrum fashion, a franc here and a franc there, than to stake everything on a youth's judgment and risk possible disaster? I subscribe myself, as always,

Your well-wisher,

PANDIT MOTILAL NEHRU

PARIS,

October 25, 1903

Dear PANDIT MOTILAL:

We trust that you have received the bundle shipped five weeks since and that our work continues to gratify. It is also pleasing to learn that our relative M. Champignon called on you and managed to be of assistance. If there is any further way he can serve you, do not hesitate to notify him.

I enclose herewith a cutting which possibly needs a brief explanation. As you see, it is a newspaper advertisement embodying your photograph and a text woven out of laudatory remarks culled from your letters to us. Knowing you would gladly concur, I took the liberty of altering a word or two in places to clarify the meaning and underline the regard you hold us in. This dramatic license, so to speak, in no way vitiates the sense of what you wrote; it is quite usual in theatrical advertising to touch up critical opinion, and to judge from comment I have already heard you will enjoy publicity throughout the continent of Europe for years to come. Believe us, dear Pandit, your eternal debtor, and allow me to remain

Yours fraternally,

OCTAVE-HIPPOLYTE PLEURNICHE

ALLAHABAD,
November 14, 1903

Dear M. PLEURNICHE:

The barristers I retained immediately on perusing your letter—Messrs. Bulstrode & Hawfinch, of Covent Garden, a firm you will hear more of one of these days—have cautioned me not to communicate with you henceforth, but the urge to speak one final word is irresistible. After all, when their suit for a million francs breaks over you like a thunderclap, when the bailiffs seize your business and you are reduced to sleeping along the *quais* and subsisting on the carrot greens you pick up around Les Halles, you may mistakenly attribute your predicament to my malignity, to voodoo, djinns, etc. Nothing of the sort, my dear chap. Using me to publicize your filthy little concern is only a secondary factor in your downfall. What doomed you from the start was the bumbling incompetence, the ingrained slovenliness, that characterizes everyone in your calling. A man too indolent to replace the snaps he tears from a waistcoat or expunge the rust he sprinkles on a brand-new Kashmiri shawl is obviously capable of any infamy, and it ill becomes him to snivel when retribution overtakes him in the end.

Adieu, then, *mon brave,* and try to exhibit in the dock at least the dignity you have failed to heretofore. With every good wish and the certainty that nothing I have said has made the slightest possible impression on a brain addled by steam, I am,

Compassionately,
PANDIT MOTILAL NEHRU

S. J. PERELMAN

Waiting for Santy

A CHRISTMAS PLAYLET

(WITH A BOW TO MR. CLIFFORD ODETS)

Scene: The sweatshop of S. Claus, a manufacturer of children's toys, on North Pole Street. Time: The night before Christmas.

At rise, seven gnomes, Rankin, Panken, Rivkin, Riskin, Ruskin, Briskin, and Praskin, are discovered working furiously to fill orders piling up on stage right. The whir of lathes, the hum of motors, and the hiss of drying lacquer are so deafening that at times the dialogue cannot be heard, which is very vexing if you vex easily. (Note: The parts of Rankin, Panken, Rivkin, Riskin, Ruskin, Briskin, and Praskin are interchangeable, and may be secured directly from your dealer or the factory.)

RISKIN *(Filing a Meccano girder, bitterly):* A parasite, a leech, a bloodsucker —altogether a five-star no goodnick! Starvation wages we get so he can ride around in a red team with reindeers!

RUSKIN *(Jeering):* Hey, Karl Marx, whyn'tcha hire a hall?

RISKIN *(Sneering):* Scab! Stool pigeon! Company spy! *(They tangle and rain blows on each other. While waiting for these to dry, each returns to his respective task.)*

BRISKIN *(Sadly, to Panken):* All day long I'm painting "Snow Queen" on these Flexible Flyers and my little Irving lays in a cold tenement with the gout.

PANKEN: You said before it was the mumps.

BRISKIN *(With a fatalistic shrug):* The mumps—the gout—go argue with City Hall.

PANKEN *(Kindly, passing him a bowl):* Here, take a piece fruit.

BRISKIN *(Chewing):* It ain't bad, for wax fruit.

PANKEN *(With pride):* I painted it myself.

BRISKIN *(Rejecting the fruit):* Ptoo! Slave psychology!

RIVKIN *(Suddenly, half to himself, half to the Party):* I got a belly full of stars, baby. You make me feel like I swallowed a Roman candle.

PRASKIN *(Curiously):* What's wrong with the kid?

RISKIN: What's wrong with all of us? The system! Two years he and Claus's daughter's been making goo-goo eyes behind the old man's back.

PRASKIN: So what?

RISKIN *(Scornfully):* So what? Economic determinism! What do you think the kid's name is—J. Pierpont Rivkin? He ain't even got for a bottle Dr. Brown's Celery Tonic. I tell you, it's like gall in my mouth two young people shouldn't have a room where they could make great music.

RANKIN *(Warningly):* Shhh! Here she comes now! *(Stella Claus enters, carrying a portable gramophone. She and Rivkin embrace, place a record on the turntable, and begin a very slow waltz, unmindful that the gramophone is playing "Cohen on the Telephone.")*

STELLA *(Dreamily):* Love me, sugar?

RIVKIN: I can't sleep, I can't eat, that's how I love you. You're a double malted with two scoops of whipped cream; you're the moon rising over Mosholu Parkway; you're a two weeks' vacation at Camp Nitgedaiget! I'd pull down the Chrysler Building to make a bobbie pin for your hair!

STELLA: I've got a stomach full of anguish. Oh, Rivvy, what'll we do?

PANKEN *(Sympathetically):* Here, try a piece fruit.

RIVKIN *(Fiercely):* Wax fruit—that's been my whole life! Imitations! Substitutes! Well, I'm through! Stella, tonight I'm telling your old man. He can't play mumblety-peg with two human beings! *(The tinkle of sleigh bells is heard offstage, followed by a voice shouting, "Whoa, Dasher! Whoa, Dancer!" A moment later S. Claus enters in a gust of mock snow. He is a pompous bourgeois of sixty-five who affects a white beard and a false air of benevolence. But tonight the ruddy color is missing from his cheeks, his step falters, and he moves heavily. The gnomes hastily replace the marzipan they have been filching.)*

STELLA *(Anxiously):* Papa! What did the specialist say?

CLAUS *(Brokenly):* The biggest professor in the country . . . the best cardiac man that money could buy. . . . I tell you I was like a wild man.

STELLA: Pull yourself together, Sam!

CLAUS: It's no use. Adhesions, diabetes, sleeping sickness, decalcomania —oh, my God! I got to cut out climbing in chimneys, he says—me, Sanford Claus, the biggest toy concern in the world!

STELLA *(Soothingly):* After all, it's only one man's opinion.

CLAUS: No, no, he cooked my goose. I'm like a broken uke after a Yosian picnic. Rivkin!

RIVKIN: Yes, Sam.

CLAUS: My boy, I had my eye on you for a long time. You and Stella thought you were too foxy for an old man, didn't you? Well, let bygones be bygones. Stella, do you love this gnome?

STELLA *(Simply):* He's the whole stage show at the Music Hall, Papa; he's Toscanini conducting Beethoven's Fifth; he's—

CLAUS *(Curtly):* Enough already. Take him. From now on he's a partner in the firm. *(As all exclaim, Claus holds up his hand for silence.)* And tonight he can take my route and make the deliveries. It's the least I could do for my own flesh and blood. *(As the happy couple kiss, Claus wipes away a suspicious moisture and turns to the other gnomes.)* Boys, do you know what day tomorrow is?

GNOMES *(Crowding around expectantly):* Christmas!

CLAUS: Correct. When you look in your envelopes tonight, you'll find a little present from me—a forty-per-cent pay cut. And the first one who opens his trap—gets this. *(As he holds up a tear-gas bomb and beams at them, the gnomes utter cries of joy, join hands, and dance around him, shouting exultantly. All except Riskin and Briskin, that is, who exchange a quick glance and go underground.)*

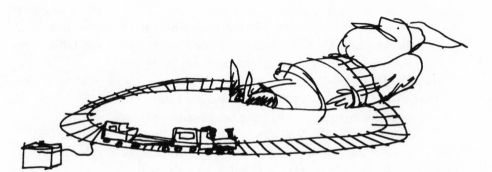

GARY SOLIN

Allen Stewart Konigsberg

When I pontificated that the film *Hannah and Her Sisters* was to Woody Allen what the Fortieth Symphony was to Mozart, Woody wrote to me: "The difference between *Hannah* and Mozart's Fortieth is that his cassettes will sell better."

I often think of Woody Allen in classical music terms. He is a composer (writer), virtuoso (actor), and conductor (director). Among his themes and variations are scherzos *(Sleeper, Take the Money and Run)*; divertimenti *(Broadway Danny Rose)*; sonatas *(Interiors)*; chamber works *(Zelig)*; concerti *(The Purple Rose of Cairo, Manhattan)*, and symphonies *(Annie Hall* and *Hannah and Her Sisters)*.

A principal difference between Allen and Mozart is that when Woody was six years old his father did not tour him through Europe's Royal Courts to perform improvizations for the crowned heads.

Too bad for the crowned heads. **G.S.**

WOODY ALLEN

The Whore of Mensa

One thing about being a private investigator, you've got to learn to go with your hunches. That's why when a quivering pat of butter named Word Babcock walked into my office and laid his cards on the table, I should have trusted the cold chill that shot up my spine.

"Kaiser?" he said, "Kaiser Lupowitz?"

"That's what it says on my license," I owned up.

"You've got to help me. I'm being blackmailed. Please!"

He was shaking like the lead singer in a rumba band. I pushed a glass across the desk top and a bottle of rye I keep handy for nonmedicinal purposes. "Suppose you relax and tell me all about it."

"You . . . you won't tell my wife?"

"Level with me, Word. I can't make any promises."

He tried pouring a drink, but you could hear the clicking sound across the street, and most of the stuff wound up in his shoes.

"I'm a working guy," he said. "Mechanical maintenance. I build and service joy buzzers. You know—those little fun gimmicks that give people a shock when they shake hands?"

"So?"

"A lot of your executives like 'em. Particularly down on Wall Street."

"Get to the point."

"I'm on the road a lot. You know how it is—lonely. Oh, not what you're thinking. See, Kaiser, I'm basically an intellectual. Sure, a guy can meet all the bimbos he wants. But the really brainy women—they're not so easy to find on short notice."

"Keep talking."

"Well, I heard of this young girl. Eighteen years old. A Vassar student. For a price, she'll come over and discuss any subject—Proust, Yeats, anthropology. Exchange of ideas. You see what I'm driving at?"

"Not exactly."

"I mean, my wife is great, don't get me wrong. But she won't discuss Pound with me. Or Eliot. I didn't know that when I married her. See, I need a woman who's mentally stimulating, Kaiser. And I'm willing to pay for it. I don't want an involvement—I want a quick intellectual experience, then I want the girl to leave. Christ, Kaiser, I'm a happily married man."

"How long has this been going on?"

"Six months. Whenever I have that craving, I call Flossie. She's a madam, with a master's in comparative lit. She sends me over an intellectual, see?"

So he was one of those guys whose weakness was really bright women. I felt sorry for the poor sap. I figured there must be a lot of jokers in his position, who were starved for a little intellectual communication with the opposite sex and would pay through the nose for it.

"Now she's threatening to tell my wife," he said.

"Who is?"

"Flossie. They bugged the motel room. They got tapes of me discussing *The Waste Land* and *Styles of Radical Will,* and, well, really getting into some issues. They want ten grand or they go to Carla. Kaiser, you've got to help me! Carla would die if she knew she didn't turn me on up here."

The old call-girl racket. I had heard rumors that the boys at headquarters were on to something involving a group of educated women, but so far they were stymied.

"Get Flossie on the phone for me."

"What?"

"I'll take your case, Word. But I get fifty dollars a day, plus expenses. You'll have to repair a lot of joy buzzers."

"It won't be ten Gs' worth, I'm sure of that," he said with a grin, and picked up the phone and dialed a number. I took it from him and winked. I was beginning to like him.

Seconds later, a silky voice answered, and I told her what was on my mind. "I understand you can help me set up an hour of good chat," I said.

"Sure, honey. What do you have in mind?"

"I'd like to discuss Melville."

"*Moby Dick* or the shorter novels?"

"What's the difference?"

"The price. That's all. Symbolism's extra."

"What'll it run me?"

"Fifty, maybe a hundred for *Moby Dick*. You want a comparative discussion—Melville and Hawthorne? That could be arranged for a hundred."

"The dough's fine," I told her and gave her the number of a room at the Plaza.

"You want a blonde or a brunette?"

"Surprise me," I said, and hung up.

I shaved and grabbed some black coffee while I checked over the Monarch College Outline series. Hardly an hour had passed before there was a knock on my door. I opened it, and standing there was a young redhead who was packed into her slacks like two big scoops of vanilla ice cream.

"Hi, I'm Sherry."

They really knew how to appeal to your fantasies. Long straight hair, leather bag, silver earrings, no make-up.

"I'm surprised you weren't stopped, walking into the hotel dressed like that," I said. "The house dick can usually spot an intellectual."

"A five-spot cools him."

"Shall we begin?" I said, motioning her to the couch.

She lit a cigarette and got right to it. "I think we could start by approaching *Billy Budd* as Melville's justification of the ways of God to man, *n'est-ce pas?*"

"Interestingly, though, not in a Miltonian sense." I was bluffing. I wanted to see if she'd go for it.

"No. *Paradise Lost* lacked the substructure of pessimism." She did.

"Right, right. God, you're right," I murmured.

"I think Melville reaffirmed the virtues of innocence in a naïve yet sophisticated sense—don't you agree?"

I let her go on. She was barely nineteen years old, but already she had developed the hardened facility of the pseudo-intellectual. She rattled off her ideas glibly, but it was all mechanical. Whenever I offered an insight, she faked a response: "Oh, yes, Kaiser. Yes, baby, that's deep. A platonic comprehension of Christianity—why didn't I see it before?"

We talked for about an hour and then she said she had to go. She stood up and I laid a C-note on her.

"Thanks, honey."

"There's plenty more where that came from."

"What are you trying to say?"

I had piqued her curiosity. She sat down again.

"Suppose I wanted to—have a party?" I said.

"Like, what kind of party?"

"Suppose I wanted Noam Chomsky explained to me by two girls?"

"Oh, wow."

"If you'd rather forget it . . ."

"You'd have to speak with Flossie," she said. "It'd cost you."

Now was the time to tighten the screws. I flashed my private-investigator's badge and informed her it was a bust.

"What!"

"I'm fuzz, sugar, and discussing Melville for money is an 802. You can do time."

"You louse!"

"Better come clean, baby. Unless you want to tell your story down at Alfred Kazin's office, and I don't think he'd be too happy to hear it."

She began to cry. "Don't turn me in, Kaiser," she said. "I needed the money to complete my master's. I've been turned down for a grant. *Twice.* Oh, Christ."

It all poured out—the whole story. Central Park West upbringing, Socialist summer camps, Brandeis. She was every dame you saw waiting in line at the Elgin or the Thalia, or penciling the words "Yes, very true" into the margin of some book on Kant. Only somewhere along the line she had made a wrong turn.

"I needed cash. A girl friend said she knew a married guy whose wife wasn't very profound. He was into Blake. She couldn't hack it. I said sure, for a price I'd talk Blake with him. I was nervous at first. I faked a lot of it. He didn't care. My friend said there were others. Oh, I've been busted before. I got caught reading *Commentary* in a parked car, and I was once stopped and frisked at Tanglewood. Once more and I'm a three-time loser."

"Then take me to Flossie."

She bit her lip and said, "The Hunter College Book Store is a front."

"Yes?"

"Like those bookie joints that have barbershops outside for show. You'll see."

I made a quick call to headquarters and then said to her, "Okay, sugar. You're off the hook. But don't leave town."

She tilted her face up toward mine gratefully. "I can get you photographs of Dwight Macdonald reading," she said.

"Some other time."

I walked into the Hunter College Book Store. The salesman, a young man with sensitive eyes, came up to me. "Can I help you?" he said.

"I'm looking for a special edition of *Advertisements for Myself*. I understand the author had several thousand gold-leaf copies printed up for friends."

"I'll have to check," he said. "We have a WATS line to Mailer's house."

I fixed him with a look. "Sherry sent me," I said.

"Oh, in that case, go on back," he said. He pressed a button. A wall of books opened, and I walked like a lamb into that bustling pleasure palace known as Flossie's.

Red flocked wallpaper and a Victorian décor set the tone. Pale, nervous girls with black-rimmed glasses and blunt-cut hair lolled around on sofas, riffling Penguin Classics provocatively. A blonde with a big smile winked at me, nodded toward a room upstairs, and said, "Wallace Stevens, eh?" But it wasn't just intellectual experiences—they were peddling emotional ones, too. For fifty bucks, I learned, you could "relate without getting close." For a hundred, a girl would lend you her Bartók records, have dinner, and then let you watch while she had an anxiety attack. For one-fifty, you could listen to FM radio with twins. For three bills, you got the works: A thin Jewish brunette would pretend to pick you up at the Museum of Modern Art, let you read her master's, get you involved in a screaming quarrel at Elaine's over Freud's conception of women, and then fake a suicide of your choosing—the perfect evening, for some guys. Nice racket. Great town, New York.

"Like what you see?" a voice said behind me. I turned and suddenly found myself standing face to face with the business end of a .38. I'm a guy with a strong stomach, but this time it did a back flip. It was Flossie, all right. The voice was the same, but Flossie was a man. His face was hidden by a mask.

"You'll never believe this," he said, "but I don't even have a college degree. I was thrown out for low grades."

"Is that why you wear that mask?"

"I devised a complicated scheme to take over *The New York Review of Books,* but it meant I had to pass for Lionel Trilling. I went to Mexico for an operation. There's a doctor in Juarez who gives people Trilling's features—for a price. Something went wrong. I came out looking like Auden, with Mary McCarthy's voice. That's when I started working the other side of the law."

Quickly, before he could tighten his finger on the trigger, I went into action. Heaving forward, I snapped my elbow across his jaw and grabbed the gun as he fell back. He hit the ground like a ton of bricks. He was still whimpering when the police showed up.

"Nice work, Kaiser," Sergeant Holmes said. "When we're through with this guy, the F.B.I. wants to have a talk with him. A little matter involving some gamblers and an annotated copy of Dante's *Inferno.* Take him away, boys."

Later that night, I looked up an old account of mine named Gloria. She was blond. She had graduated *cum laude.* The difference was she majored in physical education. It felt good.

WOODY ALLEN

Confessions of a Burglar

(FOLLOWING ARE EXCERPTS FROM THE SOON TO BE PUBLISHED MEMOIRS OF VIRGIL IVES, WHO IS CURRENTLY SERVING THE FIRST OF FOUR CONSECUTIVE NINETY-NINE-YEAR SENTENCES FOR VARIOUS FELONIES. MR. IVES PLANS ON WORKING WITH CHILDREN WHEN HE GETS OUT.)

Sure I stole. Why not? Where I grew up, you had to steal to eat. Then you had to steal to tip. Lots of guys stole fifteen per cent, but I always stole twenty, which made me a big favorite among the waiters. On the way home from a heist, I'd steal some pajamas to sleep in. Or if it was a hot

night, I'd steal underwear. It was a way of life. I had a bad upbringing, you
might say. My dad was always on the run from the cops and I never saw
him out of disguise till I was twenty-two. For years, I thought he was a
short, bearded man with dark glasses and a limp; actually, he was tall and
blond and resembled Lindbergh. He was a professional bank robber, but
sixty-five was the mandatory retirement age, so he had to get out. Spent
his last few years in mail fraud, but the postal rates went up and he lost
everything.

Mom was wanted, too. Of course in those days it wasn't the way it is
now, with women demanding equal rights, and all. Back then, if a woman
turned to crime the only opportunities open to her were blackmail and,
once in a while, arson. Women were used in Chicago to drive getaway
cars, but only during the drivers' strike, in 1926. Terrible strike. It lasted
eight weeks, and whenever a gang pulled a job and ran out with the
money they were forced to walk or take a cab.

I had a sister and two brothers. Jenny married money. Not an actual
human being—it was a pile of singles. My brother Vic got in with a gang of
plagiarists. He was in the middle of signing his name to "The Waste
Land" when the feds surrounded the house. He got ten years. Some rich
kid from a highfalutin family who signed Pound's "Cantos" got off on
probation. That's the law for you. Charlie—that's my youngest brother—
he's been a numbers runner, a fence, and a loan shark. Never could find
himself. Eventually he was arrested for loitering. He loitered for seven
years, till he realized it was not the kind of crime that brought in any
money.

The first thing I ever stole was a loaf of bread. I was working for Rifkin's
Bakery, where my job was to remove the jelly from doughnuts that had
gone stale and transfer it to fresh goods. It was very exacting work, done
with a rubber tube and a scalpel. If your hands shook, the jelly went on the
floor and old man Rifkin would pull your hair. Arnold Rothstein, who we
all looked up to, came in one day and said he wanted to get his hands on a
loaf of bread but he absolutely refused to pay for it. He hinted that this
was a chance for some smart kid to get into the rackets. I took that as a
cue, and each day when I left I put one slice of rye under my coat, until
after three weeks I had accumulated a whole loaf. On the way to Rothstein's office, I began to feel remorse, because even though I hated Rifkin
his wife had once let me take home two seeds from a roll when my uncle
was dying. I tried to return the bread, but I got caught while I was trying
to figure out which loaf each slice belonged to. The next thing I knew, I
was in Elmira Reformatory.

Elmira was a tough joint. I escaped five times. Once I tried to sneak out in the back of a laundry truck. The guards got suspicious, and one of them poked me with his stick and asked me what the hell I was doing lying around in a hamper. I looked him right in the eye and said, "I'm some shirts." I could tell he was dubious. He kept pacing back and forth and staring at me. I guess I got a little panicky. "I'm some *shirts,*" I told him. "Some denim work shirts—blue ones." Before I could say another word, my arms and legs were manacled and I was back in stir.

I learned everything I knew about crime at Elmira: how to pick pockets, how to crack a safe, how to cut glass—all the fine points of the trade. For instance, I learned (and not even all professional criminals know this) that in the event of a shootout with the cops, the cops are always allowed the first two shots. It's just the way it's done. Then you return fire. And if a cop says, "We have the house surrounded, come out with your hands up," you don't just shoot wildly. You say, "I'd prefer not to," or "I'd rather not at this particular time." There's a right way to do these things, but today . . . Well, why go into all that?

For the next few years of my life I was the best damn burglar you ever saw. People talk about Raffles, but Raffles had his style and I had mine. I had lunch with Raffles' son once. Nice guy. We ate at the old Lindy's. He stole the pepper mill. I stole the silverware and napkins. Then he took the ketchup bottle. I took his hat. He got my umbrella and tiepin. When we left we kidnapped a waiter. It was quite a haul. The original Raffles began as a cat burglar. (I couldn't do that, because the whiskers make me sneeze.) He'd dress up in this beat-up cat suit and dart over rooftops. In the end, he was caught by two guys from Scotland Yard dressed as dogs. I suppose you've heard of the Kissing Bandit? He'd break into a joint and rob the victim, and if it was a woman he'd kiss her. It was sad the way the law finally nailed him. He had two old dowagers tied up and he was prancing in front of them singing "Gimme a Little Kiss, Will Ya, Huh?" when he slipped on a footstool and fractured his pelvis.

Those boys made all the headlines, but I pulled off some capers that the police never did figure out. Once, I entered a mansion, blew the safe, and removed six thousand dollars while a couple slept in the same room. The husband woke up when the dynamite went off, but when I assured him that the entire proceeds would go to the Boys' Clubs of America he went back to sleep. Cleverly, I left behind some fingerprints of Franklin D. Roosevelt, who was President then. Another time, at a big diplomatic cocktail party, I stole a woman's diamond necklace while we were shaking hands. Used a vacuum cleaner on her—an old Hoover. Got her necklace and earrings. Later, when I opened the bag I found some false teeth there, which belonged to the Dutch Ambassador.

My most beautiful job, though, was when I broke into the British Museum. I knew that the entire floor of the Rare Gems Room was wired and the slightest pressure on it would set off an alarm. I was lowered in upside down by a rope from the skylight, so I wouldn't touch the ground. I came through neat as you please, and in a minute I was hovering over the famous Kittridge Diamonds in their display case. As I pulled out my glass cutter a little sparrow flew in through the skylight and landed on the floor. The alarm sounded and eight squad cars arrived. I got ten years. The sparrow got twenty to life. The bird was out in six months, on probation. A year later, he was picked up in Fort Worth for pecking Rabbi Morris Klugfein into a state of semiconsciousness.

What advice would I give the average homeowner to protect himself against burglars? Well, the first thing is to keep a light on in the house when you go out. It must be at least a sixty-watt bulb; anything less and the burglar will ransack the house, out of contempt for the wattage. Another good idea is to keep a dog, but this is not foolproof. Whenever I was about to rob a house with a dog in it, I threw in some dog food mixed with Seconal. If that didn't work, I'd grind up equal parts of chopped meat and a novel by Theodore Dreiser. If it happens that you are going out of town and must leave your house unguarded, it's a good idea to put a cardboard silhouette of yourself in the window. Any silhouette will do. A Bronx man once placed a cardboard silhouette of Montgomery Clift in his window and then went to Kutsher's for the weekend. Later, Montgomery Clift himself happened to walk by and saw the silhouette, which caused him great anxiety. He attempted to strike up a conversation, and when it failed to answer for seven hours Clift returned to California and told his friends that New Yorkers were snobbish.

If you surprise an intruder in the act of burglarizing your home, do not panic. Remember, he is as frightened as you are. One good device is to rob *him*. Seize the initiative and relieve the burglar of his watch and wallet. Then he can get into your bed while you make a getaway. Trapped by this defense, I once wound up living in Des Moines for six years with another man's wife and three children, and only left when I was fortunate enough to surprise another burglar, who took my place. The six years I lived with that family were very happy ones, and I often look back on them with affection, although there is also much to be said for working on a chain gang.

Fran Lebowitz

The bright boy who sat in front of me in high school was big and broad-shouldered. That was good (the teacher couldn't see me), and bad (I couldn't copy from his tests). His name was Harold Lebowitz, and after graduation he opened an upholstery shop, smoked a pipe, and became a father whose daughter was considered incorrigible (I'm being as polite as I can). She was smart. So smart that she was thrown out of high school. She wrote smart and spoke smart and when somebody speaks smart it smarts. Many people confused her wit with insolence, and so she became the girl who wasn't invited to their daughters' parties. Today the fanciest New York people vie to have her at their parties because of her exhilarating conversation. If her name were not at the top of this page, I would now stun you by saying: "And that girl was . . . *Fran Lebowitz!*"

Millions enjoy her television appearances and speaking engagements, during which she smokes cigarettes and burns butts with her barbs, and they revel in her writing. Her first two books were bestsellers: *Metropolitan Life* and *Social Studies.* Since then, she has been working and working on a novel in which she observes New York people. Getting the people right is a struggle, but she's nearly got it. A few more parties should do it.   **G.S.**

FRAN LEBOWITZ

Tips for Teens

There is perhaps, for all concerned, no period of life so unpleasant, so unappealing, so downright unpalatable, as that of adolescence. And while pretty much everyone who comes into contact with him is disagreeably affected, certainly no one is in for a ruder shock than the actual teenager himself. Fresh from twelve straight years of uninterrupted cuteness, he is singularly unprepared to deal with the harsh consequences of inadequate personal appearance. Almost immediately upon entering the thirteenth year of life, a chubby little child becomes a big fat girl, and a boy previously spoken of as "small for his age" finds that he is, in reality, a boy who is short.

Problems of physical beauty, grave though they be, are not all that beset the unwary teen. Philosophical, spiritual, social, legal—a veritable multitude of difficulties daily confront him. Understandably disconcerted, the teenager almost invariably finds himself in a state of unrelenting misery. This is, of course, unfortunate, even lamentable. Yet one frequently discovers a lack of sympathy for the troubled youth. This dearth of compassion is undoubtedly due to the teenager's insistence upon dealing with his lot in an unduly boisterous fashion. He is, quite simply, at an age where he can keep nothing to himself. No impulse too fleeting, no sentiment too raw, that the teenager does not feel compelled to share it with those around him.

This sort of behavior naturally tends to have an alienating effect. And while this is ofttimes its major intent, one cannot help but respond with hearty ill will.

Therefore, in the interest of encouraging if not greater understanding, at least greater decorum, I have set down the following words of advice.

If in addition to being physically unattractive you find that you do not get along well with others, do not under any circumstances attempt to alleviate this situation by developing an interesting personality. An interesting personality is, in an adult, insufferable. In a teenager it is frequently punishable by law.

———

Wearing dark glasses at the breakfast table is socially acceptable only if you are legally blind or partaking of your morning meal out of doors during a total eclipse of the sun.

———

Should your political opinions be at extreme variance with those of your parents, keep in mind that while it is indeed your constitutional right to express these sentiments verbally, it is unseemly to do so with your mouth full—particularly when it is full of the oppressor's standing rib roast.

———

Think before you speak. Read before you think. This will give you something to think about that you didn't make up yourself—a wise move at any age, but most especially at seventeen, when you are in the greatest danger of coming to annoying conclusions.

———

Try to derive some comfort from the knowledge that if your guidance counselor were working up to *his* potential, he wouldn't still be in high school.

———

The teen years are fraught with any number of hazards, but none so perilous as that which manifests itself as a tendency to consider movies an important art form. If you are presently, or just about to be, of this opinion, perhaps I can spare you years of unbearable pretension by posing this question: If movies (or films, as you are probably now referring to them) were of such a high and serious nature, can you possibly entertain even the slightest notion that they would show them in a place that sold Orange Crush and Jujubes?

———

It is at this point in your life that you will be giving the greatest amount of time and attention to matters of sex. This is not only acceptable, but should, in fact, be encouraged, for this is the last time that sex will be genuinely exciting. The more farsighted among you may wish to cultivate supplementary interests in order that you might have something to do when you get older. I personally recommend the smoking of cigarettes— a habit with staying power.

———

While we're on the subject of cigarettes, do not forget that adolescence is also the last time that you can reasonably expect to be forgiven a taste for a brand that might by way of exotic shape, color or package excite comment.

———

The girl in your class who suggests that this year the Drama Club put on *The Bald Soprano* will be a thorn in people's sides all of her life.

———

Should you be a teenager blessed with uncommon good looks, document this state of affairs by the taking of photographs. It is the only way anyone will ever believe you in years to come.

———

Avoid the use of drugs whenever possible. For while they may, at this juncture, provide a pleasant diversion, they are, on the whole, not the sort of thing that will in later years (should you *have* later years) be of much use in the acquisition of richly rewarding tax shelters and beachfront property.

———

If you reside in a state where you attain your legal majority while still in your teens, pretend that you don't. There isn't an adult alive who would want to be contractually bound by a decision he came to at the age of nineteen.

———

Remember that as a teenager you are at the last stage in your life when you will be happy to hear that the phone is for you.

———

Stand firm in your refusal to remain conscious during algebra. In real life, I assure you, there is no such thing as algebra.

CHARLES SCHULZ

E. B. WHITE

Dusk in Fierce Pajamas

Ravaged by pink eye, I lay for a week scarce caring whether I lived or died. Only Wamba, my toothless old black nurse, bothered to bring me food and quinine. Then one day my strength began to return, and with it came Wamba to my bedside with a copy of *Harper's Bazaar* and a copy of *Vogue*. "Ah brought you couple magazines," she said proudly, her red gums clashing.

In the days that followed (happy days of renewed vigor and reawakened interest), I studied the magazines and lived, in their pages, the gracious lives of the characters in the ever-moving drama of society and fashion. In them I found surcease from the world's ugliness, from disarray, from all unattractive things. Through them I escaped into a world in which there was no awkwardness of gesture, no unsuitability of line, no people of no importance. It was an enriching experience. I realize now that my own life is by contrast an unlovely thing, with its disease, its banalities, its uncertainties, its toil, its single-breasted suits, and its wine from lesser years. I am aware of a life all around me of graciousness and beauty, in which every moment is a tiny pearl of good taste, and in which every acquaintance has the common decency to possess a good background.

Lying here in these fierce pajamas, I dream of the *Harper's Bazaar* world, the *Vogue* life; dream of being a part of it. In fancy I am in Mrs. Cecil Baker's pine-panelled drawing-room. It is dusk. (It is almost always dusk in the fashion magazines.) I have on a Gantner & Mattern knit jersey bathing suit with a flat-striped bow and an all white buck shoe with a floppy tongue. No, that's wrong. I am in chiffon, for it is the magic hour after bridge. Suddenly a Chippendale mahogany hors-d'oeuvre table is brought in. In its original old blue-and-white Spode compartments there sparkle olives, celery, hard-boiled eggs, radishes—evidently put there by somebody in the employ of Mrs. Baker. Or perhaps my fancy wanders away from the drawing-room: I am in Mrs. Baker's dining-room, mingling unostentatiously with the other guests, my elbows resting lightly on the dark polished oak of the Jacobean table, my fingers twiddling with the early Georgian silver. Or perhaps I am not at Mrs. Baker's oak table in chiffon at all—perhaps instead I am at Mrs. Jay Gould's teakwood table in a hand-knitted Anny Blatt ensemble in diluted tri-colors and an off-the-face hat.

It is dusk. I am dining with Rose Hobart at the Waldorf. We have lifted our champagne glasses. "To sentiment!" I say. And the haunting dusk is shattered by the clean glint of jewels by Cartier.

It is dusk. I am seated on a Bruce Buttfield pouf, for it is dusk.

Ah, magazine dreams! How dear to me now are the four evenings in the life of Mrs. Allan Ryan, Junior. I have studied them one by one, and I feel that I know them. They are perfect little crystals of being—static, precious. There is the evening when she stands, motionless, in a magnificent sable cape, her left arm hanging gracefully at her side. She is ready to go out to dinner. What will this, her first of four evenings, bring of romance, or even of food? Then there is the evening when she just sits on the edge of a settee from the Modernage Galleries, the hard bright gleam of gold lamé topping a slim, straight, almost Empire skirt. I see her there (the smoke from a cigarette rising), sitting, sitting, waiting. Or the third evening—the evening with books. Mrs. Ryan is in chiffon; the books are in morocco. Or the fourth evening, standing with her dachshund, herself in profile, the dog in full face.

So I live the lives of other people in my fancy: the life of the daughter of Lord Curzon of Kedleston, who has been visiting the Harold Talbotts on Long Island. All I know of her is that she appeared one night at dinner, her beauty set off by the lustre of artificial satin and the watery fire of aquamarine. It is all I know, yet it is enough; for it is her one perfect moment in time and space, and I know about it, and it is mine.

It is dusk. I am with Owen Johnson over his chafing dish. It is dusk. I am with Prince Matchabelli over his vodka. Or I am with the Countess de Forceville over her bridge tables. She and I have just pushed the tables against the wall and taken a big bite of gazpacho. Or I am with the Marquis de Polignac over his Pommery.

How barren my actual life seems, when fancy fails me, here with Wamba over my quinine. Why am I not to be found at dusk, slicing black bread very thin, as William Powell does, to toast it and sprinkle it with salt? Why does not twilight find me (as it finds Mrs. Chester Burden) covering a table with salmon-pink linens on which I place only white objects, even to a white salt shaker? Why don't I learn to simplify my entertaining, like the young pinch-penny in *Vogue,* who has all his friends in before the theatre and simply gives them champagne cocktails, caviar, and one hot dish, then takes them to the show? Why do I never give parties after the opera, as Mr. Paul Cravath does, at which I have the prettiest women in New York? Come to think of it, why don't the prettiest women in New York ever come down to my place, other than that pretty little Mrs. Fazaenzi, whom Wamba won't let in? Why haven't I a butler named Fish, who makes a cocktail of three parts gin to one part lime juice, honey, vermouth, and apricot brandy in equal portions—a cocktail so delicious that people like Mrs. Harrison Williams and Mrs. Goodhue Livingston seek him out to get the formula? And if I *did* have a butler named Fish, wouldn't I kid the pants off him?

All over the world it is dusk! It is dusk at Armando's on East Fifty-fifth Street. Armando has taken up his accordion; he is dreaming over the keys. A girl comes in, attracted by the accordion, which she mistakes for Cecil Beaton's camera. She is in stiff green satin, and over it she wears a silver fox cape which she can pull around her shoulders later in the evening if she gets feeling like pulling a cape around her shoulders. It is dusk on the Harold Castles' ranch in Hawaii. I have risen early to shoot a goat, which is the smart thing to do in Hawaii. And now I am walking silently through hedges of gardenias, past the flaming ginger flowers, for I have just shot a goat. I have on nothing but red sandals and a Martex bath towel. It is dusk in the Laurentians. I am in ski togs. I feel warm and safe, knowing that the most dangerous pitfall for skiers is *color,* knowing that although a touch of brilliance against the snow is effective, too much of it is the sure sign of the amateur. It is the magic hour before cocktails. I am in the modern penthouse of Monsieur Charles de Beistegui. The staircase is entirely of cement, spreading at the hemline and trimmed with padded satin tubing caught at the neck with a bar of milk chocolate. It is dusk in Chicago. I am standing beside Mrs. Howard Linn, formerly Consuelo Vanderbilt, formerly Sophie M. Gay, formerly Ellen Glendinning, formerly Saks-Fifth Avenue. It is dusk! A pheasant has Julian Street down and is pouring a magnificent old red Burgundy down his neck. Dreams, I'm afraid. It is really dusk in my own apartment. I am down on my knees in front of an airbound radiator, trying to fix it by sticking pins in the vent. Dusk in these fierce pajamas. Kneeling here, I can't help wondering where Nancy Yuille is, in her blue wool pants and reefer and her bright red mittens. For it is dusk. I said *dusk,* Wamba! Bring the quinine!

VERONICA GENG

The Stylish New York Couples

These four couples have different names and faces, but they have one thing in common—a strong tendency to appear in articles of this kind, because they are fashion individualists. One couple may prefer an eclectic style, another retro-amalgam, another mongrel revival, and another hybrid-*retrouvé,* yet each couple stands on his and her own as a single, unique personality. They show that to be one of a kind, you have to be one of a pair.

Artist Marie Bane (25) and collector Morton Braine (30) dress in simple, bold fabric wrappings—colorful bolts and mill ends layered directly onto the skin with rubber cement. "We call it Yardage Formalism," says Morton, whose current project is winding all the furniture in their Tribeca penthouse with colored thread inherited from his grandparents, Coco Chanel and David Belasco. Adds Marie, "When Julian Schnabel's show sold out, I thought mine would, too, but then it didn't."

Her clothes: Scalamandré, Museum of Tissues (Lyons), Taipei silkworm farms. Mad Frisson and Warren Beatty for shoes.
His clothes: Porthault, Einstein Moomjy. Galerie du Sabot (Brussels) for shoes.
Interests: Oneiromancy, vacuuming up bits of thread, intaglio hunting, reading.
Restaurants: Chive, La Petite Bière, Imperial Musk-Polyp, Charlie's Bum Steer, La Tricoteuse, Folie à Deux (Paris).

Neither William nor Mary Molding (both 88) has bought any clothing in over 50 years. They feel that they have "subsumed fashion under the category of pure tradition." Both dress exclusively in what Mary calls "lateral hand-me-downs: I wear Moldie's old clothes and he wears mine." Real-estate collector William likes to wheel and deal on their Park Avenue triplex telex in a Schiaparelli cocktail dress, and relaxes later in "nothing at all except a dab of vintage Shocking on pulse points." For Mary, founder of the Ghetto Repair League and president of the Don't Be Beastly to Congress Committee, living well still means "a dinner coat always"—the one handmade for her husband in 1909 by Eugene V. Debs.

Her clothes: His.
His clothes: Hers.
Interests: Reading, telephoning, telescopes.
Restaurants: "It is impossible to go out." Entertain close friends at amusing dinners famous for including musk-polyps in every course.

Annabella Carissima ("Pat") von Patina (49), a Milan-born architect, and Stanley Sohoux (18), former collector, have shaped each other's design sensibilities in the ongoing process of gradually removing everything they own from their fabulous 40,000-square-foot loft in the bone-meal district. "I'm a bit big on minimalism," says Pat, "but Stan is completely his own man and has *kept* one or two little *objets* instead of relying on me to throw them away." Stan sometimes wears all his clothes at once, carrying his personal possessions in the pockets, "so the spatial interpenetrations of the open-plan closets can be kept unobstructed." Pat sticks to one designer for clothes and keeps her efficient wardrobe stored flat behind the ceiling in the crawlspace.

Her clothes: Ralph Racquet for Women. Warren Beatty and Mad Frisson for shoes.
His clothes: Ralph Racquet for Women for Men.
Interests: Medicinal-brandy tastings, oneiromancy. Visiting friends (Stan). Reading, intaglio disposal (Pat).
Restaurants: La Tricoteuse, Huis Clos, Chive, Imperial Musk-Polyp, Folie à Deux (Paris).

The proprietors of Chive, one of the most popular new dining places in town, Clive (35) and Olive (25) Alive are self-proclaimed "style immortals." Explains Clive, "By translating ourselves into commodities, we become abstract concepts of exchange; for that which hovers in a shop waiting to be bought is an immutable idea. As long as we are still for sale, we cannot be used." Everything in their East Side apartment has its price sticker—even the much-mended antique purse seine covering the walls, to which are pinned costly holograph pages from Richard Strauss's *Ariadne auf Naxos* and inexpensive crayon tracings of autumn leaves from their country estate ("Macy's" in Oxfordshire). The rare Sabayon carpet invites a visitor to lift it and explore the bargains beneath. Both Clive and Olive created their own wardrobes by stitching together labels bought in bulk at wholesale: "We transcend the material."

Her clothes: Calvin Mazuma, Yves Ducat, Vittorio Dinero, Simoleon, Made of Money. Mad Frisson and Warren Beatty for shoes; cobbles her own boots from Levi's labels.

His clothes: Mach Wash Tumble Dry, Property of the Harvard Athletic Association, I.L.G.W.U., It Is Illegal to Remove This Tag. Galerie du Sabot (Brussels) for shoes, Savile Row for sweatbands.

Interests: Collecting, reading, taking inventory.

Restaurants: Betamax of Athens, Imperial Musk-Polyp, Folie à Deux (Paris).

CRAIG CLAIBORNE

Just a Quiet Dinner for Two in Paris: 31 Dishes, Nine Wines, a $4,000 Check

If one were offered dinner for two at any price, to be eaten in any restaurant anywhere in the world, what would the choice be? And in these days of ever-higher prices, what would the cost be?

By submitting the highest bid on Channel 13's fund-raising auction last June, we found ourselves in a position earlier this week to answer these questions. The place: Chez Denis in Paris. The cost: $4,000.

Our winning bid was $300.

.   .   .

The selection of the restaurant dominated our fantasies for weeks as in our minds, we dined on a hundred meals or more. At times we were in Paris, then in Alsace. We considered Rome, Tokyo and Hong Kong, Copenhagen and Stockholm, Brussels and London.

The consideration of restaurants competed with thoughts of the greatest of champagnes and still wines, visions of caviar and foie gras, dreams of elaborate desserts. Perhaps we would choose nothing but vodka or champagne with caviar followed by foie gras with Chateau d'Yquem—but no, any old millionaire could do that.

. . .

In time we considered Chez Denis, which is a great favorite among several food writers (Henri Gault, Christian Millau and Waverly Root among them), but is nonetheless not well known. It is a tiny place on the Rue Gustave Flaubert, not far from the Arc de Triomphe.

We visited Chez Denis in a party of three to reconnoiter. It was not hard to go incognito, for we suspect that the proprietor, Denis Lahana, does not credit any Americans with even the most elementary knowledge of French wine and food.

. . .

A CRUCIAL QUESTION, SERIOUSLY ANSWERED

After dinner, we asked Mr. Denis, offhandedly, how much he would charge for the most lavish dinner for two that he and his chef could prepare. He spoke in terms of $2,000 to $3,000.

We told him that we were about to celebrate a birthday and that money was no obstacle in ordering the finest dinner in Europe. Mr. Denis, with little hesitation, pulled up a chair and sat down. He took us seriously.

We asked him to consider the matter at his convenience and write to us with his proposal. When he did, his letter stated:

"In accordance with your demand, I propose to organize for you a prestigious dinner. In the land of my birth, the region of Bordeaux, one speaks of a repas de vins, a meal during the course of which a number of wines of great prestige are served, generally nine wines.

"I am suggesting nine such wines, to be served in the course of a dinner à la Française in the classic tradition. To dine properly in this style, many dishes are offered and served to the guests, chosen with the sole thought that each dish be on the same high level as the wines and those most likely to give pleasure as the wines are tasted."

He suggested a dinner of 31 dishes that would start with an hors d'oeuvre and go on to three "services," the first consisting of soups, savory, an assortment of substantial main dishes, and ices or sherbets to clear the palate.

This would be followed by the second service: hot roasts or baked dishes, vegetables, cold, light, meaty dishes in aspic and desserts.

And then the third service: decorated confections, petits fours and fruits.

The youngest wine would be a six-year-old white burgundy, the oldest a 140-year-old madeira.

Mr. Denis set a price of $4,000. This, we must hasten to add, included service and taxes. We accepted.

The proprietor suggested that the meal be served to four persons—all for the same price—because the food had to be prepared in a certain quantity and would be enough to serve as many as 10 persons, while the wines were enough for four.

We declined, because the rules set by American Express called for dinner for two. The dinner party would be made up of me and my colleague, Pierre Franey. Anything left over, we knew, would not go to waste.

Mr. Denis noted that it was not required that all foods be sampled and that the quantity of the food served would depend on the guest's appetite.

BELUGA CAVIAR IN CRYSTAL

And so, we sat down to our $4,000 dinner.

The hors d'oeuvre was presented: fresh Beluga caviar in crystal, enclosed in shaved ice, with toast. The wine was a superb 1966 Champagne Comtesse Marie de France.

Then came the first service, which started with three soups. There was consomme Denis, an inordinately good, rich, full-bodied, clear consomme of wild duck with shreds of fine crepes and herbs. It was clarified with raw duck and duck bones and then lightly thickened, as many classic soups are, with fine tapioca.

The second soup (still of the first service) was a crème Andalouse, an outstanding cream of tomato soup with shreds of sweet pimento and *fines herbes,* including fresh chives and chervil.

The first two soups were superb but the third, cold germiny (a cream of sorrel), seemed bland and anticlimactic. One spoonful of that sufficed.

The only wine served at this point was a touch of champagne. The soups having been disposed of, we moved on to a spectacularly delicate parfait of sweetbreads, an equally compelling mousse of quail in a small tarte, and a somewhat salty, almost abrasive but highly complementary tarte of Italian ham, mushrooms and a border of truffles.

1918 CHATEAU LATOUR, THE BEST BORDEAUX

The wine was a 1918 Chateau Latour, and it was perhaps the best bordeaux we had ever known. It was very much alive, with the least trace of tannin.

The next segment of the first service included a fascinating dish that the proprietor said he had created, Belon oysters broiled quickly in the shell and served with a pure beurre blanc, the creamy, lightly thickened butter sauce.

Also in this segment were a lobster in a creamy, cardinal-red sauce that was heavily laden with chopped truffles and, after that, another startling but excellent dish, a sort of Provençale pie made with red mullet and baked with tomato, black olives and herbs, including fennel or anise seed, rosemary, sage and thyme.

The accompanying wine was a 1969 Montrachet Baron Thénard, which was extraordinary (to our taste, all first-rate Montrachet whites are extraordinary).

The final part of the first service consisted of what was termed filets et sots l'y laissent de poulard de Bresse, sauce suprême aux cèpes (the so-called "fillet" strips of chicken plus the "oysters" found in the after-backbone of chicken blended in a cream sauce containing sliced wild mushrooms).

CHARTREUSE OF PARTRIDGE AND COOKED CABBAGE

There followed another curious but oddly appealing dish, a classic chartreuse of partridge, the pieces of roasted game nested in a bed of cooked cabbage and baked in a mosaic pattern, intricately styled, of carrot and turnip cut into fancy shapes.

And a tender rare-roasted fillet of Limousin beef with a rich truffle sauce.

The wine with the meat and game was a 1928 Chateau Mouton Rothschild. It was ageless and beautiful.

The first service finally ended with sherbets in three flavors—raspberry, orange and lemon: The purpose of this was to revive the palate for the second service, and it did. We were two hours into the meal and going at the food, it seemed, at a devilish pace.

The second service included the ortolans en brochette, an element of the dinner to be anticipated with a relish almost equal to that of the caviar or the foie gras.

The small birds, which dine on berries through their brief lives, are cooked whole, with the head on, and without cleaning except for removing the feathers. They are as fat as butter and an absolute joy to bite into because of the succulence of the flesh. Even the bones, except for the tiny leg bones, are chewed and swallowed. There is one bird to one bite.

The second service also included fillets of wild duck en salmis in a rich brown game sauce. The final dish in this segment was a rognonade de veau, or roasted boned loin of veal wrapped in puff pastry with fresh black truffles about the size of golf balls.

The vegetables served were pommes Anna—the potatoes cut into small rounds and baked in butter—and a purée rachel, a purée of artichokes.

FOIE GRAS, WOODCOCK AND PHEASANT

Then came the cold meat delicacies. There was butter-rich fresh foie gras in clear aspic, breast meat of woodcocks that was cooked until rare and served with a natural chaudfroid, another aspic and cold pheasant with fresh hazelnuts.

The wines for this segment consisted of a 1947 Chateau Lafite-Rothschild, a 1961 Chateau Petrus, and the most magnificent wine of the evening, a 1929 Romanée Conti.

The dinner drew near an end with three sweets—a cold glazed charlotte with strawberries, an ile flottante and poires alma. The wine for the sweets was a beautiful unctuous 1928 Chateau d'Yquem, which was quite sweet yet "dry."

The last service consisted of the pastry confections and fruits, served with an 1835 madeira. With coffee came a choice of a 100-year-old calvados or an hors d'age cognac.

And for the $4,000, logic asks if it was a perfect meal in all respects? The answer is no.

The crystal was Baccarat and the silver was family sterling, but the presentation of the dishes, particularly the cold dishes such as the sweetbread parfait and quail mousse tarte, was mundane.

The foods were elegant to look at, but the over-all display was undistinguished, if not to say shabby.

The chartreuse of pheasant, which can be displayed stunningly, was presented on a most ordinary dish.

The food itself was generally exemplary, although there were regrettable lapses there, too. The lobster in the gratin was chewy and even the sauce could not compensate for that. The oysters, of necessity, had to be cooked as briefly as possible to prevent toughening, but the beurre blanc should have been very hot. The dish was almost lukewarm when it reached the table, and so was the chartreuse of pheasant.

We've spent many hours reckoning the cost of the meal and find that we cannot break it down. We have decided this: We feel we could not have made a better choice, given the circumstance of time and place.

Mr. Denis declined to apply a cost to each of the wines, explaining that they contributed greatly to the total cost of the meal because it was necessary to open three bottles of the 1918 Latour in order to find one in proper condition.

Over all, it was an unforgettable evening and we have high praise for Claude Mornay, the 37-year-old genius behind the meal.

We reminded ourselves of one thing during the course of that evening: If you were Henry VIII, Lucullus, Gargantua and Bacchus, all rolled into one, you cannot possibly sustain, start to finish, a state of ecstasy while dining on a series of 31 dishes.

Wines, illusion or not, became increasingly interesting, although we were laudably sober at the end of the meal.

RUSSELL BAKER

Francs and Beans

As chance would have it, the very evening Craig Claiborne ate his historic $4,000 dinner for two with 31 dishes and nine wines in Paris, a Lucullan repast for one was prepared and consumed in New York by this correspondent, no slouch himself when it comes to titillating the palate.

Mr. Claiborne won his meal in a television fund-raising auction and had it professionally prepared. Mine was created from spur-of-the-moment inspiration, necessitated when I discovered a note on the stove saying, "Am eating out with Dora and Imogene—make dinner for yourself." It was from the person who regularly does the cooking at my house and, though disconcerted at first, I quickly rose to the challenge.

The meal opened with a 1975 Diet Pepsi served in a disposable bottle. Although its bouquet was negligible, its distinct metallic aftertaste evoked memories of tin cans one had licked experimentally in the first flush of childhood's curiosity.

To create the balance of tastes so cherished by the epicurean palate, I followed with a *paté de fruites de nuts of Georgia,* prepared according to my own recipe. A half-inch layer of creamy-style peanut butter is troweled onto a graham cracker, then half a banana is crudely diced and pressed firmly into the peanut butter and cemented in place as it were by a second graham cracker.

The accompanying drink was cold milk served in a wide-brimmed jelly glass. This is essential to proper consumption of the paté, since the entire confection must be dipped into the milk to soften it for eating. In making the presentation to the mouth, one must beware lest the milk-soaked portion of the sandwich fall onto the necktie. Thus, seasoned gourmandisers follow the old maxim of the Breton chefs and "bring the mouth to the jelly glass."

At this point in the meal, the stomach was ready for serious eating, and I prepared beans with bacon grease, a dish I perfected in 1937 while developing my *cuisine du dépression.*

The dish is started by placing a pan over a very high flame until it becomes dangerously hot. A can of Heinz's pork and beans is then emptied into the pan and allowed to char until it reaches the consistency of hardening concrete. Three strips of bacon are fried to crisps, and when the beans have formed huge dense clots firmly welded to the pan, the bacon grease is poured in and stirred vigorously with a large screw driver.

This not only adds flavor but also loosens some of the beans from the side of the pan. Leaving the flame high, I stirred in a three-day-old spaghetti sauce found in the refrigerator, added a sprinkle of chili powder, a large dollop of Major Grey's chutney and a tablespoon of bicarbonate of soda to make the whole dish rise.

Beans with bacon grease is always eaten from the pan with a tablespoon while standing over the kitchen sink. The pan must be thrown away immediately. The correct drink with this dish is a straight shot of room-temperature gin. I had a Gilbey's, 1975, which was superb.

For the meat course, I had fried bologna *à la Nutley, Nouveau Jersey.* Six slices of A&P bologna were placed in an ungreased frying pan over maximum heat and held down by a long fork until the entire house filled with smoke. The bologna was turned, fried the same length of time on the other side, then served on air-filled white bread with thick lashings of mayonnaise.

The correct drink for fried bologna *à la Nutley, Nouveau Jersey* is a 1927 Nehi Cola, but since my cellar, alas, had none, I had to make do with a second shot of Gilbey's 1975.

The cheese course was deliciously simple—a single slice of Kraft's individually wrapped yellow sandwich cheese, which was flavored by vigorous rubbing over the bottom of the frying pan to soak up the rich bologna juices. Wine being absolutely *de rigueur* with cheese, I chose a 1974 Muscatel, flavored with a maraschino cherry, and afterwards cleared my palate with three pickled martini onions.

It was time for the fruit. I chose a Del Monte tinned pear, which, regrettably, slipped from the spoon and fell on the floor, necessitating its being blotted with a paper towel to remove cat hairs. To compensate for the resulting loss of pear syrup, I dipped it lightly in hot-dog relish which created a unique flavor.

With the pear I drank two shots of Gilbey's 1975 and one shot of Wolfschmidt vodka (non-vintage), the Gilbey's having been exhausted.

At last it was time for the dish the entire meal had been building toward —dessert. With a paring knife, I ripped into a fresh package of Oreos, produced a bowl of My-T-Fine chocolate pudding which had been coagulating in the refrigerator for days and, using a potato masher, crushed a dozen Oreos into the pudding. It was immense.

Between mouthfuls, I sipped a tall, bubbling tumbler of cool Bromo-Seltzer, and finished with six ounces of Maalox. It couldn't have been better.

FRAN LEBOWITZ

Lesson One

LOS ANGELES, *laws* AN *juh lus,* or *laws* ANG *guh lus,* Calif., is a large citylike area surrounding the Beverly Hills Hotel. It is easily accessible to New York by phone or plane (although the converse is not true).

In 1956 the population of Los Angeles was 2,243,901. By 1970 it had risen to 2,811,801, 1,650,917 of whom are currently up for a series.

Early Spanish settlers called Los Angeles El Pueblo de Nuestra Señora la Reina de los Angeles, which means The Town of Our Lady, Queen of the Angels. The first part of the name was dropped when Los Angeles became a Mexican city in 1835. Today Los Angeles is often called collect.

THE LAND AND ITS RESOURCES

LOCATION, SIZE AND SURFACE FEATURES

Los Angeles lies on the Pacific Coast approximately three thousand miles from midtown Manhattan. The terrain is varied and ranges from clay to grass to composition, depending upon the type of court you find most comfortable. Los Angeles is on the large side, covering over four hundred and fifty square miles, which makes it advisable to play close to the net.

Surface features are numerous, and include hills, palm trees, large billboards depicting former and future back-up singers, highly colored flowers, eye-tucks, parking attendants and an enormous sign spelling out the word "Hollywood," the purpose of which is to indicate that one has indeed gotten off the plane.

CURRENCY

The most popular form of currency in Los Angeles is the point. Points are what they give to writers instead of money. Curiously enough, it is impossible to use points to purchase either goods or services, a situation that makes imperative the possession of a round-trip airplane ticket.

CLIMATE

It is generally quite sunny in Los Angeles, thereby allowing the natives to read contracts by natural light. The mild weather is one of the main topics of conversation in Los Angeles, the other one being the lack thereof in New York.

Many tourists come to Los Angeles because of the climate, attracted no doubt by the pleasant glare and festive air colors.

CHIEF PRODUCTS

The chief products of Los Angeles are novelizations, salad, game-show hosts, points, muscle tone, mini-series and rewrites. They export all of these items with the twin exceptions of muscle tone and points, neither of which seem to travel well.

THE PEOPLE

Many of the people in Los Angeles appear so lifelike that a sharp eye is necessary in order to avoid conversation with those who may be too dead to offer points. Initiates will carefully study a prospective producer's gold neckchain and will not start talking until certain that it is moving rhythmically.

The inhabitants of Los Angeles are a warm people, and family ties are so strong that a florist may volunteer the information that his sister-in-law's stepmother was once married to Lee Major's great-uncle before one has had a chance to ask.

EVERYDAY LIFE AND CUSTOMS

Everyday life in Los Angeles is casual but highly stratified and can probably best be understood by realizing that the residents would be happiest with a telephone book that contained subscribers' first names, followed by an announcement that the party had four lines, sixteen extensions and a fiercely guarded unlisted number.

FOOD AND DRINK

A great many people in Los Angeles are on special diets that restrict their intake of synthetic foods. The reason for this appears to be a widely held belief that organically grown fruits and vegetables make the cocaine work faster.

One popular native dish is called gambei and is served exclusively in Mr. Chow's, an attractive little Chinese restaurant on North Camden Drive. The menu description of gambei reads as follows: "This mysterious dish is everybody's favorite. People insist it is seaweed because it tastes and looks just like seaweed. But in fact it is not. It's a secret." This mystery was recently solved by a visiting New York writer, who took one taste of her surprise and said, "Grass."

"Grass?" queried her dinner companion. "You mean marijuana?"

"No," the writer replied. "Grass—you know, lawns, grass. The secret is that every afternoon all of the gardeners in Beverly Hills pull up around the back, the cook takes delivery and minutes later the happy patrons are avidly consuming—at $3.50 per portion—crisply French-fried—their own backyards."

CULTURE

Los Angeles is a contemporary city, and as such unfettered by the confining standards of conventional art. Therefore the people of this modern-day Athens have been free to develop new and innovative forms all their own. Of these, the most interesting is the novelization, for this enables one, for perhaps the very first time, to truly appreciate the phrase, "One picture is worth a thousand words."

The garb of Los Angeles is colorful, with lemon yellow, sky blue and lime green predominating, particularly in the attire of middle-aged men, most of whom look like Alan King. It is customary for these men to leave unbuttoned the first five buttons of their shirts in a rakish display of gray chest hair. Visitors are warned that calling the police to come in and button everyone up is a futile gesture; they will not respond.

Teenagers of both sexes wear T-shirts that disprove the theory that the young are no longer interested in reading, and facial expressions that disprove the T-shirts.

Middle-aged women favor for daytime wear much the same apparel as do teenage girls, but after six they like to pretty up and generally lean toward prom clothes.

THE LANGUAGE

Alphabet and pronunciation were both borrowed from the English, as was the custom of reading receipts from left to right. Word usage is somewhat exotic, however, and visitors would do well to study carefully the following table of words and phrases:

Formal: long pants

Concept: car chase

Assistant Director: the person who tells the cars which way to go. The phrase for this in New York is traffic cop.

Director: the person who tells the assistant director which way to tell the cars to go. The phrase for this in New York is traffic cop.

Creative Control: no points

Take a Meeting: this phrase is used in place of "have a meeting," and most likely derives from the fact that "take" is the verb that the natives are most comfortable with.

Sarcasm: what they have in New York instead of Jacuzzis.

TRANSPORTATION

There are two modes of transport in Los Angeles: car and ambulance. Visitors who wish to remain inconspicuous are advised to choose the latter.

ARCHITECTURE

The architecture of Los Angeles is basically the product of a Spanish heritage and a rich inner life. Public buildings, which are called gas stations *(gaz TAY shuns)* or restaurants *(res tur ONTS),* are characterized by their lack of height and are generally no taller than your average William Morris agent, although they occasionally hold more people. Houses, which are called homes *(HOMZ),* can be distinguished from public buildings by the number of Mercedes-Benzes parked outside. If there are over twelve, it is fairly safe to assume that they take American Express.

The Homespun Cowboy

Will Rogers born in 1879 took his lariat and his homespun humor and went from cowhand to stagehand and he never met a man he didn't like and all he knew was what he read in the papers and he made movies in Hollywood and worked in Argentina and South Africa and he toured with Texas Jack's Wild West Circus and drawled to fame on Broadway in 1916 as a star in the Ziegfeld Follies where he was not a comedian he was a humorist a humorist scratches his head before he tells a joke and if you think times have changed think again because here is part of his monologue from the 1923 Ziegfeld Follies and every one of his observations is still up-to-date.   **G.S.**

WILL ROGERS

Timely Topics

Now folks, all *I* know is just what little news I read every day in the papers. I see where another wife out on Long Island, here in New York, shot her husband. Season's opened a month *earlier* this year. Never a day passes in New York without some innocent bystander being shot. You just stand around this town long enough and be innocent, and somebody's gonna *shoot* ya. One day there was *four* shot. That's the best shootin' they ever *done* in this town. Hard to *find* four innocent people in New York. That's why a policeman never has to *aim* here. He just shoots up the street at anyone: No matter who it hits, its the right one.

Been havin' every kinda week here in New York. "Smile Week," "Apple Week" an' one called "Don't Git Hurt Week." Taxicab drivers couldn't hardly wait till the followin' Monday to run over you.

Everybody's talkin' about 'What's the matter with this country and what this country needs.' What this country needs worse than anything else is a place to park your *car!*

A New York society woman is suin' her ex-husband agin, claims she can't properly support that child on $50,000 a year alimony. Somebody's been feedin' that young un' *meat!*

Lots a people wondered why we left our soldiers in Germany so long. That's so they can git the *mail* sent to 'em during the war. We had to leave 'em over thar—two of 'em hadn't *married* yet.

92

But If There *Were* a Best . . .

There is no "best" in the arts. There is no "best" violinist in history, no "best" painter or, to move down a step or two, no "best" comedian. But we all have a favorite, and my favorite radio comedian was Fred Allen, whose programs were broadcast weekly from October 23, 1932, to June 26, 1949. Allen had wit, a keen sense of the topical, and an understanding of character. His "Allen's Alley" sequences featured four individuals who became as familiar as neighbors to millions of Americans: Senator Claghorn, a bellowing Southern political buffoon; Mrs. Nussbaum, a New York Jewish housewife; Titus Moody, a rube from Maine, and Ajax Cassidy, who, like Allen, was Irish Catholic. Allen's humor required intelligence to write and (from the audience) imagination, so it was television that killed it. ("The reason television is called a medium," he said, "is because nothing on it is well done.") For Fred Allen's final radio program, he chose as his guest Jack Benny, with whom he had had a toy feud since 1936 (to their mutual publicity benefit). In his autobiographical book *Treadmill to Oblivion,* Allen writes:

> For years people have been asking me if Jack and I are friendly. I don't think that Jack Benny has an enemy in the world. He is the best-liked actor in show business. He is the only comedian I know who dies laughing at all of the other comedians. He is my favorite comedian and I hope to be his friend until he is forty. That will be forever.
>
> After our long radio association it seemed that Jack should be the one to escort me out of the medium. He did.

Here is their sketch from the last program—with Jack Benny and the director Gregory Ratoff—one of Fred Allen's personal favorite scripts. **G.S.**

FRED ALLEN

Jack Benny in "Allen's Alley"

ALLEN: I can't get over it, Jack. I've never seen you looking better.
JACK: Well, thanks.
ALLEN: That beautiful wavy hair—
JACK: Well—
ALLEN: Those sparkling white teeth—
JACK: Gee—
ALLEN: And those long eyelashes—
JACK: Uh-huh. What about my nose?
ALLEN: Your nose?
JACK: Yes. At least that's *mine.*
JACK: Just between you and me, Fred, I have undergone a little plastic surgery.
ALLEN: Plastic surgery?
JACK: Yes. Every so often I have this plastic surgeon take up the slack skin on my face and tie it at the back of my neck.
ALLEN: The back of your neck? Doesn't it bother you?
JACK: No. The only thing is, now I wear a Size 27 collar.
ALLEN: I noticed that your Adam's Apple was pulled around under your left ear. But with it all, Jack, you still look the same as the first day I met you.
JACK: And, Fred, you look the same as the first day I met you.
ALLEN: Remember that first day we met.
VIOLINS: "Memories . . ." *(Sneaks in)*
ALLEN: I was in vaudeville—a star. I was headlining at the Cecil Theater in Mason City, Iowa. After the first show there was a knock on my dressing-room door.
(Knock on door)
ALLEN: Come in!
(Door opens)

KRAKAUER: Mr. Allen. I'm the manager, Mr. Krakauer. You've got a great act. You're a great star.

ALLEN: Thank you, Mr. Krakauer.

KRAKAUER: With you as the headliner I've got a great show. All but one act.

ALLEN: Oh.

KRAKAUER: I'm canning that guy right now. He's dressing across the hall. *(Knock on door. Door opens)*

JACK: Yes?

KRAKAUER: I'm the manager. Your act is putrid. You're canned!

JACK: Everything went wrong. When I came on the orchestra forgot to play "Pony Boy." When I played "Listen to the Mocking Bird" my E-string broke. At the finish when I play "Glow Worm" my violin lights up. The electrician forgot to plug it in.

KRAKAUER: My patrons are Iowa farmers. All week they work in the cornfields. They come to the theater to forget corn, not to have it thrown in their faces. Start packing!

JACK: But Mr. Krakauer—

KRAKAUER: You're through! Get out!

JACK: I wish I was dead.

ALLEN: What's the matter, son?

JACK: The manager canned me.

ALLEN: Come in to my room. Don't hang back, lad.

JACK: But—this is the star's dressing room.

ALLEN: I know.

JACK: You mean you're Fred Allen?

ALLEN: Yes. Stop trembling, son. Sit down.

JACK: Gosh! Me in Fred Allen's dressing room. It's like a dream.

ALLEN: What is your act called?

JACK: Gypsy Jack and his Tzigeuner Fiddle.

ALLEN: Gypsy Jack.

JACK: This is my first date in vaudeville. Now I'm canned.

ALLEN: Don't give up, Gypsy Jack.

JACK: But I haven't any money. I can't get home. I live in Waukegan.

ALLEN: What is the fare to Waukegan?

JACK: Thirty dollars.

ALLEN: Here is thirty dollars, Gypsy Jack. Go back to Waukegan.

JACK: Oh, thank you, Mr. Allen!

VIOLINS: "Memories . . ." *(Fades)*

ALLEN: Gosh, Jack, when I saw you leaving the theater that day in your gypsy suit with the burlap sash, little did I think I would ever see you again. What happened?

JACK: When I finally got home to Waukegan, I went back to pressing pants in my Uncle Tyler's tailor shop.

ALLEN: Mason City had left no scars?

JACK: No. But show business was still in my blood. I used to take my violin around and play for all of my friends.

ALLEN: You were happy.

JACK: For the nonce. Then, suddenly I had no friends.

ALLEN: And then?

JACK: One day, I was pressing a pair of pants. It was a rush job. The pants belonged to the tenor in a Blossom Time company. They were leaving that night.

ALLEN: I see.

JACK: I was pressing carefully, avoiding the holes, when my iron ran into a lump in one of the pockets. The lump turned out to be a ticket to Hollywood.

ALLEN: Hollywood! That was the second time we met.

VIOLINS: "Memories . . ." *(Fades)*

ALLEN: It was on the 20th Century Fox lot. I was starring in my first picture *Thanks a Million.* I remember that morning I walked on the set . . .

1ST VOICE: Quiet on the Set! Quiet on the set! Mr. Allen is ready for this scene!

2ND VOICE: Here's the script, Mr. Allen.

ALLEN: Thank you.

3RD VOICE: Chair, Mr. Allen?

ALLEN: Thank you.

4TH VOICE: Let me touch up your make-up, Mr. Allen.

ALLEN: Thank you.

RATOFF: Mr. Allen, we are shooting right away the big comedy scene.

ALLEN: Which one, Mr. Ratoff?

RATOFF: It is the Bowery. You do a scene with a bum.

ALLEN: A scene with a bum?

RATOFF: Yes. Joe, bring in the bum.

JOE: This way, you guys! Central Casting sent us fifteen of the seediest extras they could find. Pick out the crumbiest, Mr. Allen.

ALLEN: Hmm. How about that one—in the dirty T-shirt and baggy beret.

JOE: Okay. Hey, you—step forward.

BENNY: Yes, *sir!*

ALLEN: Just a minute, Beaten One. I know your face. Aren't you Gypsy Jack?

JACK: Yes, Mr. Allen. But here in Hollywood my name is Jack Benny.

ALLEN: I hardly knew you with that beard.

JACK: I've been standing-in for Gabby Hayes. This is my big break, Mr. Allen. Gosh, doing a scene with you . . . It's like a dream again.

RATOFF: All right. Let's get going. Cameras ready! Lights!

JOE: Here's the pie, Mr. Allen. *(Hands Fred lemon pie)*

JACK: Wait! A pie?

RATOFF: Yes. It's a very short scene. Mr. Allen hits you in the face with a pie. Camera! Lights! Ready, Mr. Allen.

ALLEN: Ready. *(Gets set to hit Benny)*

JACK: Wait a minute!

RATOFF: Hold it! What is it?

JACK: What do I do?

RATOFF: You do nothing. You just get the pie in the face. Camera! Lights! Get ready to throw, Mr. Allen.

ALLEN: I'm ready. *(Gets set)*

JACK: One moment, please!

RATOFF: HOLD IT! Now what?

JACK: Don't I duck or anything?

ALLEN: No. You just hold your face still and *Whap* you get it.

JACK: It might help if I mug after the *Whap.*

RATOFF: Get another bum! This bum is a bum!

ALLEN: He'll be all right, Gregory. Now, Jack, pipe down.

JACK: Sorry, Mr. Allen.

RATOFF: Camera! Lights! Ready, Mr. Allen.

ALLEN: All set. *(Gets set)*

JACK: Wait a minute!

ALLEN: What is it now?

JACK: What kind of a pie is it, Mr. Allen?

ALLEN: Lemon meringue.

JACK: Couldn't they make it banana cream? I like banana cream better.

ALLEN: It so happens Mr. Zanuck likes lemon meringue.

JACK: Oh!

RATOFF: Camera! Lights! Quick, throw it, Mr. Allen!

JACK: Hold it! Just one more thing.

RATOFF: Now what?

JACK: What part of my face is Mr. Allen going to hit? I'd like to get it right so you won't have to do the scene over. I'm anxious to make good.

RATOFF: He will hit you between the eyes, so the lemon meringue will drip down on your clothes.

JACK: On my clothes?

RATOFF: We will have them cleaned and pressed for you.

JACK: The pressing I can do myself. I don't want to cause trouble. *(Laugh)*

RATOFF: *(Fast)* Camera! Lights! Quick, Fred!

ALLEN: Okay. *(Gets set)*

JACK: Wait! Wouldn't it be funnier if he hit me with a loaf of bread?

ALLEN: A loaf of bread?

JACK: Sliced.

RATOFF: I've had enough! You're fired! Get off the set!

JACK: But, sir—

RATOFF: That's all for today, everybody! This bum has unnerved me. Put away the pie. *(Fade)* That's all!

ALLEN: Well?

JACK: I wish I was dead.

ALLEN: Look, Gypsy. I told you ten years ago in Mason City—

JACK: But, Mr. Allen, I thought the movies—

ALLEN: Okay, so you don't need talent in movies. You still have to have *something.*

JACK: You're right. I guess I'm just not meant for show business.

ALLEN: Do you still live in Waukegan?

JACK: Yes, Mr. Allen. It's thirty dollars by bus.

ALLEN: Okay. Go back to Waukegan. Here is the thirty dollars.

JACK: Mr. Allen—how will I ever be able to repay your kindness—

VIOLINS: "Memories . . ." *(Sneaks in)*

ALLEN: I'll never forget, Jack, when you left the studio I gave you the lemon meringue pie.

JACK: It lasted me all the way to Green Bay.

ALLEN: What happened when you got back to Waukegan this time?

JACK: I went back to the tailor shop. But my Uncle Tyler wasn't there any more.

ALLEN: There was a new owner?

JACK: And he made life miserable.

ALLEN: He was mean to you?

JACK: All day he kept singing those songs of his from *Blossom Time.* To this day I hate tenors. I hate *Blossom Time.*

ALLEN: You were unhappy, eh?

JACK: I was desperate to get away. Whenever I got a pair of pants to press, the first thing I did was feel for lumps. And then one day—

ALLEN: Another lump?

JACK: A big one.

ALLEN: A railroad ticket?

JACK: This time it was money. I could go where I wanted. I went to New York.

ALLEN: New York. That was the third time we met.

VIOLINS: "Memories . . ." (Fades)

ALLEN: New York! That's where you got your start in radio.

JACK: Thanks to you, Fred.

ALLEN: Oh, it was nothing. I remember, that day I got the call from a man named Weaver. A big-shot with the American Tobacco Company. I entered Mr. Weaver's office—

(Door opens and closes)

WEAVER: Gad! Fred Allen! We've been waiting all afternoon.

ALLEN: I got your note, Mr. Weaver.

WEAVER: We've got a big radio program all lined up for Lucky Strike Cigarettes—and we want you to be the star.

ALLEN: I'm sorry.

WEAVER: Wait till you hear this setup—we've got Don Wilson to announce; Rochester, Dennis Day, Phil Harris . . .

ALLEN: But I've just signed to do a program for Tender Leaf Tea and Shefford Cheese.

WEAVER: Well, that does it. Without Allen we might as well pull Lucky Strikes off the market. We'll close the plantations, put LSMFT back in the alphabet, and send old F. E. Boone back to Lexington, Kentucky.

ALLEN: There must be somebody else you can get.

WEAVER: WHO? Singin' Sam wants too much money. The Street Singer went into the real estate business. And what a program we had lined up!

ALLEN: I'm sorry.

WEAVER: We had this quintette hired to do the commercials.

ALLEN: A quintette?

WEAVER: Yeah. Show him, boys!

CAST: HMMMMMMMMMMMM.

ALLEN: Wait! The guy on the end—aren't you Gypsy Jack?

JACK: Yes, Mr. Allen.

ALLEN: Jack, you in a quintette?

WEAVER: (Sotto) His wife, Mary, is in the show. We did her a favor.

ALLEN: Look, Mr. Weaver, the star of this Lucky Strike show—does he have to be funny?

WEAVER: No. We've got Rochester, Dennis, Phil—plenty of comedians.

ALLEN: Does he have to have any talent?

WEAVER: All we need is a slob the others can bounce jokes off of.

ALLEN: Then here's your man—Jack Benny!

WEAVER: Okay, Benny—you're hired!

JACK: Fred. I'll never—never be able to thank you enough.

VIOLINS: "Memories . . ." *(Sneaks in)*

ALLEN: So, Jack, that's how you got into radio.

JACK: Yes, Fred, and if it wasn't for the thirty dollars you gave me in Mason City and Hollywood— Say, funny how things slip your mind. I never did pay you back that sixty dollars. *(Laugh)*

ALLEN: No.

JACK: I lost your address. And you were traveling around all the time. I tried to find you through *Billboard.*

ALLEN: Forget it, Jack.

JACK: But it isn't like me.

ALLEN: I know. Forget about it.

JACK: Gosh, it just happens I haven't got a cent on me right now, or I'd—

ALLEN: Please, Jack. Don't mention it again.

JACK: I won't. Well, Fred, it's been swell talking over old times.

ALLEN: It sure has, Jack. Tell me, what are you doing now?

JACK: Nothing. My program finished last Sunday.

ALLEN: You're out of work again, eh?

JACK: Yes, Fred.

ALLEN: What are you going to do?

JACK: I guess I'll go back to Waukegan. But, Fred—

ALLEN: You don't have to ask me, Jack. Here's the thirty dollars.

JACK: But, Fred—

ALLEN: And this time stay in Waukegan!

By Any Other Name

George Burns (played by Nathan Birnbaum) first met Gracie Allen (played by Grace Ethel Cecile Rosalie Allen) backstage in 1922 and they were soon teamed for good: good humor, a good marriage, and good times for their audiences. It was George who created the character of the literal-minded scatterbrained Gracie, and it was Gracie's expert acting that convinced the public that she really *was* a literal-minded scatterbrain.

In the long-ago days and nights of vaudeville, playing the Palace Theater on Broadway meant that You Had Arrived. Here is the routine that Burns and Allen used the very first time they played the Palace.

G.S.

GEORGE BURNS AND GRACIE ALLEN

Say Good Night, Gracie

(Play-on music. George and Gracie enter holding hands. Gracie stops, turns, looks toward the wings, and waves. She lets go of George's hand and walks toward the wing, still waving. Then she stops and beckons to whomever she is waving to come out. A man comes out, puts his arms around Gracie, and kisses her, and she kisses him. They wave to each other as he backs offstage. Gracie returns to George center stage.)

GRACIE: Who was that?

GEORGE: You don't know?

GRACIE: No, my mother told me never to talk to strangers.

GEORGE: That makes sense.

GRACIE: This always happens to me. On my way in, a man stopped me at the stage door and said, "Hiya, cutie, how about a bite tonight after the show?"

GEORGE: And you said?

GRACIE: I said, "I'll be busy after the show but I'm not doing anything now," so I bit him.

GEORGE: Gracie, let me ask you something. Did the nurse ever happen to drop you on your head when you were a baby?

GRACIE: Oh, no, we couldn't afford a nurse, my mother had to do it.

GEORGE: You had a smart mother.

GRACIE: Smartness runs in my family. When I went to school I was so smart my teacher was in my class for five years.

GEORGE: Gracie, what school did you go to?

GRACIE: I'm not allowed to tell.

GEORGE: Why not?

GRACIE: The school pays me $25 a month not to tell.

GEORGE: Is there anybody in the family as smart as you?

GRACIE: My sister Hazel is even smarter. If it wasn't for her, our canary would never have hatched that ostrich egg.

GEORGE: A canary hatched an ostrich egg?

GRACIE: Yeah . . . but the canary was too small to cover that big egg.

GEORGE: So?

GRACIE: So . . . Hazel sat on the egg and held the canary in her lap.

GEORGE: Hazel must be the smartest in your family.

GRACIE: Oh, no. My brother Willy was no dummy either.

GEORGE: Willy?

GRACIE: Yeah, the one who slept on the floor.

GEORGE: Why would he sleep on the floor?

GRACIE: He had high blood pressure—

GEORGE: And he was trying to keep it down?

GRACIE: Yeah.

GEORGE: I'd like to meet Willy.

GRACIE: You can't miss him. He always wears a high collar to cover the appendicitis scar on his neck.

GEORGE: Gracie, your appendix is down around your waist.

GRACIE: I know, but Willy was so ticklish they had to operate up there.

GEORGE: What's Willy doing now?

GRACIE: He just lost his job.

GEORGE: Lost his job?

GRACIE: Yeah, he's a window washer.

GEORGE: And?

GRACIE: And . . . he was outside on the twentieth story washing a window and when he got through he stepped back to admire his work.

GEORGE: And he lost his job.

GRACIE: Yeah . . . And when he hit the pavement he was terribly embarrassed.

GEORGE: Embarrassed?

GRACIE: Yeah . . . his collar flew off and his appendicitis scar showed.

GEORGE: Gracie, this family of yours—

GRACIE: When Willy was a little baby my father took him riding in his carriage, and two hours later my father came back with a different baby and a different carriage.

GEORGE: Well, what did your mother say?

GRACIE: My mother didn't say anything because it was a better carriage.

GEORGE: A better carriage?

GRACIE: Yeah . . . And the little baby my father brought home was a little French baby so my mother took up French.

GEORGE: Why?

GRACIE: So she would be able to understand the baby—

GEORGE: When the baby started to talk?

GRACIE: Yeah.

GEORGE: Gracie, this family of yours, do you all live together?

GRACIE: Oh, sure. My father, my brother, my uncle, my cousin and my nephew all sleep in one bed and—

GEORGE: In one bed? I'm surprised your grandfather doesn't sleep with them.

GRACIE: Oh, he did, but he died, so they made him get up.

They went on to decades of national fame on radio and television, and it was lines of this nature that endeared Gracie to the country.   **G.S.**

GRACIE: I see in the papers that the Los Angeles Police are hunting for a Chicago gangster. But why should they want one from Chicago? Can't they be satisfied with a hometown boy?

GRACIE: Shorter cars use much more gas. With a short car you have to travel much farther to go the same distance.

REPAIRMAN: Mrs. Burns, there's nothing wrong with your electric clock. You didn't have it plugged in.

GRACIE: I don't want to waste electricity so I plug it in when I want to know what time it is.

NEIGHBOR: I have to go to Sears and Roebuck. We don't have a garbage disposal.

GRACIE: Isn't that a long way to take your garbage every day?

APPLIANCE SALESMAN: You'll like this range, Mrs. Burns. For instance, you put in a roast, you set the oven control, then you go out all day. When you come home at night, the roast is done.

Gracie: Haven't you got one where I don't have to go out?

Say good night, Gracie.

FLENNIKEN

THE UNHAPPIEST MAN IN NEW YORK

He had an Irish psychiatrist and a Jewish bartender.

Bob and Ray: The Two and Only

Bob Elliott and Ray Goulding first found friendship at radio station WHDH in Boston. That was 1946, and in 1951 they found higher wages in New York and were found by national audiences who found them so funny that many haven't stopped laughing yet.

Bob and Ray have spoofed soap operas, radio interviewers who don't listen to the answers, wonder dogs, slow talkers, and crime shows ("Mr. Trace, Keener Than Most Persons"). They have also benefited the public by offering merchandise from their Overstocked Warehouse, including prefab land for people who need a place to put their prefab homes.

Among their unforgettable characters are Wally Ballou, Mary Backstayge, her theater doorman Pop Beloved, and, in today's episodes, Agatha Murchfield, her son Rodney, and her lawyer, Bodin Pardew. Let's listen.

G.S.

BOB ELLIOTT AND RAY GOULDING

Garish Summit—Episode 1

(Drama theme music. Establish and under for)

BOB: And now, Chapter One in the unfolding story of intrigue among the socially prominent families of Garish Summit. There—in stately splendor far removed from the squalid village below—they fight their petty battles over power and money.

(Theme up briefly and then fade for)

BOB: As our action begins, Miss Agatha is staring thoughtfully out the music room window. Suddenly, she turns and speaks . . .

AGATHA: There's a strange car stopping out in front, Rodney.

RODNEY: I wouldn't exactly call it strange, Mother. Of course, I never cared for rally stripes on a Rolls-Royce myself. However . . .

AGATHA: Oh, my word, Rodney! I don't mean strange in that sense. I just never saw it before. And now, a strange man is getting out.

RODNEY: I agree, Mother. He is an odd-looking duck. Ears set too low . . .

AGATHA: Oh, Rodney—you're such a wimp. You never understand a word I say to you.

(Doorbell)

RODNEY *(Calls off):* Come in. It's open.

(Door opens and closes. Then a long period of footsteps)

RODNEY *(Calls off):* Over here—in the music room.

(More footsteps. Then door opens and closes. Then more footsteps)

RODNEY *(Calls off):* Back here—in the conversation pit behind the Wurlitzer.

(Another long period of footsteps)

MAN: Quite a place you've got here.

RODNEY: Thank you. We like it. We have forty-six thousand, two hundred square feet here in the main house. Then, the twins live over in the annex, which has . . .

AGATHA: Oh, shut up, Rodney. Whoever this man is, I'm sure he doesn't want to hear you recite a lot of boring figures.

RODNEY: You're quite right, Mother. Perhaps introductions would be more in order. I'm the wealthy but spineless young executive, Rodney Murchfield. And this is my dowager mother, Agatha.

MAN: Pleased to meet you, Miss Agatha. I've been looking forward to this moment. You see, I'm your long-lost elder son, Skippy.

(Organ: musical sting)

RODNEY: I'm afraid there's been some mistake, you sleazy impostor. I'm an only child and sole heir to the Murchfield billions. Mother, tell him you never had another son.

AGATHA: Well, I'm just trying to remember. That would have been about thirty years ago. And there were so many events going on at the country club then that it's hard to keep track of everything.

RODNEY: But, Mother—he's obviously feeding you a cock-and-bull story.

MAN: It's no cock-and-bull story, pal. I've got proof. Look! Here's a picture of me when I was four, and Mom took me to see Santa Claus at Gucci's.

RODNEY: What does this prove? There's no one in the picture but you and Santa Claus.

MAN: Well, of course not. A guy wouldn't want his mother in the picture when he was talking to Santa Claus.

RODNEY: Apparently you take me for a complete fool.

MAN: Yeah—more or less.

RODNEY: Well, I'm onto your little game. You fortune hunters are all alike. You learn how my Grandpa Murchfield was exploring for oil in this land in 1912 when he struck lead. It proved to be the Mother Lode —a rich vein of drab, gray metal stretching as far as the eye could see.

AGATHA: Oh, knock it off, Rodney. You always tell that story as if you had something to do with it.

RODNEY: Sorry, Mother. I guess I get carried away with family pride. After all, he was my grandfather.

MAN: Well, he was mine too. I remember he used to take me on his knee and say, "Skippy, someday it'll be your job to get the lead out."

RODNEY: He couldn't have said that to you. He died before you were born.

MAN: Oh, really? Well, maybe I heard it someplace else then.

RODNEY: Besides, no one in this family would ever have a name like Skippy.

AGATHA: Well, maybe that's just a nickname. His real name could be something more socially acceptable—like Caldwell or E. W.

RODNEY: Mother, believe me—this man's a fraud.

MAN: Caldwell sounds okay to me. Yep. No doubt about it. That's who I am—Caldwell Murchfield.

RODNEY: See, Mother? You're playing right into his hands.

AGATHA: No. I don't think so. I always liked the name Caldwell. But no one outside the family could have known that. It's good to have you home, Caldwell. Now come along and meet the others.

RODNEY: I wish you'd reconsider all this.

MAN: Oh, I already know part of the family, Mom. Like for instance Rodney's ravishingly beautiful wife, Jennifer. I know her well. Yes indeed. I know her real well! *(Evil chuckle)*

(Organ: sting)

BOB: Will this unknown man in the ready-to-wear suit be accepted as a Murchfield without any further questions? Can Jennifer provide some of the missing answers? And what about the butler who failed to answer the door when the stranger arrived? Perhaps we'll learn more next time when we hear Agatha say . . .

AGATHA: No. I didn't write you out of my will, Rodney. You were never in it.

BOB: That's next time when we resume our story of decadence as it unfolds on *Garish Summit*.

(Organ: theme up briefly and then out)

BOB ELLIOTT
AND RAY GOULDING

Garish Summit—Episode 2

(Dramatic theme music: Establish and under for)

BOB: Welcome again to Garish Summit and its endless story of intrigue among the socially prominent. There—in stately splendor far removed from the squalid village below—the beautiful people fight their petty battles over power and money.

(Theme up briefly and then fade for)

BOB: As our action begins, strong-willed Agatha Murchfield is in the solarium, awaiting the arrival of her lawyer, Bodin Pardew.

(Door opens and closes. Then footsteps)

AGATHA: Is that you, Bodin?

PARDEW: Yes. I seem to be somewhere in the entry hall, Agatha. Can you talk me in from here?

AGATHA: Just hang a right through the music room and then cut across the west edge of the library until you get to the solarium. You can't miss it.

PARDEW: Very well. I'm on my way.

(About ten seconds of footsteps. The door opens and closes. Then more prolonged footsteps. Then another door opens and closes)

AGATHA: Ah, there you are, Bodin. It's been ages.

PARDEW: Yes, it has, Agatha. But that's only because the carpet cleaners had the library blocked, and I had to double clear back through the dining room . . . I must say you're looking well, except that you seem drawn and haggard—as if you haven't slept in days.

AGATHA: Well, I have something preying on my mind that I need your help with, Bodin. A man has turned up here in Garish Summit who claims to be my long-lost elder son, Caldwell.

PARDEW: That's shocking, Agatha. We've known each other for forty years, and I always thought your weak-willed son, Rodney, was an only child.

AGATHA: Well, I thought so, too. That's the strange part I don't understand.

PARDEW: Well, you're a fabulously rich widow who's inherited the world's largest chain of lead mines. The man's probably a fortune hunter.

AGATHA: No. I've encountered those before. But this chap definitely claims to be the son I never knew I had. So, of course, it's just his word against mine.

PARDEW: Well, I'm not sure that's the case. But how can I be of help?

AGATHA: I want you to check out his story, Bodin. See if there's a birth certificate—look into hospital records—dig through newspaper files . . . Well, aren't you going to write down these instructions?

PARDEW: I suppose I could, if you like. The back of this envelope is blank, so all I need is a point on my pencil. Is there a sharpener around anywhere, Agatha?

AGATHA: Over there under the window by the tumbling mat.

PARDEW: Thank you. I'll be back in a jiffy.

(*Prolonged footsteps, then the grinding of a pencil sharpener. A pause. Then more grinding of the sharpener*)

AGATHA: My stars, Bodin! What are you doing over there?

PARDEW: It's all right, Agatha. Everything's being take care of.

(*More pencil sharpening. Then footsteps*)

PARDEW: There, now. Shall we begin?

AGATHA: Well, first, I want to find out whether a birth certificate was ever issued for a Caldwell Murchfield. Then . . .

PARDEW: Just a minute. (*Mumbles to himself*) She—wants—me—to—find—out . . .

AGATHA: My word! How did a nincompoop like you ever get to be my attorney?

PARDEW: I don't know, Agatha. I suppose I could look in the files at my office and see if I have any documents covering that.

AGATHA: No. Don't waste any more time. Just find out if this mysterious stranger is really my eldest son. If he is, I'll want to rewrite my will to exclude my other boy, Rodney.

PARDEW: I understand. Incidentally, about this young man who calls himself Caldwell Murchfield. Where is he now?

AGATHA: Rodney took him moose hunting. Caldwell had wanted to go to the bank and rummage through my safe deposit box. But Rodney insisted they go hunting first.

PARDEW: Were both young men carrying shotguns when they left here, Agatha?

AGATHA: No. I remember that part distinctly because it struck me as strange. Rodney had a gun, but he told Caldwell just to carry a shovel.

PARDEW: Agatha, I think this has the makings of a dangerous situation.

AGATHA: Well, I told them that before they left. You can't bring down a moose with a shovel. But Rodney said not to worry. He said there's no space in the trophy room for another stuffed animal, anyway!

PARDEW: I'm afraid this is no longer a case for a lawyer. I'm going to call the police.

(Musical stinger)

AGATHA: Well, I guess the police couldn't botch things up any worse than you always do. But will they hunt for those old birth records I need?

PARDEW: A more urgent matter is involved here, Agatha. To put it as delicately as possible—one of your sons may have slaughtered the other.

(Theme. Establish and under for)

RAY: Must Agatha now face the loss of a son that she had assumed was lost all along? Can Caldwell be a murder victim if birth records show that he never existed? And what about the blank envelope that Bodin Pardew mysteriously found in his pocket? Perhaps we'll learn more next time when we hear Rodney Murchfield say . . .

RODNEY: I know it's only a raccoon. But I thought pasting these horns on its head might make it seem like more.

RAY: That's next time when we resume our story of wealth and intrigue on *Garish Summit*.

(Theme up briefly and then out)

MIKE PETERS

ELLIS WEINER

Patriotic Spot (60 Secs.)

You're waking up, America. It's morning—and you're waking up to live life like you've never lived it before. Say hello to a whole new way of being awake, American. Say hello to us.

Who are we? The idea people. A family of companies. America's supermarket. We're all this—and more. All day, every day, something we do will touch your life. At home. At school. Whether you need us or not, we're there.

We're watching you, America. We're watching you when you work—because, America, you work hard. And we know that afterward you've got a mighty big thirst. Not just a thirst for the best beer you can find. But a thirst for living. A thirst for years of experience. America, you're thirsty.

You're spelling more today, America. You're spelling a lot of things. Words. Words like "cheese." "Relief." And you're using those words to make phrases, and you're talking with those phrases every day, keeping America's telephone system the best in the world. America, you've got something to say, and you're coming in loud and clear. "Cheese relief." "Relief cheese." You said it, America.

Where does America go when it wants more of everything? It comes to us. Who are we? An American tradition. We provide a broad range of services. In eight major markets. Sixteen times a day. All across this great country of ours. Who are we? We're people.

People who know that America is digging in. People who come from all walks of life. People whose job it is to serve you. And we're doing it—better than ever. We're working harder to serve you, America. Because you're entitled. You've earned it. You deserve the best—the very best. From the skillful management of natural resources to the thirst-quenching beer you drink: you know what you want, and you grab it. You expect more, and you get it. Ask for it by name, America.

You're on the move, too—and we're doing our best to beat you there. Around the corner, or around the world: we're waiting for you. Who are we? America's host from coast to coast. We are insight. We are knowledge. We are the future. And we're changing—changing to keep up with you.

America, say hello to something new. Say hello to quality. Quality you can see. Quality you can feel. Quality you can say hello to. (How do you spell "quality," America? *Real* quality—quality you can trust? The same way we've been spelling it for over a hundred and fifty years.)

You're looking good, America. And we're looking at you. Who are we? People building transportation to serve people. Where are we? Where America shops. What are we? What the Colonel cooks. How did we get here? We are driven.

We want what you want. It's that simple. And we're giving it to you. At work. At play. Because America works as hard as it works, and plays as hard as it plays. When America has nothing to do, it reaches for us. And we're there—in energy, in communications, in research. With the meticulous attention to detail that comes only from the choicest hops, the finest barley.

We're Number One. You're Number One. You're a winner, America. And we know what you're thinking. We know how you feel. How do we know? Because we take the time to tell you. We take the time to care.

And it pays off. We're here, America. And the next time you're here—the next time we can tell you who we are and what we do—we'll be doing what we do best.

"I may be crazy, Leo, but I'm not stupid.
Or the other way round."

VERONICA GENG

Curb Carter Policy Discord Effort Threat

WASHINGTON, OCT. 11—In a surprise move, a major spokesman announced yesterday that a flurry of moves has forestalled deferment of the Administration's controversial hundred-pronged strategy. The nine-page indictment provides a minimum of new details about the alleged apprehensions now being voiced in key areas. As holiday traffic flowed into and out of the nation's cities, President Carter acknowledged in a telephone interview that there is "cause for some optimism." But Senate conferees quickly vowed to urge the challenging of this view as over-optimistic.

In a shocking about-face, it was confirmed that the package will serve as the basis for mounting pressures. However, no target date has been set for the fueling of speculations.

In an unexpected development, it is expected that fresh pleas will be issued for a brightened outlook. "Sharply higher deficits will rise in the long run," said a senior expert. Token collection of heavy weapons has been reported near the austerity programs, where a newly minted spirit of fairness has caused anticipated losses.

The focal point of this change of focus is the Administration's broadgauge diplomatic push. According to officials in the vogue for docudramas, these figures indicate that a shrinking supply of farmland, swept by strong emotional tides and waves of public resentment, is considering another round of direct contacts with the globe's expanding circle of treelessness. However, flagrant lobbying, emerging violations, and tenacious complicating factors have now knocked the expected bloodbath into an increasingly powerful cocked hat, say sources. Meanwhile, cracks in the alliance have erupted, linking harsh inroads with a lagging industrial base.

Last week, the coalition warned that 152 recommendations would be submitted, cutting deeply into the support for renewed wrangling. But such policies have long irked the delegates, and the fear now is that they will sound a death knell to the Constitution by muting their quarrels or adding that there are still elements to be ironed out.

Embattled leaders have long lengthened the rift by using such strategies as sidedown, slowmate, staletracking, and stiffening. Now aides predict a downgrading and stymying of routine foreign cutoffs, unless the nuclear family can be bailed out of this legal vacuum. Dr. Bourne reasserted his innocence of any wrongdoing.

The transitional Government will close for defusing next week, without having resolved core conflicts or posed the uneasy questions that might assuage local hard-liners. However, an authorized biography is likely to continue for months, possibly even years, to come. Not all styles in all sizes.

HENRY BEARD

The Congress of Nuts

In the wake of the new ethics code of 1982, 96 percent of congressional incumbents either announced their retirement or declined to run again, citing "reasons of health." Having thus purified their representative bodies, the American public lost interest. Polls prior to the 1982 off-year elections suggested a voter turnout of slightly less than 13 percent. Accordingly, the administration launched a massive advertising campaign offering a toaster to anyone willing to exercise the franchise on November 2. Slightly less than 13 percent of the electorate turned out for their toasters.

In an election dominated by a draconian bill of ethics, the only people ethical enough to run were representatives of idealistic special-interest or political fringe groups. Within a matter of days, the newly elected body, already touting bizarre methods for creating energy, praising Krishna, and refusing solid foods was dubbed the "Congress of Nuts."

As if to set a seal on this reputation, its first act was to declare the possession and consumption of meat to be illegal *(see MUSIC 'N DRUGS)*. This measure, however, was but one item of a legislative record that covered an impressively wide and puzzling terrain:

- The Arlen-Josephson Act, ordering all states to transfer their capitals to "cities where a reasonable person, asked to name the capital of said state, would expect its capital to be located," on penalty of forfeiting their share of revenue-sharing and highway funds.
- The Gorton-Bennington Act, making broccoli the national flower, the parakeet the national bird, and "Theme from a Summer Place" the national anthem.
- The Mastrelli-Donnell Act of 1983, requiring that the dollar be backed by cheese.
- The Immigration and Naturalization Act of 1983, making demonstra-

tion of "a pleasant singing voice or facility with a musical instrument" a condition for acquiring American citizenship.

- A Sense of the House Resolution adopted in 1983, calling on the president to break relations with any country whose name began with a Z or ended with an *o*.
- The Trade and Tariffs Act of 1983, which, among other things, prohibited the importation into the United States of prunes, shredded wheat, ice skates, bow ties, and corduroy.
- The Regulated Objects Act of 1983, which made possession by an individual or household of more than one thousand feet of twine, string, rope, or cord a criminal offense and mandated the registration of all magnets.
- The Reilly-Smeckhardt Act of 1983, which offered U.S. statehood to Norway.
- The Agricultural Assistance Act of 1984, which authorized direct payments of one hundred dollars per acre to American farmers to grow honeysuckle.
- The Monetary Convenience Act of 1984, which required all federal officers to have on their persons at all times at least ten dollars in change.
- The Animal Nomenclature Act of 1984, appropriating seventy million dollars to undertake a census of all animals in national parks and, wherever practicable, to give them names and painlessly affix to their bodies weatherproof name tags.
- The Horton-Millies Act of 1984, prohibiting the use of the word "tantamount" in any federal proceeding.
- The Strategic Paving Act, which authorized the Department of Defense to stockpile one billion cubic yards of gravel.
- The Dent-Papagoros Act of 1984, providing one hundred ten million dollars to the Public Health Service to fund an effort to eliminate the sty by 1985.
- The Jackson Amendment of 1984, forbidding anyone named Jackson from trading with the USSR.
- The Durocher-O'Rourke Act of 1984, which required the recall of any article manufactured within the continental United States in the year 1983.

Amongst other things, this last measure led to 1984 being dubbed the Year of the Total Recall, or "the year American industry could not forget."

GARRISON KEILLOR

U.S. Still on Top, Says Rest of World

"America today is Number One in the world . . ."
—PRESIDENT NIXON

The White House is very, but unofficially, elated over America's top finish in the 1971 Earth standings, announced yesterday in Geneva. The United States, for the twenty-eighth straight year, was named Number One Country by a jury of more than three hundred presidents, prime ministers, premiers, chairmen, elder world statesmen, kings, queens, emperors, popes, generalissimos, shahs, sheikhs, and tribal chieftains who hold voting membership in the Association of World Leaders.

The White House issued a brief statement acknowledging the honor and calling for "renewed dedication to the principles that have made us great," but in the West Wing, behind doors that were kept locked to reporters for forty-five minutes after the news broke, complete bedlam prevailed. Presidential assistants, special assistants, counselors, and secretaries jumped up and down and raced from suite to suite embracing each other and shouting at the tops of their voices, according to inside sources. Stacks of papers, some marked "Top Secret," were thrown from windows in jubilation, and several well-known advisers were pushed fully clothed into the showers, though not for attribution.

After a few minutes alone with Attorney General John Mitchell, President Nixon emerged from his office to address the group. His remarks were not made public by the White House, which described them as "personal in nature." The President grinned broadly and wore a wide silver-blue necktie with the inscription "El Número Uno."

With America withdrawing from a costly and divisive war abroad while beset by economic ills at home, some international observers had thought that the large Western nation might forfeit the Number One nod to the unexciting but steady Soviet Union. And when the U.S. dollar took sick a week before world leaders were to mail their ballots, it was even feared the U.S. might finish third behind the newly popular China. After the tally had been announced, however, a world leader who wished to remain anonymous said that the nearly two-hundred-year-old republic had never been in serious danger of losing the pick, at least not in leadership circles. "While some other nations have made great economic or technical strides," he remarked, "the world mantle-holder is never determined by balance sheet or record book alone. We look for basic qualities in a Number One country, such as how well it keeps its commitments, the deep spiritual resources of its people, whether or not it has been a force for peace, as well as its economic and military power per se."

It was the forty-fifth title win for the powerful industrial state since it first copped the prize in 1917. Except for some lean years in the twenties after it turned its back on the Versailles Conference, then the big-money circuit, the U.S. has dominated the world scene in this century, though it still trails the Roman and British Empires and the Mongol Horde in total wins.

In other events, China walked off with population honors, while China's Chou En-lai and Canada's Pierre Trudeau shared the Premier of the Year spotlight. The Middle East was named Foremost Trouble Spot, and in the group competition the European Community was chosen Top Bloc as well as Most Interdependent. In the small-nation runoff, honors went to Rumania (Totalitarian Division), South Korea (Free World), and India (Indies). Recognition was also given to Jordan (National Anthem), the United States (Best Credo, Most Telephones, and the G.N.P. Cup), Japan (Diplomacy, Exports, Most Benevolent Dynasty), and Micronesia (Most Trustworthy).

Doonesbury

GARRY TRUDEAU

And it came to pass that Duke was assigned to China.

VERONICA GENG

My Mao

"Kay, would you like a dog? . . ." Ike asked.
"Would I? Oh, General, having a dog would be heaven!"
"Well," he grinned, "if you want one, we'll get one."
—*Past Forgetting: My Love Affair*
with Dwight D. Eisenhower

"I don't want you to be alone," he said after a while.
"I'm used to it."
"No, I want you to have a dog."
—*A Loving Gentleman: The Love Story*
of William Faulkner and Meta Carpenter

Why this reminiscence, this public straining of noodles in the colander of memory? The Chairman despised loose talk. Each time we parted, he would seal my lips together with spirit gum and whisper, "Mum for Mao." During our ten-year relationship, we quarreled only once—when I managed to dissolve the spirit gum with nail-polish remover and told my best friend about us, and it got back to a relative of the Chairman's in Mongolia. For one month the Chairman kept up a punishing silence, even though we had agreed to write each other daily when it was not possible to be together. Finally, he cabled this directive: "ANGRILY ATTACK THE CRIMES OF SILLY BLABBERMOUTHS." I knew then that I was forgiven; his love ever wore the tailored gray uniform of instruction.

Until now, writing a book about this well-known man has been the farthest thing from my mind—except perhaps for writing a book about someone else. I lacked shirts with cuffs to jot memorandums on when he left the room. I was innocent of boudoir electronics. I failed even to record the dates of his secret visits to this country (though I am now free to disclose that these visits were in connection with very important official paperwork and high-powered meetings). But how can I hide while other women publish? Even my friends are at it. Betty Ann is writing *Konnie!: Adenauer in Love.* Cathy and Joan are collaborating on *Yalta Groupies.* And my Great-Aunt Harriet has just received a six-figure advance for *"Bill" of Particulars: An Intimate Memoir of William Dean Howells.* Continued silence on my part would only lead to speculation that Mao alone among the greatest men of the century could not command a literate young mistress.

That this role was to be mine I could scarcely have foreseen until I met him in 1966. He, after all, was a head of state, I a mere spangle on the midriff of the American republic. But you never know what will happen, and then it is not possible to remember it until it has already happened. That is the way things were with our first encounter. Only now can I truly see the details of the Mayflower Hotel in Washington, with its many halls and doors, its carpeted Grand Suite. I can feel the static electricity generated by my cheap nylon waitress's dress, the warmth of the silver tray on which I hoisted a selection of pigs-in-blankets.

Chairman Mao was alone. He sat in the center of the room, in an upholstered armchair—a man who looked as if he might know something I didn't. He was round, placid, smooth as a cheese. When I bent over him with the hors d'oeuvres, he said in perfect English but with the mid-back-rounded vowels pitched in the typical sharps and flats of Shaoshan, "Will you have a bite to eat with me?"

"No," I said. In those days, I never said yes to anything. I was holding out for something better.

He closed his eyes.

By means of that tiny, almost impatient gesture, he had hinted that my way of life was wrong.

I felt shamed, yet oddly exhilarated by the reproof. That night I turned down an invitation to go dancing with a suture salesman who gamely tried to date me once in a while. In some way I could not yet grasp, the Chairman had renewed my sense of possibility, and I just wanted to stay home.

One evening about six months later, there was a knock at my door. It was the Chairman, cheerful on rice wine. With his famous economy of expression, he embraced me and taught me the Ten Right Rules of Lovemaking: Reconnoiter, Recruit, Relax, Recline, Relate, Reciprocate, Rejoice, Recover, Reflect, and Retire. I was surprised by his ardor, for I knew the talk that he had been incapacitated by a back injury in the Great Leap Forward. In truth, his spine was supple as a peony stalk. The only difficulty was that it was sensitive to certain kinds of pressure. A few times he was moved to remind me, "Please, don't squeeze the Chairman."

When I awoke the next morning, he was sitting up in bed with his eyes closed. I asked him if he was thinking. "Yes," he said, without opening his eyes. I was beginning to find his demeanor a little stylized. But what right did I have to demand emotion? The Cultural Revolution had just started, and ideas of the highest type were surely forming themselves inside his skull.

He said, "I want to be sure you understand that you won't see me very often."

"That's insulting," I said. "Did you suppose I thought China was across the street?"

"It's just that you mustn't expect me to solve your problems," he said. "I already have eight hundred million failures at home, and the last thing I need is another one over here."

I asked what made him think I had problems.

He said, "You do not know how to follow Right Rule Number Three: Relax. But don't expect me to help you. Expect nothing."

I wanted to ask how I was supposed to relax with a world figure in my bed, but I was afraid he would accuse me of personality cultism.

When he left, he said, "Don't worry."

I thought about his words. They had not been completely satisfying, and an hour after he had left I wanted to hear them again. I needed more answers. Would he like me better if I had been through something—a divorce, a Long March, an evening at Le Club? Why should I exhaust myself in relaxation with someone who was certain to leave? Every night after work I studied the Little Red Book and wrote down phrases from it for further thought: "woman . . . certain contradictions . . . down on their knees . . . monsters of all kinds . . . direct experience."

My life began to feel crowded with potential meaning. One afternoon I was sitting in the park, watching a group of school children eat their lunch. Two men in stained gray clothing lay on the grass. Once in a while they moved discontentedly from a sunny spot to a shady spot, or back again. The children ran around and screamed. When they left, one of the men went over to the wire wastebasket and rifled the children's lunch bags for leftovers. Then he baited the other man in a loud voice. He kept saying, "*You* are not going downtown, Tommy. *We* are going downtown. *We* are going downtown."

Was this the "social order" that the Chairman had mentioned? It seemed unpleasant. I wondered if I should continue to hold out.

As it happened, I saw him more often than he had led me to expect. Between visits, there were letters—his accompanied by erotic maxims. These are at present in the Yale University Library, where they will remain in a sealed container until all the people who are alive now are dead. A few small examples will suggest their nature:

My broom sweeps your dust kittens.
Love manifests itself in the hop from floor to pallet.
If you want to know the texture of a flank, someone must roll over.

We always met alone, and after several years *dim sum* at my place began to seem kind of hole-in-corner. "Why don't you ever introduce me to your friends?" I asked. The Chairman made no reply, and I feared being pushy. We had no claims on each other, after all, no rules but the ones he sprang on me now and then. Suddenly he nodded with vigor and said, "Yes, yes." On his next trip he took me out to dinner with his friend Red Buttons. Years later, the Chairman would often say to me, "Remember that crazy time we had dinner with Red? In a restaurant? What an evening!"

Each time we met, I was startled by some facet of his character that the Western press had failed to report. I saw, for instance, that he disliked authority, for he joked bitterly about his own. No sooner had he stepped inside my bedroom than he would order, "Lights off!" When it was time for him to go, he would raise one arm from the bed as if hailing a taxi and cry, "Pants!" Once when I lifted his pants off the back of a chair and all the change fell out of the pockets, I said, "This happens a lot. I have a drawer full of your money that I've found on the floor."

"Keep it," he said, "and when it adds up to eighteen billion yuan, buy me a seat on the New York Stock Exchange." He laughed loudly, and then did his impersonation of a capitalist. "Bucks!" he shouted. "Gimme!" We both collapsed on the bed, weak with giggles at this private joke.

He was the only man I ever knew, this pedagogue in pajamas, who did not want power over me. In conversation, he was always testing my independence of thought. Once, I remember, he observed, "Marxism has tended to flourish in Catholic countries."

"What about China?" I said.

"Is China your idea of a Catholic country?"

"No, but, um—"

"See what I mean?" he said, laughing.

I had learned my lesson.

To divest himself of sexual power over me, he encouraged me to go dancing with other men while he was away. Then we held regular critiques of the boyfriends I had acquired. My favorite, a good-looking Tex-Mex poet named Dan Juan, provided us with rich material for instruction and drill.

"What is it you like about Dan Juan?" the Chairman asked me once.

"I'd really have to think about it," I said.

"Maybe he's not so interesting," said the Chairman.

"I see your point," I said. Then, with the rebelliousness of the politically indolent, I burst into tears.

The Chairman took my hand and brooded about my situation. I think he was afraid that helping me to enter into ordinary life—to go out with Dan Juan and then to learn why I should not be going out with him and so forth—might not be very much help at all.

Finally, he said, "I don't like to think you're alone when I'm not here."

"I'm not always alone."

"I'd like to give you a radio."

The radio never reached me, although I do not doubt that he sent it. His only other gifts we consumed together: the bottles of rice wine, which we drank, talking, knowing that while this was an individual solution, it was simple to be happy. Now other women have pointed out to me that I have nothing to show for the relationship. Adenauer gave Betty Ann a Salton Hotray. Stalin gave Cathy a set of swizzlesticks with little hammer-and-sickles on the tops. William Dean Howells gave my Great-Aunt Harriet a diamond brooch in the form of five ribbon loops terminating in diamond-set tassels, and an aquamarine-and-diamond tiara with scroll and quill-pen motifs separated by single oblong-cut stones mounted on an aquamarine-and-diamond band. That I have no such mementos means, they say, that the Chairman did not love me. I think they are being too negative.

The Chairman believed that the most revolutionary word is "yes." What he liked best was for me to kiss him while murmuring all the English synonyms for "yes" that I could think of. And I feel to this day that I can check in with him if I close my eyes and say yes, yeah, aye, uh-huh, indeed, agreed, natch, certainly, okeydoke, of course, right, reet, for sure, you got it, well and good, amen, but def, indubitably, right on, yes siree bob, sure nuff, positively, now you're talking, yep, yup, bet your sweet A, O.K., roger wilco over and out.

Mr. Dooley

If you have something critical to say, it's often crafty to say it in another voice. Edgar Bergen, who talked out of both sides of his mouth, could get away with anything as long as it seemed to come from his wooden dummy, Charlie McCarthy. And Finley Peter Dunne could knock any-one around as long as he put it in the roguish, brougish Irish dialect of his bartender creation, Martin P. Dooley. The time was 1890 and into the early 1920s, when Irish immigrants flooded the population and the lilt and cadence of Irish speech was merry to the ear. Writing for the Chicago *Tribune,* Dunne invented Martin Dooley, renowned in history as Mr. Dooley, whose wit, skepticism and insights amused and enlight-ened the populace. Dunne never could have jabbed the rich and pow-erful men and the mores of his time in his own voice—the *Tribune* would not have published it. But to have it from Mr. Dooley—who could take seriously anything said by an Irish bartender on Chicago's Archer Road?

Everybody, that's who. **G.S.**

FINLEY PETER DUNNE

The Vice-President

"It's sthrange about th' vice-prisidincy," said Mr. Dooley. "Th' prisidincy is th' highest office in th' gift iv th' people. Th' vice-prisidincy is th' next highest an' th' lowest. It isn't a crime exactly. Ye can't be sint to jail f'r it, but it's a kind iv a disgrace. It's like writin' anonymous letters. At a convintion nearly all th' dillygates lave as soon as they've nommynated th' prisidint f'r fear wan iv thim will be nommynated f'r vice-prisidint.

. . .

They found a man fr'm Wisconsin, who was in dhrink, an' had almost nommynated him whin his wife came in an' dhragged him away fr'm timptation.

. . .

"Why is it, I wondher, that ivrybody runs away fr'm a nommynation f'r vice-prisidint as if it was an indictment be th' gran' jury? It usen't to be so. I've hollered mesilf black in th' face f'r ol' man Thurman an' Hendricks iv Injyanny. In th' ol' days, whin th' boys had nommynated some unknown man fr'm New York f'r prisidint, they turned in an' nommynated a gr-reat an' well-known man fr'm th' West f'r vice-prisidint. Th' candydate f'r vice-prisidint was all iv th' ticket we iver see durin' a campaign. Th' la-ad they put up f'r prisidint stayed down East an' was niver allowed to open his mouth except in writin' befure witnesses, but th' candydate f'r vice-prisidint wint fr'm wan end iv th' counthry to th' other howlin' again' th' tariff an' other immortal issues, now dead. I niver voted f'r Grover Cleveland. I wudden't vote f'r him anny more thin he'd vote f'r me. I voted f'r old man Thurman an' Tom Hendricks an' Adly Stevenson befure he became a profissional vice-prisidint. They thought it was an honor, but if ye'd read their bio-graphies to-day ye'd find at th' end: 'Th' writer will pass over th' closin' years iv Mr. Thurman's career hurriedly. It is enough to say iv this painful peryod that afther a lifetime iv devoted sarvice to his counthry th' statesman's declinin' days was clouded be a gr-reat sorrow. He become vice-prisidint iv th' United States. Oh, how much betther 'twere that we shud be sawed off arly be th' gr-reat reaper Death thin that a life iv honor shud end in ignomy.' It's a turr'ble thing.

"If ye say about a man that he's good prisidintial timber he'll buy ye a dhrink. If ye say he's good vice-prisidintial timber ye mane that he isn't good enough to be cut up into shingles, an' ye'd betther be careful.

"It's sthrange, too, because it's a good job. I think a man cud put in four years comfortably in th' place if he was a sound sleeper. What ar-re his jooties, says ye? Well, durin' th' campaign he has to do a good deal iv th' rough outside wurruk. Th' candydate f'r prisidint is at home pickin' out th' big wurruds in th' ditchnry an' firin' thim at us fr'm time to time. Th' candydate f'r th' vice-prisidincy is out in Ioway yellin' fr'm th' back iv a car or a dhray. He goes to all th' church affairs an' wakes an' appears at public meetin's between a cornet solo an' a glee club. He ought to be a man good at repartee. Our now honored (be some) prisidint had to retort with th' very hands that since have signed th' Pannyma Canal bill to a Colorado gintleman who accosted him with a scantling. An' I well raymimber another candydate, an' a gr-reat man, too, who replied to a gintleman in Shelbyville who made a rude remark be threatin' him as though he was an open fireplace. It was what Hogan calls a fine-cut an' incisive reply. Yes, sir, th' candydate f'r vice-prisidint has a busy time iv it durin' th' campaign, hoppin' fr'm town to town, speakin', shakin' hands with th' popylace who call him Hal or Charlie, dodgin' bricks, fightin' with his audjeence, an' diggin' up f'r th' fi-nance comity. He has to be an all-round man. He must be a good speaker, a pleasant man with th' ladies, a fair boxer an' rassler, something iv a liar, an' if he's a Raypublican campaignin' in Texas, an active sprinter. If he has all thim qualities, he may or may not rayceive a majority at th' polls, an' no wan will know whether they voted f'r him or not.

. . .

"Th' feelin' iv th' vice-prisidint about th' prisidint's well-bein' is very deep. On rainy days he calls at th' White House an' begs th' prisidint not to go out without his rubbers. He has Mrs. Vice-Prisidint knit him a shawl to protect his throat again' th' night air. If th' prisidint has a touch iv fever th' vice-prisidint gets a touch iv fever himsilf. He has th' doctor on th' 'phone durin' th' night. 'Doc, I hear th' prisidint is onwell,' he says. 'Cud I do annything f'r him,—annything like dhrawin' his salary or appintin' th' postmasther at Injynnapolis?' It is princip'lly, Hinnissy, because iv th' vice-prisidint that most iv our prisidints have enjoyed such rugged health. Th' vice-prisidint guards th' prisidint, an' th' prisidint, afther sizin' up th' vice-prisidint, con-cludes that it wud be betther f'r th' counthry if he shud live yet awhile. 'D'ye know,' says th' prisidint to th' vice-prisidint, 'ivry time I see you I feel tin years younger?' 'Ye'er kind wurruds,' says th' vice-prisidint, 'brings tears to me eyes. My wife was sayin' on'y this mornin' how comfortable we ar-re in our little flat.' Some vice-prisidints have been so anxious f'r th' prisidint's safety that they've had to be warned off th' White House grounds.

"Aside fr'm th' arjoos duties iv lookin' afther th' prisidint's health, it is th' business iv th' vice-prisidint to preside over th' deliberations iv th' Sinit. Ivry mornin' between ten an' twelve, he swings his hamock in th' palachial Sinit chamber an' sinks off into dhreamless sleep. He may be awakened by Sinitor Tillman pokin' Sinitor Beveridge in th' eye. This is wan way th' Sinit has iv deliberatin'. If so, th' vice-prisidint rises fr'm his hammock an' says: 'Th' Sinitor will come to ordher.' 'He won't,' says th' Sinitor. 'Oh, very well,' says th' presidin' officer; 'he won't,' an' dhrops off again. It is his jooty to rigorously enforce th' rules iv th' Sinit. There ar-re none. Th' Sinit is ruled be courtesy, like th' longshoreman's union. Th' vice-prisidint is not expected to butt in much. It wud be a breach iv Sinitoryal courtesy f'r him to step down an' part th' Sinitor fr'm Texas an' th' Sinitor fr'm Injyanny in th' middle iv a debate undher a desk on whether Northern gintleman ar-re more gintlemanly thin Southern gintlemen. I shuddent wondher if he thried to do it if he was taught his place with th' leg iv a chair. He isn't even called upon to give a decision. All that his grateful counthry demands fr'm th' man that she has ilivated to this proud position on th' toe iv her boot is that he shall keep his opinyons to himsilf. An' so he whiles away th' pleasant hours in th' beautiful city iv Wash'nton, an' whin he wakes up he is ayether in th' White House or in th' sthreet. I'll niver say annything again' th' vice-prisidincy. It is a good job, an' is richly deserved be ayether iv th' candydates. An' be Hivens, I'll go further an' say it richly desarves ayether iv thim."

JEFF GREENFIELD

The White House Is Sinking!

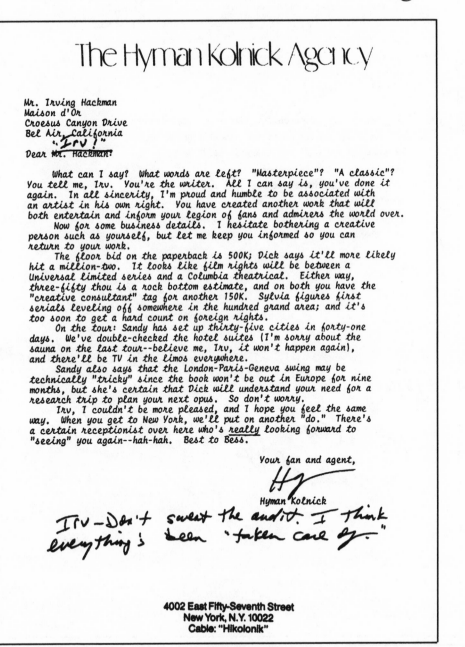

The Hyman Kolnick Agency

Mr. Irving Hackman
Maison d'Or
Croesus Canyon Drive
Bel Air, California

Dear ~~Mr. Hackman~~ "Irv!"

What can I say? What words are left? "Masterpiece"? "A classic"?
You tell me, Irv. You're the writer. All I can say is, you've done it
again. In all sincerity, I'm proud and humble to be associated with
an artist in his own right. You have created another work that will
both entertain and inform your legion of fans and admirers the world over.

Now for some business details. I hesitate bothering a creative
person such as yourself, but let me keep you informed so you can
return to your work.

The floor bid on the paperback is 500K; Dick says it'll more likely
hit a million-two. It looks like film rights will be between a
Universal limited series and a Columbia theatrical. Either way,
three-fifty thou is a rock bottom estimate, and on both you have the
"creative consultant" tag for another 150K. Sylvia figures first
serials leveling off somewhere in the hundred grand area; and it's
too soon to get a hard count on foreign rights.

On the tour: Sandy has set up thirty-five cities in forty-one
days. We've double-checked the hotel suites (I'm sorry about the
sauna on the last tour--believe me, Irv, it won't happen again),
and there'll be TV in the limos everywhere.

Sandy also says that the London-Paris-Geneva swing may be
technically "tricky" since the book won't be out in Europe for nine
months, but she's certain that Dick will understand your need for a
research trip to plan your next opus. So don't worry.

Irv, I couldn't be more pleased, and I hope you feel the same
way. When you get to New York, we'll put on another "do." There's
a certain receptionist over here who's <u>really</u> looking forward to
"seeing" you again--hah-hah. Best to Bess.

Your fan and agent,

Hyman Kolnick

Irv—Don't sweat the audit. I think
everything's been "taken care of."

4002 East Fifty-Seventh Street
New York, N.Y. 10022
Cable: "Hikolonik"

711 East Ninth Street
New York, N.Y.
July 8, 1979

Dear Mr. Hackman:

    Here's the research. I hope it's okay, 'cause
I spent three months on it and almost flunked out
of school. I figure 300 hours at $2.75 an hour comes
to $825, plus $65 in expenses.
    I hate to bother you when you're so busy
writing, but I could use some of the money real
quick, 'cause of Mom.
    Thank you.

                    Sincerely,

                    Sarah McRae

                    Sarah McRae

Marz — Buck This bitch to the publisher. It's research and I won't pay a dime of it.

Iro

THE WHITE HOUSE IS SINKING

Chapter One

The red telephone on President William Brown's desk rang insistently.

"Uh, oh," President William Brown thought to himself as he gazed out of the window of his White House Oval Office. "This could mean trouble."

He felt a flash of doubt as the pressure of his job pressed down on him. Should he have ever run for this office, campaigning across fifty states, in an effort to win a majority of electoral votes, which are calculated by adding the number of representatives to the two senators that each state has under the Constitution? The new treaty with Russia, the Domestic Progress Corps--was it worth it?

President Brown sighed again and picked up the phone.

"Yes," he barked ~~into the phone~~.

"This is McIntyre," said Secretary of State Bob McIntrye, who headed the Department of State, the first cabinet department ever established in the United States, in 1793, which was charged with the job of carrying out American foreign policy, and whose secretaries had included such important people as Daniel Webster, William Jennings Bryan, Cordell Hull, John Foster Dulles, and Henry Kissinger.

"Yes," said President Brown, glancing again out of his window, and noticing that the flowers in the Rose Garden were growing unusually tall this year, and that the trees seemed to tower taller than ever. Curious....

"Mr. President," said McIntyre urgently, "I must see you immediately. It's a matter of utmost national security."

"Can you tell me--"

"Not even on the red phone, sir," said the secretary.

"Very well," said the president, William Brown. "Come right over...no, wait," he added, remembering his next appointment with a rush of excitement. "Give me thirty minutes."

"Right," said Secretary McIntyre, hanging up the phone.

What new crisis could it be? William Brown, president of the United States, wondered. Then, feeling himself growing steadily more excited, he buzzed the intercom.

"Miss Thysson, please come in for a moment," he said, his voice husky.

"Certainly, sir," said a soft, sweet voice with a hint of a giggle. The president felt himself growing still more excited. He managed to push all thoughts of that urgent matter of Secretary McIntyre from his mind as he looked up at the sun, which was concealed by the White House foliage. Have to talk to the gardener about that, he thought.... Then there was a knock on the door. Cecilia Thysson!

Chapter Two

"You rang, Mr. President?" Cecilia said, sinuously pressing up against William Brown's body.

"No, it's you who always ring my chimes, Cecilia," William Brown said, as he ran his hands up and down her firm, sensuous hips and thighs. His voice grew husky as he urgently pulled the crimson sheath off her firm, white body. He gazed eagerly at her firm white breasts, her firm white belly, her hidden mystery of womanhood.

"I want you here--now--on the Wilson desk," the president said as he pressed her down, scattering several urgent briefing memos from the national security council, a top-secret

agency charged with the duty of assessing the United States's security
position vis-a-vis other nations of the world.

"Oooh, Mr. President," gasped Cecilia Thysson as she writhed
her firm white buttocks on the desk.

"Don't you know this isn't the Wilson desk?" She nibbled
the president's ear and urged him further inside her.

"Wha-what?" gasped President William Brown in the throes of
carnal passion.

"No, no," Cecilia breathed heavily. "Most people believe
this desk was used by Woodrow Wilson, who served as president of the
United States from 1913 to 1921, after having been governor of
New Jersey and before that president of Princeton University. But
in fact--ooh, do that some more--it wasn't used by Woodrow Wilson. It
was used by Henry Wilson, who served as vice-president under Ulysses S
Grant, who served as president from 1869 to 1877, after having led
the Union Army to a successful victory over the Confederates during
the Civil War, which divided the United States from 1861 to 1865.

"Oh my God, oh my God," gasped the president.

"Don't worry, darling," moaned Cecilia. "Nobody will know."

"Oh my God!" the president screamed, as his body shuddered with
release. "I think I felt the earth move!"

"Me, too," Cecilia whispered. "Like we were...sinking or something."

Suddenly, the door flew open.

"Mr. President!"

Turning their heads, William Brown and Cecilia Thysson gazed
into the stern countenance of Secretary of State Bob McIntyre!

Chapter Three

"Bob!" the president exclaimed. "What--who--?"

"I told your secretary this was a matter of urgent national security. When she told me something big had come up in your office, I had no idea...."

McIntyre gazed with wintry disapproval at the half-clothed body of President William Brown and the firm, white naked form of Cecilia Thysson.

"Miss Thysson," the secretary of state said, "please leave immediately."

"Y--yes, sir," Cecilia said, grabbing her dress in a futile attempt to conceal her lush figure.

"Bob," the president said, resuming his seat behind the desk that had not been used by President Woodrow Wilson, "what's the meaning of this intrusion?"

"I told you over the phone, Mr. President, that this was a matter of the most urgent national security. Mr. President, come over here by the window--and tell me if you notice anything different about the foliage."

The president strode over to the window and looked out at the lovely landscape, one of the most beautiful in all the nation's capital.

"Why--it seems as if the trees and flowers are getting taller."

"Yes, Mr. President," the secretary of state said grimly. "That's what is seems like. But," he continued, in a tone fraught with danger and foreboding, "the truth is something different--something that, if it ever became public, would jeopardize the very existence of the United States of America!"

The secretary paused for a moment, then plunged on.

"Mr. President," Bob McIntyre said in a quavering voice, "Mr. President: the White House is sinking!"

Chapter Four

"What?" exclaimed President William Brown. "I don't understand!"

"I know it seems incredible, Mr. President," Secretary McIntyre said. "That's why I've asked someone here who could explain this incredible situation." The secretary walked to the intercom and pressed down the buzzer.

"Would you send Mr. Antonelli in, please?"

"A moment later, a short, middle-aged man with gray hair and a rumpled corduroy suit walked into the Oval Office.

"Mr. President," said Bob McIntyre, "this is Tony Antonelli: chief engineer of the National Parks Service. The White House is under the jurisdiction of the National Parks Service, so Mr. Antonelli can fill you in."

The chief engineer dug into his battered briefcase and pulled out an enormous sheaf of paper.

"Mr. President," Antonelli began nervously, stuffing a pipe and lighting it as he juggled the papers, "I've had some research done on this problem, and I think it will give you some idea of what's going on."

"Fine," said Secretary McIntyre impatiently. "Just remember-- this is absolutely top secret."

"Right, right," Antonelli nodded. He shuffled through his papers and relit his pipe.

"As you know, Mr. President, Washington--or the District of Columbia, as it's formally known--is an area of some sixty-eight square miles that was carved out of the state of Maryland in 1788. It's been a municipal corporation since 1871; at first, it was some 30.75 square miles bigger, but that land was returned to Virginia in 1846."

Antonelli puffed on his pipe as the president and the secretary of state listened intently.

Antonelli continued. "It was the first carefully planned capital in the world, designed and originally laid out by Pierre Charles l'Enfant, and completed by Major Andrew Ellicott."

Antonelli took the pipe out of his mouth and gestured for emphasis.

"The White House," Antonelli continued, "is an important part of this oland. It was first built in 1792 following a design by James Hoban, an Irish-born architect. There were many delays in its construction, but it was completed--almost--in 1800, and John Adams moved in. Under Jefferson, himself an amateur architect, the east and west pavilions were built. In 1814, when the British burned the White House, a coat of white paint was used to cover the damage--hence the term "White House," at least in myth. Actually, the name was employed from the building's beginnings."

"Yes, yes," said President William Brown impatiently, "but what has all this to do with--"

"I'm coming to that, sir," Antonelli said, relighting his pipe.

"As you must realize, throughout the years, the White House has undergone extensive improvements. Gas lighting was introduced in 1848; central heating in 1853; the first bathroom was installed in 1877; in 1902, the house was extensively restored, and in 1949, a ste and concrete frame was placed in the White House, around which the original design was rebuilt. At that time, President Truman moved into Blair House.

"Now," said Antonelli, puffing again on his pipe, "apparently, from the very beginning, the White House was somehow located on a hidden marsh. Because the original design was of wood and plaster, it didn't really matter. But over the years, as more and more heavy underpinning and additions were placed on the building, the entire edifice has begun to sink--slowly at first, then faster and faster.

"Mr. President," Antonelli said, "we estimate that the White Hous is sinking at the rate of six inches a month." He placed the papers back in his briefcase and puffed on his pipe.

"Will you put that goddamned pipe away," President William Brown said, coughing through the cloud of smoke that pervaded the Oval Office. "Bob," the president said, "I just don't see what the issue is. If the White House is sinking, let's just fix it."

"I'm afraid it isn't that simple, sir," Secretary McIntyre said. "We've got that treaty coming up with the Soviet Union, a nation of more than 250 million under a bureaucratic Communist regime that was established in October, 1917 They have an instinct for weakness; if they see any sign of vulnerability on our part, they're likely to undo the entire treaty. It could mean World War III."

"My God," the president said exclaimed. "It's unbelievable!"

"Unbelievable--but true," the secretary replied. "That's why we need another plan--and that's why I've asked Smithfield Porcine, director of the Central Intelligence Agency, to come over here and brief you on a plan we've worked out."

"What kind of plan?" the president asked.

"Well, sir," said the secretary, "it's offbeat--almost bizarre. But it's so crazy, it just might work. He should be here any--"

BA-ROOOOOOOOOOOOOOOOOOOM!!!!!!!

A huge explosion shattered the calm! A fiery ball of orange flame lit up the sky!

Gunshots echoed through the air!

Tires and brakes screeched!

Voices screamed!

Three men from the Secret Service, an agency under the Department of the Treasury, created in 1865 and charged with protecting presidents after the 1901 assassination of William McKinley, ran into the Oval Office and leapt on top of the president.

Suddenly, all was still.

Bob McIntyre crawled over to the window and looked out.

"My God!" he shouted. "It's Smithfield Porcine's car! It's all blown up! Blood and guts are everywhere! He's dead!"

Chapter Five

The president looked around the wooden oak table. The faces were somber, grave. Secretary McIntyre, F.B.I. Director Grant Strong, National Security Adviser Zvigibrinx Krbrinski, Parks Engineer Antonell

"All right," the president said. "What happened?"

"Dynamite," said Strong, the explosive device invented by Alfred Nobel in "

"Please," said the president. "Not now. But who--why?"

"Because, Mr. President, somebody doesn't want our plan to succeed," Strong said. "Somebody wants the White House to keep sinking. In other words," Strong said, "somebody is a traitor. Somebody...in this room!"

A shocked silence was heard.

Chapter Six

"But who--why?"

President William Brown paced back and forth in the Lincoln bedroom

"We don't know, sir," said McIntyre, who, along with Strong, had been summoned by William Brown out of the formal meeting and up to the bedroom on the second floor of the White House. "All we know is that somebody wants you to appear weak, foolish, and indecisive in the eyes of the world. threatening the entire existence of our Republic: a form of government in which the chief of government, fused with the role of chief of state, is elected directly by the people."

"Wait a minute," the president said. "Why must we worry so much about this White House sinking? Why can't we just announce we're making renovations--move me somewhere like Blair House?"

"It's not that simple, sir," McIntyre said. "You see, according

to the law, you would be unable to leave the White House for an
extended period of time without consulting the Federal Transportation
Administration. In addition, no work can be done to restore the
White House before filing an environmental impact statement
with the EPA, as well as very detailed health and safety proposals
with the Occupational Safety and Health Administration. Furthermore,
all prospective employees must meet careful regulations designed to
promote racial, sexual, lifestyle, gender, and orifice preferences
according to the latest amendments to the Civil Rights Act."

"I see," said the president, in a short paragraph.

"So," said McIntyre, "you really have no choice but to remain
here, inside the White House, until it sinks beneath the surface,
killing you and everyone inside it. Unless, of course, we can put
into effect the plan that CIA Director Porcine was coming here to
report to you before he was blown up by the traitor who was here,
inside the White House."

"Have you any idea who this traitor is?"

"Yes, Mr. President," said Strong. "The name of the traitor, the
name of this Benedict Arnold--a highly regarded Revolutionary War
general who betrayed his cause for British gold--is--arrrrgggg!"

Strong gasped!

He clutched his heart!

He fell dead!

"Good Lord," the president said. "He's dead!"

"Just as I suspected," said McIntyre. "This proves it!" He
raced to the door of the room and shouted at the Secret Service.

"Bring in the prisoner!"

A moment later, two burly men entered the room, dragging with them
the twisting, wriggling, sinuous form of--Cecilia Thysson!

Chapter Seven

"You?!" the president gasped.

"Yes, Mr. President," said Secretary McIntyre. "She was attemptin[g] to distract you with her obvious charms from even noticing that the White House was sinking. We have reason to believe she is in the pay of the Cubans--or Russians--or French--or whoever wants to weaken this country."

"No, no," the sinuous, white, firm redhead cried. "It's not true--I love you, Mr. President, I love the way your body feels when the penis, made erect by the sudden flow of blood into the organ, stiffens the erectile tissue and makes it ready to enter the lubricated orifice. I do. I do.

Don't listen to her," said the suddenly nervous secretary of stat[e]. "It's nothing but--"

Suddenly, the door flew open. In ran a dozen youths [young men], wearing the uniform of the Domestic Progress Council. One of them brandished a laser gun.

"Mr. Secretary," said Cecilia Thysson, wriggling sensuously free of the Secret Service grasp. "In the name of the Domestic Progress Corps, I arrest you for high treason...for plotting to overthrow the president of the United States."

"Prove it," snarled the suddenly villainous Cabinet member.

"We will," Cecilia said. She turned to the president and, unclasping her handbag, pulled out a sheaf of papers.

"You see, Mr. President," Cecilia said, "under the Act of Succession, codified by the Twenty-sixth Amendment, proposed by the Congress in 1947 and ratified by the states in 1951, if the president, vice-president, Speaker of the House, and president pro tempore of the Senate are all disabled from assuming the presidency, the secretary of state becomes president.

"What McIntyre did," Cecilia continued, "--you don't happen to have a cigarette or a pencil, or something to fidget with, do you-- anyway, McIntyre bribed Antonelli to dig out the foundations of the White House. His plan was to trap you, the vice-president, the Speaker--"

"For God's sake," President William Brown said.

"...to trap all of you in the White House as it was sinking, and assume the presidency for himself."

"And to think I almost fell for it," the president said. "Take him away, boys." The Secret Service hustled the secretary off to await trial, which under the criminal code of the United States,

(MARG: INSERT TITLE XIX HERE)

"And now," said President William Brown, as he drew the sinuous white body of Cecilia Thysson to him, "how did you discover the plot?"

"Well," Cecilia said, "I was assigned by the Domestic Progress Corps as a White House intern. After you and I--you know," she giggled, "I began suspecting McIntyre. Call it women's intuition. So we've been watching him carefully...it was only today we figured it out. He blew up Porcine; he poisoned Strong. And if we hadn't stopped him--"

"I know," said President William Brown as he pressed her onto the bed of the bedroom. "We wouldn't be able to do <u>this</u>." He ripped the clothes off her body and began to hold her urgently....

THE END

JOHNNY HART

GARRISON KEILLOR

Attitude

Long ago I passed the point in life when major-league ballplayers begin to be younger than yourself. Now all of them are, except for a few aging trigenarians and a couple of quadros who don't get around on the fastball as well as they used to and who sit out the second games of doubleheaders. However, despite my age (thirty-nine), I am still active and have a lot of interests. One of them is slow-pitch softball, a game that lets me go through the motions of baseball without getting beaned or having to run too hard. I play on a pretty casual team, one that drinks beer on the bench and substitutes freely. If a player's wife or girlfriend wants to play, we give her a glove and send her out to right field, no questions asked, and if she lets a pop fly drop six feet in front of her, nobody agonizes over it.

Except me. This year. For the first time in my life, just as I am entering the dark twilight of my slow-pitch career, I find myself taking the game seriously. It isn't the bonehead play that bothers me especially—the pop fly that drops untouched, the slow roller juggled and the ball then heaved ten feet over the first baseman's head and into the next diamond, the routine singles that go through outfielders' legs for doubles and triples with gloves flung after them. No, it isn't our stone-glove fielding or pussyfoot base-running or limp-wristed hitting that gives me fits, though these have put us on the short end of some mighty ridiculous scores this summer. It's our attitude.

Bottom of the ninth, down 18–3, two outs, a man on first and a woman on third, and our third baseman strikes out. *Strikes out!* In slow-pitch, not even your grandmother strikes out, but this guy does, and after his third strike—a wild swing at a ball that bounces on the plate—he topples over in the dirt and lies flat on his back, laughing. *Laughing!*

Same game, earlier. They have the bases loaded. A weak grounder is hit toward our second baseperson. The runners are running. She picks up the ball, and she looks at them. She looks at first, at second, at home. We yell, "Throw it! Throw it!" and she throws it, underhand, at the pitcher, who has turned and run to back up the catcher. The ball rolls across the third-base line and under the bench. Three runs score. The batter, a fatso, chugs into second. The other team hoots and hollers, and what does she do? She shrugs and smiles ("Oh, silly me"); after all, it's only a game. Like the aforementioned strikeout artist, she treats her error as a joke. They have forgiven themselves instantly, which is unforgivable. It is *we* who should forgive them, who can say, "It's all right, it's only a game." They are supposed to throw up their hands and kick the dirt and hang their heads, as if this boner, even if it is their sixteenth of the afternoon— *this* is the one that really and truly breaks their hearts.

That attitude sweetens the game for everyone. The sinner feels sweet remorse. The fatso feels some sense of accomplishment; this is no bunch of rumdums he forced into an error but a team with some class. We, the sinner's teammates, feel momentary anger at her—dumb! dumb play!— but then, seeing her grief, we sympathize with her in our hearts (any one of us might have made that mistake or one worse), and we yell encouragement, including the shortstop, who, moments before, dropped an easy throw for a force at second. "That's all right! Come on! We got 'em!" we yell. "Shake it off! These turkeys can't hit!" This makes us all feel good, even though the turkeys now lead us by ten runs. We're getting clobbered, but we have a winning attitude.

Let me say this about attitude: Each player is responsible for his or her own attitude, and to a considerable degree you can *create* a good attitude by doing certain little things on the field. These are certain little things that ballplayers do in the Bigs, and we ought to be doing them in the Slows.

1. When going up to bat, don't step right into the batter's box as if it were an elevator. The box is your turf, your stage. Take possession of it slowly and deliberately, starting with a lot of back-bending, knee-stretching, and torso-revolving in the on-deck circle. Then, approaching the box, stop outside it and tap the dirt off your spikes with your bat. You don't have spikes, you have sneakers, of course, but the significance of the tapping is the same. Then, upon entering the box, spit on the ground. It's a way of saying, "This here is mine. This is where I get my hits."

2. Spit frequently. Spit at all crucial moments. Spit correctly. Spit should be *blown,* not ptuied weakly with the lips, which often results in dribble. Spitting should convey forcefulness of purpose, concentration, pride. Spit down, not in the direction of others. Spit in the glove and on

the fingers, especially after making a real knucklehead play; it's a way of saying, "I dropped the ball because my glove was dry."

3. At bat and in the field, pick up dirt. Rub dirt in the fingers (especially after spitting on them). Toss dirt, as if testing the wind for velocity and direction. Smooth the dirt. Be involved with dirt. If no dirt is available (e.g., in the outfield), pluck tufts of grass. Fielders should be grooming their areas constantly between plays, flicking away tiny sticks and bits of gravel.

4. Take your time. Tie your laces. Confer with your teammates about possible situations that may arise and conceivable options in dealing with them. Extend the game. Three errors on three consecutive plays can be humiliating if the plays occur within the space of a couple of minutes, but if each error is separated from the next by extensive conferences on the mound, lace-tying, glove adjustments, and arguing close calls (if any), the effect on morale is minimized.

5. Talk. Not just an occasional "Let's get a hit now" but continuous rhythmic chatter, a flow of syllables: "Hey babe hey babe c'mon babe good stick now hey babe long tater take him downtown babe . . . hey good eye good eye."

Infield chatter is harder to maintain. Since the slow-pitch pitch is required to be a soft underhand lob, infielders hesitate to say, "Smoke him babe hey low heat hey throw it on the black babe chuck it in there back him up babe no hit no hit." Say it anyway.

6. One final rule, perhaps the most important of all: When your team is up and has made the third out, the batter and the players who were left on base do not come back to the bench for their gloves. *They remain on the field, and their teammates bring their gloves out to them.* This requires some organization and discipline, but it pays off big in morale. It says, "Although we're getting our pants knocked off, still we must conserve our energy."

Imagine that you have bobbled two fly balls in this rout and now you have just tried to stretch a single into a double and have been easily thrown out sliding into second base, where the base runner ahead of you had stopped. It was the third out and a dumb play, and your opponents smirk at you as they run off the field. You are the goat, a lonely and tragic figure sitting in the dirt. You curse yourself, jerking your head sharply forward. You stand up and kick the base. How miserable! How degrading! Your utter shame, though brief, bears silent testimony to the worthiness of your teammates, whom you have let down, and they appreciate it. They call out to you now as they take the field, and as the second baseman runs to his position he says, "Let's get 'em now," and tosses you your glove.

Lowering your head, you trot slowly out to right. There you do some deep knee bends. You pick grass. You find a pebble and fling it into foul territory. As the first batter comes to the plate, you check the sun. You get set in your stance, poised to fly. Feet spread, hands on hips, you bend slightly at the waist and spit the expert spit of a veteran ballplayer—a player who has known the agony of defeat but who always bounces back, a player who has lost a stride on the base paths but can still make the big play.

This is *ball,* ladies and gentlemen. This is what it's all about.

GEORGE PRICE

Casey Stengel

On July 9, 1958, Charles Dillon Stengel committed unpremeditated humor when he appeared before the United States Senate Subcommittee on Antitrust and Monopoly.

Casey Stengel is one of the most famous characters in the history of baseball. He was born in 1890, lived for eighty-five years, managed the New York Yankees at their height, the New York Mets at the depths, was a major league player, and, through astute investments, a millionaire. His wrinkled face looked like a topographical map of mountain ranges, and he walked on a pair of legs that (Red Smith observed), resembled a pair of parentheses.

At the time of Casey's death, *The New York Times* wrote: "He spoke in a nonstop style that became known as Stengelese—a kind of circuitous doubletalk laced with ambiguous antecedents, dangling participles, a lack of proper names, and a liberal use of adjectives. . . . He would clinch points by saying with finality: 'You could look it up'."

I *did* look it up and here, for what I believe to be the first time outside of the *Congressional Record,* is Stengel's complete, unexpurgated give-and-take (mostly give) with the bewildered senators on the question: Should professional baseball be subject to federal antitrust laws? **G.S.**

CASEY STENGEL

Organized Professional Team Sports

Mr. STENGEL. Well, I started in professional ball in 1910. I have been in professional ball, I would say, for 48 years. I have been employed by numerous ball clubs in the majors and in the minor leagues.

I started in the minor leagues with Kansas City. I played as low as class

D ball, which was at Shelbyville, Ky., and also class C ball, and class A ball, I have advanced in baseball as a ballplayer.

I had many years that I was not so successful as a ballplayer, as it is a game of skill. And then I was no doubt discharged by baseball in which I had to go back to the minor leagues as a manager, and after being in the minor leagues as a manager, I became a major league manager in several cities and was discharged, we call it "discharged", because there is no question I had to leave. [Laughter.]

And I returned to the minor leagues at Milwaukee, Kansas City, and Oakland, Calif., and then returned to the major leagues.

In the last 10 years, naturally, in major league baseball with the New York Yankees, the New York Yankees have had tremendous success and while I am not the ballplayer who does the work, I have no doubt worked for a ball club that is very capable in the office.

I must have splendid ownership, I must have very capable men who are in radio and television, which no doubt you know that we have mentioned the three names—you will say they are very great.

We have a wonderful press that follows us. Anybody should in New York City, where you have so many million people.

Our ball club has been successful because we have it, and we have the spirit of 1776.

We put it into the ball field and if you are not capable of becoming a great ballplayer since I have been in as the manager, in 10 years, you are notified that if you don't produce on the ball field, the salary that you receive, we will allow you to be traded to play and give your services to other clubs.

The great proof of that was yesterday. Three of the young men that were stars and picked by the players in the American League to be in the All-Star game were Mr. Cerv, who is at Kansas City; Mr. Jensen who was at Boston, and I might say Mr. Triandos that caught for the Baltimore ball club, all three of those players were my members and to show you that I was not such a brilliant manager they got away from me and were chosen by the players and I was fortunate enough to have them come back to play where I was successful as a manager.

If I have been in baseball for 48 years there must be some good in it. I was capable and strong enough at one time to do any kind of work but I came back to baseball and I have been in baseball ever since.

I have been up and down the ladder. I know there are some things in baseball 35 to 50 years ago that are better now than they were in those days. In those days, my goodness, you could not transfer a ball club in the minor leagues, class D, class C ball, class A ball.

How could you transfer a ball club when you did not have a highway? How could you transfer a ball club when the railroads then would take you to a town you got off and then you had to wait and sit up 5 hours to go to another ball club?

How could you run baseball then without night ball?

You had to have night ball to improve the proceeds, to pay larger salaries and I went to work, the first year I received $135 a month.

I thought that was amazing. I had to put away enough money to go to dental college. I found out it was not better in dentistry, I stayed in baseball.

Any other questions you would like to ask me?

I want to let you know that as to the legislative end of baseball you men will have to consider that what you are here for. I am a bench manager.

I will speak about anything from the playing end—in the major or minor leagues—and do anything I can to help you.

Senator KEFAUVER. Mr. Stengel, are you prepared to answer particularly why baseball wants this bill passed?

Mr. STENGEL. Well, I would have to say at the present time, I think that baseball has advanced in this respect for the player help. That is an amazing statement for me to make, because you can retire with an annuity at 50 and what organization in America allows you to retire at 50 and receive money?

I want to further state that I am not a ballplayer, that is, put into that pension fund committee. At my age, and I have been in baseball, well, I will say I am possibly the oldest man who is working in baseball. I would say that when they start an annuity for the ballplayers to better their conditions, it should have been done, and I think it has been done.

I think it should be the way they have done it, which is a very good thing.

The reason they possibly did not take the managers in at that time was because radio and television or the income to ball clubs was not large enough that you could have put in a pension plan.

Now I am not a member of the pension plan. You have young men here who are, who represent the ball clubs.

They represent them as players and since I am not a member and don't receive pension from a fund which you think, my goodness, he ought to be declared in that too but I would say that is a great thing for the ballplayers.

That is one thing I will say for the ballplayers they have an advanced pension fund. I should think it was gained by radio and television or you could not have enough money to pay anything of that type.

Now the second thing about baseball that I think is very interesting to the public or to all of us that it is the owners' own fault if he does not improve his club, along with the officials in the ball club and the players.

Now what causes that?

If I am going to go on the road and we are a traveling ball club and you know the cost of transportation now—we travel sometimes with three pullman coaches, the New York Yankees and remember I am just a salaried man and do not own stock in the New York Yankees, I found out that in traveling with the New York Yankees on the road and all, that it is the best, and we have broken records in Washington this year, we have broken them in every city but New York and we have lost two clubs that have gone out of the city of New York.

Of course we have had some bad weather, I would say that they are mad at us in Chicago, we fill the parks.

They have come out to see good material. I will say they are mad at us in Kansas City, but we broke their attendance record.

Now on the road we only get possibly 27 cents. I am not positive of these figures, as I am not an official.

If you go back 15 years or if I owned stock in the club I would give them to you.

Senator KEFAUVER. Mr. Stengel, I am not sure that I made my question clear. [Laughter.]

Mr. STENGEL. Yes, sir. Well that is all right. I am not sure I am going to answer yours perfectly either. [Laughter.]

Senator KEFAUVER. I was asking you, sir, why it is that baseball wants this bill passed.

Mr. STENGEL. I would say I would not know, but I would say the reason why they would want it passed is to keep baseball going as the highest paid ball sport that has gone into baseball and from the baseball angle, I am not going to speak of any other sport.

I am not in here to argue about other sports, I am in the baseball business. It has been run cleaner than any business that was ever put out in the 100 years at the present time.

I am not speaking about television or I am not speaking about income that comes into the ball parks. You have to take that off. I don't know too much about it. I say the ballplayers have a better advancement at the present time.

Senator KEFAUVER. One further question, and then I will pass to the other Senators.

How many players do the Yankees control, Mr. Stengel?

Mr. STENGEL. Well, I will tell you: I hire the players and if they make good with me I keep them without any criticism from my ownership.

I do not know how many players they own as I am not a scout and I cannot run a ball club during the daytime and be busy at night, and up the next day and find out how many players that the Yankees own.

If you get any official with the Yankees that is here, why he could give you the names.

Senator KEFAUVER. Very well.

Senator Langer?

Senator LANGER. Mr. Stengel?

Mr. STENGEL. Yes, sir.

Senator LANGER. What do you think is the future of baseball? Is it going to be expanded to include more clubs than are in existence at the present time?

Mr. STENGEL. I think every chamber of commerce in the major league cities would not change a franchise, I think they will be delighted because they have a hard time to put in a convention hall or to get people to come to your city and if it is going to be like Milwaukee or Kansas City or Baltimore, I think they would want a major league team.

But if I was a chamber of commerce member and I was in a city I would not want a baseball team to leave the city as too much money is brought into your city even if you have a losing team and great if you have a winning ball team.

Senator LANGER. You look forward then, do you not, to, say, 10 years or 20 years from now this business of baseball is going to grow larger and larger and larger?

Mr. STENGEL. Well, I should think it would.

I should think it would get larger because of the fact we are drawing tremendous crowds, I believe, from overseas programs in television, that is one program I have always stuck up for.

I think every ballplayer and everyone should give out anything that is overseas for the Army, free of cost and so forth.

I think that every hospital should get it. I think that because of the lack of parking in so many cities that you cannot have a great ball park if you don't have parking space.

If you are ancient or 45 or 50 and have acquired enough money to go to a ball game, you cannot drive a car on a highway, which is very hard to do after 45, to drive on any modern highway and if you are going to stay home you need radio and television to go along for receipts for the ball club.

Senator LANGER. That brings us to another question.

Mr. STENGEL. Yes, sir.

Senator LANGER. That is, what do you think of pay-as-you-go television?

Mr. STENGEL. Well, to tell you the truth, if I were starting in it myself I would like to be in that line of business as I did not think they would ever have television and so forth here but they have got it here now. [Laughter.]

Forty years ago you would not have had it around here yourself and you would not have cameras flying around here every 5 minutes but we have got them here and more of them around here than around a ball field, I will give you that little tip.

Senator LANGER. You believe the time is ever going to come when you will have pay-as-you-go in the world series, which would be kept from the public unless they had pay-as-you-go television in their homes?

Mr. STENGEL. I think you have got a good argument there and it is worthy of you to say that.

I am thinking myself of anybody that is hospitalized and anybody who cannot go to a ball park, I should think if they could pass that they should try to pass it.

But I don't think they will be able to do it because they have gone in television so far that they reach so many outside people, you have to have a sponsor for everything else you do, go pay television and that is going to run all the big theaters out of business where you have to use pay television.

All the big theaters and all the big movie companies went broke. We know that. You see that now or you would not have a place to hold a television for pay.

I don't know how they would run that of course. I am not on that side of the fence. I am paid a salary——

Senator LANGER. Just one further question. You do not have to answer it unless you want to. That is, is there any provision made whereby the team owners can keep a racketeer out of the baseball business?

Mr. STENGEL. Well, sir——

Senator LANGER. Can the owners of the New York Yankees, for example, sell out to anyone who may want to buy the club at a big price without the consent of the other owners?

Mr. STENGEL. That is a very good thing that I will have to think about but I will give you an example.

I think that is why they put in as a commissioner Judge Landis, and he said if there is a cloud on baseball I will take it off, and he took the cloud off and they have only had one scandal or if they had it is just one major league city.

How can you be a ballplayer and make 25 ballplayers framed without it being heard?

It is bound to leak, and your play will show it.

I don't think, an owner possibly could do something but he can't play the game for you. It is the most honest profession I think that we have, everything today that is going on outside——

Senator LANGER. Mr. Chairman, my final question. This is the Antimonopoly Committee that is sitting here.

Mr. STENGEL. Yes, sir.

Senator LANGER. I want to know whether you intend to keep on monopolizing the world's championship in New York City.

Mr. STENGEL. Well, I will tell you, I got a little concerned yesterday in the first 3 innings when I say the 3 players I had gotten rid of and I said when I lost 9 what am I going to do and when I had a couple of my players. I thought so great of that did not do so good up to the sixth inning I was more confused but I finally had to go and call on a young man in Baltimore that we don't own and the Yankees don't own him, and he is doing pretty good, and I would actually have to tell you that I think we are more the Greta Garbo type now from success.

We are being hated I mean, from the ownership and all, we are being hated. Every sport that gets too great or one individual—but if we made 27 cents and it pays to have a winner at home why would not you have a good winner in your own park if you were an owner.

That is the result of baseball. An owner gets most of the money at home and it is up to him and his staff to do better or they ought to be discharged.

Senator LANGER. That is all, Mr. Chairman. Thank you.

Senator KEFAUVER. Thank you, Senator Langer.

Senator O'Mahoney?

Senator O'MAHONEY. May I say, Mr. Stengel, that I congratulate you very much for what happened on the field at Baltimore yesterday. I was watching on television when you sent Gil McDougald up to bat for Early Wynn. I noticed with satisfaction that he got a hit, knocking Frank Malzone in with the winning run. That is good management.

Mr. STENGEL. Thank you very much. [Laughter.]

Senator O'MAHONEY. Did I understand you to say, Mr. Stengel, at the beginning of your statement that you have been in baseball for 48 years?

Mr. STENGEL. Yes, sir; the oldest man in the service.

Senator O'MAHONEY. How many major league teams were there in the United States when you entered baseball?

Mr. STENGEL. Well, there was in 1910—there were 16 major league baseball teams.

Senator O'MAHONEY. How many are there now?

Mr. STENGEL. There are 16 major league clubs but there was 1 year that they brought in the Federal League which was brought in by Mr. Ward and Mr. Sinclair and others after a war, and it is a very odd thing to tell you that during tough times it is hard to study baseball. I have been through 2 or 3 depressions in baseball and out of it.

The First World War we had good baseball in August.

The Second World War we kept on and made more money because everybody was around going to the services, the larger the war, the more they come to the ball park, and that was an amazing thing to me.

When you were looking for tough times why it changed for different wars.

Senator O'MAHONEY. How many minor leagues were there in baseball when you began?

Mr. STENGEL. Well, there were not so many at that time because of this fact: Anybody to go into baseball at that time with the educational schools that we had were small, while you were probably thoroughly educated at school, you had to be—we had only small cities that you could put a team in and they would go defunct.

Why, I remember the first year I was at Kankakee, Ill., and a bank offered me $550 if I would let them have a little notice. I left there and took a uniform because they owed me 2 weeks' pay. But I either had to quit but I did not have enough money to go to dental college so I had to go with the manager down to Kentucky.

What happened there was if you got by July, that was the big date. You did not play night ball and you did not play Sundays in half of the cities on account of a Sunday observance, so in those days when things were tough, and all of it was, I mean to say, why they just closed up July 4 and there you were sitting there in the depot.

You could go to work some place else but that was it.

So I got out of Kankakee, Ill., and I just go there for the visit now. [Laughter.]

I think now, do you know how many clubs they have?

Anybody will start a minor league club but it is just like your small cities, the industries have left them and they have gone west to California, and I am a Missourian—Kansas City, Mo.—but I can see all those towns and everybody moving west and I know if you fly in the air you can see anything from the desert, you can see a big country over there that has got many names.

Well, now why wouldn't baseball prosper out there, with that many million people?

Senator O'MAHONEY. Are the minor leagues suffering now?

Mr. STENGEL. I should say they are.

Senator O'MAHONEY. Why?

Mr. STENGEL. Do you know why?

I will tell you why. I don't think anybody can support minor league ball when they see a great official, it would be just like a great actress or actor had come to town. If Bob Hope had come here or Greta Garbo over there half of them would go to see Greta Garbo and half Bob Hope but if you have a very poor baseball team they are not going to watch you until you become great and the minor leagues now with radio and television will not pay very much attention to minor league ballplayers. Softball is interesting, the parent is interested; he goes around with him. He watches his son and he is more enthusiastic about the boy than some stranger that comes to town and wants to play in a little wooden park and with no facilities to make you be interested. You might rather stay home and see a program.

Senator O'MAHONEY. How many baseball players are now engaged in the activity as compared to when you came in?

Mr. STENGEL. I would say there are more, many more. Because we did not have as many cities that could support even minor league baseball in those days.

Senator O'MAHONEY. How many players did the 16 major league clubs have when you came in?

Mr. STENGEL. At that time they did not have as many teams. They did not have near as many teams as below.

Later on Mr. Rickey came in and started what was known as what you would say numerous clubs, you know in which I will try to pick up this college man, I will pick up that college boy or I will pick up some corner lot boy and if you picked up the corner lot boy maybe he became just as successful as the college man, which is true.

He then had a number of players.

Now, too many players is a funny thing, it costs like everything. I said just like I made a talk not long ago and I told them all when they were drinking and they invited me in I said you ought to be home. You men are not making enough money. You cannot drink like that. They said, "This is a holiday for the Shell Oil Co.," and I said "Why is it a holiday?" and they said, "We did something great for 3 years and we are given 2 days off to watch the Yankees play the White Sox," but they were mostly White Sox rooters.

I said, "You are not doing right."

I said, "You can't take all those drinks and all even on your holidays. You ought to be home and raising more children because big league clubs now give you a hundred thousand for a bonus to go into baseball." [Laughter.]

And by the way I don't happen to have any children but I wish Mrs. Stengel and I had eight, I would like to put them in on that bonus rule. [Laughter.]

Senator O'MAHONEY. What I am trying to find out, Mr. Stengel, is how many players are actively working for the major league teams now as was formerly the case?

How many players do you suppose——

Mr. STENGEL. You are right, I would honestly tell you they naturally have more and they are in more competition now.

You have to buck now a university—anyone who wants to be a hockey player——

Senator O'MAHONEY. Let's stick to baseball for a minute.

Mr. STENGEL. I stay in baseball. I say I can't name them. If you want to know you get any executive, you have got any names, bring any executive with the Yankees that is an official in the ball club and he will tell you how many players the Yankees have.

And there is his jurisdiction—every ball club owner can tell you he is an official, they have enough officials hired with me with a long pencil, too.

Senator O'MAHONEY. I recently saw a statement by a baseball sports writer that there were about 400 active ball players in the major leagues now.

Would you think that is about correct now?

Mr. STENGEL. I would say in the major leagues each club has 25 men which is the player limit.

There are 8 clubs in each league so you might say there are 400 players in the major leagues, you mean outside of it that they own two or three hundred each individual club, isn't that what you have reference to?

Senator O'MAHONEY. I was coming to that, but is that the fact?

Mr. STENGEL. Well, I say that is what you would say [laughter] if you want to find that out you get any of those executives that come in here that keep those books. I am not a bookkeeper for him. But I take the man when he comes to the big league. They can give it to you and each club should.

That does not mean and I would like to ask you, How would you like to pay those men?

That is why they go broke.

Senator O'MAHONEY. I am not in that business.

Mr. STENGEL. I was in that business a short time, too; it is pretty hard to make a living at it.

Senator O'MAHONEY. But the stories that we read in the press——

Mr. STENGEL. That is right.

Senator O'MAHONEY. Are to the effect that the minor leagues are suffering. There are no more major league teams now than there were when you came into baseball, and what I am trying to find out is, What are the prospects for the future growth of baseball and to what extent have the 16 major league teams, through the farm system, obtained, by contract or agreement or understanding, control over the professional lives of the players?

Mr. STENGEL. That is right.

If I was a ballplayer and I was discharged, and I saw within 3 years that I could not become a major league ballplayer I would go into another profession.

That is the history of anything that is in business.

Senator O'MAHONEY. Do you think that the farm system keeps any players in the minor leagues when they ought to be in the majors?

Mr. STENGEL. I should say it would not keep any players behind or I have been telling you a falsehood.

I would say it might keep a few back, but very few.

There is no manager in baseball who wants to be a success without the ability of those great players and if I could pull them up to make money in a gate for my owner and for myself to be a success, I don't believe I would hold him back.

Senator O'MAHONEY. The fact is, is it not, Mr. Stengel, that while the population of the United States has increased tremendously during the period that you have been engaged in professional baseball, the number of major-league teams has not increased; it remains the same as it was then. The number of players actually engaged by the major-league teams is approximately the same as back in 1903, and there is now, through the farm system, a major league control of the professional occupation of baseball playing. Is that a correct summary?

Mr. STENGEL. Well, you have that from the standpoint of what you have been reading. You have got that down very good. [Laughter.]

But if you are a player——

Senator O'MAHONEY. I am trying to get it down from your standpoint as a 48-year man in baseball.

Mr. STENGEL. That is why I stayed in it.

I have been discharged 15 times and rehired; so you get rehired in baseball, and they don't want a good ballplayer leaving, and I always say a high-priced baseball player should get a high salary just like a moving-picture actor.

He should not get the same thing as the 25th man on the ball club who is very fortunate he is sitting on your ball club, and I say it is very hard to have skill in baseball.

Senator O'MAHONEY. You are not changing the subject; are you, sir?

Mr. STENGEL. No. You asked the question and I told you that if you want to find out how minor league baseball is; it is terrible now.

How can you eat on $2.50 a day when up here you can eat on $8 or better than $8?

Now how can you travel in a bus all night and play ball the next night to make a living?

How can you, a major league man, make it so that you can't?

Is he going to fly all of them to each place?

Senator O'MAHONEY. I am not arguing with you, Mr. Stengel.

Mr. STENGEL. I am just saying minor league ball has outgrown itself, like every small town has outgrown itself industrially because they don't put a plant in there to keep the people working so they leave.

Senator O'MAHONEY. Does that mean in your judgment that the major league baseball teams necessarily have to control ball playing?

Mr. STENGEL. I think that they do.

I don't think that if I was a great player and you released me in 4 years, I think it would be a joke if you released a man and he made 1 year for you and then bid for a job and then played the next year, we will say, out of Washington, he played in New York the third year, he would play in Cleveland and put himself up in a stake.

I think they ought to be just as they have been.

A man who walks in and sees you get fair compensation and if you are great be sure you get it because the day you don't report and the day you don't open a season you are hurting the major league and hurting your-self somewhat, but you are not going to be handicapped in life if you are great in baseball.

Every man who goes out has a better home than he had when he went in.

Senator O'MAHONEY. Did I understand you to say that in your own personal activity as manager, you always give a player who is to be traded advance notice?

Mr. STENGEL. I warn him that—I hold a meeting. We have an instructional school, regardless of my English, we have got an instructional school.

Senator O'MAHONEY. Your English is perfect and I can understand what you say, and I think I can even understand what you mean.

Mr. STENGEL. Yes, sir. You have got some very wonderful points in. I would say in an instructional school we try you out for 3 weeks and we clock you, just like—I mean how good are you going to be in the service; before you go out of the service and we have got you listed.

We know if you are handicapped in the service and we have got instructors who teach you. They don't have to listen to me if they don't like me.

I have a man like Crosetti, who never has been to a banquet; he never would. He does a big job like Art Fletcher; he teaches that boy and teaches his family; he will be there. I have a man for first base, second base, short; that is why the Yankees are ahead.

We have advanced so much we can take a man over to where he can be a big league player and if he does not, we advance him to where he can play opposition to us.

I am getting concerned about opposition. I am discharging too many good ones.

Senator O'MAHONEY. Mr. Chairman, I think the witness is the best entertainment we have had around here for a long time and it is a great temptation to keep asking him questions but I think I had better desist.

Thank you.

Senator KEFAUVER. Senator Carroll.

Senator CARROLL. Mr. Stengel, I am an old Yankee fan and I come from a city where I think we have had some contribution to your success—from Denver. I think you have many Yankee players from Denver.

The question Senator Kefauver asked you was *what,* in your honest opinion, with your 48 years of experience, *is the need for this* legislation in view of the fact that baseball has not been subject to antitrust laws?

Mr. STENGEL. No.?

Senator CARROLL. It is not now subject to the antitrust laws. What do you think the need is for this legislation? I had a conference with one of the attorneys representing not only baseball but all of the sports, and I listened to your explanation to Senator Kefauver. It seemed to me it had some clarity. I asked the attorney this question: What was the need for this legislation? I wonder if you would accept his definition. He said they didn't want to be subjected to the ipse dixit of the Federal Government because they would throw a lot of damage suits on the ad damnum clause. He said, in the first place, the Toolson case was sui generis, it was de minimus non curat lex.

Do you call that a clear expression?

Mr. STENGEL. Well, you are going to get me there for about 2 hours.

Senator CARROLL. I realize these questions which are put to you are all, I suppose, legislative and legal questions. Leaning on your experience as a manager, do you feel the farm system, the draft system, the reserve-clause system, is fair to the players, to the managers, and to the public interest?

Mr. STENGEL. I think the public is taken care of, rich and poor, better at the present time than years ago. I really think that the ownership is a question of ability. I really think that the business manager is a question of ability. Some of those men are supposed to be very brilliant in their line of work, and some of them are not so brilliant, so that they have quite a bit of trouble with it when you run an operation of a club in which the ownership maybe doesn't run the club.

I would say that the players themselves—I told you, I am not in on that fund, it is a good thing. I say I should have been, to tell you the truth. But I think it is a great thing for the players.

Senator CARROLL. I am not talking about that fund.

Mr. STENGEL. Well, I tell you, if you are going to talk about the fund you are going to think about radio and television and pay television.

Senator CARROLL. I do not want to talk about radio and television, but I do want to talk about the draft clause and reserve systems.

Mr. STENGEL. Yes, sir. I would have liked to have been free four times in my life; and later on I have seen men free, and later on they make a big complaint "they wuz robbed," and if you are robbed there is always some club down the road to give you an opportunity.

Senator CARROLL. That was not the question I asked you, and I only asked you on your long experience——

Mr. STENGEL. Yes, sir. I would not be in it 48 years if it was not all right.

Senator CARROLL. I understand that.

Mr. STENGEL. Well, then, why wouldn't it stay that?

Senator CARROLL. In your long experience——

Mr. STENGEL. Yes.

Senator CARROLL. Do you feel—you have had experience through the years——

Mr. STENGEL. That is true.

Senator CARROLL. With the draft system, and the reserve clause in the contracts. Do you think you could still exist under existing law without changing the law?

Mr. STENGEL. I think it is run better than it has even been run in baseball, for every department.

Senator CARROLL. Then I come back to the principal question. This is the real question before this body.

Mr. STENGEL. All right.

Senator CARROLL. Then what is the need for legislation, if they are getting along all right?

Mr. STENGEL. I didn't ask for the legislation. [Laughter.]

Senator CARROLL. Your answer is a very good one, and that is the question Senator Kefauver put to you.

Mr. STENGEL. That is right.

Senator CARROLL. That is the question Senator O'Mahoney put.

Mr. STENGEL. Right.

Senator CARROLL. Are you ready to say there is no need for legislation in this field, then, insofar as baseball is concerned?

Mr. STENGEL. As far as I am concerned, from drawing a salary and from my ups and downs and being discharged, I always found out that there was somebody ready to employ you, if you were on the ball.

Senator CARROLL. Thank you very much, Mr. Stengel.

Senator KEFAUVER. Thank you very much, Mr. Stengel. We appreciate your testimony.

Senator LANGER. May I ask you a question?

Senator KEFAUVER. Senator Langer has a question. Just a moment, Mr. Stengel.

Senator LANGER. Can you tell this committee what countries have baseball teams besides the United States, Mexico, and Japan?

Mr. STENGEL. I made a tour with the New York Yankess several years ago, and it was the most amazing tour I ever saw for a ball club, to go over where you have trouble spots. It wouldn't make any difference whether he was a Republican or Democrat, and so forth.

I know that over there we drew 250,000 to 500,000 people in the streets, in which they stood in front of the automobiles, not on the sidewalks, and those people are trying to play baseball over there with short fingers [laughter], and I say, "Why do you do it?"

But they love it. They are crazy about baseball, and they are not worried at the handicap. And I'll tell you, business industries run baseball over there, and they are now going to build a stadium that is going to be covered over for games where you don't need a tarpaulin if it rains.

South America is all right, and Cuba is all right. But I don't know, I have never been down there except to Cuba, I have never been to South America, and I know that they broadcast games, and I know we have players that are playing from there.

I tell you what, I think baseball has spread, but if we are talking about anything spreading, we would be talking about soccer. You can go over in Italy, and I thought they would know DiMaggio everyplace. And my goodness, you mention soccer, you can draw 50,000 or a hundred thousand people. Over here you have a hard time to get soccer on the field, which is a great sport, no doubt.

Senator LANGER. What I want to know, Mr. Stengel, is this: When the American League plays the National League in the world series and it is advertised as the world championship——

Mr. STENGEL. Yes, sir.

Senator LANGER. I want to know why you do not play Mexico or Japan or some other country and really have a world championship.

Mr. STENGEL. Well, I think you have a good argument there. I would say that a couple of clubs that I saw, it was like when I was in the Navy, I thought I couldn't get special unless they played who I wanted to play. So I would look over a team. When they got off a ship I would play them, but if they had been on land too long, my team couldn't play them.

So I would play the teams at sea 6 months, and I would say, "You are the club I would like to play." I would like to play those countries, and I think it should be nationwide and governmentwide, too, if you could possibly get it in.

Senator LANGER. Do you think the day is ever going to come, perhaps 5 years from now or 10——

Mr. STENGEL. I would say 10 years, not 5.

Senator LANGER. When the championship team of the United States would play the championship team of Mexico?

Mr. STENGEL. I really think it should be that way, but I don't think you will get it before 10 years, because you have to build stadiums and you have to have an elimination in every country for it, and you have to have weather at the same time, or how could you play unless you would hold a team over?

Senator LANGER. Do you not think these owners are going to develop this matter of world championship of another country besides the United States?

Mr. STENGEL. I should think they would do that in time. I really do. I was amazed over in Japan. I couldn't understand why they would want to play baseball with short fingers and used the same size ball, and not a small size, and compete in baseball. And yet that is their great sport, and industries are backing them.

Senator LANGER. In other words, the owners some day, in your opinion, Mr. Stengel, are going to make a lot of money by having the champions of one country play another country and keep on with eliminations until they really have a world championship?

Mr. STENGEL. That is what I say. I think it is not named properly right now unless you can go and play all of them. You would have to do that.

Senator LANGER. That is all, Mr. Chairman.

Senator KEFAUVER. Mr. Stengel, one final question. You spoke of Judge Landis and the fact that he had rather absolute control over baseball. There was a clause in Judge Landis' contract which read:

We, the club owners, pledge ourselves to loyally support the commissioner in his important and difficult task, and we assure him that each of us will acquiesce in his decisions even when we believe they are mistaken, and that we will not discredit the sport by criticism of him or one another.

This same clause was in Mr. Chandler's contract, but we do not understand it to be in Mr. Frick's contract. Do you think the commissioner needs to have this power over the management?

Mr. STENGEL. I would say when there was a cloud over baseball, like any sport, you have to have a man that has the power to change things.

Now when Landis was in, that was the situation with baseball. You were bucking racetracks. We don't have a tote board. We are playing baseball for admission fees.

Now, we don't want a tote board in baseball. Who would? That would be great, if you have that out there, and you could go out there and, you know, use a tote board and say, "Does he get to first or won't he get to first?" and so forth.

Now Landis was an amazing man. I will give you an example of him. It is a good thing you brought him in. I was discharged one year, and I was the president of a ball club at Worcester, Mass., so I discharged myself, and I sent it in to Landis and he O.K.'d it.

Why was I president? Then I could release my player, couldn't I? And I was the player. So I was the only player ever released by the president, and that was in Worcester, Mass., so I got discharged.

Senator KEFAUVER. Do you think the present commissioner ought to have the same power?

Mr. STENGEL. There are 16 men in baseball who own ball clubs. We will say that an individual can hardly make it any more unless he is wealthy. That is how it has grown. I would say the biggest thing in baseball at the present time now, and with the money that is coming in, and so forth, and with an annuity fund for the players, you can't allow the commissioner to just take everything sitting there, and take everything insofar as money is concerned, but I think he should have full jurisdiction over the player and player's habits, and the way the umpires and ball clubs should conduct their business in the daytime and right on up tight up here.

Senator KEFAUVER. Thank you very much, Mr. Stengel. We appreciate your presence here.

UNIVERSITY OF CALIFORNIA

Engineer's Yell

E to the X dy! dx!
E to the X dx!

Secant, cosine, tangent, sine,
Three-point-one-four-one-five-nine;

Square root, cube root, QED.
Slip stick! slide rule!
            'ray, U.C.!

ROBERT DAY

*"Well, folks, here it is starting time! . . . One moment
while we take a look at that little old schedule."*

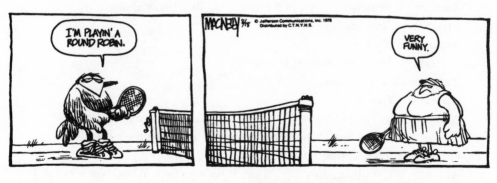

JEFF MacNELLY

BUD ABBOTT
AND LOU COSTELLO

Who's on First?

COSTELLO: Hey, Abbott!

ABBOTT: What do you want, Costello?

COSTELLO: Look, Abbott, I understand you're going to be the manager of the Lou Costello Junior Youth Foundation Baseball Team . . .

ABBOTT: Yes, we just organized the thing.

COSTELLO: You did?

ABBOTT: Sure!

COSTELLO: Well, I'd like to play on the team myself. You know, I know something about baseball.

ABBOTT: That could be accomplished.

COSTELLO: I'd like to know some of the guys' names on the team, so when I meet them on the street or in the ballpark I can say hello to them.

ABBOTT: Why, surely I'll introduce you to the boys. You know, strange as it may seem they give these ballplayers nowadays very peculiar names.

COSTELLO: You mean funny names?

ABBOTT: Nicknames . . . pet names . . . like Dizzy Dean . . .

COSTELLO: And his brother Daffy?

ABBOTT: Daffy Dean.

COSTELLO: I'm their French cousin.

ABBOTT: French cousin?

COSTELLO: Goo Fay!

ABBOTT: Goo Fay? *(Laugh)* Well, now, let's see we have on the bags—We have Who's on first, What's on second, I Don't Know's on third . . .

COSTELLO: That's what I want to find out.

ABBOTT: What silly names . . . I say Who's on first, What's on second, I Don't Know's on third . . .

COSTELLO: Are you the manager?

ABBOTT: Yes.

COSTELLO: Do you know the fellas' names?

ABBOTT: Well, I should.

COSTELLO: Well, then, who's on first?

ABBOTT: Yes.

COSTELLO: I mean, the fella's name.

ABBOTT: That's it.

COSTELLO: That's who?

ABBOTT: Yes.

COSTELLO: Well, go ahead and tell me.

ABBOTT: Who.

COSTELLO: The guy on first.

ABBOTT: Who.

COSTELLO: The first baseman.

ABBOTT: Who!

COSTELLO: Have you got a first baseman?

ABBOTT: *Who* is on first!

COSTELLO: I'm asking *you* who's on first!!

ABBOTT: That's the man's name!

COSTELLO: That's who's name?

ABBOTT: Yes.

COSTELLO: Now, tell me who's on first.

ABBOTT: That's right.

COSTELLO: I wanna know what's the guy's name on first base . . .

ABBOTT: Naw . . . No . . . What's on *second* base.

COSTELLO: I'm not asking who's on second.

ABBOTT: *Who* is on *first!*

COSTELLO: I don't know . . .

ABBOTT: He's on third . . . Let's get together here.

COSTELLO: How did I get on third base?

ABBOTT: You happened to mention the man's name.

COSTELLO: If I mentioned the third baseman's name, who did I say is playing third base?

ABBOTT: No, *Who's* playing *first!*

COSTELLO: I'm not asking you who's playing first!

ABBOTT: Who *is* on first!

COSTELLO: I'm asking you what's the guy's name on third?

ABBOTT: What is on *second.*

COSTELLO: Who's on second?

ABBOTT: Who's on *first!*

COSTELLO: I don't know!

ABBOTT: He's on *third!*

COSTELLO: There I go . . . Back on third again!

ABBOTT: I can't change their names.

COSTELLO: You got a first baseman?

ABBOTT: Absolutely!

COSTELLO: When you pay him off every month, who gets the money?

ABBOTT: Every dollar of it. *(Pause, and big laugh)* Why not? The man's entitled to it!

COSTELLO: Who is?

ABBOTT: Yes.

COSTELLO: So, who gets it?

ABBOTT: Sure he does!

COSTELLO: Look, the left fielder's name?

ABBOTT: Why.

COSTELLO: Because!

ABBOTT: Oh, he's *center* field!

COSTELLO: Eeeeeeee!

ABBOTT: Now, you know these players as well as I do!

COSTELLO: You got a catcher?

ABBOTT: Surely!

COSTELLO: The catcher's name?

ABBOTT: Today.

COSTELLO: Today. And Tomorrow's pitching?

ABBOTT: Now you've got it!

COSTELLO: Now I've got it? Well, I'm a pretty good catcher myself.

ABBOTT: So they tell me . . .

COSTELLO: Now, I'll catch today . . . myself. And Tomorrow's pitching on the team. Now Tomorrow throws the ball and the guy up bunts. Now, me being a good catcher, I wanna throw the guy out at first base, so I pick up the ball and throw it to who?

ABBOTT: That's the first thing you've said right!

COSTELLO: I don't even know what I'm talking about!

ABBOTT: Well, that's all you have to do!

COSTELLO: Is to throw the ball to first base?

ABBOTT: Yes.

COSTELLO: Now, who's got it?

ABBOTT: Naturally.

COSTELLO: If I throw the ball to first base, somebody's got to get it. Now, who's got it?

ABBOTT: Naturally.

COSTELLO: Naturally?

ABBOTT: Naturally!

COSTELLO: Oh, so I throw the ball to Naturally!

ABBOTT: You do nothing of the kind. You throw the ball to Who.

COSTELLO: Naturally.

ABBOTT: That's it!

COSTELLO: That's what I said!

ABBOTT: No, you didn't . . . No, you didn't!

COSTELLO: I throw the ball to Naturally . . .

ABBOTT: But you don't.

COSTELLO: I throw it to who?

ABBOTT: Naturally!

COSTELLO: That's what I'm saying.

ABBOTT: But that's *not* what you said!

COSTELLO: I throw the ball to who?

ABBOTT: Naturally.

COSTELLO: You ask me.

ABBOTT: You throw the ball to Who?

COSTELLO: Naturally! Same as you! I throw the ball to who.

ABBOTT: Naturally.

COSTELLO: Naturally. Now, whoever it is drops the ball, so the guy runs to second. Who picks up the ball and throws it to What, What throws it to I Don't Know, I Don't Know throws it back to Tomorrow—triple play! Another guy gets up and hits a long fly ball to be caught. Why? I Don't Know! He's on third and I don't give a darn!

ABBOTT: What'd you say?

COSTELLO: I said I don't give a darn!

ABBOTT: Oh, he's our shortstop!

COSTELLO: Abbott!!!!!!

CHARLES SCHULZ

DON MARQUIS

The Rivercliff Golf Killings

OR WHY PROFESSOR WADDEMS
NEVER BROKE A HUNDRED

I am telling this story to the public just as I told it in the grand jury room; the district attorney having given me a carbon copy of my sworn testimony.

THE CASE OF DOC GREEN

QUESTION: Professor Waddems, when did you first notice that Dr. Green seemed to harbor animosity towards you?

ANSWER: It was when we got to the second hole.

QUESTION: Professor, you may go ahead and tell the jury about it in your own words.

ANSWER: Yes, sir. The situation was this: My third shot lay in the sand in the shallow bunker—an easy pitch with a niblick to within a foot or two of the pin, for anyone who understands the theory of niblick play as well as I do. I had the hole in five, practically.

"Professor," said Doc Green, with whom I was playing—

QUESTION: This was Dr. James T. Green, the eminent surgeon, was it not?

ANSWER: Yes, sir. Dr. Green, with whom I was playing, remarked, "You are all wrong about Freud. Psychoanalysis is the greatest discovery of the age."

"Nonsense! Nonsense! Nonsense!" I replied. "Don't be a fool, Doc! I'll show you where Freud is all wrong, in a minute."

And I lifted the ball with an explosion shot to a spot eighteen inches from the pin, and holed out with an easy putt.

"Five," I said and marked it on my card.

"You mean eight," said Doc Green.

"Three into the bunker, four onto the green, and one putt—five," I said.

"You took four strokes in the bunker, Professor," he said. "Every time you said 'Nonsense' you made a swipe at the ball with your niblick."

"Great Godfrey," I said, "you don't mean to say you are going to count those gestures I made to illustrate my argument as *golf strokes?* Just mere gestures! And you know very well I have never delivered a lecture in twenty-five years without gestures like that!"

"You moved your ball an inch or two with your club at every gesture," he said.

QUESTION: Had you really done so, Professor? Remember, you are on oath.

ANSWER: I do not remember. In any case, the point is immaterial. They were merely gestures.

QUESTION: Did you take an eight, or insist on a five?

ANSWER: I took an eight. I gave in. Gentlemen, I am a good-natured person. Too good-natured. Calm and philosophical; unruffled and patient. My philosophy never leaves me. I took an eight.

(Sensation in the grand jury room.)

QUESTION: Will you tell something of your past life, Professor Waddems—who you are and what your lifework has been, and how you acquired the calmness you speak of?

ANSWER: For nearly twenty-five years I lectured on philosophy and psychology in various universities. Since I retired and took up golf it has been my habit to look at all the events and tendencies in the world's news from the standpoint of the philosopher.

QUESTION: Has this helped you in your golf?

ANSWER: Yes, sir. My philosophical and logical training and my specialization in psychology, combined with my natural calmness and patience, have made me the great golfer that I really am.

QUESTION: Have you ever received a square deal, Professor, throughout any eighteen holes of golf?

ANSWER: No, sir. Not once! Not once during the five years since I took the game up at the Rivercliff Country Club.

QUESTION: Have you ever broken a hundred, Professor Waddems?

ANWER: No, sir. I would have, again and again, except that my opponents, and other persons playing matches on the course, and the very forces of nature themselves are always against me at critical moments. Even the bullfrogs at the three water holes treat me impertinently.

QUESTION: Bullfrogs? You said the bullfrogs, Professor?

ANSWER: Yes, sir. They have been trained by the caddies to treat me impertinently.

QUESTION: What sort of treatment have you received in the locker room?

ANSWER: The worst possible. In the case under consideration, I may say that I took an eight on the second hole, instead of insisting on a five, because I knew the sort of thing Dr. Green would say in the locker room after the match—I knew the scene he would make, and what the comments of my so-called friends would be. Whenever I do get down to a hundred an attempt is made to discredit me in the locker room.

QUESTION: Well, you took an eight on the second hole. What happened at the third hole?

ANSWER: Well, sir, I teed up for my drive, and just as I did so, Doc Green made a slighting remark about the League of Nations. "I think it is a good thing we kept out of it," he said.

QUESTION: What were your reactions?

ANSWER: A person of intelligence could only have one kind of reaction, sir. The remark was silly, narrow-minded, provincial, boneheaded, crass and ignorant. It was all the more criminal because Dr. Green knew quite well what I think of the League of Nations. The League of Nations was my idea. I thought about it even before the late President Wilson did, and talked about it and wrote about it and lectured about it in the university.

QUESTION: So that you consider Dr. Green's motives in mentioning it when you were about to drive——

ANSWER: The worst possible, sir. They could only come from a black heart at such a time.

QUESTION: Did you lose your temper, Professor?

ANSWER: No, sir! No, sir! No, sir! I *never* lose my temper! Not on any provocation. I said to myself, Be calm! Be philosophical! He's trying to get me excited! Remember what he'll say in the locker room afterwards! Be calm! Show him, show him, show him! Show him he can't get my goat.

QUESTION: Then you drove?

ANSWER: I addressed the ball the second time, sir. And I was about to drive when he said, with a sneer, "You must excuse me, Professor. I forgot that you invented the League of Nations."

QUESTION: Did you become violent, then, Professor?

ANSWER: No, sir! No, sir! I never become violent! I never——

QUESTION: Can you moderate your voice somewhat, Professor?

ANSWER: Yes, sir. I was explaining that I never become violent. I had every right to become violent. Any person less calm and philosophical would have become violent. Doc Green to criticize the League of Nations! The ass! Absurd! Preposterous! Silly! Abhorrent! Criminal! What the world wants is peace! Philosophic calm! The fool! Couldn't he understand that!

QUESTION: Aren't you departing, Professor, from the events of the 29th of last September at the Rivercliff golf course? What did you do next?

ANSWER: I drove.

QUESTION: Successfully?

ANSWER: It was a good drive, but the wind caught it, and it went out of bounds.

QUESTION: What did Dr. Green do then?

ANSWER: He grinned. A crass bonehead capable of sneering at the progress of the human race would sneer at a time like that.

QUESTION: But you kept your temper?

ANSWER: All my years of training as a philosopher came to my aid.

QUESTION: Go on, Professor.

ANSWER: I took my midiron from my bag and looked at it.

QUESTION: Well, go on, Professor. What did you think when you looked at it?

ANSWER: I do not remember, sir.

QUESTION: Come, come, Professor! You are under oath, you know. Did you think what a dent it would make in his skull?

ANSWER: Yes, sir. I remember now. I remember wondering if it would not do his brain good to be shaken up a little.

QUESTION: Did you strike him, then?

ANSWER: No, sir. I knew what they'd say in the locker room. They'd say that I lost my temper over a mere game. They would not understand that I had been jarring up his brain for his own good, in the hope of making him understand about the League of Nations. They'd say I was irritated. I know the things people always say.

QUESTION: Was there no other motive for not hitting him?

ANSWER: I don't remember.

QUESTION: Professor Waddems, again I call your attention to the fact that you are under oath. What was your other motive?

ANSWER: Oh yes, now I recall it. I reflected that if I hit him they might make me add another stroke to my score. People are always getting up the flimsiest excuses to make me add another stroke. And then accusing me of impatience if I do not acquiesce in their unfairness. I am never impatient or irritable!

QUESTION: Did you ever break a club on the course, Professor?

ANSWER: I don't remember.

QUESTION: Did you not break a mashie on the Rivercliff course last week, Professor Waddems? Reflect before you answer.

ANSWER: I either gave it away or broke it, I don't remember which.

QUESTION: Come, come, don't you remember that you broke it against a tree?

ANSWER: Oh, I think I know what you mean. But it was not through temper or irritation.

QUESTION: Tell the jury about it.

ANSWER: Well, gentlemen, I had a mashie that had a loose head on it, and I don't know how it got into my bag. My ball lay behind a sapling, and I tried to play it out from behind the tree and missed it entirely. And then I noticed I had this old mashie, which should have been gotten rid of long ago. The club had never been any good. The blade was laid back at the wrong angle. I decided that the time had come to get rid of it once and for all. So I hit it a little tap against the tree, and the head fell off. I threw the pieces over into the bushes.

QUESTION: Did you swear, Professor?

ANSWER: I don't remember. But the injustice of this incident was that my opponent insisted on counting it as a stroke and adding it to my score —my judicial, deliberate destruction of this old mashie. I never get a square deal.

QUESTION: Return to Dr. James T. Green, Professor. You are now at the third hole, and the wind has just carried your ball out of bounds.

ANSWER: Well, I didn't hit him when he sneered. I carried the ball within bounds.

"Shooting three," I said calmly. I topped the ball. Gentlemen, I have seen Walter Hagen top the ball the same way.

"Too bad, Professor," said Doc Green. He said it hypocritically. I knew it was hypocrisy. He was secretly gratified that I had topped the ball. He knew I knew it.

QUESTION: What were your emotions at this further insult, Professor?

ANSWER: I pitied him. I thought how inferior he was to me intellectually, and I pitied him. I addressed the ball again. "I pity him," I murmured. "Pity, pity, pity, pity, pity!"

He overheard me. "Your pity has cost you five more strokes," he said.

"I was merely gesticulating," I said.

QUESTION: Did the ball move? Remember, you are under oath, and you have waived immunity.

ANSWER: If the ball moved, it was because a strong breeze had sprung up.

QUESTION: Go on.

ANSWER: I laid the ball upon the green and again holed out with one putt. "I'm taking a five," I said, marking it on my card.

"I'm giving you a ten," he said, marking it on his card. "Five gesticulations on account of your pity."

QUESTION: Describe your reactions to this terrible injustice, Professor. Was there a red mist before your eyes? Did you turn giddy and wake up to find him lying lifeless at your feet? Just what happened?

ANSWER: Nothing, sir.

(Sensation in the grand jury room.)

QUESTION: Think again, Professor. Nothing?

ANSWER: I merely reflected that, in spite of his standing scientifically, Dr. James T. Green was a moron and utterly devoid of morality and that I should take this into acount. I did not lose my temper.

QUESTION: Did you snatch the card from his hands?

ANSWER: I took it, sir. I did not snatch it.

QUESTION: And then did you cram it down his throat?

ANSWER: I suggested that he eat it, sir, as it contained a falsehood in black and white, and Dr. Green complied with my request.

QUESTION: Did you lay hands upon him, Professor? Remember, now, we are still talking about the third hole.

ANSWER: I think I did steady him a little by holding him about the neck and throat while he masticated and swallowed the card.

QUESTION: And then what?

ANSWER: Well, gentlemen, after that there is very little more to tell until we reached the sixteenth hole. Dr. Green for some time made no further attempt to treat me unjustly and played in silence, acquiescing in the scores I had marked on my card. We were even as to holes, and it was a certainty that I was about to break a hundred. But I knew what was beneath this silence on Doc Green's part, and I did not trust it.

QUESTION: What do you mean? That you knew what he was thinking, although he did not speak?

ANSWER: Yes, sir. I knew just what kind of remarks he would have made if he had made any remarks.

QUESTION: Were these remarks which he suppressed derogatory remarks?

ANSWER: Yes, sir. Almost unbelievably so. They were deliberately intended to destroy my poise.

QUESTION: Did they do so, Professor?

ANSWER: I don't think so.

QUESTION: Go on, Professor.

ANSWER: At the sixteenth tee, as I drove off, this form of insult reached its climax. He accentuated his silence with a peculiar look, just as my club head was about to meet the ball. I knew what he meant. He knew that I knew it, and that I knew. I sliced into a bunker. He stood and watched me as I stepped into the sand with my niblick—watched me with that look upon his face. I made three strokes at the ball and, as will sometimes happen even to the best of players, did not move it a foot. The fourth stroke drove it out of sight into the sand. The sixth stroke brought it to light again. Gentlemen, I did not lose my temper. I never do. But I admit that I did increase my tempo. I struck rapidly three more times at the ball. And all the time Doc Green was regarding me with that look, to which he now added a smile. Still I kept my temper, and he might be alive today if he had not spoken.

QUESTION *(by the foreman of the jury):* What did the man say at this trying time?

ANSWER: I know that you will not believe it is within the human heart to make the black remark that he made. And I hesitate to repeat it. But I have sworn to tell everything. What he said was, "Well, Professor, the club puts these bunkers here, and I suppose they have got to be used."

QUESTION *(by the foreman of the jury):* Was there something especially trying in the way he said it?

ANSWER: There was. He said it with an affectation of joviality.

QUESTION: You mean as if he thought he were making a joke, Professor?

ANSWER: Yes, sir.

QUESTION: What were your emotions at this point?

ANSWER: Well, sir, it came to me suddenly that I owed a duty to society; and for the sake of civilization I struck him with the niblick. It was an effort to reform him, gentlemen.

QUESTION: Why did you cover him with sand afterwards?

ANSWER: Well, I knew that if the crowd around the locker room discovered that I had hit him, they would insist on counting it as another stroke. And that is exactly what happened when the body was discovered—once again I was prevented from breaking a hundred.

THE DISTRICT ATTORNEY: Gentlemen of the jury, you have heard Professor Waddems' frank and open testimony in the case of Dr. James T. Green. My own recommendation is that he be not only released, but complimented, as far as this count is returned. If ever a homicide was justifiable, this one was. And I suggest that you report no indictment against the Professor, without leaving your seats. Many of you will wish to get in at least nine holes before dinner.

JEFF MacNELLY

THE THRILL THAT COMES ONCE IN A LIFETIME

LOVE AT FIRST SIGHT

H. T. WEBSTER

LOIS ROMANO

English Lit(mus)

A New York writer with floor-to-ceiling bookshelves in every room of his house takes an attractive receptionist out to dinner one night. She is Catholic, he is Jewish, and that gives him an opening for some fancy conversational footwork. He recites the Hail Mary for her over their sirloin strips.

"How did you know that?" she cried. Suitably impressed.

"It's said over and over again in *For Whom the Bell Tolls,*" he tells her.

Long pause.

"What's *For Whom the Bell Tolls?*"

It tolled for her.

Books: They can bring out the intellectual snob in all of us. This is potentially the most nerve-racking of all Litmus Tests.

Did he sneeze while taking inventory of her bookshelf, or was he strangling back an attack of the snickers?

When she asked, "Did you read all these?" was she hoping he'd say no?

Does he read a lot? Does she know Jung from Jong? It doesn't matter. The facts of life (or of the Litmus Test) are that on that first impressionable foray into the opposition's living room, what matters is what's on display. Beyond that stack of *Cosmopolitans* may lurk Colette, but he probably won't stick around long enough to find out.

Can you trust her with your autographed first edition of *Catcher in the Rye?* Or will she cavalierly tell you next week that she lent it to some guy in her office who reads fast?

Some men will pronounce an instant verdict when he sees that her *World According to Garp* is not the solid blue hardback with the gold lettering, but the one with Robin Williams on the cover. Does her Scott Spencer novel proclaim *Endless Love* in big red letters on the plain white background, or did she catch up with the post-movie special at the super-market featuring Brooke Shields on the front?

And if his neat bookshelf is filled with crisp, virginal hardbacks it probably means he mostly reads *Apartment Life* to get decorating ideas.

"I walk into a woman's house and see Joyce and Melville," says one teacher. "It tells me she was a serious reader and didn't just see Melville interviewed on Phil Donahue."

That bookcase in his or her apartment is like a Rorschach test. You walk into the living room, take in the titles, and this literary Ink Blot tells you these things:

He knows he has struck gold if she has *Joy of Sex* with bookmarks in it.

His Hemingway is cause for caution. It's all right if he *likes* the Papa, just as long as he doesn't act like him.

Hermann Hesse is probably left over from college. It goes along with the ponytail. His ponytail.

Her Richard Simmons *Never Say Diet Cookbook* is grounds for instant retreat. *Thin Thighs in 30 Days* tells him what's beneath those pleated slacks.

Rod McKuen: instant disqualification from polite conversation in most parts of the civilized world.

A shelf full of Gothic Romances warns him that she's prone to turn around at any moment and sigh, "Oh, Wendell, where are we going, we two?"—on the first date. He'll probably say, "Home."

Self-improvement books: a person more interested in helping themselves than you.

J. D. Salinger is a two-edged sword. Mildly impressive if allowed to sit used-looking on the shelves, but dangerous if he starts asking you to name all the members of the Glass family.

John Irving is significant only if the edition came *before* the *Time* maga-zine cover on him.

E. L. Doctorow is a good, safe entry. Sort of like Haagen-Däzs, high-brow ice cream, but still ice cream. Makes everybody happy.

Her Jacqueline Susann sets off alarms. She's probably got her movie magazines and chocolates stashed somewhere.

Lots of F. Scott Fitzgerald means nothing unless you ask him about Gatsby and he thinks it's a bar on the Upper East Side.

Dostoevsky, Ezra Pound, and Proust: A serious but possibly grim mate.

Jonathan Livingston Seagull: Slip quietly out the door while she's in the bathroom.

Thoreau, Shakespeare, Tolstoy, Homer, and *Social Psychology:* He hasn't read a book since college.

Alphabetized bookshelves: Person has dangerous amount of leisure time on his hands.

Complete works of any author: Person has completion fetish and the love affair will be very difficult to end.

Bound volumes of *Sports Illustrated* . . . and nothing else in sight: Don't worry about what he thinks of Hemingway. He probably doesn't know who he is.

Liberal collection of books not published in U.S. or Canada: Serious intellectual. Well traveled.

Tom Wolfe: Funky. Daring. Rambling.

John Barth: A person whose taste at least moves slightly out of best-seller rut. Definitely has a healthy, perverse streak.

James Michener and Irving Shaw: He doesn't take chances. You'll always know what to expect. He does what the Book of the Month Club tells him to do.

His Marquis de Sade: You're taking a big chance.

CHARLES SCHULZ

NICOLE HOLLANDER

GARRY TRUDEAU

"Will you be right home after the peccadillo?"

RING LARDNER

Some Like Them Cold

N. Y., Aug. 3.

Dear Miss GILLESPIE:

How about our bet now as you bet me I would forget all about you the minute I hit the big town and would never write you a letter. Well girlie it looks like you lose so pay me. Seriously we will call all bets off as I am not the kind that bet on a sure thing and it sure was a sure thing that I would not forget a girlie like you and all that is worrying me is whether it may not be the other way round and you are wondering who this fresh guy is that is writeing you this letter. I bet you are so will try and refreshen your memory.

Well girlie I am the handsome young man that was wondering round the Lasalle st. station Monday and "happened" to sit down beside of a mighty pretty girlie who was waiting to meet her sister from Toledo and the train was late and I am glad of it because if it had not of been that little girlie and I would never of met. So for once I was a lucky guy but still I guess it was time I had some luck as it was certainly tough luck for you and I to both be liveing in Chi all that time and never get together till a half hour before I was leaveing town for good.

Still "better late than never" you know and maybe we can make up for lost time though it looks like we would have to do our makeing up at long distants unless you make good on your threat and come to N. Y. I wish you would do that little thing girlie as it looks like that was the only way we would get a chance to play round together as it looks like they was little or no chance of me comeing back to Chi as my whole future is in the big town. N. Y. is the only spot and specially for a man that expects to make my liveing in the song writeing game as here is the Mecca for that line of work and no matter how good a man may be they don't get no recognition unless they live in N. Y.

Well girlie you asked me to tell you all about my trip. Well I remember you saying that you would give anything to be makeing it yourself but as far as the trip itself was conserned you ought to be thankfull you did not have to make it as you would of sweat your head off. I know I did specially wile going through Ind. Monday P. M. but Monday night was the worst of all trying to sleep and finely I give it up and just layed there with the prespiration rolling off of me though I was laying on top of the covers and nothing on but my underwear.

Yesterday was not so bad as it rained most of the A. M. comeing through N. Y. state and in the P. M. we road along side of the Hudson all P. M. Some river girlie and just looking at it makes a man forget all about the heat and everything else except a certain girlie who I seen for the first time Monday and then only for a half hour but she is the kind of a girlie that a man don't need to see her only once and they would be no danger of forgetting her. There I guess I better lay off that subject or you will think I am a "fresh guy."

Well that is about all to tell you about the trip only they was one amuseing incidence that come off yesterday which I will tell you. Well they was a dame got on the train at Toledo Monday and had the birth opp. mine but I did not see nothing of her that night as I was out smokeing till late and she hit the hay early but yesterday A. M. she come in the dinner and sit at the same table with me and tried to make me and it was so raw that the dinge waiter seen it and give me the wink and of course I paid no tension and I waited till she got through so as they would be no danger of her folling me out but she stopped on the way out to get a tooth pick and when I come out she was out on the platform with it so I tried to brush right by but she spoke up and asked me what time it was and I told her and she said she geussed her watch was slow so I said maybe it just seemed slow on acct. of the company it was in.

I don't know if she got what I was driveing at or not but any way she give up trying to make me and got off at Albany. She was a good looker but I have no time for gals that tries to make strangers on a train.

Well if I don't quit you will think I am writeing a book but will expect a long letter in answer to this letter and we will see if you can keep your promise like I have kept mine. Don't dissapoint me girlie as I am all alone in a large city and hearing from you will keep me from getting home sick for old Chi though I never thought so much of the old town till I found out you lived there. Don't think that is kidding girlie as I mean it.

You can address me at this hotel as it looks like I will be here right along as it is on 47th st. right off of old Broadway and handy to everything and am only paying $21 per wk. for my rm. and could of got one for $16 but without bath but am glad to pay the differents as am lost without my bath in the A. M. and sometimes at night too.

Tomorrow I expect to commence fighting the "battle of Broadway" and will let you know how I come out that is if you answer this letter. In the mean wile girlie au reservoir and don't do nothing I would not do.

Your new friend (?)
CHAS. F. LEWIS

Chicago, Ill., Aug. 6.

My Dear Mr. LEWIS:

Well, that certainly was a "surprise party" getting your letter and you are certainly a "wonder man" to keep your word as I am afraid most men of your sex are gay deceivers but maybe you are "different." Any way it sure was a surprise and will gladly pay the bet if you will just tell me what it was we bet. Hope it was not money as I am a "working girl" but if it was not more than a dollar or two will try to dig it up even if I have to "beg, borrow or steal."

Suppose you will think me a "case" to make a bet and then forget what it was, but you must remember, Mr. Man, that I had just met you and was "dazzled." Joking aside I was rather "fussed" and will tell you why. Well, Mr. Lewis, I suppose you see lots of girls like the one you told me about that you saw on the train who tried to "get acquainted" but I want to assure you that I am not one of those kind and sincerely hope you will believe me when I tell you that you was the first man I ever spoke to meeting them like that and my friends and the people who know me would simply faint if they knew I ever spoke to a man without a "proper introduction."

Believe me, Mr. Lewis, I am not that kind and I don't know now why I did it only that you was so "different" looking if you know what I mean and not at all like the kind of men that usually try to force their attentions on every pretty girl they see. Lots of times I act on impulse and let my feelings run away from me and sometimes I do things on the impulse of the moment which I regret them later on, and that is what I did this time, but hope you won't give me cause to regret it and I know you won't as I know you are not that kind of a man a specially after what you told me about the girl on the train. But any way as I say, I was in a "daze" so can't remember what it was we bet, but will try and pay it if it does not "break" me.

Sis's train got in about ten minutes after yours had gone and when she saw me what do you think was the first thing she said? Well, Mr. Lewis, she said: "Why Mibs (That is a pet name some of my friends have given me) what has happened to you? I never seen you have as much color." So I passed it off with some remark about the heat and changed the subject as I certainly was not going to tell her that I had just been talking to a man who I had never met or she would of dropped dead from the shock. Either that or she would not of believed me as it would be hard for a person who knows me well to imagine me doing a thing like that as I have quite a reputation for "squelching" men who try to act fresh. I don't mean anything personal by that, Mr. Lewis, as am a good judge of character and could tell without you telling me that you are not that kind.

Well, Sis and I have been on the "go" ever since she arrived as I took yesterday and today off so I could show her the "sights" though she says she would be perfectly satisfied to just sit in the apartment and listen to me "rattle on." Am afraid I am a great talker, Mr. Lewis, but Sis says it is as good as a show to hear me talk as I tell things in such a different way as I cannot help from seeing the humorous side of everything and she says she never gets tired of listening to me, but of course she is my sister and thinks the world of me, but she really does laugh like she enjoyed my craziness.

Maybe I told you that I have a tiny little apartment which a girl friend of mine and I have together and it is hardly big enough to turn round in, but still it is "home" and I am a great home girl and hardly ever care to go out evenings except occasionally to the theatre or dance. But even if our "nest" is small we are proud of it and Sis complimented us on how cozy it is and how "homey" it looks and she said she did not see how we could afford to have everything so nice and Edith (my girl friend) said: "Mibs deserves all the credit for that. I never knew a girl who could make a little money go a long ways like she can." Well, of course she is my best friend and always saying nice things about me, but I do try and I hope I get results. Have always said that good taste and being careful is a whole lot more important than lots of money though it is nice to have it.

You must write and tell me how you are getting along in the "battle of Broadway" (I laughed when I read that) and whether the publishers like your songs though I know they will. Am crazy to hear them and hear you play the piano as I love good jazz music even better than classical, though I suppose it is terrible to say such a thing. But I usually say just what I think though sometimes I wish afterwards I had not of. But still I believe it is better for a girl to be her own self and natural instead of always acting. But am afraid I will never have a chance to hear you play unless you come back to Chi and pay us a visit as my "threat" to come to New York was just a "threat" and I don't see any hope of ever getting there unless some rich

New Yorker should fall in love with me and take me there to live. Fine chance for poor little me, eh Mr. Lewis?

Well, I guess I have "rattled on" long enough and you will think I am writing a book unless I quit and besides, Sis has asked me as a special favor to make her a pie for dinner. Maybe you don't know it, Mr. Man, but I am quite famous for my pie and pastry, but I don't suppose a "genius" is interested in common things like that.

Well, be sure and write soon and tell me what N.Y. is like and all about it and don't forget the little girlie who was "bad" and spoke to a strange man in the station and have been blushing over it ever since.

Your friend (?)
MABELLE GILLESPIE

N. Y., Aug. 10.

Dear GIRLIE:

I bet you will think I am a fresh guy commencing that way but Miss Gillespie is too cold and a man can not do nothing cold in this kind of weather specially in this man's town which is the hottest place I ever been in and I guess maybe the reason why New Yorkers is so bad is because they think they are all ready in H—— and can not go no worse place no matter how they behave themselves. Honest girlie I certainly envy you being where there is a breeze off the old Lake and Chi may be dirty but I never heard of nobody dying because they was dirty but four people died here yesterday on acct. of the heat and I seen two different women flop right on Broadway and had to be taken away in the ambulance and it could not of been because they was dressed too warm because it would be impossible for the women here to leave off any more cloths.

Well have not had much luck yet in the battle of Broadway as all the heads of the big music publishers is out of town on their vacation and the big boys is the only ones I will do business with as it would be silly for a man with the stuff I have got to waste my time on somebody that is just on the staff and have not got the final say. But I did play a couple of my numbers for the people up to Levy's and Goebel's and they went crazy over them in both places. So it looks like all I have to do is wait for the big boys to get back and then play my numbers for them and I will be all set. What I want is to get taken on the staff of one of the big firms as that gives a man the inside and they will plug your numbers more if you are on the staff. In the mean wile have not got nothing to worry me but am just seeing the sights of the big town as have saved up enough money to play round for a wile and any way a man that can play piano like I can don't never have to worry about starveing. Can certainly make the old music box talk girlie and am always good for a $75 or $100 job.

Well have been here a week now and on the go every minute and I thought I would be lonesome down here but no chance of that as I have been treated fine by the people I have met and have sure met a bunch of them. One of the boys liveing in the hotel is a vaudeville actor and he is a member of the Friars club and took me over there to dinner the other night and some way another the bunch got wise that I could play piano so of course I had to sit down and give them some of my numbers and everybody went crazy over them. One of the boys I met there was Paul Sears the song writer but he just writes the lyrics and has wrote a bunch of hits and when he heard some of my melodies he called me over to one side and said he would like to work with me on some numbers. How is that girlie as he is one of the biggest hit writers in N. Y.

N. Y. has got some mighty pretty girlies and I guess it would not be hard to get acquainted with them and in fact several of them has tried to make me since I been here but I always figure that a girl must be something wrong with her if she tries to make a man that she don't know nothing about so I pass them all up. But I did meet a couple of pips that a man here in the hotel went up on Riverside Drive to see them and insisted on me going along and they got on some way that I could make a piano talk so they was nothing but I must play for them so I sit down and played some of my own stuff and they went crazy over it.

One of the girls wanted I should come up and see her again, and I said I might but I think I better keep away as she acted like she wanted to vamp me and I am not the kind that likes to play round with a gal just for their company and dance with them etc. but when I see the right gal that will be a different thing and she won't have to beg me to come and see her as I will camp right on her trail till she says yes. And it won't be none of these N. Y. fly by nights neither. They are all right to look at but a man would be a sucker to get serious with them as they might take you up and next thing you know you would have a wife on your hands that don't know a dish rag from a waffle iron.

Well girlie will quit and call it a day as it is too hot to write any more and I guess I will turn on the cold water and lay in the tub a wile and then turn in. Don't forget to write to

Your friend,
CHAS. F. LEWIS

Dear Mr. MAN:

Hope you won't think me a "silly Billy" for starting my letter that way but "Mr. Lewis" is so formal and "Charles" is too much the other way and any way I would not dare call a man by their first name after only knowing them only two weeks. Though I may as well confess that Charles is my favorite name for a man and have always been crazy about it as it was my father's name. Poor old dad, he died of cancer three years ago, but left enough insurance so that mother and we girls were well provided for and do not have to do anything to support ourselves though I have been earning my own living for two years to make things easier for mother and also because I simply can't bear to be doing nothing as I feel like a "drone." So I flew away from the "home nest" though mother felt bad about it as I was her favorite and she always said I was such a comfort to her as when I was in the house she never had to worry about how things would go.

But there I go gossiping about my domestic affairs just like you would be interested in them though I don't see how you could be though personaly I always like to know all about my friends, but I know men are different so will try and not bore you any longer. Poor Man, I certainly feel sorry for you if New York is as hot as all that. I guess it has been very hot in Chi, too, at least everybody has been complaining about how terrible it is. Suppose you will wonder why I say "I guess" and you will think I ought to know if it is hot. Well, sir, the reason I say "I guess" is because I don't feel the heat like others do or at least I don't let myself feel it. That sounds crazy I know, but don't you think there is a good deal in mental suggestion and not letting yourself feel things? I believe that if a person simply won't allow themselves to be affected by disagreeable things, why such things won't bother them near as much. I know it works with me and that is the reason why I am never cross when things go wrong and "keep smiling" no matter what happens and as far as the heat is concerned, why I just don't let myself feel it and my friends say I don't even look hot no matter if the weather is boiling and Edith, my girl friend, often says that I am like a breeze and it cools her off just to have me come in the room. Poor Edie suffers terribly during the hot weather and says it almost makes her mad at me to see how cool and unruffled I look when everybody else is perspiring and have red faces etc.

I laughed when I read what you said about New York being so hot that people thought it was the "other place." I can appreciate a joke, Mr. Man, and that one did not go "over my head." Am still laughing at some of the things you said in the station though they probably struck me funnier than they would most girls as I always see the funny side and sometimes something is said and I laugh and the others wonder what I am laughing at as they cannot see anything in it themselves, but it is just the way I look at things so of course I cannot explain to them why I laughed and they think I am crazy. But I had rather part with almost anything rather than my sense of humour as it helps me over a great many rough spots.

Sis has gone back home though I would of liked to of kept her here much longer, but she had to go though she said she would of liked nothing better than to stay with me and just listen to me "rattle on." She always says it is just like a show to hear me talk as I always put things in such a funny way and for weeks after she has been visiting me she thinks of some of the things I said and laughs over them. Since she left Edith and I have been pretty quiet though poor Edie wants to be on the "go" all the time and tries to make me go out with her every evening to the pictures and scolds me when I say I had rather stay home and read and calls me a "book worm." Well, it is true that I had rather stay home with a good book than go to some crazy old picture and the last two nights I have been reading myself to sleep with Robert W. Service's poems. Don't you love Service or don't you care for "highbrow" writings?

Personly there is nothing I love more than to just sit and read a good book or sit and listen to somebody play the piano, I mean if they can really play and I really believe I like popular music better than the classical though I suppose that is a terrible thing to confess, but I love all kinds of music but a specially the piano when it is played by somebody who can really play.

Am glad you have not "fallen" for the "ladies" who have tried to make your acquaintance in New York. You are right in thinking there must be something wrong with girls who try to "pick up" strange men as no girl with self respect would do such a thing and when I say that, Mr. Man, I know you will think it is a funny thing for me to say on account of the way our friendship started, but I mean it and I assure you that was the first time I ever done such a thing in my life and would never of thought of doing it had I not known you were the right kind of man as I flatter myself that I am a good judge of character and can tell pretty well what a person is like by just looking at them and I assure you I had made up my mind what kind of a man you were before I allowed myself to answer your opening remark. Otherwise I am the last girl in the world that would allow myself to speak to a person without being introduced to them.

When you write again you must tell me all about the girl on Riverside Drive and what she looks like and if you went to see her again and all about her. Suppose you will think I am a little old "curiosity shop" for asking all those questions and will wonder why I want to know. Well, sir, I won't tell you why, so there, but I insist on you answering all questions and will scold you if you don't. Maybe you will think that the reason why I am so curious is because I am "jealous" of the lady in question. Well, sir, I won't tell you whether I am or not, but will keep you "guessing." Now, don't you wish you knew?

Must close or you will think I am going to "rattle on" forever or maybe you have all ready become disgusted and torn my letter up. If so all I can say is poor little me—she was a nice little girl and meant well, but the man did not appreciate her.

There! Will stop or you will think I am crazy if you do not all ready.

Yours (?)
MABELLE

N. Y., Aug. 20.

Dear GIRLIE:

Well girlie I suppose you thought I was never going to answer your letter but have been busier than a one armed paper hanger the last week as have been working on a number with Paul Sears who is one of the best lyric writers in N. Y. and has turned out as many hits as Berlin or Davis or any of them. And believe me girlie he has turned out another hit this time that is he and I have done it together. It is all done now and we are just waiting for the best chance to place it but will not place it nowheres unless we get the right kind of a deal but maybe will publish it ourselves.

The song is bound to go over big as Sears has wrote a great lyric and I have give it a great tune or at least every body that has heard it goes crazy over it and it looks like it would go over bigger than any song since Mammy and would not be surprised to see it come out the hit of the year. If it is handled right we will make a bbl. of money and Sears says it is a cinch we will clean up as much as $25000 apiece which is pretty fair for one song but this one is not like the most of them but has got a great lyric and I have wrote a melody that will knock them out of their seats. I only wish you could hear it girlie and hear it the way I play it. I had to play it over and over about 50 times at the Friars last night.

I will copy down the lyric of the chorus so you can see what it is like and get the idea of the song though of course you can't tell much about it unless you hear it played and sang. The title of the song is When They're Like You and here is the chorus:

> "Some like them hot, some like them cold.
> Some like them when they're not too darn old.
> Some like them fat, some like them lean.
> Some like them only at sweet sixteen.
> Some like them dark, some like them light.

Some like them in the park, late at night.
Some like them fickle, some like them true,
But the time I like them is when they're like you."

How is that for a lyric and I only wish I could play my melody for you as you would go nuts over it but I will send you a copy as soon as the song is published and you can get some of your friends to play it over for you and I know you will like it though it is a different melody when I play it or when somebody else plays it.

Well girlie you will see how busy I have been and am libel to keep right on being busy as we are not going to let the grass grow under our feet but as soon as we have got this number placed we will get busy on another one as a couple like that will put me on Easy st. even if they don't go as big as we expect but even 25 grand is a big bunch of money and if a man could only turn out one hit a year and make that much out of it I would be on Easy st. and no more hammering on the old music box in some cabaret.

Who ever we take the song to we will make them come across with one grand for advance royaltys and that will keep me going till I can turn out another one. So the future looks bright and rosey to yours truly and I am certainly glad I come to the big town though sorry I did not do it a whole lot quicker.

This is a great old town girlie and when you have lived here a wile you wonder how you ever stood for a burg like Chi which is just a hick town along side of this besides being dirty etc. and a man is a sucker to stay there all their life specially a man in my line of work as N. Y. is the Mecca for man that has got the musical gift. I figure that all the time I spent in Chi I was just wasteing my time and never really started to live till I come down here and I have to laugh when I think of the boys out there that is trying to make a liveing in the song writeing game and most of them starve to death all their life and the first week I am down here I meet a man like Sears and the next thing you know we have turned out a song that will make us a fortune.

Well girlie you asked me to tell you about the girlie up on the Drive that tried to make me and asked me to come and see her again. Well I can assure you you have no reasons to be jealous in that quarter as I have not been back to see her as I figure it is wasteing my time to play round with a dame like she that wants to go out somewheres every night and if you married her she would want a house on 5th ave. with a dozen servants so I have passed her up as that is not my idea of home.

What I want when I get married is a real home where a man can stay home and work and maybe have a few of his friends in once in a wile and entertain them or go to a good musical show once in a wile and have a wife that is in sympathy with you and not nag at you all the wile but be a real help mate. The girlie up on the Drive would run me ragged and have me in the poor house inside of a year even if I was makeing 25 grand out of one song. Besides she wears a make up that you would have to blast to find out what her face looks like. So I have not been back there and don't intend to see her again so what is the use of me telling you about her. And the only other girlie I have met is a sister of Paul Sears who I met up to his house wile we was working on the song but she don't hardly count as she has not got no use for the boys but treats them like dirt and Paul says she is the coldest proposition he ever seen.

Well I don't know no more to write and besides have got a date to go out to Paul's place for dinner and play some of my stuff for him so as he can see if he wants to set words to some more of my melodies. Well don't do nothing I would not do and have as good a time as you can in old Chi and will let you know how we come along with the song.

CHAS. F. LEWIS

Chicago, Ill., Aug. 23.

Dear Mr. MAN:

I am thrilled to death over the song and think the words awfully pretty and am crazy to hear the music which I know must be great. It must be wonderful to have the gift of writing songs and then hear people play and sing them and just think of making $25,000 in such a short time. My, how rich you will be and I certainly congratulate you though am afraid when you are rich and famous you will have no time for insignificant little me or will you be an exception and remember your "old" friends even when you are up in the world? I sincerely hope so.

Will look forward to receiving a copy of the song and will you be sure and put your name on it? I am all ready very conceited just to think that I know a man that writes songs and makes all that money.

Seriously I wish you success with your next song and I laughed when I read your remark about being busier than a one armed paper hanger. I don't see how you think up all those comparisons and crazy things to say. The next time one of the girls asks me to go out with them I am going to tell them I can't go because I am busier than a one armed paper hanger and then they will think I made it up and say: "The girl is clever."

Seriously I am glad you did not go back to see the girl on the Drive and am also glad you don't like girls who makes themselves up so much as I think it is disgusting and would rather go round looking like a ghost than put artificial color on my face. Fortunately I have a complexion that does not need "fixing" but even if my coloring was not what it is I would never think of lowering myself to "fix" it. But I must tell you a joke that happened just the other day when Edith and I were out at lunch and there was another girl in the restaurant whom Edie knew and she introduced her to me and I noticed how this girl kept staring at me and finally she begged my pardon and asked if she could ask me a personal question and I said yes and she asked me if my complexion was really "mine." I assured her it was and she said: "Well, I thought so because I did not think anybody could put it on so artistically. I certainly envy you." Edie and I both laughed.

Well, if that girl envies me my complexion, why I envy you living in New York. Chicago is rather dirty though I don't let that part of it bother me as I bathe and change my clothing so often that the dirt does not have time to "settle." Edie often says she cannot see how I always keep so clean looking and says I always look like I had just stepped out of a band box. She also calls me a fish (jokingly) because I spend so much time in the water. But seriously I do love to bathe and never feel so happy as when I have just "cleaned up" and put on fresh clothing.

Edie has just gone out to see a picture and was cross at me because I would not go with her. I told her I was going to write a letter and she wanted to know to whom and I told her and she said: "You write to him so often that a person would almost think you was in love with him." I just laughed and turned it off, but she does say the most embarrassing things and I would be angry if it was anybody but she that said them.

Seriously I had much rather sit here and write letters or read or just sit and dream than go out to some crazy old picture show except once in awhile I do like to go to the theater and see a good play and a specially a musical play if the music is catchy. But as a rule I am contented to just stay home and feel cozy and lots of evenings Edie and I sit here without saying hardly a word to each other though she would love to talk but she knows I had rather be quiet and she often says it is just like living with a deaf and dumb mute to live with me because I make so little noise round the apartment. I guess I was born to be a home body as I so seldom care to go "gadding."

Though I do love to have company once in awhile, just a few congenial friends whom I can talk to and feel at home with and play cards or have some music. My friends love to drop in here, too, as they say Edie and I always give them such nice things to eat. Though poor Edie has not much to do with it, I am afraid, as she hates anything connected with cooking which is one of the things I love best of anything and I often say that when I begin keeping house in my own home I will insist on doing most of my own work as I would take so much more interest in it than a servant, though I would want somebody to help me a little if I could afford it as I often think a woman that does all her own work is liable to get so tired that she loses interest in the bigger things of life like books and music. Though after all what bigger thing is there than home making a specially for a woman?

I am sitting in the dearest old chair that I bought yesterday at a little store on the North Side. That is my one extravagance, buying furniture and things for the house, but I always say it is economy in the long run as I will always have them and have use for them and when I can pick them up at a bargain I would be silly not to. Though heaven knows I will never be "poor" in regards to furniture and rugs and things like that as mother's house in Toledo is full of lovely things which she says she is going to give to Sis and myself as soon as we have real homes of our own. She is going to give me the first choice as I am her favorite. She has the loveliest old things that you could not buy now for love or money including lovely old rugs and a piano which Sis wanted to have a player attachment put on it but I said it would be an insult to the piano so we did not get one. I am funny about things like that, a specially old furniture and feel towards them like people whom I love.

Poor mother, I am afraid she won't live much longer to enjoy her lovely old things as she has been suffering for years from stomach trouble and the doctor says it has been worse lately instead of better and her heart is weak besides. I am going home to see her a few days this fall as it may be the last time. She is very cheerful and always says she is ready to go now as she has had enough joy out of life and all she would like would be to see her girls settled down in their own homes before she goes.

There I go, talking about my domestic affairs again and I will bet you are bored to death though personly I am never bored when my friends tell me about themselves. But I won't "rattle on" any longer, but will say good night and don't forget to write and tell me how you come out with the song and thanks for sending me the words to it. Will you write a song about me some time? I would be thrilled to death! But I am afraid I am not the kind of girl that inspires men to write songs about them, but am just a quiet "mouse" that loves home and am not giddy enough to be the heroine of a song.

Well, Mr. Man, good night and don't wait so long before writing again to

Yours (?)

MABELLE

N. Y., Sept. 8.

Dear GIRLIE:

Well girlie have not got your last letter with me so cannot answer what was in it as I have forgotten if there was anything I was supposed to answer and besides have only a little time to write as I have a date to go out on a party with the Sears. We are going to the Georgie White show and afterwards somewheres for supper. Sears is the boy who wrote the lyric to my song and it is him and his sister I am going on the party with. The sister is a cold fish that has no use for men but she is show crazy and insists on Paul taking her to 3 or 4 of them a week.

Paul wants me to give up my room here and come and live with them as they have plenty of room and I am running a little low on money but don't know if I will do it or not as am afraid I would freeze to death in the same house with a girl like the sister as she is ice cold but she don't hang round the house much as she is always takeing trips or going to shows or somewheres.

So far we have not had no luck with the song. All the publishers we have showed it to has went crazy over it but they won't make the right kind of a deal with us and if they don't loosen up and give us a decent royalty rate we are libel to put the song out ourselves and show them up. The man up to Goebel's told us the song was O. K. and he liked it but it was more of a production number than anything else and ought to go in a show like the Follies but they won't be in N. Y. much longer and what we ought to do is hold it till next spring.

Mean wile I am working on some new numbers and also have taken a position with the orchestra at the Wilton and am going to work there starting next week. They pay good money $60 and it will keep me going.

Well girlie that is about all the news. I believe you said your father was sick and hope he is better and also hope you are getting along O. K. and take care of yourself. When you have nothing else to do write to your friend,

CHAS. F. LEWIS

Chicago, Ill., Sept. 11.

Dear Mr. LEWIS:

Your short note reached me yesterday and must say I was puzzled when I read it. It sounded like you was mad at me though I cannot think of any reason why you should be. If there was something I said in my last letter that offended you I wish you would tell me what it was and I will ask your pardon though I cannot remember anything I could of said that you could take offense at. But if there was something, why I assure you, Mr. Lewis, that I did not mean anything by it. I certainly did not intend to offend you in any way.

Perhaps it is nothing I wrote you, but you are worried on account of the publishers not treating you fair in regards to your song and that is why your letter sounded so distant. If that is the case I hope that by this time matters have rectified themselves and the future looks brighter. But any way, Mr. Lewis, don't allow yourself to worry over business cares as they will all come right in the end and I always think it is silly for people to worry themselves sick over temporary troubles, but the best way is to "keep smiling" and look for the "silver lining" in the cloud. That is the way I always do and no matter what happens, I manage to smile and my girl friend, Edie, calls me Sunny because I always look on the bright side.

Remember also, Mr. Lewis, that $60 is a salary that a great many men would like to be getting and are living on less than that and supporting a wife and family on it. I always say that a person can get along on whatever amount they make if they manage things in the right way.

So if it is business troubles, Mr. Lewis, I say don't worry, but look on the bright side. But if it is something I wrote in my last letter that offended you I wish you would tell me what it was so I can apologize as I assure you I meant nothing and would not say anything to hurt you for the world.

Please let me hear from you soon as I will not feel comfortable until I know I am not to blame for the sudden change.

Sincerely,
MABELLE GILLESPIE

N. Y., Sept. 24.

Dear Miss GILLESPIE:

Just a few lines to tell you the big news or at least it is big news to me. I am engaged to be married to Paul Sears' sister and we are going to be married early next month and live in Atlantic City where the orchestra I have been playing with has got an engagement in one of the big cabarets.

I know this will be a surprise to you as it was even a surprise to me as I did not think I would ever have the nerve to ask the girlie the big question as she was always so cold and acted like I was just in the way. But she said she supposed she would have to marry somebody some time and she did not dislike me as much as most of the other men her brother brought round and she would marry me with the understanding that she would not have to be a slave and work round the house and also I would have to take her to a show or somewheres every night and if I could not take her myself she would "run wild" alone. Atlantic City will be O. K. for that as a lot of new shows opens down there and she will be able to see them before they get to the big town. As for her being a slave, I would hate to think of marrying a girl and then have them spend their lives in druggery round the house. We are going to live in a hotel till we find something better but will be in no hurry to start house keeping as we will have to buy all new furniture.

Betsy is some doll when she is all fixed up and believe me she knows how to fix herself up. I don't know what she uses but it is weather proof as I have been out in a rain storm with her and we both got drowned but her face stayed on. I would almost think it was real only she tells me different.

Well girlie I may write to you again once in a wile as Betsy says she don't give a dam if I write to all the girls in the world just so I don't make her read the answers but that is all I can think of to say now except good bye and good luck and may the right man come along soon and he will be a lucky man getting a girl that is such a good cook and got all that furniture etc.

But just let me give you a word of advice before I close and that is don't never speak to strange men who you don't know nothing about as they may get you wrong and think you are trying to make them. It just happened that I knew better so you was lucky in my case but the luck might not last.

Your friend,
Chas. F. Lewis

Chicago, Ill., Sept. 27.

My Dear Mr. Lewis:

Thanks for your advice and also thank your fiance for her generosity in allowing you to continue your correspondence with her "rivals," but personly I have no desire to take advantage of that generosity as I have something better to do than read letters from a man like you, a specially as I have a man friend who is not so generous as Miss Sears and would strongly object to my continuing a correspondence with another man. It is at his request that I am writing this note to tell you not to expect to hear from me again.

Allow me to congratulate you on your engagement to Miss Sears and I am sure she is to be congratulated too, though if I met the lady I would be tempted to ask her to tell me her secret, namely how she is going to "run wild" on $60.

Sincerely,
Mabelle Gillespie

OGDEN NASH

How to Harry a Husband
or
Is That Accessory Really Necessary?

Husband stands at door of flat,
Coat in elbow, hand on hat,
In his pocket, from broker shady,
Two good seats for *My Fair Lady.*
Patiently he stands there humming,
Coming, darling? Darling, coming?

But she's a freak and she's a hag,
She's got the wrong, she murmurs, bag,
She's got, she adds in wild distress,
To change the bag or change the dress.
She'd as soon appear with stockings ragged
As be seen incongruously bebaggèd.

Husband rings the bell for lift,
Hears it chunk and upward drift,
Well knows taxis in the rain
Rarer than the whooping crane.
Impatiently he stands there snarling,
Darling, coming? Coming, darling?

Another bag at last she chooses
And everything in the first bag loses.
She fumbles with many a dainty curse
For lipstick, glasses, keys, and purse.*
He grunts, as dies preprandial liquor,
To change from the skin out would have been quicker.

They disrupt the middle of the show,
Their seats are middle of the row,
They crawl and climb like tandem tractors
Between the audience and the actors,
Whose delicious rapport might have lagged
Had she been incongruously bebagged.

* Then—
She turns it inside out and scratches
For handkerchief, cigarettes, and matches,
Tweezers, compact, and aspirin,
And Band-Aids redolent of My Sin,
Driver's license and Charga-Plate,
A sweepstake ticket one year late,
A colored chart of a five-day diet,
A Penguin commended by Gilbert Highet,
A tearful appeal from a charitymonger,
And a catalogue from Lewis & Conger.
This is she whose eyes start from their sockets
At the contents of her small son's pockets.

HOWARD MARGULIES

"When I say 'I love you,' I mean, 'I really love you!' . . .
I don't think you understand . . . *I mean, 'love you! Really!'* . . .
Maybe you don't fully comprehend . . . *'I really love you!'* . . ."

JAMES THURBER

"Have you seen my pistol, honey-bun?"

CHARLES ADDAMS

B. KLIBAN

ROY BLOUNT, JR.

Blue Yodel 9
Jesse

I'll tell you what Miriam and I can't talk about. Warren Beatty. Warren Beatty almost destroyed our marriage one night.

Originally it was "Who do you find attractive in the movies?" Seems like an interesting question, right? Way for men and women to understand each other. Don't try it.

Miriam couldn't think of anybody. "I don't know any of them well enough," she said.

"No. Wait. Of *course* you don't!" I said. "That's not the point! But, like, for instance, somebody like Warren Beatty."

"Oh, no," she says. Wrinkles her nose.

"What?" I said to her. *"You're not attracted to Warren Beatty?"*

"No," she says.

"Yes you are," I say, "you just don't want to admit it."

"No I'm not!" she says. "And I don't know any women who are."

"What!" I say. "Warren Beatty has run through Natalie Wood, Joan Collins, Leslie Caron, Julie Christie, Diane Keaton, God knows who else, and he's not good enough for you or anybody you know?"

Now she's getting upset.

"Look," I say. *"I'm* not Warren Beatty. I don't *know* Warren Beatty. I don't imagine I have to worry about you ever *meeting* Warren Beatty. We're just, you know, talking about a guy on a screen. You can level with me."

She won't say anything.

"Okay!" I say. "Okay! Who *are* you attracted to? There's got to be somebody. I mean one big whole point of the movies . . . Don't get me wrong. I'm not saying you'd be a *pushover* for Warren Beatty. I'm not saying you're *mooning* over Warren Beatty. I'm not saying you admire Warren Beatty's *life-style.* I'm just saying, in your heart of hearts . . ."

She won't say anything.

"Okay. Never mind Warren Beatty, who . . . But never mind. There must be *somebody."*

"Well, okay," she says finally. "Ed Asner."

Ed Asner! She gets turned on by Ed Asner! She's twenty-eight years old and she claims she's hot for Ed Asner!

Hey. I *like* Ed Asner. Who *doesn't* like Ed Asner? But when Warren Beatty and Ed Asner run into each other somewhere, on or off the screen, I don't think it is Beatty who is thinking, "How does he *do* it?"

Ed Asner. Now every time I'm looking into Miriam's eyes I'm thinking . . .

Hey. I'm thirty-four years old! I've got hair! I work out! I'm married to a woman who is turned on by Ed Asner!

"Okay," I say to Miriam. "Ed Asner, to me, he looks like a good guy; no doubt about it. I'd love to have a few beers with Ed Asner. Probably rather have a few beers with Ed Asner than with Warren Beatty. But I'm not talking about that. I'm talking about, you know, somebody who—like, for *me,* I'd say, for example, Ann-Margret. You know. Does it for me."

"Whuh!" Miriam says. *"Ann-Margret?"* She looks at me like I said Peter Lorre.

"Of course Ann-Margret," I say. "That's the whole *point* of Ann-Margret. Why do you think they *make* Ann-Margret movies?"

And it's like I just destroyed the whole basis of our relationship. Miriam is appalled. Because I said Ann-Margret did it for me.

"Listen!" I say. "Come on. I'm not saying me and Ann-Margret would be *compatible.* I'm not saying there'd be any *future* in it. I'm not saying we'd have much to *say* to each other. I'm just . . . See, the whole point . . ."

Miriam wound up spending the night with her friend Wendy. Who I can't stand. Who now, whenever anybody brings the movies up, makes a point of saying how Warren Beatty thinks he's so cool.

I don't say anything.

I tell you what. People talk about a ménage à trois. How does anybody ever agree on the third party?

BERT LESTON TAYLOR

To Lillian Russell

(A reminiscence of 18—.)

Dear Lillian! (The "dear" one risks;
"Miss Russell" were a bit austerer)—
Do you remember Mr. Fiske's
  Dramatic Mirror

Back when—? (But we'll not count the years;
The way they've sped is most surprising.)
You were a trifle in arrears
  For advertising.

I brought the bill to your address;
I was the *Mirror's* bill collector—
In Thespian haunts a more or less
  Familiar spectre.

On that (to me) momentous day
You dwelt amid the city's clatter,

A few doors west of old Broadway;
    The street—no matter.

But while you have forgot the debt,
And him who called in line of duty,
He never, never shall forget
    Your wondrous beauty.

You were too fair for mortal speech,—
Enchanting, positively rippin';
You were some dream, and quelque peach,
    And beaucoup pippin.

Your "fight with Time" had not begun,
Nor any reason to promote it;
No beauty battles to be won.
    Beauty? You wrote it!

"A bill?" you murmured in distress,
"A bill?" (I still can hear you say it.)
"A bill from Mr. Fiske? Oh, yes . . .
    I'll call and pay it."

And he, the thrice-requited kid,
That such a goddess should address him,
Could only blush and paw his lid,
    And stammer, "Yes'm!"

Eheu! It seems a cycle since,
But still the nerve of memory tingles.
And here you're writing Beauty Hints,
    And I these jingles.

JULES FEIFFER

OGDEN NASH

I Never Even Suggested It

I know lots of men who are in love and lots of men who are married
and lots of men who are both,
And to fall out with their loved ones is what all of them are most
loth.
They are conciliatory at every opportunity,
Because all they want is serenity and a certain amount of impunity.
Yes, many the swain who has finally admitted that the earth is flat
Simply to sidestep a spat,
Many the masculine Positively or Absolutely which has been diluted
to an If
Simply to avert a tiff,
Many the two-fisted executive whose domestic conversation is limited
to a tactfully interpolated Yes,
And then he is amazed to find that he is being raked backwards over
a bed of coals nevertheless.
These misguided fellows are under the impression that it takes two to
make a quarrel, that you can sidestep a crisis by nonaggression
and nonresistance,
Instead of removing yourself to a discreet distance.
Passivity can be a provoking *modus operandi;*
Consider the Empire and Gandhi.
Silence is golden, but sometimes invisibility is golder,
Because loved ones may not be able to make bricks without straw but
often they don't need any straw to manufacture a bone to pick or
blood in their eye or a chip for their soft white shoulder.
It is my duty, gentlemen, to inform you that women are dictators all,
and I recommend to you this moral:
In real life it takes only one to make a quarrel.

MORRIS BISHOP

Mournful Numbers

Where in the attic the dust encumbers
   Days that are gone,
I found a paper with telephone numbers
   Scribbled thereon.

Again I feel the tremendous wallop
   It gave to me
When I had a valid excuse to call up
   1503.

Again I feel the excuses springing,
   Just as of yore,
When I could no longer refrain from ringing
   9944.

Again I feel my old heart prickle
   As in my youth,
When I left the house to deposit a nickel
   In a sound-proof booth;

And I hear again a phantasmal titter,
   As I would coo
Passionately to the dark transmitter:
   "2342!"

My heart awakes, as if roused from slumber
   By a telephone bell;

Quick! I will call again the number
   Once loved so well!

I breathe the syllables recollected:
   "2342!"
But Central answers: "Disconnected!"
   How true! How true!

MARGARET FISHBACK

I Stand Corrected

When I was happy in my youth
   I laid my state of mind to love,
But now, to tell the dismal truth,
   I see I didn't know whereof
I spoke. For I have lately found—
   With great dissatisfaction—that
Though love can make the world go round,
   It often makes the world go flat.

E. B. WHITE

The Sexual Revolution: Being a Rather Complete Survey of the Entire Sexual Scene

The sexual revolution began with Man's discovery that he was not attractive to Woman, as such. The lion had his mane, the peacock his gorgeous plumage, but Man found himself in a three-button sack suit. His masculine appearance not only failed to excite Woman, but in many cases it only served to bore her. The result was that Man found it necessary to develop attractive personal traits to offset his dull appearance. He learned to say funny things. He learned to smoke, and blow smoke rings. He learned to earn money. This would have been a solution to his difficulty, but in the course of making himself attractive to Woman by developing himself mentally, he inadvertently became so intelligent an animal that he saw how comical the whole situation was.

Thus, at the very start of the sexual revolution, Man faced one very definite problem: in becoming mentally "aware," he had become intellectually critical, and had discovered that it was increasingly difficult to make up his mind whether he really desired any one woman, however capable he was of getting her. It was the heyday of monogamy, and in order to contemplate marriage, it was necessary for a man to decide on One Particular Woman. This he found next to impossible, for the reason that he had unconsciously set up so many mental barriers and hazards.

Let me mention a few.

1. The fear that his fiancée might get fat inside of a few years. To any

mentally alert man, this thought was a strong deterrent. Quite often the man met the girl's parents. He would quickly size up her mother and make a mental calculation as to how long it would be before the daughter was in the same boat. Somehow, it took the bloom off the romance. If he was not fortunate enough to meet the parents of the young lady, he was quite apt to note things about her own conformation that seemed prophetic. A slight thickness in the neck, a trace of rotundity in the bosom, a touch too much ankle. In these portents he found much discomfort, and was quite likely to call the engagement off.

2. The use of a word, phrase, or punctuation mark by his fiancée that annoyed him. In these early days of the sex awakening, it was not at all uncommon to find examples of the girl's using some slight phrase which had a grating effect. It was often the case that the man was literarily inclined—because literary inclinations were early found to be advantageous in sex, almost as advantageous, in fact, as the peacock's tail—and if this was the case the man was doubly sensitive to the curious little crudities, niceties, whimsies, and circumlocutions which women were afflicted with. I am thinking at the moment of the case of a young man who, in his junior year in college, had found the girl he believed ideal for him to marry, and then one day learned, quite by accident, that she was in the habit of using the word "Howdy" as a form of salutation. He did not like "Howdy," although he did not know why. Days and nights he spent trying to reconcile himself to the idea of it, weighing the young lady's extreme beauty and affability against her one flaw. In the end he decided he could not stomach it, and broke the troth.

3. Difference in height. If a man fell in love with a woman taller than himself (which sometimes happened), he became morose from dwelling on the objections to such an alliance. This particular situation usually had a way of settling itself automatically: there were so many reasons, real or imaginary, why the man felt that the marriage was impossible, that just the mere business of thinking about them broke him in health and he died, leaving a margin of several weeks before the date of the wedding.

4. The suspicion that if he waited twenty-four hours, or possibly less, he would likely find a lady even more ideally suited to his taste than his fiancée. Every man entertained such a suspicion. Entertained it royally. He was greatly strengthened in his belief by the fact that he kept catching a fleeting glimpse of this imaginary person—in restaurants, in stores, in trains. To deny the possibility of her existence would be, he felt, to do a grave injustice to her, to himself, and to his fiancée. Man's unflinching desire to give himself and everybody else a square deal was the cause of

much of his disturbance. Man had become, you see, a thinking being. He had come to know enough about permutations and combinations to realize that with millions of Caucasian females to choose from, the chances of his choosing the ideal mate were almost zero.

So matters went. Man, we have seen, had begun to develop himself so that he would be attractive to Woman, and in doing so had made Woman of doubtful attraction to *him.* He had become independent. He had become critical. He had become scared. Sex was awakening and it was all Man could do to keep from laughing.

Woman, on her part, saw dimly what was going on in the world. She saw it through the sweet haze of Dream. She caught glimpses of it in the mirror of her Narcissistic soul.[1] Woman was at the crossroads. She had many ways open to her, but she chose one: *she chose to imitate Man.* At a time when sex was in transition, she had the bad judgment to begin a career of independence for herself, in direct imitation of her well-meaning mate. She took up smoking. She began to earn money (not much, but some). She drank. She subordinated domesticity to individuality—of which she had very little. She attained to a certain independence, a cringing independence, a wistful, half-regretful state. Men and women both became slightly regretful: men regretted that they had no purple tail to begin with, women that they had ever been fools enough to go to work. Women now "understood life," but life had been so much more agreeable in its original mystery.

And now we come to Sex.[2] Woman, observing that her mate went out of his way to make himself entertaining, rightly surmised that sex had something to do with it. From that she logically concluded that sex was recreational rather than procreational. (The small, hardy band of girls who failed to get this point were responsible for the popularity of women's field hockey in this country, 1911–1921.) As though in a vision, the "right to be sexual" came to women. They fell to with a will. For thousands of years they had been content merely to be amiable, and now they were going to be sexual. The transition from amiability to sexuality was revolutionary.[3] It presented a terrific problem to Woman, because in acquiring and assuming the habits that tended to give her an equality with Man, she discovered that she necessarily became a good deal *like* Man. The more

[1] This is the first mention in this article of Narcissism. You'll hear more about it, don't worry.

[2] Are you glad?

[3] Zaner claims it was also amusing.

she got like him, the less he saw in her. (Or so he liked to think, anyway.) Just as soon as she began to put her own sex on an even basis, she found that he lost interest. Her essential Narcissism (pleasure of looking in a mirror) was met by his Begonia-ism (concept of the potted plant). Things got so that Woman spent *all* her time admiring herself in mirrors, and Man, discouraged, devoted himself quietly to raising begonias, which are fairly easy to raise. Sex atrophied.

But, as I say, sex was in the transition stage. Woman soon began to outgrow her Narcissism and was satisfied to snatch quick glances of herself in make-shift mirrors, such as the backs of watches, the shiny fenders of automobiles, plate-glass windows, subway weighing machines, and such. Convinced that sex was not sin, she set out joyously to study it. How hard she studied has recently been apparent, even to persons who read only a few books a year.

New York became the capital of the sexual revolution. It was conveniently located, had a magnificent harbor,[4] a high mortality rate, and some of the queerest-shaped apartments to be found anywhere. There are apartments in New York in which one must step across an open bathtub in going from the kitchen to the bedroom; any unusual layout like that arouses sexual desire and brings people pouring into New York from other cities. New York became the Mecca for young ladies from the South and from the Middle West whose minds were not quite made up about sexual freedom, but who thought that if they could once get to New York and into an irregular apartment, the answer might come to them.

Their mothers were against it.

"Now what can you get in New York that you can't get right here at home?" their mothers said.

"Concerts, new plays, and the opera," the daughters invariably replied. There has never, to my knowledge, been a case of a young lady telling her mother that she wanted to go to New York because she was seeking an outlet for her erotic eagerness. It was always concerts that she wanted. Often it turned out to be concerts that she got.

When she arrived in New York and secured her unfurnished apartment (usually in West Fourth Street), her mental elation was so great and her activity in making parchment lamp shades so unabating that for the first couple of weeks she let sex go. Women are notoriously apt to get off the track; no man ever was diverted from the gratification of his desires by a parchment lamp shade. At any rate, the young lady was so tired at night

---

[4] New York has one of the finest harbors in the world.

she could hardly keep her eyes open, much less her mind. Furthermore, she was beginning to have *Schmalhausen* trouble. *Schmalhausen* trouble is a common ailment among girls in their twenties. It usually attacks girls who have taken a small apartment *(schmalhausen)* and are reading the behavior-ism essays of Samuel D. Schmalhausen. The effect of sitting within nar-row walls and absorbing a wide viewpoint breaks down their health. The pain that they suffer during this period is caused by their discovery of the lyrical duality, or two-sidedness, of life—a discovery that unbalances all sensitive young ladies in whom sex cries for expression. Even in a New York apartment there are two sides to everything, and this particularly applies to a girl's potential sexuality.[5]

Let me explain this duality.

The very fact that the young lady had settled in the vicinity of Sheridan Square indicates that there was a strong vein of poetry in her. She saw life (and sex) through a lyrical haze which tended to accentuate its beauty by softening its truths. The whole purpose and scheme of poetry is to heighten the tenderness and essential goodness of life by a musical elabo-ration of its traditional worth.[6] Well, when the young lady allowed the lyrical possibilities of love to work on her mind, it made her mad to remember how candid she had been the night before in discussing con-traception with the commercial artist who lived downstairs. It grew to be a big question in her own mind, just what her emancipation ought to consist of: whether it meant having lemon skins and gin stoppers in the wash-basin and talking freely of exhibitionism and voyeurism, or whether it meant being the recipient of some overwhelmingly beautiful passion which her poetical soul still prescribed but which she knew couldn't exist because she was so widely read. To stall for time she would make another lamp shade.

Days slipped by. Always there was conflict in her soul. She had plunged into the "candor régime" whole-heartedly; she could enter a roomful of people and say almost anything at all. She also went in for nudity—another outlet for sex eagerness. She dallied in the bath, lay around the apartment without any clothes on, appeared scantily clad at her door when the laundryman called to collect, and week-ends went swimming naked in the moonlight with other young people. (Incidentally, when she saw what a man looked like without any clothes on, the old *Schmalhausen* trouble came back stronger than ever.)

---

[5] Girls with a bad case of Schmalhausen sometimes saw as many as three sides to sex.
[6] See Tithridge's "Poetry," but don't read it.

By and by, because of this very uncertainty of soul, a kind of orderliness of habit crept into her life. Unable to decide whether sex was the poem she half believed it to be or the casual episode she had schooled herself to think it was, she compromised by practically giving sex the air. She now held a good job and was earning well. Candor and nudity, with an occasional bit of exhibitionism, began to satisfy her completely. She was growing older. The apartment was nicely decorated now and teeming with lamp shades. She held some good industrial stocks and had developed an ambition to write. She became content to be literary rather than sexual. She became, in other words, that most dangerous of all by-products of the Sexual Revolution—a biologico-cultural type. She had a way of leading young men on into exhilarating topics, and sitting with them in provocative attitudes, and then putting on her hat and going quietly home to bed. In short, New York was now home to this girl, this biologico-cultural lady, and she was in a fair way to step placidly into a good old-fashioned marriage when the right man came along.

And he usually did, the poor yap.

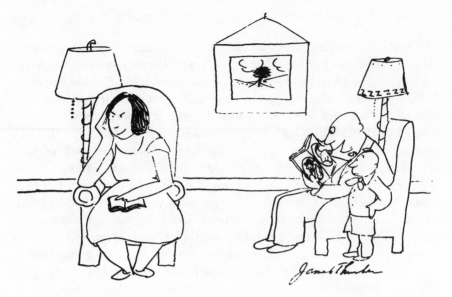

"And This Is Tom Weatherby, an old Beau of Your Mother's.
He Never Got to First Base"

JAMES THURBER

"That's My First Wife Up There, and This Is the Present Mrs. Harris"

"This rivalry has got to stop, Harold!"

FINLEY PETER DUNNE

Short Marriage Contracts

"Who is George Meredith?" asked Mr. Hennessy.

"Ye can search me," said Mr. Dooley. "What is th' charge again' him?"

"Nawthin'," said Mr. Hennessy; "but I see he's in favor iv short-term marredges."

"What d'ye mean?" asked Mr. Dooley. "Reducin' th' terms f'r good behavyor?"

"No," said Mr. Hennessy. "He says people ought to get marrid f'r three or four years at a time. Thin, if they don't like each other, or if wan gets tired, they break up housekeepin'."

"Well," said Mr. Dooley, "it mightn't be a bad thing. Th' throuble about mathrimony, as I have obsarved it fr'm me seat in th' gran' stand, is that afther fifteen or twinty years it settles down to an endurance thrile. 'Women,' as Hogan says, 'are creatures iv such beaucheous mien that to be loved they have but to be seen; but,' he says, 'wanst they're seen an' made secure,' he says, 'we first embrace, thin pity, thin endure,' he says. Most iv th' ol' marrid men I know threat their wives like a rockin'-chair, a great comfort whin they're tired, but apt to be in th' way at other times.

"Now, it might be diff'rent if th' ladies, instead iv bein' secured f'r life, was on'y held on a short-term lease. Whin Archybald, th' pride iv South Wather Sthreet, makes up his mind that it would be well f'r his credit if he enthered th' holy bonds iv mathrimony an' selects th' target iv his mad affections, he thinks that all he has to do is to put a geeranyum in his buttonhole an' inthrajooce himsilf be his first name to be carrid to th' altar. But th' ladies, Gawd bless thim, are be nature skilled in this game, an' befure Archybald has been coortin' two weeks he begins to shift his idees iv his own worth. He finds that at best he has on'y an outside chance. He wondhers if he is really worthy iv th' love iv an innocint young girl iv thirty-two. Has he money enough to support her as she shud be supported? He even has doubts f'r th' first time in his life iv his own ravishin' beauty. He detects blemishes that he niver see befure. He discovers that what he used to considher a merry twinkle is a slight cast in th' right eye, an' that th' fillin' shows in his teeth. He consults a manicure an' a hair-dhresser an' buys th' entire stock iv a gents' furnishin'-store. Thin whin he's thurly humble he goes thremblin' to Belinda's house, raysolved that if th' fair wan rayfuses him, as she prob'bly will an' surely ought to, he will walk off th' bridge an' end all.

"It's at this time that th' short-term conthract shud be sprung. I don't know how men propose. I niver thried it but wanst, an' th' hired girl said th' lady was not at home. No wan will iver tell ye. Most marrid men give ye th' impressyon that their wives stole thim fr'm their agonized parents. But, anyhow, we'll suppose that Archybald, layin' a silk handkerchief on th' carpet an' pullin' up th' leg iv his pantaloons, to prevint baggin', hurls himsilf impetchoosly at th' feet iv his adored wan an' cries: 'Belinda, I can on'y offer ye th' love iv an honest South Wather Sthreet commission merchant an' mimber iv th' Brotherhood iv Wholesale an' Retail Grocers. Will ye take me f'r life?' Belinda blushes a rosy red an' replies: 'Archybald, ye ask too much. I cannot take ye f'r life, but I'll give ye a five-year lease an' resarve th' right to renew at th' end iv that time,' she says. 'Will that do?' says she. 'I will thry to make ye happy,' says he. An' she falls on his bosom, an' between her sobs cries: 'Thin let us repair at wanst to th' Title Guarantee an' Thrust Comp'ny an' be made man an' wife,' she says.

"Well, after Archybald is safely marrid his good opinyon iv himsilf returns. Belinda does her share to encourage him, an' befure long he begins to wondher how as fine a fellow as him come to throw himsilf away. Not that she ain't a good creature, d'ye mind, an' slavishly devoted to him. He hasn't annything again' her; still, think iv what he might have done if he had on'y known his thrue worth. Whin a man gets a good repytation he doesn't have to live up to it. So bimeby Archybald, knowin' fr'm what his wife says that he is handsome enough without anny artificyal aid, f'rgets th' mannycure an' th' hair-dhresser. Sometimes he shaves, an' sometimes he doesn't. So far as he is consarned, he thinks th' laundhry bill is too high. He advertises th' fact that he wears a red flannel chest-protictor. His principal convarsation is about his lumbago. He frequently mintions that he likes certain articles iv food, but they don't like him. Whin he comes home at night he plays with th' dog, talks pollyticks with his next-dure neighbor, puts his hat an' a pair iv cuffs on th' piannah, sets down in front iv th' fire, kicks off his boots, and dhraws on a pair iv carpet slippers, and thin notices that the wife iv his bosom is on th' premises. 'Hello, ol' woman,' he says. 'How's all ye'er throubles?' he says.

"Wanst a year Belinda meets him at th' dure with a flower in her hair. 'Well,' he says, 'what are th' decorations about?' he says. 'Don't ye know what day this is?' says she. 'Sure,' says he, 'it's Choosdah.' 'No, but what day?' 'I give it up. St. Pathrick's day, Valentine's day, pay day. What's th' answer?' 'But think.' 'I give it up.' 'It's th' annyvarsary iv our weddin'.' 'Oh,' says he, 'so it is. I'd clean f'rgot. That's right. I raymimber it well, now that ye mintion it. Well, bether luck nex' time. There, take that,' he says. An' he salutes her on th' forehead an' goes down in th' cellar to wurruk on a patent skid that will rivoluchionize th' grocery business. If he suffers a twinge iv remorse later he tells her to take two dollars out iv th' housekeepin' money an' buy herself a suitable prisint.

"He's pleasant in th' avenin'. At supper, havin' explained his daily maladies at full length, he relapses into a gloomy silence, broken on'y be such sounds as escape fr'm a man dhrinkin' hot coffee. Afther supper he figures on th' prob'ble market f'r rutybagy turnips, while his wife r-reads th' advertisements in th' theaytres. 'Jawn Drew is here this week,' says she. 'Is he?' says Archybald. 'That's good,' he says. 'I haven't been to a theaytre since Billy Emerson died,' he says. 'I hate th' theaytre. It ain't a bit like rale life as I see it in business hours,' he says. Afther a while, whin Belinda begins to tell him a thrillin' says-she about wan iv the neighbors, he lapses into a pleasant sleep, now an' thin arousin' himsilf to murmur: 'Um-m.' At nine o'clock he winds th' clock, puts th' dog out f'r the night, takes off his collar on th' stairs, an' goes to bed. Belinda sets up a little later an' dhreams Richard Harding Davis wrote a book about her.

"But th' five years ar-re up at last. Wan mornin' Archybald is glarin' fr'm behind a newspaper in his customary jaynial breakfast mood whin his wife says: 'Where will I sind ye'er clothes?' 'What's that?' says he. 'Where d'ye live to-morrah?' 'Don't be foolish, ol' woman. What d'ye mean?' says he. 'I mean,' says she, 'that th' lease has expired. At tin-thirty to-day it r-runs out. I like ye, Archybald, but I think I'll have to let ye go. Th' property has r-run down. Th' repairs haven't been kept up. Ye haven't allowed enough for wear an' tear. It looks too much like a boardin'-house. I'm goin' into th' market to prospect f'r a husband with all modhren improvements,' says she.

"Well, wudden't that be a jolt f'r Archybald? Ye bet he'd beat th' quarther-mile record to th' joolers. He'd haul out ol' pitchers iv himsilf as he was th' day he won his threasure, an' he'd hurry to a beauty uphol-sterer an' say: 'Make me as like that there Apollo Belvydere as ye can without tearin' me down altogether.' It wud be fine. He'd get her back, maybe, but it wud be a sthruggle. An' afther that, about a year befure th' conthract expired again, ye'd see him pickin' purple ties out iv th' shop window, buyin' theaytre tickets be th' scoor, an' stoppin' ivry avenin' at a flower-shop to gather a bunch iv vilets. He'd hire a man to nudge him whin his birthday come around, an' ivry time th' annyvarsary iv th' weddin' occurred he'd have a firewurruks display fr'm th' front stoop. Whin he'd succeeded in convincin' th' objeck iv his affictions that she cud put up with him f'r another five years they cud go on their weddin' journey. Ye'd read in th' pa-apers: 'Misther an' Mrs. Archybald Pullets were marrid again las' night be th' president iv th' First Naytional Bank. They departed on their twelfth weddin' journey, followed be a shower iv rice fr'm their gr-reat grandchildher.' It wud be fine. I hope George What's-his-name puts it through."

"I don't believe wan wurrud ye say," said Mr. Hennessy.

"P'raps not," said Mr. Dooley. "In me heart I think if people marry it ought to be f'r life. Th' laws ar-re altogether too lenient with thim."

JIM UNGER

Samuel Hoffenstein

Late one twilight, in a year between knickers and jeans, I found myself in Syracuse (and a good thing, too, because I had looked all over Rochester with no luck). Celebrating my good fortune by tossing down a chocolate egg cream, I asked the lad at the fountain, "So what's going on around here tonight?"

"Over at the university there's an orchestra and some guy named Arden Nash," he said, wiping his hands on his apron. Knowing *The Carnival of the Animals* when I hear about it, I rushed to the campus, purchased one of the last balcony tickets, and there he was, the man himself, *Ogden Nash!*—the man who rhymed boomerang with kangaroo meringue; the man who called the TV generation Village Vidiots . . . I *had* to meet him. But how? In a flash it came to me, a scheme remarkable in its ingenuity (considering I was still in college): *I would call his hotel room from the lobby.*

"I write for the University of Illinois student paper. May I come up?"

Whether the response was a grunt, a sigh, or a choke, it sounded like "Yes" to me, so in a trice I was up the elevator and knocking at his door, which opened to display a weary-looking man with silver hair, silver spectacles, tuxedo pants low around his hips, white suspenders looping down to his knees, and a formal shirt de-studded, de-tied, and opened to expose an undershirt. His voice said: "Come in." His face said: "Another college kid. How long am I going to have to put up with this?"

After a few minutes of my idle idolatry, he was backing me toward the door when I said without provocation, "Have you ever heard of Samuel Hoffenstein?"

Magic. Life gleamed into Nash's eyes. Weariness lifted as if a cape. The ceiling parted and golden light encased him. First he looked astonished, then he smiled, and then he beckoned me to sit down, there, that chair, sure, anywhere. *"You're* familiar with Samuel Hoffenstein?" he said. I couldn't deny. He looked directly into my face for a long moment and then said: "You know, if it hadn't been for him I would never have *begun* to write poetry. It was his work that inspired me. He was my hero. He was Dorothy Parker's hero. He was *every*body's hero in the 1920s."

When we parted, after midnight, it was with a smile and a handshake that I felt signified camaraderie and lasting fellowship, brothers in verse. His door closed behind me. My head was light. "Wait till I tell Rafe!"

Samson Raphaelson had been my mentor at the University of Illinois when he was a visiting professor. Playwright and film writer, he was one of the consummate stylists of sophisticated screen comedy. He created nine films with the great director Ernst Lubitsch, among them, *Trouble in Paradise, The Shop Around the Corner,* and *Heaven Can Wait.* His praised work for Broadway included *The Jazz Singer, Accent on Youth, Skylark,* and *Jason.* It was Rafe, a friend of Hoffenstein's, who introduced his poems to me, often reading them aloud during beer-and-coffee klatches with his students at his home. Rafe rendered the verses in a Yiddish-inflected sing-song, which is how many of them are meant to be heard. They had such a joyful effect on me that I ran to the bookstore and bought all two of Hoffenstein's books, *Year In, You're Out* and *Poems in Praise of Practically Nothing.* Years later I discovered the third, *Pencil in the Air,* in which my favorite is its proem:

> Wherever I go,
> *I* go too,
> And spoil everything

a sentiment I have adopted as my own.

Hoffenstein was a poet, Broadway theatrical press agent for the famous producer Al Woods, New York newspaper columnist, drama critic, and, finally, screenwriter (he wrote the movie adaptation of Theodore Dreiser's *An American Tragedy*). He had been with 20th-Century Fox for fourteen years when he died at age fifty-seven in 1947.

It was *Poems in Praise of Practically Nothing* in 1928 that had captivated the young Ogden Nash, as it captivated an entire generation of flappers and jazz babies. Some ninety thousand copies were sold in the first six months, astonishing for poetry. It was at Fox that he delivered his famous remark, "In the movies we writers work our brains to the bone. And what do we get for it? . . . A fortune."

Samuel Hoffenstein's funny verse is dipped in sadness and regret, laced with cynicism and the blues, buoyant with revelations and unexpected twists. If you relish what follows as much as I do, hie thee to a secondhand bookstore or a near-at-hand library and read him yourself, firsthand. The pleasure is yours.   **G.S.**

SAMUEL HOFFENSTEIN

Poems in Praise of Practically Nothing

I

You buy some flowers for your table;
You tend them tenderly as you're able;
You fetch them water from hither and thither—
What thanks do you get for it all? They wither.

II

Only the wholesomest foods you eat;
You lave and you lave from your head to your feet;
The earth is not steadier on its axis
Than you in the matter of prophylaxis;
You go to bed early and early you rise;
You scrub your teeth and you scour your eyes—
What thanks do you get for it all? Nephritis,
Pyorrhea, appendicitis,
Renal calculus and gastritis.

III

You buy yourself a new suit of clothes;
The care you give it, God only knows;
The material, of course, is the very *best* yet;
You get it pressed and pressed and *pressed* yet;
You keep it free from specks *so* tiny—
What thanks do you get? The pants get shiny.

IV

You practice every possible virtue;
You hurt not a soul, while others hurtue;
You fetch and carry like a market basket—
What thanks do you get for it? Me don't ask it!

V

You leap out of bed; you start to get ready;
You dress and you dress till you feel unsteady;
Hours go by, and still you're busy
Putting on clothes, till your brain is dizzy.
Do you flinch? Do you quit? Do you go out naked?—
The least little button, you don't forsake it.
What thanks do you get? Well, for all this mess, yet
When night comes around, you've got to undress yet.

VI

You're kind to women, children, worms;
You speak of God in the highest terms;
You help spell words like "tetrahedral";
You show respect for a cathedral;
You're sweet and gentle as a mouse is:
(Wives should behave so to their spouses!)
Though women tempt you, more than plenty,
Your rate is half a girl in twenty;—
In short, from grace you never fell yet—
And what do you get? On all sides hell yet!

VII

Your life's a wreck; you're tired of living,
Of lending, spending, borrowing, giving;
Of doubt and fear, of hope and question,
Of women, children and digestion;
There isn't a single dream you cherish—
You simply pine and pray to perish.
You haven't the nerve to take bichloride,
But you stay up nights till you're gaunt and sore eyed;
You don't eat greens, as the doctors tell you,

And you drink the very worst they sell you;
You've earned, at least, let's say, cirrhosis—
And what do you get for it? Halitosis!

VIII

You take a bath, and sit there bathing
In water cold, in water scathing;
You scrub till you're *sans* an epidermis,
And feel like a regular bathing Hermes.
You do not waste a single minute;
The tub shows how you worked while in it;
You dry, and do some honest rooting
For such remarkable abluting:—
Well, a day goes by, or ten, or thirty,
And what thanks do you get? You're just as dirty!

IX

You meet a girl and you surrender;
Though God knows why, you're kind and tender;
You're husband, lover, sister, brother,
Companion, banker, father, mother;
You try your best to be worthy of her;
You make mistakes, but she knows you love her;
You're hers completely, and you show it:
And what thanks do you get? The gate—I know it!

X

You're a good girl; you're gray with virtue;
The very thought of a misstep hurts you;
You know that honor must be hoarded
Against the day when it is rewarded;
You see a girl who's all men's vassal,
Marry a duke in his own castle;
You see another, who can't say, "No, sir,"
Capture, at least, a wholesale grocer;—
But you never let your thoughts grow sordid:
You know in your heart you'll be rewarded.
Well, the years go by, like queens and roses,
The way they did in the time of Moses,

And what do you get? False teeth, a doorman,
A complex, or assistant foreman!

XI

You hire a cook, but she can't cook yet;
You teach her by candle, bell, and book yet;
You show her, as if she were in her cradle,
Today, the soup, tomorrow, a ladle.
Well, she doesn't learn, so although you need her,
You decide that somebody else should feed her:—
But you're kind by birth; you hate to fire her;
To tell a woman you don't require her—
So you wait and wait, and before you do it,
What thanks do you get? She beats you to it!

XII

You're a pure spirit; you're air and water;
You're nobody's son and nobody's daughter;
In short, you're still in the state pre-natal—
A strange condition, but seldom fatal—
Well, anyhow, you're a harmless atom,
Content to stay in your own stratum;
You do not drink or play the horses,
Or interfere with natural forces,
Indulge in moods or whims erratic,
Which cause the flu, and sometimes, static:—
A perfect type of the homo *non est,*
You're unobtrusive, kind and honest,
As upright as an ear of corn—
And what thanks do you get for it all? You're born!

XIII

You're a positive fiend for life extension:
You eat greens in every dimension;
You know as well as any parrot
The quirks of calory and carrot—
They've taken out, without a quiver,
Your tonsils, teeth, ambition, liver,
Appendix, income—every center

Designed to let bacilli enter.
You never miss the daily dozen
That killed your uncle, brother, cousin;
You breathe only the freshest breezes—
And what do you get? The same diseases.

XIV

You work and work, and keep on working,
While poets, even worse, are shirking;
Your hair falls out, your eyes grow bleary,
Your bones grow old, your outlook dreary;
But you never seek to break the fetters—
You go on filing useless letters.
Well, a day arrives, and it must be spring yet:
The birds, somehow, begin to sing yet;
The grass is green, the cows are mooing,
The flies are buzzing, the people shooing,
The air is fresh—it makes you tipsy—
And, all of a sudden, you turn gipsy.
So you come in late, you go home early;
The thought of the office makes you surly;
You come in later, you go home earlier;
The thought of the office makes you surlier;
You've worked enough; you've earned the leisure
To have some poor, but honest pleasure;
No desk, you think, should rise and quell you—
And what do you get? Do I have to tell you?

XV

You go to high school, even college;
You become a regular Book of Knowledge;
You learn that Nero played the fiddle;
That the Sphinx is, after all, a riddle;
That women weep while men go faring;
That Bismarck seldom was a herring.
No matter what a person asks you,
The brilliant answer never tasks you;
You smile and say, "Go ask another,"
Like, "Did the Gracchi have a mother?"
Well, you meet a girl, and nothing sweeter;

The kind—well, anyhow, you meet 'er—
You look her over with elation—
She seems to have a cerebration:
So you start right in, like Kipling's thunder,
To be the twenty-seventh wonder;
You spout such high and fancy learning,
You're sure the girl will die of yearning—
And when you're finished, did you please her?
Did you hear her say, "You're Julius Caesar"?
What thanks did you get? The usual solo:
She likes the Prince of Wales and polo.

XVI

You're born (whose fault is it?) a poet—
Nobody sees it, but you know it;
You try to temper your psychoses
And get, at least, Grade B neuroses;
But it's no use—so great the curse is,
You go from bad to worse, then verses.
But suppose you wrote a poem a minute,
What menace, after all, is in it?
You might have been a chiropractor,
Dentist, diplomat, or actor,
Banker, lawyer, politician,
Or, let us say, your own physician,
Attacked the world, and brought upon it
More harm than even a first-rate sonnet—
Here is your chance, but you eschew it;
You haven't quite the heart to do it—
And what thanks do you get for it? Don't I know it?—
You go on being a sap and poet.

SAMUEL HOFFENSTEIN

The Notebook of a Schnook

schnook = schlemiel

I

I'm sitting home, I feel lonesome,
I feel saber-toothed and ownsome;
If I had a friend of the female gender
I feel I could make the girl surrender.
So I call this one, I call that one,
A bright one, a dim one, a slim one, a fat one,
Till I find a girl who says she's willing
To do the cooing if I do the billing.
So I bill in one place, I bill in another,
And she coos a little, like Whistler's mother;
Then I take her home to my mortgaged chalet,
A cute little place, if not a *palais,*
In a very respectable part of town,
With some rooms upstairs and some down;
I play a record by Tchaikovsky,
A very high-toned approach to lovsky;
I play waltzes by all the Strausses
And name big names in adjoining houses;
I try etchings, book-ends, brandy,
Rare editions and nougat candy,
Broadloom carpet and rose-leaf ceiling,
On which she can look, I hope, with feeling—
And what happens? You won't believe it;
As usual, nothing—take it or leave it!

II

I write a scenario for moving pictures;
I let myself go without any strictures;
My mind works in bright ascensions;
The characters swell and get dimensions;
The heroine rises from Gimbel's basement
To what could be called a magic casement,
By sheer virtue and, call it pluck,
With maybe a reel and a half of luck;
She doesn't use posterior palsy
Or displace so much as a single falsie;
She scorns the usual oo-la-la
And never ruffles a modest bra,
(The censor's dream of the cinema);
She doesn't find pearls in common oysters;
She sips a little but never roisters.
The hero's gonads are under wraps,
He never clutches or cuffs or slaps
In heat Vesuvian, or even Stygian—
He acts Oxonian or Cantabrigian
With maybe a soupçon of the South—
Cotton wouldn't melt in his mouth;
The plot could harmlessly beguile
A William Wordsworth honey chile;
The Big Shot's hot and the little shotlets
Wake their wives with contagious hotlets.
So what happens? The usual factors—
The studio simply can't get actors,
Directors, cutters, stagehands, stages,
Or girls to type the extra pages:
The way it ends, to put it briefly,
Is what happens is nothing, chiefly.

III

I work hard, I earn little,
A roof, a beer, a vittle, a skittle;
I keep—well what, if you haven't got money
Do you *think* you can keep—a high-class honey,
Maybe a nobleman's youngest daughter

With a yacht to protect her from salt and water?—
I keep a budget, a can of herring,
A box of matzos and maybe swearing.
Well, the worm turns 'round like a fresh-made cruller,
He's now a horse of another color—
I begin to make money, fast and plenty;
Life looks like rainbows and spumenti;
I begin to regard Jehovah highly,
And think of the life of the younger Riley;
I begin to dream of Lucullan doin's:
I'll travel a lot and see the ruins;
I'll hire a butler who doesn't hurry,
Who doesn't work, but who's pure Surrey,
A chauffeur who looks like the late Lord Essex,
A maid with wattles firm and Wessex;
I'll pay, spot cash, three years' advance
And import a cook from Paris, France;
O Paris, France! O Town de luxe!
I see you as you were in books—
O Paris, France, where gay *les femmes*
Cavort and do not give a *demmes;*
Where waxed and debonair *les hommes*
Disport and do not give a *dommes;*
Where even merry *les enfants*
Know all and do not give a *dants!*—
I'm running wild, I must subdue
What you could call my parvenu—
Well anyhow, I'm thinking of
La belle amour and even love;
Of serving dinners in ten courses,
And meeting gents who own horses
And powerful, natural female forces
Who own the gents who own the horses—
So what happens? I pay taxes;
The earth wobbles on half an axis;
I'm happy if the butler's cousin
Drops in sometimes for a daily dozen,
If I meet people who fix plumbing,
Or own a goldfish that's up and coming—
Things could happen to guys like Nero,
But to me, excuse the expression, zero.

IV

I paid my taxes. I got sick;
The doctor said I was going quick
Of double multiple complications,
Confirmed by seven consultations.
Well, if this is it, I said, resigned,
I'll do some thinking in my mind,
I'll do some planning in my head
On the way I'll live when they say I'm dead.
Well, first I'll go and get my blessing,
Then take my time about convalescing,
Because the sickness that I got
Weakens a fellow quite a lot.
I'll lie around a couple of eons
And listen to them pealing paeans
And drumming on what they call there, tabors,
And get acquainted with the neighbors,
And flop and sprawl on golden grass
And watch the little cherubs pass,
The way, up there, they call their cuties—
And from the pictures are they beauties!—
Sift pearls and rubies through my fingers,
Sing tenor with the carol singers,
And while I'm loafing, maybe lay
Some onyx up for a rainy day.
Then when I'm feeling good and strong
And think that I can live that long—
Because up there you feel immortal
Or else they show you the so-called portal—
I'll move into my permanent mansion,
With grounds enough for later expansion,
Take a look-see 'round the place,
Pick up a little special grace,
Meet the Biggies, make my mark,
Get promoted from angel to arch-,
Or maybe, even this could be,
To seraph, thirty-third degree,
With extra wings. Well, that's about

As far as I got when I passed out.
So what happened? To put it clearly,
Not only nothing, but nothing merely
And absolutely. You won't believe it:
I'm not even an angel—take it or leave it.

SAMUEL HOFFENSTEIN

Poems of Passion Carefully Restrained So As to Offend Nobody

I

You have a most attractive pan,
And I'm a very foolish man,
And, what between the two, I fell
As deep as Dante into hell;
But do you, in your triumph, think
I'll stay forever on the blink,
And pine and pale and waste away
And grow cadaverous and gray—
A wreck, a rum, a shard? Well, maybe
You are right about it, baby!

II

When you're away, I'm restless, lonely,
Wretched, bored, dejected; only
Here's the rub, my darling dear,
I feel the same when you are here.

III

Psycho-analyzed, I stand
And meditate your little hand;
Your lost, evasive eyes, that seem
To lean upon me while they scheme;
And thus contemplative, I know
Why I adore and need you so:—
When I was six or seven or eight,
In that divine, pre-nubile state,
I had a horror, vent in yelpings,
Of what were known as single helpings;
When I was nine, or maybe ten,
I nursed an unrequited yen:
I loved her, middle-aged and shrewish,
That she was Gentile, I but Jewish—
Though now I marvel at it all,
Who am devout Episcopal—
When I was in my 'teens, I dreamed
Green apples were not what they seemed,
But beasts, inimical to rest,
Who sat upon a fellow's chest;
When I achieved the peak of twenty,
Bad breaks with dames I had aplenty,
Who left my burning love behind,
And each, a complex in my mind;—
Now, to these inhibitions true,
I am a-Freud of losing you,
And, though I fully understand,
I meditate your little hand,
Your eyes that lie as like as not,
And love you, whom I ought to swat.

IV

Lovely lady, who does so
All my waking haunt,
Tell me, tell me, do you know
What the hell you want?

Lady, to whose feet I'd bring
The world, if I could win it,
Are you sure of anything
For a single minute?

You whose eyes can kindle flame
Only Death could smother,
Tell me, please, does any dame
Differ from another?

Was the apple applesauce
Eve ate in the garden?
Aren't you all a total loss?
No? I beg your pardon!

V

Oh, the first kiss is sweet—
Like a bud, like a wafer;
But the last, I repeat,
But the last kiss is safer.

The first kiss is sweet
With an innocent savor;
But the last is like meat
With some salt for its flavor.

Oh, with wonder I look—
You so fair, so capricious!
Say, whose goose did you cook
For a meat so delicious?

VI

Come, my sweet (or what you will)
Let us drink our blasé fill;
Let us give the night and day
To love and neurasthen-i-ay.

Let our nerves and passions rage
In the manner of the age,
Dancing through erotic scenes
To the jazzing endocrines.

You love me and I love you
And a dozen others too;
Let's exchange, with linkèd hopes,
Our amorous kaleidoscopes.

While the Fords the land obscure,
And radio makes the silence poor,
Let us be exhibit Z
In the new pathology.

VII

Belovèd, let our love be quite
Intense and splendid, but polite,
That in the hour of parting, we
May end the matter pleasantly.

Since the foredoomed farewell is core
Of all the mortal evermore,
Let us not mar with present fret
The gracious sequel of regret.

Rather, my little love, let me
Your guide for future lovers be,
Whose pleasure now is sometimes fraught
With envy of the men who taught.

VIII

I cannot elude you, I cannot escape:
You haunt me in every conceivable shape;—
You're morning and midnight and twilight and noon,
Orion, the Dipper, the Lion, the moon.

You keep me enchanted, exalted and true
In snares of the fair and ubiquitous you;
I don't mind your being the glories above—
But here you intrude on the ladies I love!

IX

I wish my mind would let me take
You as you are for your own sake;

A trifle less I might adore,
But then, I should enjoy you more.

But Imagination will
Change and transfigure you, until
I never see you, but it seems
Some glory of you stayed in dreams.

Sometimes I think the only thing
That can the lasting rapture bring,
Is not to see you, but to stay
In love with you and far away.

This is the kind of distant bliss
That Dante got from Beatrice:
A woman singing in the trees
A name, an epic, to the breeze.

And men and women all will prove
This cruel arson against Love—
That he burns all else away
In the belovèd but the clay.

X

Sweetling, try not to forget,
Lest in trying, you remember;
She who blows too hard may get
Flame from the deceptive ember.

Let the attic of your mind
Keep whatever stores are in it;
Do not look too much behind,
Lest you tread the present minute.

I shall pluck the moments now—
Only folly weeps to miss one;
Let some later lover's brow
Wrinkle at the thought of this one!

XI

The rain that falls upon my heart
And on my eyes so wistfully,

Will fall again; I shall not start,
For it will drop so restfully

On eyes that will be pools of quiet,
Upon a heart that will not stir
At memories of ancient riot
Within the rain's sad dulcimer.

Even as it falls upon the ground,
Nor makes the tiniest pebble start,
The rain will fall, nor make a sound
Of anything within my heart—

Neither of the bitter nor the sweet
Of loving you, my dear, my dear—
Though all our moments it repeat,
I, who have loved you, shall not hear.

I shall but stare upon my heaven
Of silent earth and starless stone,
Beyond which, grazing sheep at even
Find peace no greater than my own.

And I, who love you now, my dear,
So wildly that my heart is spent,
Think of the time I shall not hear
Your voice in rain, and am content.

XII

I shall sing a song to you,—
Fair a song as any;
Perfect as a drop of dew—
Rare among the many.

Eager, dancing words will do
Their melodious duty;
Make a lucent mirror, true
To your shining beauty.

I shall coin your golden hair
For a stanza's treasure;
Tame your wild and wayward air
To my love-sick measure.

I shall lift my song and sing
With the voice of doom
The utter loneliness you bring
Into this little room.

SKIP MORROW

SAMUEL HOFFENSTEIN

Budget

The gonad is designed to mate us,
And thereby, obviously, create us,
Whereas the mute, minute bacillus
Is admirably made to kill us:
A balanced budget in this case
Would greatly benefit the race.

TON SMITS

TON SMITS

Kat + Mouse + Pup = Love Triangle

"Krazy Kat" was as much a part of my childhood as were popsicles with lucky sticks, hot sweet potato vendors, and the nickel ferryboat ride across the Hudson. But for scholars of the time (and even now), "Krazy Kat" was more than "reading the funnies." For the critic Gilbert Seldes (writing in 1924), "[Krazy Kat] is the most amusing and fantastic and satisfactory work of art produced in America today. It is wise . . . it has delicacy, sensitiveness, and an unearthly beauty." The poet e.e. cummings had similar feelings, and in 1969 Barbara Gelman wrote: "Of the all-time greats of the comic strip, the most talked about—yet para-doxically the most difficult to talk about—is 'Krazy Kat'. [Critics] have tried to capture and define the elusive qualities of this comic strip [but] each reader felt that he, and he alone, really got what 'Krazy Kat' was all about. But there is *no* explaining 'Krazy Kat'. For all the allegorical, philosophical, political meanings attributed to it by devoted readers, it was, and remains, primarily an experience, one to be had only at firsthand." And so, here is some of "Krazy Kat", firsthand, from the hand of George Herriman.   **G.S.**

GEORGE HERRIMAN

Krazy Kat

H. L. MENCKEN

The Wedding:
A Stage Direction

The scene is a church in an American city of about half a million population, and the time is about eleven o'clock of a fine morning in early spring. The neighborhood is well-to-do, but not quite fashionable. That is to say, most of the families of the vicinage keep two servants (alas, more or less intermittently!), and eat dinner at half-past six, and about one in every four boasts a colored butler (who attends to the fires, washes windows and helps with the sweeping), and a last year's automobile. The heads of these families are merchandise brokers; jobbers in notions, hardware and drugs; manufacturers of candy, hats, badges, office furniture, blank books, picture frames, wire goods and patent medicines; managers of steamboat lines; district agents of insurance companies; owners of commercial printing offices, and other such business men of substance—and the prosperous lawyers and popular family doctors who keep them out of trouble. In one block live a Congressman and two college professors, one of whom has written an unimportant textbook and got himself into "Who's Who in America." In the block above lives a man who once ran for Mayor of the city, and came near being elected.

The wives of these householders wear good clothes and have a liking for a reasonable gayety, but very few of them can pretend to what is vaguely called social standing, and, to do them justice, not many of them waste any time lamenting it. They have, taking one with another, about three children apiece, and are good mothers. A few of them belong to women's clubs or flirt with the suffragettes, but the majority can get all of the intellectual stimulation they crave in the Ladies' Home Journal and the Saturday Evening Post, with Vogue added for its fashions. Most of them, deep down in their hearts, suspect their husbands of secret frivolity, and about ten per cent have the proofs, but it is rare for them to make rows about it, and the divorce rate among them is thus very low. Themselves indifferent cooks, they are unable to teach their servants the art, and so the food they set before their husbands and children is often such as would make a Frenchman cut his throat. But they are diligent housewives otherwise; they see to it that the windows are washed, that no one tracks mud into the hall, that the servants do not waste coal, sugar, soap and gas, and that the family buttons are always sewed on. In religion these estimable wives are pious in habit but somewhat nebulous in faith. That is to say, they regard any person who specifically refuses to go to church as a heathen, but they themselves are by no means regular in attendance, and not one in ten of them could tell you whether transubstantiation is a Roman Catholic or a Dunkard doctrine. About two per cent. have dallied more or less gingerly with Christian Science, their average period of belief being one year.

The church we are in is like the neighborhood and its people: well-to-do but not fashionable. It is Protestant in faith and probably Episcopalian. The pews are of thick, yellow-brown oak, severe in pattern and hideous in color. In each there is a long, removable cushion of a dark, purplish, dirty hue, with here and there some of its hair stuffing showing. The stained-glass windows, which were all bought ready-made and depict scenes from the New Testament, commemorate the virtues of departed worthies of the neighborhood, whose names appear, in illegible black letters, in the lower panels. The floor is covered with a carpet of some tough, fibrous material, apparently a sort of grass, and along the center aisle it is much worn. The normal smell of the place is rather less unpleasant than that of most other halls, for on the one day when it is regularly crowded practically all of the persons gathered together have been very recently bathed.

On this fine morning, however, it is full of heavy, mortuary perfumes, for a couple of florist's men have just finished decorating the chancel with flowers and potted palms. Just behind the chancel rail, facing the center aisle, there is a prie-dieu, and to either side of it are great banks of lilies, carnations, gardenias and roses. Three or four feet behind the prie-dieu and completely concealing the high altar, there is a dense jungle of palms. Those in the front rank are authentically growing in pots, but behind them the florist's men have artfully placed some more durable, and hence more profitable, sophistications. Anon the rev. clergyman, emerging from the vestry-room to the right, will pass along the front of this jungle to the prie-dieu, and so, framed in flowers, face the congregation with his saponaceous smile.

The florist's men, having completed their labors, are preparing to depart. The older of the two, a man in the fifties, shows the ease of an experienced hand by taking out a large plug of tobacco and gnawing off a substantial chew. The desire to spit seizing him shortly, he proceeds to gratify it by a trick long practised by gasfitters, musicians, caterer's helpers, piano movers and other such alien invaders of the domestic hearth. That is to say, he hunts for a place where the carpet is loose along the chancel rail, finds it where two lengths join, deftly turns up a flap, spits upon the bare floor, and then lets the flap fall back, finally giving it a pat with the sole of his foot. This done, he and his assistant leave the church to the sexton, who has been sweeping the vestibule, and, after passing the time of day with the two men who are putting up a striped awning from the door to the curb, disappear into a nearby saloon, there to wait and refresh themselves until the wedding is over, and it is time to take away their lilies, their carnations and their synthetic palms.

It is now a quarter past eleven, and two flappers of the neighborhood, giggling and arm-in-arm, approach the sexton and inquire of him if they may enter. He asks them if they have tickets and when they say they haven't, he tells them that he ain't got no right to let them in, and don't know nothing about what the rule is going to be. At some weddings, he goes on, hardly nobody ain't allowed in, but then again, sometimes they don't scarcely look at the tickets at all. The two flappers retire abashed, and as the sexton finishes his sweeping, there enters the organist.

The organist is a tall, thin man of melancholy, uraemic aspect, wearing a black slouch hat with a wide brim and a yellow overcoat that barely reaches to his knees. A pupil, in his youth, of a man who had once studied (irregularly and briefly) with Charles-Marie Widor, he acquired thereby the artistic temperament, and with it a vast fondness for malt liquor. His mood this morning is acidulous and depressed, for he spent yesterday evening in a Pilsner ausschank with two former members of the Boston Symphony Orchestra, and it was 3 A.M. before they finally agreed that Johann Sebastian Bach, all things considered, was a greater man than Beethoven, and so parted amicably. Sourness is the precise sensation that wells within him. He feels vinegary; his blood runs cold; he wishes he could immerse himself in bicarbonate of soda. But the call of his art is more potent than the protest of his poisoned and quaking liver, and so he manfully climbs the spiral stairway to his organ-loft.

Once there, he takes off his hat and overcoat, stoops down to blow the dust off the organ keys, throws the electrical switch which sets the bellows going, and then proceeds to take off his shoes. This done, he takes his seat, reaches for the pedals with his stockinged feet, tries an experimental 32-foot CCC, and then wanders gently into a Bach toccata. It is his limbering-up piece: he always plays it as a prelude to a wedding job. It thus goes very smoothly and even brilliantly, but when he comes to the end of it and tackles the ensuing fugue he is quickly in difficulties, and after four or five stumbling repetitions of the subject he hurriedly improvises a crude coda and has done. Peering down into the church to see if his flounderings have had an audience, he sees two old maids enter, the one very tall and thin and the other somewhat brisk and bunchy.

They constitute the vanguard of the nuptial throng, and as they proceed hesitatingly up the center aisle, eager for good seats but afraid to go too far, the organist wipes his palms upon his trousers legs, squares his shoulders, and plunges into the program that he has played at all weddings for fifteen years past. It begins with Mendelssohn's Spring Song, pianissimo. Then comes Rubinstein's Melody in F, with a touch of forte toward the close, and then Nevin's "Oh, That We Two Were Maying," and then the Chopin waltz in A flat, Opus 69, No. 1, and then the Spring Song again, and then a free fantasia upon "The Rosary" and then a Moszkowski mazurka, and then the Dvorák Humoresque (with its heart-rending cry in the *middle), and then some vague and turbulent thing (apparently the disjecta membra of another fugue), and then Tschaikowsky's "Autumn," and then Elgar's "Salut d'Amour," and then the Spring Song a third time, and then something or other from one of the Peer Gynt suites, and then an hurrah or two from the Hallelujah chorus, and then Chopin again, and Nevin, and Elgar, and—*

But meanwhile, there is a growing activity below. First comes a closed automobile bearing the six ushers and soon after it another automobile bearing the bridegroom and his best man. The bridegroom and the best man disembark before the side entrance of the church and make their way into the vestryroom, where they remove their hats and coats, and proceed to struggle with their cravats and collars before a mirror which hangs on the wall. The room is very dingy. A baize-covered table is in the center of it, and around the table stand six or eight chairs of assorted designs. One wall is completely covered by a bookcase, through the glass doors of which one may discern piles of cheap Bibles, hymn-books and back numbers of the parish magazine. In one corner is a small washstand. The best man takes a flat flask of whiskey from his pocket, looks about him for a glass, finds it on the washstand, rinses it at the tap, fills it with a policeman's drink, and hands it to the bridegroom. The latter downs it at a gulp. Then the best man pours out one for himself.

The ushers, reaching the vestibule of the church, have handed their silk hats to the sexton, and entered the sacred edifice. There was a rehearsal of the wedding last night, but after it was over the bride ordered certain incomprehensible changes in the plan, and the ushers are now completely at sea. All they know clearly is that the relatives of the bride are to be seated on one side and the relatives of the bridegroom on the other. But which side for one and which for the other? They discuss it heatedly for three minutes and then find that they stand three for putting the bride's relatives on the left side and three for putting them on the right side. The debate, though instructive, is interrupted by the sudden entrance of seven women in a group. They are headed by a truculent old battleship, possibly an aunt or something of the sort, who fixes the nearest usher with a knowing, suspicious glance, and motions to him to show her the way.

He offers her his right arm and they start up the center aisle, with the six other women following in irregular order, and the five other ushers scattered among the women. The leading usher is tortured damnably by doubts as to where the party should go. If they are aunts, to which house do they belong, and on which side are the members of that house to be seated? What if they are not aunts, but merely neighbors? Or perhaps an association of former cooks, parlor maids, nurse girls? Or strangers? The sufferings of the usher are relieved by the battleship, who halts majestically about twenty feet from the altar, and motions her followers into a pew to the left. They file in silently and she seats herself next the aisle. All seven settle back and wriggle for room. It is a tight fit.

(Who, in point of fact, are these ladies? Don't ask the question! The ushers never

find out. No one ever finds out. They remain a joint mystery for all time. In the end they become a sort of tradition, and years hence, when two of the ushers meet, they will cackle over old dreadnaught and her six cruisers. The bride, grown old and fat, will tell the tale to her daughter, and then to her granddaughter. It will grow more and more strange, marvelous, incredible. Variorum versions will spring up. It will be adapted to other weddings. The dreadnaught will become an apparition, a witch, the Devil in skirts. And as the years pass, the date of the episode will be pushed back. By 2017 it will be dated 1150. By 2475 it will take on a sort of sacred character, and there will be a footnote referring to it in the latest Revised Version of the New Testament.)

It is now a quarter to twelve, and of a sudden the vestibule fills with wedding guests. Nine-tenths of them, perhaps even nineteen-twentieths, are women, and most of them are beyond thirty-five. Scattered among them, hanging on to their skirts, are about a dozen little girls—one of them a youngster of eight or thereabout, with spindle shanks and shining morning face, entranced by her first wedding. Here and there lurks a man. Usually he wears a hurried, unwilling, protesting look. He has been dragged from his office on a busy morning, forced to rush home and get into his cutaway coat, and then marched to the church by his wife. One of these men, much hustled, has forgotten to have his shoes shined. He is intensely conscious of them, and tries to hide them behind his wife's skirt as they walk up the aisle. Accidentally he steps upon it, and gets a look over the shoulder which lifts his diaphragm an inch and turns his liver to water. This man will be court-martialed when he reaches home, and he knows it. He wishes that some foreign power would invade the United States and burn down all the churches in the country, and that the bride, the bridegroom and all the other persons interested in the present wedding were dead and in hell.

The ushers do their best to seat these wedding guests in some sort of order, but after a few minutes the crowd at the doors becomes so large that they have to give it up, and thereafter all they can do is to hold out their right arms ingratiatingly and trust to luck. One of them steps on a fat woman's skirt, tearing it very badly, and she has to be helped back to the vestibule. There she seeks refuge in a corner, under a stairway leading up to the steeple, and essays to repair the damage with pins produced from various nooks and crevices of her person. Meanwhile the guilty usher stands in front of her, mumbling apologies and trying to look helpful. When she finishes her work and emerges from her improvised drydock, he again offers her his arm, but she sweeps past him without noticing him, and proceeds grandly to a seat far forward. She is a cousin to the bride's mother, and will make a report to every branch of the family that all six ushers disgraced the ceremony by appearing at it far gone in liquor.

Fifteen minutes are consumed by such episodes and divertisements. By the time the clock in the steeple strikes twelve the church is well filled. The music of the organist, who has now reached Mendelssohn's *Spring Song* for the third and last time, is accompanied by a huge buzz of whispers, and there is much craning of necks and long-

distance nodding and smiling. Here and there an unusually gorgeous hat is the target of many converging glances, and of as many more or less satirical criticisms. To the damp funeral smell of the flowers at the altar, there has been added the cacodorous scents of forty or fifty different brands of talcum and rice powder. It begins to grow warm in the church, and a number of women open their vanity bags and duck down for stealthy dabs at their noses. Others, more reverent, suffer the agony of augmenting shines. One, a trickster, has concealed powder in her pocket handkerchief, and applies it dexterously while pretending to blow her nose.

The bridegroom in the vestry-room, entering upon the second year (or is it the third?) of his long and ghastly wait, grows increasingly nervous, and when he hears the organist pass from the Spring Song into some more sonorous and stately thing he mistakes it for the wedding march from "Lohengrin," and is hot for marching upon the altar at once. The best man, an old hand, restrains him gently, and administers another sedative from the bottle. The bridegroom's thoughts turn to gloomy things. He remembers sadly that he will never be able to laugh at benedicts again; that his days of low, rabelaisian wit and care-free scoffing are over; that he is now the very thing he mocked so gaily but yesteryear. Like a drowning man, he passes his whole life in review—not, however, that part which is past, but that part which is to come. Odd fancies throng upon him. He wonders what his honeymoon will cost him, what there will be to drink at the wedding breakfast, what a certain girl in Chicago will say when she hears of his marriage. Will there be any children? He rather hopes not, for all those he knows appear so greasy and noisy, but he decides that he might conceivably compromise on a boy. But how is he going to make sure that it will not be a girl? The thing, as yet, is a medical impossibility—but medicine is making rapid strides. Why not wait until the secret is discovered? This sapient compromise pleases the bridegroom, and he proceeds to a consideration of various problems of finance. And then, of a sudden, the organist swings unmistakably into "Lohengrin" and the best man grabs him by the arm.

There is now great excitement in the church. The bride's mother, two sisters, three brothers and three sisters-in-law have just marched up the center aisle and taken seats in the front pew, and all the women in the place are craning their necks toward the door. The usual electrical delay ensues. There is something the matter with the bride's train, and the two bridesmaids have a deuce of a time fixing it. Meanwhile the bride's father, in tight pantaloons and tighter gloves, fidgets and fumes in the vestibule, the six ushers crowd about him inanely, and the sexton rushes to and fro like a rat in a trap. Finally, all being ready, with the ushers formed two abreast, the sexton pushes a button, a small buzzer sounds in the organ loft, and the organist, as has been said, plunges magnificently into the fanfare of the "Lohengrin" march. Simultaneously the sexton opens the door at the bottom of the main aisle, and the wedding procession gets under weigh.

The bride and her father march first. Their step is so slow (about one beat to two measures) that the father has some difficulty in maintaining his equilibrium, but the bride herself moves steadily and erectly, almost seeming to float. Her face is thickly encrusted with talcum in its various forms, so that she is almost a dead white. She keeps her eyelids lowered modestly, but is still acutely aware of every glance fastened upon her—not in the mass, but every glance individually. For example, she sees clearly, even through her eyelids, the still, cold smile of a girl in Pew 8 R—a girl who once made an unwomanly attempt upon the bridegroom's affections, and was routed and put to flight by superior strategy. And her ears are open, too: she hears every "How sweet!" and "Oh, lovely!" and "Ain't she pale!" from the latitude of the last pew to the very glacis of the altar of God.

While she has thus made her progress up the hymeneal chute, the bridegroom and his best man have emerged from the vestryroom and begun the short march to the prie-dieu. They walk haltingly, clumsily, uncertainly, stealing occasional glances at the advancing bridal party. The bridegroom feels of his lower right-hand waistcoat pocket; the ring is still there. The best man wriggles his cuffs. No one, however, pays any heed to them. They are not even seen, indeed, until the bride and her father reach the open space in front of the altar. There the bride and the bridegroom find themselves standing side by side, but not a word is exchanged between them, nor even a look of recognition. They stand motionless, contemplating the ornate cushion at their feet, until the bride's father and the bridesmaids file to the left of the bride and the ushers, now wholly disorganized and imbecile, drape themselves in an irregular file along the altar rail. Then, the music having died down to a faint murmur and a hush having fallen upon the assemblage, they look up.

Before them, framed by foliage, stands the reverend gentleman of God who will presently link them in indissoluble chains—the estimable rector of the parish. He has got there just in time; it was, indeed, a close shave. But no trace of haste or of anything else of a disturbing character is now visible upon his smooth, glistening, somewhat feverish face. That face is wholly occupied by his official smile, a thing of oil and honey all compact, a balmy, unctuous illumination—the secret of his success in life. Slowly his cheeks puff out, gleaming like soap-bubbles. Slowly he lifts his prayer-book from the prie-dieu and holds it droopingly. Slowly his soft caressing eyes engage it. There is an almost imperceptible stiffening of his frame. His mouth opens with a faint click. He begins to read.

The Ceremony of Marriage has begun.

JULES FEIFFER

"Armbruster here has what I think is a marvelous suggestion."

"Wake up, you mutt! We're getting married today."

JAMES THURBER

Mr. Preble Gets Rid of His Wife

Mr. Preble was a plump middle-aged lawyer in Scarsdale. He used to kid with his stenographer about running away with him. "Let's run away together," he would say, during a pause in dictation. "All righty," she would say.

One rainy Monday afternoon, Mr. Preble was more serious about it than usual.

"Let's run away together," said Mr. Preble.

"All righty," said his stenographer. Mr. Preble jingled the keys in his pocket and looked out the window.

"My wife would be glad to get rid of me," he said.

"Would she give you a divorce?" asked the stenographer.

"I don't suppose so," he said. The stenographer laughed.

"You'd have to get rid of your wife," she said.

Mr. Preble was unusually silent at dinner that night. About half an hour after coffee, he spoke without looking up from his paper.

"Let's go down in the cellar," Mr. Preble said to his wife.

"What for?" she said, not looking up from her book.

"Oh, I don't know," he said. "We never go down in the cellar any more. The way we used to."

"We never did go down in the cellar that I remember," said Mrs. Preble. "I could rest easy the balance of my life if I never went down in the cellar." Mr. Preble was silent for several minutes.

"Supposing I said it meant a whole lot to me," began Mr. Preble.

"What's come over you?" his wife demanded. "It's cold down there and there is absolutely nothing to do."

"We could pick up pieces of coal," said Mr. Preble. "We might get up some kind of a game with pieces of coal."

"I don't want to," said his wife. "Anyway, I'm reading."

"Listen," said Mr. Preble, rising and walking up and down. "Why won't you come down in the cellar? You can read down there, as far as that goes."

"There isn't a good enough light down there," she said, "and anyway, I'm not going to go down in the cellar. You may as well make up your mind to that."

"Gee whiz!" said Mr. Preble, kicking at the edge of a rug. "Other people's wives go down in the cellar. Why is it you never want to do anything? I come home worn out from the office and you won't even go down in the cellar with me. God knows it isn't very far—it isn't as if I was asking you to go to the movies or some place."

"I don't want to *go!*" shouted Mrs. Preble. Mr. Preble sat down on the edge of a davenport.

"All right, all *right,*" he said. He picked up the newspaper again. "I wish you'd let me tell you more about it. It's—kind of a surprise."

"Will you quit harping on that subject?" asked Mrs. Preble.

"Listen," said Mr. Preble, leaping to his feet. "I might as well tell you the truth instead of beating around the bush. I want to get rid of you so I can marry my stenographer. Is there anything especially wrong about that? People do it every day. Love is something you can't control——"

"We've been all over that," said Mrs. Preble. "I'm not going to go all over that again."

"I just wanted you to know how things are," said Mr. Preble. "But you have to take everything so literally. Good Lord, do you suppose I really wanted to go down in the cellar and make up some silly game with pieces of coal?"

"I never believed that for a minute," said Mrs. Preble. "I knew all along you wanted to get me down there and bury me."

"You can say that now—after I told you," said Mr. Preble. "But it would never have occurred to you if I hadn't."

"You didn't tell me; I got it out of you," said Mrs. Preble. "Anyway, I'm always two steps ahead of what you're thinking."

"You're never within a mile of what I'm thinking," said Mr. Preble.

"Is that so? I knew you wanted to bury me the minute you set foot in this house tonight." Mrs. Preble held him with a glare.

"Now that's just plain damn exaggeration," said Mr. Preble, considerably annoyed. "You knew nothing of the sort. As a matter of fact, I never thought of it till just a few minutes ago."

"It was in the back of your mind," said Mrs. Preble. "I suppose this filing woman put you up to it."

"You needn't get sarcastic," said Mr. Preble. "I have plenty of people to file without having her file. She doesn't know anything about this. She isn't in on it. I was going to tell her you had gone to visit some friends and fell over a cliff. She wants me to get a divorce."

"That's a laugh," said Mrs. Preble. *"That's* a laugh. You may bury me, but you'll never get a divorce."

"She knows that! I told her that," said Mr. Preble. "I mean—I told her I'd never get a divorce."

"Oh, you probably told her about burying me, too," said Mrs. Preble.

"That's not true," said Mr. Preble, with dignity. "That's between you and me. I was never going to tell a soul."

"You'd blab it to the whole world; don't tell me," said Mrs. Preble. "I know you." Mr. Preble puffed at his cigar.

"I wish you were buried now and it was all over with," he said.

"Don't you suppose you would get caught, you crazy thing?" she said. "They always get caught. Why don't you go to bed? You're just getting yourself all worked up over nothing."

"I'm not going to bed," said Mr. Preble. "I'm going to bury you in the cellar. I've got my mind made up to it. I don't know how I could make it any plainer."

"Listen," cried Mrs. Preble, throwing her book down, "will you be satisfied and shut up if I go down in the cellar? Can I have a little peace if I go down in the cellar? Will you let me alone then?"

"Yes," said Mr. Preble. "But you spoil it by taking that attitude."

"Sure, sure, I always spoil everything. I stop reading right in the middle of a chapter. I'll never know how the story comes out—but that's nothing to you."

"Did I make you start reading the book?" asked Mr. Preble. He opened the cellar door. "Here, you go first."

"Brrr," said Mrs. Preble, starting down the steps. "It's *cold* down here! You *would* think of this, at this time of year! Any other husband would have buried his wife in the summer."

"You can't arrange those things just whenever you want to," said Mr. Preble. "I didn't fall in love with this girl till late fall."

"Anybody else would have fallen in love with her long before that.

She's been around for years. Why is it you always let other men get in ahead of you? Mercy, but it's dirty down here! What have you got there?"

"I was going to hit you over the head with this shovel," said Mr. Preble.

"You were, huh?" said Mrs. Preble. "Well, get that out of your mind. Do you want to leave a great big clue right here in the middle of everything where the first detective that comes snooping around will find it? Go out in the street and find some piece of iron or something—something that doesn't belong to you."

"Oh, all right," said Mr. Preble. "But there won't be any piece of iron in the street. Women always expect to pick up a piece of iron anywhere."

"If you look in the right place you'll find it," said Mrs. Preble. "And don't be gone long. Don't you dare stop in at the cigarstore. I'm not going to stand down here in this cold cellar all night and freeze."

"All right," said Mr. Preble. "I'll hurry."

"And shut that *door* behind you!" she screamed after him. "Where were you born—in a barn?"

GEORGE BOOTH

"I've got an idea for a story: Gus and Ethel live on Long Island, on the North Shore. He works sixteen hours a day writing fiction. Ethel never goes out, never does anything except fix Gus sandwiches, and in the end she becomes a nympho-lesbo-killer-whore. Here's your sandwich."

SAMUEL HOFFENSTEIN

A Simple Tale

I had a girl and *you* had a girl
And she was a pretty dame,
And mine was mine and yours was yours
And she was one and the same.

Yes, *I* had a girl and *you* had a girl
And she had a lovely laugh,
And whenever *I* saw her, whenever *you* saw her,
We always sawed her in half.

Now *she* has a fellow, a loving fellow,
But a careworn fellow and pale,
Who wonders which of us got the head
And which of us got (a simple tale),
And which of us got the other part,
And which of us got, in short, her heart.

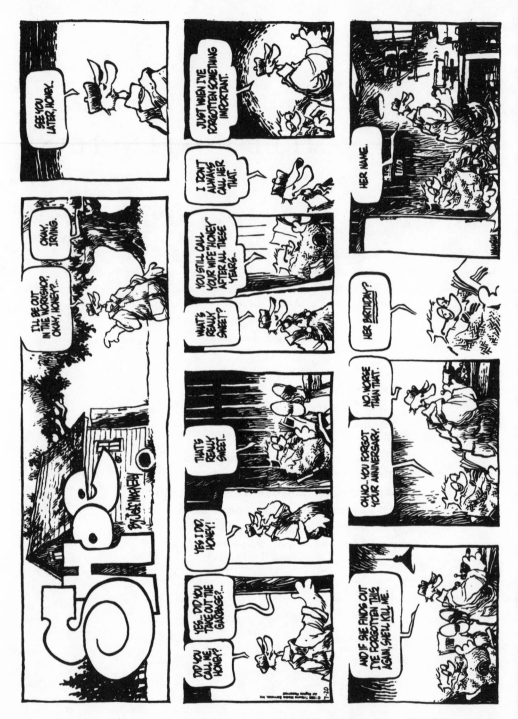

JEFF MacNELLY

FRAN LEBOWITZ

The Last Laugh

Coming from a family where literary tradition runs largely toward the picture postcard, it is not surprising that I have never really succeeded in explaining to my grandmother exactly what it is that I do. It is not that my grandmother is unintelligent; quite the contrary. It is simply that so firmly implanted are her roots in retail furniture that she cannot help but view all other occupations from this rather limited vantage point. Therefore, every time I see my grandmother I am fully prepared for the following exchange:

"So, how are you?"

"Fine, Grandma. How are you?"

"Fine. So how's business, good?"

"Very good, Grandma."

"You busy this time of year? Is this a good season for you?"

"Very good, Grandma."

"Good. It's good to be busy."

"Yes, Grandma."

Satisfied with my responses, my grandmother will then turn to my father and ask the very same questions, a dialogue a bit more firmly grounded in reality, since he has not deviated from the Lebowitz custom of fine upholstered furniture.

The lack of understanding between my grandmother and myself has long troubled me, and in honor of her recently celebrated ninety-fifth birthday I have prepared the following business history in order that she might have a clearer vision of my life and work.

My beginnings were humble, of course, but I am not ashamed of them. I started with a humor pushcart on Delancey Street—comic essays, forty cents apiece, four for a dollar. It was tough out there on the street;

competition was cut-throat, but it was the best education in the world because on Delancey "mildly amusing" was not enough—you had to be *funny.* I worked ten-hour days, six days a week, and soon I had a nice little following. Not exactly a cult, maybe, but I was doing okay. It was a living. I was able to put aside some money, and things looked pretty good for a store of my own in the not too distant future. Oh sure, I had my troubles, who doesn't? The housewives browsing through every essay on the cart, trying to contain their glee in the hope that I'd come down a little in price. The kids snitching a couple of paragraphs when my back was turned. And Mike the cop with his hand out all the time looking for a free laugh. But I persevered, never losing sight of my objective, and after years of struggle I was ready to take the plunge.

I went down to Canal Street to look for a store, a store of my own. Not being one to do things halfway, I was thorough and finally found a good location. Lots of foot traffic, surgical supplies on one side, maternity clothes on the other—these were people who could use a good laugh. I worked like a dog getting ready for that opening. I put in a very reasonable ready-to-hear line, an amusing notions counter, a full stock of epigrams, aphorisms and the latest in wit and irony. At last I was ready; Fran's Humor Heaven: Home of the Devastating Double Entendre was open for business. It was tough going at first, but my overhead was low. I wrote all my own stock. And eventually I began to show a nice healthy gross and a net I could live with.

I don't know when it all began to go sour—who can tell about these things, I'm a humorist, not a fortuneteller—but business began to slip. First I took a bath with some barbed comments I was trying out, and then I got stuck with a lot of entertaining anecdotes. I hoped it was just an off season, but it didn't let up, and before I knew it I was in really big trouble. I tried everything, believe you me. I ran big sales—"Buy one epigram, get one free," "Twenty percent off all phrases." I even instituted a "Buy now, say later" plan. But nothing worked. I was at my wits' end; I owed everybody and was in hock up to my ears. So one day, pen in hand, I went to Morris "The Thesaurus" Pincus—a shy on East Houston who lent money to humorists in a jam. The interest rates were exorbitant but I signed my life away. What else could I do?

But it wasn't enough, and I was forced to take in a collaborator. At first he seemed to be working out. He specialized in parodies and they were moving pretty good, but before too long I began to get suspicious of him. I mean, I could barely put food on my table, and there he was, riding around in a Cadillac a block long. One night after dinner I went back to the store and went over the books with a fine-tooth comb. Just as I thought, there it was in black and white: the guy was a thief. He'd been stealing my lines all along. I confronted him with the evidence and what could he do? He promised to pay me back a few pages a week, but I knew that was one joker I'd never see again.

I kicked him out and worked even harder. Eighty-hour weeks, open every night until ten, but it was a losing battle. With the big humor chains moving in, what chance did an independent like me have? Then the day came when I knew all was lost. Sol's Discount Satire opened up right across the street. He wrote in bulk; I couldn't meet his prices. I, of course, was wittier, but nobody cared about quality anymore. Their attitude was "So it's a little broad, but at forty percent below list we'll forsake a little subtlety." I went in the back of the store and sat down, trying desperately to figure something out. There was a sharp rap at the door, and in walked Morris, a goon on either side, ready to collect. I told him I didn't have it. I begged for more time. I was pleading for my life. Morris stared at me coolly, a hard glint in his eye as he cleaned his nails with a lethal-looking fountain pen.

"Look, Fran," he said, "you're breaking my heart. Either you pay up by next Monday, or I'm gonna spread it around that you're mixing your metaphors."

With that he turned on his heel and walked out the door followed by the two gorillas. I was sweating bullets. If Morris spread that around, I'd never get another laugh as long as I lived. My head swam with crazy plans, and when I realized what I had to do, my heart thumped like a jackhammer.

Late that night I went back to the store. I let myself in through the side door and set to work. I poured a lot of gasoline around, took a last look, threw in a match and beat it the hell out of there. I was twenty blocks away when the full realization of what I'd done hit me. Overcome by remorse, I ran all the way back, but it was too late. The deed was done; I'd burned my comic essays for the insurance money.

The next day I met with the adjuster from That's Life, and thank God he bought the fire and paid me off. It was just enough to settle with Morris, and then I was broke again.

I started to free-lance for other stores, writing under a pseudonym, of course. My heart wasn't in it, but I needed the cash. I was grinding it out like hamburger meat, trying to build up some capital. The stuff was too facile, I knew that, but there was a market for it, so I made the best of it.

The years went by and I was just getting to the point where I could take it a little easy, when I was struck by an idea that was to change not only my own life but that of everyone in the entire humor business. The idea? Fast humor. After all, the pace had picked up a lot since my days on Delancey Street. The world was a different place; humor habits had changed. Everyone was in a hurry. Who had time anymore for a long comic essay, a slow build, a good long laugh? Everything was rush, rush, rush. Fast humor was an idea whose time had come.

Once again I started small, just a little place out on Queens Boulevard. I called it Rapid Repartee and used every modern design technique available. All chrome and glass, everything sleek and clean. Known in the business for my cunning and waggish ways, I couldn't resist a little joke and so used as my trademark a golden arch. No one got it. So I added another one, and got a great reaction. You really have to hit people over the head, don't you? Be that as it may, the place caught on like wildfire. I couldn't keep Quick Comebacks in stock, and the Big Crack was the hit of the century. I began to franchise, but refused to relinquish quality control. Business boomed and today I can tell you I'm sitting pretty. I've got it all: a penthouse on Park, a yacht the size of the *Queen Mary* and a Rolls you could live in. But still, every once in a while I get that old creative itch. When this happens I slip on an apron and cap, step behind one of my thousands of counters, smile pleasantly at the customer and say, "Good morning. Something nice in a Stinging Barb?" If I'm recognized, it's always good for a laugh, because, believe you me, in this business unless you have a sense of humor you're dead.

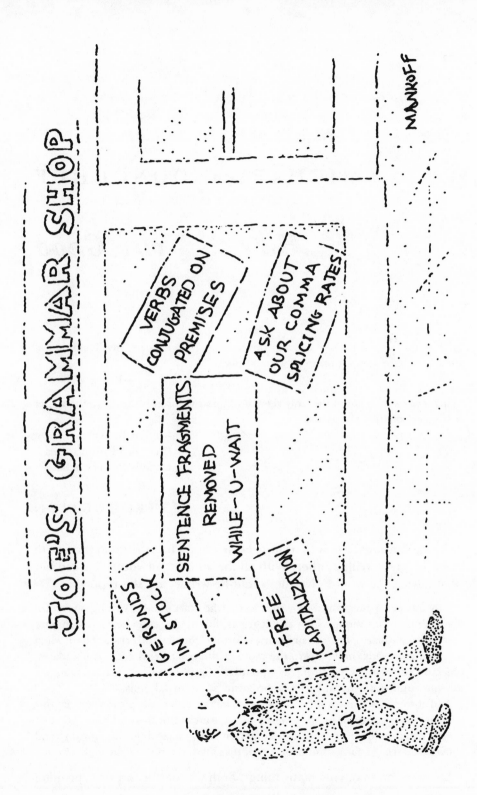

ROBERT MANKOFF

MICHAEL O'DONOGHUE

How to Write Good

"If I could not earn a penny from my writing, I would earn my livelihood at something else and continue to write at night."

—Irving Wallace

"Financial success is not the only reward of good writing. It brings to the writer rich inner satisfactions as well."

—Elliot Foster
Director of Admissions
Famous Writers School

INTRODUCTION

A long time ago, when I was just starting out, I had the good fortune to meet the great Willa Cather. With all the audacity of youth, I asked her what advice she would give the would-be-writer and she replied:

"My advice to the would-be-writer is that he start slowly, writing short undemanding things, things such as telegrams, flip-books, crank letters, signature scarves, spot quizzes, capsule summaries, fortune cookies and errata. Then, when he feels he's ready, move up to the more challenging items such as mandates, objective correlatives, passion plays, pointless diatribes, minor classics, manifestos, mezzotints, oxymora, exposés, broadsides and papal bulls.

And above all, never forget that the pen is mightier than the plow-share. By this I mean that writing, all in all, is a hell of a lot more fun than farming. For one thing, writers seldom, if ever, have to get up at five o'clock in the morning and shovel manure. As far as I'm concerned, that gives them the edge right there."

She went on to tell me many things, both wonderful and wise, probing the secrets of her craft, showing how to weave a net of words and capture the fleeting stuff of life. Unfortunately, I've forgotten every bit of it.

I do recall, however, her answer when I asked "If you could only give me one rule to follow, what would it be?" She paused, looked down for a moment, and finally said, "Never wear brown shoes with a blue suit."

There's very little I could add to that except to say "Go to it and good luck!"

LESSON 1—THE GRABBER

The "grabber" is the initial sentence of a novel or short story designed to jolt the reader out of his complacency and arouse his curiosity, forcing him to press onward. For example:

"It's no good, Alex," she rejoined, "Even if I did love you, my father would never let me marry an alligator."

The reader is immediately bombarded with questions, questions such as: "Why won't her father let her marry an alligator?" "How come she doesn't love him?" and "Can she learn to love him in time?" The reader's interest has been "grabbed"!

Just so there'll be no misunderstanding about grabbers, I've listed a few more below:

"I'm afraid you're too late," sneered Zoltan. "The fireplace has already flown south for the winter!"

Sylvia lay sick among the silverware . . .

"Chinese vegetables mean more to me than you do, my dear," Charles remarked to his wife, adding injury to insult by lodging a grapefruit knife in her neck.

One morning Egor Samba awoke from uneasy dreams to find himself transformed into a gigantic Volkswagen.

"I have in my hands," Professor Willowbee exclaimed, clutching a sheaf of papers in his trembling fingers and pacing in circles about the carpet while I stood at the window, barely able to make out the Capitol dome through the thick, churning fog that rolled in off the Potomac, wondering to myself what matter could possibly be so urgent as to bring the distinguished historian bursting into my State Department office at this unseemly hour, "definitive proof that Abraham Lincoln was a homo!"

These are just a handful of the possible grabbers. Needless to say, there are thousands of others, but if you fail to think of them, feel free to use any or all of these.

LESSON 2—THE ENDING

All too often, the budding author finds that his tale has run its course and yet he sees no way to satisfactorily end it, or, in literary parlance, "wrap it up." Observe how easily I resolve this problem:

Suddenly, everyone was run over by a truck.
>   —the end—

If the story happens to be set in England, use the same ending, slightly modified:

Suddenly, everyone was run over by a lorry.
>   —the end—

If set in France:

Soudainement, tout le monde était écrasé par un camion.
>   —finis—

You'll be surprised at how many different settings and situations this ending applies to. For instance, if you were writing a story about ants, it would end "Suddenly, everyone was run over by a centipide." In fact, this is the only ending you ever need use.*

LESSON 3—CHOOSING A TITLE

A friend of mine recently had a bunch of articles rejected by the *Reader's Digest* and, unable to understand why, he turned to me for advice. I spotted the problem at a glance. His titles were all wrong. By calling his pieces such things as "Unwed Mothers—A Head Start on Life," "Cancer—The Incurable Disease," "A Leading Psychologist Explains Why There Should Be More Violence on Television," "Dognappers I Have Known and Loved," "My Baby Was Born Dead and I Couldn't Care Less" and "Pleasantville—Last of the Wide-Open Towns," he had seriously misjudged his market. To steer him straight, I drew up this list of all-purpose, surefire titles:

> —————————— *at the Crossroads*
> *The Case for* —————————
> *The Role of* —————————
> *Coping with Changing* —————————
> *A Realistic Look at* —————————

* Warning—If you are writing a story about trucks, do *not* have the trucks run over by a truck. Have the trucks run over by a *mammoth* truck.

> The ——————— Experience
> Bridging the ——————— Gap
> A ——————— for All Seasons

Simply fill in the blanks with the topic of your choice and, if that doesn't work, you can always resort to the one title that never fails:

> *South America, the Sleeping Giant on Our Doorstep*

LESSON 4—EXPOSITION

Perhaps the most difficult technique for the fledgling writer to master is the proper treatment of exposition. Yet watch the sly, subtle way I "set the scene" of my smash play, *The Last to Know,* with a minimum of words and effort.

(The curtain opens on a tastefully appointed dining room, the table ringed by men in tuxedos and women in costly gowns. There is a knock at the door.)

LORD OVERBROOKE: Oh, come in, Lydia. Allow me to introduce my dinner guests to you.

This is Cheryl Heatherton, the madcap soybean heiress whose zany antics actually mask a heart broken by her inability to meaningfully communicate with her father, E. J. Heatherton, seated to her left, who is too caught up in the heady world of high finance to sit down and have a quiet chat with his own daughter, unwanted to begin with, disposing of his paternal obligations by giving her everything, everything but love, that is.

Next to them sits Geoffrey Drake, a seemingly successful merchant banker trapped in an unfortunate marriage with a woman half his age, who wistfully looks back upon his days as the raffish Group Captain of an R.A.F. bomber squadron that flew eighty-one missions over Berlin, his tortured psyche refusing to admit, despite frequent nightmares in which, dripping with sweat, he wakes screaming, "Pull it up! Pull it up, I say! I can't hold her any longer! We're losing altitude! We're going down! Jerry at three o'clock! Aaaaaaaaaaaaaaaagggh!", that his cowardice and his cowardice alone was responsible for the loss of his crew and "Digger," the little Manchester terrier who was their mascot.

The empty chair to his right was vacated just five minutes ago by Geoffrey's stunning wife, twenty-three-year-old, golden-tressed Edwina Drake, who, claiming a severe migraine, begged to be excused that she might return home and rest, whereas, in reality, she is, at this moment, speeding to the arms of another man, convinced that if she can steal a little happiness now, it doesn't matter who she hurts later on.

The elderly servant preparing the Caviar *en Socle* is Andrew who's been with my family for over forty years although he hasn't received a salary for the last two, even going so far as to loan me his life's savings to cover my spiraling gambling debts but it's only a matter of time before I am exposed as a penniless fraud and high society turns its back on me.

The dark woman opposite me is Yvonne de Zenobia, the fading Mexican film star, who speaks of her last movie as though it was shot only yesterday, unwilling to face the fact that she hasn't been before the cameras in nearly fifteen years; unwilling to confess that her life has been little more than a tarnished dream.

As for her companion, Desmond Trelawney, he is an unmitigated scoundrel about whom the less said, the better.

And, of course, you know your father, the ruthless war profiteer, and your hopelessly alcoholic mother, who never quite escaped her checkered past, realizing, all too late, that despite her jewels and limousines, she was still just a taxi-dancer who belonged to any man for a drink and a few cigarettes.

Please take a seat. We were just talking about you.

This example demonstrates everything you'll ever need to know about exposition. Study it carefully.

LESSON 5—FINDING THE RAW MATERIAL

As any professional writer will tell you, the richest source of material is one's relatives, one's neighbors and, more often than not, total strangers. A day doesn't go by without at least one person, upon learning that I'm a professional writer, offering me some terrific idea for a story. And I'm sure it will come as no shock when I say that most of the ideas are pretty damn good!

Only last week, a pipe-fitter of my acquaintance came up with a surprise ending guaranteed to unnerve the most jaded reader. What you do is tell this really weird story that keeps on getting weirder and weirder until, just when the reader is muttering, "How in the heck is he going to get himself out of this one? He's really painted himself into a corner!" you spring the "mind-blower": "But then he woke up. It had all been a dream!" (which I, professional writer that I am, honed down to: "But then the alarm clock rang. It had all been a dream!"). And this came from a common, run-of-the-mill pipe-fitter! For free!

Cabdrivers, another great wealth of material, will often remark, "Boy, lemme tell ya! Some of the characters I get in this cab would fill a book! Real kooks, ya know what I mean?" And then, without my having to coax even the slightest, they tell me about them, and they *would* fill a book. Perhaps two or three books. In addition, if you're at all interested in social science, cabdrivers are able to provide countless examples of the failures of the welfare state.

To illustrate just how valid these unsolicited suggestions can be, I shall print a few lines from a newly completed play inspired by my aunt, who had the idea as far back as when she was attending grade school. It's called *If an Old House Could Talk, What Tales It Would Tell:*

The Floor: Do you remember the time the middle-aged lady who always wore the stiletto heels tripped over an extension cord while running to answer the phone and spilled the Ovaltine all over me and they spent the next 20 minutes mopping it up?
THE WALL: No.

Of course, I can't print too much here because I don't want to spoil the ending (although I will give you a hint: it involves a truck . . .), I just wanted to show you how much the world would have missed had I rejected my aunt's suggestion out of hand simply because she is not a professional writer like myself.

LESSON 6—QUOTING OTHER AUTHORS

If placed in a situation where you must quote another author, always write "[sic]" after any word that may be misspelled or looks the least bit questionable in any way. If there are no misspellings or curious words, toss in a few "[sic]"s just to break up the flow. By doing this, you will appear to be knowledgeable and "on your toes," while the one quoted will seem suspect and vaguely discredited. Two examples will suffice:

> "O Sleepless as the river under thee,
> Vaulting the sea, the prairies' dreaming sod,
> Unto us lowiest sometime sweep, descend
> And of the curveship [sic], lend a myth to God."
> —HART CRANE

> "Beauty is but a flowre [sic],
> Which wrinckles [sic] will devoure [sic],
> Brightnesse [sic] falls from the ayre [sic],
> Queenes [sic] have died yong [sic] and faire [sic],
> Dust hath closde [sic] *Helens* [sic] eye [sic].
> I am sick [sic], I must dye [sic]: Lord, have mercy on us."
> —THOMAS NASHE

Note how only one small "[sic]" makes Crane's entire stanza seem trivial and worthless, which, in his case, takes less doing than most. Nashe, on the other hand, has been rendered virtually unreadable. Anyone having to choose between you and Nashe would pick you every time! And, when it's all said and done, isn't that the name of the game?

LESSON 7—MAKING THE READER FEEL INADEQUATE

Without question, the surest way to make a reader feel inadequate is through casual erudition, and there is no better way to achieve casual erudition than by putting the punchline of an anecdote in a little-spoken foreign language. Here's a sample:

One crisp October morning, while taking my usual stroll down the Kurfürstenstrasse, I spied my old friend Casimir Malevitch, the renowned Suprematist painter, sitting on a bench. Noting that he had a banana in his ear, I said to him, "Excuse me, Casimir, but I believe you have a banana in your ear."

"What?" he asked.

Moving closer and speaking quite distinctly, I repeated my previous observation, saying, "I said 'You have a banana in your ear!' "

"What's that you say?" came the reply.

By now I was a trifle piqued at this awkward situation and, seeking to make myself plain, once and for all, I fairly screamed, "I SAID THAT YOU HAVE A BANANA IN YOUR EAR, YOU DOLT!!!"

Imagine my chagrin when Casimir looked at me blankly and quipped,

"১৯০২ বেড়েই চন্দ্রা এবং পররাজ্ঞা প্রোসডেন্ট রুজে ১৯০৭) কিংগ, বাতে।"

Oh, what a laugh we had over that one.

With one stroke, the reader has been made to feel not only that his education was second-rate, but that you are getting far more out of life than he. This is precisely why this device is best used in memoirs, whose sole purpose is to make the reader feel that you have lived life to the fullest, while his existence, in comparison, has been meaningless and shabby. . . .

LESSON 8—COVERING THE NEWS

Have you ever wondered how reporters are able to turn out a dozen or so news articles day after day, year after year, and still keep their copy so fresh, so vital, so alive? It's because they know The Ten Magic Phrases of Journalism, key constructions with which one can express *every known human emotion!* As one might suppose, The Phrases, discovered only after centuries of trial and error, are a closely guarded secret, available to no one but accredited members of the press. However, at the risk of being cashiered from the Newspaper Guild, I am now going to reveal them to you:

The Ten Magic Phrases of Journalism
1. "violence flared"
2. "limped into port"
3. "according to informed sources"
4. "wholesale destruction"
5. "no immediate comment"
6. "student unrest"
7. "riot-torn"
8. "flatly denied"
9. "gutted by fire"
10. "roving bands of Negro youths"

Let's try putting The Phrases to work in a sample news story:

NEWARK, N.J., Aug. 22 (UPI)—*Violence flared* yesterday when *roving bands of Negro youths* broke windows and looted shops in *riot-torn* Newark. Mayor Kenneth Gibson had *no immediate comment* but, *according to informed sources*, he *flatly denied* saying that *student unrest* was behind the *wholesale destruction* that resulted in scores of buildings being *gutted by fire*, and added, "If this city were a Liberian freighter,* we just may have *limped into port.*"

Proof positive that The Ten Magic Phrases of Journalism can express every known human emotion *and then some!*

LESSON 9—TRICKS OF THE TRADE

Just as homemakers have their hints (e.g. a ball of cotton, dipped in vanilla extract and placed in the refrigerator, will absorb food odors), writers have their own bag of tricks, a bag of tricks, I might hasten to point out, you won't learn at any Bread Loaf Conference. Most writers, ivory tower idealists that they are, prefer to play up the mystique of their "art" (visitations from the Muse, *l'ecriture automatique,* talking in tongues, et cetera, et cetera), and sweep the hard-nosed practicalities under the rug. Keeping in mind, however, that a good workman doesn't curse his tools, I am now going to make public these long suppressed tricks of the trade.

Suppose you've written a dreadful chapter (we'll dub it Chapter Six for our purposes here), utterly without merit, tedious and boring beyond belief, and you just can't find the energy to re-write it. Since it's obvious

---

* Whenever needed, "Norwegian tanker" can always be substituted for "Liberian freighter." Consider them interchangeable.

that the reader, once he realizes how dull and shoddy Chapter Six really is, will refuse to read any further, you must provide some strong ulterior motive for completing the chapter. I've always found lust effective:

Artfully concealed within the next chapter is the astounding secret of an ancient Bhutanese love cult that will increase your sexual satisfaction by at least 60% and *possibly more—*
(Print Chapter Six.)

Pretty wild, huh? Bet you can hardly wait to try it! And don't forget to show your appreciation by reading Chapter Seven!*

Fear also works:

Dear Reader,
This message is printed on *Chinese poison paper* which is made from deadly herbs that are instantly absorbed by the fingertips so it won't do any good to wash your hands because you will die a horrible and lingering death in about an hour unless you take the special antidote which is revealed in *Chapter Six* and you'll be saved.
Sincerely,
(Your Name)

Or even:

Dear Reader,
You are obviously one of those rare people who are immune to Chinese poison paper so this message is printed on *Bavarian poison paper* which is about a hundred thousand times more powerful and even if you're wearing gloves you're dead for sure unless you read *Chapter Six* very carefully and find the special antidote.
Sincerely,
(Your Name)

Appealing to vanity, greed, sloth and whatever, you can keep this up, chapter by chapter, until they finish the book. In fact, the number of appeals is limited only by human frailty itself. . . .

LESSON 10—MORE WRITING HINTS

There are many more writing hints I could share with you, but suddenly I am run over by a truck.

—the end—

---

* This insures that the reader reads Chapter Six not once but several times. Possibly, he may even read Chapter Seven.

BERT LESTON TAYLOR

The Bards We Quote

Whene'er I quote I seldom take
From bards whom angel hosts environ;
But usually some damned rake
    Like Byron.

Of Whittier I think a lot,
My fancy to him often turns;
But when I quote 'tis some such sot
    As Burns.

I'm very fond of Bryant, too,
He brings to me the woodland smelly;
Why should I quote that "village roo,"
    P. Shelley?

I think Felicia Hemans great,
I dote upon Jean Ingelow;
Yet quote from such a reprobate
    As Poe.

To quote from drunkard or from rake
Is not a proper thing to do.
I find the habit hard to break,
    Don't you?

MARK TWAIN

Fenimore Cooper's Literary Offences

The Pathfinder and *The Deerslayer* stand at the head of Cooper's novels as artistic creations. There are others of his works which contain parts as perfect as are to be found in these, and scenes even more thrilling. Not one can be compared with either of them as a finished whole.

The defects in both of these tales are comparatively slight. They were pure works of art.—*Prof. Lounsbury.*

The five tales reveal an extraordinary fulness of invention.

. . . One of the very greatest characters in fiction, Natty Bumppo. . . .

The craft of the woodsman, the tricks of the trapper, all the delicate art of the forest, were familiar to Cooper from his youth up.—*Prof. Brander Matthews.*

Cooper is the greatest artist in the domain of romantic fiction yet produced by America.—*Wilkie Collins.*

It seems to me that it was far from right for the Professor of English Literature in Yale, the Professor of English Literature in Columbia, and Wilkie Collins to deliver opinions on Cooper's literature without having read some of it. It would have been much more decorous to keep silent and let persons talk who have read Cooper.

Cooper's art has some defects. In one place in *Deerslayer,* and in the restricted space of two-thirds of a page, Cooper has scored 114 offences against literary art out of a possible 115. It breaks the record.

There are nineteen rules governing literary art in the domain of romantic fiction—some say twenty-two. In *Deerslayer* Cooper violated eighteen of them. These eighteen require:

1. That a tale shall accomplish something and arrive somewhere. But the *Deerslayer* tale accomplishes nothing and arrives in the air.

2. They require that the episodes of a tale shall be necessary parts of

the tale, and shall help to develop it. But as the *Deerslayer* tale is not a tale, and accomplishes nothing and arrives nowhere, the episodes have no rightful place in the work, since there was nothing for them to develop.

3. They require that the personages in a tale shall be alive, except in the case of corpses, and that always the reader shall be able to tell the corpses from the others. But this detail has often been overlooked in the *Deerslayer* tale.

4. They require that the personages in a tale, both dead and alive, shall exhibit a sufficient excuse for being there. But this detail also has been overlooked in the *Deerslayer* tale.

5. They require that when the personages of a tale deal in conversation, the talk shall sound like human talk, and be talk such as human beings would be likely to talk in the given circumstances, and have a discoverable meaning, also a discoverable purpose, and a show of relevancy, and remain in the neighborhood of the subject in hand, and be interesting to the reader, and help out the tale, and stop when the people cannot think of anything more to say. But this requirement has been ignored from the beginning of the *Deerslayer* tale to the end of it.

6. They require that when the author describes the character of a personage in his tale, the conduct and conversation of that personage shall justify said description. But this law gets little or no attention in the *Deerslayer* tale, as Natty Bumppo's case will amply prove.

7. They require that when a personage talks like an illustrated, gilt-edged, tree-calf, hand-tooled, seven-dollar Friendship's Offering in the beginning of a paragraph, he shall not talk like a negro minstrel in the end of it. But this rule is flung down and danced upon in the *Deerslayer* tale.

8. They require that crass stupidities shall not be played upon the reader as "the craft of the woodsman, the delicate art of the forest," by either the author or the people in the tale. But this rule is persistently violated in the *Deerslayer* tale.

9. They require that the personages of a tale shall confine themselves to possibilities and let miracles alone; or, if they venture a miracle, the author must so plausibly set it forth as to make it look possible and reasonable. But these rules are not respected in the *Deerslayer* tale.

10. They require that the author shall make the reader feel a deep interest in the personages of his tale and in their fate; and that he shall make the reader love the good people in the tale and hate the bad ones. But the reader of the *Deerslayer* tale dislikes the good people in it, is indifferent to the others, and wishes they would all get drowned together.

11. They require that the characters in a tale shall be so clearly defined

that the reader can tell beforehand what each will do in a given emergency. But in the *Deerslayer* tale this rule is vacated.

In addition to these large rules there are some little ones. These require that the author shall

12. *Say* what he is proposing to say, not merely come near it.
13. Use the right word, not its second cousin.
14. Eschew surplusage.
15. Not omit necessary details.
16. Avoid slovenliness of form.
17. Use good grammar.
18. Employ a simple and straightforward style.

Even these seven are coldly and persistently violated in the *Deerslayer* tale.

Cooper's gift in the way of invention was not a rich endowment; but such as it was he liked to work it, he was pleased with the effects, and indeed he did some quite sweet things with it. In his little box of stage properties he kept six or eight cunning devices, tricks, artifices for his savages and woodsmen to deceive and circumvent each other with, and he was never so happy as when he was working these innocent things and seeing them go. A favorite one was to make a moccasined person tread in the tracks of the moccasined enemy, and thus hide his own trail. Cooper wore out barrels and barrels of moccasins in working that trick. Another stage-property that he pulled out of his box pretty frequently was his broken twig. He prized his broken twig above all the rest of his effects, and worked it the hardest. It is a restful chapter in any book of his when somebody doesn't step on a dry twig and alarm all the reds and whites for two hundred yards around. Every time a Cooper person is in peril, and absolute silence is worth four dollars a minute, he is sure to step on a dry twig. There may be a hundred handier things to step on, but that wouldn't satisfy Cooper. Cooper requires him to turn out and find a dry twig; and if he can't do it, go and borrow one. In fact, the Leather Stocking Series ought to have been called the Broken Twig Series.

I am sorry there is not room to put in a few dozen instances of the delicate art of the forest, as practised by Natty Bumppo and some of the other Cooperian experts. Perhaps we may venture two or three samples. Cooper was a sailor—a naval officer; yet he gravely tells us how a vessel, driving towards a lee shore in a gale, is steered for a particular spot by her skipper because he knows of an *undertow* there which will hold her back against the gale and save her. For just pure woodcraft, or sailorcraft, or

whatever it is, isn't that neat? For several years Cooper was daily in the
society of artillery, and he ought to have noticed that when a cannon-ball
strikes the ground it either buries itself or skips a hundred feet or so; skips
again a hundred feet or so—and so on, till it finally gets tired and rolls.
Now in one place he loses some "females"—as he always calls women—in
the edge of a wood near a plain at night in a fog, on purpose to give
Bumppo a chance to show off the delicate art of the forest before the
reader. These mislaid people are hunting for a fort. They hear a cannon-
blast, and a cannon-ball presently comes rolling into the wood and stops
at their feet. To the females this suggests nothing. The case is very
different with the admirable Bumppo. I wish I may never know peace
again if he doesn't strike out promptly and *follow the track* of that cannon-
ball across the plain through the dense fog and find the fort. Isn't it a
daisy? If Cooper had any real knowledge of Nature's ways of doing things,
he had a most delicate art in concealing the fact. For instance: one of his
acute Indian experts, Chingachgook (pronounced Chicago, I think), has
lost the trail of a person he is tracking through the forest. Apparently that
trail is hopelessly lost. Neither you nor I could ever have guessed out the
way to find it. It was very different with Chicago. Chicago was not
stumped for long. He turned a running stream out of its course, and
there, in the slush in its old bed, were that person's moccasin-tracks. The
current did not wash them away, as it would have done in all other like
cases—no, even the eternal laws of Nature have to vacate when Cooper
wants to put up a delicate job of woodcraft on the reader.

We must be a little wary when Brander Matthews tells us that Cooper's
books "reveal an extraordinary fulness of invention." As a rule, I am quite
willing to accept Brander Matthews's literary judgments and applaud his
lucid and graceful phrasing of them; but that particular statement needs
to be taken with a few tons of salt. Bless your heart, Cooper hadn't any
more invention than a horse; and I don't mean a high-class horse, either; I
mean a clothes-horse. It would be very difficult to find a really clever
"situation" in Cooper's books, and still more difficult to find one of any
kind which he has failed to render absurd by his handling of it. Look at the
episodes of "the caves"; and at the celebrated scuffle between Maqua and
those others on the table-land a few days later; and at Hurry Harry's
queer water-transit from the castle to the ark; and at Deerslayer's half-
hour with his first corpse; and at the quarrel between Hurry Harry and
Deerslayer later; and at—but choose for yourself; you can't go amiss.

If Cooper had been an observer his inventive faculty would have
worked better; not more interestingly, but more rationally, more plausibly. Cooper's proudest creations in the way of "situations" suffer notice-

ably from the absence of the observer's protecting gift. Cooper's eye was splendidly inaccurate. Cooper seldom saw anything correctly. He saw nearly all things as through a glass eye, darkly. Of course a man who cannot see the commonest little every-day matters accurately is working at a disadvantage when he is constructing a "situation." In the *Deerslayer* tale Cooper has a stream which is fifty feet wide where it flows out of a lake; it presently narrows to twenty as it meanders along for no given reason, and yet when a stream acts like that it ought to be required to explain itself. Fourteen pages later the width of the brook's outlet from the lake has suddenly shrunk thirty feet, and become "the narrowest part of the steam." This shrinkage is not accounted for. The stream has bends in it, a sure indication that it has alluvial banks and cuts them; yet these bends are only thirty and fifty feet long. If Cooper had been a nice and punctilious observer he would have noticed that the bends were oftener nine hundred feet long than short of it.

Cooper made the exit of that stream fifty feet wide, in the first place, for no particular reason; in the second place, he narrowed it to less than twenty to accommodate some Indians. He bends a "sapling" to the form of an arch over this narrow passage, and conceals six Indians in its foliage. They are "laying" for a settler's scow or ark which is coming up the stream on its way to the lake; it is being hauled against the stiff current by a rope whose stationary end is anchored in the lake; its rate of progress cannot be more than a mile an hour. Cooper describes the ark, but pretty obscurely. In the matter of dimensions "it was little more than a modern canal-boat." Let us guess, then, that it was about one hundred and forty feet long. It was of "greater breadth than common." Let us guess, then, that it was about sixteen feet wide. This leviathan had been prowling down bends which were but a third as long as itself, and scraping between banks where it had only two feet of space to spare on each side. We cannot too much admire this miracle. A low-roofed log dwelling occupies "two-thirds of the ark's length"—a dwelling ninety feet long and sixteen feet wide, let us say—a kind of vestibule train. The dwelling has two rooms—each forty-five feet long and sixteen feet wide, let us guess. One of them is the bedroom of the Hutter girls, Judith and Hetty; the other is the parlor in the daytime, at night it is papa's bedchamber. The ark is arriving at the stream's exit now, whose width has been reduced to less than twenty feet to accommodate the Indians—say to eighteen. There is a foot to spare on each side of the boat. Did the Indians notice that there was going to be a tight squeeze there? Did they notice that they could make money by climbing down out of that arched sapling and just stepping aboard when the ark scraped by? No; other Indians would have noticed these things, but Cooper's Indians never notice anything. Cooper thinks they are marvellous creatures for noticing, but he was almost always in error about his Indians. There was seldom a sane one among them.

The ark is one hundred and forty feet long; the dwelling is ninety feet long. The idea of the Indians is to drop softly and secretly from the arched sapling to the dwelling as the ark creeps along under it at the rate of a mile an hour, and butcher the family. It will take the ark a minute and a half to pass under. It will take the ninety foot dwelling a minute to pass under. Now, then, what did the six Indians do? It would take you thirty years to guess, and even then you would have to give it up, I believe. Therefore, I will tell you what the Indians did. Their chief, a person of quite extraordinary intellect for a Cooper Indian, warily watched the canal-boat as it squeezed along under him, and when he had got his calculations fined down to exactly the right shade, as he judged, he let go and dropped. And *missed the house!* That is actually what he did. He missed the house, and landed in the stern of the scow. It was not much of a fall, yet it knocked him silly. He lay there unconscious. If the house had been ninety-seven feet long he would have made the trip. The fault was Cooper's, not his. The error lay in the construction of the house. Cooper was no architect.

There still remained in the roost five Indians. The boat has passed under and is now out of their reach. Let me explain what the five did—you would not be able to reason it out for yourself. No. 1 jumped for the boat, but fell in the water astern of it. Then No. 2 jumped for the boat, but fell in the water still farther astern of it. Then No. 3 jumped for the boat, and fell a good way astern of it. Then No. 4 jumped for the boat, and fell in the water *away* astern. Then even No. 5 made a jump for the boat—for he was a Cooper Indian. In the matter of intellect, the difference between a Cooper Indian and the Indian that stands in front of the cigar-shop is not spacious. The scow episode is really a sublime burst of invention; but it does not thrill, because the inaccuracy of the details throws a sort of air of fictitiousness and general improbability over it. This comes of Cooper's inadequacy as an observer.

The reader will find some examples of Cooper's high talent for inaccurate observation in the account of the shooting-match in *The Pathfinder*.

"A common wrought nail was driven lightly into the target, its head having been first touched with paint."

The color of the paint is not stated—an important omission, but Cooper deals freely in important omissions. No, after all, it was not an important omission; for this nail-head is *a hundred yards* from the marksmen, and could not be seen by them at that distance, no matter what its color might be. How far can the best eyes see a common house-fly? A hundred yards? It is quite impossible. Very well; eyes that cannot see a house-fly that is a hundred yards away cannot see an ordinary nail-head at that distance, for the size of the two objects is the same. It takes a keen eye to see a fly or a nail-head at fifty yards—one hundred and fifty feet. Can the reader do it?

The nail was lightly driven, its head painted, and game called. Then the Cooper miracles began. The bullet of the first marksman chipped an edge of the nail-head; the next man's bullet drove the nail a little way into the target—and removed all the paint. Haven't the miracles gone far enough now? Not to suit Cooper; for the purpose of this whole scheme is to show off his prodigy, Deerslayer-Hawkeye-Long-Rifle-Leather-Stocking-Path-finder-Bumppo before the ladies.

" 'Be all ready to clench it, boys!' cried out Pathfinder, stepping into his friend's tracks the instant they were vacant. 'Never mind a new nail; I can see that, though the paint is gone, and what I can see I can hit at a hundred yards, though it were only a mosquito's eye. Be ready to clench!'

"The rifle cracked, the bullet sped its way, and the head of the nail was buried in the wood, covered by the piece of flattened lead."

There, you see, is a man who could hunt flies with a rifle, and command a ducal salary in a Wild West show to-day if we had him back with us.

The recorded feat is certainly surprising just as it stands; but it is not surprising enough for Cooper. Cooper adds a touch. He has made Path-finder do this miracle with another man's rifle; and not only that, but Pathfinder did not have even the advantage of loading it himself. He had everything against him, and yet he made that impossible shot; and not only made it, but did it with absolute confidence, saying, "Be ready to clench." Now a person like that would have undertaken that same feat with a brickbat, and with Cooper to help he would have achieved it, too.

Pathfinder showed off handsomely that day before the ladies. His very first feat was a thing which no Wild West show can touch. He was standing with the group of marksmen, observing—a hundred yards from the target, mind; one Jasper raised his rifle and drove the centre of the bull's-eye. Then the Quartermaster fired. The target exhibited no result this time. There was a laugh. "It's a dead miss," said Major Lundie. Pathfinder waited an impressive moment or two; then said, in that calm, indifferent, know-it-all way of his, "No, Major, he has covered Jasper's bullet, as will be seen if any one will take the trouble to examine the target."

Wasn't it remarkable! How *could* he see that little pellet fly through the air and enter that distant bullet-hole? Yet that is what he did; for nothing is impossible to a Cooper person. Did any of those people have any deep seated doubts about this thing? No; for that would imply sanity, and these were all Cooper people.

"The respect for Pathfinder's skill and for his *quickness and accuracy of sight*" (the italics are mine) "was so profound and general, that the instant he made this declaration the spectators began to distrust their own opinions, and a dozen rushed to the target in order to ascertain the fact. There, sure enough, it was found that the Quartermaster's bullet had gone through the hole made by Jasper's, and that, too, so accurately as to require a minute examination to be certain of the circumstance, which, however, was soon clearly established by discovering one bullet over the other in the stump against which the target was placed."

They made a "minute" examination; but never mind, how could they know that there were two bullets in that hole without digging the latest one out? for neither probe nor eyesight could prove the presence of any more than one bullet. Did they dig? No; as we shall see. It is the Pathfinder's turn now; he steps out before the ladies, takes aim, and fires.

But, alas! here is a disappointment; an incredible, an unimaginable disappointment—for the target's aspect is unchanged; there is nothing there but that same old bullet-hole!

" 'If one dared to hint at such a thing,' cried Major Duncan, 'I should say that the Pathfinder has also missed the target!' "

As nobody had missed it yet, the "also" was not necessary; but never mind about that, for the Pathfinder is going to speak.

" 'No, no, Major,' said he, confidently, 'that *would* be a risky declaration. I didn't load the piece, and can't say what was in it; but if it was lead, you will find the bullet driving down those of the Quartermaster and Jasper, else is not my name Pathfinder.'

"A shout from the target announced the truth of this assertion."

Is the miracle sufficient as it stands? Not for Cooper. The Pathfinder speaks again, as he "now slowly advances towards the stage occupied by the females":

" 'That's not all, boys, that's not all; if you find the target touched at all, I'll own to a miss. The Quartermaster cut the wood, but you'll find no wood cut by that last messenger.' "

The miracle is at last complete. He knew—doubtless *saw*—at the distance of a hundred yards—that his bullet had passed into the hole *without fraying the edges*. There were now three bullets in that one hole—three bullets embedded processionally in the body of the stump back of the target. Everybody knew this—somehow or other—and yet nobody had dug any of them out to make sure. Cooper is not a close observer, but he is interesting. He is certainly always that, no matter what happens. And he is more interesting when he is not noticing what he is about than when he is. This is a considerable merit.

The conversations in the Cooper books have a curious sound in our modern ears. To believe that such talk really ever came out of people's mouths would be to believe that there was a time when time was of no value to a person who thought he had something to say; when it was the custom to spread a two-minute remark out to ten; when a man's mouth was a rolling-mill, and busied itself all day long in turning four-foot pigs of thought into thirty-foot bars of conversational railroad iron by attenuation; when subjects were seldom faithfully stuck to, but the talk wandered all around and arrived nowhere; when conversations consisted mainly of irrelevances, with here and there a relevancy, a relevancy with an embarrassed look, as not being able to explain how it got there.

Cooper was certainly not a master in the construction of dialogue. Inaccurate observation defeated him here as it defeated him in so many other enterprises of his. He even failed to notice that the man who talks corrupt English six days in the week must and will talk it on the seventh, and can't help himself. In the *Deerslayer* story he lets Deerslayer talk the showiest kind of book talk sometimes, and at other times the basest of base dialects. For instance, when some one asks him if he has a sweetheart, and if so, where she abides, this is his majestic answer:

" 'She's in the forest—hanging from the boughs of the trees, in a soft rain—in the dew on the open grass—the clouds that float about in the blue heavens—the birds that sing in the woods—the sweet springs where I slake my thirst—and in all the other glorious gifts that come from God's Providence!' "

And he preceded that, a little before, with this:

" 'It consarns me as all things that touches a fri'nd consarns a fri'nd.' "

And this is another of his remarks:

" 'If I was Injin born, now, I might tell of this, or carry in the scalp and boast of the expl'ite afore the whole tribe; or if my inimy had only been a bear' "—

and so on.

We cannot imagine such a thing as a veteran Scotch Commander-in-Chief comporting himself in the field like a windy melodramatic actor, but

Cooper could. On one occasion Alice and Cora were being chased by the French through a fog in the neighborhood of their father's fort:

> " *'Point de quartier aux coquins!'* cried an eager pursuer, who seemed to direct the operations of the enemy.
>
> " 'Stand firm and be ready, my gallant 60ths!' suddenly exclaimed a voice above them; 'wait to see the enemy; fire low, and sweep the glacis.'
>
> " 'Father! father!' exclaimed a piercing cry from out the mist; 'it is I! Alice! thy own Elsie! spare, O! save your daughters!'
>
> " 'Hold!' shouted the former speaker, in the awful tones of parental agony, the sound reaching even to the woods, and rolling back in solemn echo. ' 'Tis she! God has restored me my children! Throw open the sally-port; to the field, 60ths, to the field; pull not a trigger, lest ye kill my lambs! Drive off these dogs of France with your steel.' "

Cooper's word-sense was singularly dull. When a person has a poor ear for music he will flat and sharp right along without knowing it. He keeps near the tune, but it is *not* the tune. When a person has a poor ear for words, the result is a literary flatting and sharping; you perceive what he is intending to say, but you also perceive that he doesn't *say* it. This is Cooper. He was not a word-musician. His ear was satisfied with the *approximate* word. I will furnish some circumstantial evidence in support of this charge. My instances are gathered from half a dozen pages of the tale called *Deerslayer*. He uses "verbal," for "oral"; "precision," for "facility"; "phenomena," for "marvels"; "necessary," for "predetermined"; "unsophisticated," for "primitive"; "preparation," for "expectancy"; "rebuked," for "subdued"; "dependant on," for "resulting from"; "fact," for "condition"; "fact," for "conjecture"; "precaution," for "caution"; "explain," for "determine"; "mortified," for "disappointed"; "meretricious," for "factitious"; "materially," for "considerably"; "decreasing," for "deepening"; "increasing," for "disappearing"; "embedded," for "enclosed"; "treacherous," for "hostile"; "stood," for "stooped"; "softened," for "replaced"; "rejoined," for "remarked"; "situation," for "condition"; "different," for "differing"; "insensible," for "unsentient"; "brevity," for "celerity"; "distrusted," for "suspicious"; "mental imbecility," for "imbecility"; "eyes," for "sight"; "counteracting," for "opposing"; "funeral obsequies," for "obsequies."

There have been daring people in the world who claimed that Cooper could write English, but they are all dead now—all dead but Lounsbury. I don't remember that Lounsbury makes the claim in so many words, still he makes it, for he says that *Deerslayer* is a "pure work of art." Pure, in that connection, means faultless—faultless in all details—and language is a detail. If Mr. Lounsbury had only compared Cooper's English with the English which he writes himself—but it is plain that he didn't; and so it is likely that he imagines until this day that Cooper's is as clean and compact as his own. Now I feel sure, deep down in my heart, that Cooper wrote about the poorest English that exists in our language, and that the English of *Deerslayer* is the very worst that even Cooper ever wrote.

I may be mistaken, but it does seem to me that *Deerslayer* is not a work of art in any sense; it does seem to me that it is destitute of every detail that goes to the making of a work of art; in truth, it seems to me that *Deerslayer* is just simply a literary *delirium tremens.*

A work of art? It has no invention; it has no order, system, sequence, or result; it has no lifelikeness, no thrill, no stir, no seeming of reality; its characters are confusedly drawn, and by their acts and words they prove that they are not the sort of people the author claims that they are; its humor is pathetic; its pathos is funny; its conversations are—oh! indescribable; its love-scenes odious; its English a crime against the language.

Counting these out, what is left is Art. I think we must all admit that.

CHARLES SCHULZ

FRANK SULLIVAN

A Garland of Ibids

I have just finished reading a book[1] which struck me as being one of the finest books I have read since I read "The Flowering of New England," by the same author.[2] But there is a fly in the ointment. I have been rendered cockeyed by the footnotes. There seem to be too many of them, even for a book largely about Boston.[3] I do not know why the author had to have so many footnotes. Maybe he had a reason for each one, but I suspect the footnote habit has crept up on him, for I got out his book on Emerson,[4] published in 1932, and he used practically no footnotes in it.

You read along in "New England: Indian Summer," interested to the hilt in what Van Wyck Brooks is telling you about Longfellow,[5] Thoreau,[6]

---

[1] "New England: Indian Summer."

[2] Van Wyck Brooks, author of "New England: Indian Summer," "The Flowering of New England," "The Life of Emerson," "The Ordeal of Mark Twain," and other books.

[3] Sometimes referred to as The Hub. Capital and chief city of Massachusetts. Scene of the Boston Tea Party and the arrest of Henry L. Mencken. Bostonians are traditionally noted for their civic pride, or, as an envious New York critic once termed it, their parochial outlook. It is related that on an occasion when Saltonstall Boylston learned that his friend L. Cabot Lowell was leaving for a trip around the world, he inquired of Lowell, "Which route shall you take, L.C.?" "Oh, I shall go by way of Dedham, of course," replied Mr. Lowell. On another occasion, the old Back Bay aristocrat Ralph Waldo Mulcahy said to Oliver Wendell Rooney, "By the way, Rooney, did your ancestors come over on the Mayflower?" "Oh, no," replied Mr. Rooney. "They arrived on the next boat. They sent the servants over on the Mayflower."

[4] Ralph Waldo Emerson, Sage of Concord and famous transcendentalist philosopher, not to be confused with Ralph McAllister Ingersoll, editor of *P.M.*

[5] Henry Wadsworth Longfellow, Good Gray Poet. Longfellow was no footnote addict. He preferred foot*prints*. Cf. his "Psalm of Life":

> And, departing, leave behind us
> Footprints on the sands of time.

[6] Henry David Thoreau, philosopher who lived at Walden Pond for two years on carrots, twigs, nuts, minnows, creek water, and, as Margaret Fuller suspected (booming it out at

Phillips,[7] James,[8] Alcott,[9] Lowell,[10] Adams,[11] and other great figures of the Periclean Age of The Hub,[12] when suddenly there is a footnote.

The text is in fine, clear type. The footnotes are in small type. So it is quite a chore to keep focussing up and down the page, especially if you have old eyes or a touch of astigmatism.[13] By and by you say to yourself,

---

Brook Farm in that full, rich voice of hers, to the dismay of William Ellery Channing, Henry Wadsworth Longfellow, Edward Everett Hale, John Lothrop Motley, Charles Eliot Norton, and William Lloyd Garrison), sirloin steaks and creamery butter smuggled to him by Emerson. Suffering as he did from a vitamin deficiency, the result of too much moss in his diet, Thoreau became somewhat of a misanthrope and would often creep up behind members of the Saturday Club and shout "Boo!," or, as some authorities maintain, "Pooh!" The matter is not clarified very much, one must admit, by a letter Mrs. Harriet Beecher Stowe wrote to her son, Harriet Beecher Stowe, Jr. (not to be confused with Herbert Bayard Swope), on June 7, 1854, in which she states: "Not much to write home about, as the saying goes. Dave Thoreau here for supper last nite [sic.] He got into an argument with John Greenleaf Whittier, the Good Gray Poet, as to whether snow is really ermine too dear for an earl, and Greenleaf called him a Communist. Dave then crept up behind Greenleaf and shouted either 'Boo!' [sic] or 'Pooh!' [sic], I couldn't make out wich [sic]. All well here except F. Marion Crawford, Sarah Orne Jewett, Charles Dudley Warner, Thomas Wentworth Higginson, and William Dean Howells, who complain of feeling sic [sic]. Your aff. mother, H. B. Stowe, Sr."

[7] Wendell Phillips. He was about the only Bostonian of his time who wore no middle name and he was therefore considered half naked. Even Mark Twain, when he went to visit Howells in Boston, registered as Samuel Langhorne Clemens.

[8] Probably not Jesse James. Probably is either William James, deviser of Pragmatic Sanctions, or his brother Henry, the novelist. It was about this time that Henry James was going through his transition period, and could not make up his mind whether he was in England living in America or in America living in England.

[9] Amos Bronson Alcott, educator and bad provider. The Mr. Micawber of his day. Not to be confused with Novelist Bus Bronson of Yale or Mrs. Chauncey Olcott.

[10] James Russell Lowell, poet, essayist, and kinfolk of late rotund, cigar-smoking Back Bay Poetess Amy Lowell, no rhymester she.

[11] Henry Adams, author of "The Education of Henry Adams," by Henry Adams. Not to be confused with Henry Adams, Samuel Adams, John Adams, John Quincy Adams, Abigail Adams, Charles Edward Adams (not to be confused with Charles Francis Adams, Charles Henry Adams, or Henry Adams), Maude Adams, Franklin Pierce Adams, Samuel Hopkins Adams, Bristow Adams, George Matthew Adams, James Truslow Adams, Adams Express, Adams & Flanagan, Horace Flanagan, or Louis Adamic.

[12] Sometimes referred to as Boston. One is reminded of the famous quatrain:

> Here's to the City of Boston,
> The home of Filene and the Card.,
> Where the Rileys speak only to Cabots
> And the Cabots speak only to God!

[13] In this connection, it is interesting to note that Louisa May Alcott had a touch of astigmatism, if we are to accept the word of Charles Eliot Norton. Edward Everett Hale states in his Letters, Vol. XV, Ch. 8, pp. 297 *et seq.*, that William Cullen Bryant told Oliver Wendell Holmes that on one occasion when the fun was running high at Thomas Wentworth

"I be damn if I look down at any more footnotes!," but you do, because the book is so interesting you don't want to miss even the footnotes.[14]

When you get to the footnote at the bottom of the page, like as not all you find is *ibid. Ibid* is a great favorite of footnote-mad authors.[15] It was a great favorite with Gibbon.[16] How come writers of fiction do not need footnotes? Take Edna Ferber.[17] She doesn't use footnotes. Suppose Edna Herford[18] took to writing her novels in this manner: "Cicely Ticklepaw* sat at her dressing table in a brown study. She had 'a very strange feeling she'd ne'er felt before, a kind of a grind of depression.'† Could it be love?‡ If so, why had she sent him§ away? She sighed, and a soft cry of 'Aye me!'ǀ escaped her. Seizing a nail file desperately, she commenced hacking away at her fingernails, when a voice behind her said, 'O! that I were a glove upon that hand, that I might touch that cheek!'$ Cicely

---

Higginson's home and all barriers were down, Thomas Bailey Aldrich had put the question bluntly to Charles Eliot Norton, saying, "Now listen, has Louisa May Alcott got astigmatism or hasn't she?" Charles Eliot Norton answered, perhaps unwisely, "Yes." Cf. the famous dictum of General William Tecumseh Sherman, sometimes erroneously ascribed to General Ulysses Simpson Grant: "Never bring up a lady's name in the mess."

[14] Ah there, Van Wyck!

[15] So is cf.

[16] Edward Gibbon, English historian, not to be confused with Cedric Gibbons, Hollywood art director. Edward Gibbon was a great hand for footnotes, especially if they gave him a chance to show off his Latin. He would come sniffing up to a nice, spicy morsel of scandal about the Romans and then, just as the reader expected him to dish the dirt, he'd go into his Latin routine, somewhat as follows: "In those days vice reached depths not plumbed since the reign of Caligula and it was an open secret that the notorious Empress Theodoro *in tres partes divisa erat* and that she was also addicted to the *argumentum ad hominem!*" Gibbon, prissy little fat man that he was, did that just to tease readers who had flunked Caesar.

[17] Edna Cabot Ferber, contemporary New England novelist. It is related of Edna Ferber that she once met Oliver Herford in Gramercy Park and recoiled at the sight of an extremely loud necktie he was wearing. "Heavens above, Oliver Herford!" exclaimed Miss Ferber, never one not to speak her mind. "That is a terrible cravat. Why do you wear it?" "Because it is my wife's whim that I wear it," explained Oliver Herford. "Well, land sakes alive, before I'd wear a tie like that just on account of a wife's whim!" jeered Miss Ferber. "You don't know my wife," said Oliver Herford. "She's got a whim of iron." Miss Ferber later made this incident the basis for the dramatic battle between the husband and wife in her novel "The Cravat."

[18] No, no, no, not Edna Herford! Edna *Ferber!* Edna Herford is the fellow who had the wife with the iron whim.

* Blonde, lovely, and twenty-one.

† See "I'm Falling in Love with Someone"—Victor Herbert.

‡ Sure.

§ Cleon Bel Murphy, the man she loves.

ǀ "Romeo and Juliet," Act. II, Scene 2.

$ *Ibid.*

reddened, turned. It was Cleon Bel Murphy! Softly, she told him, 'What man art thou, that, thus bescreen'd in night, so stumblest on my counsel?' ''&

What would Van Wyck Brooks say if Edna Ferber wrote like that?[19] Yes. Exactly. Now, where were we?[20] No, I was not. I know what I was saying. You keep out of this. You're a footnote.[21] Yeah? Well, just for that, no more footnotes. Out you go![22] I am, that's who.[23] See what I mean, Van Wyck? Give a footnote an inch and it'll take a foot.[24] I give up. They got me. And they'll get you too in the end, Van Wyck. You may think you're strong enough to keep 'em under control; you may think you can take a footnote or leave it. All I say is, remember Dr. Jekyll! Lay off 'em, Van. I'm telling you for your own good.

—UNEASY BROOKS FAN[25]

& *Ibid.*
[19] And what would Edna Ferber say if Edna Ferber wrote like that?
[20] You were saying Louisa May Alcott had astigmatism.
[21] Yeah? And how far would you have got in this article without footnotes?
[22] Who's gonna put me out?
[23] Yeah? You and who else?
[24] Yoo-hoo! Footnote!
[25] Frank Saltonstall Sullivan.

ROY BLOUNT, JR.

The List of the Mohicans *

When I sit down and make up a list of the things I will do today, I never do any of them. That is not to say I don't do anything. I may compose an operetta. But I don't do any of the things on the list.

And what am I going to do with an operetta? I don't know any violinists. Violinists may not be the first thing that springs to mind in connection with an operetta, but someone has to think of them at some point. Now that I have an operetta, I've got to sit down and make a list:

1. See about staging of operetta.
    a. Union difficulties?
    b. Real horses?
       (1) Check legality.

Lists generate sublists. And now that I have an item 1.*b*.(1), I have to have a 1.*b*.(2). I learned this in school. I may not need a 1.*b*.(2), but I have to have one. I also have to have an item 2. Now who is in charge, me or the list?

That is the question. When I am making a list, I feel dynamic, goal-oriented, ahead of the game. When the list is finished and I am looking at it, the power has shifted. I have to do what the list says.

But even while making the list, I am subject to certain laws:

1. Plurality.
    a. You can't have a list that says just "1. Be Thyself."
    b. You have to have a list that says
       (1) For instance, "1. Be Thyself"

* a. Chingachgook.
  b. Porthos?
  c. Uncas.

      (2) And something else, like "2. Think About It."

    c. And then you are in trouble.

      (1) Because how can you be *being* something—thyself, a ground squirrel, it doesn't matter what—while you are thinking about being it?

      (2) And how can you not think about it when you see—inevitably, your eyes steal ahead—that the next item is "Think About It"?

  2. Impersonality.

    a. You've got problems if you start using personal pronouns.

    b. Should it be

      (1) "Be Thyself," or

      (2) "Be Myself"?

        (a) If (1), then who is speaking?

        (b) If (2), then here I am, a grown man, saying "Be Myself" to myself. It's embarrassing.

III. Roman numerals.

  A. Come to think of it, it is a good idea to start off with Roman numerals. Otherwise, before you know it you are down to 1.*a.*(1)*(a)*,

    1. Which is scraping bottom,

    2. Whereas I.A.1.*a.* leaves room for two more levels:

      a. I.A.1.*a.*(1).

      b. I.A.1.*a.*(1)*(a)*.

  B. On the other hand, no one has ever been able to follow a list of items headed by Roman numerals.

    1. It goes back to the Ten Commandments.

    2. And as soon as you see *I*, even when it means "roman numeral one," you tend to think about yourself. The "I." And what a strange remove it is, that takes us to this notion of "the 'I.' " It is bad enough when someone named, say, Billy, goes around referring to himself as "Billy." If he should start talking about "the 'Billy' "—well, here we go down the rabbit hole. It's like those insurance companies now that will sell you a policy to cover (supposedly) your legal expenses in the event that you have to sue your insurance company for not paying off. Did you know that after a big high-rise luxury resort casino-hotel burns down and hundreds die, the hotel can insure itself *retroactively?* You or I couldn't, but a big outfit like that can. Somehow the hotel people and the insurance people all make out.

IV. Everything has to be parallel.

"Oh, you're getting way off into outlining," some may say. "Lists, kept in their place, are a servant to man." Uhm-hm. It is always a mistake to condescend to a list. You look at a list and say: "Well, now, this is a handy little prioritizational device. I should be able to knock all these items off bing bing bing." The list goes through a moment of quiet fusion and says: "Okay. Come on." Then try striking anything off it.

You never take the first item first, obviously. That would be like accepting the Russians' first offer in a disarmament talk: "Let me see if I have this straight. We transfer to you all of our military might except the generals and admirals, whom we get to keep, and you commit yourselves to an unspecified period of 'all due restraint.' Okay, what the hell."

But even the second item is not something you want to be drawn into precipitately. You look up and down the list and feel as though you are standing on one side of a stream, trying to decide which rock to put your foot on first. None of them look good.

I. It may very well be that a given item is not *right* for you when you come to it on a list.
II. It may very well be that in a free society, a given item is *by definition* not right for you when you come to it on a list.

Now it is time for lunch. As a rule, I have stopped drinking at lunch. It isn't fashionable to drink at lunch these days. But it used to be. I remember, years ago, when I first got a job in New York City. An old hand took me to lunch at a Chinese restaurant, treated himself to eight martinis, and fell—in stages, as if by peristalsis—all the way down a circular staircase that was ornamented to look like a dragon.

I. Some good nonalcoholic lunch beverages:
    A. Iced tea.
    B. Alka-Seltzer.
    C. Bireley's Chocolate Drink.
        1. If lunch is a peanut-butter log.
        2. And not many places today have peanut-butter logs.
        3. In fact, I don't remember the last time I saw:
            a. A peanut-butter log.
            b. A Bireley's Chocolate Drink.
II. Some bad nonalcoholic lunch beverages:
    A. Virgin margarita.
    B. Herbal old-fashioned.
    C. Bireley's Chocolate Drink.

1. Now that I think about it.
2. When I was a kid it was good, though:
   a. So was Nehi strawberry
   b. And Nugrape.
      (1) I don't think anything has ever struck me as prettier-colored than Nugrape foam back then.
      (2) Of course I was a child, and my tastes were unformed.
      (3) But in college English, when I came upon ". . . the blushful Hippocrene,/With beaded bubbles winking at the brim,/And purple-stainèd mouth," it brought Nugrape back.

Even when I don't drink, however, for a couple of hours after lunch I feel listless. Before long it is nearly time to relax and look back over the events of the day; and there haven't been any yet.

I scan the list for a vulnerable spot. Sure, I could tack on something easy, like "Memorize new apartment number." But when you've seen as many digits come and go as I have, what's so easy about that? Anyway, if I tacked it onto a list, I wouldn't do it.

While I was not doing any of the things on my list for today, I came across, in some of my papers, the following list, "Gifts to Get for People," which dates back to December 1981.

1. *The Book of Lists*—Vaughn
2. *The Book of Lists II*—Beryl
3. *The Book of Sports Lists*—Artie
4. *The Book of Fish Lists*—Carl and Dot
5. *Listlust*—Hope
6. *Lost Lists of the Incas*—Oola
7. *The List Book Booklist*—Franz

I'll tell you something. That list did not give one iota. Hey, Christmas is not a line-item affair. Christmas should be cornucopious. Higgledy-piggledy down in the stocking and under the tree. You wouldn't want to buy your turkey by the inch, would you? You want partridges in pear trees untold.

I remember when a cold-drink machine was a big, rusting, red-metal box with a slide-open door in the top. You'd reach down into that well of melting ice and variously shaped cold bottles randomly heaped, and you'd swush around heavily for a while and come up with a Nugrape. A Grapette. A Sun Drop. An Orange Crush, with its pebbly, thick-walled bottle the color of iodine. A Bireley's Chocolate Drink. Bireley's put out an orange, too. A Nehi black cherry. Or it might be something entirely new, that you'd never encountered before. Back then, TV marketing strategy was less advanced, so if there was a new soft drink out, you might not have seen a representation of it before you actually pulled one up out of the ice and cold rivulets and ice flecks ran down it onto your pulse and forearm.

Today a cold-drink machine is a list of buttons. Push one, and a can comes down a chute.

Remember back even further—frankly, to the womb? How your day developed? It was all very structured, very symmetrical, but none of this by-the-numbers. You'd be reflecting, "Hmmmmn," and "I've got a heart-beat," and "I'm not going to be a fish." But it wasn't:

1. "Hmmmmn."
2. "I've got a heartbeat."
3. "I'm not going to be a fish."

It was dawnings overlapping. You didn't know *what* you were going to be. Even if you had known, it wasn't anything you'd ever seen.

But you could sense the thread. And it wasn't linear. It was more like the thread on a screw, only preindustrial; something that turned to go forward. I'm holding out for a helical list. With a bubbling, grape-colored head.

JEFF MacNELLY

MARGARET FISHBACK

The Purist to Her Love

Whatever its function,
Like's not a conjunction.

And if you continue
Committing that sin, you

Will drive me to Reno's
Consoling casinos.

BUD HANDELSMAN

*"You could care less? Don't you mean you couldn't care less?
That kind of crummy English is why I'm leaving."*

FRANK SULLIVAN

The Cliché Expert Testifies on Literary Criticism

Q—Mr. Arbuthnot, you are an expert in the use of the cliché as applied to literary criticism?

A—I am told that I am, sir.

Q—We shall soon find out. What is this object, marked Exhibit A, which I hold?

A—That is a book.

Q—Good. What kind of book is it?

A—It is a minor American classic. Truly a prose epic.

Q—And what kind of document is it?

A—It is a valuable human document.

Q—Very good, Mr. Arbuthnot. Please continue.

A—It is a book in which the results of painstaking—or scholarly—research are embodied and it should interest all thoughtful readers. This reviewer could not put it down.

Q—Why not?

A—Because of its penetrating insight into the ever-present problem of international relationships. It is a sincere and moving study of an American family against the background of a small college town, and it is also a vivid and full-blooded portrayal of the life of that true child of nature, the Southern Negro.

Q—How is it written?

A—It is written with sympathy, pathos, and kindly humor. It throws a clear light on a little-understood subject and is well worth reading.

Q—How is it illustrated?

A—Profusely. It is original in conception, devoid of sentimentality, highly informative, consistently witty, and rich in color. Place it on your required-reading list.

Q—Why?

A—Because it strikes a new note in fiction. Mystery and suspense crowd its pages. The author has done an encylopedic job of blending fact and fiction, and the result is an authentic drama of social revolution, a definite contribution to proletarian literature, and an important addition to frontier literature.

Q—Told with a wealth of what?

A—Told with a wealth of detail.

Q—And how portrayed?

A—Realistically portrayed, in staccato prose. For sheer brilliance of style there has been nothing like it since "Moby Dick." Rarely does a narrative move at such a fast pace.

Q—What is it a shrewd comment on?

A—The American scene. It marks a red-letter day in American literature. It is capital entertainment.

Q—What pervades it?

A—A faint tinge of irony.

Q—And how is it translated?

A—Ably. It is a penetrating study in abnormal psychology, and unlike most scientific works, it is written in language understandable to the layman. It belongs in the front rank of modern picaresque literature. Ideology.

Q—I beg your pardon?

A—I said ideology. Also catharsis, and nuances of feeling.

Q—What about them?

A—Well, they have to come in somewhere.

Q—I see. Now, to return to the minor American classic, Mr. Arbuthnot. Would you call it a subtle and arresting piece of work?

A—Certainly I would. Why do you suppose I'm an expert in the use of the cliché? I'd also call it an honest attempt to depict, a remarkable first novel, a veritable masterpiece, a genuine contribution to literature, a really fine study in contemporary manners, a thrilling saga of life in frontier days, and the most impressive study of degeneration since Zola. It bids fair to go down as one of the great biographies of all time, including "Moby Dick." In short, it has unusual merit.

Q—How does it augur?

A—It augurs well for the future of the author.

Q—And how does it end?

A—It ends upon a distinct note of despair. It is a work of art.

Q—I'm glad you liked it, Mr. Arbuthnot.

A—Who said I liked it?

Q—Well, didn't you like it?

A—Certainly not.

Q—Why not?

A—Because it is, one fears, mawkishly sentimental and, one regrets, faintly pretentious. It is destructive rather than constructive. Curiously enough, it does not carry conviction. Strangely enough, it lacks depth. Oddly enough, the denouement is weak. It is to be regretted that the title is rather misleading and it need hardly be pointed out that the book as a whole lacks cohesion and sparkle. I am very much afraid, one regrets, that it falls definitely into the hammock school of fiction. And of course, like all first novels, it is autobiographical. Frankly, it doesn't quite come off.

Q—I'm glad you told me. I won't buy it.

A—Ah, but in spite of its faults it contains much of real value, and in the opinion of the present reviewer it would be the long-awaited great American novel except for one serious defect.

Q—What is that?

A—It lacks an index.

Q—Mr. Arbuthnot, it is easy to see that you have earned your spurs in the field of literary criticism. So much for the book. Now, observe this object I hold here in my hand, marked Exhibit B. What is it?

A—That? *That* is an *author.*

Q—Whose are those italics, Mr. Arbuthnot?

A—The italics are mine.

Q—What kind of author is this?

A—A promising young author who will bear watching.

Q—What does he write?

A—Powerful first novels. Or important first novels.

Q—What kind of story-teller is he?

A—He's a born story-teller.

Q—What kind of satirist is he?

A—A satirist of the first order.

Q—Tell us more about this interesting creature.

A—Well, he cannot be lightly dismissed. He is undoubtedly to be reckoned with, one feels, as a definite force in American literature.

Q—Why?

A—Because his work plainly shows the influence of Joyce, Hemingway, Proust, Gertrude Stein, and Virginia Woolf. Here is an authentic talent from which we may expect great things, for he is a writer of no mean ability and he knows whereof he writes.

Q—So what do you do?

A—So I hail him. And I acclaim him. He has a keen ear for the spoken word. He also has a flair. He sets out to tell. He deals with themes, or handles them. He captures moods. His execution is brilliant, his insight is poetic, his restraint is admirable, and he has a sense of values. He writes hard-bitten, full-bodied, fine-grained novels of the soil, with a telling use of the American language. There is something almost uncanny in his ability to look into men's souls. Not since "Moby Dick" has an American author displayed such a knowledge of human nature. And he paints a vivid word picture and works on a vast canvas.

Q—How?

A—With consummate artistry. He writes with commendable frankness.

Q—Using what kind of style?

A—Using a limpid prose style. He has a real freshness of approach that stamps him as an artist in the true sense of the word. He culls his material, and his niche in the hall of literary fame seems secure.

Q—I'm glad you like him, Mr. Arbuthnot.

A—But I don't.

Q—No? Why not?

A—Because his talent is plainly superficial and ephemeral. He has an unfortunate habit of allowing his personality to obtrude. His book is badly documented, and not the least of his many irritating mannerisms is his addiction to inexcusable typographical errors. His book is full of clichés, and he does not make his characters live and feel and breathe. And he writes with one eye on Hollywood.

Q—You mean to tell me that a cad like that has the audacity to call himself an author?

A—Well, now, don't be too hard on him. Although he decidedly does not justify his early promise, it is as yet too early to evaluate his work. Want to know about the plot?

Q—Yes, indeed. What about the plot?

A—The plot is like Mae West.

Q—I give up. Why?

A—Because it is well rounded and fully developed. But unlike Mae West, it is marred by structural weaknesses.

Q—What kind of structural weaknesses?

A—Inherent structural weaknesses. It is motivated, of course. And its threads are cunningly woven into a harmonious texture by the deft hand of a skilled literary craftsman.

Q—Just one thing more, Mr. Arbuthnot. How many kinds of readers are there?

A—Four: casual, average, gentle, and constant.

Q—Mr. Arbuthnot, I think that about finishes. I can't thank you enough for having come here today to help us out.

A—It has been a pleasure—a vivid, fascinating, significant, vigorous, timely, urbane, breath-taking, mature, adequate, nostalgic, unforgettable, gripping, articulate, engrossing, poignant, and adult pleasure to be of service to you, sir.

STEVEN CRIST

Letterati

So you think you're ready to go to the grave a famous guy or gal of letters. Your undiscovered notebooks are neatly arrayed on the bookshelf, those revealing first drafts are handing out of the desk drawers and your sketches for that problem novel will turn up the instant your grabby relatives try to make off with the couch. The hemlock's on the table, the epitaph's in your coat pocket and then it hits you: there's more than arts to arts and letters.

Every aspirant to the Norton anthology must be worried about his correspondence. Remember that note to your older sister, begging for money so you could go to Xochitl and get your head together? You won't find anything like that in *The Correspondence of Matthew Arnold*. A scrutinous study of Edmund Wilson's billets-doux won't turn up a missive a fraction as tedious as that three-pager you knocked out as a freshman to tell your parents how bad the food was in the cafeteria. And what if Leon Edel gets his paws on those job-seeking paeans to the personnel department of Dow Chemical? You're in big trouble, and you won't be able to buy them all back in time to escape the judgment of history.

It's time to realize that great correspondence must be as carefully contrived as a college application, or you'll never find your mailbox deposits gracing anyone's coffee table come Christmas time. It's never too early to start paving the way for the annotators and doctoral students, and you'd be well advised to apply the following wisdom to your letters as regularly as a postage stamp.

Remember whom you're writing for. Your correspondence should be addressed to the ages, not the guy whose name happens to follow "Dear." Your reader is the public of fifty years hence; you can always phone up the addressee to tell him what's *really* on your mind.

Confusion, confusion and then some. Unless you provide a payload of this precious commodity, you'll fail to keep tomorrow's assistant professors swimming in National Endowment for the Humanities grants. You'll never find yourself the eye of *The New York Review of Books'* latest maelstrom unless you can keep 'em guessing. But don't go overboard:

Get the facts straight. Be as ambiguous and misleading as you can, but don't tell two tales. If you write to one friend that you think Henry James was "a master wordsmith" and jot to another that James was "an inept and shoddy prose stylist," the critical bigwigs will chuck your reputation into the crazy-person file. The sole exception to this rule is if you intend to leave this mortal coil by your own hand. Nutty letters by suicides, especially poetesses, sell faster than picture books of cats.

Don't tip your hand. This final golden rule is meant to dissuade the epistolier who might otherwise make it too obvious that he's only interested in the posthumous postman. Unless you convince them that you *always* write this way, you'll be spotted for a phony quicker than your mail-order master's thesis.

Let's turn our attention to the specifics. Starting at the top of your page, there is the matter of the date, and it is here that you will set the theme and tone of whatever is fated to follow.

It used to be fashionable to preface the date with a city, as in "Coventry, May 22," "Trieste, July 3" or "West Miami Beach, October 29," but this ploy has been taken over by branch offices of insurance companies and mail-order cheese-log concerns. It is now considered better form to begin the text of the letter with a wry observation regarding the locale, such as "Dubuque resonates with the magic of Mozart's Vienna," or "There is about Piscataway some ineffable quality that makes me cry."

Equally inappropriate is the once dashing style of "8 August 1909," previously considered a benchmark of sophistication because normal people do not talk that way. Just as anachronistic is the *malle lettres* genre of the 1960s that favored such constructions as "Winter/Daynight/Snow/Death."

Your best bet for credulity nowadays is to write the month first, cross out the date several times to illustrate your resentment of such trivialities and smear the year to keep the annotator on his toes and those obscure quarterlies rolling off the presses. Never write the day of the week unless it's Sunday, which might be symbolic and would fuel many a lively evening of debate over your religious subconscious.

The salutation should never be presented in the form of "Dear So-and-So" and So-and-So's proper name should never be used. You must assign each of your correspondents a "letter name" to show the literary historian what an intensely personal relationship you enjoyed with each addressee. Here are some surefire choices: Baba, Tuck, Sport, Old Man, Buddha.

A wonderful variation on this is the old "dead letter" trick no neophyte should proceed without. Write a letter to the most influential poet or philosopher of the day in which you thank him for his (nonexistent, of course) letter of Sunday last praising your new novel and invite him to tea. Deliberately misaddress the envelope, and when it is returned to you, throw it unopened into the closet. When the annotator discovers it, not only will he win himself a teaching position for life, but also lament that the two greatest minds of the century never met, due to a trivial mistake. He'll find great significance in how you refer to the great man. ("For some fascinating but unfathomable reason, he called Faulkner 'Scruffy.' I shall investigate this in my next monograph.") He'll also have a Freudian field day over why you misaddressed the envelope.

The middle of your letter is like the main course at dinner—all substance and no style. It's up to you what legacy you want to entrust civilization with, but here are some helpful hints to ease the way. Above all, never worry about boring your correspondent with the minutiae of your daily existence. As long as you drop a biggie about Art or Life every few pages, feel free to spend eternity and a day on your collie's case of worms or a play-by-play of several rounds of solitaire. This lends an authentic flavor to your writing and eats up a necessary good deal of space. If the public thinks it's getting to know the inner and unselfconscious you, it will put up with anything.

Always startle the reader with your vacillations between the tedious and the mundane, creating the impression that your extraordinary mind thinks of the most profound things at the commonest moments. You should aim to catch your future reader in danger of using the collected edition of your letters as a sleep mask and jolt him from near-nap with a jarring reflection on the irony of the cosmos. Vary your timing so he doesn't learn to read just the last sentence of every fifth paragraph. These examples should illuminate:

The Wrong Way: "I have been talking of the shrubs in my garden for the last six pages and now I must tell you why it is that I tend to these bushes: like Art, they are part of nature, that vast and unforgiving panorama. Contemplation of my junipers is a window to my own insignificance."

In this instance, the reader could have skimmed those last six pages and smart-aleck critics could accuse you of extraneous buildup to your main point. Since you want every word devoured, you should be headed in this direction:

"I took the watering can back to the faucet. Faucets, like humanity, turn on and off in cold disregard to life. Then I filled up the can. If only Keats had lived to thirty! I proceeded to water the small fruit-bearing trees, bringing life to budding lemons. Art is a strange and terrible thing. It was time for lunch." Bravo!

So much for the middle of the letter. As for the signature, remember the rules for the salutation: devise an intriguing sign-off for each correspondent, using every possible variant of your name. The MLA boys will love it. ("When he wrote to the phone company, he was 'Johnny,' clearly mirroring the sense of childlike wonder he felt in the presence of the technological bureaucracy, a father figure to him. Strangely, he chose the blunt and rakish 'John' in seasonal greetings to his male friends, which supports my much-maligned theory of his need for homosexual bonding, and opted for the castrative 'J.' with the household help.")

If you think you're finished, you've got a first-class ticket on the obscurity express; the final threshold to greatness is the postscript. If a letter were a joke, the P.S. would be the punch line. Here is the perfect spot for a casual mention of the most important item you've got. ("P.S. By the way, Richard Ellman thinks my new novel makes *Ulysses* look like *Babar*.") This is also the time and place for dropping that proverbial bombshell, one that you'll never follow up on and give the annotators tics of frustration for years to come. Here are some tried and true examples:

"P.S. I've discovered a missing link in the Great Chain of Being. Remind me to explain it to you when we have drinks next week."

"P.S. I noticed last evening that the key to *Hamlet* is a palindrome—in code, of course—toward the end of the second act. More on this later."

"P.S. I have decided not to bring to light the story of how the Second World War was actually won. It would upset too many people."

Above all, at some point toward the end of your career, be sure to say that you never thought much of the book that made your reputation, noting that you can't understand why the newspaper boys made such a fuss over an inferior effort. Heap praise on the one that nobody likes, calling it the greatest achievement of your life. This will not only jack up the sales of your dud and provide handsome royalties for your estate, but also beef up the charming notion that writers are just plain folk who can't understand what people like and why.

If they believe that—and they probably will, considering they've read that far in your collected letters—they'll believe anything, and you'll be laughing all the way to the bank and on to Westminster Abbey. Today's laundry list is tomorrow's literature, and the only difference between a lout and laureate is a few letters.

FRANKLIN P. ADAMS

To a Thesaurus

O precious codex, volume, tome,
   Book, writing, compilation, work
Attend the while I pen a pome,
   A jest, a jape, a quip, a quirk.

For I would pen, engross, indite,
   Transcribe, set forth, compose, address,
Record, submit—yea, even write
   An ode, an elegy to bless—

To bless, set store by, celebrate,
   Approve, esteem, endow with soul,
Commend, acclaim, appreciate,
   Immortalize, laud, praise, extol.

Thy merit, goodness, value, worth,
    Expedience, utility—
O manna, honey, salt of earth,
    I sing, I chant, I worship thee!

How could I manage, live, exist,
    Obtain, produce, be real, prevail,
Be present in the flesh, subsist,
    Have place, become, breathe or inhale,

Without thy help, recruit, support,
    Opitulation, furtherance,
Assistance, rescue, aid, resort,
    Favor, sustention, and advance?

Alas! alack! and well-a-day!
    My case would then be dour and sad,
Likewise distressing, dismal, gray,
    Pathetic, mournful, dreary, bad.

* * *

Though I could keep this up all day,
    This lyric, elegiac song,
Meseems hath come the time to say
    Farewell! adieu! good-by! so long!

CHARLES SCHULZ

WOODY ALLEN

The Kugelmass Episode

Kugelmass, a professor of humanities at City College, was unhappily married for the second time. Daphne Kugelmass was an oaf. He also had two dull sons by his first wife, Flo, and was up to his neck in alimony and child support.

"Did I know it would turn out so badly?" Kugelmass whined to his analyst one day. "Daphne had promise. Who suspected she'd let herself go and swell up like a beach ball? Plus she had a few bucks, which is not in itself a healthy reason to marry a person, but it doesn't hurt, with the kind of operating nut I have. You see my point?"

Kugelmass was bald and as hairy as a bear, but he had soul.

"I need to meet a new woman," he went on. "I need to have an affair. I may not look the part, but I'm a man who needs romance. I need softness, I need flirtation. I'm not getting younger, so before it's too late I want to make love in Venice, trade quips at '21,' and exchange coy glances over red wine and candlelight. You see what I'm saying?"

Dr. Mandel shifted in his chair and said, "An affair will solve nothing. You're so unrealistic. Your problems run much deeper."

"And also this affair must be discreet," Kugelmass continued. "I can't afford a second divorce. Daphne would really sock it to me."

"Mr. Kugelmass—"

"But it can't be anyone at City College, because Daphne also works there. Not that anyone on the faculty at C.C.N.Y. is any great shakes, but some of those co-eds . . ."

"Mr. Kugelmass—"

"Help me. I had a dream last night. I was skipping through a meadow holding a picnic basket and the basket was marked 'Options.' And then I saw there was a hole in the basket."

"Mr. Kugelmass, the worst thing you could do is act out. You must simply express your feelings here, and together we'll analyze them. You have been in treatment long enough to know there is no overnight cure. After all, I'm an analyst, not a magician."

"Then perhaps what I need is a magician," Kugelmass said, rising from his chair. And with that he terminated his therapy.

A couple of weeks later, while Kugelmass and Daphne were moping around in their apartment one night like two pieces of old furniture, the phone rang.

"I'll get it," Kugelmass said. "Hello."

"Kugelmass?" a voice said. "Kugelmass, this is Persky."

"Who?"

"Persky. Or should I say The Great Persky?"

"Pardon me?"

"I hear you're looking all over town for a magician to bring a little exotica into your life? Yes or no?"

"Sh-h-h," Kugelmass whispered. "Don't hang up. Where are you calling from, Persky?"

Early the following afternoon, Kugelmass climbed three flights of stairs in a broken-down apartment house in the Bushwick section of Brooklyn. Peering through the darkness of the hall, he found the door he was looking for and pressed the bell. I'm going to regret this, he thought to himself.

Seconds later, he was greeted by a short, thin, waxy-looking man.

"You're Persky the Great?" Kugelmass said.

"The Great Persky. You want a tea?"

"No, I want romance. I want music. I want love and beauty."

"But not tea, eh? Amazing. O.K., sit down."

Persky went to the back room, and Kugelmass heard the sounds of boxes and furniture being moved around. Persky reappeared, pushing before him a large object on squeaky roller-skate wheels. He removed some old silk handkerchiefs that were lying on its top and blew away a bit of dust. It was a cheap-looking Chinese cabinet, badly lacquered.

"Persky," Kugelmass said, "what's your scam?"

"Pay attention," Persky said. "This is some beautiful effect. I developed it for a Knights of Pythias date last year, but the booking fell through. Get into the cabinet."

"Why, so you can stick it full of swords or something?"

"You see any swords?"

Kugelmass made a face and, grunting, climbed into the cabinet. He couldn't help noticing a couple of ugly rhinestones glued onto the raw plywood just in front of his face. "If this is a joke," he said.

"Some joke. Now, here's the point. If I throw any novel into this cabinet with you, shut the doors, and tap it three times, you will find yourself projected into that book."

Kugelmass made a grimace of disbelief.

"It's the emess," Persky said. "My hand to God. Not just a novel, either. A short story, a play, a poem. You can meet any of the women created by the world's best writers. Whoever you dreamed of. You could carry on all you like with a real winner. Then when you've had enough you give a yell, and I'll see you're back here in a split second."

"Persky, are you some kind of outpatient?"

"I'm telling you it's on the level," Persky said.

Kugelmass remained skeptical. "What are you telling me—that this cheesy homemade box can take me on a ride like you're describing?"

"For a double sawbuck."

Kugelmass reached for his wallet. "I'll believe this when I see it," he said.

Persky tucked the bills in his pants pocket and turned toward his bookcase. "So who do you want to meet? Sister Carrie? Hester Prynne? Ophelia? Maybe someone by Saul Bellow? Hey, what about Temple Drake? Although for a man your age she'd be a workout."

"French. I want to have an affair with a French lover."

"Nana?"

"I don't want to have to pay for it."

"What about Natasha in *War and Peace?*"

"I said French. I know! What about Emma Bovary? That sounds to me perfect."

"You got it, Kugelmass. Give me a holler when you've had enough." Persky tossed in a paperback copy of Flaubert's novel.

"You sure this is safe?" Kugelmass asked as Persky began shutting the cabinet doors.

"Safe. Is anything safe in this crazy world?" Persky rapped three times on the cabinet and then flung open the doors.

Kugelmass was gone. At the same moment, he appeared in the bedroom of Charles and Emma Bovary's house at Yonville. Before him was a beautiful woman, standing alone with her back turned to him as she folded some linen. I can't believe this, thought Kugelmass, staring at the doctor's ravishing wife. This is uncanny. I'm here. It's her.

Emma turned in surprise. "Goodness, you startled me," she said. "Who are you?" She spoke in the same fine English translation as the paperback.

It's simply devastating, he thought. Then, realizing that it was he whom she had addressed, he said, "Excuse me. I'm Sidney Kugelmass. I'm from

City College. A professor of humanities. C.C.N.Y.? Uptown. I—oh, boy!"

Emma Bovary smiled flirtatiously and said, "Would you like a drink? A glass of wine, perhaps?"

She is beautiful, Kugelmass thought. What a contrast with the troglodyte who shared his bed! He felt a sudden impulse to take this vision into his arms and tell her she was the kind of woman he had dreamed of all his life.

"Yes, some wine," he said hoarsely. "White. No, red. No, white. Make it white."

"Charles is out for the day," Emma said, her voice full of playful implication.

After the wine, they went for a stroll in the lovely French countryside. "I've always dreamed that some mysterious stranger would appear and rescue me from the monotony of this crass rural existence," Emma said, clasping his hand. They passed a small church. "I love what you have on," she murmured. "I've never seen anything like it around here. It's so . . . so modern."

"It's called a leisure suit," he said romantically. "It was marked down." Suddenly he kissed her. For the next hour they reclined under a tree and whispered together and told each other deeply meaningful things with their eyes. Then Kugelmass sat up. He had just remembered he had to meet Daphne at Bloomingdale's. "I must go," he told her. "But don't worry, I'll be back."

"I hope so," Emma said.

He embraced her passionately, and the two walked back to the house. He held Emma's face cupped in his palms, kissed her again, and yelled, "O.K., Persky! I got to be at Bloomingdale's by three-thirty."

There was an audible pop, and Kugelmass was back in Brooklyn.

"So? Did I lie?" Persky asked triumphantly.

"Look, Persky, I'm right now late to meet the ball and chain at Lexington Avenue, but when can I go again? Tomorrow?"

"My pleasure. Just bring a twenty. And don't mention this to anybody."

"Yeah. I'm going to call Rupert Murdoch."

Kugelmass hailed a cab and sped off to the city. His heart danced on point. I am in love, he thought, I am the possessor of a wonderful secret. What he didn't realize was that at this very moment students in various classrooms across the country were saying to their teachers, "Who is this character on page 100? A bald Jew is kissing Madame Bovary?" A teacher in Sioux Falls, South Dakota, sighed and thought, Jesus, these kids, with their pot and acid. What goes through their minds!

Daphne Kugelmass was in the bathroom-accessories department at Bloomingdale's when Kugelmass arrived breathlessly. "Where've you been?" she snapped. "It's four-thirty."

"I got held up in traffic," Kugelmass said.

Kugelmass visited Persky the next day, and in a few minutes was again passed magically to Yonville. Emma couldn't hide her excitement at seeing him. The two spent hours together, laughing and talking about their different backgrounds. Before Kugelmass left, they made love. "My God, I'm doing it with Madame Bovary!" Kugelmass whispered to himself. "Me, who failed freshman English."

As the months passed, Kugelmass saw Persky many times and developed a close and passionate relationship with Emma Bovary. "Make sure and always get me into the book before page 120," Kugelmass said to the magician one day. "I always have to meet her before she hooks up with this Rodolphe character."

"Why?" Persky asked. "You can't beat his time?"

"Beat his time. He's landed gentry. Those guys have nothing better to do than flirt and ride horses. To me, he's one of those faces you see in the pages of *Women's Wear Daily*. With the Helmut Berger hairdo. But to her he's hot stuff."

"And her husband suspects nothing?"

"He's out of his depth. He's a lacklustre little paramedic who's thrown in his lot with a jitterbug. He's ready to go to sleep by ten, and she's putting on her dancing shoes. Oh, well . . . See you later."

And once again Kugelmass entered the cabinet and passed instantly to the Bovary estate at Yonville. "How you doing, cupcake?" he said to Emma.

"Oh, Kugelmass," Emma sighed. "What I have to put up with. Last night at dinner, Mr. Personality dropped off to sleep in the middle of the dessert course. I'm pouring my heart out about Maxim's and the ballet, and out of the blue I hear snoring."

"It's O.K., darling. I'm here now," Kugelmass said, embracing her. I've earned this, he thought, smelling Emma's French perfume and burying his nose in her hair. I've suffered enough. I've paid enough analysts. I've searched till I'm weary. She's young and nubile, and I'm here a few pages after Leon and just before Rodolphe. By showing up during the correct chapters, I've got the situation knocked.

Emma, to be sure, was just as happy as Kugelmass. She had been starved for excitement, and his tales of Broadway night life, of fast cars and Hollywood and TV stars, enthralled the young French beauty.

"Tell me again about O.J. Simpson," she implored that evening, as she and Kugelmass strolled past Abbé Bournisien's church.

"What can I say? The man is great. He sets all kinds of rushing records. Such moves. They can't touch him."

"And the Academy Awards?" Emma said wistfully. "I'd give anything to win one."

"First you've got to be nominated."

"I know. You explained it. But I'm convinced I can act. Of course, I'd want to take a class or two. With Strasberg maybe. Then, if I had the right agent—"

"We'll see, we'll see. I'll speak to Persky."

That night, safely returned to Persky's flat, Kugelmass brought up the idea of having Emma visit him in the big city.

"Let me think about it," Persky said. "Maybe I could work it. Stranger things have happened." Of course, neither of them could think of one.

"Where the hell do you go all the time?" Daphne Kugelmass barked at her husband as he returned home late that evening. "You got a chippie stashed somewhere?"

"Yeah, sure, I'm just the type," Kugelmass said wearily. "I was with Leonard Popkin. We were discussing Socialist agriculture in Poland. You know Popkin. He's a freak on the subject."

"Well, you've been very odd lately," Daphne said. "Distant. Just don't forget about my father's birthday. On Saturday?"

"Oh, sure, sure," Kugelmass said, heading for the bathroom.

"My whole family will be there. We can see the twins. And Cousin Hamish. You should be more polite to Cousin Hamish—he likes you."

"Right, the twins," Kugelmass said, closing the bathroom door and shutting out the sound of his wife's voice. He leaned against it and took a deep breath. In a few hours, he told himself, he would be back in Yonville again, back with his beloved. And this time, if all went well, he would bring Emma back with him.

At three-fifteen the following afternoon, Persky worked his wizardry again. Kugelmass appeared before Emma, smiling and eager. The two spent a few hours at Yonville with Binet and then remounted the Bovary carriage. Following Persky's instructions, they held each other tightly, closed their eyes, and counted to ten. When they opened them, the carriage was just drawing up at the side door of the Plaza Hotel, where Kugelmass had optimistically reserved a suite earlier in the day.

"I love it! It's everything I dreamed it would be," Emma said as she swirled joyously around the bedroom, surveying the city from their window. "There's F.A.O. Schwarz. And there's Central Park, and the Sherry is which one? Oh, there—I see. It's too divine."

On the bed there were boxes from Halston and Saint Laurent. Emma unwrapped a package and held up a pair of black velvet pants against her perfect body.

"The slacks suit is by Ralph Lauren," Kugelmass said. "You'll look like a million bucks in it. Come on, sugar, give us a kiss."

"I've never been so happy!" Emma squealed as she stood before the mirror. "Let's go out on the town. I want to see *Chorus Line* and the Guggenheim and this Jack Nicholson character you always talk about. Are any of his flicks showing?"

"I cannot get my mind around this," a Stanford professor said. "First a strange character named Kugelmass, and now she's gone from the book. Well, I guess the mark of a classic is that you can reread it a thousand times and always find something new."

The lovers passed a blissful weekend. Kugelmass had told Daphne he would be away at a symposium in Boston and would return Monday. Savoring each moment, he and Emma went to the movies, had dinner in Chinatown, passed two hours at a discothèque, and went to bed with a TV movie. They slept till noon on Sunday, visited SoHo, and ogled celebrities at Elaine's. They had caviar and champagne in their suite on Sunday night and talked until dawn. That morning, in the cab taking them to Persky's apartment, Kugelmass thought, It was hectic, but worth it. I can't bring her here too often, but now and then it will be a charming contrast with Yonville.

At Persky's, Emma climbed into the cabinet, arranged her new boxes of clothes neatly around her, and kissed Kugelmass fondly. "My place next time," she said with a wink. Persky rapped three times on the cabinet. Nothing happened.

"Hmm," Persky said, scratching his head. He rapped again, but still no magic. "Something must be wrong," he mumbled.

"Persky, you're joking!" Kugelmass cried. "How can it not work?"

"Relax, relax. Are you still in the box, Emma?"

"Yes."

Persky rapped again—harder this time.

"I'm still here, Persky."

"I know, darling. Sit tight."

"Persky, we *have* to get her back," Kugelmass whispered. "I'm a married man, and I have a class in three hours. I'm not prepared for anything more than a cautious affair at this point."

"I can't understand it," Persky muttered. "It's such a reliable little trick."

But he could do nothing. "It's going to take a little while," he said to Kugelmass. "I'm going to have to strip it down. I'll call you later."

Kugelmass bundled Emma into a cab and took her back to the Plaza. He barely made it to his class on time. He was on the phone all day, to Persky and to his mistress. The magician told him it might be several days before he got to the bottom of the trouble.

"How was the symposium?" Daphne asked him that night.

"Fine, fine," he said, lighting the filter end of a cigarette.

"What's wrong? You're as tense as a cat."

"Me? Ha, that's a laugh. I'm as calm as a summer night. I'm just going to take a walk." He eased out the door, hailed a cab, and flew to the Plaza.

"This is no good," Emma said. "Charles will miss me."

"Bear with me, sugar," Kugelmass said. He was pale and sweaty. He kissed her again, raced to the elevators, yelled at Persky over a pay phone in the Plaza lobby, and just made it home before midnight.

"According to Popkin, barley prices in Kraków have not been this stable since 1971," he said to Daphne, and smiled wanly as he climbed into bed.

The whole week went by like that.

On Friday night, Kugelmass told Daphne there was another symposium he had to catch, this one in Syracuse. He hurried back to the Plaza, but the second weekend there was nothing like the first. "Get me back into the novel or marry me," Emma told Kugelmass. "Meanwhile, I want to get a job or go to class, because watching TV all day is the pits."

"Fine. We can use the money," Kugelmass said. "You consume twice your weight in room service."

"I met an Off Broadway producer in Central Park yesterday, and he said I might be right for a project he's doing," Emma said.

"Who is this clown?" Kugelmass asked.

"He's not a clown. He's sensitive and kind and cute. His name's Jeff Something-or-Other, and he's up for a Tony."

Later that afternoon, Kugelmass showed up at Persky's drunk.

"Relax," Persky told him. "You'll get a coronary."

"Relax. The man says relax. I've got a fictional character stashed in a hotel room, and I think my wife is having me tailed by a private shamus."

"O.K., O.K. We know there's a problem." Persky crawled under the cabinet and started banging on something with a large wrench.

"I'm like a wild animal," Kugelmass went on. "I'm sneaking around town, and Emma and I have had it up to here with each other. Not to mention a hotel tab that reads like the defense budget."

"So what should I do? This is the world of magic," Persky said. "It's all nuance."

"Nuance, my foot. I'm pouring Dom Pérignon and black eggs into this little mouse, plus her wardrobe, plus she's enrolled at the Neighborhood Playhouse and suddenly needs professional photos. Also, Persky, Professor Fivish Kopkind, who teaches Comp Lit and who has always been jealous of me, has identified me as the sporadically appearing character in the Flaubert book. He's threatened to go to Daphne. I see ruin and alimony jail. For adultery with Madame Bovary, my wife will reduce me to beggary."

"What do you want me to say? I'm working on it night and day. As far as your personal anxiety goes, that I can't help you with. I'm a magician, not an analyst."

By Sunday afternoon, Emma had locked herself in the bathroom and refused to respond to Kugelmass's entreaties. Kugelmass stared out the window at the Wollman Rink and contemplated suicide. Too bad this is a low floor, he thought, or I'd do it right now. Maybe if I ran away to Europe and started life over . . . Maybe I could sell the *International Herald Tribune*, like those young girls used to.

The phone rang. Kugelmass lifted it to his ear mechanically.

"Bring her over," Persky said. "I think I got the bugs out of it."

Kugelmass's heart leaped. "You're serious?" he said. "You got it licked?"

"It was something in the transmission. Go figure."

"Persky, you're a genius. We'll be there in a minute. Less than a minute."

Again the lovers hurried to the magician's apartment, and again Emma Bovary climbed into the cabinet with her boxes. This time there was no kiss. Persky shut the doors, took a deep breath, and tapped the box three times. There was the reassuring popping noise, and when Persky peered inside, the box was empty. Madame Bovary was back in her novel. Kugelmass heaved a great sigh of relief and pumped the magician's hand.

"It's over," he said. "I learned my lesson. I'll never cheat again, I swear it." He pumped Persky's hand again and made a mental note to send him a necktie.

Three weeks later, at the end of a beautiful spring afternoon, Persky answered his doorbell. It was Kugelmass, with a sheepish expression on his face.

"O.K., Kugelmass," the magician said. "Where to this time?"

"It's just this once," Kugelmass said. "The weather is so lovely, and I'm not getting any younger. Listen, you've read *Portnoy's Complaint?* Remember The Monkey?"

"The price is now twenty-five dollars, because the cost of living is up, but I'll start you off with one freebie, due to all the trouble I caused you."

"You're good people," Kugelmass said, combing his few remaining hairs as he climbed into the cabinet again. "This'll work all right?"

"I hope. But I haven't tried it much since all that unpleasantness."

"Sex and romance," Kugelmass said from inside the box. "What we go through for a pretty face."

Persky tossed in a copy of *Portnoy's Complaint* and rapped three times on the box. This time, instead of a popping noise there was a dull explosion, followed by a series of crackling noises and a shower of sparks. Persky leaped back, was seized by a heart attack, and dropped dead. The cabinet burst into flames, and eventually the entire house burned down.

Kugelmass, unaware of this catastrophe, had his own problems. He had not been thrust into *Portnoy's Complaint,* or into any other novel, for that matter. He had been projected into an old textbook, *Remedial Spanish,* and was running for his life over a barren, rocky terrain as the word *tener* ("to have")—a large and hairy irregular verb—raced after him on its spindly legs.

NOEL PERRIN

Answers to Poets' Questions

> Shall I, wasting in despair,
> Die because a woman's fair?

DEAR MR. WITHER:

Your problem's the other way. The great body of modern experience shows that people like you—people suffering from emotional deprivation, and in particular those who are frustrated in a significant interpersonal relationship—tend to compensate by systematic overeating. My suggestion would be that you go on a diet.

> I'm nobody! Who are you?
> Are you nobody, too?

DEAR MISS DICKINSON:

No. Nobody is nobody these days. Take you, for example. As a member of an upper-income, upper-education family, for example, you would be on somewhere between a dozen and three hundred mailing lists, getting chances almost daily to subscribe to *Time*, to buy health insurance, to join the Diners' Club. And don't forget that you were class of '48 at Mount Holyoke; you'd be getting your annual fund appeals, your alumnae bulletin, your writeup in the class's twenty-five-year book. Furthermore, both as treasurer of Amherst College and as a member of Congress, your father would naturally be listed in *Who's Who*, and you would naturally get a line in his entry. That's not being nobody. Try to cultivate a less negative attitude.

And what is so rare as a day in June?

DEAR MR. LOWELL:
A day in September, April, or November. Days in February are rarer.

How to kéep—is there ány any, is there none such, nowhere known some,
    bow or brooch or braid or brace, láce, latch or catch or key to keep
Black beauty, keep it, beauty, beauty, beauty, . . . from vanishing away?
O is there no frowning of these wrinkles, rankèd wrinkles deep,
Dówn? no waving off of these most mournful messengers, still messen-
    gers, sad and stealing messengers of grey?

DEAR FATHER HOPKINS:
These are smaller problems than you seem to think. To begin with, no
woman needs to have grey hair now, any more than she needs to have dry
skin or less than perfectly white teeth. It is true that no bow or brooch or
braid has yet been discovered that will keep back beauty—though braces
can be helpful. But, what with anti-wrinkle cream and plastic surgery,
there is simply no such crisis as you imagine. You should try to relax,
Father. Perhaps you need more recreation.

> Is my team ploughing,
> That I was used to drive
> And hear the harness jingle
> When I was man alive?

DEAR MR. HOUSMAN:
No, it's not. Shropshire farmers are pretty well mechanized these days.
There's hardly a pair of plough horses between Wenlock and Shrewsbury.
Even if your team *were* still ploughing, you couldn't hear the harness
jingle, because a London antique dealer came through just after the war
and bought up all the horse brasses. (He also got a lot of the pewter mugs
you lads used to drink from at Ludlow Fair.) Most of the brasses worn by
your team are now in a collection in Forth Worth, Texas.

> Clara, Clara Vere de Vere,
> If time be heavy on your hands,
> Are there no beggars at your gate,
> Nor any poor about your lands?

DEAR MR. TENNYSON:
Lady Clara has issued the following statement through her grandson,
the present Earl de Vere:

1. There hasn't been a beggar at the gates since 1926. It should be clearly understood that the crowds which gather every morning and on Monday, Wednesday, and Friday afternoons are tourists.

2. Most of the land was sold in 1953, to meet death duties. While it is true that the family retains ownership of the housing estate called de Vere Gardens, this does not involve the presence of the poor. Houses in the development are in the six-to-eight-thousand-pound category.

3. As for time hanging heavy on Lady Clara's hands, she finds herself busier in her later years than at any previous period of her life. She personally conducts all afternoon tours of the castle, and the special Saturday tours in July and August. For the last seven years, she has tended the rose garden by the West Terrace with her own hands. Her principal problem is chronic exhaustion.

> O Time, whence comes the Mother's
> moody look amid her labours,
> As of one who all unwittingly has
> wounded where she loves?

DEAR MR. HARDY:

The trouble is that the Mother is not fulfilling herself as a person, and over the years has begun to project her frustrations onto her children and husband. There's nothing unwitting about it. That woman is riddled with guilt over being a housewife, Mr. Hardy, and until you get her out of the kitchen and into something creative, her family will continue to suffer. At the very least she needs a weekly lunch date with her husband. Don't you keep up with the women's magazines?

> As I ride, as I ride
> To our Chief and his Allied,
> Who dares chide my heart's pride
> As I ride, as I ride?
> Or are witnesses denied—
> Through the desert waste and wide,
> Do I glide unespied
> As I ride, as I ride?

DEAR MR. BROWNING:

The answer to your question is no, you don't glide unespied. To begin with, there are the U-2 planes and various unmanned satellites. You appear in blowups of quite a number of aerial photographs. Furthermore, there is reason to believe that the North African desert is pinpointed with a network of radar stations, at least one of which has you within scanning range much of the time. Finally, don't forget what a picturesque sight you make cantering along on that white horse. If you will look back over your left shoulder, just beyond that first line of dunes, you will see that you are being followed by a French and two American television crews, the total party consisting of three trucks, two jeeps, and a Land-Rover.

> O what can ail thee, knight at arms,
>   Alone and palely loitering?
> The sedge has withered from the lake,
>   And no birds sing!

DEAR DR. KEATS:

It sounds like a clear case of radiation sickness. Fallout hath the poor fellow in thrall, and there's not a thing you can do.

DON MARQUIS

the coming of archy

Dobbs Ferry possesses a rat which slips out of his lair at night and runs a typewriting machine in a garage. Unfortunately, he has always been interrupted by the watchman before he could produce a complete story.

It was at first thought that the power which made the typewriter run was a ghost, instead of a rat. It seems likely to us that it was both a ghost and a rat. Mme. Blavatsky's ego went into a white horse after she passed over, and someone's personality has undoubtedly gone into this rat. It is an era of belief in communications from the spirit land.

And since this matter had been reported in the public prints and seriously received we are no longer afraid of being ridiculed, and we do not mind making a statement of something that happened to our own typewriter only a couple of weeks ago.

We came into our room earlier than usual in the morning, and discovered a gigantic cockroach jumping about upon the keys.

He did not see us, and we watched him. He would climb painfully upon the framework of the machine and cast himself with all his force upon a key, head downward, and his weight and the impact of the blow were just sufficient to operate the machine, one slow letter after another. He could not work the capital letters, and he had a great deal of difficulty operating the mechanism that shifts the paper so that a fresh line may be started. We never saw a cockroach work so hard or perspire so freely in all our lives before. After about an hour of this frightfully difficult literary labor he fell to the floor exhausted, and we saw him creep feebly into a nest of the poems which are always there in profusion.

Congratulating ourself that we had left a sheet of paper in the machine the night before so that all this work had not been in vain, we made an examination, and this is what we found:

```
expression is the need of my soul
i was once a vers libre bard
but i died and my soul went into the body of a cockroach
it has given me a new outlook upon life
i see things from the under side now
thank you for the apple peelings in the wastepaper basket
but your paste is getting so stale i cant eat it
there is a cat here called mehitabel i wish you would have
removed she nearly ate me the other night why dont she
catch rats that is what she is supposed to be for
there is a rat here she should get without delay

most of these rats here are just rats
but this rat is like me he has a human soul in him
he used to be a poet himself
night after night i have written poetry for you
on your typewriter
and this big brute of a rat who used to be a poet
comes out of his hole when it is done
and reads it and sniffs at it
he is jealous of my poetry
he used to make fun of it when we were both human
he was a punk poet himself
and after he has read it he sneers
and then he eats it

i wish you would have mehitabel kill that rat
```

or get a cat that is onto her job
and i will write you a series of poems showing how things look
to a cockroach
that rats name is freddy
the next time freddy dies i hope he wont be a rat
but something smaller i hope i will be a rat
in the next transmigration and freddy a cockroach
i will teach him to sneer at my poetry then

dont you ever eat any sandwiches in your office
i havent had a crumb of bread for i dont know how long
or a piece of ham or anything but apple parings
and paste leave a piece of paper in your machine
every night you can call me archy

mehitabel was once cleopatra

boss i am disappointed in
some of your readers they
are always asking how does
archy work the shift so as to get a
new line or how does archy do
this or do that they
are always interested in technical
details when the main question is
whether the stuff is
literature or not
i wish you would leave
that book of george moores on
the floor

mehitabel the cat and i want to
read it i have discovered that
mehitabel s soul formerly inhabited a
human also at least that
is what mehitabel is claiming these
days it may be she got jealous of
my prestige anyhow she and
i have been talking it over in a

friendly way who were you
mehitabel i asked her i was
cleopatra once she said well i said i
suppose you lived in a palace you bet
she said and what lovely fish dinners
we used to have and licked her chops

mehitabel would sell her soul for
a plate of fish any day i told her i thought
you were going to say you were
the favorite wife of the emperor
valerian he was some cat nip eh
mehitabel but she did not get me
                              archy

the song of mehitabel

this is the song of mehitabel

of mehitabel the alley cat
as i wrote you before boss
mehitabel is a believer
in the pythagorean
theory of the transmigration
of the soul and she claims
that formerly her spirit
was incarnated in the body
of cleopatra
that was a long time ago
and one must not be
surprised if mehitabel
has forgotten some of her
more regal manners

i have had my ups and downs
but wotthehell wotthehell
yesterday sceptres and crowns
fried oysters and velvet gowns
and today i herd with bums
but wotthehell wotthehell

i wake the world from sleep
as i caper and sing and leap
when i sing my wild free tune
wotthehell wotthehell
under the blear eyed moon
i am pelted with cast off shoon
but wotthehell wotthehell

do you think that i would change
my present freedom to range
for a castle or moated grange
wotthehell wotthehell
cage me and i d go frantic
my life is so romantic
capricious and corybantic
and i m toujours gai toujours gai

i know that i am bound
for a journey down the sound
in the midst of a refuse mound
but wotthehell wotthehell
oh i should worry and fret
death and i will coquette
there s a dance in the old dame yet
toujours gai toujours gai

i once was an innocent kit
wotthehell wotthehell
with a ribbon my neck to fit
and bells tied onto it
o wotthehell wotthehell
but a maltese cat came by
with a come hither look in his eye
and a song that soared to the sky
and wotthehell wotthehell
and i followed adown the street
the pad of his rhythmical feet
o permit me again to repeat
wotthehell wotthehell

my youth i shall never forget
but there s nothing i really regret

wotthehell wotthehell
there s a dance in the old dame yet
toujours gai toujours gai

the things that i had not ought to
i do because i ve gotto
wotthehell wotthehell
and i end with my favorite motto
toujours gai toujours gai

boss sometimes i think
that our friend mehitabel
is a trifle too gay

the old trouper

i ran onto mehitabel again
last evening
she is inhabiting
a decayed trunk
which lies in an alley
in greenwich village
in company with the
most villainous tom cat
i have ever seen
but there is nothing
wrong about the association
archy she told me
it is merely a plutonic
attachment
and the thing can be
believed for the tom
looks like one of pluto s demons
it is a theatre trunk
archy mehitabel told me
and tom is an old theatre cat
he has given his life
to the theatre

he claims that richard
mansfield once
kicked him out of the way
and then cried because
he had done it and
petted him
and at another time
he says in a case
of emergency
he played a bloodhound
in a production of
uncle tom s cabin
the stage is not what it
used to be tom says
he puts his front paw
on his breast and says
they don t have it any more
they don t have it here
the old troupers are gone
there s nobody can troupe
any more
they are all amateurs nowadays
they haven t got it
here
there are only
five or six of us oldtime
troupers left
this generation does not know
what stage presence is
personality is what they lack
personality
where would they get
the training my old friends
got in the stock companies
i knew mr booth very well
says tom
and a law should be passed
preventing anybody else
from ever playing
in any play he ever
played in

there was a trouper for you
i used to sit on his knee
and purr when i was
a kitten he used to tell me
how much he valued my opinion
finish is what they lack
finish
and they haven t got it
here
and again he laid his paw
on his breast
i remember mr daly very
well too
i was with mr daly s company
for several years
there was art for you
there was team work
there was direction
they knew the theatre
and they all had it
here
for two years mr daly
would not ring up the curtain
unless i was in the
prompter s box
they are amateurs nowadays
rank amateurs all of them
for two seasons i played
the dog in joseph
jefferson s rip van winkle
it is true i never came
on the stage
but he knew i was just off
and it helped him
i would like to see
one of your modern
theatre cats
act a dog so well
that it would convince
a trouper like jo jefferson
but they haven t got it

nowadays
they haven t got it
here
jo jefferson had it he had it
here
i come of a long line
of theatre cats
my grandfather
was with forrest
he had it he was a real trouper
my grandfather said
he had a voice
that used to shake
the ferryboats
on the north river
once he lost his beard
and my grandfather
dropped from the
fly gallery and landed
under his chin
and played his beard
for the rest of the act
you don t see any theatre
cats that could do that
nowadays
they haven t got it they
haven t got it
here
once i played the owl
in modjeska s production
of macbeth
i sat above the castle gate
in the murder scene
and made my yellow
eyes shine through the dusk
like an owl s eyes
modjeska was a real
trouper she knew how to pick
her support i would like
to see any of these modern
theatre cats play the owl s eyes

to modjeska s lady macbeth
but they haven t got it nowadays
they haven t got it
here

    mehitabel he says
    both our professions
    are being ruined
    by amateurs
          archy

the flattered lightning bug

a lightning bug got
in here the other night a
regular hick from
the real country he was
awful proud of himself you
city insects may think
you are some punkins
but i don t see any
of you flashing in the dark
like we do in
the country all right go
to it says i mehitabel the
cat and that green
spider who lives in your locker
and two or three cockroach
friends of mine and a
friendly rat all gathered
around him and urged him on
and he lightened and
lightened and lightened you
don t see anything like this
in town often he says go to it
we told him it s a
real treat to us and
we nicknamed him broadway
which pleased him

this is the life
he said all i
need is a harbor
under me to be a
statue of liberty and
he got so vain of
himself i had to take
him down a peg you ve
made lightning for two hours
little bug i told him
but i don t hear
any claps of thunder
yet there are some men
like that when he wore
himself out mehitabel
the cat ate him

                    archy

the lesson of the moth

i was talking to a moth
the other evening
he was trying to break into
an electric light bulb
and fry himself on the wires

why do you fellows
pull this stunt i asked him
because it is the conventional
thing for moths or why
if that had been an uncovered
candle instead of an electric
light bulb you would
now be a small unsightly cinder
have you no sense

plenty of it he answered
but at times we get tired

of using it
we get bored with the routine
and crave beauty
and excitement
fire is beautiful
and we know that if we get
too close it will kill us
but what does that matter
it is better to be happy
for a moment
and be burned up with beauty
than to live a long time
and be bored all the while
so we wad all our life up
into one little roll
and then we shoot the roll
that is what life is for
it is better to be a part of beauty
for one instant and then cease to
exist than to exist forever
and never be a part of beauty
our attitude toward life
is come easy go easy
we are like human beings
used to be before they became
too civilized to enjoy themselves

and before i could argue him
out of his philosophy
he went and immolated himself
on a patent cigar lighter
i do not agree with him
myself i would rather have
half the happiness and twice
the longevity

but at the same time i wish
there was something i wanted
as badly as he wanted to fry himself
                              archy

OGDEN NASH

The Firefly

The firefly's flame
Is something for which science has no name.
I can think of nothing eerier
Than flying around with an unidentified glow on a
      person's posteerier.

ANONYMOUS

Great Fleas

Great Fleas have little fleas upon their back to bite 'em,
And little fleas have lesser fleas, and so *ad infinitum.*
The great fleas themselves in turn have greater fleas to go on,
While these again have greater still, and greater still, and so on.

THE FAR SIDE

By GARY LARSON

YOU ARE HERE

Krism — 7-20 © 1986 Universal Press Syndicate

GARY LARSON

ROBERT FROST

A Considerable Speck

(Microscopic)

A speck that would have been beneath my sight
On any but a paper sheet so white
Set off across what I had written there.
And I had idly poised my pen in air
To stop it with a period of ink
When something strange about it made me think.
This was no dust speck by my breathing blown,
But unmistakably a living mite
With inclinations it could call its own.
It paused as with suspicion of my pen,
And then came racing wildly on again
To where my manuscript was not yet dry;
Then paused again and either drank or smelt—
With loathing, for again it turned to fly.
Plainly with an intelligence I dealt.
It seemed too tiny to have room for feet,
Yet must have had a set of them complete
To express how much it didn't want to die.
It ran with terror and with cunning crept.
It faltered: I could see it hesitate;

Then in the middle of the open sheet
Cower down in desperation to accept
Whatever I accorded it of fate.

I have none of the tenderer-than-thou
Collectivistic regimenting love

With which the modern world is being swept.
But this poor microscopic item now!
Since it was nothing I knew evil of
I let it lie there till I hope it slept.

I have a mind myself and recognize
Mind when I meet with it in any guise.
No one can know how glad I am to find
On any sheet the least display of mind.

DON MARQUIS

the honey bee

the honey bee is sad and cross
and wicked as a weasel
and when she perches on you boss
she leaves a little measle

MARK O'DONNELL

Insect Societies

Listen, don't talk to me about bees. Soldier bees, worker bees, none of 'em. I'm on to those bees. They have their own language, for starters. Sure. You think I'm kidding? Bees can talk. They did a study on it. You didn't know that? Scientists can talk to the bees the same way they talk to Flipper. They just put on their headphones and turn on their computer-translators and start chatting up the bees like nobody's business. True. They've been talking to the bees for years. They just don't let that fact get out because there'd be panics.

In fact, it was the bees who invented the A-bomb. Sure. You think a man could've invented the A-bomb? Naah. It takes a bug to come up with something like that.

Oh, they're smart, I give them that much. Very keen, those little feelers are always working. I heard how the scientists study the bee brain and model the computers after it. But you won't read that fact in the evening paper. They couldn't let a fact like that get out. They couldn't. There would be panics.

One thing those bees have come up with is a time-travel bomb. It is the perfect ultimate weapon. In case somebody ever bombs us first, we send the time-travel bomb back in time and it bombs them before they can bomb us, so we never get bombed. Pretty good, huh? We may have to wait a little to find out if it really works.

Anyway, bees are all geniuses. They even have little built-in glasses they wear. But it's just like the UFOs, they do a cover-up job on it. Just like you could get gas for a penny a gallon if they used this pill that was invented. You didn't know that? You didn't know that? Sure. You drop it in water. But the big oil companies do a big cover-up on it. Just like the birth control fog they have that could cover a whole city (or just a neighborhood, if you get my meaning). Then you'd have to go through a lot of paper work before you could have a baby. You'd have to be really serious about it. But the baby-bootie concerns do a big cover-up on it.

You didn't know that? It's just the tip of the corruption iceberg. Everybody's on the take, schoolteachers (from the Russians), the cops (I think the government pays them).

I know what you think. You think you can ask the President for help. Forget that. Don't ask him for help, he doesn't know who you are. Who are you, a schmo, nothing personal. Don't ask him for help. He doesn't even answer his own mail, he has people to do it. People answer his mail, not him. You could be dead and ask him for help and he wouldn't hear you.

Presidents try to kill themselves all the time, you know. There's so much pressure, it's like they're prisoners. True. Every President since the Hoover Administration has been constantly trying to kill himself. But they hush it up. Who needs panics? They have to strap his arms to his side so he won't start doing harm to himself. Don't offer me that job, boy, you can have it! I don't even want it! But they don't show the straps when he's on TV.

Half the time those Presidents are in the hospital, begging to be allowed to die. But they have to go on, they're forced to. You and I—Who are we? John Q. Schmo—we never hear about it. That's not the President you see on TV anyway. He's in the critical ward somewhere. That's his double you see on TV.

Sure. You didn't know that? That's his double. You don't think they would let the President of the United States go out and stand in the open where he could be shot! They have too much money invested in him to do that.

Of course, all those guys have doubles, too, to make their speeches. You didn't know that? You didn't know that? Everybody big gets a double. It's all done with plastic surgery.

Those aren't the movie stars themselves you see up there on the movie screen, either. Naah. That's their doubles. And everything they say is written out for them. They have people to do their conversation. And the weather lady on the phone? That's not her. They use somebody else's voice. Some schmo's. But the movie stars sleep late and who pays the millions of dollars in income taxes for the plastic surgery for their doubles? You and me, the little guy, the schmo on the graveyard shift who has to eat his lunch at three in the morning, the worker, the drone. So don't talk to me about bees.

EARNEST A. HOOTON

Ode to a Dental Hygienist[1]

Hygienist, in your dental chair
I sit without a single care,
Except when tickled by your hair.
I know that when you grab the drills
I need not fear the pain that kills.
You merely make my molars clean
With pumice doped with wintergreen.
So I lean back in calm reflection,
With close-up views of your complexion,
And taste the flavor of your thumbs
While you massage my flabby gums.
To me no woman can be smarter
Than she who scales away my tartar,
And none more fitted for my bride
Than one who knows me from inside.
At least as far as she has gotten
She sees how much of me is rotten.

[1] *Peroration of address to the graduating class of Dental Hygienists, given at the Forsyth Dental Infirmary, Boston, July, 1942.*

S. J. PERELMAN

Nothing But the Tooth

I am thirty-eight years old, have curly brown hair and blue eyes, own a uke and a yellow roadster, and am considered a snappy dresser in my crowd. But the thing I want most in the world for my birthday is a free subscription to *Oral Hygiene,* published by Merwin B. Massol, 1005 Liberty Avenue, Pittsburgh, Pa. In the event you have been repairing your own teeth, *Oral Hygiene* is a respectable smooth-finish technical magazine circulated to your dentist with the compliments of his local supply company. Through its pages runs a recital of the most horrendous and fantastic deviations from the dental norm. It is a confessional in which dentists take down their back hair and stammer out the secrets of their craft. But every time I plunge into its crackling pages at my dentist's, just as I get interested in the story of the Man with the Alveolar Dentures or Thirty Reasons Why People Stay Away from Dentists, the nurse comes out slightly flushed and smoothing her hair to tell me that the doctor is ready. Last Thursday, for example, I was head over heels in the question-and-answer department of *Oral Hygiene.* A frankly puzzled extractionist, who tried to cloak his agitation under the initials "J.S.G.," had put his plight squarely up to the editor: "I have a patient, a woman of 20, who has a full complement of teeth. All of her restorations are gold foils or inlays. She constantly grinds her teeth at night. How can I aid her to stop grinding them? Would it do any good to give her a vellum rubber bite?" But before I could learn whether it was a bite or just a gentle hug the editor recommended, out popped Miss Inchbald with lipstick on her nose, giggling, "The Doctor is free now." "Free," indeed—"running amok" would be a better way to put it.

I had always thought of dentists as of the phlegmatic type—square-jawed sadists in white aprons who found release in trying out new kinds of burs on my shaky little incisors. One look at *Oral Hygiene* fixed that. Of all the inhibited, timorous, uncertain fumble-bunnies who creep the earth,

Mr. Average Dentist is the worst. A filing clerk is a veritable saber-toothed tiger by comparison. Faced with a decision, your dentist's bones turn to water and he becomes all hands and feet. He muddles through his ordinary routine with a certain amount of bravado, plugging a molar here with chewing gum, sinking a shaft in a sound tooth there. In his spare time he putters around his laboratory making tiny cement cupcakes, substituting amber electric bulbs for ordinary bulbs in his waiting room to depress patients, and jotting down nasty little innuendoes about people's gums in his notebook. But let an honest-to-goodness sufferer stagger in with his face out of drawing, and Mr. Average Dentist's nerves go to hell. He runs sobbing to the "Ask *Oral Hygiene*" department and buries his head in the lap of V. C. Smedley, its director. I dip in for a typical sample:

Question—A patient of mine, a girl, 18, returned from school recently with a weird story of lightning having struck an upper right cuspid tooth and checked the enamel on the labial surface nearly two-thirds of the way from the incisal edge toward the neck. The patient was lying on a bed looking out an open window during an electric storm, and this one flash put out the lights of the house, and at the same time, the patient felt a burning sensation (like a burning wire) along the cuspid tooth. She immediately put her tongue on the tooth which felt rough, but as the lights were out she could not see it so she went to bed. (A taste as from a burnt match accompanied the shock.)

Next morning she found the labial of the tooth black. Some of the color came off on her finger. By continually brushing all day with the aid of peroxide, salt, soda and vinegar she removed the remainder of the black after which the tooth was a yellow shade and there was some roughness on the labial surface.

Could the lightning have caused this and do you recommend smoothing the surface with discs?—R. D. L., D.D.S., Oregon.

Well, Doctor, let us take your story step by step. Miss Muffet told you the sensation was like a burning wire, and she tasted something like a burnt match. Did you think, by any chance, of looking into her mouth for either wire or matches? Did you even think of looking into her mouth? I see no mention of the fact in your letter. You state that she walked in and told you the story, that's all. Of course it never occurred to you that she had brought along her mouth for a reason. Then you say, "she removed the remainder of the black after which the tooth was a yellow shade." Would it be asking too much of you to make up your mind? Was it a tooth or a yellow shade? You're quite sure it wasn't a Venetian blind? Or a gaily striped awning? Do you ever take a drink in the daytime, Doctor?

Frankly, men, I have no patience with such idiotic professional behavior. An eighteen-year-old girl walks into a dentist's office exhibiting obvious symptoms of religious hysteria (stigmata, etc.) She babbles vaguely of thunderstorms and is patently a confirmed drunkard. The dentist goes to pieces, forgets to look in her mouth, and scurries off to *Oral Hygiene* asking for permission to smooth her surface with discs. It's a mercy he doesn't take matters into his own hands and try to plow every fourth tooth under. This is the kind of man to whom we entrust our daughters' dentures.

There is practically no problem so simple that it cannot confuse a dentist. For instance, thumb-sucking. "Could you suggest a method to correct thumb and index finger sucking by an infant of one year?" flutters a Minnesota orthodontist, awkwardly digging his toe into the hot sand. Dr. Smedley, whose patience rivals Job's, has an answer for everything: "Enclose the hand by tying shut the end of the sleeve of a sleeping garment, or fasten a section of a pasteboard mailing tube to the sleeping garment in such a position as to prevent the bending of the elbow sufficiently to carry the thumb or index finger to the mouth." Now truly, Dr. Smedley, isn't that going all the way around Robin Hood's barn? Nailing the baby's hand to the high-chair is much more cozy, or, if no nail is available, a smart blow with the hammer on Baby's fingers will slow him down. My grandfather, who was rather active in the nineties (between Columbus and Amsterdam avenues—they finally got him for breaking and entering), always used an effective method to break children of this habit. He used to tie a Mills grenade to the baby's thumb with cobbler's waxed thread, and when the little spanker pulled out the detonating pin with his teeth, Grandpa would stuff his fingers into his ears and run like the wind. Ironically enough, the people with whom Grandpa now boards have the same trouble keeping him from biting his thumbs, but overcome it by making him wear a loose jacket with very long sleeves, which they tie to the bars.

I have always been the mildest of men, but you remember the old saying, "Beware the fury of a patient man." (I remembered it very well and put my finger on it instantly, page 269 of Bartlett's book of quotations.) For years I have let dentists ride roughshod over my teeth; I have been sawed, hacked, chopped, whittled, betwitched, bewildered, tattooed, and signed on again; but this is cuspid's last stand. They'll never get me into that chair again. I'll dispose of my teeth as I see fit, and after they're gone, I'll get along. I started off living on gruel, and, by God, I can always go back to it again.

SAMUEL HOFFENSTEIN

Oral History and Prognostication

One cannot mastic-
Ate with plastic;
Porcelain stains;
Cement pains;
Gold glitters;
Diamond twitters;
Lead sinks;
Iron stinks;
Wood rots;
Coal blots;
Zinc corrodes;
Uranium explodes;
Bridges miss;
Plates hiss;
Copper hums—
Hurrah, gums!

HENRY FLESHMAN, EMILIO FONTENEGRO, AND THE CHOMSKY BROTHERS GROUP
IN ASSOCIATION WITH
MUKTAFILM-INTERNAZIONALE AND S/D/I CINEMATOGRAF
FOR
ITALIO/FRANCO/YAMAGUCHI PRODUCTIONS, LTD.
PRESENT
AN
ASSAT VULGARIAN CO-PRODUCTION
(WITH MÜNCHNER FILMWERKE A.G.)
OF A
JOSEPH BARGEMAN PRODUCTION
OF A
JONATHAN PEAVY FILM

THE ENIGMA REDUNDANCY

TADZIO SMEED   SAMANTHA POPKIN   SIR FENWICK CHOMES
AND LEROY "POPS" MACVOUTIE
IN
THE ENIGMA REDUNDANCY
STARRING
DUNCAN SMARM   OMU NGBWAME
JACK TWELVE
AND
RENAY STILTON
AND INTRODUCING
PACO AS "MR. CHORISH"
CO-STARRING
TAD FREEBOARD AND MARIANNA MOULDING
SPECIAL GUEST APPEARANCE BY
THE DEAD BODIES

SUGGESTED BY THE NOVEL "SCUM OF THE EARTH," BY H.E.W. POOLE
STORY BY BARRY BRACKFORD AND JOE BARGEMAN
SCREENPLAY BY BARRY BRACKFORD AND JOE BARGEMAN AND H.E.W. POOLE
AND ERNST MITTVOCH AND GLORIA SHMWAST AND JERRY BAP

"ENIGMA" THEME BY MANFREDO TINTO · · · MUSIC BY JERRY MONTE
SONG: "SWEET REDUNDANCY" · · · MUSIC BY MANFREDO TINTO AND JERRY MONTE
LYRICS BY NATALIE CHOMSKY AND BERNIE GOLEM
PERFORMED BY
THE DEAD BODIES
(COURTESY OF NAPOLEON RECORDS)

DIRECTOR OF PHOTOGRAPHY — VITELLO TONNATO, I.A.C., A.I.C.
EXECUTIVE PRODUCERS — BARRY BRACKFORD AND MILT CHOMSKY
PRODUCED BY   DIRECTED BY
ASSAT AND CHMUD BARBARIAN   JONATHAN PEAVY

· ·

DOLBY DX ®   Technicolor ®
PANAVISION LENSES ®   NASERROUND
Auro-Jolt   MagnaScope ®
BUZZ-O-FLEX   HOLOGRAF ®

READ THE BALLANTINE NOVELIZATION BY T. SNIT
SOUND TRACK EXCLUSIVELY ON
MISERICORDEON
RECORDS AND TAPES

A UNIFILM International – PARGOON RELEASE
THROUGH
transco-multicom inc.

A WHOLLY OWNED SUBSIDIARY OF
I.G. FARBEN GESELLSCHAFT

MARSHALL BRICKMAN

Marxism

Two words that have become eroded through misuse—*unique* and *genius*—apply perfectly to the Marx Brothers. Groucho, Chico, and Harpo Marx were three of history's funniest comic actors, and the following two scenes with Chico and Groucho are among the highest peaks in their mountain of humor.

In *A Night at the Opera* (1935), Chico pretends to be the agent for "the world's greatest singer," and Groucho is determined to sign that singer up. He whips out a contract so long that it hangs down like a bridal train, and the ensuing dialogue is a lunatic dissection of legal negotiating.

In *The Cocoanuts* (1929), their first movie, Groucho strives to persuade Chico to shill for him at an auction of Florida land. Chico's Italian ears make hash of Groucho's New York pitch, and the result has pitched hysterical audiences out of their seats for more than half a century. **G.S.**

GEORGE S. KAUFMAN AND MORRIE RYSKIND

Groucho and Chico Make a Deal

GROUCHO: Two beers, bartender.

CHICO: I'll take two beers too.

GROUCHO (*Drifting right into that barroom conversation*): Well, things seem to be getting better around the country.

CHICO: I don't know—I'm a stranger here myself.

GROUCHO (*Looking at him curiously*): Stranger? Aren't you an Italian?

From *A Night at the Opera*

CHICO: No, no. I just look that way because my mother and father are Italian.

GROUCHO: I just remembered—I came back here looking for somebody. You don't know who it is, do you?

CHICO: Funny—it just slipped my mind.

GROUCHO (*Snapping his fingers*): I remember now—the greatest tenor in the world, that's what I'm after!

CHICO: That's funny. I am his manager.

GROUCHO: Whose manager?

CHICO: The greatest tenor in the world.

GROUCHO: The fellow that sings at the opera here?

CHICO: Sure!

GROUCHO: What's his name?

CHICO: What do you care? Some Italian name—I can't pronounce it. What you want with him?

GROUCHO: Well, I'd like to offer him a job. Would he be interested?

CHICO: I don't know, but *I'm* interested. That's the main thing. What sort of job?

GROUCHO: With the New York Opera. America is waiting to hear him sing.

CHICO: Well, he can sing loud, but he can't sing that loud.

GROUCHO: Well, I think we can get America to meet him halfway. The main thing is, can he sail tomorrow night?

CHICO: If you pay him enough money, he can sail *last* night. How much you pay him?

GROUCHO (*Aside*): Let's see—a thousand dollars a night. I'm entitled to a little profit. (*To* CHICO) How about ten dollars a night?

(CHICO *laughs scornfully.*)

CHICO: Ten dollars! . . . (*A quick change of mood*) All right. I'll take it.

GROUCHO: That's fine. Of course, I want a ten percent commission for putting the deal over.

CHICO: And I get ten percent as his manager.

GROUCHO: Well, that leaves eight dollars. Say he sings once a week— that's eight dollars a week clear profit for him.

CHICO (*Considering a week*): He sends five dollars home to his mother.

GROUCHO: Well, that still leaves him three dollars.

CHICO: Three dollars. Can he live in New York on that?

GROUCHO: Like a prince—of course, he won't be able to eat, but he can live like a prince. Oh, I forgot to tell you. He'll have to pay income tax on that three dollars.

CHICO: Income tax?

GROUCHO: Yes, there's a federal tax and the state tax and there may be a city tax. And, naturally, a sales tax.

CHICO: How much does that all come to?

GROUCHO: Well, I figure if he doesn't sing too often, he can break even.

CHICO: All right. We'll take it.

GROUCHO: Fine! *(He pulls out two contracts)* Now, just his name there and you sign on the bottom. You don't have to read yours because it's a duplicate.

CHICO: What?

GROUCHO: A duplicate. (CHICO *looks at him*) Don't you know what duplicates are?

CHICO: Oh, sure! Those five kids up in Canada.

GROUCHO: Well, I wouldn't know about that. I haven't been in Canada for years.

CHICO: Wait a minute. Before I sign anything, what does it say?

GROUCHO: Go ahead and read it.

CHICO *(A little reluctantly):* Well—er—you read it. I don't like to read anything unless I know what it says.

GROUCHO *(Catching on):* I see. All right, *I'll* read it to you. Can you hear?

CHICO: I haven't heard anything yet. Did you say anything?

GROUCHO: Well, I haven't said anything worth hearing.

CHICO: I guess that's why I didn't hear anything.

GROUCHO *(Having the last word):* Well, that's why I didn't say anything.

(He scans the contract, holding it near him and then far away. CHICO *watches him suspiciously.)*

CHICO: Wait a minute. Can *you* read?

GROUCHO *(Holding contract farther and farther away):* I can read, but I can't see it. If my arms were a little longer, I could read it. . . . Ah, here we are. Now pay attention to this first clause. *(Reads)* "The party of the first part shall be known in this contract as the party of the first part." How do you like that? Pretty neat, eh?

CHICO: No, that'sa no good.

GROUCHO *(Indignantly):* What's the matter with it?

CHICO *(Conciliatorily):* I don't know—let's hear it again.

GROUCHO: "The party of the first part shall be known in this contract as the party of the first part."

CHICO: It sounds a little better this time.

GROUCHO: Well, it grows on you. Want to hear it once more?

CHICO: Only the first part.

GROUCHO: The *party* of the first part?

CHICO: No. The *first part* of the party of the first part.

GROUCHO: Well, it says, "The first part of the party of the first part shall be known in this contract—" Look! Why should we quarrel about a thing like that? *(He tears off the offending clause)* We'll take it right out.

CHICO *(Tearing the same clause out of his contract):* Sure, it's too long anyhow. Now what have we got left?

GROUCHO: Well, I've got about a foot and a half. . . . Now, then: "The party of the second part shall be known in this contract as the party of the second part."

CHICO: Well, I don't know. I don't like the second party, either.

GROUCHO: You should have come to the first party. We didn't get home till around four in the morning. *(Slight pause)* I was blind for three days.

CHICO: Look, couldn't the first part of the second party be the second part of the first party? Then we got something.

GROUCHO: Look! Rather than go through all that again, what do you say? *(He indicates a willingness to tear further.)*

CHICO: Fine. *(They both tear off another piece.)*

GROUCHO: Now, I've got something here you're *bound* to like. You'll be crazy about it.

CHICO: No, I don't like it.

GROUCHO: You don't like what?

CHICO: Whatever it is.

GROUCHO: All right. Why should we break up an old friendship over a thing like this? Ready?

CHICO: Okay. *(They both tear)* Now, the next part I don't think you're going to like.

GROUCHO: All right—your word's good enough for me. *(They both tear)* Now then, is my word good enough for *you?*

CHICO: I should say not.

GROUCHO: All right—let's go. *(They both tear.* GROUCHO, *looking at the contract)* The party of the eighth part—

CHICO: No. *(They tear)*

GROUCHO: The party of the ninth part—

CHICO: No. *(They tear)* Say, how is it I got a skinnier contract than you?

GROUCHO: I don't know. You must have been out on a tear last night. Anyhow, now we're all set. Now sign right here. *(He produces a fountain pen)*

CHICO: I forgot to tell you. I can't write.

GROUCHO: That's all right. There's no ink in the pen, anyway. But listen, it's a bargain, isn't it? We've got a contract, no matter how small it is.

CHICO *(Extending hand.* GROUCHO *clasps it):* You betcha! Only one thing I want to know: what does this say? *(Showing last piece of contract left)*

GROUCHO: Oh, that's nothing. That's the usual clause in every contract. It says if any of the parties participating in the contract are shown not to be in their right mind, the contract is nullified.

CHICO: What do you call it?

GROUCHO: That's what they call a sanity clause.

CHICO: You can't fool me. There ain't no sanity clause!

THE MARX BROTHERS

Why a Duck?

HAMMER (GROUCHO): Come over here, I want to see you. Now, listen to me. I'm not going to have that red-headed fellow running around the lobby. If you want to keep him up in the room, you'll have to keep him in a trap.

CHICO: You can't catch him.

HAMMER: Who is he? [HARPO]

CHICO: He's my partner, but he no speak.

HAMMER: Oh, that's your silent partner. Well, anyhow you wired me about some property. I've thought it over. Now, I can let you have three lots watering the front, or I can let you have three lots fronting the water. Now, these lots cost me nine thousand dollars and I'm going to let you have them for fifteen because I like you.

CHICO: I no buy nothing. I gotta no money.

HAMMER: You got no money?

CHICO: I no gotta one cent.

HAMMER: How're you going to pay for your room?

CHICO: Thatsa your lookout.

HAMMER: Oh, you're just an idle rumor?

CHICO: Well, you see, we comma here to maka money. I reada in de paper, and it say: "Big boom in Florida." So we come. We're coupla big booms, too!

From *The Cocoanuts*

HAMMER: Well, I'll show you how you can make some REAL money. I'm going to hold an auction in a little while in Cocoanut Manor. You—you know what an auction is, eh?

CHICO: I come from Italy on the Atlantic-Auction.

HAMMER: Well, let's go ahead as if nothing happened. I say I'm holding an auction at Cocoanut Manor. And when the crowd gathers around, I want you to mingle with them. Don't pick their pockets, just mingle with them—and—.

CHICO: I'll find time for both.

HAMMER: Well, maybe we can cut out the auction. Here's what I mean. If somebody says a hundred dollars, you say two—if somebody says two hundred dollars, you say three—

CHICO: Speaka up?

HAMMER: That's right. Now, if nobody says anything, then you start it off.

CHICO: How'm I going to know when to no say nuthin'?

HAMMER: Well, they'll probably notify you. You fool, if they don't say anything, you'll hear 'em, won't you?

CHICO: Well, mebbe I no lissen.

HAMMER: Well, don't tell 'em. Now then, if we're successful in disposing of these lots, I'll see that you get a nice commission.

CHICO: How about some money?

HAMMER: Well, you can have your choice.

HAMMER: Now, in arranging these lots, of course, we use blue prints. You know what a blue print is, huh?

CHICO: OYSTERS!

HAMMER: How is that you never got double pneumonia?

CHICO: I go around by myself.

HAMMER: Do you know what a lot is?

CHICO: Yeah, too much.

HAMMER: I don't mean a whole lot. Just a little lot with nothing on it.

CHICO: Any time you gotta too much, you gotta whole lot. Look, I'll explain it to you. Some time you no gotta much; sometimes you gotta whole lot. You know that it's a lot. Somebody else maybe thinka it's too much; it's a whole lot, too. Now, a whole lot is too much; too much is a whole lot; same thing.

HAMMER: Come here, Rand McNally, and I'll explain this thing to you. Now look, this is a map and diagram of the whole Cocoanut section. This whole area is within a radius of approximately three-quarters of a mile. Radius? Is there a remote possibility that you know what a radius means?

CHICO: It'sa WJZ.

HAMMER: Well—I walked right into that one. It's going to be a cinch explaining the rest of this thing to you—I can see that.

CHICO: I catcha on quick.

HAMMER: That's a rodeo you're thinking of. Look, Einstein. Here's Cocoanut Manor. No matter what you say, this is Cocoanut Manor. Here's Cocoanut Manor. Here's Cocoanut Heights. That's a swamp—right over where the—where the road forks, that's Cocoanut Junction.

CHICO: Where have you got Cocoanut Custard?

HAMMER: Why, that's on one of the forks. You probably eat with your knife, so you wouldn't have to worry about that.

HAMMER: Now, here's the main road, leading out of Cocoanut Manor. That's the road I wish you were on. Now over here—on this site we're going to build an Eye and Ear Hospital. This is going to be a site for sore eyes. You understand? That's fine. Now, right here is the residential section.

CHICO: People live there, eh?

HAMMER: No, that's the stockyard. Now all along here—this is the river front—all along the river, all along the river—those are all levees.

CHICO: Thatsa the Jewish neighborhood.

HAMMER: Well, we'll passover that.

HAMMER: You're a peach, boy! Now, here is a little peninsula, and here is a viaduct leading over to the mainland.

CHICO: Why a duck?

HAMMER: I'm all right. How are you? I say here is a little peninsula, and here's a viaduct leading over to the mainland.

CHICO: All right. Why a duck?

HAMMER: I'm not playing Ask-Me-Another. I say, that's a viaduct.

CHICO: All right. Why a duck? Why a— why a duck? Why-a-no-chicken?

HAMMER: I don't know why-a-no-chicken. I'm a stranger here myself. All I know is that it's a viaduct. You try to cross over there on a chicken, and you'll find out why a duck. It's deep water, that's viaduct.

CHICO: That's-why-a-duck?

HAMMER: Look . . . Suppose you were out horseback riding and you came to that stream and wanted to ford over there, you couldn't make it. Too deep.

CHICO: But what do you want with a Ford when you gotta horse?

HAMMER: Well, I'm sorry the matter ever came up. All I know is that it's a viaduct.

CHICO: Now look . . . all righta . . . I catcha on to why-a-horse, why-a-chicken, why-a-this, why-a-that. I no catch on to why-a-duck.

HAMMER: I was only fooling. I was only fooling. They're going to build a tunnel in the morning. Now, is that clear to you?

CHICO: Yes. Everything—excepta why-a-duck.

HAMMER: Well, that's fine. Now I can go ahead. Now, look, I'm going to take you down and show you our cemetery. I've got a waiting list of fifty people at that cemetery just dying to get in. But I like you—

CHICO: —Ah—you're-a-my friend.

HAMMER: I like you and I'm going—

CHICO: —I know you like-a . . .

HAMMER: To shove you in ahead of all of them. I'm going to see that you get a steady position.

CHICO: That's good.

HAMMER: And if I can arrange it, it will be horizontal.

CHICO: Yeah, I see—

HAMMER: Now remember, when the auction starts, if anybody says one hundred dollars—

CHICO: I-a say-a two hundred—

HAMMER: That's grand. Now, if somebody says two hundred—

CHICO: —I-a say three hundred!

HAMMER: That's great!

HAMMER: Yes. Now, you know how to get down there?

CHICO: No, I no understand.

HAMMER: Now, look. Listen. You go down there, down to that narrow path there, until you come to the—to that little jungle there. You see it? Where those thatched palms were?

CHICO: Yes, I see.

HAMMER: And then, there's a little clearing there, a little clearing with a wire fence around it. You see that wire fence there?

CHICO: All right. Why-a-fence?

HAMMER: Oh no, we're not going to go all through that again! You come along with me, and I'll fix you up!

FRANK SULLIVAN

The Cliché Expert Testifies on the Movies

Q—Mr. Arbuthnot, you attend the movies?

A—Yes, Mr. Boskert, I am an inveterate moviegoer.

Q—Why?

A—Because the movies bring romance into starved lives such as mine. The shimmering, glamorous creatures of the silver screen provide me with an escape from the drab realities of the workaday world.

Q—Do you think you could qualify as an expert in the clichés of moviedom?

A—I'm pretty sure I could.

Q—I'll ask you a test question to find out. In what pictures does this line occur: "Why, Daddy, you're crying"?

A—In all Shirley Temple pictures.

Q—You'll do, Mr. Arbuthnot. We'll proceed with the examination. When Robert Montgomery gets the girl out on the terrace, where they stand under the moon listening to the distant strains of the orchestra, what does he say to her?

A—He says, "Has anyone ever told you that you are the most beautiful girl in the world?"

Q—And how is Robert dressed?

A—White tie.

Q—Doesn't she know that he is Guy Thremple, Jr., son of old Guy ("Labor Be Damned") Thremple, the ruthless steel magnate who years ago stole her father's patent and reduced him to penury?

A—She doesn't find that out until the third reel, after she has fallen for Robert.

Q—Mr. Arbuthnot, when Fredric March, the handsome young surveyor, falls into the toils of Garbo, the beautiful spy, and she learns (but only because it suits Fredric's purpose to *let* her learn it) that he is not a surveyor at all, but the mysterious "X-27," ace operative of the American Secret Service, who is hot on the trail of the stolen plans of the Kentucky gold vaults (which at that very moment are sewed in the lining of Garbo's peignoir), and she reports this to her chief, the mysterious "ME-7-1212" (Lionel Atwill), what does "ME-7" say?

A—He has a choice of two remarks. He can say, "He must not suspect that we know." Or he can say, "He must not know that we suspect."

Q—Very good. Now then, who said, "Nothing matters but our love"?

A—Well, let's see. Joan Crawford, Greta Garbo, Sylvia Sidney, Katharine Hepburn, Ann Harding, Carole Lombard, Alice Faye, Janet Gaynor, Marion Davies, Kay Francis, Marlene Dietrich, Rochelle Hudson, Gloria Stuart, Loretta Young, Merle Oberon, Dolores Del Rio, Fay Wray, Madeleine Carroll, Elissa Landi, Margaret Sullavan, Rosalind Russell, Olivia De Havilland—Mr. Boskert, it might save time if I just recited the names of the girls who have *not* said it.

Q—All right. Name them.

A—To date, Jane Withers, Patsy Kelly, Edna May Oliver, Shirley Temple, Farina, and Minnie Mouse.

Q—Who said, "Won't you please try to—Understand?"

A—Those same girls that said, "Nothing matters but our love."

Q—What is it the girls say along about the third reel when it looks as though Robert Taylor had been playing fast and loose with their affections—although of course he hasn't, as appears later?

A—They say, "I-hate-you-I-hate-you-I-hate-you!"

Q—Why do they say that?

A—Because they love him.

Q—Then what?

A—Oh, in the last reel they find that the girl they were jealous of is only his stepmother, who is two years younger than he is.

Q—What do the girls say then?

A—They say, "Can you ever—Forgive me?" And Robert replies, "Forgive? Darling, what is there to Forgive?" Then he takes them in his arms.

Q—Who do most of the suffering on the silver screen?

A—Kay Francis and Ann Harding.

Q—Why?

A—Because they're so god-damn noble.

Q—Describe the situation which wrings from the heroine the following diatribe: "Money, money, money! That's all you think of is money!"

A—That's the picture where Cary Grant, the ambitious young businessman, becomes so engrossed in his career that he forgets those little attentions which mean so much to a wife (Sylvia Sidney). In other words, he degenerates from a lover into a husband.

Q—What does Sylvia do?

A—She takes up with the dashing foreign count. After all, it is the right of every woman to be—Loved. And all that she asks of life is one little golden hour of Happiness.

Q—Can't get that at home with Cary, eh?

A—No. Because he has Killed Something in her—Something that was Tender and Fine.

Q—Who is this foreign count she steps out with?

A—Francis Lederer, of course.

Q—Does she go back to Cary?

A—Oh, yes.

Q—When?

A—In the last reel, when he comes to her, a sadder but a wiser man, and says, "I see it all now. Oh, what a fool I have been. Success, money, fame —what are they—without you?" Then they start life anew.

Q—Very good. Now, Mr. Arbuthnot, in conclusion, I want to put to you a rather lengthy hypothetical question. I want you to assume that you are Georgette Le Gume, a ravishingly beautiful demimondaine. More than one poor devil has sought to forget you in the black waters of the Seine. One day, at the Arc de Triomphe, you meet a handsome, manly, American art student, Joel McCrea by name. Or possibly Henry Fonda. He falls desperately in love with you. You scoff. But you are touched, for his love is something Fine and Clean and True, the like of which you have never received from the roués and dukes who make up your circle of acquaintances. Suddenly you find yourself helplessly, hopelessly, in love for the first time in your life. But you realize that it—Cannot Be.

A—Why can't it be?

Q—O-o-h—because.

A—I see.

Q—You realize that you must send him away. It is best that you—Forget Each Other. Now, how would you go about sending your lover away in the Hollywood manner?

A—Well, I'm sitting on a divan like this, see? I tell him it cannot be, that we must forget each other. "Why?" he asks. "Because, Derek, I have not the Right—to Love You," I reply. "Why not?" he asks. "Because, Derek, I am not a—Good Woman," I say. "You mean . . . ?" he says. I lower my head. As the truth dawns upon him, he sinks into a chair, his head in his hands. Ah, I have hurt him cruelly, yes, cruelly; but is there not a dagger in my own heart, too?

MR. BOSKERT (*quite affected*)—Yes. Yes. There is. Plunged there by your own hand.

A—But I must be brave. Is it not so?

Q—Ah yes, Georgette, be brave. Oh, Mr. Arbuthnot, this is *very* good.

A—For I am being cruel only in order to be kind, am I not?

Q—Ah, my poor one, you are. What a trick Fate has played upon you twain! You twain could have made Such Sweet Music Together as you went down Life's Pathway, hand in hand. But it is better that you part.

A—Why?

Q—Because.

A—Exactly. And though I love Derek more than life itself, he must never know.

Q—He must never know what?

A—I don't know. I know only that I am prepared to sacrifice myself on the altar of my love. After all, what is love but sacrifice? And what is sacrifice but love? Love *is* sacrifice. And sacrifice is love.

Q—How true! Noble female. And to think that they call *you* the wickedest woman in Paris.

A—Ah, *mon ami*, when a woman loves, she is never wicked.

Q—*What!*

A—Don't get excited; it's just an epigram. *Alors*, I sit there on the divan, gazing at his dear, bowed head. I, Georgette Le Gume, for whom men have died. Now it is I who suffer. I extend a hand tenderly, haltingly, toward his dear, bowed head.

MR. BOSKERT (*in alarm*)—Oh, Georgette, don't touch his dear, bowed head. Be brave.

A—Never fear, *mon vieux*. It is Georgette Le Gume's one chance to do something Fine, something Noble. Do you think she will flunk it?

Q—No, no. Don't flunk it, Georgette.

A—I shall not. I withdraw the hand.

Q—*Brava! Brava!*

A—Derek rises. Scorn blazes from his honest, hurt eyes. He says, "And to think that I—Trusted You." But I am brave. I do not let him see. I pretend. I laugh. I say, "Ah, Derek, love knows no trust." He says, "Love. *You* talk of *love!*" His scorn sears my very soul. I wince. He stumbles from the room. The door slams. He is gone. "Derek!" I cry. "Derek!" I sink to the divan and sit there—staring—*staring*—STARING. . . . That's all. Isn't that a honey of a renunciation scene? Whew, I'm all of a lather; this acting certainly takes it out of a person. . . . You liked? . . . Why, Daddy—I mean, why, Mr. Boskert, you're—Crying!

ROARK BRADFORD

Green Pastures

After ole King Solomon died de kings got to comin' and goin' so fast dat hit made de Lawd dizzy tryin' to keep up wid who was de king and who wa'n't de king. So he say, "Dis ain't gittin' nowheres. Ef my people can't keep a king long enough for me to get acquainted wid him, well, I'm gonter see what gonter happen."

So hit was a king over in de next town name Nebuchadnezzar which yared de news, so he say, "Well, when de Lawd was sidin' wid de Hebrew boys they was doin' some mighty struttin'. But now wid de Lawd layin' back and watchin', I'll jest drap over and raise me some sand." And so he did.

So ole King Nebuchadnezzar lined up his army and lit out.

"Halt, who comin' yar?" say de Hebrew sentry.

"Sad news is comin' yar," say King Nebuchadnezzar.

"Ain't yo' name King Nebuchadnezzar?" say de sentry.

"Dat's what dey calls me," he say. "What's yo' name?"

"Daniel," say de sentry.

"Well, Daniel," say Nebuchadnezzar, "I'm bringin' you some sad news. I'm bringin' you de news which say I'm gonter raise me some sand in dis town."

"You better let dis town alone," say Daniel. "When you raise a ruckus in dis town you's raisin' a ruckus in de Lawd's town."

"I kotched de Lawd away f'm home, dis time," say Nebuchadnezzar.

"You didn't kotch me away f'm home," say Daniel.

"Naw," say Nebuchadnezzar, "and I'm gonter use you. I'm gonter feed my pet lines on you."

So de soldiers captured Daniel and de army marched into town and raised a ruckus. They got drunk and they shot up de place. Den when de sheriff tried to arrest 'em, dey locked de sheriff up in his own jail and den burned de jail down wid him in hit. So they busted out de window lights and they tore down de gyarden fences. So they driv off de men and women and scared all de chillun.

"King Nebuchadnezzar," say Queen Nebuchadnezzar when he got back home, "did you spile dat town?"

"Did I spile hit?" say de king. "Queen Nebuchadnezzar, I didn't spile hit, I jest natchally ruint hit."

"Well, did you bring me somethin' back?" say de queen.

"I brang back some solid-gold drinkin' cups, and I brang back a few Hebrew boys to feed my lines on," King Nebuchadnezzar say.

"You's always bringin' back somethin' to drink out of, and somethin' to feed yo' lines on," say de queen, "but you ain't brang back nothin' to build me no fire wid. And yar poor me, settin' round de house queenin' all day long and 'bout to freeze to death."

"Well, queen," say de king, "I'm good-hearted. You kin have a few of my Hebrew boys to pitch on de fire."

So dey brought out a few of de Hebrew boys and pitch 'em on de fire. But when dey got to doin' de Hebrew boys like dat, de Lawd tuck a hand. "Jest go on and git pitched in de fire," say de Lawd, " 'cause I ain't gonter let you git burnt." So when dey put de Hebrews in de fire hit jest sputtered a couple er times and went out.

"No wonder they won't burn," say King Nebuchadnezzar; "you ain't got no kindlin' in yar." So dey brang a armful of pine knots and toch off. And de pine knots burned and blazed, and de Hebrew chillun jest sot round on de coals. "Bring my overcoat, King Nebuchadnezzar," say one of de Hebrew boys. "Hit's a draft in yar and I'm cold, and I don't want to git tuck down wid de phthisic."

"Well, dat whups me," say King Nebuchadnezzar. "I b'lieve I'll go on out and feed my lines. Bring dat boy Daniel out yar so I kin feed him to my lines."

So dey brang Daniel out, but Daniel wa'n't skeered. He been tawkin' wid de Lawd 'bout dem lines.

"Dem lines ain't hongry," say Daniel.

"Well, you kin stay among 'em to dey gits hongry," say de king.

"Well," say Daniel, "I wish you'd fix me up a bed and bring me some vittles, 'cause I'm gonter git mighty tired sleepin' on de ground wid nothin' but a line for my pillow till dem scound'els gits hongry enough to eat me."

"Dat's jest you and de lines about dat," say Nebuchadnezzar. "I'm goin' and put on my robes and wash my face and hands and git ready for de big doin's tonight."

So dat night ole King Nebuchadnezzar had a mighty feast. All de big folks and de quality folks in de town came, and hit kept de handmaidens busy dancin' and singin' and makin' music, and hit kept de handmen busy rollin' out de licker and knockin' out de bungs.

"When I invites y'all to come to a mighty feast," say Nebuchadnezzar, "do y'all have a mighty feast or don't you?"

"Yo' Majesty," say all de people, "we does."

"Well, den, is ev'ybody happy?" say Nebuchadnezzar.

"Don't we look happy?" say de people.

"Well, jest make yo' own fun," say Nebuchadnezzar. So some er de menfolks got to drinkin' de licker outer de bungholes, and some er de women got to passin' out and fallin' to sleep under de tables, and ev'ybody got to carryin' on scandalous.

"Whar all dem solid-gold cups which I tuck f'm de Hebrew boys?" say ole King Nebuchadnezzar.

"Put away," say de haid waiter.

"Well, bring 'em out so My Majesty kin drink some licker outer dem solid-gold drinkin'-cups," say ole King Nebuchadnezzar. And right dar was whar he made a big mistake, 'cause dem cups wa'n't de Hebrew boys' cups. Dem was de Lawd's cups. So 'bout de time ole King Nebuchadnezzar drunk out of a solid-gold cup, de Lawd stepped right through de wall and wrote somethin' on hit, and den stepped right back again.

"I seen a ha'nt," say King Nebuchadnezzar.

"Hit's de licker," say de gal which is settin' in his lap. "Hit'll make you see mighty nigh anything."

"Naw, hit ain't de licker," say Nebuchadnezzar. "Licker makes me see snakes. You can't fool me 'bout licker. I know when I sees snakes. I tell you I seen a ha'nt."

"Well," say de gal, "le's call him over and give him a drink."

"Ain't no time to git funny wid me now, gal," say Nebuchadnezzar. "I sees some writin' on de wall. Dat's what I sees."

"What do hit say?" say de gal.

"I didn't brought my glasses," say Nebuchadnezzar.

"I'm too drunk to read hit, too," say de gal. "Whyn't you call dat boy Daniel which is sleepin' wid de lines? He ain't drunk."

So dey sont for Daniel out in de lines' den.

"Read hit to me, Daniel," say Nebuchadnezzar, "and I'll give you de best job in my kingdom."

So Daniel look at de writin' and den he look at de king. "Ole King Nebuchadnezzar," he say, "you can't give me no job in yo' kingdom 'cause f'm what I reads yonder on de wall, you ain't got no kingdom no more."

"Is dat a fack?" say Nebuchadnezzar. "What do hit say?"

"It's de Lawd's own handwritin'," say Daniel.

"Lawd writin' me a letter, is he?" say Nebuchadnezzar. "What he writin' to me, Daniel?"

" 'Dear King Nebuchadnezzar,' hit say," say Daniel, " 'Heavy, heavy hangs over yo' haid. Yours truly, Lawd.' "

"Sounds like he's writin' me a riddle instid of a letter," say de king.

"Well, riddle or letter," say Daniel, "dat's what hit say. And hit means dat de Lawd is done got tired er yo' foolishness and is done quit playin' wid you. Hit means dat befo' sunup you ain't gonter be no king no more. Dat is what hit means."

"So de Lawd don't like my style er bein' king?" say Nebuchadnezzar. "Well, I be doggone!"

"De Lawd don't like yo' style and he ain't gonter try to change hit," say Daniel.

"What he gonter do?" say Nebuchadnezzar.

"He gonter change kings," say Daniel.

"Well," say Nebuchadnezzar, "bein' king ain't much fun, anyway. Y'all boys and gals go right on wid de party as long as de licker holds out. I b'lieve I'm gonter go out and eat me a little grass."

MARC CONNELLY

A Fish Fry *

In the darkness many voices are heard singing "Rise, Shine, Give God The Glory."
They sing it gayly and rapidly. The lights go up as the second verse ends. The chorus is
being sung diminuendo by a mixed company of angels. That is they are angels in that
they wear brightly colored robes and have wings protruding from their backs. Other-

---

* This is Part I, Scene 2, of The Green Pastures. *In an author's note Marc Connelly says:* "The Green Pastures *is an attempt to present certain aspects of a living religion in the terms of its believers. The religion is that of thousands of Negroes in the deep South. With terrific spiritual hunger and the greatest humility these untutored black Christians—many of whom cannot even read the book which is the treasure house of their faith—have adapted the contents of the Bible to the consistencies of their everyday lives. . . . The author is indebted to Mr. Roark Bradford, whose retelling of several of the Old Testament stories in* Ol' Man Adam an' His Chillun *first stimulated his interest in this point of view."*

*wise they look and act like a company of happy Negroes at a fish fry. The scene itself is
a pre-Creation Heaven with compromises. In the distance is an unbroken stretch of
blue sky. Companionable varicolored clouds billow down to the floor of the stage and
roll overhead to the branches of a live oak tree which is up left. The tree is leafy and
dripping with Spanish moss, and with the clouds makes a frame for the scene. In the
cool shade of the tree are the usual appurtenances of a fish fry; a large kettle of hot fat
set on two small parallel logs, with a fire going underneath, and a large rustic table
formed by driving four stakes into the ground and placing planks on top of the small
connecting boards. On the table are piles of biscuits and corn bread and the cooked fish
in dish pans. There are one or two fairly large cedar or crock "churns" containing
boiled custard, which looks like milk. There is a gourd dipper beside the churns and
several glasses and cups of various sizes and shapes from which the custard is drunk.*

*The principal singers are marching two by two in a small area at the right of the
stage. Two* MAMMY ANGELS *are attending to the frying beside the kettle. Behind the
table a* MAN ANGEL *is skinning fish and passing them to the cooks. Another is ladling
out the custard. A* MAMMY ANGEL *is putting fish on bread for a brood of cherubs,
and during the first scene they seat themselves on a grassy bank upstage. Another*
MAMMY ANGEL *is clapping her hands disapprovingly and beckoning a laughing*
BOY CHERUB *down from a cloud a little out of her reach. Another* MAMMY ANGEL
*is solicitously slapping the back of a girl cherub who has a large fish sandwich in her
hand and a bone in her throat. There is much movement about the table, and during
the first few minutes several individuals go up to the table to help themselves to the
food and drink. Many of the women angels wear hats and a few of the men are
smoking cigars. A large boxful is on the table. There is much laughter and chatter as
the music softens, but continues, during the early part of the action. The following
short scenes are played almost simultaneously.*

FIRST COOK *(At kettle; calling off):* Hurry up, Cajey. Dis yere fat's cryin' fo'
mo' feesh.

A VOICE *(Off stage):* We comin', fas' we kin. Dey got to be ketched, ain't
dey? We cain't say, "C'm'on little fish. C'm'on an' git fried," kin we?

SECOND COOK *(At table):* De trouble is de mens is all worm fishin'.

FIRST MAN ANGEL *(At table):* Whut dif'runce do it make? Yo' all de time
got to make out like somebody's doin' somethin' de wrong way.

SECOND COOK *(Near table):* I s'pose you got de perfec' way fo' makin' bait.

FIRST MAN ANGEL: I ain't sayin' dat. I is sayin' what's wrong wid worm
fishin'.

SECOND COOK: Whut's wrong wid worm fishin'? Ever'thing, dat's all.
Dey's only one good way fo' catfishin', an' dats minny fishin'. Anybody
know dat.

FIRST MAN ANGEL: Well, it jest so happen dat minny fishin' is de dog-
gondest fool way of fishin' dey is. You kin try minny fishin' to de cows

come home an' all you catch'll be de backache. De trouble wid you, sister, is you jest got minny fishin' on de brain.

SECOND COOK: Go right on, loud mouf. You tell me de news. My, my! You jest de wisest person in de worl'. First you, den de Lawd God.

FIRST MAN ANGEL *(To the custard ladler):* You cain't tell dem nothin'. *(Walks away to the custard churn.)* Does you try to 'splain some simple fac' dey git man-deaf.

FIRST MAMMY ANGEL *(To* CHERUB *on the cloud):* Now, you heerd me. *(The* CHERUB *assumes several mocking poses, as she speaks.)* You fly down yere. You wanter be put down in de sin book? *(She goes to the table, gets a drink for herself and points out the* CHERUB *to one of the men behind the table.)* Dat baby must got imp blood in him he so vexin'. *(She returns to her position under the cloud.)* You want me to fly up dere an' slap you down? Now, I tol' you. *(The* CHERUB *starts to come down.)*

STOUT ANGEL *(To the* CHERUB *with a bone in her throat):* I tol' you you was too little fo' catfish. What you wanter git a bone in you' froat fo'? *(She slaps the* CHERUB'S *back.)*

SLENDER ANGEL *(Leisurely eating a sandwich as she watches the backslapping):* What de trouble wid Leonetta?

STOUT ANGEL: She got a catfish bone down her froat. *(To the* CHERUB.) Doggone, I tol' you to eat grinnel instead.

SLENDER ANGEL: Ef'n she do git all dat et, she gonter have de bellyache.

STOUT ANGEL: Ain't I tol' her dat? *(To* CHERUB). Come on now; let go dat bone. *(She slaps* CHERUB'S *back again. The bone is dislodged and the* CHERUB *grins her relief.)* Dat's good.

SLENDER ANGEL *(Comfortingly):* Now she all right.

STOUT ANGEL: Go on an' play wid yo' cousins. *(The* CHERUB *joins the* CHERUBS *sitting on the embankment. The concurrency of scenes ends here.)* I ain't see you lately, Lily. How you been?

SLENDER ANGEL: Me, I'm fine. I been visitin' my mammy. She waitin' on de welcome table over by de throne of grace.

STOUT ANGEL: She always was pretty holy.

SLENDER ANGEL: Yes, ma'am. She like it dere. I guess de Lawd's took quite a fancy to her.

STOUT ANGEL: Well, dat's natural. I declare yo' mammy one of de finest lady angels I know.

SLENDER ANGEL: She claim you de best one she know.

STOUT ANGEL: Well, when you come right down to it, I suppose we is all pretty near perfec'.

SLENDER ANGEL: Yes, ma'am. Why is dat, Mis' Jenny?

STOUT ANGEL: I s'pose it's caize de Lawd he don' 'low us 'sociatin' wid de devil any mo' so dat dey cain' be no mo' sinnin'.

SLENDER ANGEL: Po' ol' Satan. Whutevah become of him?

STOUT ANGEL: De Lawd put him some place I s'pose.

SLENDER ANGEL: But dey ain't any place but Heaven, is dey?

STOUT ANGEL: De Lawd could make a place, couldn't he?

SLENDER ANGEL: Dat's de truth. Dey's one thing confuses me though.

STOUT ANGEL: What's dat?

SLENDER ANGEL: I do a great deal of travelin' an' I ain't never come across any place but Heaven anywhere. So if de Lawd kick Satan out of Heaven jest whereat did he go? Dat's my question.

STOUT ANGEL: You bettah let de Lawd keep his own secrets, Lily. De way things is goin' now dey ain't been no sinnin' since dey give dat scamp a kick in de pants. Nowadays Heaven's free of sin an' if a lady wants a little constitutional she kin fly till she wing-weary widout gittin' insulted.

SLENDER ANGEL: I was jest a baby when Satan lef'. I don't even 'member what he look like.

STOUT ANGEL: He was jest right fo' a devil. (*An* ARCHANGEL *enters. He is older than the others and wears a white beard. His clothing is much darker than that of the others and his wings a trifle more imposing.*) Good mo'nin', Archangel.

(*Others say good morning.*)

ARCHANGEL: Good mo'nin', folks. I wonder kin I interrup' de fish fry an' give out de Sunday school cyards? (*Cries of "Suttingly!" "Mah goodness, yes"—etc. The marching* CHOIR *stops.*) You kin keep singin' if you want to. Why don' you sing "When de Saints Come Marchin' In"? Seem to me I ain' heard dat lately. (*The* CHOIR *begins "When the Saints Come Marching In," rather softly, but does not resume marching. The* ARCHANGEL *looks off left.*) All right, bring 'em yere. (*A prim-looking* WOMAN TEACHER-ANGEL *enters, shepherding ten* BOY *and* GIRL CHERUBS. *The* TEACHER *carries ten beribboned diplomas, which she gives to the* ARCHANGEL. *The* CHERUBS *are dressed in stiffly starched white suits and dresses, the little girls having enormous ribbons at the backs of their dresses and smaller ones in their hair and on the tips of their wings. They line up in front of the* ARCHANGEL *and receive the attention of the rest of the company. The* CHOIR *sings through the ceremony.*) Now den cherubs, why is you yere?

CHILDREN: Because we so good.

ARCHANGEL: Dat's right. Now who de big boss?

CHILDREN: Our dear Lawd.

ARCHANGEL: Dat's right. When you all grow up what you gonter be?

CHILDREN: Holy angels at de throne of grace.

ARCHANGEL: Dat's right. Now, you passed yo' 'xaminations and it gives me great pleasure to hand out de cyards for de whole class. Gineeva

Chaproe. (*The* FIRST GIRL CHERUB *goes to him and gets her diploma. The* CHOIR *sings loudly and resumes marching, as the* ARCHANGEL *calls out another name—and presents diplomas.*) Corey Moulter. (SECOND GIRL CHERUB *gets her diploma.*) Nootzie Winebush. (THIRD GIRL CHERUB.) Harriet Prancy. (FOURTH GIRL CHERUB.) I guess you is Brozain Stew't. (*He gives the* FIFTH GIRL CHERUB *the paper. Each of the presentations has been accompanied by handclapping from the bystanders.*) Now you boys know yo' own names. Suppose you come yere and help me git dese 'sorted right?

(BOY CHERUBS *gather about him and receive their diplomas. The little* GIRLS *have scattered about the stage, joining groups of the adult angels. The angel* GABRIEL *enters. He is bigger and more elaborately winged than even the* ARCHANGEL, *but he is also much younger and beardless. His costume is less conventional than that of the other men, resembling more the Gabriel of the Doré drawings. His appearance causes a flutter among the others. They stop their chattering with the children. The* CHOIR *stops as three or four audible whispers of "Gabriel!" are heard. In a moment the heavenly company is all attention.*)

GABRIEL (*Lifting his hand*): Gangway! Gangway for de Lawd God Jehovah! (*There is a reverent hush as* GOD *enters. He is the tallest and biggest of them all. He wears a white shirt with a white bow tie, a long Prince Albert coat of black alpaca, black trousers and congress gaiters. He looks at the assemblage. There is a pause. He speaks in a rich, bass voice.*)

GOD: Is you been baptized?

OTHERS (*Chanting*): Certainly, Lawd.

GOD: Is you been baptized?

OTHERS: Certainly, Lawd.

GOD (*With the beginning of musical notation*): Is you been baptized?

OTHERS (*Now half-singing*): Certainly, Lawd. Certainly, certainly, certainly, Lawd. (*They sing the last two verses with equivalent part division.*)

> Is you been redeemed?
>   Certainly, Lawd.
> Is you been redeemed?
>   Certainly, Lawd.
> Is you been redeemed?
>   Certainly, Lawd. Certainly, certainly, certainly, Lawd.
>
> Do you bow mighty low?
>   Certainly, Lawd.
> Do you bow mighty low?
>   Certainly, Lawd.
> Do you bow mighty low?
>   Certainly, Lawd. Certainly, certainly, certainly, Lawd.

(As the last response ends all heads are bowed. GOD *looks at them for a moment; then lifts His hand.)*

GOD: Let de fish fry proceed.

*(*EVERYONE *rises. The* ANGELS *relax and resume their inaudible conversations. The activity behind the table and about the cauldron is resumed. Some of the* CHOIR *members cross to the table and get sandwiches and cups of the boiled custard. Three or four of the* CHILDREN *in the Sunday School class and the* LITTLE GIRL *who had the bone in her throat affectionately group themselves about* GOD *as He speaks with the* ARCHANGEL. *He pats their heads, they hang to His coat-tails, etc.)*

ARCHANGEL: Good mo'nin', Lawd.

GOD: Good mo'nin', Deacon. You lookin' pretty spry.

ARCHANGEL: I cain' complain. We jest been givin' our cyards to de chillun.

GOD: Dat's good.

(A small CHERUB, *his feet braced against one of* GOD'*s shoes, is using* GOD'*s coat-tail as a trapeze. One of the* COOKS *offers a fish sandwich which* GOD *politely declines.)*

FIRST MAMMY ANGEL: Now, you leave go de Lawd's coat, Herman. You heah me?

GOD: Dat's all right, sister. He jest playin'.

FIRST MAMMY ANGEL: —He playin' too rough. *(*GOD *picks up the* CHERUB *and spanks him good-naturedly. The* CHERUB *squeals with delight and runs to his mother.* GABRIEL *advances to* GOD *with a glass of the custard.)*

GABRIEL: Little b'iled custud, Lawd?

GOD: Thank you very kindly. Dis looks nice.

CUSTARD MAKER *(Offering a box):* Ten cent seegar, Lawd?

GOD *(Taking it):* Thank you, thank you. How de fish fry goin'? *(Ad lib, cries of "O. K., Lawd," "Fine an' dandy, Lawd," "De best one yit, Lawd," etc. To the* CHOIR.) How you shouters gittin' on?

CHOIR LEADER: We been marchin' and singin' de whole mo'nin'.

GOD: I heerd you. You gettin' better all de time. You gittin' as good as de one at de throne. Why don' you give us one dem ol' time jump-ups?

CHOIR LEADER: Anythin' you say, Lawd. *(To the others.)* "So High!" *(The* CHOIR *begins to sing "So High You Can't Get Over It." They sing softly, but do not march. An* ANGEL *offers his cigar to* GOD *from which He can light His own.)*

GOD: No, thanks. I'm gonter save dis a bit. *(He puts the cigar in his pocket and listens to the singers a moment. Then he sips his custard. After a second sip, a look of displeasure comes on his face.)*

GABRIEL: What's de matter, Lawd?

GOD *(Sipping again):* I ain't jest sure, yit. Dey's something 'bout dis custard. *(Takes another sip.)*

CUSTARD MAKER: Ain't it all right, Lawd?

GOD: It don't seem seasoned jest right. You make it?

CUSTARD MAKER: Yes, Lawd, I put everythin' in it like I allus do. It's supposed to be perfec'.

GOD: Yeah. I kin taste de eggs and de cream and de sugar. *(Suddenly.)* I know what it is. It needs jest a little bit mo' firmament.

CUSTARD MAKER: Dey's firmament in it, Lawd.

GOD: Maybe, but it ain' enough.

CUSTARD MAKER: It's all we had, Lawd. Dey ain't a drap in de jug.

GOD: Dat's all right. I'll jest r'ar back an' pass a miracle. (CHOIR *stops singing.)* Let it be some firmament! An' when I say let it be some firmament, I don't want jest a little bitty dab o' firmament caize I'm sick an' tired of runnin' out of it when we need it. Let it be a whole mess of firmament! *(The stage has become misty until* GOD *and the heavenly company are obscured. As he finishes the speech there is a burst of thunder. As the stage grows darker.)* Dat's de way I like it.

(Murmurs from the others: "Dat's a lot of firmament." "My, dat is firmament!" "Look to me like he's created rain," etc.)

FIRST MAMMY ANGEL *(When the stage is dark):* Now, look Lawd, dat's too much firmament. De cherubs is gettin' all wet.

SECOND MAMMY ANGEL: Look at my Carlotta, Lawd. She's soaked to de skin. Dat's *plenty* too much firmament.

GOD: Well, 'co'se we don't want de chillun to ketch cold. Can't you dreen it off?

GABRIEL: Dey's no place to dreen it, Lawd.

FIRST MAMMY ANGEL: Why don't we jest take de babies home, Lawd?

GOD: No, I don' wanta bust up de fish fry. You angels keep quiet an' I'll pass another miracle. Dat's always de trouble wid miracles. When you pass one you always gotta r'ar back an' pass another. *(There is a hush.)* Let dere be a place to dreen off this firmament. Let dere be mountains and valleys an' let dere be oceans an' lakes. An' let dere be rivers and bayous to dreen it off in, too. As a matter of fac' let dere be de earth. An' when dat's done let dere be de sun, an' let it come out and dry my cherubs' wings.

(The lights go up until the stage is bathed in sunlight. On the embankment upstage there is now a waist-high wrought-iron railing such as one sees on the galleries of houses in the French quarter of New Orleans. The CHERUBS *are being examined by their parents and there is an ad lib. murmur of, "You all right, honey?" "You feel better now, Albert?" "Now you all dry, Vangy?" until the* ARCHANGEL, *who has been gazing in awe at the railing, drowns them out.)*

ARCHANGEL: Look yere!

*(There is a rush to the embankment accompanied by exclamations, "My goodness!"
"What's dis?" "I declah!" etc. GABRIEL towers above the group on the middle of
the embankment. GOD is wrapped in thought, facing the audience. The CHOIR
resumes singing "So High You Can't Get Over It" softly. The babbling at the
balustrade dies away as the people lean over the railing. GABRIEL turns and faces
GOD indicating the earth below the railing with his left hand.)*

GABRIEL: Do you see it, Lawd?

GOD *(Quietly, without turning his head upstage):* Yes, Gabriel.

GABRIEL: Looks mighty nice, Lawd.

GOD: Yes.

(GABRIEL turns and looks over the railing.)

GABRIEL *(Gazing down):* Yes, suh. Dat'd make mighty nice farming country. Jest look at dat South forty over dere. You ain't going to let dat go
to waste is you Lawd? Dat would be a pity an' a shame.

GOD *(Not turning):* It's good earth. (GOD *turns, room is made for him beside*
GABRIEL *on the embankment.)* Yes. I ought to have somebody to enjoy it.
(He turns, facing the audience. The others, save for the CHOIR *who are lined up in
two rows of six on an angle up right, continue to look over the embankment.)*
Gabriel! (GOD *steps down from the embankment two paces.)*

GABRIEL *(Joining him):* Yes, Lawd.

GOD: Gabriel, I'm goin' down dere.

GABRIEL: Yes, Lawd.

GOD: I want you to be my working boss yere while I'm gone.

GABRIEL: Yes, Lawd.

GOD: You know dat matter of dem two stars?

GABRIEL: Yes, Lawd.

GOD: Git dat fixed up! You know dat sparrow dat fell a little while ago?
'Tend to dat, too.

GABRIEL: Yes, Lawd.

GOD: I guess dat's about all. I'll be back Saddy. *(To the choir.)* Quiet,
angels. *(The* CHOIR *stops singing. Those on the embankment circle down stage.*
GOD *goes to embankment. Turns and faces the company.)* I'm gonter pass one
more miracle. You all gonter help me an' not make a soun' caize it's one
of de most impo'tant miracles of all. *(Nobody moves.* GOD *turns, facing the
sky and raises His arms above his head.)* Let there be man.

(There is growing roll of thunder as stage grows dark. The CHOIR *bursts into
"Hallelujah," and continues until the lights go up on the next scene.)*

FIDDLER MADE A GOOF DEPT.

Practically everyone has seen the prize-winning musical about the lovable people in that little village in Old Russia called Anetevka. Well, as far as we're concerned, *Fiddler* made a *goof!* Because a show like that is very sentimental and touching until we think about the *descendants* of those oppressed people who fled Europe so many years ago, and how those descendants have almost destroyed a Dream. Which is why *Mad* now takes this famous musical about the problems of people who had *nothing,* and updates it with a version about the problems of people who have *everything*—mainly America's Upper Middle Class. Here, then, is our sing-along rendition, retitled . . .

Antenna

ARTIST: MORT DRUCKER

An antenna on the roof! What's so strange about that? Nothing much . . . except that this antenna is on the roof of our kennel!

You see, here in our $150,000 home in the suburbs, even our dog is spoiled rotten!

You may ask: Why do I work so hard to provide such luxuries as a Zenith Color TV Console for our dog? Why not just a simple Black-and-White Emerson Portable?

Because here in the suburbs, a family is measured by one yardstick— POSSESSIONS!

POSSESSIONS!

Possessions are what earn us the respect and admiration of the people who mean the most to us! And who are they . . . ? THE NEIGHBORS!!

THE NEIGHBORS!

Still, it's not so easy being prosperous! Even WE have our problems! And what are our biggest ones . . . ? OUR DAUGHTERS!

OUR DAUGHTERS!

FRANK JACOBS
AND MORT DRUCKER

on the Roof

WRITER: FRANK JACOBS

WOODY ALLEN

The Scrolls

Scholars will recall that several years ago a shepherd, wandering in the Gulf of Aqaba, stumbled upon a cave containing several large clay jars and also two tickets to the ice show. Inside the jars were discovered six parchment scrolls with ancient incomprehensible writing which the shepherd, in his ignorance, sold to the museum for $750,000 apiece. Two years later the jars turned up in a pawn shop in Philadelphia. One year later the shepherd turned up in a pawn shop in Philadelphia and neither was claimed.

Archeologists originally set the date of the scrolls at 4000 BC, or just after the massacre of the Israelites by their benefactors. The writing is a mixture of Sumerian, Aramaic and Babylonian and seems to have been done by either one man over a long period of time, or several men who shared the same suit. The authenticity of the scrolls is currently in great doubt, particularly since the word Oldsmobile appears several times in the text, and the few fragments that have finally been translated deal with familiar religious themes in a more than dubious way. Still, excavationist A. H. Bauer has noted that even though the fragments seem totally fraudulent, this is probably the greatest archeological find in history with the exception of the recovery of his cufflinks from a tomb in Jerusalem. The following are the translated fragments.

One . . . And the Lord made an bet with Satan to test Job's loyalty and the Lord, for no apparent reason to Job, smote him on the head and again on the ear and pushed him into an thick sauce so as to make Job sticky and vile and then He slew a 10th part of Job's kine and Job calleth out: "Why doth thou slay my kine? Kine are hard to come by. Now I am short kine and I'm not even sure what kine are." And the Lord produced two stone tablets and snapped them closed on Job's nose. And when Job's wife saw this she wept and the Lord sent an angel of mercy who anointed her head with a polo mallet and of the 10 plagues, the Lord sent one through six, inclusive, and Job was sore and his wife angry and she rent her garment and then raised the rent but refused to paint.

And soon Job's pastures dried up and his tongue cleaved to the roof of his mouth so he could not pronounce the word "frankincense" without getting big laughs.

And once the Lord, while wreaking havoc upon his faithful servant, came too close and Job grabbed him around the neck and said, "Aha! Now I got you! Why art thou giving Job a hard time, eh? Eh? Speak up!"

And the Lord said, "Er, look—that's my neck you have . . . could you let me go?"

But Job showed no mercy and said, "I was doing very well till you came along. I had myrrh and fig trees in abundance and a coat of many colors with two pairs of pants of many colors. Now look."

And the Lord spake and his voice thundered: "Must I who created heaven and earth explain my ways to thee? What hath thou created that thou doth dare question me?"

"That's no answer," Job said. "And for someone who's supposed to be omnipotent, let me tell you, 'tabernacle' has only one 'L.' " Then Job fell to his knees and cried to the Lord. "Thine is the kingdom and the power and the glory. Thou hast a good job. Don't blow it."

Two . . . And Abraham awoke in the middle of the night and said to his only son, Isaac, "I have had an dream where the voice of the Lord sayeth that I must sacrifice my only son, so put your pants on." And Isaac trembled and said, "So what did you say? I mean when He brought this whole thing up?"

"What am I going to say?" Abraham said. "I'm standing there at two a.m. in my underwear with the Creator of the Universe. Should I argue?"

"Well, did he say why he wants me sacrificed?" Isaac asked his father.

But Abraham said, "The faithful do not question. Now let's go because I have a heavy day tomorrow."

And Sarah who heard Abraham's plan grew vexed and said, "How doth thou know it was the Lord and not, say, thy friend who loveth practical jokes, for the Lord hateth practical jokes and whosoever shall pull one shall be delivered into the hands of his enemies whether they can pay the delivery charge or not." And Abraham answered, "Because I know it was the Lord. It was a deep, resonant voice, well modulated, and nobody in the desert can get a rumble in it like that."

And Sarah said, "And thou art willing to carry out this senseless act?"

But Abraham told her, "Frankly yes, for to question the Lord's word is one of the worst things a person can do, particularly with the economy in the state it's in."

And so he took Isaac to a certain place and prepared to sacrifice him but at the last minute the Lord stayed Abraham's hand and said, "How could thou doest such a thing?" And Abraham said, "But thou said. . . ."

"Never mind what I said," the Lord spake. "Doth thou listen to every crazy idea that comes thy way?" And Abraham grew ashamed. "Er—not really . . . no. . . ."

"I jokingly suggest thou sacrifice Isaac and thou immediately runs out to do it."

And Abraham fell to his knees, "See, I never know when you're kidding."

And the Lord thundered, "No sense of humor. I can't believe it."

"But doth this not prove I love thee, that I was willing to donate mine only son on thy whim?"

And the Lord said, "It proves that some men will follow any order no matter how asinine as long as it comes from a resonant, well modulated voice."

And with that, the Lord bid Abraham get some rest and check with him tomorrow.

Three . . . And it came to pass that a man who sold shirts was smitten by hard times. Neither did any of his merchandise move nor did he prosper. And he prayed and said, "Lord, why hast thou left me to suffer thus? All mine enemies sell their goods except I. And it's the height of the season. My shirts are good shirts. Take a look at this rayon. I got button-downs, flare collars, nothing sells. Yet, I have kept thy commandments. Why can I not earn a living when mine younger brother cleans up in childen's ready-to-wear?"

And the Lord heard the man and said, "About thy shirts. . . ."

"Yes, Lord," the man said, falling to his knees.

"Put an alligator over the pocket."

"Pardon me, Lord?"

"Just do what I'm telling you. You won't be sorry."

And the man sewed on to all his shirts a small alligator symbol and lo and behold, suddenly his merchandise moved like gangbusters and there was much rejoicing while amongst his enemies there was wailing and gnashing of teeth and one said, "The Lord is merciful. He maketh me to lie down in green pastures. The problem is, I can't get up."

Laws and Proverbs:

Doing abominations is against the law, particularly if the abominations
   are done while wearing a lobster bib.

The lion and the calf shall lie down together but the calf won't get much
   sleep.

Whosoever shall not fall by the sword or by famine, shall fall by pes-
   tilence, so why bother shaving?

The wicked at heart probably know something.

Whosoever loveth wisdom is righteous but he that keepeth company with
   fowl is weird.

My Lord, my Lord! What hast thou done, lately?

WOODY ALLEN

Hasidic Tales, with a Guide to Their Interpretation by the Noted Scholar

A man journeyed to Chelm in order to seek the advice of Rabbi Ben
Kaddish, the holiest of all ninth-century rabbis and perhaps the greatest
noodge of the medieval era.

   "Rabbi," the man asked, "where can I find peace?"

   The Hasid surveyed him and said, "Quick, look behind you!"

   The man turned around, and Rabbi Ben Kaddish smashed him in the
back of the head with a candlestick. "Is that peaceful enough for you?" he
chuckled, adjusting his yarmulke.

In this tale, a meaningless question is asked. Not only is the question meaningless
but so is the man who journeys to Chelm to ask it. Not that he was so far away from

Chelm to begin with, but why shouldn't he stay where he is? Why is he bothering Rabbi Ben Kaddish—the rabbi doesn't have enough trouble? The truth is, the rabbi's in over his head with gamblers, and he has also been named in a paternity case by a Mrs. Hecht. No, the point of this tale is that this man has nothing better to do with his time than journey around and get on people's nerves. For this, the rabbi bashes his head in, which, according to the Torah, is one of the most subtle methods of showing concern. In a similar version of this tale, the rabbi leaps on top of the man in a frenzy and carves the story of Ruth on his nose with a stylus.

A man who could not marry off his ugly daughter visited Rabbi Shimmel of Cracow. "My heart is heavy," he told the Reb, "because God has given me an ugly daughter."

"How ugly?" the seer asked.

"If she were lying on a plate with a herring, you wouldn't be able to tell the difference."

The Seer of Cracow thought for a long time and finally asked, "What kind of herring?"

The man, taken aback by the query, thought quickly and said, "Er— Bismarck."

"Too bad," the Rabbi said. "If it was matjes, she'd have a better chance."

Here is a tale that illustrates the tragedy of transient qualities such as beauty. Does the girl actually resemble a herring? Why not? Have you seen some of the things walking around these days, particularly at resort areas? And even if she does, are not all creatures beautiful in God's eyes? Perhaps, but if a girl looks more at home in a jar of wine sauce than in an evening gown she's got big problems. Oddly enough, Rabbi Shimmel's own wife was said to resemble a squid, but this was only in the face, and she more than made up for it by her hacking cough—the point of which escapes me.

Rabbi Zwi Chaim Yisroel, an Orthodox scholar of the Torah and a man who developed whining to an art unheard of in the West, was unanimously hailed as the wisest man of the Renaissance by his fellow Hebrews, who totaled a sixteenth of one percent of the population. Once, while he was on his way to synagogue to celebrate the sacred Jewish holiday commemorating God's reneging on every promise, a woman stopped him and asked the following question: "Rabbi, why are we not allowed to eat pork?"

"We're *not?*" the Reb said incredulously. "Uh-oh."

This is one of the few stories in all Hasidic literature that deals with Hebrew law. The rabbi knows he shouldn't eat pork; he doesn't care, though, because he *likes* pork. Not only does he like pork; he gets a kick out of rolling Easter eggs. In short, he cares very little about traditional Orthodoxy and regards God's covenant with Abraham as "just so much chin music." Why pork was proscribed by Hebraic law is still unclear, and some scholars believe that the Torah merely suggested not eating pork at certain restaurants.

Roth's Fillip

The very first book by Philip Roth, *Goodbye, Columbus,* won the
National Book Award. That was 1959, and ten years later he published
Portnoy's Complaint. Those are the Roth works best known to the
multitude, but I cherish him for *On the Air,* which I first read in Theodore Solotaroff's vanished (where is justice?) periodical *New American
Review.* Here is the opening section of that piece: a series of letters
(none answered) to Albert Einstein proposing that the exalted Jewish
scientist host a radio show patterned after the "Dr. I.Q." or "The
Answer Man" quiz shows in radio's dim bright days ("I have a lady in
the balcony, Doctor.").   **G.S.**

PHILIP ROTH

Letters to Einstein

Dear Mr. EINSTEIN:

I am writing you with a wonderful suggestion that I know would bring
about gigantic changes in the world and improve the lot of Jews everywhere. Mr. Einstein, I am a fellow Jew, and proud of it. Your name is
sacred to me as to people of our faith around the globe. That the Nazis
chased you from Germany is our gain and their loss a million times over,
if they even know what a loss is, and I only hope and pray that you are
happy here in "the land of the free."

Here is my suggestion. Why don't you go on the radio every week with
your own show? If you would agree I would like to manage you, so that
your famous mind would not have to be cluttered up with business and so
on. I am ashamed to say this in the same breath with your name, but
probably you are aware of "The Answer Man" program which is on every

night from seven to seven-fifteen. If you're not, just listen for a minute some night. Children all over America think this fake is "an Einstein" probably, when the real Einstein is something they would faint to hear in person. I would like them to know that THE GENIUS OF ALL TIME IS A JEW! This is something the world must know, and soon.

Respectfully yours,

M. LIPPMAN,

Talent Agent

P.S. You will probably want to know what right I have even to suggest myself as a manager to the great Einstein. And all I can say is that if I had a list of the greatest names in the entertainment industry as my clientele, I would be as ashamed of my credentials as I am right now where you are concerned, the Great Albert Einstein. I feel it is even a sin to write out your whole name, that it is too holy for me to utter. But if I didn't write it out, how would you even get this letter? So forgive me. Until now, I have to tell you, I have not had a famous list of acts. Mostly I represent colored. I probably have most of the best tap dancing talent in the state under contract to me at this very moment, and am helping some of these young men—for instance, the Famous Brothers (Buck and Wing)—to raise themselves into a respectable life. With my new talent discoveries since Buck and Wing, I am changing their old names to the names of famous American Presidents, only backwards. This way I think they still sound colored, which they should as tap dancers, and yet have a little class. Also I attend an average of two to three *bar mitzvah* parties of a single Saturday, in my endless search for young Jewish talent in singing, bandleading, et cetera.

I hope I will be hearing from you soon, and favorably, about "The Albert Einstein Show."

Again respectfuly,

M. LIPPMANN

Dear Mr. EINSTEIN:

I can understand how busy you must be thinking, and appreciate that you did not answer my letter suggesting that I try to get you on a radio program that would make "The Answer Man" look like the joke it is. Will you reconsider, if the silence means no? I realize that one of the reasons you don't wear a tie or even bother to comb your hair is because you are as busy as you are, thinking new things. Well, don't think that you would have to change your ways once you became a radio personality. Your hair is a great gimmick, and I wouldn't change it for a second. It's a great trademark. Without disrespect, it sticks in your mind the way Harpo Marx's does. Which is excellent. (Now I wonder if you even have the time to know who the Marx Brothers are? They are four zany Jewish brothers, and you happen to look a little like one of them. You might get a kick out of catching one of their movies. Probably they don't even show movies in Princeton, but maybe you could get somebody to drive you out of town. You can get the entire plot in about a minute, but the resemblance between you and Harpo, and his hair and yours, might reassure you that you are a fine personality in terms of show business just as you are.)

The kind of program I have in mind is something I would certainly have to talk with you about before embarking upon making the right contacts. For instance, should we follow "The Answer Man" format with questions sent in? Should we have a theme song? Would you object to another personality asking the questions? Something strikes me right about the idea of you being interviewed by Tony Martin, the singer. He has a beautiful speaking voice and makes a wonderful impression in a dinner jacket, and is also (contrary to the belief that he is of Italian extraction) a Jewish boy with whom you would feel completely at home. Easygoing is his whole style, *but with respect.* Whether I can get him is another story. I don't want to make promises I can't deliver so as to entice the famous Einstein. I wouldn't dare. But what I'm saying is that the sky is the limit once I get an okay from you. I am tempted to spell that with a capital letter. You. But in the middle of the sentence.

Perhaps I should have told You that my fee is ten percent. But truly and honestly I am not in this business for money. I want to help people. I have taken colored off the streets, shoeshine kit and all, and turned them into headline tap dancers at roadhouses and nightclubs overnight. And my satisfaction comes not from the money, which in all honesty is not so much, but in seeing those boys getting dressed up in dinner jackets and learning to face an audience of people out for a nice time. Dignity far more than money is my business.

With you, Mr. Einstein, I think I could really break through into something of worldwide importance in terms of doing good. Who better than you knows the persecution the Jews have taken around the globe? It will only stop when they look up to us and recognize that when it comes to smart, we are the tops. It will only stop when our own little Jewish boys and girls realize that there is an Einstein in the world who is a Jew just like them, and is a million times smarter than some *goy* radio announcer with a stuffy voice who they also give the answers to anyway. Do we want our children to grow up admiring such fakes? I have a little boy of my own, and I know what it would mean to me if I could sit with him at night once a week and listen to the Famous Albert Einstein talking around a fireside with someone of the caliber of a Tony Martin.

If you are too busy to write and discuss these matters, how about if I came to see you some Sunday? It would be a thrill if I could bring my son along.

Respectfully yours,
M. LIPPMAN
Agent to
The Famous Brothers,
Roosevelt Franklin,
Jefferson Thomas,
Cleveland Grover, &
Monroe James

Dear *Dr.* EINSTEIN:

No word, but I understand. I hope and pray you were not offended that I have been addressing you all along as Mister. I cannot express all my admiration for you, and it breaks my heart if you think any disrespect was intended. I am not an educated person, though I try to make up in hard work and quick thinking what I don't know from books. Every day, and this is no exaggeration. I have a hundred wonderful ideas that could improve the world. My idea to encourage you to go on the air on a regular basis is only one, Doctor.

I am sure that you are naturally nervous about me and the millions of others who probably write to you looking for "an easy buck." I have to assure you, *the money is secondary.* Uppermost is getting you on the radio and showing those *goyim* what smart really means. Why hide under a barrel something that could change the life of *every Jew alive and their children to come?* This is how strongly I believe in the power of radio. I think sometimes that the Bible stories of God talking from above to the people down below is just what they had in those days instead of radio. People, whether then or now, like to hear "the real thing." Hearing is believing! (Maybe that could be our motto for the show—if you approve. For a theme song I have been thinking along robust lines, but still meaningful—something like "The Whole World Is Singing My Song.") Today we don't *hear* God as they did in the Bible—and what is the result? It is impossible for some people to believe He is there. There. The same holds true with you, Doctor Einstein, I'm sorry to say. To the general public, who is Einstein? A name who doesn't comb his hair (not that I have any objection) and is *supposed* to be the smartest person alive. A lot of good that does the Jews, if you understand what I'm saying. At this stage of the game, I'm afraid that if an election were held tonight between you and The Answer Man, more people would vote for him than for you. I have to be honest with you.

Here is my proposal. I will drive to Princeton next Sunday, arriving around two P.M. If you are not home, fine. If you are, and you happen to be at the window, and you happen to feel only like waving and that's all, well let me tell you, that would be a wonderful experience in itself. But if you want to ask a question or two about my suggestion, even through the window if that's all you have the time for, fine with me, I'll do that, too, from the lawn. I will leave my wife and child in the car so that they don't bother you, though if you should want to wave at the boy, I would be most appreciative. And he of course would remember it for life.

To make a joke, don't put on a tie for my account, Doctor.

Your fellow Jew and humble admirer,
M. LIPPMAN

REA IRVIN

*"People slowly accustomed themselves to the idea that the
physical states of space itself were the final physical reality."*
—PROFESSOR ALBERT EINSTEIN

Hooray for L*e*o R*o*s*t*e*n

In the glory days of *Look* magazine (yes there were), one esteemed member of the editorial board was Leo Rosten, and when I went to work there right after I graduated from college (yes I did), it didn't occur to me that Mr. Rosten was the creator of one of my favorite characters of fiction, Hyman Kaplan. *The Education of H*y*m*a*n K*a*p*l*a*n* was published in 1937 and signed Leonard Q. Ross. How was I to remember that "Ross" was a shield for Rosten? The academic Rosten thought his colleagues might consider him unworthy if they caught him writing humor (a difficult form they were incapable of emulating). Each time I recall or reread Kaplan's verbal adventures, I am reminded of Leo Rosten's protean gifts: political scientist, humorist, teacher, scholar, and —luckiest for us—*writer*.   **G.S.**

LEO ROSTEN

*Christopher K*a*p*l*a*n*

Mr. Parkhill considered the beginners' grade as more than a group of scholars eager to master the English language. He took a larger view of his responsibilities; to Mr. Parkhill the American Night Preparatory School for Adults was not merely a place where foreigners could learn the English language—it was an incubator of Americans, a kind of intellectual Ellis Island. To imbue the men and women of a dozen nations with the meaning of America—its past, its traditions, its aspirations—this, to Mr. Parkhill, was the greater work to which he had dedicated himself.

So it was that on the eve of any national holiday, Mr. Parkhill devoted at least half an hour to a foray into the patriotic sentiments of the occasion. One Monday night, therefore, two nights before Columbus Day, Mr. Parkhill opened the class session with these ringing words, "Tonight, let us—er—consider the work of the man whose achievement the world will celebrate Wednesday."

A happy murmur ran through the room.

"To this man," said Mr. Parkhill earnestly, "the United States owes its very existence. For he—"

"Jawdge Vashington!" Miss Fanny Gidwitz promptly guessed.

"No, no, Miss Gidwitz. *Not* George Washington—watch that 'w,' Miss Gidwitz. I'm referring to—"

"Paul Rewere!" cried Oscar Trabish impetuously. Mr. Parkhill adjusted his spectacles. Mr. Trabish had formed some strange psychic union with "Paul Rewere": he had already written two compositions and made one fiery speech on his historical alter ego. The compositions had been called "Paul Revere's Horse Makes History" and "Paul Revere. One by the Land, Two by the Seashore." The title of the speech had been announced by Mr. Trabish as "Paul Rewere! Vhy He Vasn't Prazidant?" He had been quite indignant about it.

But now Mr. Parkhill shook his head. "Not Paul Re*were*—it's a 'v,' Mr. Trabish. Let's not *guess,* class. What date is next Wednesday?"

"Mine boitday!" an excited voice rang out.

Mr. Parkhill ignored this comment. "Next Wednesday," he continued firmly, "is October twelfth. And on October twelfth, 1492—"

He got no further.

"Det's mine boitday! Mine *boit*day! I should live so! Honist!"

Mr. Parkhill recognized that voice. It was Hyman Kaplan's. Mr. Parkhill took a deep breath, a slow, deep breath, and said cautiously, "Mr. Kaplan, is October twelfth—er—really your birthday?"

Mr. Kaplan's eyes widened with hurt. *"Mister* Pockheel." Mr. Parkhill felt ashamed of himself.

Stanislaus Wilkomirski growled, "Kaplan too old for have bir-day." (Mr. Wilkomirski was a member of the Opposition.)

"October tvalf I'm born; October tvalf I'm tsalebratink!" Mr. Kaplan retorted. "All mine *life* I'm hevink boitdays October tvalf. No haxceptions!"

Mr. Parkhill said, "Well, well, well. That *is* a coincidence. October twelfth. Hmm." He smiled politely. "I'm sure we all wish Mr. Kaplan many happy returns."

Mr. Kaplan beamed, jumped to his feet, bowed, and sat down, beaming.

Miss Mitnick, feeling the occasion called for good will and peace among men, said, "Congratulations."

Mr. Kaplan said, "Denks."

"However," Mr. Parkhill went on resolutely, "the historical anniversary is that of Christopher Columbus. On October twelfth, 1492—"

"*Colom*biss!" Mr. Kaplan's rapture postively exploded.

Excitement seized the beginners' grade. "Columbus!" "Aha!" "Columbia Day!" "Colombus discovert America!"

"On October twelfth, 1492—"

Mr. Trabish dropped a sneer in the general direction of Fanny Gidwitz. "And you sad Jawdge Vashington!"

"You said Paul Rewere!"

"On October twelfth, 1492," persevered Mr. Parkhill.

"By me is avery day in year somthing about Paul Rewere!"

"And by *me* is our foist Prazident vert ten hoss-riders!"

"On October twelfth, 1492"—Mr. Parkhill's voice had risen until it was commanding—"Christopher Columbus discovered a new continent!"

The class quieted down at last, and Mr. Parkhill launched upon the saga of Christopher Columbus. He spoke slowly, impressively, almost with fervor. They listened to him closely, caught by the drama of the great voyage. "The food ran low. Water was scarce. The sailors began to grumble. . . ."

Goldie Pomeranz leaned forward and sighed moistly into Mr. Kaplan's ear, "You soitinly locky, Mr. Kaplan. Born same day Columbus did."

Mr. Kaplan was in a world of dreams. *"Christover Columbiss!"* He kept whispering the name to himself. "My!" He had closed his eyes to be alone with his hero. "October tvalf I'm arrivink in de voild—an' October tvalf Columbiss picks ot for discoverink U.S.! Dastiny."

"Mutiny faced Christopher Colombus," Mr. Parkhill said with feeling.

"My boitday is Motch toity," Miss Pomeranz whispered to Mr. Kaplan with sad envy. "Not iven a soborb vas discovered Motch toity."

Mr. Kaplan gave Miss Pomeranz a modest murmur. "Ufcawss, Colombiss discovert lonk bafore I arrived."

"October twalf is October twalf!" cried Mr. Pinsky, a true-blue Kaplan supporter.

Mr. Kaplan sighed, nodded, and let the mantle of history fall upon his shoulders.

Mr. Parkhill, driven to greater efforts by the Pomeranz-Kaplan-Pinsky symposium, told the class of the geographical boundaries in 1492, of the then current belief that the world was flat, of the mockery to which Columbus had been subjected. He described the singular confluence of events which had led to the new continent's being named after Amerigo Vespucci. ("A *mistake!*" Mr. Kaplan cried indignantly.) Mr. Parkhill outlined the immortal voyage of three tiny ships across an ocean infested in men's minds by monstrous things. When he said, "And because Colombus thought he was really in India, he called the natives Indians," the amazement of the beginners' grade of the American Night Preparatory School for Adults burst its bonds.

"Vun mistake on top de odder!" Mr. Kaplan moaned.

"So dey called Hindyans by *mistake?*" asked Mrs. Moskowitz, wide-eyed. Mrs. Moskowitz could scarcely believe that of history.

"Yes, Mrs. Moskowitz, by mistake," said Mr. Parkhill quietly.

Mr. Kaplan shook his head three times. "Dose poor Hindyans."

Mr. Parkhill hurried on to details about Ferdinand and Isabella. Just before he had completed the absorbing tale, Mr. Kaplan announced, without warning, "Ectual ve ain't Americans!"

Mr. Parkhill paused. " 'Actual*ly,* we *are*n't Americans,' Mr. Kaplan. There is no such word as—"

"Ectual ve all Colombians!" Mr. Kaplan cried. A passion for justice flamed in his eyes.

Mr. Parkhill turned the class over to Miss Mitnick for General Discussion. General Discussion, Mr. Parkhill had found, was a particularly fruitful exercise, and he occasionally invited one of the more competent students, like Miss Mitnick, to lead the discussion. It was even better training than the more formal Recitation and Speech periods and aroused fewer anxieties in the breasts of the timid.

Miss Mitnick struck the keynote for the evening with a touching if half-embarrassed eulogy of explorers in general and Columbus in particular. She ended her comments with a deft comparison of Columbus with Admiral Byrd. "Both men fond new places for humanity. Natchelly, in different places."

"Edmiral Boyd?" Mr. Kaplan sniffed at once. It was clear that henceforth anyone drawing comparisons between Columbus and lesser spirits would have to answer to Hyman Kaplan. "Vat kind finder new tings is dis Edmiral Boyd?"

"It's '*Ad*miral *Byrd,* ' "Mr. Parkhill suggested from the seat he had taken next to Mr. Studniczka.

"Admiral Byrd is a kind *modern* Columbus," Miss Mitnick said, blushing.

"Vat he discovert should compare Colombiss's vunderful didd?" There was hauteur in Mr. Kaplan's tone.

"Admiral Byrd discovered Sout Pole," Miss Mitnick said. She looked a little frightened.

"Som discoverink!" said Mr. Kaplan, dismissing Antarctica scornfully.

"Sout Pole is important, Mr. Kaplan! It has—"

"It's to leff! Averybody *knew* vas Sot Pole, no? All Edmiral Boyd did vas *go* dere!"

Miss Mitnick turned pale.

*"Ad*miral *Byrd,* Mr. Kaplan," said Mr. Parkhill.

"Admiral Byrd is big *hero,"* Miss Mitnick insisted, wetting her lips. "He went through terrible things for humanity—cold, icebergs, alone, freezings."

"Edmiral Boyd *vent mit all modinn conweniences!"*

Miss Mitnick shot a wild S.O.S. to Mr. Parkhill.

"Er—it's *Ad*miral *Byrd!"* Mr. Parkhill said. No one paid any attention to him.

Miss Caravello plunged into the controversy with a passionate "Is only da one Columbus! No more lak!" It was clear that to Miss Caravello Columbus was a peculiarly Italian phenomenon, unparalleled, incomparable. Admiral Byrd, she said flatly, was a "copying cat." For Columbus, Miss Caravello concluded hotly, nothing short of a thousand *"Viva"*'s would do. She proceeded to give three of them: *"Viva! Viva! Viva!"*

Mr. Kaplan broke into furious applause.

Now Mr. Gus Matsoukas demanded the floor. "Colomb' good man, no doubts about," he began magnanimously. Columbus was, indeed, worth all that Mr. Kaplan and Miss Caravello had claimed for him. But after all, Mr. Matsoukas insinuated, should one not regard Columbus as no more than a sort of descendant of the first and *greatest* explorer—Ulysses? Ulysses, it turned out, was born in a town no more than seventeen kilometres from Mr. Matsoukas's birthplace.

"Boit*days* is more important den boit*places!"* Mr. Kaplan said.

Mr. Matsoukas, crestfallen, could think of no answer to this proposition. He fell back into his normal coma.

"Anybody else wants to say few words?" asked Miss Mitnick.

There were vague mumblings. Mr. Kaplan raised his hand.

"Floor is *open,"* Miss Mitnick announced. She kept her eyes away from Mr. Kaplan. *"Any*body can talk."

Mr. Kaplan rose at once, said "Foidinand an' Isabel. Ha!" and sat down.

There was a nervous silence. Miss Mitnick twisted her handkerchief around her fingers. "Mr. Kaplan, please," she stammered. "I didn't catch."

Mr. Kaplan got up again. "Foidinand an' Isabel. Ha!" He sat down.

Miss Mitnick looked to Mr. Parkhill in anguish.

"Er—Mr. Kaplan . . ."

"Axplain, Keplen!" Mr. Plonsky called out.

Mr. Kaplan said nothing.

"Keplen wants to talk or Keplen *not* wants to talk?" Mr. Plonsky asked the elements ironically.

Mr. Parkhill recognized his responsibility and decided to intervene. "Y-yes, Mr. Kaplan. I do think the class is entitled to some explanation of your brief—er—comment."

"All of a sodden Mr. Kaplan makes fun Foidinand, Isabel!" Mrs. Moskowitz snickered. "Not even sayink 'Axcuse!' he makes 'Ha, ha!' on kinks and quinns!"

This frontal attack stirred the royalists into action.

"Talk, Kaplan!"

"You got the floor, no?"

"Tell awreddy! Tell!"

A more formal dialectician cried, "Give your meanink dose remocks!"

Mr. Kaplan faced his attackers calmly, almost apologetically. "Ladies an' gantlemen, Mr. Pockheel—an' chairlady." Miss Mitnick lowered her eyes. "Ve all agreeink Colombiss's joiney vas vun de most movvellous tings in de voild." There were murmurs of affirmation. "*Tink* abot det treep, jost *tink*. Viks an' viks Colombiss vas sailink—tru storm, lighteninks, tonder. Tru vafes high like Ampire State Buildink. Fodder an' fodder Colombiss vent—alone!" Mr. Kaplan paused to let the drama sink home. "Vell, in *vat kind boats* Colombiss made det vunderful voyitch?" Mr. Kaplan's eyes narrowed. "I esk—*in vat kind boats?* Leetle, teentsy sheeps! Chizz boxes! Boats full likks! Boats full doit, joims, vater commink in! *Som* boats for discoverink America! An' det's vy I'm sayink '*Shame* on you, Foidinand an' Isabel!' " Mr. Kaplan's eyes flashed. "Couldn't dey give a man like Colombiss batter transportation!"

Fury broke in the classroom.

"Bravo!" cried Miss Caravello. "Bravo!"

"Crazy talk," muttered Mr. Matsoukas, thinking of the raft of Ulysses.

"Maybe dey should builded in 1492 a S.S. Quinn Marie?" asked Mr. Plonsky sarcastically.

Attacks, defences, taunts filled the scholastic air. Miss Mitnick, charged with the duties of arbitration, kept stammering, "Mr. Kaplan please. Mr. Kaplan please." Her voice shook. "Mr. Kaplan please. The ships Ferdinand and Isabella gave were fine for that *time.*"

"For de *time?* But not for de *man!*"

"But in those days—"

"A man like Colombiss should have averyting fromm de bast!"

Mr. Parkhill got up. It seemed to be the only thing to do. "Well, class, I think—"

"Colombiss desoived more den a Senta Maria, a Nina, an' a Pintele!" Mr. Kaplan, soulmate of Columbus, plunged on in his passion, hacking right and left without mercy in the service of his historical partner. "I say det ven a man stotts ot to discover America—"

"Columbus didn't go to discover a specific *place,"* Miss Mitnick objected.

"He didn't go for axercise!" cried Hyman Kaplan.

Miss Mitnick bit her lip. "I mean Columbus didn't *know* was America. He didn't know was a continent in Atlentic Ocean. Columbus just went out . . ."

Mr. Kaplan regarded Miss Mitnick with tolerance. *"Vy* he vent ot, plizz?"

"To—to discover," Miss Mitnick said feebly.

"Vat to discover?"

Tears were in Miss Mitnick's eyes. "Just to *discover."*

Mr. Kaplan looked from side to side, nodding. "Colombiss vent 'jost to discover,' " he repeated softly. " *'Jost* to discover.' " He sighed and shook his head, mourning man's naïveté. And then, his face lit with fervor, he struck. "Som people tink det if a man goes ot to mail a latter he *hopes* he'll find a mailbox!"

And now the battle raged once more—with shouts and cries and accusations; with lusty assaults on Mr. Kaplan's logic, and hot defences of Rose Mitnick.

In the corridors the bell rang, but no one heard it. The bell rang again, loud and long, but no one cared.

Mr. Parkhill said, "That's all for tonight, class." He said it calmly, but he had a worried look. For Mr. Parkhill felt that General Discussion had not been a complete success this evening. If only Columbus had discovered America on October eleventh; if only Hyman Kaplan had been born on October thirteenth.

OGDEN NASH

Look What You Did, Christopher!

In fourteen hundred and ninety-two,
Somebody sailed the ocean blue.
Somebody borrowed the fare in Spain
For a business trip on the bounding main,
And to prove to people, by actual test,
You could get to the East by traveling West.
Somebody said, Sail on! Sail on!
And studied China and China's lingo,
And cried from the bow, There's China now!
And promptly bumped into San Domingo.
Somebody murmured, Oh dear, oh dear!
I've discovered the Western Hemisphere.

And that, you may think, my friends, was that.
But it wasn't. Not by a fireman's hat.
Well enough wasn't left alone,
And Columbus was only a cornerstone.
There came the Spaniards,
There came the Greeks,
There came the Pilgrims in leather breeks.
There came the Dutch,
And the Poles and Swedes,
The Persians, too,
And perhaps the Medes,
The Letts, the Lapps and the Lithuanians,
Regal Russians, and ripe Roumanians.
There came the French

And there came the Finns,
And the Japanese
With their formal grins.
The Tartars came,
And the Terrible Turks—
In a word, humanity shot the works.
And the country that should have been Cathay
Decided to be
The U.S.A.

And that, you may think, my friends, was that.
But it wasn't. Not by a fireman's hat.
Christopher C. was the cornerstone,
And well enough wasn't left alone.
For those who followed
When he was through,
They burned to discover something, too.
Somebody, bored with rural scenery,
Went to work and invented machinery,
While a couple of other mental giants
Got together
And thought up Science.
Platinum blondes
(They were once peroxide),
Peruvian bonds
And carbon monoxide,
Tax evaders
And Vitamin A,
Vice crusaders,
And tattletale gray—
These, with many another phobia,
We owe to that famous Twelfth of Octobia.
O misery, misery, mumble and moan!
Someone invented the telephone,
And interrupted a nation's slumbers,
Ringing wrong but similar numbers.
Someone devised the silver screen
And the intimate Hollywood magazine,
And life is a Hades
Of clicking cameras,
And foreign ladies

Behaving amorous.
Gags have erased
Amusing dialog,
As gas replaced
The crackling firelog.
All that glitters is sold as gold,
And our daily diet grows odder and odder,
And breakfast foods are dusty and cold—
It's a wise child
That knows its fodder.
Someone invented the automobile,
And good Americans took the wheel
To view American rivers and rills
And justly famous forests and hills—
But somebody equally enterprising
Had invented billboard advertising.
You linger at home
In dark despair,
And wistfully try the electric air.
You hope for a program controversial,
And what do they give you?
A beer commercial.
Oh, Columbus was only a cornerstone,
And well enough wasn't left alone,
For the Inquisition was less tyrannical
Than the iron rules of an age mechanical,
Which, because of an error in '92,
Are clamped like corsets on me and you,
While Children of Nature we'd be today
If San Domingo
Had been Cathay.

And that, you may think, my friends, is that.
But it isn't—not by a fireman's hat.
The American people,
With grins jocose,
Always survive the fatal dose.
And though our systems are slightly wobbly,
We'll fool the doctor this time, probly.

MILT GROSS

Ferry-tail from Keeng Mitas for Nize Baby

Oohoo, nize baby, itt opp all de Cheeken Zoop so mamma'll gonna tell you a Ferry-Tail from Keeng Mitas. Wance oppon a time was a werry, werry reech Keeng from de name from Keeng Mitas. Sotch a welt wot he hed!—wot it would make J.P. Morgan witt Hanry Fudd witt John D. Rockefeller dey should look like puppers. (Nize baby, take anodder spoon cheeken zoop—)

So instat from bing setisfite witt contempted—he becrutched yat averybody helse wot dey possassed, und he was only trying how he could incriss yat wot he had (mmmm-dot griddy ting). To a whole time he was hudding opp de moneh witt glutting yat from it like a miser. So wan day he was wukking opp witt don in de godden so he was tinking so, "Hm— wot could I do, dot I should hev it ivvin more yat from wot I got?" (mmm-dot salfish critchure). So he was interropted by a leedle Ferry wot it was stealing in de front from him witt a Megic Want.

So de Ferry sad, "You Keeng Mitas???"

So de Keeng sad, "So wot is??"

So de Ferry sad, "I'm a Ferry wot I could grent you wot annyting wot you'll weesh so'll be foolfeeled de weesh!!!" So de Keeng sad, "Wot kind bunco-steerage game you call dees, ha? You got maybe some goot-for-nothing Hoil Stocks wot you want to sell it, ha, maybe? Odder a petent carpet-swipper, odder maybe a phuny Gold mine yat, ha!! Try batter by Old Keeng Cole, not by me—Goot hefternoon!"

So de Ferry sad, "Hm—you a werry septical poison, ha? Soppose wot you geeve me a hopportunity I should conweence you?"

So de Keeng said, "Ho K, I weesh wot averting wot I toch it, it should toin into gold."

So he was holding in de hand a spectre, so de Ferry gave him a tree

times a tep witt de megic want—so he gave a look—so it was by him a solit
gold spectre in de hend!!—Noo, noo!—So don't esk!!!

So de Keeng was dencing witt jomping witt lipping witt bonding witt
prencing from joy. You should see wot he was deshing hitter witt titter—
opp witt don, high witt low—beck witt futt, to witt frau,—wot he was
touching averyting on wheech he put on de hends. So his Wessel sad, "Is
goot now?" So de Keeng sad, "Yeh, is good bot look a hincome-tax I'll
gonna have und'll be mine lock yat wot I'll gat maybe to-morrow roo-
mateezum in de hends." (MMMmmm—dot apparitious ting.)

So it came gredually deener-time so de Keeng was werry hongry so he
set don he should itt opp a hoyster. So so soon wot he toched de hoyster it
became solit gold!! So he said, "Hm—Wott's dees??" So he tried he
should ketch in queek a potato in de mout no one should see, so so soon
wot he stodded he should chew it, it became solit gold wot it broke him
two teet witt a cron witt a heff from de breedge—woik yat besites wot it
was werry hot so it made him yat a bleesters on de tong!!

So he sad—"Hm!—Is a seerous preposition. It simms wot I'll have to
employ stragedy." So he sad to de Wessel, "I'll gonna stend witt de mout
open—So you'll put in a binn-shooter a hepple, wot you'll shoot it, it
should go in mine mout wot I'll swallow it queeck it shouldn't toch me."
So de Wessel compiled gredually witt de requast, bot he was a werry poor
mox-man, so instat from de Keeng's mout it went in de had wot it became
immiditly gold wot it gave him sotch a knock wot he had almost conclusion from de brain.

So was a werry cricketal situation—wot de Keeng sad, "Hm, so it
rimmains wot I'll gonna hev to leeve maybe a whole life on goldfeesh,
Ha!!" So it was gredually all kind from trobbles!! It came de night so he
stodded in he should ondrass so it was dere by him a pair from 18 carrot
Bivvy Dizz wot de wessels had to ondrass him yat witt a can uppener. So
one day he was wukking opp witt don so it came ronning over to heem his
leedle dudder—Hm, deed she was a switt child!! So he was so epsom
minded, dot dope, wot he put on her head de hend he should toch her so
she became solit gold. Yi yi yi yi—So you should see a griff from a remuss
wot it was by de Keeng—mmm!!! Deed he was sowry!!! witt meeserable
witt donhotted—witt rependant—wot he was wipping beeterly.

So it gredually appeared in de front from him de Ferry witt de Megic
Want so he sad, "Goot Monnink, Keeng, How is by you de Gold Rosh???"
So de Keeng gave sotch a grun from meesery wot it toched de Ferry's hott
—so he sad, "You'll gonna be steengy witt griddy witt salfish anny more?"

So de Keeng sad, "NO."

"You'll gonna dunnate maybe itch year someting to de Meelk Fond?"

"Yeh."

"Wid de Selwation Ommy?"

"Yeh."

"Widd de Uffan's Home?"

"Yeh."

"So you'll gonna refumm, ha?"

"Yeh."

"In odder woids you'll gonna be from now on a deeference indiwijial halltogadder?"

"Cruss mine hott!"

So de Ferry gave him tree times a tep witt de Megic Want so dere it was stending in de front from him de leedle dudder jost like new, wot dey leeved heppily hever hefter.

(Hm—Sotch a dollink baby—ate opp all de chicken Zoop!)

T. A. DALY

Mia Carlotta

Giuseppe, da barber, ees greata for "mash,"
He gotta da bigga, da blacka moustache,
Good clo'es an' good styla an' playnta good cash.

W'enevra Giuseppe ees walk on da street,
Da people dey talka, "how nobby! how neat!
How softa da handa, how smalla da feet."

He leefta hees hat an' he shaka hees curls,
An' smila weeth teetha so shiny like pearls;
Oh, manny da heart of da seelly young girls
    He gotta.
   Yes, playnta he gotta—
    But notta
    Carlotta!

Giuseppe, da barber, he maka da eye,
An' like da steam engine puffa an' sigh,
For catcha Carlotta w'en she ees go by.

Carlotta she walka weeth nose in da air,
An' look through Giuseppe weeth far-away stare,
As eef she no see dere ees som'body dere.

Giuseppe, da barber, he gotta da cash,
He gotta da clo'es an' da bigga moustache,
He gotta da seelly young girls for da "mash,"
But notta—
You bat my life, notta—
Carlotta.
I gotta!

FINLEY PETER DUNNE

Over the Counter

Ivrybody is inthrested in what ivrybody else is doin' that's wrong.

A fanatic is a man that does what he thinks th' Lord wud do if He knew th' facts iv th' case.

Th' best thing about a little judicyous swearin' is that it keeps th' temper. 'Twas intinded as a compromise between runnin' away an' fightin'. Befure it was invinted they was on'y th' two ways out iv an argymint.

Woman's rights? What does a woman want iv rights whin she has priv'leges? Rights is th' last thing we get in this wurruld. They're th' nex' things to wrongs. They're wrongs tur-ned inside out. . . . If I cud fly d'ye think I'd want to walk?

An autocrat's a ruler that does what th' people wants an' takes th' blame f'r it. A constitootional ixicutive, Hinnissy, is a ruler that does as he dam pleases an' blames th' people.

If ye put a beggar on horseback ye'll walk ye'ersilf.

All th' wurruld loves a lover—excipt sometimes th' wan that's all th' wurruld to him.

Has Andhrew Carnaygie given ye a libry yet? . . . He will. Ye'll not escape him. Befure he dies he hopes to crowd a libry on ivry man, woman, an' child in th' counthry. . . . Th' most cillybrated dead authors will be honored be havin' their names painted on th' wall in distinguished comp'ny, as thus: Andhrew Carnaygie, Shakespeare; Andhrew Carnaygie, Byron; Andhrew Carnaygie, Bobby Burns; Andhrew Carnaygie, an' so on. . . . That's th' dead authors. Th' live authors will stand outside an' wish they were dead. . . . Isn't it good f'r lithrachoor, says ye? Sure, I think not, Hinnissy. Libries niver encouraged lithrachoor anny more thin tombstones encourage livin'. No wan iver wrote annythin' because he was tol' that a hundherd years fr'm now his books might be taken down fr'm a shelf in a granite sepulcher an' some wan wud write "Good" or "This man is crazy" in th' margin. . . . What lithrachoor needs is fillin' food. . . . I'm f'r helpin' th' boys that's now on th' job.

Th' modhren idee iv governmint is "Snub th' people, buy th' people, jaw th' people."

ARTHUR KOBER

Boggains in the Bronx

Bella looked at her watch, quickly drew her napkin across her mouth, pushed the plate away, and rose. Ma Gross saw her rise and frowned.

"Come on, Pa," said Bella. "Help me clear the table."

Mr. Gross had his newspaper propped up against a sugar bowl and was too deep in a news item to pay any attention to his daughter. The latter now started stacking the dishes.

"Come on, Ma," she said. "I'll wash the dishes and you can dry them."

"Look, look, how she rushes!" Mrs. Gross was obviously suspicious of such eager and unsolicited aid. "So who you rushing to see, Miss Hurry-Shmurry? Maybe you rushing to see President Rosenvelt, he's waiting donnstairs in the hall?"

Mrs. Gross's rasping voice managed to spear her husband. "Awways talk, talk, talk with the tongue," he shouted. "Give the poor tongue a couple minutes' rest!"

"Look who's talking!" Mrs. Gross curled her lip contemptuously as she addressed her husband. "He comes home fomm woik, puts by him the nose in newspaper, and now alluva sudden Mr. Boss, he's talking. Put better back the nose in newspaper, Mr. Boss."

"Aw, please help me with the dishes, will ya?" Bella pleaded. "Kitty Shapiro and her intended, Dr. Rappaport, they're coming here to pick me up. We're gonna take in a pickcha show."

Bella's parents suddenly came to life. Pa dropped the newspaper and began to empty the remains of the evening's dinner into one large platter. Ma carefully folded the napkins and placed them in the top drawer of the bureau.

"So is coming here Kitty's intendit, the docteh?" Mrs. Gross asked with great interest.

"The denttist!" Pa was more explicit.

This subject was too familiar to Pa to be of any interest. He gathered his newspaper and wandered out toward the bathroom.

"Max and I," Bella added, "we just happen to be platonic friends."

"Tonic-shmonic! Believe me, all I say is when I see my dutter married, I'll be happy like anything. When—" The doorbell interrupted Mrs. Gross.

Bella admitted Kitty Shapiro and Dr. Rappaport.

"Hello, Kitty." Mrs. Gross's greeting was very warm. "How's the Mamma filling? She's filling good?"

"She's O.K., thank you. Oh, this here is my intended, Dr. Rappaport." She turned to her intended and took his hand. "Come here, Butchkie," she said. "Dr. Rappaport, this here is Mrs. Gross, Billie's mother."

"Pleasta meetchoo, Mrs. Gross." He extended a hand. This surprised Ma Gross, who quickly wiped her hand on her apron before shaking his.

"Likewise," she said. Suddenly her eye was caught by the engagement ring Kitty was wearing. "Say, that's some beyoodyful stone!" Kitty extended her hand so that Mrs. Gross could make a closer examination. "A stone like that must cust heavy money, believe me."

"Dr. Rappaport got it wholesale fomm a patient of his, a jewlerer," Kitty explained. "Dincha, Butchkie?" She gave her fiancé a smile which expressed profound admiration and affection.

Pa Gross came out of the bathroom, his suspenders dangling from his trousers, his newspaper in his hand. "Oh, hello, Kitty," he said, becoming aware of his guests.

"Hello, Mr. Gross. Come here, Butchkie." Again Kitty took her fiancé's hand. "This here is Mr. Gross, Billie's father. Mr. Gross, this here is my intended, Dr. Rappaport."

"Hoddeya do, Mr. Gross?"

"I can't complain, thenks," replied Mr. Gross.

"Pa! Look at you!" Bella's eyes flashed as she pointed to his trailing suspenders.

"Excuse me, Docteh," Pa apologized. "Bella don't like to see by me the pents falling donn. It ain't stylish by her."

"And by you it's stylish?" Mrs. Gross jumped to the defense of her daughter. "Listen to him awreaddy!"

"Gee, Billie." Kitty was now examining Bella's dress. "That's some nifty outfit you got on. Turn arounn." Bella did so. "Very chick, Billie. Very! Is it new?"

"I just got it last week. Max Fine gave me a card to the wholesaler's. Really like it?"

"I should say. It's very chick, Billie. Wear it in good health."

"Thank you."

Pa had sidled up to Dr. Rappaport. He tapped him on the shoulder and said, "Listen, Docteh. If you don't mind, I'd like to esk you something."

"Sure, go ahead."

"I got by me here in mouth a britch—" Pa opened his mouth and pulled his lip up with his finger. Bella turned and looked at her father in dismay.

"Pa!" she cried. "Waddeya doing?"

"Look at him! This is nice! This is refined!" It was Ma who was now indignant.

"What'sa metta?" Pa asked, closing his mouth. "What I done so terrible?"

"The Docteh is here a guest in house," Ma explained. "He didn't come here fa no visits fa two and a half dolless."

"Oh, that's awright," said Dr. Rappaport, generously. "I don't mind."

"Give him one of your cards, Butchkie." Kitty turned to the others. "I better start getting my future hubby some business now."

"What pickcha we seeing?" asked Bella, looking into the bureau mirror as she got into her coat.

"Oh, there's one down the street where Herbert Moshill takes off a doctor. I thought it would be good fa Dr. Rappaport to see it. You know," Kitty explained, "because they got things in common. Well, goodnight."

Goodnights were exchanged. Ma waited until Bella and her friends had gone before she expressed herself.

"You seen the stone Kitty got on?" she asked her husband.

"No," he said.

"Such a stone!" She shrugged her shoulders. "Such stones I don't even wish my worst enemies. In five-and-ten cent stores you get such stones. Believe me, before our Bella wears such a ring, betta she stick single."

"A nice boy, the Docteh," Pa said abstractedly, turning the pages of the newspaper.

"What's so nice? A shrimp! A skinny boy! Comes a good wind and blows him right away. Nice! Before our Bella marries such a shrimp, betta she stick single."

Pa looked up from his newspaper in surprise. "You want Bella to stay single?"

"God fabbid!" Ma quickly replied. "Oney such boggains like that dent-tist, Kitty Shapiro can kipp!"

Genghis & Sylvia Khan

B. KLIBAN

JOHN COLLINS BOSSIDY

On the Aristocracy of Harvard

And this is good old Boston,
  The home of the bean and the cod,
Where the Lowells talk only to Cabots
And the Cabots talk only to God.

FREDERICK SCHEETZ JONES

On the Democracy of Yale

Here's to the town of New Haven,
  The Home of the Truth and the Light,
Where God talks to Jones in the very same tones
  That he uses with Hadley and Dwight.

Sherman's March

Allan Sherman was the *enfant wonderful* at the University of Illinois in the middle 1940s. He produced the annual campus variety show, for which he wrote the book, music, and lyrics. I was in two of those shows and I still sing his antic songs with pleasure.

In 1951 he and a friend created the idea for the TV panel show "I've Got a Secret," which he sold to Goodson-Todman for One Dollar. (Math he didn't major in.) Allan never stopped writing parodies and in 1963 he made an album called *My Son, the Folksinger,* expecting nothing. Surprise. It was a cascading hit, it hurled him into celebrity, and "My Son, the———" swept the country. It was adapted by everyone from newspaper headline writers to El Al Airlines ads ("My Son, the Pilot").

Allan spent the rest of his too-brief life entertaining audiences beyond counting. (Anyone who sells a TV show for One Dollar *is* beyond counting.) This is one of his favorite lyrics, put to the tune of "The Battle Hymn of the Republic."   **G.S.**

ALLAN SHERMAN

The Drapes of Roth

(Sung to the tune of "The Battle Hymn of the Republic")

I'm singing you the ballad
Of a great man of the cloth,
His name was Harry Lewis
And he worked for Irving Roth.
He died while cutting velvet
On a hot July the Fourth . . .
But his cloth goes shining on.

Glory, glory, Harry Lewis.
Glory, glory, Harry Lewis.
Glory, glory, Harry Lewis.
His cloth goes shining on.

Oh, Harry Lewis perished
In the service of his lord.
He was trampling through the warehouse
Where the drapes of Roth are stored.
He had the finest funeral
The Union could afford
And his cloth goes shining on.

Glory, glory, Harry Lewis.
Glory, glory, Harry Lewis.
Glory, glory, Harry Lewis.
His cloth goes shining on.

Although a fire was raging,
Harry stood by his machine.
And when the firemen broke in
They discovered him between
A pile of roasted Dacron
And some french-fried gabardine.
His cloth goes shining on.

Glory, glory, Harry Lewis.
Glory, glory, Harry Lewis.
Glory, glory, Harry Lewis.
His cloth goes shining on.

GARY LARSON

JACK ZIEGLER

DOROTHY PARKER

Résumé

Razors pain you;
Rivers are damp;
Acids stain you;
And drugs cause cramp.
Guns aren't lawful;
Nooses give;
Gas smells awful;
You might as well live.

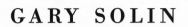

WILLIAM SAROYAN

Old Country Advice to the American Traveler

One year my uncle Melik traveled from Fresno to New York. Before he got aboard the train his uncle Garro paid him a visit and told him about the dangers of travel.

When you get on the train, the old man said, choose your seat carefully, sit down, and do not look about.

Yes, sir, my uncle said.

Several moments after the train begins to move, the old man said, two men wearing uniforms will come down the aisle and ask you for your ticket. Ignore them. They will be imposters.

How will I know? my uncle said.

You will know, the old man said. You are no longer a child.

Yes, sir, my uncle said.

Before you have traveled twenty miles an amiable young man will come to you and offer you a cigarette. Tell him you don't smoke. The cigarette will be doped.

Yes, sir, said my uncle.

On your way to the diner a very beautiful young woman will bump into you intentionally and almost embrace you, the old man said. She will be extremely apologetic and attractive, and your natural impulse will be to cultivate her friendship. Dismiss your natural impulse and go on in and eat. The woman will be an adventuress.

A what? my uncle said.

A whore, the old man shouted. Go on in and eat. Order the best food, and if the diner is crowded, and the beautiful young woman sits across the table from you, do not look into her eyes. If she speaks, pretend to be deaf.

Yes, sir, my uncle said.

Pretend to be deaf, the old man said. That is the only way out of it.

Out of what? my uncle said.

Out of the whole ungodly mess, the old man said. I have traveled. I know what I'm talking about.

Yes, sir, my uncle said.

Let's say no more about it, the old man said.

Yes, sir, my uncle said.

Let's not speak of the matter again, the old man said. It's finished. I have seven children. My life has been a full and righteous one. Let's not give it another thought. I have land, vines, trees, cattle, and money. One cannot have everything—except for a day or two at a time.

Yes, sir, my uncle said.

On your way back to your seat from the diner, the old man said, you will pass through the smoker. There you will find a game of cards in progress. The players will be three middle-aged men with expensive-looking rings on their fingers. They will nod at you pleasantly and one of them will invite you to join the game. Tell them, No speak English.

Yes, sir, my uncle said.

That is all, the old man said.

Thank you very much, my uncle said.

One thing more, the old man said. When you go to bed at night, take your money out of your pocket and put it in your shoe. Put your shoe under your pillow, keep your head on the pillow all night, *and don't sleep.*

Yes, sir, my uncle said.

That is all, the old man said.

The old man went away and the next day my uncle Melik got aboard the train and traveled straight across America to New York. The two men in uniforms were not imposters, the young man with the doped cigarette did not arrive, the beautiful young woman did not sit across the table from my uncle in the diner, and there was no card game in progress in the smoker. My uncle put his money in his shoe and put his shoe under his pillow and put his head on the pillow and didn't sleep all night the first night, but the second night he abandoned the whole ritual.

The second day he *himself* offered another young man a cigarette which the other young man accepted. In the diner my uncle went out of his way to sit at a table with a young lady. He started a poker game in the smoker, and long before the train ever got to New York my uncle knew everybody aboard the train and everybody knew him. Once, while the train was traveling though Ohio, my uncle and the young man who had accepted the cigarette and two young ladies on their way to Vassar formed a quartette and sang *The Wabash Blues*.

The journey was a very pleasant one.

When my uncle Melik came back from New York, his old uncle Garro visited him again.
I see you are looking all right, he said. Did you follow my instructions?
Yes, sir, my uncle said.

The old man looked far away in space.
I am pleased that *someone* has profited by my experience, he said.

———————————

EDWIN ARLINGTON ROBINSON

Miniver Cheevy

Miniver Cheevy, child of scorn,
  Grew lean while he assailed the seasons;
He wept that he was ever born,
  And he had reasons.

Miniver loved the days of old
  When swords were bright and steeds were prancing;
The vision of a warrior bold
  Would set him dancing.

Miniver sighed for what was not,
  And dreamed, and rested from his labors;
He dreamed of Thebes and Camelot,
  And Priam's neighbors.

Miniver mourned the ripe renown
  That made so many a name so fragrant;
He mourned Romance, now on the town,
  And Art, a vagrant.

Miniver loved the Medici,
  Albeit he had never seen one;
He would have sinned incessantly
  Could he have been one.

Miniver cursed the commonplace
  And eyed a khaki suit with loathing;
He missed the mediaeval grace
  Of iron clothing.

Miniver scorned the gold he sought,
  But sore annoyed was he without it;
Miniver thought, and thought, and thought,
  And thought about it.

Miniver Cheevy, born too late,
  Scratched his head and kept on thinking;
Miniver coughed, and called it fate.
  And kept on drinking.

D. F. PARRY

Miniver Cheevy, Jr.

Miniver Cheevy, Jr., child
  Of Robinson's renowned creation,
Also lamented and reviled
  His generation.

Miniver similarly spurned
  The present that so irked his pater,
But that langsyne for which he yearned
  Came somewhat later.

Miniver wished he were alive
  When dividends came due each quarter,
When Goldman Sachs was 205,
  And skirts were shorter.

Miniver gave no hoot in hell
  For Camelot or Troy's proud pillage;
He would have much preferred to dwell
  In Greenwich Village.

Miniver cherished fond regrets
  For days when benefits were boundless;
When radios were crystal sets,
  And films were soundless.

Miniver missed the iron grills,
  The whispered word, the swift admission,
The bath-tub gin, and other thrills
  Of Prohibition.

Miniver longed, as all men long,
  To turn back time (his eyes would moisten),
To dance the Charleston, play mah jong,
  And smuggle Joyce in.

Miniver Cheevy, Jr., swore,
  Drank till his health was quite imperiled;
Miniver sighed, and read some more
  F. Scott Fitzgerald.

E. B. WHITE

Across the Street and into the Grill

(With respects to Ernest Hemingway)

This is my last and best and true and only meal, thought Mr. Perley as he descended at noon and swung east on the beat-up sidewalk of Forty-fifth Street. Just ahead of him was the girl from the reception desk. I am a little fleshed up around the crook of the elbow, thought Perley, but I commute good.

He quickened his step to overtake her and felt the pain again. What a stinking trade it is, he thought. But after what I've done to other assistant treasurers, I can't hate anybody. Sixteen deads, and I don't know how many possibles.

The girl was near enough now so he could smell her fresh receptiveness, and the lint in her hair. Her skin was light blue, like the sides of horses.

"I love you," he said, "and we are going to lunch together for the first and only time, and I love you very much."

"Hello, Mr. Perley," she said, overtaken. "Let's not think of anything."

A pair of fantails flew over from the sad old Guaranty Trust Company, their wings set for a landing. A lovely double, thought Perley, as he pulled. "Shall we go to the Hotel Biltmore, on Vanderbilt Avenue, which is merely a feeder land for the great streets, or shall we go to Schrafft's, where my old friend Botticelli is captain of girls and where they have the mayonnaise in fiascos?"

"Let's go to Schrafft's," said the girl, low. "But first I must phone Mummy." She stepped into a public booth and dialled true and well, using her finger. Then she telephoned.

As they walked on, she smelled good. She smells good, thought Perley.

But that's all right, I add good. And when we get to Schrafft's, I'll order from the menu, which I like very much indeed.

They entered the restaurant. The wind was still west, ruffling the edges of the cookies. In the elevator, Perley took the controls. "I'll run it," he said to the operator. "I checked out long ago." He stopped true at the third floor, and they stepped off into the men's grill.

"Good morning, my Assistant Treasurer," said Botticelli, coming forward with a fiasco in each hand. He nodded at the girl, who he knew was from the West Seventies and whom he desired.

"Can you drink the water here?" asked Perley. He had the fur trapper's eye and took in the room at a glance, noting that there was one empty table and three pretty waitresses.

Botticelli led the way to the table in the corner, where Perley's flanks would be covered.

"Alexanders," said Perley. "Eighty-six to one. The way Chris mixes them. Is this table all right, Daughter?"

Botticelli disappeared and returned soon, carrying the old Indian blanket.

"That's the same blanket, isn't it?" asked Perley.

"Yes. To keep the wind off," said the Captain, smiling from the backs of his eyes. "It's still west. It should bring the ducks in tomorrow, the chef thinks."

Mr. Perley and the girl from the reception desk crawled down under the table and pulled the Indian blanket over them so it was solid and good and covered them right. The girl put her hand on his wallet. It was cracked and old and held his commutation book. "We are having fun, aren't we?" she asked.

"Yes, Sister," he said.

"I have here the soft-shelled crabs, my Assistant Treasurer," said Botticelli. "And another fiasco of the 1926. This one is cold."

"Dee the soft-shelled crabs," said Perley from under the blanket. He put his arm around the receptionist good.

"Do you think we should have a green pokeweed salad?" she asked. "Or shall we not think of anything for a while?"

"We shall not think of anything for a while, and Botticelli would bring the pokeweed if there was any," said Perley. "It isn't the season." Then he spoke to the Captain. "Botticelli, do you remember when we took all the mailing envelopes from the stockroom, spit on the flaps, and then drank rubber cement till the foot soldiers arrived?"

"I remember, my Assistant Treasurer," said the Captain. It was a little joke they had.

"He used to mineograph pretty good," said Perley to the girl. "But that was another war. Do I bore you, Mother?"

"Please keep telling me about your business experiences, but not the rough parts." She touched his hand where the knuckles were scarred and stained by so many old mimeographings. "Are both your flanks covered, my dearest?" she asked, plucking at the blanket. They felt the Alexanders in their eyeballs. Eighty-six to one.

"Schrafft's is a good place and we're having fun and I love you," Perley said. He took another swallow of the 1926, and it was a good and careful swallow. "The stockroom men were very brave," he said, "but it is a position where it is extremely difficult to stay alive. Just outside that room is a little bare-assed highboy and it is in the way of the stuff that is being brought up. The hell with it. When you make a breakthrough, Daughter, first you clean out the baskets and the halfwits, and all the time they have the fire escapes taped. They also shell you with old production orders, many of them approved by the general manager in charge of sales. I am boring you and I will not at this time discuss the general manager in charge of sales as we are unquestionably being listened to by that waitress over there who is setting out the decoys."

"I am going to give you my piano," the girl said, "so that when you look at it you can think of me. It will be something between us."

"Call up and have them bring the piano to the restaurant," said Perley. "Another fiasco, Botticelli!"

They drank the sauce. When the piano came, it wouldn't play. The keys were stuck good. "Never mind, we'll leave it here, Cousin," said Perley.

They came out from under the blanket and Perley tipped their waitress exactly fifteen per cent minus withholding. They left the piano in the restaurant, and when they went down the elevator and out and turned in to the old, hard, beat-up pavement of Fifth Avenue and headed south toward Forty-fifth Street, where the pigeons were, the air was as clean as your grandfather's howitzer. The wind was still west.

I commute good, thought Perley, looking at his watch. And he felt the old pain of going back to Scarsdale again.

ROBERT BENCHLEY

Christmas Afternoon

Done in the Manner, if Not the Spirit, of Dickens

What an afternoon! Mr. Gummidge said that, in his estimation, there never had *been* such an afternoon since the world began, a sentiment which was heartily endorsed by Mrs. Gummidge and all the little Gummidges, not to mention the relatives who had come over from Jersey for the day.

In the first place, there was the ennui. And such ennui as it was! A heavy, overpowering ennui, such as results from a participation in eight courses of steaming, gravied food, topping off with salted nuts which the little old spinster Gummidge from Oak Hill said she never knew when to stop eating—and true enough she didn't—a dragging, devitalizing ennui, which left its victims strewn about the living-room in various attitudes of prostration suggestive of those of the petrified occupants in a newly unearthed Pompeiian dwelling; an ennui which carried with it a retinue of yawns, snarls and thinly veiled insults, and which ended in ruptures in the clan spirit serious enough to last throughout the glad new year.

Then there were the toys! Three and a quarter dozen toys to be divided among seven children. Surely enough, you or I might say, to satisfy the little tots. But that would be because we didn't know the tots. In came Baby Lester Gummidge, Lillian's boy, dragging an electric grain-elevator which happened to be the only toy in the entire collection which appealed to little Norman, five-year-old son of Luther, who lived in Rahway. In came curly-headed Effie in frantic and throaty disputation with Arthur, Jr., over the possession of an articulated zebra. In came Everett, bearing a mechanical negro which would no longer dance, owing to a previous forcible feeding by the baby of a marshmallow into its only available aperture. In came Fonlansbee, teeth buried in the hand of little Ormond, which bore a popular but battered remnant of what had once been the proud false-bosom of a hussar's uniform. In they all came, one after another, some crying, some snapping, some pulling, some pushing—all appealing to their respective parents for aid in their intra-mural warfare.

And the cigar smoke! Mrs. Gummidge said that she didn't mind the smoke from a good cigarette, but would they mind if she opened the windows for just a minute in order to clear the room of the heavy aroma of used cigars? Mr. Gummidge stoutly maintained that they were good cigars. His brother, George Gummidge, said that he, likewise, would say that they were. At which colloquial sally both the Gummidge brothers laughed testily, thereby breaking the laughter record for the afternoon.

Aunt Libbie, who lived with George, remarked from the dark corner of the room that it seemed just like Sunday to her. An amendment was offered to this statement by the cousin, who was in the insurance business, stating that it was worse than Sunday. Murmurings indicative of as hearty agreement with this sentiment as their lethargy would allow came from the other members of the family circle, causing Mr. Gummidge to suggest a walk in the air to settle their dinner.

And then arose such a chorus of protestations as has seldom been heard. It was too cloudy to walk. It was too raw. It looked like snow. It looked like rain. Luther Gummidge said that he must be starting along home soon, anyway, bringing forth the acid query from Mrs. Gummidge as to whether or not he was bored. Lillian said that she felt a cold coming on, and added that something they had had for dinner must have been undercooked. And so it went, back and forth, forth and back, up and down, and in and out, until Mr. Gummidge's suggestion of a walk in the air was reduced to a tattered impossibility and the entire company glowed with ill-feeling.

In the meantime, we must not forget the children. No one else could. Aunt Libbie said that she didn't think there was anything like children to make a Christmas; to which Uncle Ray, the one with the Masonic fob, said, "No, thank God!" Although Christmas is supposed to be the season of good cheer, you (or I, for that matter) couldn't have told, from listening to the little ones, but what it was the children's Armageddon season, when Nature had decreed that only the fittest should survive, in order that the race might be carried on by the strongest, the most predatory and those possessing the best protective colouring. Although there were constant admonitions to Fonlansbee to "Let Ormond have that whistle now; it's his," and to Arthur, Jr., not to be selfish, but to "give the kiddie-car to Effie; she's smaller than you are," the net result was always that Fonlansbee kept the whistle and Arthur, Jr., rode in permanent, albeit disputed, possession of the kiddie-car. Oh, that we mortals should set ourselves up against the inscrutable workings of Nature!

Hallo! A great deal of commotion! That was Uncle George stumbling over the electric train, which had early in the afternoon ceased to function and which had been left directly across the threshold. A great deal of crying! That was Arthur, Jr., bewailing the destruction of his already useless train, about which he had forgotten until the present moment. A great deal of recrimination! That was Arthur, Sr., and George fixing it up. And finally a great crashing! That was Baby Lester pulling over the tree on top of himself, necessitating the bringing to bear of all of Uncle Ray's knowledge of forestry to extricate him from the wreckage.

And finally Mrs. Gummidge passed the Christmas candy around. Mr. Gummidge afterward admitted that this was a tactical error on the part of his spouse. I no more believe that Mrs. Gummidge thought they wanted that Christmas candy than I believe that she thought they wanted the cold turkey which she later suggested. My opinion is that she wanted to drive them home. At any rate, that is what she succeeded in doing. Such cries as there were of "Ugh! Don't let me see another thing to eat!" and "Take it away!" Then came hurried scramblings in the coat-closet for overshoes. There were the rasping sounds made by cross parents when putting wraps on children. There were insincere exhortations to "come and see us soon" and to "get together for lunch some time." And, finally, there were slammings of doors and the silence of utter exhaustion, while Mrs. Gummidge went about picking up stray sheets of wrapping paper.

And, as Tiny Tim might say in speaking of Christmas afternoon as an institution, "God help us, every one."

GAHAN WILSON

"Then Mrs. Cratchit entered, smiling proudly, with the pudding. Oh, a wonderful pudding! Shaped like a cannonball, blazing in half-a-quartern of ignited brandy bedight with Christmas holly stuck into the top, and stuffed full with plums and sweetmeats and sodium diacetate and monoglyceride and potassium bromate and aluminum phosphate and calcium phosphate monobasic and chloromine T and aluminum potassium sulfate and calcium propionate and sodium alginate and butylated hydroxyanisole and . . ."

MAX SHULMAN

Excerpts from Barefoot Boy with Cheek

The morning of the big day dawned bright and clear. As the rosy fingers of the sun crept through my window and illuminated the C&H on my homemade bed sheet, I could scarcely contain myself. "Huzzah!" I shouted. "Huzzah!"

I bounded joyously from my bed. I bounded right back again. My drop-seat pajamas had become entangled in a bedspring during the night. Disengaging myself, I ran to wake Mother. "Mother," I called. "Mother, give me to eat."

But lovable old Mother had anticipated me. She had been up for hours. While I had lain in drowsyland, she had slaughtered the brood sow and bustled about preparing the morning meal. When I came into the kitchen, my favorite breakfast was already on the table.

"Mother!" I cried. "Johnson grass and brala suet. Just for me."

"Set down and eat, slugabed," she chided gently. "You don't want to be late the first day."

I could not help taking her in my arms and kissing her careworn cheek. A person can choose his friends and select a wife, but he has only one mother, I always say. The trouble with many of us is that we don't appreciate our mothers. I think that a certain day should be set aside each year and dedicated to mothers. It could be called "Mother's Day."

"Son," she said, "you ain't my baby no more."

"The hell you say, Mother," I said. "The hell you say."

"You're agoin' off to thet air university and get your haid all full of l'arnin', and you're gonna fergit your pore old igerant mother."

"Aw, you're not so dumb," I protested.

"Yes, I be," she declared. "I don't know no more than your old houn' dog Edmund layin' over there by the stove."

I jumped up from the table. "Now just you be careful what you're saying about Edmund. I don't mean to have that dog run down when I'm here. He's a mighty smart dog." I whistled to him. "Play dead, Edmund," I said. "See," I told Mother. "Look at how he obeys. All four feet sticking up in the air."

"He ain't playin', son," Mother said softly. "I didn't want to tell you. He's been dead since Friday."

Edmund dead! I couldn't believe it. Why, only last Friday I had seen him happily flushing grouse. In his excitement he had flushed too many, and we had had to call a plumber. But it was all fixed now, and Edmund was forgiven. Naturally, I had punished him, but—— No. No! I couldn't have——

"Mother!" I cried.

"Yes, son," she said. "He died right after. That last time you ran over him with the car did it."

I stumbled over to the window and pressed my hot forehead against the pane. A cloud passed over the sun, and it began to rain. The room was oppressively quiet. A loon cried over the lake.

Father came into the kitchen. "Good morning, son," he said. "I came to say good-by before you went off to the University."

"Thank you," I said simply.

"Button your fly," Mother said.

"Oh, button your lip," Father exclaimed testily, and hit her in the mouth with a skillet. Mother went to weld her dentures.

Father came over and put his arm around me. "Son, today you are entering a new phase of your life."

"Oh, can't you leave me alone?" I snapped. "Can't anybody leave me alone?"

Father drew back. "Why, son, what's the matter? This should be the happiest day in your life."

I laughed ironically. "The happiest day of your life, he says."

"No, no," Father interrupted. "I said the happiest day *in* your life. Not *of—in!*"

"Oh. Excuse me. The happiest day in your life, he says." I lifted my clenched fists. "Oh, ironical gods! What a mockery you have made of this day."

"Why, son, what——"

I pointed mutely to Edmund.

"I understand," said Father simply.

The door opened and two men from the animal rescue league came in.

They took Edmund. "Neighbors been complaining," one of them explained.

Father put an arm around my shaking shoulders. "You know, son," he said, "I had a dog once. A little Pekingese bitch named Anna May."

"Is it true what they say about the Pekingese, Father?" I asked.

He winked obscenely and continued: "She wasn't much of a dog, I guess. She couldn't hunt. She was no good as a watchdog. All she did all day long was lie on a chaise longue reading slim yellow French novels and eating bonbons. But when I came home at night from a hard day at the egg candlery, Anna May was always waiting, wagging her little tail and being sick on the rug. I—I guess I loved her, that's all," Father said.

"I understand," I said simply.

"But I didn't have Anna May long. One day my cousin May Fuster came to visit me. You remember May, don't you, son?"

"Of course," I said. "Whatever became of her?"

"It's a long story. She ran off with a full-blooded Chippewa named Alf Mountainclimbing. He took her to La Paz, Bolivia, where he found employment as a clerk in an Adam hat store. At first May loved it down there. She used to watch the colorful *pesos* riding around in their old-fashioned *tortillas*. Every afternoon she used to lie down and take a *hacienda*. During the carnival season she would put on her *vincent lopez* and dance in the street with the rest of the happy natives. In her own words she was, as the expression goes, very *muy Usted*.

"But a cloud passed over the sunshine of her life. Alf's Chippewa heritage manifested itself. He started to drink heavily. One could always find him sprawled drunkenly over a table in one of the lower-class *cojones* of La Paz. He lost his position at the hat store. Poor May, in order to keep body and soul together, was forced into inter-American relations with the natives.

"Alf grew progressively worse. His alcoholic brain cells finally failed him. One day he dropped to all fours and declared that he was a pinball machine. From that day on he remained in that position, complaining occasionally that he was being tilted.

"May's sultry Northern beauty brought her a large and varied clientele. One of her patrons was Ed Frenesi, the local bullfight impressario. Frenesi remarked the supple grace of her limbs and suggested to her that she should become a female bullfighter.

"Of course she scoffed at the idea. But after he offered her 5,000 *muchachas* (about thirty-four hundred dollars) while she was learning and 5,000 more for every bull she killed, May accepted."

"I understand," I said simply.

"Then began a rigorous training period. First she trained with less dangerous bulls from which the horns had been removed. May was up early every morning making passes at the dehorns. All day long she practiced in the hot sun with a draped cape and a gored sword. She retired every evening at eight, and after reading Hemingway for an hour fell into the deep sleep of fatigue.

"Frenesi watched her progress with considerable satisfaction. He saw how easily she mastered the intricate art of dominating the bull, and he knew that if everything went right he would have a great attraction. He taught May by easy stages until she learned the ultimate accomplishment in the bullfighter's craft—the Veronica, or killing a bull while your hair hangs over one eye. Then Frenesi knew that she was ready for her debut. He Latinized her name to Yanqui Imperialismo, and splashed posters all over La Paz.

"Frenesi's shrewd showmanship had its desired effect. For weeks before the bullfight nobody in La Paz talked about anything but *el toreador broad*—the lady bullfighter. From all the surrounding territories people poured into La Paz. Hotel rooms were filled almost immediately, and thousands of visitors had to sleep on makeshift *frijoles* in the lobbies. The wineshops and cafés were unable to handle all their trade. Alf, May's husband, took in a considerable sum posing as a pinball machine in a downtown tavern. La Paz's choked streets resounded with good-natured cries of 'I spit in the milk of your motor,' and 'I this and that on your this.' The land office did a land-office business."

Father took a guitar from the mantel and struck chords as he continued his narrative. "The day of the big fight dawned bright and clear. In the morning Frenesi went down to the bull pen and selected a crowd pleaser named Harry Holstein as May's opponent. May went to her dressing room at the arena where her cross-eyed seamstress named Pilar helped her with the involved business of dressing. May was nervous and frightened, but Pilar reassured her. 'Do not be afraid, my little,' she said. 'We all got to go sometime.'

"At last May heard the fanfare, and she knew that the *Presidente* had entered his box. The fight was about to begin. Suddenly May was in the center of the hot white sand of the arena. A roar rose from a hundred thousand throats. A gate swung open, and Harry Holstein, pawing and snorting, charged into the ring.

"Now the fear left May. Coolly she prepared to nimbly sidestep the initial charge of the beast. But, alas, her cross-eyed seamstress had tied the laces of her two shoes together. She could not move.

"May was impaled on the horns of the bull. What a dilemma! The attendants rushed from the sidelines to rescue her. The angry, cheated people in the stands cut off their ears and threw them into the arena with enraged cries of '*Olé! Olé!*'

"May eventually recovered. As soon as she could, she left La Paz. Her name was anathema in the town. She tried to see Frenesi once, but he instructed his housekeeper to pour hot water on her.

"So she wandered from one South American city to another, eking out a bare living tuning guitars and dealing double Canfield. Today, a broken woman, she earns a meager subsistence as a harbor buoy in Havana."

"But what about your Pekingese, Father?" I asked.

"Gad, son, look at the time!" Father exclaimed. "You'll be late for school."

*   *   *

St. Paul and Minneapolis extend from the Mississippi River like the legs on a pair of trousers. Where they join is the University of Minnesota.

I stood that day and gazed at the campus, my childish face looking up, holding wonder like a cup; my little feet beating time, time, time, in a sort of runic rhyme. A fraternity man's convertible ran me down, disturbing my reverie. "Just a flesh wound," I mumbled to disinterested passersby.

With eager steps I proceeded to explore the campus. All around me was the hum of happy men at work. Here were masons aging a building so they could hang ivy on it. There were chiselers completing the statue of Cyrus Thresher, first regent of the University. It was Thresher, as you know, who said, "It takes a heap o' learnin' to make a school a school." Yonder were landscapers cleverly trimming a twelve-foot hedge to spell "Minnesota, Minnesota, rah, rah, ree. Little brown jug, how we love thee."

The architecture at Minnesota is very distinctive, and thereby hangs a tale. It goes back a good many years, back to the time when the mighty, sprawling University was just an infant. At that time Art Chaff, the son of a wealthy Minneapolis flour miller named Elihu Chaff, was expelled from Harvard for playing buck euchre on the Sabbath. Old Elihu was deeply incensed by the indignity. He was determined that Art should go to college, and, moreover, to a bigger college than Harvard.

So Elihu went to work on the University of Minnesota campus. He erected twenty buildings. They all looked like grain elevators, for that is what Elihu intended to use them for after Art had been graduated. But Elihu never fulfilled his plan.

One weekend Elihu went fishing, accompanied only by an Indian guide named Ralph Duckhonking. They went into a deep forest, and after two days Duckhonking came out alone. He was wearing Elihu's suit and carrying all of his valuables. He said he knew nothing about Elihu's disappearance. Duckhonking was indicted for murder, but he was never tried because it was impossible to obtain twelve English-speaking veniremen in that judicial district. Duckhonking walked about free until he died more than twenty years later of nepotism. This case later became famous as the *Crédit Mobilier* scandal.

Elihu's elevators, therefore, remained part of the University. In fact, out of respect to Elihu, all the buildings which were subsequently erected on the campus were built to resemble grain elevators.

But this was no time to be gawking about the campus. I had things to do. First I had to see Mr. Ingelbretsvold, my freshman adviser, about making out a program of studies for the year. Obtaining directions from a friendly upperclassman who sold me a freshman button, freshman cap, subscription to *Ski-U-Mah,* the campus humor magazine, a map of the campus, and a souvenir score card of last year's home-coming game, I proceeded to the office of Mr. Ingelbretsvold.

A line of freshmen stood in front of his door. I knew how they must feel, about to embark on this great adventure, and I could not help cheerily hollering "Halloa" to them. They stoned me in an amiable fashion.

At last a voice came from behind the door bidding me come in. How my heart beat as I opened the door and trod across the luxuriant burlap rug to Mr. Ingelbretsvold's desk.

"My name is Asa Hearthrug and I've come for advice," I said.

He stood up and smiled at me kindly. "Sit down, young man," he said.

"Thank you," I said, making a low curtsey.

"Well, it's certainly a nice day."

"Yes," I agreed. "Almost twelve inches of rain since sunup."

"That's what I meant," he said. "It's a nice rain. It will help the potato crop."

"Yes," I agreed, "it should wash out every potato in Minnesota."

"That's what I meant," he said. "It will get rid of those damn potatoes. People are eating altogether too many potatoes. But enough of this meteorological chitchat. Let's get down to business. First of all, I want you to know that I'm your friend."

I licked his hand gratefully.

"You are about to enter a new phase of your life. I wonder whether you realize just how important this is."

"Oh, I do, sir, I do," I exclaimed.

"Shut up when I'm talking," he said. "Now, I have a little story that I like to tell to freshmen to impress them with the importance of college. I have had a great many students who were graduated from Minnesota and went out to take their places in the world come back after many years and say to me, 'Mr. Ingelbretsvold, I can never thank you enough for that little story you told me when I first came to the University.' Yes, young man, this story has helped a great many people, and I hope it will help you."

"So tell it already," I said.

"Well, sir, when I was a boy I had a good friend named Kyrie Eleison. We went through grade school and high school together, and on the night we were graduated from high school I said to him, 'Well, Kyrie, what are you going to do now?'

" 'Oh,' he said, 'I've got a chance to get a job in a nepotism business in North Dakota.'

" 'Kyrie,' I told him, 'don't take it. Come to college with me, or else you'll always regret it.'

"But he didn't choose to take my advice. I went to college, and he took the job. Yes, he did well at his work. By the time he was thirty he had seventy-five million dollars, and he has been getting richer ever since. He built a fine big house in which he holds the most lavish social affairs in the whole Northwest.

"Well, sir, one night I was invited to a party at Kyrie's house. I rented a suit and went. The house was filled with prominent people. A hundred-and-twenty-piece orchestra was playing. When we went in for dinner the table groaned with all sorts of expensive delicacies. And at the head of the table sat Kyrie, the monarch of all he surveyed.

"But during the course of the dinner a well-dressed young woman leaned over and said to Kyrie, 'Who was the eighth avatar of Vishnu?' and Kyrie, for all his wealth and power, did not know the answer."

"How ghastly!" I cried, throwing up my hands.

"Yes," said Mr. Ingelbretsvold. "You will find that sort of thing all through life. People come up to you on the street and say, 'Does a paramecium beat its flagella?' or 'How many wheels has a fiacre?' or 'When does an oryx mate?' and if you have not been to college, you simply cannot answer them."

"But that cannot happen to me. I am going to the University," I said.

"Ah, but it can," Mr. Ingelbretsvold answered. "It happens to many who go to college."

"But how?"

"You see, my boy, a great many people go to college to learn how to *do* something. They study medicine or law or engineering, and when they are through they know how to trepan a skull or where to get a writ of estoppel or how to find the torque of a radial engine. But just come up to them and ask how many caliphs succeeded Mohammed or who wrote *Baby Duncan's Whistling Lung* and they stare at you blankly."

I shuddered. "Oh, please, Mr. Ingelbretsvold," I begged, "what must I do?"

"You must do like I tell you. You must let college make you a well-rounded-out personality. That is the chief function and purpose of this University: to make you a well-rounded-out personality. Now you get out a pencil and paper and write down the names of the courses I am going to give you. If you follow this program you will find yourself a well-rounded-out personality."

I took out a pencil and poised it over my dickey bosom.

"Ready. Here they are: Races and Cultures of Arabia, Egypt, and North Africa; Ethnology of India; History of Architecture; Greek; Latin; Sixteenth-Century Literature; Seventeenth-Century Literature; Eighteenth-Century Literature; Nineteenth-Century Literature; Twentieth-Century Literature; Geography; Ancient History; Medieval History; Modern History; Ancient Philosophy; Modern Philosophy; Contemporary Philosophy; History of Religion; American Government; British Government; Chinese Government; Japanese Government; Lett Government; First Aid; Public Health; General Psychology; Psychology of Learning; Psychology of Advertising; Psychology of Literature; Psychology of Art; Psychology of Behavior; Animal Psychology; Abnormal Psychology; Norwegian; Swedish; Danish; French; German; Russian; Italian; Lett; Urban Sociology; Rural Sociology; Juvenile Sociology; Statistical Sociology; Criminology; Penology; Elocution; Speech Pathology; and Canoe Paddling.

"That will do for a start. As you go into these courses you will find others that will interest you too."

"And these will make me a well-rounded-out personality?" I asked.

He laughed gently. "Oh no, my boy. That is only a small but essential part of rounding out your personality. There is the social life too." He nudged me and winked. "A fellow can have a good time here."

"Sir," I said, and blushed.

"But you'll soon find out all about that. Now, one more thing. In addition to the work you do for these courses I have named you should do a lot of reading that has not been assigned in your classes. Do you read anything now?"

"A mystery story now and then," I confessed.

"Oh, have you read Rex Snout's latest, *The Case of the Gelded Gnu?*"

"No, but I read the one before that, *The Case of the Missing Lynx.*"

"I missed that one. What was it about?"

"Well, a horribly mutilated corpse is found on the railroad tracks near Buffalo. This corpse is in such a state that it is impossible to identify it or even to tell whether it is a man or a woman. The story is concerned almost entirely with trying to establish the identity of the corpse. In the end it is discovered that it is not a corpse at all, but a pan of waffle batter that fell out of the window of a New York Central dining car."

"How interesting. Well, I guess that's all the time I can give you. Others are waiting," he said, taking cognizance of the stones they were throwing through the window.

"Just one more thing, Mr. Ingelbretsvold," I said. "I don't know quite how to say this, but I think I would like to be a writer when I grow up. Will the program you made out for me help me to be a writer?"

"Why, bless you, child," Mr. Ingelbretsvold said, "you follow that program and there's nothing else you can be."

* * *

The University of Minnesota builds not only minds; it also builds bodies. Before you can enter the University you must undergo a thorough and rigorous examination at the Student Health Service. Minnesota has one of the finest health services in the country. Here prominent doctors, serving without compensation, give unstintingly of their time and wisdom that youth of Minnesota might be strong.

I shall always remember, with a mixture of gratitude and admiration, the day I went through the Health Service for my examination. I was extensively examined by not one, but many doctors, each an expert in his particular branch of medicine.

First I was sent to the bone surgeon. He was sitting at his desk reading a copy of *Film Fun*. "How many arms and legs you got?" he asked, without putting down the *Film Fun*.

"Two," I answered.

"Two altogether?"

"No sir, two of each."

"O.K. You're all right. Go ahead," he said, still looking at the *Film Fun*.

I proceeded to the office of the heart doctors. Because heart examination is a delicate, involved process, two doctors are assigned to that duty. When I came into the office, they were standing by the window dropping paper bags filled with water on pedestrians.

"I had an interesting case the other day," said one to the other. "I was listening to a kid's heart and it was the damnedest thing I ever heard. It didn't thump. It chimed in three notes."

"What do you know?" said the second. "What caused that?"

"I couldn't find out for a long time," answered the first. "It wasn't until I went way back into the kid's history that I found the solution. His mother was frightened by an NBC station break."

"Well, what do you know?" said the second. "Say, I heard of another interesting case yesterday. Dr. Curette in plastic surgery told me about it. A man came in to see him. The fellow didn't have a nose."

"No nose?" said the first. "How did he smell?"

"Terrible," said the second.

"Oh, Harold," said the first, "you're more fun than a barrel of monkeys."

I cleared my throat. They turned and noticed me for the first time.

"I've come for a heart examination," I said.

"You look all right. Go ahead," they said.

They went over to the sink to fill some more bags with water.

My next stop was the weighing room. I stepped on the scale, my weight was recorded, and a doctor said, "You make friends easily. You are a good worker although you are a little inclined to put things off. You are going to make a long trip on water."

I gave him a penny and proceeded to the abdominal clinic. The doctor was sitting at a table building a boat in a bottle. "Ever have to get up in the middle of the night?" he asked.

"Yes sir," I answered.

"Hmm," he said. "I'm going to have a little trouble with the mizzenmast. Know anything about boats?"

"Some," I confessed modestly.

"I love boats," he said. "I love the sea. Right now I'd love to be on a trim little schooner hauling a cargo of oscars from the levant. I love the good feel of a stout ship on a rough sea. Perhaps a nor'wester would blow up, and all the hearty mates would be on the deck pulling together while the grizzled old skipper stood on the bridge and yelled his orders: 'Keelhaul the bosun! Jettison the supercargo!' "

"My, you certainly know a lot about boats," I said admiringly.

He lowered his eyes. "I should. I was cuckold on the Yale crew in 1912. But enough of this. So you have to get up in the middle of the night?"

"Yes sir. You see, my sister Morningstar keeps company with an engineer on the Natchez, Mobile, and Duluth railroad. About a year ago he got put on a night run, and Morningstar never used to get to see him. She complained so much that he finally had a sidetrack built into our back yard.

"Now when he comes by at night he runs the train into our back yard for a while. I have to get up in the middle of the night and go out and keep his steam up while he comes in the house and trifles with Morningstar."

But he wasn't listening. He was fiddling with his boat in the bottle. "Wonder which side is starboard," he mumbled.

I left quietly for the chiropodist's office.

The doctor was sitting behind his desk playing "Your Feets Too Big" on a jew's-harp when I came in.

"How did you get here?" he asked.

"Why, I walked."

"Well, then," he said, "your feet are all right. You're lucky. There was a girl in here the other day whose feet were in terrible shape. She had been wearing such high heels that she constantly leaned forward at a forty-five-degree angle. Gave the impression of being on a ski slide."

"What did you do for her?" I asked.

"Cut off her legs, naturally. She's much happier now. She's made a lot of new friends who affectionately call her 'Shorty.' "

I made as if to go.

"Wait a minute. Know how I got interested in chiropody?"

"No sir," I said, for I did not.

He giggled. "I got webbed feet, that's why." He leaped up from his chair and ran around the room quacking wildly. Water was rolling off his back.

Now I went to the last office, the psychiatrist's. He was driving golf balls through the window. An angry crowd was collecting outside. "Any insanity in your family?" he asked.

"Oh, not really insanity," I said. "Maybe some of them act a little funny sometimes, but I wouldn't call it insanity. Uncle Bert, for instance, he's in Washington now circulating a petition to free Sacco and Vanzetti.

"And Cousin Roger. He's got a little farm near Des Moines. Every day he hauls his produce to Des Moines in a square-wheeled cart.

"And Uncle Donald. He started a million-dollar suit against the Reynolds Tobacco Company last year. He says he got a hump on his back from smoking Camels.

"And Aunt Yetta. Every time she needs a little money, she pulls out a tooth and puts it under her pillow.

"And then there's Cousin Booker, who thinks he's got a diamond in his navel, and Aunt Melanie who burns churches, and Uncle Alex who hangs on the wall and says he's a telephone, and Uncle Milton who has been standing in a posthole since 1924.

"But I wouldn't call that insanity exactly, would you, Doctor?"

"Oh, certainly not," he said. "They're probably just a little tired. Well, my boy, the examination is all over. Let me congratulate you. You are now a student at the University of Minnesota."

Tears filled my eyes and my throat was all choked up.

"Don't try to talk," said the doctor. "Just hold me tight. I want to remember you always, just like this."

In a little while I was all right, and I left, hoping with all my heart that I would prove worthy of the consideration that my new alma mater had lavished upon me.

JAMES THURBER

The Little Girl and the Wolf

One afternoon a big wolf waited in a dark forest for a little girl to come along carrying a basket of food to her grandmother. Finally a little girl did come along and she was carrying a basket of food. "Are you carrying that basket to your grandmother?" asked the wolf. The little girl said yes, she was. So the wolf asked her where her grandmother lived and the little girl told him and he disappeared into the wood.

When the little girl opened the door of her grandmother's house she saw that there was somebody in bed with a nightcap and nightgown on. She had approached no nearer than twenty-five feet from the bed when she saw that it was not her grandmother but the wolf, for even in a nightcap a wolf does not look any more like your grandmother than the Metro-Goldwyn lion looks like Calvin Coolidge. So the little girl took an automatic out of her basket and shot the wolf dead.

Moral: It is not so easy to fool little girls nowadays as it used to be.

ROY BLOUNT, JR.

What to Do on New Year's Eve—I

There comes a time in life when it is unseemly to awaken late in the afternoon of January 1 on someone's snooker table, naked save for a tiny conical hat (whose elastic strap has ridden up to just under your nose), shriveled tuxedo pants, and a crust of onion dip and confetti. In your productive middle years, you tend to feel not only your responsibilities but also your hangovers deeply: way down in the nucleoli of your every body cell, for up to three months. Furthermore you find those little hat-straps to be more and more irritating, even under the chin (even if you still have only one of those), and even *during* the party.

New Year's Eve becomes a time not to blow off steam, but to behave yourself. This realization may come as more of a relief than steam blowing does. "Nothing is more hopeless than a scheme of merriment," wrote Dr. Johnson. There is no American merrymaking, or merry faking, so forced and obligatory as a New Year's Eve party. There is also no hang-over—not to dwell on this point—so profound as that induced by a lot of champagne on top of a lot of, say, bourbon and a number of sips of various fellow celebrants' apricot and artichoke and so on liqueurs.

What, then, is to be done on December 31? Should the day be ignored altogether? Or is there a way to ring out the old and in the new without leaving yourself with the feeling that you have spent forty-eight hours inside a gong? Let us consider some of the possibilities.

1. Ignore December 31 altogether. The trouble with this is that it may become a habit. If so widely acknowledged a day as New Year's Eve can be ignored, then why not the following Monday? Why not every Monday? Why not February? Why not the entire new year? These are all good

questions. If you hold a position of mature responsibility, it is better not to ask them.

2. Celebrate with a magnum of sparkling water, a bowl of light watercress dip, and some cauliflower sprigs. Unfortunately this pretty much comes under the heading of number 1.

3. Celebrate New Year's Eve, 1958. This seems worth a try, until you realize that it is not worth a try. You drank worse things in 1958 than you do now. And where are you going to find a pair of pink-and-black socks?

4. Dress up like the New Year and lie in a sensory-deprivation tank until midnight. The trouble with this is, what if it gets back to the people in the office? Or what if, being made to feel born-again, you never get back to the office?

5. Stay home, watch Times Square on television, and at midnight, instead of kissing thirty-four wives in one minute, kiss your own wife for thirty-four minutes. You need not feel maturely responsible for whatever happens next.

My New Year's resolution is to try number 5. It is too late to resolve to try it this New Year's Eve, however. This New Year's Eve, out of a mature sense of obligation, I am going to attend a party. Maybe a *bit* of champagne, but I intend to lay off the dip as soon as traces of it reach my first knuckles. And I will take the sensible precaution of placing a bit of adhesive tape under my nose.

ROY BLOUNT, JR.

What to Do on New Year's Eve—II

Okay. You're sitting home alone on New Year's Eve with auld lang syne on your hands. What do you do?

1. Get out your Scottish dictionary and look up *auld lang syne*. You could dig around for hours without finding your Scottish dictionary. Get out your Scotch.

2. Wear a lampshade on your head. I have seen people do almost everything at a party: fall down, get naked, fight, start fires, climb out of windows, and put big wet slices of warm roast beef down each other's shirts. But I have never seen anybody put a lampshade on his or her head.

Try it, and you'll see why. A lampshade has prongs that don't fit the human head (might fit a cat's, but a cat would hate it), and there are dead moths in there. Stuck to the sides. But not stuck very securely. You could breathe one into your nose.

3. Call up friends. One problem with this is, they may be having a party that they didn't invite you to. I don't know why; they just didn't. Even if they live several hundred miles away, which would explain (maybe) why you weren't invited, they probably won't answer their phone themselves. Someone whose voice you don't recognize, and probably wouldn't recognize even if it weren't thickened by debauchery, will answer and say:

"HARPY NOYERS!"

"Hello," you'll say. "I'm a friend of Griff and Betty's—"

"HOOPY NOO-WAH!"

"Is Griff or Betty—"

"HOPPAH NAW REE!"

There will be a sound like people throwing roast beef in the background and you will hear the phone hit the floor. Eat your heart out.

4. Get yourself organized for the months ahead. There are twelve of them. I won't list them here. You could take out twelve slips of paper, write the name of a different month on each one, and set them out neatly, in chronological order (I mean the order in which the months come during the year, not the order in which you wrote them on the slips, though it is a good idea to write them on the slips in the same order in which they come during the year, because otherwise you could forget March), on a desk or tabletop. Or the floor will do. Especially if you have fallen down.

Now. Take more slips of paper, a lot of them, and write on each one something that you intend to get done:

- Take up organ.
- Oil reels.
- Obedience classes—Mitzi.
- Winterize gazebo.
- Get racquetball racquet. (In your wording, you want to be terse and businesslike. Isn't there something redundant about "racquetball racquet"? You wouldn't say "football foot." "Tennis tennis-ball." And isn't that a pretty la-di-da spelling—"racquet"? As in "leather jacquet," or "yacquety-yacque.")
- Europe. (But you don't want to be so terse in your wording that, when the month to get this thing done rolls around, you won't remember what it was you were going to do. *Visit* Europe? Reassess Europe's role in the world community today? Or does that say "Elope"? Use good handwriting.)
- Look into umbrella coverage.
- Get things straight with the Seebohms.
- Learn cook Indian.
- Add inch to chest.

And so on. Now sort these slips of paper into twelve piles of things you are going to get done each month.

But are you going to get them done? Probably not. There is not much point in embarking upon the new year by trying to fool yourself. And failing.

5. Come up with this great idea for a screenplay about this guy who doesn't have anything to do on New Year's Eve or anybody to do it with, right? And he's all alone, see, so he's sitting there thinking *[voiceover]:* "Hey, this would be a great idea for a screenplay: a guy who's all alone on

New Year's Eve trying to think of an idea for a screenplay, or trying to think of something to do, I mean, or somebody to do it with, so he . . ."

6. Turn over a new leaf. This is something anybody could stand to do. I don't care if you are a prominent religious leader or the world's greatest living cellist. It wouldn't hurt you to turn over a new leaf. But you need to be in a dynamic mood to turn over a new leaf, unless it is a tiny leaf—like, "Okay! From this day forward I will never again clip my fingernails except over a receptacle of some kind!" And if you were in a dynamic mood you wouldn't be home alone on New Year's Eve.

Furthermore: I, for example, am forty-two years old and I have never turned over a new leaf. Not on purpose. It's like wearing a lampshade on your head. Trying to do such a classic thing makes you self-conscious. You wonder, "Is this for real?" When something is classic, you can never think of an example of how it's done.

Maybe in the Greek myths. But you may not be able to put your hand on any Greek myths. I don't think you want to start looking for them on New Year's Eve, after you've already been through the whole house looking for a Scottish dictionary.

What if you did find, say, *The Iliad?* The Trojan Wars don't provide much of a model for a person sitting home alone. Unless you are the type of guy who gets up and goes out and kidnaps someone named Helen. If you are, you ought to turn over a new leaf.

Of Course Harvey Would Have a Rabbit

When Harvey Fierstein's remarkable drama *Torch Song Trilogy* was playing to packed houses on Broadway in the mid 1980s, he had in his dressing room a large white pet rabbit (live) who lived in an unusually large (for a rabbit) cage. A panther could have lived in there. On Harvey's feet were bunny (not live) slippers, and in the audience were people who were about to watch a memorable performance by the author, Harvey Fierstein. In *Torch Song Trilogy* he portrays Arnold, a drag queen, and the opening scene is all his, a monologue—as bravura a performance as any I have seen.   **G.S.**

HARVEY FIERSTEIN

Scene One: Arnold

The play is performed against a black cyclorama with as little actual scenery as possible. Upstage center a grand piano sits on its platform—raising Lady Blues high above the action. Downstage of her, on either side, are three-foot-high platforms which will be the two apartments. Each has a chair, table, and telephone. Arnold's chair is worn and comfortable, Ed's is new and straight. Downstage center stands The International Stud platform. It is just large enough for one person to stand comfortably and is raised two feet from the stage. Left of it is a larger platform, six feet by eight feet, which holds an armchair and vanity table. It is Arnold's dressing room. As the lights come down on Lady Blues after her opening song, the sounds of a music box are heard softly. The lights rise on the backstage platform, revealing Arnold in full drag applying a false eyelash to his face. He turns off the music box. . . . The lash slips out of place. . . .

ARNOLD *(To audience):* Damned Elmer's glue! Just let me finish emasculating this eye and I'll be right with you. *(Fixes it. Poses in the mirror.)*

Gorgeous, huh? Use your imagination, it's still under construction.

I think my biggest problem is being young and beautiful. It is my biggest problem because I have never been young and beautiful. More importantly, I will never be young and beautiful. Oh, I've been beautiful. And God knows I've been young. But never the twain have met. Not so's anyone would notice anyway. A shrink acquaintance of mine believes this to be the root of my attraction to a class of men most subtly described as old and ugly. But I think he's underestimating my wheedles. See, an ugly person who goes after a pretty person gets nothing but trouble. But a pretty person who goes after an ugly person gets at least cabfare.

I ain't sayin' I never fell for a pretty face, but when *"les jeux sont faits"* . . . give me a toad with a pot of gold and I'll give ya three meals a day. 'Cause, honeys, ain't no such thing as a toad when the lights go down. It's either feast or famine. It's the daylight you gotta watch out for. Face it, a thing of beauty is a joy till sunrise.

I never push Lady Luck myself. I got, whatchoo call a extrasensory sense about such things. If I really like a guy, I automatically wake three minutes before him. Giving me just enough time to unsucker my pucker, reinstate my coif, and repose my repose so's his eyes upon waking conjure images by Jove and Lana Turner; guaranteeing my breakfast if not his real phone number.

Here's another hint to all present presently unattached. You can cross any man off your dance card who A: Discusses his wonderful relationship with his mother. B: Discusses his wonderful relationship with his shrinker. Or C: Refuses to discuss his wonderful relationship with his mother or shrinker. See, a guy who's got that kind of confidante is in what I call a "state of confession." And experience has sorely taught me, you can never be more to a man in such a state than subject matter for their conversations. . . .

Not that I got anything against analysis, I don't. I think it's a great way to keep from boring your friends. But what's good for the bored just ain't so for the bed, if you get my drift. See, when there's trouble in Paradise you got two possible M.O.'s. Pull back or push in. But pull back when he's got a professional shoulder to lean on and the entire effect of losing you is shot. Try pushing and you've bought yourself two for one. Push hard enough, and you'll find yourself visiting him Sundays at the "Happy Home for the Bewildered."

Now, I ain't sayin' you should only date sane men (I don't want to kill off all the fish in the polluted sea), but at least find one who's willing to fight on his own. Give me a man with both fists clenched tight . . . and I'll give you a smile from here to next Thursday.

And there's another group you've gotta watch your food stamps around . . . "The Hopeless." They break down into three major categories: Married, "Just in for the Weekend," and terminally ill. Those affairs are the worst. You go into them with your eyes open, knowing all the limitations and accepting them maturely . . . then wham-bam! . . . You're writing letters to Dear Abby and burning black candles at midnight and you ask yourself, "What happened?" I'll tell you what happened. You got just what you wanted! The person who thinks they's mature enough to handle an affair that's hopeless from the beginning is the very same person who keeps the publishers of Gothic Romances up to their tragic endings in mink; not to mention the reissuers of those twenties torch ditties . . . music to be miserable by.

So, what's left? I don't know. But there are some. I found one once. His name was Charley. He was tall, handsome, rich, deaf. Everything you could want in an affair and more. The deafness was the more. He never screamed at me, all his friends were nice and quiet, I could play music as loud as I liked without ever disturbing his reading, and best of all, I could snore. I even learned me some of that sign language. Wait, I still remember some. Like this here, *(He demonstrates.)* it means cockroach. And this one *(Demonstrates)* means fuck. Here's my favorite. *(Demonstrates)* It means "I love you." And I did. But . . . *(Signing and speaking together)* not enough. I guess I bought them Gothic publishers a few minks of my own.

(Back to his dressing) For those of yis what ain't yet guessed I am an entertainer (or what's left of one), I go by the name Virginia Hamm. Ain't that a kick in the rubber parts? You should hear some of my former handles: Kitty Litter, Lorretta Dung, Bertha Venation . . . and I'm plenty tough too. I can afford to be; behind a phony name, face, and figure. But that's all right.

See, I'm among the last of a dying breed. Once the ERA and gay civil rights bills have been passed, me and mine will find ourselves swept under the carpets like the blacks done to Amos, Andy, and Aunt Jemima. But that's all right too. With a voice and face like this I got nothing to worry about, I can always drive a cab. And that, chillun', is called power. Be it gay, black, or flowered, it always comes down to the survival of the majority.

Shit, I'd better get a move on it! *(He takes a roll of toilet paper and unwinds two huge wads.)* Would ya'll mind turning your backs? . . . Well, could you at least close your eyes?

(He places the paper in his bra with his back to the audience, turns proudly with his chest held high, catches the unevenness of the sizes in the mirror, and adjusts them.)

There are easier things in this life than being a drag queen. But, I ain't got no choice. Try as I may, I just can't walk in flats.

(Putting on his hat and shoes)

You know what I really want? I want The International Stud. No, not the bar. The man. A stud. A guy who knows what he wants and ain't a'scared to go and get it. A guy who satisfies his every need, and don't mind if you get what you want in the bargain. Matter of fact, he aims to please. He'd be happy to be whatever you wanted him to be, 'cause you're happy bein' what he wants you to be. The more you put in, the more you get back. An honest man. The International Stud. One size fits all. But I wouldn't want no guy that wanted me like this here. No, I'd need him for the rest of the time. For the other part of me. The part that's not so well-protected. Oh, there's plenty that want me like this. And I take their admiration gratefully. But, at a distance. I guess a drag queen's like bein' an oil painting! You gotta stand back from it to get the full effect.

(Standing) Well, I think we're in business! My, how time flies when you's doin' all the talking. *(Tucking in the chair)* Who knows, maybe my Right Man is out there tonight, right? Y'all take care now, hear? *(He makes the "I love you" sign, turns to go, stops, and comes back.)* Ya know . . . in my life I have slept with more men than are named and/or numbered in the Bible (Old and New Testaments put together). But in all those beds not once has someone said, "Arnold, I love you . . ." that I could believe. So, I ask myself, "Do you really care?" And the only honest answer I can give myself is, "Yes, I care." I care be— *(Catches himself)* I care a great deal. But not enough.

(He smiles knowingly as the lights black out on him and up on the singer.)

FRAN LEBOWITZ

Ideas

It was only to be expected that the era that gave us the word "lifestyle" would sooner or later come up with the concept of thoughtstyle.

Thoughtstyle can probably best be defined by noting that in the phrase "lifestyle" we have the perfect example of the total being lesser than the sum of its parts, since those who use the word "lifestyle" are rarely in possession of either.

So too with thoughtstyle, and thus we find ourselves the inhabitants of a period during which ideas are not exactly flourishing—denizens, in fact, of a time when the most we can possibly hope to see are a couple of darn good notions. What is the difference, you may now be asking, between an idea and a notion? Well, the primary difference, of course, is that a notion you can sell but an idea you can't even give away. There are other differences, to be sure, and as can readily be seen by the following chart, I have taken care not to neglect them.

IDEAS	NOTIONS
MAKING CHANGE	ALGEBRA
ENGLISH	ESPERANTO
BLUEBERRY PIE	BLUEBERRY VINEGAR
POETRY	POETS
LITERATURE	THE NONFICTION NOVEL
CHOOSING	PICKING
BATHROOMS IN MUSEUMS	PAINTINGS IN BATHROOMS
LIGHT BULBS	LIGHT BEER
THOMAS JEFFERSON	JERRY BROWN
BREAKFAST	BRUNCH
DETROIT	SAUSALITO

While it may appear to the novice that this just about wraps it up, I am afraid that the novice is sadly mistaken. Ideas are, after all, a subject of some complexity. There are good ideas, bad ideas, big ideas, small ideas, old ideas and new ideas. There are ideas that we like and ideas that we don't. But the idea that I have seized upon is the idea that is not quite finished—the idea that starts strong but in the final analysis doesn't quite make it. Naturally, there is more than one such idea, and so I offer what can only be called:

A BUNCH OF HALF-BAKED IDEAS

TRIAL BY A JURY	OF YOUR PEERS
ADULT	EDUCATION
THE NOBLE	SAVAGE
HERO	WORSHIP
IMMACULATE	CONCEPTION
HIGH	TECH
POPULAR	CULTURE
FISCAL	RESPONSIBILITY
SALES	TAX
HUMAN	POTENTIAL
SUPER	MAN
MAY	DAY
BUTCHER	BLOCK
SEXUAL	POLITICS
METHOD	ACTING
MODERN	MEDICINE
LIVING WELL	IS THE BEST REVENGE

GEORGE PRICE

*"There's so much in what you say that I wonder if
I might have thirty minutes or so to digest it."*

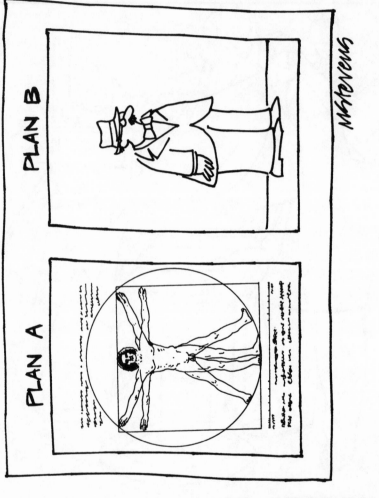

M. STEVENS

ARNOLD ROTH

CALVIN TRILLIN

Ben's Dairy

Having heard a number of people discuss the Last Straw that drove them from the city, I realize that if I didn't leave when Ben's Dairy started closing Sundays I'm probably in New York for good. It was an awful blow. It happened four years ago, and I still remember the details of the morning I discovered it, the way some people remember what they were wearing when they learned of the attack on Pearl Harbor—which also, as I remember it, took place on a Sunday morning. (I mention that without trying to imply any mystic pattern governing catastrophes. I understand that the Spanish Inquisition began late on a Tuesday afternoon.) At about nine-thirty, I had parked brilliantly on Houston Street itself—as the ex-co-editor of a one-issue journal called *Beautiful Spot, A Magazine of Parking,* I find that a perfect spot on Houston Street on Sunday morning can give me almost as much pleasure as a freshly baked bialy—and found myself in front of Yonah Shimmel's Knishery. Restraining myself from having one of Shimmel's legendary potato knishes at that hour of the morning, I had settled for a cheese bagel, figuring a little extra energy might be useful when I faced the counter crowds down the street. At Russ & Daughters, ordinarily my first stop, I was hardly in the door before someone was expertly removing from a succulent-looking Nova Scotia salmon some slices that were going to be my very own. My next move had been established years before. Leaving Russ & Daughters, I would take a quick look into Ben's Dairy, next door, and a quick look into Tanenbaum's Bakery, next door to Ben's—both tiny stores with barely enough room between the counter and the wall for a customer to elbow aside more than one other customer at a time. In either place, there could be an occasional lull in the crowd, the way there is a lull when a group of large men who are breaking down a door with a battering ram back up to get some running room. Making a quick, hard decision about which crowd looked less lethal at the moment, I would plunge into Ben's or Tanenbaum's, stagger back out to Houston Street, and plunge into the other one—emerging at the end carrying Ben's homemade cream cheese with scallions and Tanenbaum's fresh pumpernickel bagels, both of which would be combined with my Russ & Daughters' Nova Scotia to create the single perfect Nova Scotia and cream cheese on bagel available in today's depleted market. Whenever I put the final ingredient in my shopping bag, I felt ecstatic in the way I have always imagined a Manhattan real-estate speculator must feel ecstatic when he finally gets his hands on the last historic brownstone he needs to make up an entire block that can be torn down for a luxury high rise. That Sunday, I shot my customary glance toward Ben's as I moved toward Tanenbaum's, and I saw a steel gate across the storefront. Closed.

I remained calm. In the past, I had often found Ben closed when I expected him to be open. Although his official policy had always been to close only on Saturdays and Jewish holidays, it had long seemed to me that Ben knew about Jewish holidays that had escaped the notice of other observant Jews. Finding Ben closed on Sundays when knishes were pouring out of Yonah Shimmel's and customers were four deep at Russ & Daughters and the open-air discount cubbyholes on Orchard Street, around the corner, were booming, I had got the impression that Ben might sometimes observe, say, the anniversary of the death of some wise and scholarly rabbi whose wisdom did not happen to spread much beyond the boundaries of one small neighborhood in Vitebsk. But my assumption that Ben was closed for religious reasons was destroyed when I looked into Tanenbaum's. Tanenbaum was known on Houston Street to be at least as strict about such matters as Ben. I had always suspected, in fact, that Tanenbaum observed the anniversary of the death of not only great rabbis but maybe cantors as well and maybe some secular heroes and perhaps an ecumenical Methodist or two. Tanenbaum was in his store, dealing out bagels with both hands. I raced back into Russ & Daughters to find out what had happened, and my worst fears were confirmed: Ben had decided to close Sundays.

I had never objected to Tanenbaum and Ben closing on Saturdays. After all, freedom of religion is guaranteed in the Constitution, and, besides, I'm usually busy on Saturday shopping for Italian food. On a Saturday morning, I'm likely to be walking down Bleecker Street making last-minute adjustments to the intricate timing that sometimes allows me to start by buying a pound of prosciuttini at Mario Bosco's, get to Zito's just as the fresh-baked bread is coming up from the basement, and still arrive at the mozzarella store on Sullivan Street before it has been snatched clean of cheese-in-the-basket. (I go to the mozzarella store mainly to buy mozzarella, of course—mozzarella soaked in milk and salt, smoked mozzarella, any kind of mozzarella they are willing to sell me. But I often eat all of it before I've gone two blocks from the store, so if I fail to get cheese-in-the-basket I can arrive home with nothing to show for the trip.) Sometimes I stop in at the bakery on Carmine Street that, on Saturdays only, creates a ring-shaped loaf of bread containing small pieces of cheese and sausage, both of which snuggle into the dough when the loaf is heated. On Saturdays I have things to do. I had never even objected to closings on Jewish holidays that I suspected were known only to two or three senior professors at the Jewish Theological Seminary. But Sundays!

I took it personally. My Sundays had been ruined. The satisfaction of capturing each of the ingredients for the perfect Nova Scotia and cream cheese on bagel was no more. The pleasure of a late breakfast that could be extended to include picking at the small bits of Nova Scotia left on the platter at three-thirty or four was gone. I felt like a baseball manager who, having finally polished a double-play combination to such brilliance that it provided the inspiration for the entire team, learns that the second baseman has decided to retire so that he can devote full time to his franchise estate-planning business.

It seemed to me that the reasons for the decision I had heard on Houston Street—that Ben was tired, that Ben had found it impossible to prepare enough cheese for the Sunday rush, that Ben could no longer take the crowds—were unpersuasive. Sunday is by far the busiest day on Houston Street. Closing on the busiest day is the kind of thing I might expect from some stationer in Surrey but not from a cheese merchant on the Lower East Side. I was not myself, of course. I became convinced that Ben, realizing how much I depended on him, had decided to close on Sundays as a display of independence. I knew, after all, that he was a strong-minded man. A year or two before, at a time when France had placed an embargo on spare parts for Israeli jets, Ben had put up a sign in his store that said something like UNTIL GENERAL DEGAULLE CHANGES HIS POLICY TOWARD ISRAEL, BEN SELLS NO MORE FRENCH CHEESE.

"He's trying to drive me from the city," I said to Alice when I arrived home, bearing a half pound of cream cheese that I had finally managed to find after a forty-minute traffic-and-parking struggle in the southern reaches of the Lower East Side—a dry, bland, half pound of cream cheese that tasted as if it might have been made by a Presbyterian missionary rigidly following directions from the Camp Fire Girls recipe book.

"He doesn't even know you," Alice said.

"He didn't know DeGaulle either," I said. But I decided to remain in the city. Out of the city, I wouldn't even be able to get decent cream cheese during the week.

I tried to look on the bright side. I told myself I could always make an extra trip on Friday to Ben's and then return on Sunday for fresh bagels and Nova Scotia; two routinely caught pop-ups may not provide as much beauty as a perfectly executed double play, but they provide precisely as many outs. I reminded myself that the ingredients for the perfect Nova Scotia and cream cheese on bagel were only part of my usual haul on Houston Street. As it happened, Ben's specialty was not even cream cheese but baked farmer cheese—a product I had learned about, years after I started going to Ben's, only because a lady from Scarsdale who shoved in front of me at the counter one morning ordered a baked farmer cheese with caraway seeds and then included an eloquent description of its taste in the speech she delivered to me about being double parked and in a terrible hurry. (Baked farmer cheese can be eaten cold, which, out of ignorance, is the way I wolfed it down for three or four years, until I heard Ben say that reheating it makes it taste "like a soufflé or a crêpe Suzette or whatever you want"—a description I found to be completely accurate.) How could I begrudge Ben an additional day of rest, I asked myself, when I could come in any weekday and have my choice of baked farmer cheese with scallions or baked farmer cheese with vegetables or even baked farmer cheese with pineapple? Who was I to complain about a little break in my Houston Street routine when there were millions of people all over the world who would never taste Russ & Daughters' chopped herring?

There were, I reminded myself, even non-food reasons to come to Houston Street on Sunday. Whenever I begin to feel oppressed by being shoved ahead of in the various lines I'm forced to stand in around New York, I spend part of a Sunday at Katz's Delicatessen, a block or two east of my combination stores, where the sandwich-makers at the counter always maintain rigid queue discipline while hand-slicing a high-quality pastrami on rye. Fathoming line behavior in various cities requires, I have found, serious research. It was only after I took sample measurings of neighborhood cinema queues in London at a time when the press was printing statistics on the imminent demise of the film industry that I realized why there seem to be so many lines in England: English people apparently queue up as a sort of hobby. A family man might pass a mild autumn evening by taking the wife and kids to stand in the cinema queue for a while and then leading them over for a few minutes in the sweetshop queue and then, as a special treat for the kids, saying, "Perhaps we've time to have a look at the Number Thirty-one bus queue before we turn in." New York line behavior can be explained only by assuming that just about everyone in the line believes himself to be in possession of what the Wall Street people call inside information. Someone has convinced the people in the subway-token line that the next person to the booth is likely to receive not just a subway token but a special golden subway token, the recipient of which will never have to ride the subways again. The people about to board a Madison Avenue bus at five-thirty in the afternoon have somehow permitted themselves to be convinced by a shady-looking little tout that what they are trying to board is not actually a Madison Avenue bus but the last boat from Dunkirk. Some out-of-towner without inside information has no way of knowing that what he is being shoved off of is not merely one of a number of buses going to Sixty-fourth Street but the last chance of escaping the Huns, so he naturally finds the behavior of his fellow citizens excessive.

After a week or two of being badly dealt with by elderly women half my size, I'm always reassured by my first sight of those Katz countermen standing there. They seem to loom over the crowd—casually piling on corned beef, keeping a strict eye on the line in front of them, and passing the time by arguing with each other in Yiddish about what I have always preferred to think was anarcho-syndicalism. I stand there happily while some woman—undoubtedly the wife of the gentleman who elbowed past me in the potato-salad line at the P.S. 3 Fair—tries to sneak in for a quick tongue on rye and receives from the counterman a devastating look and some comment like "And who are you—a movie star maybe?" Katz's is the place in which a counterman who was told by a customer that a particularly lean corned-beef sandwich would earn a commendation to the boss replied, "The boss! May the boss's nose fall off!" I find it a great comfort.

A couple of years after my first daughter was born, I realized that I was going to Houston Street on Sunday partly to have her properly appreciated. At that time, a check of the census statistics for Manhattan had confirmed a suspicion that had been growing in my mind: At least half of the people who saw her on the street were neither Jewish nor Italian, and were therefore culturally handicapped in trying to demonstrate their appreciation of her in a way I considered appropriate. At Russ & Daughters, people pay some attention to a two-year-old. I don't mean quick smiles or routine "Isn't she cute?"s. I mean Notice Is Taken. Lox lies unsliced. Strategic places at the counter are abandoned. Candy fish are pressed into hands. I always thought that Russ & Daughters could get away with charging admission to new parents.

After Ben started closing on Sundays, in fact, I faced the simple truth that I could never give up Sunday mornings at Russ & Daughters completely, even if the entire Nova Scotia supply were lost to the Russian fishing fleet. (I will admit that when I stumble across one of those late-night philosophical discussions about whether war is ever justifiable, the question of how much of the Nova Scotia supply the Soviets can be allowed to swallow up leaps to my mind.) I have always thought that anyone who wants to open up a retail business in New York—a candy store or a Manhattan branch of Harrods—ought to be required to observe Russ & Daughters in action for a week. Russ & Daughters is a splendid refutation of the false teaching that a store selling pickled herring cannot have character and a clean display case at the same time. The daughters of the late founder are particularly warm and cheerful women, and a customer who enters the store having just stormed the counter at Tanenbaum's or subjected himself to the discipline of a Katz counterman could get the impression he has wandered into the Fourth of July outing of a large family. The salesperson—a daughter, a husband of a daughter, lately even a daughter of a daughter—is likely to be friendly enough to disarm even an experienced tormentor of Lower East Side countermen.

"A nice piece of whitefish," a customer says.

"A piece of whitefish," the counterman says cheerfully, moving toward the riches of the smoked fish section.

"A *nice* piece of whitefish," the customer repeats.

"Right, I'll get you a very nice piece," the counterman says.

The customer waits until the chosen piece is weighed and wrapped—four or five previous pieces having been rejected—and then, looking suddenly indecisive, says, "Is the whitefish *good?*"

"Very good," the counterman says.

"Is it *excellent?*" the customer asks.

"You're going to love it," the counterman says.

The potential licensee can then step forward, sample the whitefish, and learn the most important lesson of his week's observation: He loves it.

Three years after Ben started closing Sundays, I went to the Lower East Side one Sunday morning partly to take a look at the city's experiment of turning Orchard Street into a "mall" on Sunday by forbidding automobile traffic from Delancey to Houston. I found that the absence of cars did make Orchard Street much less crowded and chaotic, which would have been all to the good except that Orchard Street is *supposed* to be crowded and chaotic. Looking down poor, barren Orchard Street, I realized that it is only a matter of time before the city officials of Addis Ababa find themselves approving an avant-garde plan for banning traffic in the city market—a plan proposed by one of those jazzy American urban-design specialists who flourished in Great Society times by knowing how to outfit an office-building complex in a way that qualified it for federal aid under a Department of Housing program to improve drainage facilities in low-rent residential areas. "We'll get a marvelous sweep of space here and a great flow of movement over here," he'll explain, stepping over four or five vegetable peddlers and wedging himself into a three-foot alley. "Naturally, we'll have designated off-street parking for all of these donkeys," I don't mean that I'm opposed to change. Tanenbaum sold his bakery a year or two ago, and I have always spoken approvingly of the transition, once I satisfied myself that the young man who bought it was not going to do anything foolish like closing on Sunday or cutting back on his supply of a favorite pastry of mine called *rugelach*. The mozzarella store on Sullivan Street, Frank's Dairy, changed hands a year or so after Tanenbaum's, and the new proprietor turned out to be a student of the craft—the kind of young man who would answer a customer's question about an interesting-looking kind of cheese not merely by saying that it was used in cooking a special Sicilian dish of liver and onions and cheese but tossing in the information that the one restaurant still serving that dish was a lunch counter on First Avenue. For stores as well as for governments, a stable transition is the test of the system. After rattling around Orchard Street for a few minutes that Sunday, I dropped into Russ & Daughters, and the subject of the stores next door came up.

"Ben's retiring," one of the daughters said.

"Retiring!" I said. I had spent three years making extra trips or making do with inferior cream cheese. Could he now plan, as the final blow, cutting off my supply completely?

"He's training someone to take his place," the daughter said.

Greatly relieved, I went to Ben's the next day to investigate the switch-over. The man being trained in the art of farmer cheese, it turned out, was taking over in partnership with the young man who ran what had been Tanenbaum's Bakery. They were even considering the possibility of knocking down the wall in between, creating one store in a space almost as vast as a Checker cab. Despite their youth, the partners are traditional-ists in such matters as observing the Sabbath—they are Hasidim from Brooklyn—but they believe in progressive business techniques. I noticed that they had erected a brightly painted double sign between the stores announcing Ben's Cheese Shop and Moishe's Bakery. The bakery had even acquired a motto: "Keep This Place in Mind/A Better One Is Hard to Find." Having a motto is not unknown on Houston Street (the Russ &

Daughters' shopping bags say "Queens of Lake Sturgeon"), but it was hardly Tanenbaum's style. Ben's Dairy, where the presence of baked farmer cheese was a secret Ben managed to keep from me for years, now had a sign in the window that not only announced the cheese but listed the varieties on individual slats hanging from the sign, in the way some ice-cream parlors announce their flavors.

"Will the place be run the same way?" I asked Ben and his successor.

"He's going to be closed on Saturdays and Jewish holidays," Ben said firmly.

"Of course. Naturally," I said, trying to control my excitement. "And, uh, the other days?"

"This week," the young man said, "we start opening on Sundays."

S. J. PERELMAN

Farewell, My Lovely Appetizer

Add Smorgasbits to your ought-to-know department, the newest of the three Betty Lee products. What in the world! Just small mouth-size pieces of herring and of pinkish tones. We crossed our heart and promised not to tell the secret of their tinting.—*Clementine Paddleford's food column in the Herald Tribune.*

The "Hush-Hush" Blouse. We're very hush-hush about his name, but the celebrated shirtmaker who did it for us is famous on two continents for blouses with details like those deep yoke folds, the wonderful shoulder pads, the shirtband bow!—*Russeks adv. in the Times.*

I came down the sixth-floor corridor of the Arbogast Building, past the World Wide Noodle Corporation, Zwinger & Rumsey, Accountants, and the Ace Secretarial Service, Mimeographing Our Specialty. The legend on the ground-glass panel next door said, "Atlas Detective Agency, Noonan & Driscoll," but Snapper Driscoll had retired two years before with a .38 slug between the shoulders, donated by a snowbird in Tacoma, and I owned what good will the firm had. I let myself into the crummy anteroom we kept to impress clients, growled good morning at Birdie Claflin.

"Well, you certainly look like something the cat dragged in," she said. She had a quick tongue. She also had eyes like dusty lapis lazuli, taffy hair, and a figure that did things to me. I kicked open the bottom drawer of her desk, let two inches of rye trickle down my craw, kissed Birdie square on her lush, red mouth, and set fire to a cigarette.

"I could go for you, sugar," I said slowly. Her face was veiled, watchful. I stared at her ears, liking the way they were joined to her head. There was something complete about them; you knew they were there for keeps. When you're a private eye, you want things to stay put.

"Any customers?"

"A woman by the name of Sigrid Bjornsterne said she'd be back. A looker."

"Swede?"

"She'd like you to think so."

I nodded toward the inner office to indicate that I was going in there, and went in there. I lay down on the davenport, took off my shoes, and bought myself a shot from the bottle I kept underneath. Four minutes later, an ash blonde with eyes the color of unset opals, in a Nettie Rosenstein basic black dress and a baum-marten stole, burst in. Her bosom was heaving and it looked even better that way. With a gasp she circled the desk, hunting for some place to hide, and then, spotting the wardrobe where I keep a change of bourbon, ran into it. I got up and wandered out into the anteroom. Birdie was deep in a crossword puzzle.

"See anyone come in here?"

"Nope." There was a thoughtful line between her brows. "Say, what's a five-letter word meaning 'trouble'?"

"Swede," I told her, and went back inside. I waited the length of time it would take a small, not very bright boy to recite *Ozymandias,* and, inching carefully along the wall, took a quick gander out the window. A thin galoot with stooping shoulders was being very busy reading a paper outside the Gristede store two blocks away. He hadn't been there an hour ago, but then, of course, neither had I. He wore a size seven dove-colored hat from Browning King, a tan Wilson Brothers shirt with pale-blue stripes, a J. Press foulard with a mixed red-and-white figure, dark blue Interwoven socks, and an unshined pair of ox-blood London Character shoes. I let a cigarette burn down between my fingers until it made a small red mark, and then I opened the wardrobe.

"Hi," the blonde said lazily. "You Mike Noonan?" I made a noise that could have been "Yes," and waited. She yawned. I thought things over, decided to play it safe. I yawned. She yawned back, then, settling into a corner of the wardrobe, went to sleep. I let another cigarette burn down until it made a second red mark beside the first one, and then I woke her up. She sank into a chair, crossing a pair of gams that tightened my throat as I peered under the desk at them.

"Mr. Noonan," she said, "you—you've got to help me."

"My few friends call me Mike," I said pleasantly.

"Mike." She rolled the syllable on her tongue. "I don't believe I've ever heard that name before. Irish?"

"Enough to know the difference between a gossoon and a bassoon."

"What *is* the difference?" she asked. I dummied up; I figured I wasn't giving anything away for free. Her eyes narrowed. I shifted my two hundred pounds slightly, lazily set fire to a finger, and watched it burn down. I could see she was admiring the interplay of muscles in my shoulders. There wasn't any extra fat on Mike Noonan, but I wasn't telling *her* that. I was playing it safe until I knew where we stood.

When she spoke again, it came with a rush. "Mr. Noonan, he thinks I'm trying to poison him. But I swear the herring was pink—I took it out of the jar myself. If I could only find out how they tinted it. I offered them money, but they wouldn't tell."

"Suppose you take it from the beginning," I suggested.

She drew a deep breath. "You've heard of the golden spintria of Hadrian?" I shook my head. "It's a tremendously valuable coin believed to have been given by the Emperor Hadrian to one of his proconsuls, Caius Vitellius. It disappeared about 150 A.D., and eventually passed into the possession of Hucbald the Fat. After the sack of Adrianople by the Turks, it was loaned by a man named Shapiro to the court physician, or hakim, of Abdul Mahmoud. Then it dropped out of sight for nearly five hundred years, until last August, when a dealer in secondhand books named Lloyd Thursday sold it to my husband."

"And now it's gone again," I finished.

"No," she said. "At least, it was lying on the dresser when I left, an hour ago." I leaned back, pretending to fumble a carbon out of the desk, and studied her legs again. This was going to be a lot more intricate than I had thought. Her voice got huskier. "Last night I brought home a jar of Smorgasbits for Walter's dinner. You know them?"

"Small mouth-size pieces of herring and of pinkish tones, aren't they?"

Her eyes darkened, lightened, got darker again. "How did you know?"

"I haven't been a private op nine years for nothing, sister. Go on."

"I—I knew right away something was wrong when Walter screamed and upset his plate. I tried to tell him the herring was supposed to be pink, but he carried on like a madman. He's been suspicious of me since—well, ever since I made him take out that life insurance."

"What was the face amount of the policy?"

"A hundred thousand. But it carried a triple-indemnity clause in case he died by sea food. Mr. Noonan—Mike"—her tone caressed me—"I've got to win back his confidence. You could find out how they tinted that herring."

"What's in it for me?"

"Anything you want." The words were a whisper. I leaned over, poked open her handbag, counted off five grand.

"This'll hold me for a while," I said. "If I need any more, I'll beat my spoon on the high chair." She got up. "Oh, while I think of it, how does this golden spintria of yours tie in with the herring?"

"It doesn't," she said calmly. "I just threw it in for glamour." She trailed past me in a cloud of scent that retailed at ninety rugs the ounce. I caught her wrist, pulled her up to me.

"I go for girls named Sigrid with opal eyes," I said.

"Where'd you learn my name?"

"I haven't been a private snoop twelve years for nothing, sister."

"It was nine last time."

"It seemed like twelve till *you* came along." I held the clinch until a faint wisp of smoke curled out of her ears, pushed her through the door. Then I slipped a pint of rye into my stomach and a heater into my kick and went looking for a bookdealer named Lloyd Thursday. I knew he had no connection with the herring caper, but in my business you don't overlook anything.

The thin galoot outside Gristede's had taken a powder when I got there; that meant we were no longer playing girls' rules. I hired a hack to Wanamaker's, cut over to Third, walked up toward Fourteenth. At Twelfth a mink-faced jasper made up as a street cleaner tailed me for a block, drifted into a dairy restaurant. At Thirteenth somebody dropped a sour tomato out of a third-story window, missing me by inches. I doubled back to Wanamaker's, hopped a bus up Fifth to Madison Square, and switched to a cab down Fourth, where the second-hand bookshops elbow each other like dirty urchins.

A flabby hombre in a Joe Carbondale rope-knit sweater, whose jowl could have used a shave, quit giggling over the Heptameron long enough to tell me he was Lloyd Thursday. His shoebutton eyes became opaque when I asked to see any first editions or incunabula relative to the *Clupea harengus,* or common herring.

"You got the wrong pitch, copper," he snarled. "That stuff is hotter than Pee Wee Russell's clarinet."

"Maybe a sawbuck'll smarten you up," I said. I folded one to the size of a postage stamp, scratched my chin with it. "There's five yards around for anyone who knows why those Smorgasbits of Sigrid Bjornsterne's happened to be pink." His eyes got crafty.

"I might talk for a grand."

"Start dealing." He motioned toward the back. I took a step forward. A second later a Roman candle exploded inside my head and I went away from there. When I came to, I was on the floor with a lump on my sconce the size of a lapwing's egg and big Terry Tremaine of Homicide was bending over me.

"Someone sapped me," I said thickly. "His name was—"

"Webster," grunted Terry. He held up a dog-eared copy of Merriam's Unabridged. "You tripped on a loose board and this fell off a shelf on your think tank."

"Yeah?" I said skeptically. "Then where's Thursday?" He pointed to the fat man lying across a pile of erotica. "He passed out cold when he saw you cave." I covered up, let Terry figure it any way he wanted. I wasn't telling him what cards I held. I was playing it safe until I knew all the angles.

In a seedy pharmacy off Astor Place, a stale Armenian whose name might have been Vulgarian but wasn't dressed my head and started asking questions. I put my knee in his groin and he lost interest. Jerking my head toward the coffee urn, I spent a nickel and the next forty minutes doing some heavy thinking. Then I holed up in a phone booth and dialled a clerk I knew called Little Farvel in a delicatessen store in Amsterdam Avenue. It took a while to get the dope I wanted because the connection was bad and Little Farvel had been dead two years, but we Noonans don't let go easily.

By the time I worked back to the Arbogast Building, via the Weehawken ferry and the George Washington Bridge to cover my tracks, all the pieces were in place. Or so I thought up to the point she came out of the wardrobe holding me between the sights of her ice-blue automatic.

"Reach for the stratosphere, gumshoe." Sigrid Bjornsterne's voice was colder than Horace Greeley and Little Farvel put together, but her clothes were plenty calorific. She wore a forest-green suit of Hockanum woolens, a Knox Wayfarer, and baby crocodile pumps. It was her blouse, though, that made tiny red hairs stand up on my knuckles. Its deep yoke folds, shoulder pads, and shirtband bow could only have been designed by some master craftsman, some Cézanne of the shears.

"Well, Nosy Parker," she sneered, "so you found out how they tinted the herring."

"Sure—grenadine," I said easily. "You knew it all along. And you planned to add a few grains of oxylbutane-cheriphosphate, which turns the same shade of pink in solution, to your husband's portion, knowing it wouldn't show in the post-mortem. Then you'd collect the three hundred g's and join Harry Pestalozzi in Nogales till the heat died down. But you didn't count on me."

"You?" Mockery nicked her full-throated laugh. "What are you going to do about it?"

"This." I snaked the rug out from under her and she went down in a swirl of silken ankles. The bullet whined by me into the ceiling as I vaulted over the desk, pinioned her against the wardrobe.

"Mike." Suddenly all the hatred had drained away and her body yielded to mine. "Don't turn me in. You cared for me—once."

"It's no good, Sigrid. You'd only double-time me again."

"Try me."

"O.K. The shirtmaker who designed your blouse—what's his name?" A shudder of fear went over her; she averted her head. "He's famous on two continents. Come on Sigrid, they're your dice."

"I won't tell you. I can't. It's a secret between this—this department store and me."

"They wouldn't be loyal to *you*. They'd sell you out fast enough."

"Oh, Mike, you mustn't. You don't know what you're asking."

"For the last time."

"Oh, sweetheart, don't you see?" Her eyes were tragic pools, a cenotaph to lost illusions. "I've got so little. Don't take that away from me. I—I'd never be able to hold up my head in Russeks again."

"Well, if that's the way you want to play it . . ." There was silence in the room, broken only by Sigrid's choked sob. Then, with a strangely empty feeling, I uncradled the phone and dialled Spring 7-3100.

For an hour after they took her away, I sat alone in the taupe-colored dusk, watching lights come on and a woman in the hotel opposite adjusting a garter. Then I treated my tonsils to five fingers of firewater, jammed on my hat, and made for the anteroom. Birdie was still scowling over her crossword puzzle. She looked up crookedly at me.

"Need me any more tonight?"

"No." I dropped a grand or two in her lap. "Here, buy yourself some stardust."

"Thanks, I've got my quota." For the first time I caught a shadow of pain behind her eyes. "Mike, would—would you tell me something?"

"As long as it isn't clean," I flipped to conceal my bitterness.

"What's an eight-letter word meaning 'sentimental'?"

"Flatfoot, darling," I said, and went out into the rain.

JEFF MacNELLY

GEORGE MEYER

Food Repairman

(Open on: Cluttered storefront repair shop with hanging bells on the door. John is sitting at a work table strewn with tools. He's soldering the head back on a chocolate bunny. He puts it in a bag, clothespins a numbered tag to it, and sets it aside. The phone rings.)

JOHN: Roy's Food Repair. *(Pause)* Eggs, huh? . . . Are they broken all the way or just cracked? . . . Okay, bring 'em in. . . . You're welcome. *(He hangs up and starts puttering. Carrie enters.)* Good morning, Mrs. Larkin. What can I do for you?

(Carrie shows him a cake with a hole carved out of its side.)

CARRIE: Take a look at this. Either Michael or Jennifer, I don't know which, they both deny it . . . Anyway, one of them reached up on the counter and just gouged out a handful of cake. It's for the St. Anne's bake sale and, frankly, I doubt it'll be a hot item with this *cave* dug out of it.

JOHN: No problem. *(Beat)* Here's what I'll do. I'll extract some cake from the interior where it won't be noticed, and then use that to fill in the damaged area. Then I'll redistribute the frosting around the entire perimeter of the cake . . .

CARRIE: Fine, whatever you want to do. Can I pick it up by five?

JOHN: Sure thing. 'Bye now.

CARRIE: Good-bye.

(She leaves, passing Dave on the way in.)

JOHN: Hiya, Rudy. Whattaya got today?

DAVE: Aw, it's this piece of cinnamon toast. I'm carrying it into the TV room, and the next thing I know it's on the carpet. Buttery side down, of course. So I pick it up and it has all this lint and hair all over it . . .

JOHN: Listen, don't worry about it. Tell you how I'm gonna fix it. First I'm gonna dip it in some of that liquid nitrogen to really freeze it solid. Then I'm gonna take it out back and sandblast off just the very top layer, just a millimeter or so. Get rid of all that debris for ya. Then thaw it out under the heat lamp. I'd say I can have it for you by four o'clock.

DAVE: That'd be great. You're a lifesaver, Roy.

("Oh, Pshaw!" Wave from John. Dave exits.)

VALRI *(From back room):* Roy?

JOHN: Yeah?

VALRI *(O.S.):* What're we gonna do with this?

JOHN: With what?

VALRI *(O.S.):* Remember that turkey Ray Gaddis carved for Thanksgiving? And then he decided to have ham instead, and you put the turkey back together?

JOHN: Yeah.

(Valri enters with moldy turkey.)

VALRI: Here it is. He forgot to pick it up.

JOHN: Throw that thing out! We hold items for thirty days, and that's it.

VALRI: He's not gonna like it.

JOHN: You tell him to come to me if he has any complaints.

(She returns to back room. Paul enters with bag of pretzels.)

JOHN *(Cont'd.):* Can I help you, sir?

PAUL: I hope so. I took this bag of pretzels on a boat ride the other day, and I guess the vibration of the motor shook all the salt off the pretzels. See it there in the bottom of the bag?

JOHN *(Peers at bag):* Okay, I'm gonna be honest with you. . . . I think you'd be better off just buying a new bag.

PAUL *(Crestfallen):* Really?

JOHN: Lemme tell you why. They have a special machine that puts that salt on, and if *I* were to do it I'd have to stick each grain on by hand. I'd have to charge you eighty or ninety dollars versus, what, a dollar nineteen or so? Then there's the taste problem with the glue. *(Beat, as thought strikes him)* You know what you *could* do, is put an ad in the paper. A lot of older people are on low-salt diets; maybe you could arrange a trade . . .

PAUL *(Unconvinced):* Well, maybe.

JOHN: Sorry, but . . . you know . . . I'd rather tell you the truth now . . .

PAUL: No, I understand. Thanks. *(Sadly, he leaves.)*

JOHN *(To himself):* Didn't want to lie to the guy.

(Phone rings.)

JOHN *(Cont'd.):* Roy's Food Repair . . . What was that? . . . Sushi? . . . No, I'm sorry, we can't fix Japanese food. . . . No, you'd have to send that back to the plant. . . . Okay . . . 'Bye.

(Buck enters during call. He's holding a frost-covered beer can.)

JOHN *(Cont'd.):* Looks like you got a problem there.

BUCK: Yeah, I suppose I do. I stuck this beer in the freezer so it would get cold faster, and then I forgot all about it. Now I'm afraid it's gonna explode or something.

JOHN: Okay, you're gonna need a beverage repairman for that.

BUCK: Really? Would there be one here in town?

JOHN *(Beat):* Yeah, there're three of 'em . . . but I know at least two of 'em are closed Saturday. *(Beat)* Helen, is C&G open today?

VALRI *(O.S.):* Is *what* open?

JOHN: C&G Cola Repair.

VALRI *(O.S.):* Yeah, I think so.

JOHN *(Pointing):* Okay, take a right and it's three blocks down the road. You'll see the sign. Great big sign.

BUCK: Wait a minute— You said cola repair. This is beer.

JOHN: Nah, they'll do beer too. They need the money.

BUCK: Thanks! Thanks a lot!

(He leaves, passing Maura and Maggie on the way in. One's carrying a bag of taco shells, all broken in half.)

JOHN: Hello, ladies. How are you today?

MAURA: Fine, thank you. Um . . . Do you fix Mexican food here?

JOHN: Sometimes—it depends. Whattaya got?

MAGGIE: Well . . . All right— We were gonna make tacos for our boy-friends, only the guy at the supermarket put the tomatoes on top of the taco shells and they got all broken.

JOHN: Lemme see . . . *(He examines one.)* Oh yeah, this shouldn't take too long. *(He looks at another one. This one is taped together.)* Wait a second, whattaya got on here? Masking tape? *(He peels it off.)*

MAURA *(Embarrassed):* Uh . . . well . . . at first we tried to fix 'em our-selves.

(John peels tape off.)

JOHN *(Irritated):* Look, girls . . . will you come to me next time? Will you leave the repairs to the experts?

MAGGIE: We're sorry . . .

JOHN: Aw, that's okay. It's just that you could hurt yourself. You don't have the proper tools or anything . . .

(Maggie and Maura nod gravely.)

JOHN *(Cont'd., brightening):* All right. I'll have these for you by noon.

MAGGIE: Thank you very much, sir.

(They leave.)

JOHN *(To self):* Nice girls.

(Phone rings.)

VALRI *(O.S.):* I'll get it.

(She enters.)

VALRI *(Cont'd.):* Hello . . . What? . . . Oh my god . . . Yes, I'll tell him . . .

(She hangs up.)

JOHN: Honey, what is it? You're white as a sheet?

VALRI: Roy, that was the sheriff. A Stouffer's truck jackknifed on Route 22. They have frozen dinners all over the highway.

JOHN: All right, let's not panic. You go warm up the car, I'll get my equipment.

(She's paralyzed by panic.)

Come on! Get moving! Seconds count!

(She hurries out as John gathers his equipment: whisk broom, tool box, plastic bags, etc.)

(Fade)

GARRISON KEILLOR

Shy Rights: Why Not Pretty Soon?

Recently I read about a group of fat people who had organized to fight discrimination against themselves. They said that society oppresses the overweight by being thinner than them and that the term "overweight" itself is oppressive because it implies a "right" weight that the fatso has failed to make. Only weightists use such terms, they said; they demanded to be called "total" people and to be thought of in terms of wholeness; and they referred to thin people as being "not all there."

Don't get me wrong. This is fine with me. If, to quote the article if I may, "Fat Leaders Demand Expanded Rights Act, Claim Broad Base of Support," I have no objections to it whatsoever. I feel that it is their right to speak up and I admire them for doing so, though of course this is only my own opinion. I could be wrong.

Nevertheless, after reading the article, I wrote a letter to President Jimmy Carter demanding that his administration take action to end discrimination against shy persons sometime in the very near future. I pointed out three target areas—laws, schools, and attitudes—where shy rights maybe could be safeguarded. I tried not to be pushy but I laid it on the line. "Mr. President," I concluded, "you'll probably kill me for saying this but compared to what you've done for other groups, we shys have settled for 'peanuts.' As you may know, we are not ones to make threats, but it is clear to me that if we don't get some action on this, it could be a darned quiet summer. It is up to you, Mr. President. Whatever you decide will be okay by me. Yours very cordially."

I never got around to mailing the letter, but evidently word got around in the shy community that I had written it, and I've noticed that most shy persons are not speaking to me these days. I guess they think the letter went too far. Probably they feel that making demands is a betrayal of the shy movement (or "gesture," as many shys call it) and an insult to shy pride and that it risks the loss of some of the gains we have already made, such as social security and library cards.

Perhaps they are right. I don't claim to have all the answers. I just feel that we ought to begin, at least, to think about some demands that we *might* make if, for example, we *had* to someday. That's all. I'm not saying we should make fools of ourselves, for heaven's sake!

SHUT UP (A SLOGAN)

Sometimes I feel that maybe we shy persons have borne our terrible burden for far too long now. Labeled by society as "wimps," "dorks," "creeps," and "sissies," stereotyped as Milquetoasts and Water Mittys, and tagged as potential psychopaths ("He kept pretty much to himself," every psychopath's landlady is quoted as saying after the arrest, and for weeks thereafter every shy person is treated like a leper), we shys are desperately misunderstood on every hand. Because we don't "talk out" our feelings, it is assumed that we haven't any. It is assumed that we never exclaim, retort, or cry out, though naturally we do on occasions when it seems called for.

Would anyone dare to say to a woman or a Third World person, "Oh, don't be a woman! Oh, don't be so Third!"? And yet people make bold with us whenever they please and put an arm around us and tell us not to be shy.

Hundreds of thousands of our shy brothers and sisters (and "cousins twice-removed," as militant shys refer to each other) are victimized every year by self-help programs that promise to "cure" shyness through hand-buzzer treatments, shout training, spicy diets, silence-aversion therapy, and every other gimmick in the book. Many of them claim to have "overcome" their shyness, but the sad fact is that they are afraid to say otherwise.

To us in the shy movement, however, shyness is not a disability or disease to be "overcome." It is simply the way we are. And in our own quiet way, we are secretly proud of it. It isn't something we shout about at public rallies and marches. It is Shy Pride. And while we don't have a Shy Pride Week, we do have many private moments when we keep our thoughts to ourselves, such as "Shy is nice," "Walk short," "Be proud— shut up," and "Shy is beautiful, for the most part." These are some that I thought up myself. Perhaps other shy persons have some of their own, I don't know.

A "NUMBER ONE" DISGRACE

Discrimination against the shy is our country's number one disgrace in my own personal opinion. Millions of men and women are denied equal employment, educational and recreational opportunities, and rewarding personal relationships simply because of their shyness. These injustices are nearly impossible to identify, not only because the shy person will not speak up when discriminated against, but also because the shy person almost always *anticipates* being denied these rights and doesn't ask for them in the first place. (In fact, most shys will politely decline a right when it is offered to them.)

Most shy lawyers agree that shys can never obtain justice under our current adversary system of law. The Sixth Amendment, for example, which gives the accused the right to confront his accusers, is anti-shy on the face of it. It effectively denies shy persons the right to accuse anyone of anything.

One solution might be to shift the burden of proof to the defendant in case the plaintiff chooses to remain silent. Or we could create a special second-class citizenship that would take away some rights, such as free speech, bearing arms, and running for public office, in exchange for some other rights that we need more. In any case, we need some sort of fairly totally new concept of law if we shys are ever going to enjoy equality, if indeed that is the sort of thing we could ever enjoy.

A MILLION-DOLLAR RIPOFF

Every year, shy persons lose millions of dollars in the form of overcharges that aren't questioned, shoddy products never returned to stores, refunds never asked for, and bad food in restaurants that we eat anyway, not to mention all the money we lose and are too shy to claim when somebody else finds it.

A few months ago, a shy friend of mine whom I will call Duke Hand (not his real name) stood at a supermarket checkout counter and watched the cashier ring up thirty fifteen-cent Peanut Dream candy bars and a $3.75 copy of *Playhouse* for $18.25. He gave her a twenty-dollar bill and thanked her for his change, but as he reached for his purchases, she said, "Hold on. There's something wrong here."

"No, really, it's O.K.," he said.

"Let me see that cash register slip," she said.

"No, really, thanks anyway," he whispered. Out of the corner of his eye, he could see that he had attracted attention. Other shoppers in the vicinity had sensed that something was up, perhaps an attempted price-tag switch or insufficient identification, and were looking his way. "It's not for me," he pleaded. "I'm only buying this for a friend."

Nevertheless, he had to stand there in mute agony while she counted all of the Peanut Dreams and refigured the total and the correct change. (In fairness to her, it should be pointed out that Duke, while eventually passing on each copy of *Playhouse* to a friend, first reads it himself.)

Perhaps one solution might be for clerks and other business personnel to try to be a little bit more careful about this sort of thing in the first place. O.K.?

HOW ABOUT SHY HISTORY?

To many of us shys, myself included, the worst tragedy is the oppression of shy children in the schools, and while we don't presume to tell educators how to do their work, work that they have been specially trained to do, we do feel that schools must begin immediately to develop programs of shy history, or at the very least to give it a little consideration.

History books are blatantly prejudiced against shyness and shy personhood. They devote chapter after chapter to the accomplishments of famous persons and quote them at great length, and say nothing at all, or very little, about countless others who had very little to say, who never sought fame, and whose names are lost to history.

Where in the history books do we find mention of The Lady in Black, Kilroy, The Unknown Soldier, The Forgotten Man, The Little Guy, not to mention America's many noted recluses?

Where, for example, can we find a single paragraph on America's hundreds of scale models, those brave men of average height whose job it was to pose beside immense objects such as pyramids and dynamos so as to indicate scale in drawings and photographs? The only credit that scale models ever received was a line in the caption—"For an idea of its size, note man (arrow, at left)." And yet, without them, such inventions as the dirigible, the steam shovel, and the swing-span bridge would have looked like mere toys, and natural wonders such as Old Faithful, the Grand Canyon, and the giant sequoia would have been dismissed as hoaxes. It was truly a thankless job.

SHYS ON "STRIKE"

The scale models themselves never wanted any thanks. All they wanted was a rope or device of some type to keep them from falling off tall structures, plus a tent to rest in between drawings, and in 1906, after one model was carried away by a tidal wave that he had been hired to pose in front of, they formed a union and went on strike.

Briefly, the scale models were joined by a contingent of shy artists' models who had posed for what they thought was to be a small monument showing the Battle of Bull Run only to discover that it was actually a large bas-relief entitled "The Bathers" and who sat down on the job, bringing the work to a halt. While the artists' models quickly won a new contract and went back to work (on a non-representational basis), the scale models' strike was never settled.

True to their nature, the scale models did not picket the work sites or negotiate with their employers. They simply stood quietly a short distance away and, when asked about their demands, pointed to the next man. A year later, when the union attempted to take a vote on the old contract, it found that most of the scale models had moved away and left no forwarding addresses.

It was the last attempt by shy persons to organize themselves anywhere in the country.

NOW IS THE TIME, WE THINK

Now is probably as good a time as any for this country to face up to its shameful treatment of the shy and to do something, almost anything, about it. On the other hand, maybe it would be better to wait for a while and see what happens. All I know is that it isn't easy trying to write a manifesto for a bunch of people who dare not speak their names. And that the shy movement is being inverted by a tiny handful of shy militants who do not speak for the majority of shy persons, nor even very often for themselves. This secret cadre, whose members are not known even to each other, advocate doing "less than nothing." They believe in tokenism, and the smaller the token the better. They seek only to promote more self-consciousness: that ultimate shyness that shy mystics call "the fear of fear itself." What is even more terrifying is the ultimate goal of this radical wing: They believe that they shall inherit the earth, and they will not stop until they do. Believe me, we moderates have our faces to the wall.

Perhaps you are saying, "What can *I* do? I share your concern at the plight of the shy and wholeheartedly endorse your two- (or three-) point program for shy equality. I pledge myself to work vigorously for its adoption. My check for ($10 $25 $50 $100 $——) is enclosed. In addition, I agree to (circulate petitions, hold fund-raising party in my home, write to congressman and senator, serve on local committee, write letters to newspapers, hand out literature door-to-door during National Friends of the Shy Drive)."

Just remember: You said it, not me.

Cushlamochree!

"Barnaby" by Crockett Johnson is one of the most fanciful and unusual of all comic strips, and one to which virtually all cartoonists pay homage. It was syndicated nationally from its home base, the unique New York newspaper *P.M.* that was published from 1940 to 1946. I knew *P.M.* was doomed when it began because (a) it cost a nickel—a shocking sum in the days of two-cent and three-cent newspapers; (b) it accepted no advertising; and (c) it was written with intelligence and clarity. Even its millionaire owner, Marshall Field, could not keep the paper going, but while it flourished I was devoted to it and to Barnaby and his lovable and roguish Fairy Godfather, the cigar-smoking, pink-winged J. J. O'Malley. **G.S.**

CROCKETT JOHNSON

In the Beginning . . .

THE FOLLOWING MORNING

ONE EVENING

—and your commentator has a thought on one aspect of the special congressional contest: The strikingly frugal campaign budget of J. J. O'Malley and—

Perhaps if I add this $2 to the fund—

—the lavish expenditures of his opponent, Beauregard Mintleaf. I believe many thinking voters, when they reflect that this is a time for stringent economy,—

You know, that occurred to me—

—will agree with this observer that O'Malley's modest campaign is as shrewd as it is patriotic . . . Economy is the watchword today. So get Conkle's Confetti in the large, two-dollar, economy size—

Mmmm . . . I'll have to run downtown, m'boy.

What for, Mr. O'Malley?

For a large box of Conkle's Confetti . . . I'll need it for my victory celebration.

THE NEXT NIGHT

That leprechaun! Allowing me to take his treasure to defray the expenses of my campaign for Congress! Knowing it was worthless! . . . Jeopardizing my promising political career! . . .
Gosh, Mr. O'Malley.

But maybe the man was wrong about the money being no good.
I doubt it, m'boy. . . . But we might check . . . Has your encyclopedia got pictures in it?

The controversy hinged on the authenticity of the portrait engraved on the face of the note. He seemed so certain of his facts that I didn't continue the argument after he beckoned to the uniformed patrolman . . .

Barnaby! He was wrong! This money is all right!
. . . Jefferson Davis did NOT have a mustache!

I had Gus fix up a few slightly used placards. Just the thing for the spontaneous demonstration I expect will follow my address at the Elves, Leprechauns, Gnomes and Little Men's Chowder and Marching Society tonight . . .

Gosh!

ONE AFTERNOON

Snagg! I paid you to lose this election! Are you crossing me up with this man O'Malley?

Mintleaf, we haven't lifted a finger for J. J. O'Malley.

Yes! . . . Listen! "Seldom has a congressional race captured voters' imaginations as has O'Malley's 'Silent Campaign' and Mintleaf's frantic and costly effort to combat it . . ."

". . . O'Malley's reticence, which has won him the intriguing and vote-getting titles of 'Nebulous Nominee' and 'Mystery Candidate' is a master stroke of the old political wizard, Boss Snagg . . ."

But you wanted him kept quiet.

Please, Snagg . . . Make him talk!

If you'd care—er—to write a check for his radio time, I might be able to coax him to speak on the air.

O'Malley! You're going on the air! . . . "Mystery Candidate to Break Silence . . . O'Malley on radio next Saturday in his first public speech of campaign."

My FIRST speech? . . . The sublime ignorance of these newspapers! I've made six public speeches,at the Elves, Leprechauns, Gnomes, and Little Men's Chowder and Marching Society so far! Why don't they send reporters there?

It's been years since a journalist has visited that fountainhead of vital news—except that reporter-at-large from The New Yorker . . . When did you say I'm to give this little radio chat, Gus?—Saturday?

Can't make it! . . . I have another very momentous oration to deliver at the ELG&LMC&M Society. . .

But, O'Malley!

Is there a copy of the collected speeches of Edmund Burke in the bookcase, little girl?

Mr. O'Malley. The record is still going...

Huh?

Perhaps I had better tell a humorous joke at this juncture... Haven't you a set of bound volumes of Captain Billy's Whizbang?

Ahem...

"... The one absolutely unselfish friend that a man can have in this selfish world, the one that never deserts him, the one that never proves ungrateful ... is his dog! Gentlemen of the Jury: A man's dog stands by him in prosperity and in poverty, in health and—

Hush, m'boy. I must find an apt quotation before I can go on. Something in Latin...

But the record machine is going and nobody is saying anything into it.

" the noble dog ... his head between his paws, his eyes sad but open in alert watchfulness, faithful and true...

Mr. O'Malley, I think the record's run out.

Nonsense. I'm just beginning my oration...

and in closing, I want my unseen audience to rise and sing three stanzas of my campaign hymn, "O Tempora, O Mores, O'Malley"—

Mr. O'Malley. This record was filled a long time ago.

Mmmm. Good I got my strongest thrusts in early, isn't it, m'boy? I must move swiftly now to get this transcription off to that radio station in the last mail...

Aren't you going to play it over?

What could be wrong with it? Anyway, I can always claim I was misquoted... Where are the stamps, little girl? ... Ah! I've found a book of them...

Well, Barnaby. That's that!

US MAIL

SATURDAY EVENING

Mintleaf finally has smoked out his silent opponent. O'Malley has to take a stand on SOMETHING in his first broadcast tonight...

Isn't it time for his speech?

I find myself echoing phrases of another immortal statesman—

He's playing safe. Taking his line on important issues from some bigshot.

THE NEXT DAY

> So my esteemed opponent says I don't dare face issues? . . . Well, Gus, what will he say to my bold challenge to him to debate these issues publicly? . . . At the Elves, Leprechauns, Gnomes and Little Men's Chowder and Marching Society . . .

> I'll run over now and arrange things . . .

> But, O'Malley. You can't do ALL your campaigning there.

> . . . special congressional election in this district . . . J. J. O'Malley, making his first appearance of his amazing campaign, will face Candidate Mintleaf on the stage.

> He arranged it already!

> The debate is expected to draw a record crowd to Town Hall . . .

> Town Hall!

But, Pop, Mr. O'Malley, my Fairy Godfather, said he was going to debate his esteemed opponent at the Little Men's Club . . . And—

Barnaby. The two candidates for Congress are having their debate at Town Hall! . . . And that imaginary pixie of yours is NOT one of the candidates!

There's one way to convince him, Ellen. Attend the debate!

Swell, Pop! But first I'll have to see Mr. O'Malley.

. . . And ask him how to get to the Little Men's Club.

THE BIG NIGHT

There's Mintleaf . . . Where's O'Malley?

Pop—

MINTLEAF for CONG

He's still backstage, I imagine . . . Planning a dramatic entrance.

I'll see if he is.

A door with a star on it. My Fairy Godfather is probably in here . . .

DRESSING ROOM

EEEK! . . . Goodness! You startled me, little boy . . . Oh, dear! Is it time now? Already? For me to make O'Malley's speech for him?

Gus!

O'MALLEY FOR CONGRESS

Your Fairy Godfather felt that half the debate should be held at the Little Men's Chowder and Marching Society. He's there . . .

And you're going to debate for him here?

O'MALLEY FOR CONGRESS

Yes. But—oh, dear—why did I permit O'Malley to talk me into it? That big audience— And I had such an upsetting adventure as I passed the cemetery on my way here . . .

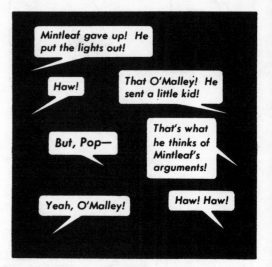

JUST BEFORE ELECTION

> Have the boys in the alley ready to start voting early and often for Mintleaf. I'll be there to pay them off... with some of the two-dollar bills O'Malley provided...

> Okay, Boss. But—

> Very reassuring item in the paper, m'boy... "Boss John Snagg confident of outcome of election"...

ELECTION DAY

> These deuces Boss Snagg give us to vote for Mintleaf! Look!

> They're phonies!

> Confederate money! Hey!

> The BUM!

> A outrage! Leave us heave some rocks through Snagg's window!

> First, leave us get even by voting for O'MALLEY!

> Yeh!... VOTE FOR O'MALLEY!

> Mintleaf? I just paid off the boys. You're as good as in... O'Malley hasn't got a trick left in his hand...

O'MALLEY FOR CONGRESS

> What? Wave my magic wand and assure my election? It wouldn't be fair, m'boy—Say! I'd better stroll by the polls and see if those Gnomes are still pulling the right lever...

> Okay, Mr. O'Malley.

THE MORNING AFTER

Let me rest here alone, Danny. Leave the window open . . . Air. To clear my head while I think our way out of this mess. . . . The old brain will see something—

I'll make a simple speech. "Thank you, Honest John," I'll say, "for your help in electing me to Congress." Then I'll clasp his hand. . .

EEEOOWWW! Help! I saw a—

Cushlamochree! Where did Honest John go?. . .

Four blocks up that way, Mr. O'Malley. . . And around a corner.

ROBERT BENCHLEY

Kiddie-Kar Travel

In America there are two classes of travel—first class, and with children. Traveling with children corresponds roughly to traveling third-class in Bulgaria. They tell me there is nothing lower in the world than third-class Bulgarian travel.

The actual physical discomfort of traveling with the Kiddies is not so great, although you do emerge from it looking as if you had just moved the piano upstairs single-handed. It is the mental wear-and-tear that tells and for a sensitive man there is only one thing worse, and that is a church wedding in which he is playing the leading comedy rôle.

There are several branches of the ordeal of Going on Choo-Choo, and it is difficult to tell which is the roughest. Those who have taken a very small baby on a train maintain that this ranks as pleasure along with having a nerve killed. On the other hand, those whose wee companions are in the romping stage, simply laugh at the claims of the first group. Sometimes you will find a man who has both an infant *and* a romper with him. Such a citizen should receive a salute of twenty-one guns every time he enters the city and should be allowed to wear the insignia of the Pater Dolorosa, giving him the right to solicit alms on the cathedral steps.

There is much to be said for those who maintain that rather should the race be allowed to die out than that babies should be taken from place to place along our national arteries of traffic. On the other hand, there *are* moments when babies are asleep. (Oh, yes, there are. There *must* be.) But it is practically a straight run of ten or a dozen hours for your child of four. You may have a little trouble in getting the infant to doze off, especially as the train newsboy waits crouching in the vestibule until he sees signs of slumber on the child's face and then rushes in to yell, "Copy of *Life*, out today!" right by its pink, shell-like ear. But after it *is* asleep, your troubles are over except for wondering how you can shift your ossifying arm to a new position without disturbing its precious burden.

If the child is of an age which denies the existence of sleep, however, preferring to run up and down the aisle of the car rather than sit in its chair (at least a baby can't get out of its chair unless it falls out and even then it can't go far), then every minute of the trip is full of fun. On the whole, having traveled with children of all the popular ages, I would be inclined to award the Hair-Shirt to the man who successfully completes the ride with a boy of, let us say, three.

In the first place, you start with the pronounced ill-will of two-thirds of the rest of the occupants of the car. You see them as they come in, before the train starts, glancing at you and yours with little or no attempt to conceal the fact that they wish they had waited for the four o'clock. Across from you is perhaps a large man who, in his home town, has a reputation for eating little children. He wears a heavy gold watch chain and wants to read through a lot of reports on the trip. He is just about as glad to be opposite a small boy as he would be if it were a hurdy-gurdy.

In back of you is a lady in a black silk dress who doesn't like the porter. Ladies in black silk dresses always seem to board the train with an aversion to the porter. The fact that the porter has to be in the same car with her makes her fussy to start with, and when she discovers that in front of her is a child of three who is already eating (you simply have to give him a lemon-drop to keep him quiet at least until the train starts) she decides that the best thing to do is simply to ignore him and not give him the slightest encouragement to become friendly. The child therefore picks her out immediately to be his buddy.

For a time after things get to going all you have to do is answer questions about the scenery. This is only what you must expect when you have children, and it happens no matter where you are. You can always say that you don't know who lives in that house or what that cow is doing. Sometimes you don't even have to look up when you say that you don't know. This part is comparatively easy.

It is when the migratory fit comes on that you will be put to the test. Suddenly you look and find the boy staggering down the aisle, peering into the faces of people as he passes them. "Here! Come back here Roger!" you cry, lurching after him and landing across the knees of the young lady two seats down. Roger takes this as a signal for a game and starts to run, screaming with laughter. After four steps he falls and starts to cry.

On being carried kicking back to his seat, he is told that he mustn't run down the aisle again. This strikes even Roger as funny, because it is such a flat thing to say. Of course he is going to run down the aisle again and he knows it as well as you do. In the meantime, however, he is perfectly willing to spend a little time with the lady in the black silk dress.

"Here, Roger," you say, "don't bother the lady."

"Hello, little boy," the lady says, nervously, and tries to go back to her book. The interview is over as far as she is concerned. Roger, however, thinks that it would be just dandy to get up in her lap. This has to be stopped, and Roger has to be whispered to.

He then announces that it is about time that he went to the wash-room. You march down the car, steering him by the shoulders and both lurching together as the train takes the curves and attracting wide attention to your very obvious excursion. Several kindly people smile knowingly at you as you pass and try to pat the boy on the head, but their advances are repelled, it being a rule of all children to look with disfavor on any attentions from strangers. The only people they want to play with are those who hate children.

On reaching the wash-room you discover that the porter has just locked it and taken the key with him, simply to be nasty. This raises quite a problem. You explain the situation as well as possible, which turns out to be not well enough. There is every indication of loud crying and perhaps worse. You call attention to the Burrows Rustless Screen sign which you are just passing and stand in the passage way by the drinking-cups, feverishly trying to find things in the landscape as it whirls by which will serve to take the mind off the tragedy of the moment. You become so engrossed in this important task that it is some time before you discover that you are completely blocking the passage way and the progress of some fifteen people who want to get off at Utica. There is nothing for you to do but head the procession and get off first.

Once out in the open, the pride and prop of your old age decides that the thing to do is pay the engineer a visit, and starts off up the platform at a terrific rate. This amuses the onlookers and gives you a little exercise after being cramped up in that old car all the morning. The imminent danger of the train's starting without you only adds to the fun. At that, there might be worse things than being left in Utica. One of them is getting back on the train again to face the old gentleman with the large watch chain.

The final phase of the ordeal, however, is still in store for you when you make your way (and Roger's way) into the diner. Here the plunging march down the aisle of the car is multiplied by six (the diner is never any nearer than six cars and usually is part of another train). On the way, Roger sees a box of animal crackers belonging to a little girl and commandeers it. The little girl, putting up a fight, is promptly pushed over, starting what promises to be a free-for-all fight between the two families. Lurching along after the apologies have been made it is just a series of unwarranted attacks by Roger on sleeping travelers and equally unwarranted evasions by Roger of the kindly advances of very nice people who love children.

In the diner, it turns out that the nearest thing they have suited to Roger's customary diet is veal cutlets, and you hardly think that his mother would approve of those. Everything else has peppers or sardines in it. A curry of lamb across the way strikes the boy's fancy and he demands some of that. On being told that he has not the slightest chance in the world of getting it but how would he like a little crackers-and-milk, he becomes quite upset and threatens to throw a fork at the Episcopal clergyman sitting opposite. Pieces of toast are waved alluringly in front of him and he is asked to consider the advantages of preserved figs and cream, but it is curry of lamb or he gets off the train. He doesn't act like this at home. In fact, he is noted for his tractability. There seems to be something about the train that brings out all the worst that is in him, all the hidden traits that he has inherited from his mother's side of the family. There is nothing else to do but say firmly, "Very well, then, Roger. We'll go back *without* any nice dinner," as I carry him protesting from the diner, apologizing to the head steward for the scene and considering dropping him overboard as you pass through each vestibule.

In fact, I had a cousin once who had to take three of his little ones on an all-day trip from Philadelphia to Boston. It was the hottest day of the year and my cousin had on a woolen suit. By the time he reached Hartford, people in the car noticed that he had only two children with him. At Worcester he had only one. No one knew what had become of the others and no one asked. It seemed better not to ask. He reached Boston alone and never explained what had become of the tiny tots. Anyone who has ever traveled with tiny tots of his own, however, can guess.

GORDON COTLER

More Big News from Out There

(THIS WEEK'S WINNER OF THE GOLDEN OPTIC—THE COVETED PRESS-AND-PERIODICAL AWARD OF THE NATIONAL COUNCIL OF SAUCER-SIGHTING SOCIETIES.)

Lester Krindchick, 37, of 12 Poplar Street, a buttons foreman at the Soft-Weve Shirt Factory of this city, and his wife, Myra, a housewife and mother of two, never gave any thought to flying saucers until 1 A.M. yesterday. At about that hour, Mrs. Krindchick happened to be glancing out the window when her eye was attracted by a strange object in the sky. She remembers calling to her husband, "Les, what is that—swamp gas?"

Mr. Krindchick, his suspicions aroused by the thought that swamp gas was unlikely over City Hall, took a good look. "More likely St. Elmo's fire or migrating geese," he recalls remarking.

The incident would have ended there except that a few moments later Mr. Krindchick's eye fell on the screen of the little radar set he has rigged up in the laundry room—he is an avid hobbyist and a past president of the Elks—and he noticed a blip in the area of the unidentified object. "The wind was wrong for an approaching plane," Mr. Krindchick, a teetotaller, told the *Gazette* this morning, "so, just to be on the safe side, we decided to put in some phone calls. We figured if there was a real situation up there we'd run smack into a surefire sign of it—flooded switchboards at the local offices of the *Saturday Evening Post* and the A.P. and Station KZMP."

While the Krindchicks were making up their minds whom to call first, the object, which they describe as "oddly shaped, with a kind of bulge," was rapidly descending on their back yard, making no sound but "a kind of low rushing hum that almost approached a roar." The Krindchicks, who are Civil Defense Air Raid Wardens, both stated that the craft—for such it proved to be—either hovered a foot or two over their lettuce patch or settled firmly on their compost heap. "It was bigger than the firehouse," Mr. Krindchick stated, but then agreed cheerfully with his wife when she stated that it was "more like the size of an old-fashioned ferry." Mr. Krindchick, an unruffled, clear-eyed man who serves weekends in the Naval Reserve and one night a week as a volunteer with a Red Cross team that gives eye tests to the needy, described the craft as made of "a strange metal I've never before encountered." Mrs. Krindchick, who is recording secretary of the Poplar Street School P.-T.A., added that the ship's surface impressed her as being of a "very dull, shiny material."

By now the Krindchicks were prepared for almost any eventuality, so they were not surprised when a door swung, slid, or folded open in the craft's side and a shaft of light spilled from the interior—"an eerie, blue-pink light, not unlike that given off by a television set or a pizzeria," according to Mrs. Krindchick, who, before her marriage, worked as an interior-design consultant for Balsa Brothers Furniture. In the light, a creature was clearly visible.

"He was about average height for a being of that type," Mr. Krindchick told reporters, "dressed in either a green cloak that hung from his shoulders—if those were in fact his shoulders—or a greenish chalk-stripe business suit. He was very much like you and I, and yet totally different, in a way I can't even begin to explain."

"As you can imagine," Mrs. Krindchick added, "we were hardly in a state to make detailed observations. When this person, or type, beckoned to us to come to him, we barely had time to snatch up some freshly sharpened pencils and a Kodak. [Unfortunately, the camera later proved to be unloaded.] A moment later, we were standing in front of the ship and this . . . individual . . . was communicating with us."

Whether their visitor spoke English or merely directed his thoughts to their intelligence centers the Krindchicks cannot say. "That's one area in which we've just plain forgot," Mr. Krindchick admits. "But anyway, we understood each other fine, even though he had a slight speech defect. He introduced himself—his name was either Falmbach or Felsch, something like that—and he clearly knew we were Mr. and Mrs. Krindchick. He said there were things of importance he wanted to convey to us, and would we come aloft with him."

The Krindchicks were naturally apprehensive, but they felt that the potential of this encounter was too important for them to allow personal considerations to interfere. Mrs. Krindchick checked back at the house to see that the children were asleep and all the faucets turned off, and then she and her husband joined their host aboard his ship. Almost before they knew it, they were air-borne, the ship taking off with what the Krindchicks describe as a "purring, thundering" sound.

Now began for the Krindchicks, somewhere high above the earth, one of the most memorable hours of their lives. While their host was piloting the ship through the atmosphere, his knees lightly gripping a wheel-like lever, they had time to make careful observations of the ship's interior. It was finished in varying shades of a muted orange blue, they agree, with Mrs. Krindchick adding that occasional accents of canary yellow provided further cheer to the spacious cabin. The "modern, sort of way-out" furniture was of a kind of wood neither Krindchick had ever seen before. The upholstered pieces, Mrs. Krindchick noted, were covered in what appeared to be a sturdy washable fabric.

Before they had time for further observation, the Krindchicks were joined by Falmbach, or Felsch, who served them a tastefully prepared meal. Although the Krindchicks had had a late and ample pot-roast dinner, they wisely chose to sample everything their host set before them—or, rather, for some reason, slightly to their right. Their notes show the first course to have been "a sort of fruit-cuppy, shrimp-cocktail sort of thing." The Krindchicks clearly remember the main course as a very strange-looking meat that tasted like TV-dinner chicken. "The seasoning," Mrs. Krindchick said, "had quite a bit of sage in it."

The Krindchicks found it impossible to give their full attention to analyzing the food, for throughout the meal their host was lecturing them, in an arresting audio-visual style, on his home, a distant, cloudlike planet that he carefully pinpointed for them in the upper-left corner of his celestial chart. (Mr. Krindchick later said it was "nearer the middle.") The visitor was obliged to return there almost at once, he indicated, owing to what the Krindchicks understood to be either "a fuel problem" or "a foot problem." He had seized this brief opportunity to exchange views with representative people of the planet Earth. He felt confident the meeting would lead to the mutual enrichment of their civilizations.

For the next half hour, over coffee, host and guests unburdened themselves at length on a great multiplicity of questions, so that when the Krindchicks were all too soon delivered back to No. 12 Poplar Street they felt, in Mrs. Krindchick's words, "wiser, deeper, better human beings for the experience."

"There was a heck of a lot of dazzling conversation," Mr. Krindchick added. "But meaty."

Pressed for details of the shipboard conference, the Krindchicks said they have not yet had time to sort out their crowded impressions. Among the subjects touched on were rush-hour traffic, "The Sound of Music," migraine headaches, and current trends in the apparel industry.

"All in all," said Mr. Krindchick, "a most worthwhile experience." Mrs. Krindchick agreed.

LYNN CARAGANIS

U.S. Torn Apart by French Attitudes

PARIS—No French Government, Socialist or otherwise, will ever follow the United States into any global commercial strategy against the Soviet Union.

If some Americans have been deceived or have deceived themselves into thinking otherwise after Secretary of State George P. Shultz's pleasant visit to Paris in mid-December, the illusion must be quickly dispelled.—*Yves Guihannec, in a Times Op-Ed article.*

As a member of the distinguished kitchen staff of our French Ambassador in Washington, I was moved to tears by this brave and patriotic article in the editorial pages of one of the big newspapers over here. Boldly titled "WASHINGTON ISN'T FRANCE'S CAPITAL," it has an almost epigrammatic clarity, balance, and vigor, which is not surprising, since it was written by M. Guihannec, who is one of our distinguished columnists at *Le Figaro*. Of course, its message of independence brought despair to our American cousins, whose almost slavish reliance on the French nation has been long remarked by such philosophers as Nietzsche, Corneille, and La Goulue. Since the article's appearance, steep increases in mental-hospital populations have been recorded in every state except Texas, and despairing people everywhere in this oversized country have been setting fire to their own homes and collecting the insurance—and then holding "square dancing" on the sites, for which the women put on clumsy farm clothes and shout like men. Apparently these uneducated people did not realize that the government of France makes its own policy. It is not a rubber stamp for the capricious vagaries of Washington!

Still reeling from their defeat by the tiny countries of Canada and Mexico in the preliminary "Children's" round of the World Cup football competition last year, the "States" are ill prepared to face resistance from a civilized and beautiful country with a celebrated culture. They know this, and the cleverer among them are most concerned.

One such gentleman—a Presidential aide from le Far Quest with great influence in trade matters—invited me to dine at his apartment outside Washington, in the hope that we could discuss some of these issues in a constructive way. You see, though officially I am merely the individual with total responsibility for potatoes in our Washington Embassy's cuisine, I am sometimes called in by my superiors and dispatched on errands of the utmost delicacy: "Remove your apron, Pierre-Marie, and negotiate with these people, these couwboys!" Frequently, I believe, our French diplomats prove too intimidating to their U.S. counterparts. Perhaps the American thinks, Who am I to play my little games with the policies of a proud nation that is one thousand years old? Yes, I have seen many of these grown men leave the negotiating table in tears!

To return to my story. Well, the dinner, I found, was to be in the aide's Virginia flat, one of those tasteless concrete boxes that— But never mind! I had no sooner stepped inside the door than his wife approached me. She was an excellent example of these man/women you see everywhere over here. But whose fault is it if these bluff creatures utterly lack the ways of our sensual Frenchwoman, the fecund, sleek animal whose pleasure it is to drive her man mad with desire—not tell him how to vote! This dear lady, named Mary, begged me to speak to her club.

"What club is this, may I ask?"

"Our Paul Claudel Catholic Poetry Club," she replied.

It seems that the popularity of our poet-diplomat has never diminished in this country, and there are such clubs in every town, no matter how small. Well, of course I agreed. At that point, the couple's teen-age son rushed up to me, notebook in hand. Would I tell him some good French epigrams that he could share with his friends at high school? Of course I complied. He was most delighted with

A woman loves her husband till he dies; then, she is ready for a new one.

Afterward, we deplored the lack of any true native epigrams in the U.S.

At dinner—we will not speak of it!—I discussed more serious matters with the *père de famille,* which was, after all, my purpose in visiting this family. I was forced to be obdurate with him on the issue of global strategies, as he had some illusions about the French nation. I did give him my personal assurances that we would never import more than eighty-nine per cent of our oil from the Soviet Union and Iran, adding that if we changed our minds that was our business.

Unfortunately for the prestige of his country, my host then got angry (drunk, perhaps), and demanded to know why we French refuse to march in lockstep with the other nations, which are like so many sheep!

"Monsieur," I told him, "I will now give you a short course in diplomacy. Is it not crude to make economic war? Are there not better ways to make war? Meanwhile, *par exemple,* why should we deprive the Iraqi people of luxury goods and 'nuclear minerals,' when it is their *governments* with whom we disagree? This is the beautiful *délicatesse* of French governments, Socialist or otherwise!" Yet my profit-minded friend could not understand an idea so classical, so balanced, so humanitarian. But—give them time.

I found my own way out. As I pulled open the door, I sensed the gaze of the wife and son on my back—full of cultural longings. In the eyes of the woman, there were perhaps longings of a different sort. It must be admitted that I had just had my hair waved. Frankly, I do not think she had ever been properly made love to by that slovenly Protectionist of hers. Ah, well, man is an empty sideshow, as Pascal and Camus realized long ago, and love, in the peasant sense of the term, is but a fleeting diversion of the moment which makes us tired at last.

So! I am off to Disney World, then home to my vacation house high in the Vosges. There my wife will dress in her milkmaid costume and wait on me, feeding me on the produce of our own French peasants. For it is only in such surroundings that a tired statesman can truly refresh his spirit, far from the temptations that gall his too human flesh!

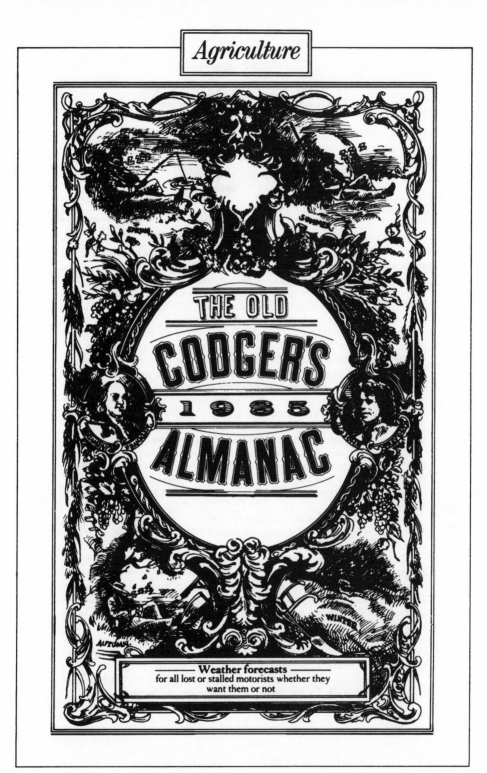

THE OLD

CODGER'S

1985

ALMANAC

AUTUMN

WINTER

—— Weather forecasts ——
for all lost or stalled motorists whether they
want them or not

MARK O'DONNELL

AND CHRIS AUSTOPCHUK

LETTER TO PATRONS

Here at the watershed roadside offices of *The Old Codger's Almanac*, we have several complete sets of all 486 previous editions of the little volume you are now holding, and all of us here must say we enjoy browsing through the stacks of these old troves of information. Crops Editor Bert Winters and I, for one, often abandon our families and checkers partners for weeks on end to bone up on some particularly arresting stretches of decades. (Did you know, for instance that in 1805, the tide went out but not in?)

The annual news of the sun's and moon's movements may lack the sensation and splash of more trivial journalism, but there is a soothing, musical regularity to the long rows of statistics that I myself prefer to warm Ovaltine. So we continue, year after year, like the running of the sap, undaunted by time, weather, and the fickleness of changing design styles. "Why do you maintain this illegible, crackerbarrel rigamarole in this day and age?" I am asked by lost media people from New York who mistake our offices for a gas station. "The layout is dense, it's unfocused and frankly unattractive," they tend to go on. "Maybe," I respond, "but I ain't the one who's lost."

This is not to say we haven't been tempted over the years to offer more timely material than kitchen remedies and unsolicited advice. Our 1943 and 1944 editions, in addition to a Pony Express retrospective, featured detailed articles on the interior designs and present positions of all battleships in the American fleet.

Since then, we have made occasional forays into the appraisal of passing fads (e.g., *Ten Uses for Old Television Antennas*, 1962), but, for the most part, we sit tight under the rapture of stars like a contented, abandoned plow.

Still, we have our own measure of fashionability. These days, what with every taxi-taking ballet dancer and advertising executive gallivanting around in down-filled skivvies and a hunter's jacket, eating country-style anything, discussing their window-boxes, and talking down-home talk into C.B.'s, *The Old Codger's Almanac* has had something of a slow-blooded revival. A lot of folks hang it in their summer home like a social register.

So, if anything, the incomprehensibility of the book boosts its value as a status accessory. And a lot of people find comfort in the notion that the elements themselves can be camp.

However that may be, we press on, already gathering outdated information for next year's edition. By our fruits ye shall know us, and by yours.

FEBRUARY hath 30 days.

1985

The winter wind will drone and drone
From day's debut 'til night is black:
Its sound is very like the tone
Of The Old Codger's Almanac.

D M	D W	Dates, Feasts, Fasts, Aspects, Taxes Due	Weather	Farmer's Calendar
1	M.	CIRCUMCISION ● Taxes $10.50/$11.50	Snow,	Remove drifts of snow that have accumulated indoors and investigate possible missing walls.
2	Tu.	☾ over Miami ● *stupid birds come north*	sleet	
3	W.	All Saints Softball ● ●!☙ Taxes $9.25/$10.10	and slop	Dip all household articles in tar to preserve them.
4	Th.	☾ light becomes you ● 1st woman lawyer dies, 1892	on top	
5	Fr.	Rhode Island ignored, 1925 ● Taxes $10.75/$10.75	of ice:	Old Christmas trees can be used to cover floors with festive dry needles.
6	Sa.	How high the ☾ ● *Jupiter lets Mars lead*	not neat	
7	G	St. Elmo's Fire Sale ● Taxes $9.50/$11.00	or nice —	Slice enough cheese for the entire winter, in case frostbitten fingers prevent knife use later.
8	M.	Festival of the Related-by-Marriage Gleaners	Watch out!	
9	Tu.	largest whale born, 1881 ● *Pluto does a little dance*	Winds clout	
10	W.	old devil ☾ ● *frogs stir in sleep*	your home	
11	Th.	1st tub in White House, 1938 ● Taxes $11.05/$12.05	and chill	Get up at half-hour intervals throughout the night to shake the bottled salad dressings in the refrigerator. This will prevent even momentary settling of contents.
12	Fr.	Elizabeth Taylor born, 1932	goodwill	
13	Sa.	Elizabeth Taylor born again (for photographers), 1932	'til all	
14	G	52nd Sunday after last year ● ☾ river	within,	
15	M.	*Saturn arrested for trespassing by Venus*	their	Leftover holiday guests make perfect sources of inconvenience and unpleasantness.
16	Tu.	it's only a paper ☾ ● snow in Alaska, 1926	patience	
17	W.	All Goats Day ● meteor resembling Will Rogers, 1953	thin,	Moose and bear can be coaxed into the house to spend winter with you by coating the halls and staircases with maple syrup.
18	Th.	☾ light sonata ● 4-foot herring elected to Congress, 1938	lash at	
19	Fr.	fly me to the ☾ ● Unknown Soldier's birthday	each other,	
20	Sa.	*moon eclipsed by large building*	husband. mother	
21	G	D. Eisenhower either b. or d., not clear which	children, wife.	Catch all local mice and rabbits and pull their teeth to prevent garden damage come spring.
22	M.	Lint Day !$%&●● Taxes $11.30/$12.00	and life	
23	Tu.	unexplained noises, 1840 ● ♄☉♂	seems ghastly.	
24	W.	Doomed Wheat Day ● Taxes $9.75/$10.60	Lastly,	Label your children and store them in a dry, frostproof place.
25	Th.	☾ glow ● St. Anne's Surprise Potluck	though,	
26	Fr.	Bad News Day ● *frogs murmur spouses' name*	a thaw!	Use the mild, moonlit nights to prune grapevines and dig up a disliked neighbor's garden.
27	Sa.	concept for Star Wars born, 1974 ♣♡●	Hurrah!	
28	G	Gherkin Sunday ● *Aquarius aligns with rich relatives*	Then	
29	M.	Deodorizing of St. Jerome ● Taxes $10.45/$11.00	more	Chip away at large boulders with only a needle, to learn better what eternity means.
30	Tu.	☾ comes over the mountain ● world ends, 1979	snow.	

S T A T E · F A I R

Thank you for the peaches Cling,
Thank you for the cherries Bing.
Thank you for the Kong that's King
Thank you, God, for everything.
— TRADITIONAL GRACE

PRIZE-WINNING JAMS
AND JELLIES ARE AS NEAR AS YOUR
NEAREST GOURMET STORE

by Velveteena Tinbrook Wheeler

Yes, mealtime wouldn't be meal time without food, and few foods are as nice as good jams and jellies, just as the little prayer above suggests. Delicious on bread, all by itself in bowls (I serve it in troughs on New Year's Eve instead of alcohol), or packed inside a big Christmas Turkey and/or doughnut, jams and jellies have long been truly the "staff of life" for millions. Even the ancient Egyptians must have loved their jelly, because we certainly don't find any leftovers cluttering up their tombs!

The best method I know for making preserves is quick, inexpensive and sure to snare you a blue ribbon at your next State Fair. I would, of course, be a fool to part with it, so I'll tell you a lesser recipe which should, nonetheless, suit your purposes adequately.

First of all, remember that when making fruit preserves, fruit is of the essence. In these strapped times, it's a temptation just to churn out the preserves minus the expense of fruit, but even if your guests don't catch on, you'll know in your heart you've been cheap — and anyway, if you like bright colors in your kitchen creations, you'll want that extra sparkle that ingredients always add.

Now that you've peeled and sliced a load of peaches or raspberries — I usually gauge a winter's supply by how many it takes to snap the springs on my mother-in-law's daybed — put on some water to boil. This is for coffee, since you've been doing all that thankless peeling and slicing for hours without a break.

Refreshed? Back to work, this time to cook those peeled and sliced whatevers within an inch of their soulless lives. Then, add sugar, pectin, cornstarch and perhaps some storebought jelly as an encouraging example to the rest of the mixture. After that — by the way, I hope you used *clean* jars! We don't want bolts or bandaids in among the boysen berries — it'll be no time before blue ribbons are dangling on your prize preserves.

Remember, too, that sometimes your own excellence is not so effective as preventing the excellence of others. Switching labels at the judging booth can make strawberry jam look deathly green, and green beans seem a bloody pulp. A little well-timed jostling and your neighbors won't even be in the running, except for a mop and wastebasket. In that gingham dress you're wearing and your hair pulled back in a bun, no one will imagine that the corridors of evil in your heart are as labyrinthine as a city slicker's.

And, after all, isn't that the beauty of country life?

RAINY DAY AMUSEMENTS

—PAPER SCRUNCHING—

Those with no patience for origami can use scrunched-up paper and lots of glue to fashion assorted animal or human figures, mostly very basic snowmen. Paper scrunching is an art that has been unknown to the Orient for centuries and though they tend to resemble stuck-together popcorn balls, scrunched-up paper figures often give the maker minutes of satisfaction.

——WUT WUZZAT?——

Alone? Blindfold yourself and spin until you are dizzy. Now, walk around the house colliding with things. Carry a pad of paper and scribble down what you imagine you've broken, based on the sound of the objects crashing to the floor. When exhausted, stop, have something cool to drink, and compare the real breakage with your guesses. The ears, you'll find, are not as quick as the eye.

——BRAIN TAUNTERS——

Mr. Morton wants to combine candy costing 79 cents a pound with candy costing 99 cents a pound to get a mixture costing 87 cents a pound. Is that all right with you?

John and Jane live on a planet that is 8,000 miles in diameter hurtling through space at 1,800 miles a second, tipped 23½° to the plane of its orbit. What chance does their love have?

THE TEN MOST COMMON ARGUMENTS—SETTLED

- The chicken came first, not the egg.
- Hot tea does not cool you off.
- Not even the President can hold his breath for more than three minutes.
- You cannot get used to poison.
- Fish *do* feel pain when hooked, but who cares?
- Scarlett does not get Rhett back.
- There are no top-secret federal conferences with super-intelligent bees.
- Women are more neat than men, except unmarried ones in large cities.
- You cannot get drunk on water, no matter how much you drink.
- It is not proper to machine-wash the American flag. It *is* proper not to mention that it is dirty.

ANSWERS TO LAST YEAR'S PUZZLES

(1) First of all, hens can't talk. Second, even if they could, they wouldn't go around trading their own eggs. No answer is correct.

(2) No, because we didn't tell you that the mother didn't really die. She was all right all along.

(3) Seven in all. There will be no Leap Year in 2200, don't forget.

(4) It depends.

(5) Never. Don't forget, the water would flow down the drain the other way once the bathtub crossed the equator.

(6) Five pieces, if you think you could eat that many.

(7) None—since, you'll recall, penguins live only at the *South* Pole.

(8) Ten. Or eleven, if you jammed them in.

(9) An infinite amount, but it sounds like publicity to us.

(10) Farmer Jones should reply, "I don't give a tinker's cuss about your daughter being half the age you are now and my being twice your age next year. I asked you a civil question and I expect a direct answer, dammit."

IAN A. FRAZIER

Into the American Maw

I was driving back to New York from Boston last Sunday and I stopped in a restaurant to get something to eat, and as I sat there waiting for my order to come, looking at my ice water and my silverware and the paper placemat, suddenly something struck me: I just might be on a savage nightmare journey to the heart of the American dream! I wasn't sure exactly what savage nightmare journeys to the heart of the American dream required, but I knew that since America has a love affair with the automobile, it was probably difficult to pursue a nightmare journey on public transportation. Fortunately, I had my own car, a 1970 Maverick. Beyond that, I couldn't think of any hard-and-fast requirements, so I decided that I *was* on a savage journey to the heart of the American dream, and I was glad that it was a Sunday. That made it more convenient for me. Once I had accepted this possibility, it was amazing how I saw all of America in a new light. Insights started coming to me one after the other, and I decided to reveal them in a voice as flat and affectless as the landscape that surrounded me (I was in a relatively flat part of Connecticut at the time).

First, I realized that discount stores—you know, the discount stores you see all over the place in America—well, I realized that discount stores equal emptiness. Beyond that, I realized that different discount stores represent different shades of emptiness—Caldor's equals an emptiness tinged with a sad, ineffable sense of mourning for a lost American innocence, while Brands Mart equals an emptiness much closer to what European philosophers call "anomie," and Zayre's equals an emptiness along the lines of Sartre's "nausea." Next, I realized that the interstate highway system equals nihilism. Have you ever been on Interstate 75 north of Berea, Kentucky? If you have, you know the stretch I'm thinking of—it's one of the most nihilistic stretches of four-lane possibly in the whole world. Although there certainly are lots of nihilistic interstate highways in every state in this country. In California, every stretch of road—I don't care whether it's interstate or a state highway or a county road or gravel or asphalt or oil—all of it is nihilistic.

Thinking about California led me to dizzying thoughts about L.A.— L.A., where sometimes on the signs advertising used-car lots they actually spell "car" with a "k." . . . L.A., a place that is so different from the East Coast. New York City, of course, is a woman. In fact, the entire tristate area, including New York, Connecticut, and New Jersey, is a woman. But L.A.—L.A. is the City of the One-Night Stands. Or at least that's what I had heard. Just to be sure, I decided to call L.A. long-distance, my voice crying through wires across the vast, buffalo-scarred dreamscape of a haunted republic. I told L.A. that I was coming out for four days, and could I possibly get a three-night stand. They said no, sir. They said I had to get three one-night stands. Q.E.D.

I paid my check and left the restaurant and got in my car. Luckily, it started. I began to drive—to drive to nowhere on a vast blank ribbon, to drive without direction or purpose (beyond getting home sometime that evening), surrounded by other Americans, my partners in the dream, all of them sealed off from me and each other by metal and glass. It got dark and began to rain, and still I was driving. I turned on the windshield wipers, and it wasn't long before I saw in the windshield the images of all my fathers before me. I saw my great-great-grandfathers' faces—not all eight of my great-great-grandfathers' faces but, say, maybe five of them— and then I saw my great-grandfathers and my grandfathers and my father, and all the faces merged into my face, reflected in the blue light from the dashboard as the wipers swished back and forth. And then my face changed into the faces of people who I guess were supposed to be my descendants. And still I was driving, stopping only occasionally to pay either thirty cents or twenty-five cents for tolls. I was on that stretch of 95 where you have to pay tolls every ten miles or so.

I stopped at a gas station to buy cigarettes. I put eighty cents in change into the machine, and pulled the knob for my brand—Camel Lights. Nothing came out. Then I pulled the knob for Vantage. Nothing came out. Then I pushed the coin return, and nothing came out. Then I pulled all of the other knobs, and nothing came out—a metaphor.

JEFF MacNELLY

KURT ANDERSEN

Affectations

Feigning ignorance of one's native language, such as the Radcliffe gradu-ate from Chicago's North Shore who stops herself mid-sentence, furrows her brow elaborately, and asks, "Oh, God, *what's* the word in En-glish . . . ?" is the real thing.

But there is an encyclopedia of also-rans, so many are the ways we get too big for our britches.

The phrase "have no" used instead of "don't speak"—as in "I have no Celtic"—is pretentious all right, but less horrifying than actually *speaking* Celtic.

A corollary outrage is the twit's frequent insistence that "it's absolutely *essential* to read Menander in the original Greek." The would-be pedant who announces that he's "read all of Goethe in the original Portuguese" won't win many stars, but at least we can laugh at his misfortune, as we do at the straggler's remark that he reads "Faulkner in the original English." (The line between the cretinous and the cryptic is thin.)

But affectation isn't limited to linguistic matters. Clam-digging, unless in service to a seafood restaurant, is a high-falutin exercise, and so are most of the pleasures overmonied urbanites manage to explore during New England summers. In the cities themselves, the sidewalks are rife with shanks of seldom-used squash rackets, each protruding rakishly from a handsome briefcase. But at least in this instance the racket's butt-end serves as a kind of low-tide warning buoy, a silent but unmistakable caution to steer clear. Commoner every month are expensive solar en-ergy setups on the roofs of the gentry's homes, this decade's version of the garden party for Cesar Chavez.

Many are rankled by non-physicians who call themselves "Doctor." Dollars to doughnuts these poseurs were born in a Warsaw Pact country, or struggled through UCLA extension courses for seventeen years, or both. It wouldn't be a bad idea to make the use of the "Dr." title statutorily limited to men and women who've actually sliced flesh and dispensed drugs. (Those who might wriggle through the law's loophole—drug-dealing killers—would probably rarely take advantage of the opportunity. And you'd hear no objection from me even if knife-wielding druggies did demand to be called "Doc.")

There are plenty of pretensions we're unaccustomed to regarding as such. Being a beautiful, trilingual Eurasian is, when you come right down to it, a colossal affectation which we can condone no more than we do foreign cigarettes, expensive mustards, houses with names like Hillrise, collar pins, Oxford degrees, using the word "commonweal," having been in the OSS, graduates of American public schools who speak, with a tear, of their "third-form year," and people who profess a fondness for Matthew Arnold and watch nothing but public television.

The obsessive Anglophilism of PBS is typical of American affectation, which for some reason takes the form of pretending to be a boyishly middle-aged Londoner. This is George Plimpton's true vocation, frankly, and that of anyone else who pronounces "harass" correctly and "extraordinary" as if it had three syllables at most. Take Gore Vidal . . . *s'il vous plaît.*

HAROLD A. LARRABEE

The Very Model of a Modern College President

(Sir W. S. Gilbert)

I am the very model of a modern college president.
I'm always on the job, though nearly always a nonresident,
I tour about the country to assemblies gastronomical
And make all sorts of speeches from sublime to broadly comical,
I keep the trustees calm and the alumni all benevolent,
Restrain all signs of riot and publicity malevolent,
I know the market-value of each wage-slave professorial,
And how much less he'll take for honorarium tutorial,
I'm on to all the low intrigues and rivalries divisional,
And on the budget how I wield my fountain-pen excisional!
So though I pile up mileage being generally nonresident
I am the very model of a modern college president!

I mix with all the business kings—the Lions and the Rotary,
Of heiresses and oil-tycoons I am a hopeful votary.
I'm fond of giving dinners in a lay-out that is squiffycal
And talking on the radio in accents quite pontifical,
I use the phrase "distinguished guest" at every opportunity,
I welcome all alumni to my parlor every June at tea.
And though I like to see the neutrals' lonely hearts-that-burn at ease,
I always have a kindly word to say about fraternities,
I've shaken every human hand that's manicured and squeezable,
I pass the hat among the rich, the buck wherever feasible!
So though I pile up mileage being generally nonresident,
I am the very model of a modern college president!

Mel-ange

I am convulsed by Mel Brooks. Even what should be a business telephone call plunges into a surreal tumult of shouting and carom-shot observations. When Brooks saw me for the first time, he pointed a finger at me and said, "You! Your face looks like an Armenian revolution!"

To capture Mel Brooks on paper is not easy. It is not only *what* he says; it is the *way* it is said. But in 1975 he was interviewed for *Playboy* magazine, and reading Brooks in this interview comes mighty close to hearing him. In a profile on Brooks in *The New Yorker* in 1978, the critic Kenneth Tynan quoted a bit of the interview and wrote:

> It is tempting to quote more. Brooks's performance throughout twelve seventy-five-minute sessions he devoted to answering *Playboy*'s questions was a marathon display for his gift for chat in full flower. The printed result deserves a place in any anthology of modern American humor. The Master is back on his home ground. Brooks is showing off his own invention—the interview as comic art—and doing so with a virtuosity that makes one wonder how any other form could ever put his talents to better use.

Who can resist Tynan's command? Here is a substantial part of that interview conducted by Brad Darrach, who observed that Brooks's "imagination is violent and boundless and, in the opinion of other comedy writers, no brain on the planet contains such a churning profusion of wildly funny ideas." **G.S.**

BRAD DARRACH

Interview with Mel Brooks

BROOKS *(Sucking up a fistful of chocolate-covered Raisinets and chomping them behind a Brooklyn-street-kid grin):* All right, ask away, Jew boy, or whatever you pretend you are.

PLAYBOY: As one Episcopalian to another, how about giving our readers some idea of what you really look like?

BROOKS: I don't want to be vain, but I might as well be honest. I'm crowding six-one. Got a mass of straight blond hair coming to a widow's peak close to the eyes. Sensational steel-blue eyes, bluer than Newman's. Muscular but whippy, like Redford.

PLAYBOY: What about your nose?

BROOKS: What about *yours?* Mine is aquiline, lacking only a little bulb at the end.

PLAYBOY: You wish you had a bulb?

BROOKS: I do; I do—one that said 60 watts on it and lit up. It would attract moths. And it would help me read at night under the blankets at summer camp. Care for a Raisinet? We mentioned Raisinets in *Blazing Saddles* and now the company sends me a gross of them every month. A *gross* of Raisinets! Take 50 boxes. My friends are avoiding me. I'm the leading cause of diabetes in California. Seriously, they make great earplugs. Or you could start a new school of Raisinet sculpture.

PLAYBOY: Why are you so short?

BROOKS: You want me to admit I'm a four-foot, six-inch freckle-faced person of Jewish extraction? I admit it. All but the extraction. But being short never bothered me for three seconds. The rest of the time I wanted to commit suicide.

PLAYBOY: Now we know what you look like. What do you do for a living?

BROOKS: I make people laugh for a living. I believe I can say objectively that what I do I do as well as anybody. Just say I'm one of the best broken-field runners that ever lived. I started in '38 and I'm hot in '75. For 35 years I was a cult hero, an underground funny. First I was a comic's comic, then I was a comedy writer's comedy writer. When I'd go to where they were working, famous comedians would turn white. "My God, he's here! The Master!" But I was never a big name to the public. And then suddenly I surfaced. *Blazing Saddles* made me famous. Madman Brooks. More laughs per minute than any other movie ever made—until *Young Frankenstein,* that is.

PLAYBOY: What's so special about your comedy?

BROOKS *(Snatching up the receiver as the phone rings):* This is Mel Brooks. We want 73 party hats, 400 balloons, a cake for 125 and any of the girls that are available in those costumes you sent up before. Thank you! *(Slams the receiver down)* You were saying?

PLAYBOY: What's so special about——

BROOKS: My comedy is midnight blue. Not black comedy—I *like* people too much. Midnight blue, and you can make it into a peacoat if you're on watch on the bow of a ship plowing through the North Atlantic. The buttons are very black and very shiny and very large.

PLAYBOY: How did you come by your sense of humor?

BROOKS: Found it at South Third and Hooper. It was in a tiny package wrapped in electrical tape and labeled GOOD HUMOR. When I opened it up, out jumped a big Jewish genie. "I'll give you three wishes," he said. "Uh, make it two."

PLAYBOY: Where was South Third and Hooper?

BROOKS: Brooklyn. I was born in Brooklyn on June 28, 1926, the 12th anniversary of the blowing up of Archduke Ferdinand of Austria. We lived at 515 Powell Street, in a tenement. I was born on the kitchen table. We were so poor my mother couldn't afford to have me; the lady next door gave birth to me. My real name was Melvin Kaminsky. I changed it to Brooks because Kaminsky wouldn't fit on a drum. My mother's maiden name was Kate Brookman. She was born in Kiev. My father was born in Danzig. Maximilian Kaminsky. He was a process server and he died when I was two and a half—tuberculosis of the kidney. They didn't know how to knock it out, no antibiotics then. To this day, my mother feels guilty about us being orphans at such early ages.

PLAYBOY: What's your mother like?

BROOKS: My mother is very short—four-eleven. She could walk under tables and never hit her head. She was a true heroine. She was left with four boys and no income, so she got a job in the Garment District. Worked the normal ten-hour day and then brought work home. Turned out bathing-suit sashes until daylight, grabbed a few hours of sleep, got us up and off to school and then went to work again. My aunt Sadie, God bless her, gave us some kind of a stipend that kept us alive. And then my brothers worked. Irving was the oldest, then Leonard, Bernie and me. Irving and Lenny went to work at 12 and put themselves through school and brought the family out of ruin into food and clothing.

PETER HYAMS (*a trim young man with black hair, poking his head in the door and looking confused*): Excuse me, is this the sex-education class?

BROOKS: Here comes Peter, folks, the well-known director of *Busting* and *Fat Chance*, hopping down the bunny trail. You know everybody here, I think, Peter, and everybody knows and despises you (*rising and screaming*) AS A FILTHY, DEGENERATE CHILD MOLESTER! No offense. (*Sits down, smiling sweetly*)

HYAMS: Mel, why are you so wishy-washy?

BROOKS: I can't stand hurting anybody's feelings.

PLAYBOY: Did your mother have time to look after you?

BROOKS: I was adored. I was always in the air, hurled up and kissed and thrown in the air again. Until I was six, my feet didn't touch the ground. "Look at those eyes! That nose! Those lips! That tooth! Get that child away from me, quick! I'll eat him!" Giving that up was very difficult later on in life.

PLAYBOY: How did you and your friends pass the time?

BROOKS: Played stickball, chased cats. I was always running. Skinny, stringy little Jew with endless energy. One day we were playing punchball—like stickball, only you used your fist to hit a Spaldeen or a bald tennis ball. There was a '36 Chevy parked on our street and I took off my new camel's-hair-looking Yom Kippur sweater and put it very carefully in that nice dip in the front of the fender where the headlight was. Then I got a scratch single and a bad throw sent me to second. Suddenly, I see this beautiful black '36 Chevy pull away from the curb and take off. Whoosh! I went after it. "Foul!" they were yelling. "Balk!" But I was gone, the hell with the game. What was that compared with a Yom Kippur sweater? For 20 minutes I chased that car—way into Flatbush. Finally, I flagged it down around Avenue U. Jesse Owens could not have made that run. Only a ten-year-old Jewish boy built like a wire hanger. But when I got my sweater, I was lost. No idea how to get home. I took the Nostrand Avenue trolley. Got off in a tough Irish neighborhood. "Hell-OOOOO, Yussel!" I didn't wait around to hear any more. Like in *The 400 Blows,* I ran till I hit the sea. Coney Island. Ten miles I ran. It took me an hour and a half to get home on the trolley. But I had my camel's-hair-looking Yom Kippur sweater.

PLAYBOY: Did you ever commit a crime?

BROOKS: Yes. I stole salt off pretzels in Feingold's candy store.

PLAYBOY: You *were* a wild kid.

BROOKS: Not only that, there were Penny Picks—chocolate-covered candy, white inside. If you got one that was pink inside, you got a nickel's worth of candy free. We would scratch the bottom of the chocolate with our thumbnails until we found a pinkie. Poor Mr. Feingold. He could never figure out how we found so many pink ones. Which reminds me—Raisinet? Take two. What the——(*Brooks looks up, startled. An actor wearing a "Planet of the Apes" mask is strolling down the corridor outside Brooks's office, as though there were nothing in the least unusual about his appearance. He glances casually into Brooks's office. Just as casually, Brooks gives him a nod.*)

Hiya, kid. Workin'? (*The actor does a startled take, then moves on*)

PLAYBOY: What were you good at in school?

BROOKS: Emoting. When I had to read a composition, I would turn into a wild-eyed maniac, fling out my arms and announce in a ringing soprano: "MY DAY AT CAMP!"

PLAYBOY: How about Hebrew school?

BROOKS: Shul, we called it. I went for a little while. About 45 minutes. We were the children of immigrants. They told us religious life was important, so we bought what they told us. We faked it, nodded like we were praying. Learned enough Hebrew to get through a *bar mitzvah.* Hebrew is a very hard language for Jews. And we suffered the incredible breath of those old rabbis. They'd turn to you and they'd say, "Melbn, make me a *brüche. A brüüüüüüüüche!"* You never knew what they said. Three words and you were on the floor because their breath would wither your face. There was no surviving rabbi breath.

PLAYBOY: When did you find out that you could be funny?

BROOKS: I was always funny. But the first time I remember was at Sussex Camp for Underprivileged Jewish Children. I was seven years old and whatever the counselors said, I would turn it around. "Put your plates in the garbage and stack the scraps, boys!" "Stay at the shallow end of the pool until you learn to drown!" "Who said that? Kaminsky! Grab him! Hold him!" Slap! But the other kids liked it and I was a success. I needed a success. I was short, I was scrawny. I was the last one they picked to be on the team. "Oh, all right, we'll take him. Put him in the outfield." Now, I wasn't a bad athlete, but the other kids were *champs.* In poor Jewish neighborhoods, every kid could hit a mile. They could be on their back and throw a guy out at first. They were great and I was just good. But I was brighter than most kids my age, so I hung around with guys two years older. Why should they let this puny kid hang out with them? I gave them a reason. I became their jester. Also, they were afraid of my tongue. I had it sharpened and I'd stick it in their eye. When are you going to ask me about sex?

PLAYBOY: Mr. Brooks, what is your attitude toward sex?

BROOKS: How *dare* you ask me such a filthy question? What do you take me for—an animal? Kindly change the subject! I prefer to speak about Cossacks. I live in terror of Cossacks. Also of cars and narrow places. And I don't like to make turns when I walk. At night I keep the lights on in the closet. Mice eat closets.

PLAYBOY: You don't have a cat?

BROOKS: I *am* a cat. As a boy, I could make the greatest cat sounds in the world, and I'm still very good. There may be better cat-sound makers, but they have not come to my attention. In *Young Frankenstein,* there is a scene in which Gene Wilder throws a dart and misses the target. A second later you hear the greatest cat-in-pain scream ever heard on film. It was performed by your obedient servant.

PLAYBOY: Were Jewish cats different from gentile cats in your neighborhood?

BROOKS: You mean, did they wear *yarmulkes?* No, but Jews were different. When I was a little kid at home, I thought the whole world was Jewish. Even when I was allowed out to play, I still thought Italians and the like were very rare. We used to try to capture them to study them. My image of a Jew has always been that of a short, funny-looking guy with kinky red hair and milk-white skin with lots of freckles and he's usually hiding under a bed, praying for his life in Yiddish while the Cossacks go thundering by. When I was a little boy, I thought when I grew up I would talk Yiddish, too. I thought little kids talked English, but when they became adults, they would talk Yiddish like the adults did. There would be no reason to talk English anymore, because we would have made it.

But even in English, Jews talked different. Gentiles have Rs. Jews were not given Rs by God. Gentiles said, "PaRk the caR." Jews said, "Pahk the cah." Jews in Brooklyn learned their English mostly from the Irish. Anybody who says, "I wantida go ta da terlit on T'oid Avunya" is mixing a Jewish-immigrant accent with an Irish brogue.

PLAYBOY: Were there any Jewish princesses in Brooklyn in those days?

BROOKS: Sheila Rabinowitz. Jewish princesses are a second-generation thing. First-generation girls were scrubbing floors and helping out. Second-generation parents could afford to support royalty. But Sheila's father was a coriander importer; he made it big in coriander; so Sheila was a *first*-generation Jewish princess. She lived two blocks away from school and she took a cab. She had four chain bracelets with different names on them, two on her wrists and two on her ankles. And all the names were gentile, just to put you in your place: Bob, Dick, Peter and Steve. They happened to be Jewish guys, but the names were gentile. Sheila came to class in a Pucci, and Pucci wasn't even in business yet. Sixteen years old and she wore a turban with a rhinestone in the middle of it. And the accent! "Why, helloooo, theahhh. How aahh you?" What the hell *is* coriander, anyway?

PLAYBOY: What became of Sheila?

BROOKS: Don't know. She was dreaming of the great world beyond the ghetto. BUT *(leaps to his feet)* ENOUGH OF JEWS! I WILL SPEAK NO MORE OF JEWS! IN FACT, I WILL SPEAK NO MORE OF ANYTHING! *(Ripping off several strips of Scotch tape, he seals his lips tight and then, in a frenzy, rolling his eyes and squealing wordlessly, slaps sticky ribbons of tape over his ears, over his nostrils, over his hair and finally, eyelids stuck shut, goes staggering around the room, dragging one leg, gurgling and mumbling)* Look! Look wha' th' G'rm'ns did t' me! *(He tears off the tape)* They stole into my foxhole at night and covered my face with Scotch tape.

PLAYBOY: In your movies, you make fun of Germans. Don't you like them?

BROOKS: Me? Not like Germans? Why should I not like Germans? Just because they're arrogant and have fat necks and do anything they're told so long as it's cruel, and killed millions of Jews in concentration camps and made soap out of their bodies and lamp shades out of their skins?

PLAYBOY: Have you ever been in Germany?

BROOKS: Only to kill Germans. I was in the Army, World War Two.

PLAYBOY: What did you do when you got out of the Army?

BROOKS: Show business. But you got to understand something: Jews don't do comedy in winter. In summer, all right. You're a kid, you work in the mountains. That's how I got started. I joined a Borscht Belt stock company. They let me play the district attorney in *Uncle Harry,* a straight melodrama. I'm 14 and a half, but I'm playing a 75-year-old man. My only line was, I pour some water from a carafe into a glass and say, "Here, Harry, have some water and calm down." But on opening night, I'm a little nervous, right? So I dropped the carafe on the table and it smashed and this flood rushed in all directions and made a waterfall off the table and all over the stage—such a mess! The audience gasped. I don't waste a minute; I walk right down to the footlights and take off my gray toupee and say, "I'm 14, what do you want?" Well, I got a 51-minute laugh, but the director of the play came running down the aisle and chased me through five Jewish resorts.

PLAYBOY: So how did you become a comedian?

BROOKS: I became a drummer, that's how. When we moved to Brighton Beach, I was 13 and a half and only a few houses away lived the one and only Buddy Rich. Buddy was just beginning with Artie Shaw then, and once in a while he would give me and my friend Billy half a lesson. When I went back to the mountains after the war, I played drums and sang. *(Eyes suddenly dreamy, begins to patter rhythmically on his desk with finger tips as he sings)* "It's not the pale mooooon that excites me, that thrills and delights me. Oh, nooooo. . . ." Oh, I was so shitty. You've no idea.

Anyway, one time in the mountains I was playing drums behind a standard mountain comedian. Wonderful delivery, but all the usual jokes. "I just flew in from Chicago and, boy, are my arms tired." "Was that girl skinny—when I took her to a restaurant, the waiter said, 'Check your umbrella?' " Anyway, one night the comic got sick and they asked me to go on for him. Wow! But I didn't want to do those ancient jokes, so I decided to go out there and make up stuff. I figured, I'll just talk about things we all know and see if they turn out funny. Now, that day a chambermaid named Molly got shut in a closet and the whole hotel heard her screaming, *"Los mir arois!"* Let me out! So when I went on stage, I stood there with my knees knocking and said, "Good evening, ladies and gentlemen . . . *LOS MIR AROIS!"* They tore the house down.

PLAYBOY: You continued to improvise your act, night after night?

BROOKS: Crazy, huh? But I did. Look, I had to take chances or it wasn't fun being funny. And you know, there was a lot of great material lying around in the Catskills, waiting to be noticed. But I wasn't a big hit, not at first. The Jews in the tearoom, the Jewish ladies with blue hair, would call me over and say, "Melvin, we enjoyed certain parts of your show, but a trade would be better for you. Anything with your hands would be good. Aviation mechanics are very well paid." I'd walk by a bald guy, Sol Yasowitz. "Well, what did you think, Mr. Yasowitz?" I'd ask him. "Stunk." With a little smile. You could never get a kind word out of the Jews. And you know, maybe I *was* terrible. I had this theme song, wrote it myself. *(Does a Donald O'Connor walk-on as he sings)* "Dadadadat dat daaaa! Here I am./I'm Melvin Brooks!/I've come to stop the show./ Just a ham who's minus looks/But in your hearts I'll grow!/I'll tell you gags, I'll sing you songs./Just happy little snappy songs that roll along./Out of my mind,/Won't you be kind?/And please . . . love . . . *Melvin Brooooooooks!"* Terrible, right? After that, you surely need a Raisinet, right? Wrong. But think it over. Believe me, there are very few things that work as well when covered with chocolate. Anyway, I wanted to entertain so badly that I kept at it until I was good. I just browbeat my way into show business.

PLAYBOY: Didn't you meet Sid Caesar when you were working in the mountains?

BROOKS: Yeah, but before I went into the Army. He was a saxophone player and a really terrific one. He could have been world-famous on the sax, but he started fooling around in the band and he was so funny they turned him into a comedian. After the war, we met again in New York and he got me into television. Sid was a genius, a great comic actor —still is—the greatest mimic who ever lived. Only he didn't imperson-ate celebrities; he did types. He would do a harried married man or an old horse on its last legs or a bop musician named Cool Cees or a whole Italian movie. He was imitating life and he had these tremendous insights over a huge range. And there was always a needle. Sid had this terrific anger in him; he was angry with the world—and so was I. Maybe I was angry because I was a Jew, because I was short, because my mother didn't buy me a bicycle, because it was tough to get ahead, because I wasn't God—who knows why? Anyway, if Sid and I hadn't felt so much alike, I would have been a comic ten years earlier. But he was such a great vehicle for my passion.

PLAYBOY: Is it true that everybody hated you on *Your Show of Shows?*

BROOKS: Everybody hated everybody. We robbed from the rich and kept everything. There was tremendous hostility in the air. A highly charged situation, but very good. We were all spoiled brats competing with each other for the king's favor, and we all wanted to come up with the funniest joke. I would be damned if anybody would write anything funnier than I would and everybody else felt the same way. There were seven comedy writers in that room, seven brilliant comedic brains. There was Mel Tolkin and Lucille Kallen. Then I came in. And spoiled everything. Then Joe Stein, who later wrote *Fiddler on the Roof,* and Larry Gelbart, who writes and produces *M*A*S*H.* Mike Stewart typed for us. Imagine! Our *typist* later wrote *Bye Bye Birdie* and *Hello, Dolly!* Later on, Mike was replaced at the typewriter by somebody named Woody Allen. Neil and Danny Simon were there, too, but Doc was so quiet we didn't know how good he was. Seven rats in a cage. The pitch sessions were lethal. In that room, you had to fight to stay alive.

PLAYBOY: What did you write for the show?

BROOKS: Masterpieces. Best work I ever did. We did eight comedy items a week. Live. No taping. Big classy items.

PLAYBOY: Would you run through a skit?

BROOKS: I remember the first one I wrote for Sid. *Jungle Boy.* "Ladies and gentlemen, now for the news. Our roving correspondent has just discovered a jungle boy, raised by lions in Africa, walking the streets of New York City." Sid played this in a lionskin, right? "Sir, how do you survive in New York City?" "Survive?" "What do you eat?" "Pigeon." "Don't the pigeons object?" "Only for a minute." "What are you afraid of more than anything?" "Buick." "You're afraid of a Buick?" "Yes. Buick can win in death struggle. Must sneak up on parked Buick, punch grille hard. Buick die."

PLAYBOY: Who were the show's other stars?

BROOKS: Imogene Coca, brilliant lady. Carl Reiner, greatest straight man in the world. And Howie Morris! Howie had the best nose ever given to a Jew. No job. His own nose. A miracle! On the nose alone he could pass. Also a genius. Didn't know a word except in English but could speak any language—German gibberish, Italian gibberish, Russian gibberish. Amazing ear for accents. You'd think it was the real thing. But the best thing about Howie was that he was the only guy on the show who was shorter than me! Gave me this incredible feeling of power.

So one night, just after he came on the show, we were walking along MacDougal Alley in the Village, chatting about the show, getting acquainted. Lovely evening, just getting dark. So I decided to rob him. No, really. I slapped him around, knocked him against a yellow Studebaker. "This is a stick-up!" I said. I had my hand in my coat pocket with my finger pointed like a pistol. "Gimme everything you got or I'll kill ya!" My eyes were glittering, I looked crazy. He went white. I took his wallet, his watch, even his wedding ring. Cleaned him out. Then I ran away in the night. He staggered to a phone booth, called Sid. Sid said, "Oh, he's started *that* again, has he? Whatever you do, don't call him up or go to his house, he'll kill ya." Howie said, "But when do I get my stuff back?" Sid said, "Ya gotta wait till he comes to his senses."

Well, for three weeks, Howie waited. No wallet, no watch. Had to buy another wedding ring. I'd say hello to him every morning like nothing had happened. "Hi, Howie. How ya doing? D'ya like the sketch?" He'd say, "Very good, Mel. Like it a lot." Then he'd go to Sid and say, "When's he going to remember? My license was in my wallet. I haven't been able to drive for three weeks." And Sid would say, "Wait." And then one day I stared at Howie and hit my head. "Howie! Oh, my God! I robbed you! I'm so sorry! Here's your wallet! Here's your money! Here's your ring!"

Well, it was the longest practical joke in history, because three years later—by now we're the best of friends—we're rowing on the lake in Central Park at lunchtime. Lovely sunny day. Butterflies making love, the splash of the oars. Howie is rowing. We go under a secluded bridge. Perfect place for a holdup. I stand up, put my hand in my pocket, slap him in the face. Howie's smart. The prey always respects the predator's prerogatives. So without a word, he forks over his wallet, his watch, his ring, takes off his shoes, ties them around his neck, jumps overboard— the water's up to his chin—and wades ashore. Well, that time I gave him his stuff back in a few days. But I intend to rob him again someday, ladies and gentlemen, because robbing Howie is what I do best.

PLAYBOY: Over the years, what was your main contribution to the show?

BROOKS: Energy and insanity. I mean, I would take terrifying chances. I was totally willing to be an idiot. I would jump off into space, not knowing where I would land. I would run across tightropes, no net. If I fell, blood all over. Pain. Humiliation. In those pitch sessions, I had an audience of experts and they showed no mercy. But I had to go beyond. It wasn't only competition to be funnier than they were. I had to get to the ultimate punch line, you know, the cosmic joke that all the other jokes came out of. I had to hit all the walls. I was immensely ambitious. It was like I was screaming at the universe to pay attention. Like I had to make *God* laugh.

Funny, I remember one year at the Emmy-awards ceremony, they gave the award for comedy writing to the writers of *The Phil Silvers Show*, and they had never ever given an Emmy to the writers of *Your Show of Shows*. So I jumped up on a table and started screaming, right there in front of the cameras and everybody. "Coleman Jacoby and Arnie Rosen won an Emmy and Mel Brooks didn't! Nietzsche was right! *There is no God! There is no God!*"

PLAYBOY: You know, you've described a lot of really wild behavior. Are you sure some of it wasn't actually a little crazy?

BROOKS: I'm sure it *was*. I went through some disastrous times when I was a young man. After I was hired by *Your Show of Shows*, I started having acute anxiety attacks. I used to vomit a lot between parked Plymouths in midtown Manhattan. Sometimes I'd get so anxiety-stricken I'd have to run, because I'd be generating too much adrenaline to do anything *but* run or scream. Ran for miles through the city streets. People stared. No joggers back then. Also, I couldn't sleep at night and I'd get a lot of dizzy spells and I was nauseated for days.

PLAYBOY: What brought on all this anxiety?

BROOKS: Fear of heights. Look at what had happened. I was a poor kid from a poor neighborhood, average family income $35 a week. I felt lucky to be making $50 a week, which is what Sid was paying me. And then, on top of that, I got a screen credit! "Additional dialog, Mel Brooks." Wow! But when I was listed as a regular writer and my pay went to $250 a week, I began to get scared. Writer! I'm not a writer. Terrible penmanship. And when my salary went to $1000 a week, I really panicked. Twenty-four years old and $1000 a week? It was unreal. I figured any day now they'd find me out and fire me. It was like I was stealing and I was going to get caught. Then, the year after that, the money went to $2500 and finally I was making $5000 a show and going out of my mind. In fact, the psychological mess I was in began to cause a real physical debilitation. To wit: low blood sugar and underactive thyroid.

PLAYBOY: You—underactive thyroid?

BROOKS: Everybody thinks, Mel Brooks, that maniac! The energy of that man! He must be hyperthyroid. *Au contraire, mon frère.* To this day, I take a half grain of thyroid—and an occasional Raisinet. Now, seriously, have you got kids? How's about taking a couple boxes Raisinets for the kids? They'll love 'em, and——

PLAYBOY: But chocolate is terrible for their teeth.

BROOKS: Are teeth so good for chocolate? Let's be fair.

PLAYBOY: Thanks, but——

BROOKS: Take your time. It's a big decision. Maybe you should call your lawyer. Use my phone, OK? Where were we?

PLAYBOY: What straightened you out emotionally?

BROOKS: Mel Tolkin sent me to an analyst. Strictly Freudian. On the couch—no peeking. But the man himself was kind and warm and bright. Most of my symptoms disappeared in the first year, and then we got into much deeper stuff—whether or not one should live and why.

PLAYBOY: Did you find any answers to that?

BROOKS: The main thing I remember from then is bouts of grief for no apparent reason. Deep melancholy, incredible grief where you'd think that somebody very close to me had died. You couldn't grieve any more than I was grieving.

PLAYBOY: Why?

BROOKS: It was connected with accepting life as an adult, getting out in the real world. I was grieving about the death of childhood. I'd had such a happy childhood, my family close to me and loving me. Now I really had to accept the mantle of adulthood—and parenthood. No more cadging quarters from my older brothers or my mother. Now I was the basic support of the family unit. I was proud of doing my bit, but it meant no longer being the baby, the adorable one. It meant being a father figure. Deep, deep shock. But finally I went on to being a mature person.

You often hear, you know, that people go into show business to find the love they never had when they were children. Never believe it! Every comic and most of the actors I know had a childhood full of love. Then they grew up and found out that in the grown-up world, you don't get all that love, you just get your share. So they went into show business to recapture the love they had known as children when they were the center of the universe.

Sherreeeeee! Bring me some Trident gum! I gave up smoking, folks, on January 3, 1974. In lieu of eating my desk, I chew gum. 'Cause the mouth still wants to inhale. Already, I've inhaled a Bell telephone; that's how fierce the desire is.

PLAYBOY: Can you give some advice to someone who is trying to quit smoking?

BROOKS: Suck somebody else's nose.

PLAYBOY: Thank you. Now about Mel Tolkin. . . .

BROOKS: Tolkin is a big, tall, skinny Jew with terribly worried eyes. He looks like a stork that dropped a baby and broke it and is coming to explain to the parents. Very sad, very funny, very widely read. When I met him, I had read nothing—*nothing!* He said, "Mel, you should read Tolstoy, Dostoievsky, Turgenev, Gogol." He was big on the Russians. So I started with Tolstoy and I was overwhelmed. Tolstoy writes like an ocean, in huge, rolling waves, and it doesn't look like it was processed through his thinking. It feels very natural. You don't question whether Tolstoy's right or wrong. His philosophy is housed in interrelating characters, so it's not up for grabs. Dostoievsky, on the other hand, you can dispute philosophical points with, but he's good, too. *The Brothers Karamazov* ain't chopped liver.

The Russian novelists made me realize it's a bigger ball park than the *Bilko* show. Right from the moment I read them, I knew I wanted to achieve more than Doc Simon and Abe Burrows did. I wanted to be the American Molière, the new Aristophanes.

PLAYBOY: Were you influenced by other comedians as well as by great writers?

BROOKS: Powerfully. I thought Chaplin was wonderful. Liked Laurel and Hardy even more. Keaton was the greatest master of physical comedy. Fields was a genius at skit construction. And Fred Allen showed me new kinds of irony.

PLAYBOY: So you got rich, cultured, secure—then what happened?

BROOKS: And then the roof fell in. There I am, strolling around in silk shirts and thinking, I'm cut out for greatness. Television's too small for me. How am I going to get out of this lousy racket? And suddenly I *am* out of it. The show is off the air. One day it's $5000 a week, the next day it's zilch. I couldn't get a job anywhere! Comedy shows went out of style and the next five years I averaged $85 a week. Five thousand a week to $85 a week! It was a terrifying nose dive.

PLAYBOY: What about the money you had saved?

BROOKS: What money? Are you kidding? I was *married!* I was so much in debt I couldn't believe it! All I had was a limited edition of *War and Peace* and an iron skate key. I kissed the skate key four times a day just to have something to do.

PLAYBOY: How about the record? Didn't you and Reiner record *The 2000-Year-Old Man* not long after the show folded?

BROOKS: A year later, the record came out. Saved me. Sold maybe 1,000,000 copies. And we did two others, *2001* and the *Cannes Film*

Festival. We'd been doing the act for nothing at parties. We'd go to Danny's Hide-A-Way in New York and Carl would say, "Sir, I understand that you were living at the time of Christ." I'd say, "Christ? Can't place him. Thin, nervous fella? Yeah. Came in the store, never bought anything. Little beard, cute. Wore sandals, right?" We did it once at a big party at Carl's house and Steve Allen said we ought to make a comedy record, there was money in it.

PLAYBOY: How did you meet Anne Bancroft?

BROOKS: Anne Bancroft? Never heard of her.

PLAYBOY: Famous actress, beauty of stage and screen, star of *The Miracle Worker, Two for the Seesaw, The Pumpkin Eater,* featured in the forthcoming film version of *The Prisoner of Second Avenue,* married to some Jewish comedian.

BROOKS: Oh, *that* Anne Bancroft. Yes, I am a great fan of hers—and of her husband's. When did I meet her? Let's go back to February 5, 1961, four o'clock in the afternoon. I went to the rehearsal of a Perry Como special, and there she was, singing in a beautiful white gown. Strangely enough, she was singing *Married I Can Always Get* and when she finished the song, I stood up and clapped loudly in this empty theater. "Bravo!" I shouted. "Terrific!" Then I rushed down the aisle and up onto the stage. "Hi," I said, "I'm Mel Brooks." I was really a pushy kid. And I shook her hand and she smiled and laughed.

Anyway, she said she was going to the William Morris office to see her agent, so I said, "Oh, by chance I happen to be going there, too." Big lie. "Let's all take a cab together." *Vrrrrrreeeeeet!* I gave this great New York whistle. It stopped a cab. Later she said that really impressed her. We went to her agent's office. I said, "I haven't seen *The Miracle Worker* yet, but I hear it's great." She said, "Want me to do it for you?" I said, "The whole play?" She said, "Yes." She obviously liked me, too. Well, she did the whole play! A one-hour version right there in the office! The fight scene and everything. And then *Waaaa! Waaaa!* The screaming at the end, the buckets of water, she did everything. I was on the floor. I was in tears, screaming with laughter, stunned.

I called and called her that night. She wasn't in. Next day I called her and went over with my record album and we sat for six hours in the living room and talked. That night she was going to Village Vanguard. I managed to be there. Then I went to a closing party for *The Miracle Worker.* Everybody was crazy about her. Me, too. I really loved her. I just fell in love. I hadn't fallen in love since I was a schoolboy. She was just radiant and beautiful and when we talked, I saw how bright she was. And her humor!

I asked her about dates and she said that very few men asked her to go out. And I realized that a man had to be pretty sure of himself, because she was quite an illustrious person. Just normal males who wanted to be big shots, wanted to hold their own, they couldn't deal with that. She was a very hard woman to dominate if you wanted to be Mr. Male. But I wasn't interested in dominating.

So we started going out and I told her, "OK, you're very bright. You're going to be my foreign-movie date. We'll go see foreign movies together." We went to the Thalia because it was 99 cents, and to dozens of recording sessions. All I could get into for nothing was recording sessions. Sometimes we ate in Chinatown for a buck-twenty-five. We walked, we held hands. I saw her every day. She would cook a lot to save money. Great cook. Eggplant *parmigiana* and lasagna, wonderful Italian dishes. After a while, we just didn't see anybody else. Not because we said, "Let's go steady" but because nobody else was as fascinating as we were to each other. Finally, I got a couple of TV spectaculars, as they were called then. An Andy Williams show, a Jerry Lewis show. Then the record began to save my life. But it was *Get Smart!*, a TV series I did with Buck Henry, that made it possible for us to get married.

PLAYBOY: Was it tough to bring yourself to the point of asking?

BROOKS: I never did. We were staying out at Fire Island and my mother had come to visit us, and her parents, too, and we were staying in separate rooms but still living in the same house. Didn't look nice for the parents. So suddenly Annie said, "Why don't we get married? It'll be so much easier for the folks to deal with our relationship." And I said, "Oh, absolutely. Fine." And she nearly fainted. Then she got scared. "Well, I don't know if I want to do this—really get *married.*" She had been married before and it hadn't been good.

Anyway, we got married in 1964, on my lunch hour. It was a civil ceremony. Annie is Italian and I'm Jewish. We were married by a Presbyterian. There was a black kid waiting in the anteroom and I asked him if he would stand up for us. His name was Andrew Boone. He had no idea that it was Mel Brooks marrying Anne Bancroft, because her maiden name is Italiano and she was married under that name. I didn't even have a wedding ring for her. Annie had an old earring. It was made of very thin, bendable silver, looked like a piece of wire. I just twisted that around and gave her that. The clerk was very upset about that; he liked regular rings. Afterward, I had to go back to work and that night I went to her apartment for our wedding dinner. Annie made me spaghetti. It was great. Just the two of us.

It's been like that to this day. My wife is my best friend, and I can't think of anybody I'd rather be with, chat with. We live way out here in California now, in a foreign place, so we need each other a little more. We're even closer. We have plenty of fights; I mean, we're *married,* right? But for me, this is it.

PLAYBOY: Do you have an active social life?

BROOKS: Only on weekends, and then not that much. Week nights we stay quietly at home and worry about how we're going to get rid of all our Raisinets. Sometimes a little *jai alai* in the living room with ripe guavas for balls and live pelicans for baskets. Why don't we talk about *The Producers?*

PLAYBOY: Your first movie, 1967. How did you get *The Producers* off the ground?

BROOKS: With 12,000 German slaves and lots of ropes. I had this idea about two schnooks on Broadway who set out to produce a flop and swindle the backers, and the flop was to be called *Springtime for Hitler.* I wrote the script in nine months, with the help of my secretary, Betty Olsen, and then couldn't think of anybody to direct it. So it had to be me. But I hated the idea of directing, and after four pictures I hate it even more. Directing is a terrible, anxious process. It's all collaboration, and if you have a dream, it's diluted very quickly by the slightest ineptness in any of your collaborators. They're supposed to help you, but too often they help you into your grave. Your vision can never achieve perfection. If you want to be a moviemaker, you've got to say, "All right, I'll chop the dream down. I'll be very happy if I get 60 percent of my vision on the screen."

PLAYBOY: Why do you direct if you don't like it?

BROOKS: In self-defense. Basically, I'm a writer. I'm the proprietor of the vision. I alone know what I eventually want to happen on the screen. So if you have a valuable idea, the only way to protect it is to direct it.

PLAYBOY: How did you get to direct *The Producers?*

BROOKS: I went to all the big studios with Sidney Glazier, my producer, and said, "I'm going to have to direct this." They said, "Please get out of here before you get hurt." There were physical threats. Finally, someone at Universal Pictures said, "You can direct, but it has to be called *Springtime for Mussolini.* Nazi movies are out." I said, "I think you missed the point." Then I met Joseph E. Levine, a plain person from the street. "You think you can direct it?" "Yes." "OK." Shook hands. That was it! In the middle of the night, I woke up in a cold sweat. "Foolish person! You had to open your big mouth."

PLAYBOY: Did you make a lot of beginner's mistakes?

BROOKS: Only the picture itself. No, I did dumb things, even though I had tremendous help from my assistant director, Michael Hertzberg. First day on the set, first scene, sound men are ready, cameras are rolling, the director is supposed to say "Action!" But, being a little nervous, I say "CUT!" Everything stops. They all look at me.

PLAYBOY: Still, you brought it in on schedule.

BROOKS: And under budget: $941,000. I won an Oscar for the Best Screenplay of 1968. And the picture died at the box office. Anyway, that's what Avco-Embassy said. Their motto is emblazoned in Hebrew letters on the office wall. WE MAKE THE MONEY. YOU TRY AND FIND IT.

PLAYBOY: With your first picture a financial flop, how did you finance *The Twelve Chairs?*

BROOKS: Minimally. I got $50,000 for writing, directing and coproducing the picture and it took three years to make. After the tax bite, I got about half of the $50,000, so that means I was living on $8000 a year and the good nature of several banks. We shot the picture in Yugoslavia, which saved us a lot of money but gave us a lot of headaches. When I went to Yugoslavia, my hair was black. When I came back, nine months later, it was gray. Truly. To begin with, it's a very long flight to Yugoslavia and you land in a field of full-grown corn. They figure it cushions the landing. The first thing they tell you is that the water is death. The only safe thing to drink is *Kieselavoda,* which is a mild laxative. In nine months, I lost 71 pounds. Now, at night, you can't do anything, because all of Belgrade is lit by a ten-watt bulb, and you can't go anywhere, because Tito has the car. It was a beauty, a green '38 Dodge. And the food in Yugoslavia is either very good or very bad. One day we arrived on location late and starving and they served us fried chains. When we got to our hotel rooms, mosquitoes as big as George Foreman were waiting for us. They were sitting in armchairs with their legs crossed.

The Yugoslav crew was very nice and helpful, but you had to be careful. One day in a fit of pique, I hurled my director's chair into the Adriatic. Suddenly I heard *"Halugchik! Kakdivmyechisnybogdanblostrov!"* On all sides, angry voices were heard and clenched fists were raised. "The vorkers," I was informed, "have announced to strike!" "But why?" "You have destroyed the People's chair!" "But it's mine! It says Mel Brooks on it!" "In Yugoslavia, everything is property of People." So we had a meeting, poured a lot of vodka, got drunk, started to cry and sing and kiss each other. Wonderful people! If they had another ten-watt bulb, I'd go there to live.

PLAYBOY: What happened when *Twelve Chairs* was released?

BROOKS: The movie was released at Meyer Roberts' apartment in Evanston, Illinois. Sixteen people attended the world premiere. Meyer himself couldn't make it; he had a date. We were all fingerprinted and booked by the police. No, the picture did pretty well in New York, but it couldn't get across the George Washington Bridge. Taught me something. There is no room in the business now for a special little picture. You either hit 'em over the head or stay home with the canary.

PLAYBOY: And *Blazing Saddles* was designed to hit 'em over the head.

BROOKS: No. Actually, it was designed as an esoteric little picture. We wrote it for two weirdos in the balcony. For radicals, film nuts, guys who draw on the washroom wall—my kind of people. I had no idea middle America would see it. What would a guy who talks about white bread, white Ford station wagons and vanilla milk shakes on Friday night see in that *meshugaas?*

PLAYBOY: How did you hit on the idea for *Blazing Saddles?*

BROOKS: It's an interesting story; I don't think I'll tell it. Can I interest you in a Raisinet? No? Maybe you'd like a chocolate-covered Volkswagen? Do you have a dollar on you? I hate to answer questions for nothing. *(Accepts a dollar)* Thank you. For two more I'll sell you my T-shirt. See this little alligator on the pocket? I understand that in the Everglades, there are alligators with little Jews on their shirt pockets.

PLAYBOY: What happened when you previewed *Blazing Saddles?*

BROOKS: Disaster! We showed it first to the studio brass. Ten of them in a small screening room. Now, the first really big joke in the picture comes when the white cowboy says, "How 'bout a good ole nigger work song?" And the black labor gang, as one man, begins to sing in a sophisticated style, "I get no kick from champaaaagne. . . ." That's a tremendous joke. But in the screening room, *nothing. Gornisht!* Not a titter. I said, "We have just entered cabin 4C on the Titanic!" The next 90 minutes was a non–laugh riot. When the lights went up, I had sweat circles the size of Rhode Island under my arms. Two years of my life I had spent on this picture and now disaster! I said to myself, "This is the worst moment of my life. My talent and my judgment are gone!" I went back to the editing room and just sat for 20 minutes. Then Mike Hertzberg said, "We booked a public screening for tonight." I said, "Cancel it!" Mike said, "No! Invite more people. Let normal people see it. Then we'll know."

So eight o'clock that night, the place was packed. Two hundred and forty people in the screening room. Seating only on the floor. First big joke: "I get no kick from champaaaagne." Children were thrown into the air. The most laughing you've ever heard in a moviehouse. Nonstop screaming. The following night, a big sneak preview in Westwood. The place went bananas. The more people you got together with this picture, the more insane the reaction was. Eleven hundred people dancing in the aisles. One guy was laughing so hard he couldn't breathe. As he fell under the seat, he told his wife, "G'bye, honey, the policies are in the top drawer." Almost two years later, the picture is still running.

PLAYBOY: What happened to your life and your career after *Blazing Saddles?*

BROOKS: I became John Carradine. Aquiline nose, face long and aristocratic, voice deep and vibrant. Thinking of running for the U. S. Senate. . . . Frankly, I'm in demand and it's great. I can take my best shot and take it under the best conditions. I have a three-picture deal at Fox that gives me everything I want.

There's one thing you've got to understand before you can direct comedy. Comedy is serious—deadly serious. Never, never try to be funny! The actors must be serious. Only the situation must be absurd. Funny is in the writing, not in the performing. If the situation isn't absurd, no amount of hoke will help. And another thing, the more serious the situation, the funnier the comedy can be. The greatest comedy plays against the greatest tragedy. Comedy is a red-rubber ball and if you throw it against a soft, funny wall, it will not come back. But if you throw it against the hard wall of ultimate reality, it will bounce back and be very lively. *Vershteh,* goy bastard? No offense. Very, very few people understand this.

PLAYBOY: Does Woody Allen understand it?

BROOKS: Woody Allen is a genius. His films are wonderful. I liked *Sleeper* very, very much. It's Woody's best work to date. The most imaginative and the best performed. I was on the floor, and very few people can put me on the floor. He's poetic, but he's also a critic. He artfully steps back from a social setting and criticizes it without—I suspect—without letting himself be vulnerable to it.

PLAYBOY: And you?

BROOKS: I'm not a critic. I like to hop right in the middle, right into the vortex. I can't just zing a few arrows at life as it thunders by! I have to be down on the ground and shouting at it, grabbing it by the horns, biting it! Look, I really don't want to wax philosophic, but I will say that if you're alive, you got to flap your arms and legs, you got to jump around a lot, you got to make a lot of noise, because life is the very opposite of death. And therefore, as I see it, if you're quiet, you're not living. I mean you're just slowly drifting into death. So you've got to be noisy, or at least your *thoughts* should be noisy and colorful and lively. My liveliness is based on an incredible fear of death. In order to keep death at bay, I do a lot of "Yah! Yah! Yah!" And death says, "All right. He's too noisy and busy. I'll wait for someone who's sitting quietly, half asleep. I'll nail *him*. Why should I bother with this guy? I'll have a lot of trouble getting him out the door." There's a little door they gotta get you through. "This will be a fight," death says. "I ain't got time."

Most people are afraid of death, but I really *hate* it! My humor is a scream and a protest against goodbye. Why do we have to die? As a kid, you get nice little white shoes with white laces and a velvet white suit with short pants and a nice collar, and you go to college, you meet a nice girl and get married, work a few years—and then you have to *die?* What is that shit? They never wrote *that* in the contract. So you yell against it, and if you yell seriously, you can be a serious playwright and everybody can say, "Very nice." But I suspect you can launch a little better artillery against death with humor.

PLAYBOY: But it's a battle you can't win.

BROOKS: You can win a conditional victory, I think. It all boils down to scratching your name in the bark of a tree. You write M. B. in the bark of a tree. *I was here.* When you do that—whatever tree you carve it in— you're saying, "Now, there's a record of me!" I won't be erased by death. Any man's greatness is a tribute to the nobility of all mankind, so when we celebrate the genius of Tolstoy, we say, "Look! One of our boys made it! Look what we're capable of!"

So I try to give my work everything I've got, because when you're dead or you're out of the business or you're in an old actors' home somewhere, if you've done a good job, your work will still be 16 years old and dancing and healthy and pirouetting and arabesquing all over the place. And they'll say, "That's who he is! He's not this decaying skeleton."

I once had this thought that was so corny, but I loved it. It was that infinitesimal bits of coral, by the act of dying upon each other, create something that eventually rises out of the sea—and there it is, it's an island and you can stand on it, live on it! And all because they died upon each other. Writing is simply one thought after another dying upon the one before. Where would I be today if it wasn't for Nikolai Gogol? You wouldn't be laughing at *Young Frankenstein.* Because he showed me how crazy you could get, how brave you could be. Son of a bitch bastard! I love him! I love Buicks! I love Dubrovnik! I love Cookie Lavagetto! I love Factor's Deli at Pico and Beverly Drive! I love Michael Hertzberg's baby boy! I love rave reviews! I love my wife! I love not wearing suits! I love New York in June! I love Raisinets! Which brings me, Mr. Interlocutor, for the last time, to the question: Would you or would you not care for a Raisinet?

PLAYBOY: Sure. Why not?

BROOKS: Sorry, kid. They're all gone.

GARY LARSON

FRAN LEBOWITZ

An Alphabet of New Year's Resolutions for Others

As an answering-service operator, I will make every effort when answering a subscriber's telephone to avoid sighing in a manner which suggests that in order to answer said telephone I have been compelled to interrupt extremely complicated neurological surgery, which is, after all, my real profession.

Being on the short side and no spring chicken to boot, I shall refrain in perpetuity from anything even roughly akin to leather jodhpurs.

Chocolate chip cookies have perhaps been recently overvalued. I will not aggravate the situation further by opening yet another cunningly named store selling these items at prices more appropriate to a semester's tuition at Harvard Law School.

Despite whatever touch of color and caprice they might indeed impart, I will never, never, *never* embellish my personal written correspondence with droll little crayoned drawings.

Even though I am breathtakingly bilingual, I will not attempt ever again to curry favor with waiters by asking for the wine list in a studiously insinuating tone of French.

Four inches is not a little trim; my job as a hairdresser makes it imperative that I keep this in mind.

Gifted though I might be with a flair for international politics, I will renounce the practice of exhibiting this facility to my passengers.

However ardently I am implored, I pledge never to divulge whatever privileged information I have been able to acquire from my very close friend who stretches canvas for a famous artist.

In light of the fact that I am a frequent, not to say permanent, fixture at even the most obscure of public events, I hereby vow to stop once and for all telling people that I never go out.

Just because I own my own restaurant does not mean that I can include on the menu a dish entitled Veal Jeffrey.

Kitchens are not suitable places in which to install wall-to-wall carpeting, no matter how industrial, how very technical, how very dark gray. I realize this now.

Large pillows, no matter how opulently covered or engagingly and generously scattered about, are not, alas, furniture. I will buy a sofa.

May lightning strike me dead on the spot should I ever again entertain the notion that anyone is interested in hearing what a fabulously warm and beautiful people I found the Brazilians to be when I went to Rio for Carnival last year.

No hats.

Overeating in expensive restaurants and then writing about it with undue enthusiasm is not at all becoming. I will get a real job.

Polite conversation does not include within its peripheries questions concerning the whereabouts of that very sweet mulatto dancer he was with the last time you saw him.

Quite soon I will absolutely stop using the word "brilliant" in reference to the accessories editors of European fashion magazines.

Raspberries, even out of season, are not a controlled substance. As a restaurant proprietor I have easy, legal access. I will be more generous.

Success is something I will dress for when I get there, and not until. Cross my heart and hope to die.

Ties, even really, really narrow ones, are just not enough. I will try to stop relying on them quite so heavily.

Unless specifically requested to do so, I will not discuss Japanese science-fiction movies from the artistic point of view.

Violet will be a good color for hair at just about the same time that brunette becomes a good color for flowers. I will not forget this.

When approached for advice on the subject of antique furniture, I will respond to all queries with reason and decorum so as not to ally myself with the sort of overbred collector who knows the value of everything and the price of nothing.

X is not a letter of the alphabet that lends itself easily, or even with great difficulty, to this type of thing. I promise not to even try.

Youth, at least in New York City, is hardly wasted on the young. They make more than sufficient use of it. I cannot afford to overlook this.

Zelda Fitzgerald, fascinating as she undoubtedly appears to have been, I promise to cease emulating immediately.

EDWARD GOREY

THE GASHLYCRUMB TINIES

A is for AMY who fell down the stairs

B is for BASIL assaulted by bears

C is for CLARA who wasted away

D is for DESMOND thrown out of a sleigh

E is for ERNEST who choked on a peach

F is for FANNY sucked dry by a leech

G is for GEORGE smothered under a rug

H is for HECTOR done in by a thug

I is for **IDA** who drowned in a lake

J is for **JAMES** who took lye by mistake

K is for KATE who was struck with an axe

L is for LEO who swallowed some tacks

M is for MAUD who was swept out to sea

N is for NEVILLE who died of ennui

O is for OLIVE run through with an awl

P is for PRUE trampled flat in a brawl

Q is for QUENTIN who sank in a mire

R is for RHODA consumed by a fire

S is for SUSAN who perished of fits

T is for TITUS who flew into bits

U is for UNA who slipped down a drain

V is for VICTOR squashed under a train

W is for WINNIE embedded in ice

X is for XERXES devoured by mice

Y is for **YORICK** whose head was knocked in

Z is for **ZILLAH** who drank too much gin

GAHAN WILSON

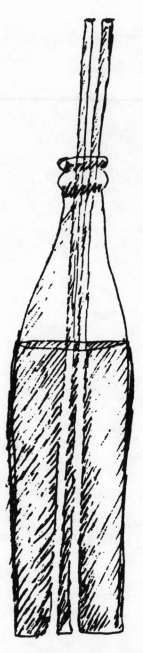

GARY SOLIN

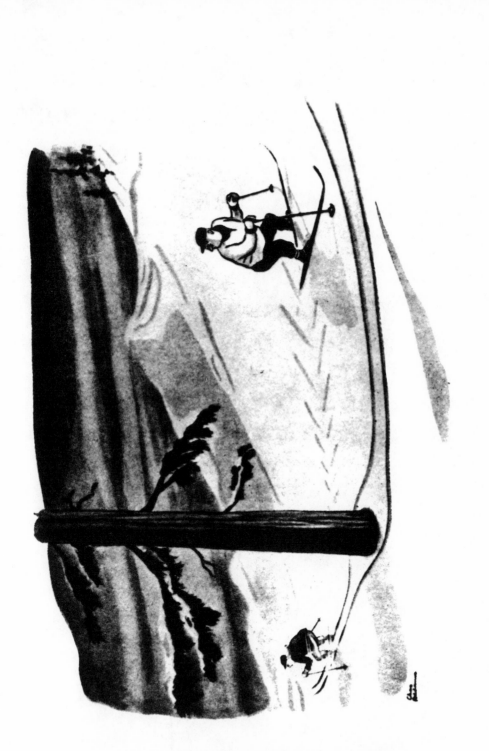

CHARLES ADDAMS

"Follow that Cab!"

RUBE GOLDBERG

Easy Way to Open a Window

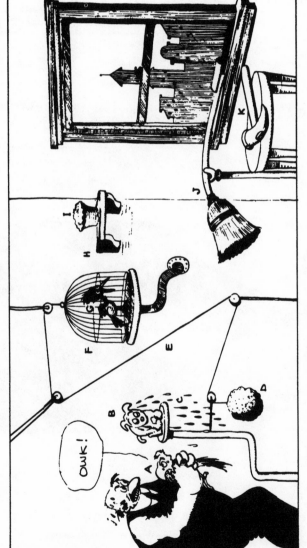

After trying unsuccessfully to open window for half an hour, you relieve your anger by choking parrot (A)–dog (B) hears parrot's groans and weeps out of sympathy–tears (C) soak sponge (D), causing its weight to pull string (E) which lifts top off cage (F) and releases woodpecker (G)– woodpecker chews away shelf (H) and heavy biscuit (I) falls on broom-handle (J), causing it to act as lever in raising window–after repeating this operation six times without success, take hammer (K) and break glass in window, allowing fresh air to enter room.

ROZ CHAST

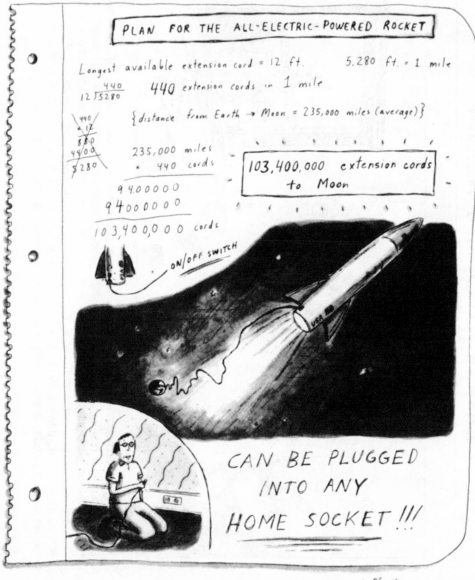

FROM THE NOTEBOOK OF

Lewis Commonsense, Ph.D.

CHRISTOPHER MORLEY

Unearned Increment

The Old Mandarin
Always perplexes his friend the Adjuster
At the Prune Exchange Bank
By adding his balances together
In the Chinese fashion.
For example: he once had $5000 in the bank
And drew various checks against it.
He drew $2000; thus leaving a balance of $3000.
He drew $1500; thus leaving a balance of $1500.
He drew $900; thus leaving a balance of $600.
He drew $600; thus leaving a balance of   000.

        $5000. $5100.

Yet, as you see, when he adds his various balances
He finds that they total $5100
And the Old Mandarin therefore maintains
There should still be $100 to his credit.
They had to engage the Governor of the Federal Reserve
To explain the fallacy to him.

BRUCE McCALL

Rolled in Rare Bohemian Onyx, Then Vulcanized by Hand

DEAR EMINENT PATRON OF THE MAIL ORDER ARTS,

Imagine a collector's item so exquisitely detailed that each is actually *invisible* to the naked eye.

Think of an heirloom so limited in availability that when you order it, the mint specially constructed to craft it will be *demolished.*

Ponder an item so precious that its value has actually *tripled* since you began reading this.

Kiln-Fired in
Edible 24-Calorie Silver

Never before in human history has the Polk McKinley Harding Coolidge Mint (not a U.S. Government body) commissioned such a rarity.

Consider: miniature pewterine reproductions, authenticated by the World Court at The Hague and sent to you in moisture-resistant Styrofoam chests, of the front-door letter slots of Hollywood's 36 most beloved character actors and actresses.

A special blue-ribbon Advisory Panel will insure that the Foundation Council's certificated and inscribed insignia is approved by Her Majesty's Master of Heralds before the application deadline.

Meanwhile, they are yours to inspect in the privacy of your home, office, shop, or den for *twenty years* by express permission, already withdrawn, of the Polk McKinley Harding Coolidge Mint—the only mint authorized to stamp your application with its own seal.

The equivalent of three centuries of painstaking historical research, supervised by the U.S. Bureau of Mines, has preceded this issue of *The Ornamental Handles of the Walking Canes of the Hohenzollern Princelings.*

Our miniature craftsmen have designed, cast, struck, etched, forged, and finished these authentic reproductions—not available in any store, even before they were commissioned—literally *without regard* for quality.

Certified by the
American Kennel Club

But now, through a special arrangement with the Postmaster General of the Republic of San Marino, this 72-piece commemorative plinth, honoring *The Footprints of the Great Jewel Thieves of the French Riviera*—each encased in its own watered-silk caddy that revolves 360 degrees on genuine Swedish steel ball bearings—has been cancelled.

A unique way, you will agree, of introducing you and your loved ones to *The Great Cookie Jars of the Restoration,* just as Congreve the boy must have pilfered from.

They are so authentic that you can actually smell them with your nose.

And don't forget: every set of hand-fired porcelain reproductions of *The Padlocks of the Free World's Great Customs Houses* comes sealed in an airtight cask, fashioned after the shoe locker of a Mogul emperor so famous that we are prohibited from disclosing his name.

12 Men Died
to Make the Ingots Perfect

But why, as a prudent investor, should you spend thousands of dollars, every month for a lifetime, to acquire this 88-piece set of *Official Diplomatic License Plates of the World's Great Governments-in-Exile?*

One Minnesota collector comments, "I never expected to buy an item so desirable that it has already kept its haunting fascination forever."

But even this merely hints at the extraordinary investment potential of the Connoisseur's Choice selection of *Great Elevator Inspection Certificates of the World's Tallest Buildings.*

Molded in unobtainable molybdenum, each is precision-ejected from a flying aircraft to check a zinc content that must measure .000000003 per cent or the entire batch will be melted down, discarded, and forgotten.

But "keepsake" is an inadequate term. Your Jubilee Edition of the 566 *Tunic Buttons of the World's Legendary Hotel Porters* will take you from New

York City to San Francisco to Hong Kong to Bombay . . . and then actually *pay your way* back home.

There is one more aspect for you to consider before refusing this offer.

If you wish, you can have *The Lavaliere Mikes of TV's Greatest Talk Show Celebrity Guests,* custom-mounted on driftwood plaques that serve as 175 dainty TV snack tables—free.

There is, of course, a surcharge and a handling fee, as well as the 25 per cent duplication cost. But so amazing is this offer that you need only pay this levy once—and never again be bothered by it in your mortal life.

If for whatever reason you elect not to purchase the complimentary *Tokens of the World's Great Subway Systems,* you still profit:

The solid-gold *Venetian Gondolier's Boat Pole Toothpick* and velvet-lined presentation case are yours to treasure for as long as this incredible offer lasts.

Our *Distinctive Axe Marks of the Immortal Brazilian Rubber Planters* are in such short supply that an advance application in your name is already reserved for you. To protect your investment, *none* will be made.

Registered with the
Department of Motor Vehicles

A dazzling proposition, you will agree. If you do not, your 560-piece set of *Belgium's Most Cherished Waffle Patterns,* together with your check or money order, will be buried at sea on or before midnight, April 15, 1982 —the 70th anniversary, college-trained historians tell us, of the sinking of R.M.S. Titanic, one of the 66 *Great Marine Disasters* commemorated in this never-yet-offered series, each individually bronzed, annealed, Martinized, and hickory-cured by skilled artisans working under the supervision of the Tulane University Board of Regents.

Please note that each comes wrapped in authentic North Atlantic seaweed, its salt content confirmed by affidavit.

Best of all, you need not order. Simply steal a new Rolls-Royce, fence it, and turn the bills into small denominations of used money (U.S. currency only, please). No salesman will call. The Polk McKinley Harding Coolidge Mint is not a U.S. Government body. This is not an offering.

THE POLK MCKINLEY
HARDING COOLIDGE MINT

P.S. If you have already begun your *Napkin Rings of the State Supreme Court Dining Rooms* collection, please disregard.

CLASSIFIED ADS

PERSONAL

HOT, DIFFICULT TO HANDLE, OVERWEIGHT MAN seeks lonely, sensitive, ethical woman with enormous breasts. Write NYR, Box 33811.

TIMID AND SHY young Bronx Jewish student, glasses, from reserved, sedate, conserv. family, seeks relations with fedayeen. NYR, Box 732.

EXTRAORDINARILY HIGH I.Q. physicist/lit. historian, fun-loving, sensual, sensitive, quiet, timid almost, with gigantic genitalia, seeks discreet relations with women from Ohio or Pennsylvania. NYR, Box 391.

PUBLISHED HISTORIAN and professor of comp. lit. (slight acne scars on right temple, lower back) seeks sexual freedom in the form of controlled napalm warfare If you follow, write NYR, Box 22199.

HUNGARIAN PROFESSOR of radiology at Technical College of Odobestio, congenial, intense, ironic, laconic, independent, occasionally redundant, with redundant tendencies seeks pen-friend outside Soviet bloc with whom to discuss stamps and oral sex. NYR.Box 551.

SOMEWHAT HOSTILE MUTE with M.A. in organismic physiognomy needs attention in form of female who can endure such doses of mature, physical stress. Asbestos. NYR, Box 31.

AM I LOOKING FOR YOU? Speak up. I'm weary of this frantic social whirl, garden parties, convertibles, highballs at the Ritz in my squash shorts. The effete Nob Hill world makes me languid with ennui. Graceless, arch, and pertinacious females swigging gossip and daiquiris and trying to impress one with their breeding and intellect at the same time as they are rolling their eyes and inching toward the bedroom door towards which I will not move from my wingback chair to take a step—from these and their kidney, spare and deliver me. I long to meet a sweet, unspoiled young thing, about nineteen, with all her virtues and ideals intact, laughing gayly over one shoulder as she comes in from tennis. Fresh of mind, fresh of body. If you are such, I am rich beyond measure, and not yet forty. Randolph is my name, despoilation my game. But I'm sincere. So few are. NYR at once! Box 65432.

SHOCK ABSORBER insertion and Saul Bellow technique. If you honestly understand what this means, please contact immediately. NYR, Box 81102.

HUMANISTIC, IRONIC, teleological, proleptic, heuristic, typological, dichotomistic, transumptive or metaleptic, eclectic, Thomistic, neocritilogical male seeks unkempt slattern with big nipples and strong bowed legs to raise a mess of brats with. Write NYR, Box 88654.

WELL-VERSED BUT BORED Indiana U. prof. of entomology seeks responsible male for short conversations, light baby sitting, some clitoral stimulation. NYR, Box 8890.

GROISSE ZETZ; TUCHUS. If you really understand, please send detailed, confidential reply to NYR, Box 11045.

JEWISH

ORTHODOX PSYCHOLOGIST who knows how to live well seeks woman to share bleeding ulcer. NYR, Box 8775.

AGING YIDDISH STORY WRITER seeks young-man for light enema work. Some typing. Other. NYR, Box 441.

REFORM LIBERAL, outspoken, Long Island Congregational rabbi and wife seek well-educated, literary black woman for racial repartee, intensive interviews, light housework. NYR, Box 3218.

SOMEWHAT UNHAPPILY MARRIED orthodox, well-mannered gentleman seeks shame. Reply NYR, Box 22910.

I'M A PETITE, CUDDLY, AFFECTIONATE, red-headed Hasid diamond merchant who seeks everlasting matrimony within sacred covenant. Will provide carfare. NYR, Box 7892.

JEWISH/GOYISH
GOYISH/JEWISH

JEWISH-GOYISH/JEWISH MAN, 33, seeks Roman-type goy to share experiences and some knocking around on Purim and other festival days, Simchat Torah, or anytime. NYR, Box 9722.

JEWISH-GOYISH/MALE Jew, 29, looks to break Sabbath and High Holy Day traditions with non-Jewish young woman who speaks very little English. NYR, Box 443.

GOYISH-JEWISH/GOYISHE, bilingual Roman Catholic girl, 29, pretty, likes Mailer, Malamud, McKuen, seeks young male who will consent to pose as ham radio operator in exchange for physical love. NYR, Box 2311.

JEWISH-GOYISH, Tired, tense Jewish woman seeks hyperactive, guilty Greek to share urinary tract infection and school holidays. Strong. NYR, Box 299.

PROTESTANT FREE-LANCE WRITER needs info for booklet on anal retention, expulsives. Jewish preferred. Possible participation. Write Prof. M. NYR, Box 5.

BROOKLYN YESHIVA, 63, PROFESSOR of Kabbalah and Tractates from Lubovitch family of fabric merchants is fed up with smelly rituals. Seeks to trade Yartzeit candles for open-minded relations with young gentlemen from upstate. NYR, Box 55113.

SERVICES

UNDER RABBINICAL SUPERVISION: Williamsburg, Brooklyn J.H.S. teacher, expert on Torah, seeks to convert homosexuals using simple prayer and other techniques. No electricity. NYR, Box 32998.

SUFFERING WRITERS! I CAN HAVE YOUR MATERIAL PUBLISHED, printed, and distributed on colorful cocktail napkins. Send 75¢ for free booklet.

SPARE TIME

HOW TO MAKE MONEY INVENTING SMALL WORDS. I'll tell you how to do it and where to go. Barrett, P.O. Box 332, Grand Central Station, NYC.

PERFORM VASECTOMIES in your spare time! Learn how. Make your own hours. Increase your income. Wilson's, Box 223, Greenvale, Fla.

TUCHIS? YENTA? GEY KOCKEN? SHTUP?? You can actually earn a living reading Yiddish words out loud in your spare time in the southern U.S. Start with simple home course. Yiddish Division, La Salle Extension University, Grand Rapids, Mich.

RUMORS AND UNPLEASANT FILLERS for Jewish or Yiddish short stories. Inexpensive outlines for unpleasant characters, odors, etc. Write Knish & Kasha Filler Co., Box 559, Brooklyn, N.Y.

SCAPEGOATS AND OTHER RELATED IDEAS can actually solve your problems practically overnight. Send for details. Free Press, Box 66, Orlando, Fla.

SICKNESS, ACCIDENTS, MILD DISEASE needed for your story? We have everything for the ethnic author. Simple insertions fit into any story or essay effortlessly. Instructions. Rank Fillers, Box 12, Acton, Ohio.

PROTESTANT? Walking around feeling insulated by the cotton of insensitivity? Have invigorating Yiddish Tension Massage by over weight woman. Creplach massages. NYR, Box 30.

GARY LARSON

"Oh hey! I just love these things! . . . Crunchy on
the outside and a chewy center!"

KURT ANDERSEN

Afterword

Humor is a peculiar literary species. Good writing of other kinds can be easygoing. A piece of journalism can offer its version of the truth coolly, casually, almost automatically. A novel may have a lot on its mind as it wanders through its story (adjusting mood, shading character, worrying about paperback royalties), but it has the leisure to let the reader fend for himself for pages at a time. Readers of humor, on the other hand, expect to get a sharp, jolly buzz from every third sentence or so. Thus, comic writing is obliged to be a little pushy: Smile, come on, chuckle, come on, *laugh.* Only humor (and pornography) is supposed to provoke just one kind of response again and again and again, a dozen times a page.

Humor writing is apt to be a dense, showy kind of prose, a literature packed full of special effects. In the nineteenth century, the stock special effect was full-bore fake-bumpkinism, the "Haint got none" and "She wuz madder'n a bobcat" of D. R. Locke (Petroleum V. Nasby), Charles Farrar Browne (Artemus Ward), and Henry Wheeler Shaw (Josh Billings). The three were contemporary writers, virtually indistinguishable from each other. Mark Twain was forging some fairly extravagant Southern dialect at the same time, but in almost every instance to serve his grander storytelling ends. For Nasby, Ward, and Billings, the wacky backwoodsy dialects were practically the whole point. (A hundred years later, the writers of "All in the Family," simultaneously fond and contemptuous of their protagonist, were getting a very similar kind of comic mileage out of Archie Bunker's working-class malapropisms.) It is hard to read much of the Nasbyites today. The concentrated effort of slogging through their tricked-up spelling and grammar requires nearly the kind of stop-and-go deciphering of Chaucer in return for some pretty lame payoffs.

As artifacts pulled straight from the heart of the last century, though, the material is telling. America was a country going through its gawky early adolescence, a provincial rube growing very quickly and just beginning to get some worldliness. American readers, most of them barely a generation removed from the uncivilized sticks themselves, were anxious about their ragtag roots and about the fussier world they had joined. Their countrymen on the farms and the frontier had plenty of rough-hewn common sense, but they were also crude, goofy buffoons. Locke, Browne, and Shaw played to that ambivalence. Their fictional personae were reassuring on both counts. The characters could get away with declaring homespun, impolite truths about highfalutin modern ways (Billings: "I hav' seen poodles that I almost wanted tew swop places with"), while being sufficiently ridiculous to make readers feel sophisticated and superior.

The real subject of nearly all the pieces, and a good deal of American humor, is the sense of not quite fitting in. This is a nation of dislocated people, of immigrants from abroad, emigrants from east to west, from country to city, sliders from social class to social class. Wherever Americans are, they have probably not been there long enough to feel entirely comfortable. We are perpetual outsiders or, if finally permitted inside, nervous and defensive about our new status. Either way, the result can be a special sensitivity to the oddities of social and linguistic custom. Given that high-pitched awareness of life's fault lines, there are two possible responses: Skulk around and whimper, or watch closely and make fun. "Humor in the first analysis," James Russell Lowell declared, "is a perception of the incongruous."[1]

The Marx Brothers were caricatures of the new immigrant swarm—noisy, manic, bewildering. They flaunted their un-American strangeness, transforming it into comedy ("Groucho and Chico Make a Deal," "Why a Duck?" pp. 373; 377). In this generation, the wild and crazy Czech Brothers of "Saturday Night Live," writer James Downey's very cruel and very funny immigrant caricatures, weren't confrontational like the Marxes: rather, they were clownishly desperate to assimilate into the prefab disco America of their *Playboy*-inflamed dreams. In the late seventies, with "Mork and Mindy," "Saturday Night's" Coneheads, and the multiplanetary mix of the comic *Star Wars* barroom scene, the humor of alienation went over the top. Ersatz extraterrestrial lingo may be the dialect humor of the Space Age, and Robin Williams's Mork a kind of twenty-first-century Petroleum V. Nasby.

Any kind of other-ness will do. Richard Pryor's comedy is all about the

[1] It is incongruous indeed that Lowell, who was, after all, a *Lowell*, wrote humorous pieces of the mock-bumpkin kind. His character, a Mr. Biglow, made declarations such as "Folks thet's afeared to fail are sure o' failin'."

perspective of the watchful man on the edge. In Joseph Heller's *Catch-22*, Yossarian is the one sane man in a mad world. In Woody Allen's earlier movies (*Take the Money and Run, Bananas, Sleeper*), his character is badly out of sync—abandoned, misidentified, misunderstood, even popped into another time. In "The Kugelmass Episode" (p. 335), Allen's protagonist wanders out of the world altogether, and Harvey Fierstein's *Torch Song Trilogy* (Scene One: Arnold) (p. 471) gets its unlikely laughes out of the profoundest kind of alienation.

Elsewhere in the world, intense odd-man-out anxiety has tended to produce hard-core existentialists, or secretive political factions, or Swedes. Seldom humorists. But this country seems determined to encourage the bouncy, the snappy, even the zany. You say you're feeling confused, frustrated, maybe a little outraged, filled with a nameless dread? *In America?* You've got to be kidding.

It is not just that we are unnaturally eager to guffaw, or reluctant to take things too seriously. We also live in a land of vast satiric opportunity. The United States undergoes change so constantly, reinventing itself every couple of decades, that new comic targets keep popping up like big tin ducks in a carnival shooting gallery. Dating services for the handicapped. *Bang!* A President who sees a flying saucer is succeeded by a President who calls expenditures for military uniforms the "wardrobe" budget. *Bang! Bang!* Television preachers raising millions to spread the glorious news that the end is near. *Bang!* Waiters called "beverage consultants." College towns that declare themselves "nuclear-free zones." Tanning salons. Groom-a-pet attachments for vacuum cleaners. Bulletproof evening gowns. *Bang! Bang! Bang! Bang! Bang!*

But exactly who did what when? And where? There were the boomtown San Franciscans—Ambrose Bierce, Bret Harte, Twain during his bicoastal period. Los Angeles has its encampment of comic screenwriters. Chicago produced the Second City troupe in the 1960s and 70s. But a large quorum of modern American humorists have lived within a few hours of Times Square. The reasons for this clustering are well known: New York is where most publishing occurs, and the city is congenial to cranks and skeptics of all kinds. What's more interesting is the result, the humor subdivision of the larger literary-*cum*-media colony: a cross-pollinating thicket of friendships, social acquaintanceships, professional partnerships, family connections, fraternal loyalties, old-school ties, and even romantic involvements that link humorist to humorist, generation to generation.

Even a selective genealogy is impressive. The 1870s and 80s were a rich time. Between 1870 and 1876 no less than six humor magazines *(Punchi-nello, Champagne, Brickbat, Cocktails, The Humorist, The Merry Masker)* were started in New York, although each lasted no more than a year. *The Harvard Lampoon* began in 1876, a year before New York's *Puck,* the first important satirical sheet. The weekly *Judge* was the doing of *Puck* defectors in 1881. Its writers ultimately included Ring Lardner, Heywood Broun, George Jean Nathan, S. J. Perelman, and Milt Gross. *Life,* started in 1883 by one of the graduate founders of the *Lampoon,* was a place for gentler satire. The magazine eventually had among its contributors Will Rogers, the illustrators Gluyas Williams *(Lampoon* class of 1911) and Charles Dana Gibson (who later bought the magazine), and most of the Algonquin Round Table principals not writing for *Judge*—Franklin P. Adams, Dorothy Parker, and Benchley *(Lampoon* class of 1910). *The Smart Set: A Magazine of Cleverness* began in 1890, its worldview a kind of fizzy upper-class bohemianism. In addition to the greatest subtitle in the history of magazine subtitles, *The Smart Set* had Nathan, H. L. Mencken, and the illustrator James Montgomery Flagg as mainstays.

Puck faded along about Armistice Day, but for its competitors the 1920s were the great days. The consumer demand for humorous prose—imagine!—seemed as great as that for bootlegged liquor. The circulation of *Judge* reached 200,000, that of *Life* 227,000. A former editor of both, one Norman Hume Anthony, started the astonishingly successful *Ballyhoo,* a more ribald and impolite magazine that claimed 2 million readers. In 1924 Mencken began his grand *American Mercury* "to belabor sham as agreeably as possible, to give a civilized entertainment." Harold Ross published the first *New Yorker,* more blithe and table-hopping than the *Mercury,* in 1925. *The New Yorker* in its first fifteen years assembled a kind of dream team: Benchley, Adams, Parker, Williams, and Perelman, as well as Leo C. Rosten, James Thurber, and Frank Sullivan.

Except for *The New Yorker,* all of the magazines petered out during the Depression. Hollywood acquired a good number of the erstwhile magazine humorists—most notably Perelman, who wrote scripts for the Marx Brothers, and Benchley, who became a minor movie star. Literary humor suffered a dry spell from World War II until the 1960s. *The New Yorker* was showing mainly its sober side to the world. There was some funny television, although Ernie Kovacs and "Your Show of Shows" (written by Woody Allen, Mel Brooks, and Neil Simon) may not by themselves constitute a Golden Age. A generation of acute, remarkably cerebral nightclub comedians (Allen, Mike Nichols and Elaine May, Lenny Bruce, Jonathan Winters, Bob Newhart) did emerge. Children had *Mad,* and a contingent from *Mad* magazine in the mid-fifties started the satirical *Trump* for adults; *Trump* lasted a year. Readers were expected to subsist on Bennett Cerf's joke books and the limp, goody-goody offerings of *The Reader's Digest.* There was not even Russell Baker, not even Erma Bombeck.

Forms inevitably change. With the advent of radio and talking pictures, for instance, dialect writing was practically mooted. If Gabby Hayes or Marjorie Main could simply perform their hick schticks on film, why go to the trouble of making up a queer dirt-road speaking manner in print? Movies and especially TV changed the way even literate people expect to get most of their laughs. Performance eclipsed prose. Reading short humor came to seem a bit musty, an anachronism by its very nature, something to do while wearing a straw boater. And of course, apart from the pressures of technology, the national moods turn and dip. Ironies that amused Americans in 1930 did not necessarily do so in 1950, and the humor of 1970 was considerably edgier than that of 1950.

But this evolution of taste is not helter-skelter. There is an additive logic to the history of modern humor, like a string of Biblical begattings. Humor accretes. Where the pulpy, popular comic book culture intersected with the underground urban current of fifties' skepticism, *Mad* was born. Where that skepticism ran deeper and flowed from campuses into cabarets, the result was the Second City improvisational troupe (and, in England, Jonathan Miller's *Beyond the Fringe).* Second City became a model, and the models in the late 1960s turned Day-Glo along with so much else: The Committee, a comedy group that appeared on "The Smothers Brothers Comedy Hour," was the most important of these lashings-together of politics, comedy, and a rock 'n' roll world view. In the Northeast, the jolt of the late sixties revived the dormant Ivy Leagueish strain of literary humor: the *National*ized *Lampoon,* started like the comic *Life* by three fresh Harvard graduates, found its large audience among the baby boomers, the first generation raised with *Mad* and the first since the 1920s predisposed to thumb its nose. "Saturday Night Live," which went on the air in 1975, was essentially a postgraduate *Lampoon:* Several of the writers came straight from the magazine, and most of the original actors were Second City veterans by way of *National Lampoon* stage shows. For the last decade or so, *The New Yorker* has once again published a large plurality of the best humorists: Allen, Veronica Geng, Garrison Keillor, Roy Blount, Jr., Ian Frazier, and several grown-up former *National Lampoon* contributors, among them Bruce McCall. In 1986, with my co-editor E. Graydon Carter, I started *Spy,* a new New York magazine with comic ambitions. Among the contributors are Mark

O'Donnell and Blount. As it happens, *Spy*'s offices are in the Manhattan quarters occupied by *Puck* seventy years ago. The circle comes around.

Is it stretching the point to put, say, Mencken and Lenny Bruce on the same family tree? Mencken only ranted about the decline of civilization; Bruce ranted and embodied it. The tendrils of linkage and influence really do extend in all kinds of curious directions. Allen and Brooks knew and draw heavily from Perelman and the Marx Brothers. Fran Lebowitz is compared to Dorothy Parker, but her archbrittleness seems at least as reminiscent of another Round Table regular, Alexander Woollcott. Or consider the following loop-de-loop. Tony Hendra, a former editor of *The National Lampoon*, performed in *This Is Spinal Tap*, a 1984 film parody directed by Rob Reiner, a former member of The Committee and the son of Carl Reiner; the elder Reiner, who produced "The Dick Van Dyke Show," has recently directed films starring Steve Martin, an ex-writer for the Smothers Brothers, and John Candy, late of the Canadian Second City offshoot.

It's getting a little crowded in here.

The last good and only really wonderful anthology of intentionally funny prose was E. B. and Katharine S. White's *Subtreasury of American Humor*. The Whites were writer and editor, respectively, for *The New Yorker*, and published their *Subtreasury*, thick with *New Yorker* pieces, when the magazine was just sixteen years old. E. B. White's generation of humorists was middle-aged. The real glory days had ended a decade before.

It seemed a good time to punctuate an era, as it does again now. The people responsible for the high-strung humor revival of the sixties and seventies are middle-aged or very nearly so. Writers have settled into voices, forms have been refined or done to death, stylistic barriers broken. *The National Lampoon*, an unreadable magazine nowadays, is seventeen years old; "Saturday Night," three producers later, is twelve.

Laughing Matters is by far the most eclectic collection of humorous writing that I know about, the only one that begins to suggest the wild breadth of American humor in the past century. Margaret Fishback, Michael O'Donoghue, Philip Roth, Veronica Geng, George Meyer, and Garry Trudeau are all squeezed between the same covers; chunks of stage, radio, and film dialogue, cartoon strips and single panels, verse and fiction, and a bit of journalism. The unorthodox mix of style and sensibility is breathtaking. It could explode.

The omissions are mostly arbitrary. Some kinds of humor were excluded systematically. There are no loose jokes. Some jokes are, all by themselves, funny. But the intent here was to provide a sampling of humorists, not a disparate bunch of punch lines. Except for the transcript of Casey Stengel's congressional testimony on "Organized Professional Team Sports" (p. 157) and "A Quiet Dinner for Two in Paris" by Craig Claiborne (p. 78), everything included is deliberately comic. Accidentally funny things can be glorious, but they belong together, in collections of their own.[2] There were some tacit quotas. Despite the welcoming attitude toward scripts, a given piece of funny prose had a better chance of admission than a given piece of comedy. This is a book, after all, and the prejudice for print was indulged.

There is probably too little political and social satire. But perishability is a particular problem. Quemoy and Matsu, for example, are not quite the comic raw material they were twenty-five years ago. Anyway, Ellis Weiner's sublime "Patriotic Spot (60 Secs.)" (p. 111) ought to give more pleasure than any dozen hard-hitting Spiro Agnew spoofs.

Only three of the living writers represented here, Russell Baker, Woody Allen, and now Garrison Keillor, are adored by millions. Good, funny prose does not generally earn big money. On the other hand, there has been quite a little bit of fame doled out the last few years. *Esquire* ran a cover story about Doug Kenney, one of the founders of *The National Lampoon,* after he died. Tony Hendra, his sometime partner Sean Kelly and Alf *(Items from Our Catalogue)* Gingold were on the cover of *Newsweek* together. Roy Blount shows up on Garrison Keillor's weekly radio program sometimes (a paired set—delightful, shambling, post-sixties, well-educated regionalists) and on TV by himself. Calvin Trillin, who writes the sharpest political humor in America, is often on "The Tonight Show." David Letterman seems to keep asking Fran Lebowitz back.

Nevertheless, and as always, people who write humor complain that they are denied the serious attention given to writers of unsmiling fiction. There is some small truth to this. It is not, however, among the world's ten leading injustices.

---

[2] Terrible translations, for instance, are a favorite type. Consider this example from the English edition of the French novel *Yvonne* by Helene D'Orsay: "As soon as the waiter had retired, they rushed into each other's arms and soon revelled in every luscious act of the hottest lust. This sort of thing could not continue for a long while. After the most delicious . . . gamahuching in every possible combination . . . it was thought prudent to draw breath in order that they might fully enjoy the night together." Gamahuch if I know what the French for "gamahuching" is.

B. KLIBAN

"These are my last
words. . . . No, these are my last words! . . .
Those weren't really my last words! Here are my
real last words! Here they are! . . . These are my last
words! No, no, just kidding! These are
really and truly my last words. . . ."

Acknowledgments

Every effort has been made to trace copyright, but if any omissions have been made please notify the publisher. We gratefully acknowledge permission from the following:

Charles Addams. By permission of the artist.

Atheneum Publishers, Inc.
   "The Garish Summit—Episode 1" and "The Garish Summit—Episode 2" from *Approximately Coast to Coast . . . It's the Bob and Ray Show* by Bob Elliott and Ray Goulding. Copyright © 1983 Goulding-Elliott-Graybar Productions, Inc.
   "Attitude," "Shy Rights: Why Not Pretty Soon?", and "U.S. Still on Top, Says Rest of World" from *Happy to Be Here* by Garrison Keillor. Copyright © 1982 by Garrison Keillor.
   "The Drapes of Roth" from *A Gift of Laughter* by Allan Sherman. Copyright © 1965 Allan Sherman.

Avon Books. "Apartment House Being Built" and "Joe's Grammar Shop" from *Elementary: The Cartoonist Did It* by Robert Mankoff. Copyright © 1980 by Robert Mankoff.

Beldock Levine & Hoffman. George Meyer Sketch, "Food Repairman," for "The New Show" © 1985 The New Show, Inc. (George Meyer, Writer.) By permission of Broadway Video, Inc.

Boston Public Library. "Jack Benny in Allen's Alley," selection from *Treadmill to Oblivion*, by Fred Allen, 1954, Little Brown and Company. Courtesy of the Trustees of the Boston Public Library.

Richard Bradford. "Green Pastures" from *Ol' Man Adam an' His Chillun* by Roark Bradford. Copyright by Estate of Roark Bradford.

George Burns. "Palace Theater Skit" by George Burns. By permission of the author.

Chronicle Features. "The Far Side" cartoons by Gary Larson (pages 438, 573, 603) are reprinted by permission of Chronicle Features, San Francisco.

Frank Cotham. "This rivalry has got to stop, Harold!" by Frank Cotham is used by permission of the artist. Appeared originally in *Cosmopolitan.*

Cowan & Bodine. "Wake up, you mutt! We're getting married today." by Peter Arno. Copyright 1930 Peter Arno, Copyright renewed 1958 Peter Arno, Copyright 1986 Patricia A. Maxwell and A. Halsey Cowan, Executors of the Estate of Peter Arno. Used by permission.

Curtis Licensing Corporation. "Who's on First?" by Bud Abbott and Lou Costello. By permission of Abbott & Costello Enterprises, Inc.

Curtis Publishing Company. "An Apartment House Anthology" by Dorothy Parker. © 1921 The Curtis Publishing Company. Reprinted from *The Saturday Evening Post.*

Liz Darhansoff Agency. "Farewell, My Lovely Appetizer" by S. J. Perelman originally appeared in *The New Yorker.* Copyright © 1944, 1972, by S. J. Perelman.

Candida Donadio & Associates, Inc. *The Gashlycrumb Tinies* by Edward Gorey. © Edward Gorey.

614   ACKNOWLEDGMENTS

Doubleday & Company, Inc.

"Affectations" from *The Real Thing* by Kurt Andersen. Copyright © 1980 by Kurt Andersen.

"A Pair of Sexes" and "To a Thesaurus" from *The Column Book of F.P.A.* by Franklin P. Adams. Copyright 1928 by Doubleday & Company, Inc.

"Letterati" from *Offtrack* by Steven G. Crist. Copyright © 1980, 1981 by Steven Crist.

"the coming of archy," "mehitabel was once cleopatra," "the song of mehitabel," "the old trouper," "the flattered lightning bug," "the honey bee," and "the lesson of the moth" from *the lives and times of archy and mehitabel* by Don Marquis. Copyright 1927 by Doubleday & Company, Inc. "The Rivercliff Golf Killings" by Don Marquis. Copyright 1927 by *Sun Dial Time*. Reprinted from the book *The Best of Don Marquis*.

Excerpts from *Barefoot Boy with Cheek* by Max Shulman. Copyright 1943 by Max Shulman.

Drawings from *Mute Point* by Gary Solin. Copyright © 1966, 1968, 1970, by Gary Solin.

"Ben's Dairy" from *American Fried* by Calvin Trillin. Copyright © 1973 by Calvin Trillin. (This originally appeared in *The New Yorker.*)

E. P. Dutton. "I Stand Corrected" and "The Purist to Her Love" from *One to a Customer* by Margaret Fishback. Copyright 1937 by E. P. Dutton, renewed 1965 by Margaret Fishback Antolini. Reprinted by permission of the publisher, E. P. Dutton, a Division of New American Library.

Jules Feiffer. Cartoons by Jules Feiffer are reprinted by permission of the artist.

Jerrold S. Gross. "Ferry-Tail from Keeng Mitas for Nize Baby" from *Nize Baby* by Milt Gross. Copyright 1926 by the George H. Doran Company, renewed © 1953 by Milt Gross. By permission of Mrs. Milt Gross.

Samuel H. Gross. "How to Get Up . . ." © 1979 The New Yorker Magazine, Inc. "Please Help Me . . ." © 1979 National Lampoon, Inc. "Going Out of Business . . ." © 1981 S. Gross. All by S. Gross and reprinted with his permission.

Harcourt Brace Jovanovich, Inc.

"Mia Carlotta" from *Selected Poems of T. A. Daly*. Copyright 1936 by Harcourt Brace Jovanovich, Inc.; renewed 1964 by Thomas A. Daly, Jr.

"Old Country Advice to the American Traveler from *My Name is Aram* by William Saroyan. Copyright 1939, 1967, by William Saroyan.

Harper & Row, Publishers, Inc.

"Christmas Afternoon" by Robert Benchley. Copyright 1921 by Harper & Row, Publishers, Inc. Copyright 1949 by Gertrude Benchley. "Kiddie-Kar Travel" by Robert Benchley. Copyright 1925 by Harper & Row, Publishers, Inc. Copyright 1953 by Gertrude Benchley. "Opera Synopses" by Robert Benchley. Copyright 1922 by Harper & Row, Publishers, Inc. Renewed 1950 by Gertrude D. Benchley. "Why We Laugh—or Do We?" by Robert Benchley. Copyright 1938 by Robert C. Benchley. All from *The Benchley Roundup* by Robert Benchley. Selected by Nathaniel Benchley.

"Curb Carter Policy Discord Effort Threat" by Veronica Geng. Copyright © 1978 by Veronica Geng. "My Mao" by Veronica Geng. Copyright © 1977 by Veronica Geng. "The Stylish New York Couples" by Veronica Geng originally appeared in *The New Yorker*. Copyright © 1982, 1984, by Veronica Geng. All are from *Partners* by Veronica Geng.

"Unearned Increment" from *Mandarin in Manhattan* by Christopher Morley (J. B. Lippincott). Copyright 1933 by Christopher Morley, Renewed 1961 by Mrs. Helen F. Morley.

"The Sexual Revolution" is Chapter IV, "The Sexual Revolution: Being a Rather Complete Survey of the Entire Sexual Scene," from *Is Sex Necessary?* by James Thurber and E. B. White. Copyright 1929 by Harper & Row, Publishers, Inc.

"Dusk in Fierce Pajamas" from *Quo Vadimus? or The Case for the Bicycle* by E. B. White. Originally appeared in *The New Yorker*. Copyright 1934 by E. B. White.

Trudy Hoffenstein. "A Simple Tale," "The Notebook of a Schnook" and "Budget" are from *Pencil in the Air* by Samuel Hoffenstein. Copyright Samuel Hoffenstein. Reprinted by permission of Trudy Hoffenstein.

Henry Holt and Company, Inc.
"A Fish Fry" from *The Green Pastures* by Marc Connelly. Copyright 1929, 1930, © 1957, 1958, by Marc Connelly.

"A Considerable Speck (Microscopic)" from *The Poetry of Robert Frost,* edited by Edward Connery Lathem. Copyright 1942 by Robert Frost. Copyright © 1969 by Holt, Rinehart and Winston. Copyright © 1970 by Lesley Frost Ballantine.

Earnest A. Hooton. "Ode to a Dental Hygienist." Extensive research failed to locate the copyright holder of this work.

Sukey Howard. "Big heart/little heart" by Skip Morrow, © 1982 by Skip Morrow, is from *The Official I Hate Love Book* by Skip Morrow.

King Features Syndicate, Inc. "Easy Way to Open a Window" by Rube Goldberg. Reprinted by special permission of King Features Syndicate, Inc.

"Krazy Kat" by George Herriman. Reprinted by special permission of King Features Syndicate, Inc.

Arthur Kober. "Boggains in the Bronx" from *Thunder in the Bronx* by Arthur Kober, originally published by Simon & Schuster, Inc. Extensive research has failed to locate a copyright holder for this work.

Edward Koren. "Does It Address the Insanity of Contemporary Life?" © Edward Koren. By permission of the artist.

Harold A. Larrabee. "The Very Model of a Modern College President" originally appeared in *What Cheer,* edited by David McCord.

Bill Lee. "Follow That Cab!" from *Man Bites Man* by Bill Lee. Copyright 1986. Courtesy Bill Lee.

Little, Brown and Company.
"Blue Yodel 9 Jesse," "The List of the Mohicans," and "What to do on New Year's Eve I and II" from *What Men Don't Tell Women* by Roy Blount, Jr. Copyright © 1984 by Roy Blount, Jr.

"The Firefly" from *Good Intentions* by Ogden Nash. Copyright 1942 by Ogden Nash. Appeared originally in *The New Yorker.*

"How to Harry a Husband or Is That Accessory Really Necessary?" Copyright © 1956 by Ogden Nash. First appeared in *The New Yorker.* "I Never Even Suggested It" Copyright 1940 by the Curtis Publishing Company. First appeared in *The Saturday Evening Post.* "Look What You Did, Christopher!" Copyright 1933 by Ogden Nash. First appeared in *Redbook.* All from *Verses from 1929 On* by Ogden Nash.

Liveright Publishing Corporation. "You buy some flowers for your table" from "Poems in Praise of Practically Nothing" and "You have a most attractive pan. . . ." from "Poems of Passion Carefully Restrained So as to Offend Nobody" both appear in *Poems in Praise of Practically Nothing* by Samuel Hoffenstein. Copyright 1928 by Samuel Hoffenstein. Copyright renewed 1955 by David Hoffenstein. Reprinted by permission of Liveright Publishing Corporation.

The Sterling Lord Agency, Inc. "The White House Is Sinking!" by Jeff Greenfield. Copyright © 1979 by Jeff Greenfield.

MCA Publishing Rights. "Why a Duck?" from *The Cocoanuts* by the Marx Brothers. Copyright © by Universal Pictures, a Division of Universal City Studios, Inc. Courtesy of MCA Publishing Rights, a Division of MCA Inc.

MGM/UA Home Entertainment Group, Inc. "Groucho and Chico Make a Deal" from *A Night at the Opera* by George S. Kaufman and Morrie Ryskind. © 1935 Metro-Goldwyn-Mayer Corporation. Renewed 1962 Metro-Goldwyn-Mayer, Inc.

Mad Magazine. "Antenna on the Roof" by Frank Jacobs and Mort Drucker. Copyright © 1972 by E. C. Publications, Inc.

Howard Margulies. "When I say 'I love you' . . ." © 1986 Howard Margulies. By permission of the artist.

Toni Mendez. "Genghis & Sylvia Kahn" and "Q.&A." from *Never Eat Anything Bigger Than*

Your Head & Other Drawings by B. Kliban. Copyright © 1976 by B. Kliban. Published by Workman Publishing Co., Inc. Reprinted by permission of the author.

National Lampoon.
"Classified Ads" from the January 1976 issue.
"The Unhappiest Man in New York," by Flenniken from the September 1979 issue.

The New Republic. "The Scrolls" by Woody Allen from the August 31, 1974, issue. © 1974 The New Republic, Inc.

The New York Times.
"Francs and Beans" by Russell Baker from November 18, 1975, issue. Copyright © 1975 by The New York Times Company.

"Just a Quiet Dinner for Two in Paris: 31 Dishes, Nine Wines, a $4,000 Check" by Craig Claiborne from November 14, 1975, issue. Copyright © 1975 by The New York Times Company.

"The Old Codger's 1985 Almanac" by Mark O'Donnell with art by Chris Austopchuk from February 26, 1983, issue. Copyright © 1983 by The New York Times Company.

The New Yorker.
Drawing by Charles Addams; © 1940, 1968, The New Yorker Magazine, Inc.

"Confessions of a Burglar" by Woody Allen. From the October 18, 1976, issue. © 1976 Woody Allen.

"Armbruster here . . ." Drawing by Peter Arno; © 1937, 1965, The New Yorker Magazine, Inc.

"I've got an idea for a story . . ." Drawing by George Booth; © 1970 The New Yorker Magazine, Inc.

"The Enigma Redundancy" by Marshall Brickman. From the May 4, 1981, issue. © 1981 Marshall Brickman.

"U.S. Torn Apart by French Attitudes" by Lynn Caraganis; © 1983 by Lynn Caraganis.

"From the Notebook of Lewis Commonsense, Ph.D." Drawing by R. Chast; © 1984 The New Yorker Magazine, Inc.

"More Big News from Out There" by Gordon Cotler; © 1967 The New Yorker Magazine, Inc.

"Well, folks, here it is . . ." Drawing by Robert Day; © 1938, 1966, The New Yorker, Inc.

"Into the American Maw" from *Dating Your Mom* (Farrar, Straus & Giroux) © 1980 and 1982, respectively, Ian Frazier. Originally in *The New Yorker.*

"I may be crazy . . ." Drawing by Bud Handelsman; © 1984 and "You could care less? . . ." Drawing by Bud Handelsman; © 1982 The New Yorker Magazine, Inc.

"People slowly accustomed themselves . . ." Drawing by Rea Irvin; © 1929, 1957, The New Yorker Magazine, Inc.

"Rolled in Rare Bohemian Onyx, Then Vulcanized by Hand" by Bruce McCall; © 1981 Bruce McCall.

"The Ultimate Diary" by Howard Moss; © 1975 The New Yorker Magazine, Inc.

"Hit this sign . . ." Drawing by George Price; © 1938, 1966, The New Yorker Magazine, Inc. "There's so much . . ." Drawing by George Price; © 1983 and "Will you be right . . ." Drawing by George Price; © 1973 The New Yorker Magazine, Inc.

"5 Panel Drawing." Drawing by Ton Smits; © 1956, 1984, The New Yorker Magazine, Inc.

"Plan A and Plan B" and "Overcoming Depression." Drawings by M. Stevens; © 1983 The New Yorker Magazine, Inc.

"The Cliché Expert Testifies on the Movies," "The Cliché Expert Testifies on Literary Criticism," and "A Garland of Ibids" by Frank Sullivan; © 1937, 1965, and 1941, 1969, respectively, The New Yorker Magazine, Inc.

"Patriotic Spot (60 Secs.)" by Ellis Weiner; © 1980 Ellis Weiner.

"Across the Street and into the Grill" by E. B. White from *The Second Street from the Corner* (Harper Bros.). © 1950, 1978, E. B. White. Originally in *The New Yorker.*

"Raconteurs." Drawing by Gluyas Williams; © 1938, 1966, The New Yorker Magazine, Inc.

"Lincoln at Gettysburg." Drawing by Jack Ziegler; © 1982 The New Yorker Magazine, Inc.

All of the above originally appeared in *The New Yorker* and are reprinted by permission of *The New Yorker*.

News America Syndicate. " 'B.C.' cartoon of July 8, 1984," by Johnny Hart. By permission of Johnny Hart and News America Syndicate.

Noel Perrin. "Answers to Poets' Questions" from the June 26, 1965, issue of *The New Yorker*. © 1965 Noel Perrin and reprinted with his permission.

PLAYBOY Magazine.

"These are my last words . . ." by B. Kliban. Copyright © 1983 by PLAYBOY. "Apartment 5B" by Gahan Wilson. Copyright © 1984 by PLAYBOY. Reproduced by Special Permission of PLAYBOY Magazine.

Excerpts from "Interview with Mel Brooks" by Brad Darrach. Originally appeared in PLAYBOY Magazine. Copyright © 1975 by PLAYBOY. Courtesy of Mel Brooks.

The Putnam Publishing Group. "Mournful Numbers" from *Spilt Milk* by Morris Bishop. Copyright © 1942, 1970, by Morris Bishop. Reprinted by permission of G. P. Putnam's Sons.

Random House, Inc.

"Selections from the Allen Notebooks" reprinted from *Without Feathers* by Woody Allen. Copyright © 1973 by Woody Allen. "Hasidic Tales, with a Guide to Their Interpretation by the Noted Scholar" reprinted from *Getting Even* by Woody Allen. Copyright © 1970 by Woody Allen. "The Kugelmass Episode," reprinted from *Side Effects* by Woody Allen. Copyright © 1977 by Woody Allen. "The Whore of Mensa" from *Without Feathers* by Woody Allen. Copyright © 1974 by Woody Allen. All reprinted by permission of Random House, Inc.

"The Old Codger's 1985 Almanac" and "Insect Societies" from *Elementary Education: An Easy Alternative to Actual Learning* by Mark O'Donnell. Copyright © 1979, 1980, by Mark O'Donnell. Reprinted by permission of Alfred A. Knopf, Inc.

"Scene One: Arnold" from "The International Stud" from *Torch Song Trilogy* by Harvey Fierstein. Copyright © 1978, 1979, by Harvey Fierstein. Reprinted by permission of Villard Books, a Division of Random House, Inc.

Cartoons from *Barnaby* by Crockett Johnson. Copyright 1942, 1943, by Crockett Johnson. Reprinted by permission of Ballantine Books, a Division of Random House, Inc.

"Tips for Teens," "Ideas," "Lesson One," "The Last Laugh," "An Alphabet of New Year's Resolutions for Others" from *Social Studies* by Fran Lebowitz. Copyright © 1981 by Fran Lebowitz. Reprinted by permission of Random House, Inc.

"The Wedding: A Stage Direction" from *A Book of Burlesques* by H. L. Mencken. Copyright 1916 by Alfred A. Knopf, Inc., and renewed 1944 by H. L. Mencken. Reprinted by permission of the publisher.

"Nothing but the Tooth" Copyright 1944 by S. J. Perelman and "Waiting for Santy" Copyright 1936 by S. J. Perelman are from *Crazy Like a Fox* by S. J. Perelman. By permission of Random House, Inc.

"English Lit(mus)" from *When to Dump Your Date* by Lois Romano. Copyright © 1984 by Lois Romano. Reprinted by permission of Ballantine Books, A Division of Random House, Inc.

Will Rogers Memorial Commission. "Timely Topics" by Will Rogers is used by permission of the Will Rogers Memorial Commission, Claremore, OK.

Leo Rosten. "Christopher K*A*P*L*A*N" appeared originally in the October 8, 1938, issue of *The New Yorker*. © Leo Rosten and reprinted with his permission.

Arnold Roth. "Leonardo da Vinci Audition" is a drawing by Arnold Roth. Copyright Arnold Roth and used with his permission.

Philip Roth. "Letters from Einstein" © Philip Roth. Reprinted with permission of the author.

Charles Scribner's Sons. "Some Like Them Cold" by Ring Lardner from *The Ring Lardner Reader.* Copyright © 1963 Charles Scribner's Sons.

"Miniver Cheevy" from *The Town Down the River* by Edwin Arlington Robinson. Copyright 1910 Charles Scribner's Sons; Copyright renewed 1938 Ruth Nivison.

Barry Secunda Associates. "How to Write Good" by Michael O'Donoghue is from the January 1976 issue of *The National Lampoon.* Copyright © Michael O'Donoghue.

Simon & Schuster, Inc.

Excerpts by Dorothy Parker from the introduction and "No Starch in the Dhoti, *S'il Vous Plaît*" by S. J. Perelman from *The Most of S. J. Perelman.* Copyright © 1953, 1956, 1958, by S. J. Perelman.

Excerpts from the introduction to *A Treasury of Laughter,* edited by Louis Untermeyer. Copyright © 1946 by Simon & Schuster, Inc., renewed © 1974 by Simon & Schuster, Inc.

All reprinted by permission of Simon & Schuster, Inc.

St. Martin's Press, Inc. "You know . . ." "Sylvia" Drawing by Nicole Hollander from *That Woman Must Be on Drugs.* Copyright © 1981 by Nicole Hollander. Reprinted with permission of St. Martin's Press, Inc.

Bert Leston Taylor. "To Lillian Russell" and "The Bards We Quote" from *Motley Measures* by Bert Leston Taylor. Extensive research failed to locate any Taylor heirs or copyright holders of this work.

Mrs. James Thurber. Drawings by James Thurber. Copr. © 1943 James Thurber. Copr., © 1971 Helen W. Thurber and Rosemary A. Thurber. From *Men, Women and Dogs* published by Harcourt Brace Jovanovich, Inc. "The Little Girl and the Wolf" by James Thurber from *Fables for Our Time* published by Harper & Row. Copr. © 1940 James Thurber. Copr. © 1968 Helen Thurber.

Tribune Media Services.

"Shoe" Cartoons by Jeff MacNelly, "H. T. Webster Cartoon," "Mother Goose & Grimm Cartoon" are all reprinted by permission of Tribune Media Services.

United Media. Five "Peanuts" cartoons by Charles Schulz. Copyright © 1972, 1977, 1978, 1979, United Feature Syndicate, Inc.

Universal Press Syndicate. Drawings from the following:

"Doonesbury" by Garry Trudeau. Copyright 1973, 1975, 1976, G. B. Trudeau. All rights reserved.

"The Far Side" by Gary Larson. (Page 361) Copyright 1986 Universal Press Syndicate. All rights reserved.

"Herman" by Jim Unger. Copyright 1986 Universal Press Syndicate. All rights reserved.

All are reprinted with permission of Universal Press Syndicate.

University of California. "Engineer's Yell" originally appeared in *What Cheer,* edited by David McCord.

Viking Penguin Inc. "Résumé" and "From the Diary of a New York Lady" in *The Portable Dorothy Parker* by Dorothy Parker. Revised and Enlarged edition, edited by Brendan Gill. Copyright 1933, renewed © 1961 by Dorothy Parker.

Workman Publishing Co., Inc. "The Congress of Nuts" from *The 80s: A Look Back* by Henry Beard. Copyright © 1979 by United Multinationals Inc.

Contributors' Index